ATLAS ROUTIER *et* TOURISTIQUE
TOURIST *and* MOTORING ATLAS
STRASSEN- *und* REISEATLAS
TOERISTISCHE WEGENATLAS

Europe

Sommaire

IV **Grands axes routiers**
VIII **Tableau des distances**
X **Conduire en Europe**

1 **Légende multilingue**
2 **L'Europe**

130 **Index des localités**
73 plans de ville

Verso de couverture
Tableau d'assemblage

Index

IV **Main road map**
VIII **Distances**
X **Driving in Europe**

1 **Legend**
2 **Europe**

130 **Place name index**
73 Town Plans

Back cover
Key to map pages

Inhaltsübersicht

IV **Durchgangsstraßen**
VIII **Entfernungstabelle**
X **Autofahren in Europa**

1 **Mehrsprachige Legende**
2 **Europa**

130 **Ortsregister**
mit 73 Stadtplänen

Einband-Rückseite
Übersicht

Inhoud

IV **Grote verbindingswegen**
VIII **Afstandstabel**
X **Autorijden in Europa**

1 **Meertalige verklaring van de tekens**
2 **Europa**

130 **Register van plaatsnamen**
73 stadsplattegronden

Binnenzijde voorplat
Overzichtskaart met Kaartnummers

Plans de villes · Town plans · Stadtpläne · Stadsplattegronden

131 Amsterdam	144 Bruxelles	158 Hamburg	173 Manchester	194 Rotterdam
133 Antwerpen	143 Budapest	159 Hannover	174 Marseille	195 Salzburg
134 Athena	148 Dijon	159 Helsinki	175 Milano	197 Sevilla
135 Barcelona	149 Dublin	160 Istanbul	176 Monaco	198 Stockholm
136 Basel	148 Düsseldorf	162 Köln	177 München	200 Strasbourg
136 Belfast	150 Edinburgh	163 København	179 Nantes	201 Stuttgart
137 Berlin	151 Essen	164 Lausanne	180 Napoli	203 Torino
138 Bern	151 Firenze	165 Liège	181 Nice	204 Toulouse
139 Birmingham	152 Frankfurt am Main	166 Lille	182 Nürnberg	206 Valencia
140 Bologna	153 Genève	167 Lisboa	183 Oslo	207 Venezia
140 Bonn	154 Genova	170 Liverpool	184 Palermo	209 Warszawa
141 Bordeaux	154 Gent	168 London	186 Paris	210 Wien
142 Bratislava	155 Glasgow	170 Luxembourg	190 Porto	211 Zürich
142 Bremen	156 Göteborg	171 Lyon	191 Praha	
143 Brugge	157 Den Haag	172 Madrid	193 Roma	

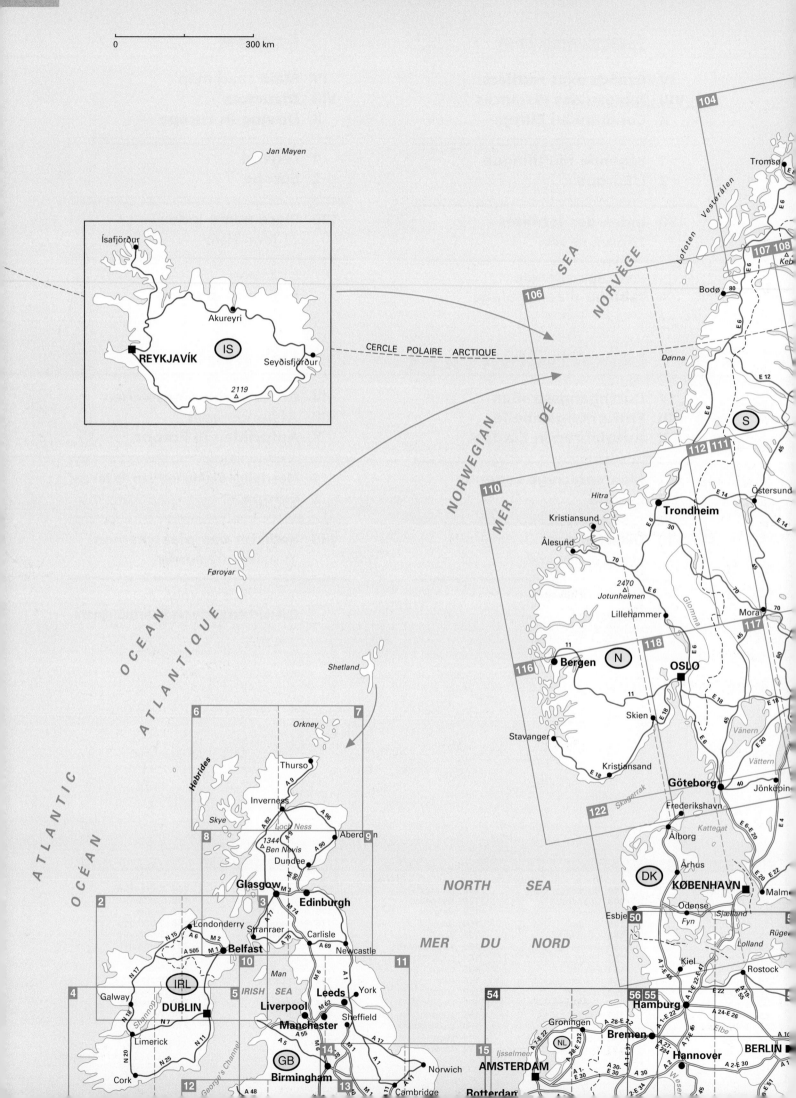

0   300 km

Jan Mayen

Ísafjörður

Akureyri

IS

REYKJAVÍK

Seyðisfjörður

2119

CERCLE POLAIRE ARCTIQUE

O C E A N

A T L A N T I Q U E

Føroyar

A T L A N T I C

O C É A N

Shetland

Hebrides

Orkney

Thurso

Inverness

Skye

Loch Ness

1344
Ben Nevis

Aberdeen

Dundee

Glasgow

Edinburgh

Londonderry

Stranraer

Carlisle

Belfast

Newcastle

Man

IRL

Galway

DUBLIN

Leeds

York

Liverpool

Sheffield

Manchester

Limerick

GB

Birmingham

Norwich

Cork

Cambridge

IRISH SEA

George's Channel

NORTH   SEA

MER   DU   NORD

SEA

NORVÈGE

DE

NORWEGIAN

MER

Tromsø

Lofoten

Vesterålen

Bodø

Keb

Dønna

Hitra

Östersund

Kristiansund

Trondheim

Ålesund

2470
Jotunheimen

Lillehammer

Mora

Bergen

N

OSLO

Skien

Stavanger

Vänern

Kristiansand

Vättern

Göteborg

Jönköping

Frederikshavn

Kattegat

Ålborg

Skagerrak

Århus

DK

KØBENHAVN

Odense

Sjælland

Esbjerg

Fyn

Malmö

Rügen

Lolland

Kiel

Rostock

Hamburg

Groningen

Bremen

NL

Hannover

BERLIN

AMSTERDAM

Ijsselmeer

Elbe

Weser

Rotterdam

S

Keb

104

106

107 108

112 111

110

118

116

117

122

50

54

56 55

15

2

3

4

5

6

7

8

9

10

11

12

13

14

1:1 000 000	Ⓐ	Österreich	1:3 000 000	BY	Belarus'	1:1 000 000	E	España	1:700 000	GR	Elláda
1:700 000	AL	Shqipëria	1:1 000 000	CH	Schweiz, Suisse, Svizzera	1:3 000 000	EST	Eesti	1:3 000 000	H	Magyarország
1:1 000 000	AND	Andorra	1:3 000 000	CZ	Česká Republika	1:1 000 000	F	France	1:1 000 000	HR	Hrvatska
1:1 000 000	B	Belgique, België				1:1 500 000	FIN	Suomi, Finland	1:1 000 000	I	Italia
1:3 000 000	BG	Bǎlgarija	1:1 000 000	D	Deutschland	1:1 000 000	FL	Liechtenstein	1:1 000 000	IRL	Ireland
1:1 000 000	BIH	Bosna i Hercegovina	1:1 500 000	DK	Danmark	1:1 000 000	GB	Great Britain	1:2 400 000	IS	Ísland

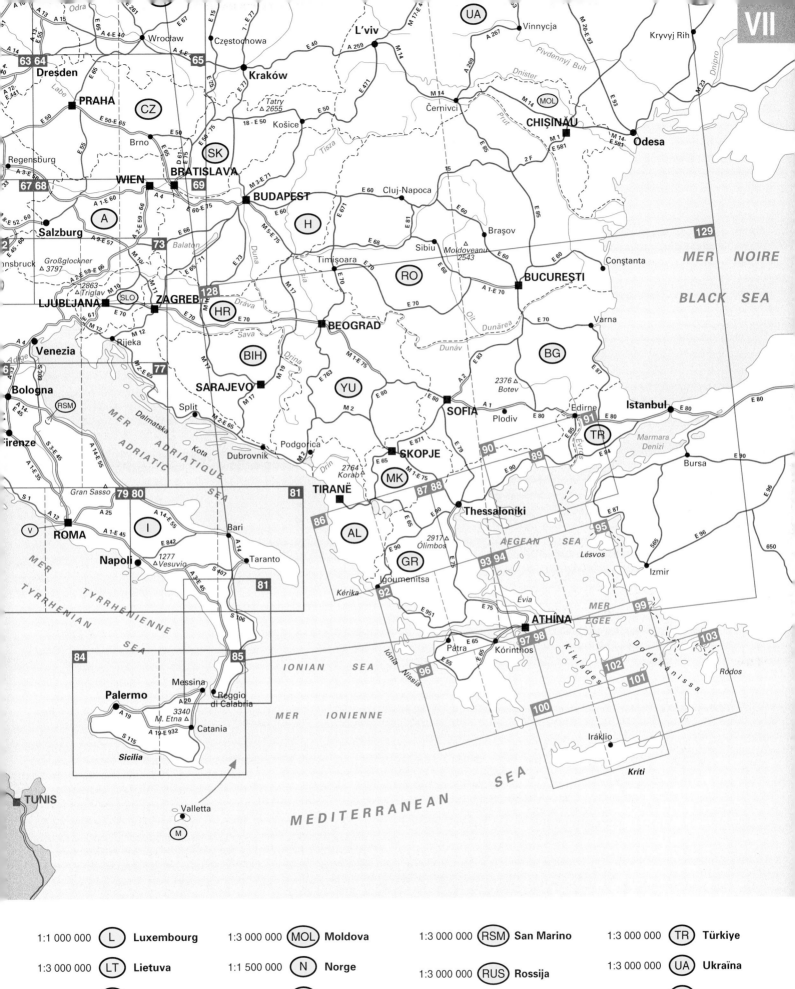

1:1 000 000	L	Luxembourg	1:3 000 000	MOL	Moldova	
1:3 000 000	LT	Lietuva	1:1 500 000	N	Norge	
1:3 000 000	LV	Latvija	1:1 000 000	NL	Nederland	
1:1 000 000	M	Malta	1:1 000 000	P	Portugal	
1:1 000 000	MC	Monaco	1:3 000 000	PL	Polska	
1:1 000 000	MK	Makedonija	1:3 000 000	RO	România	

1:3 000 000	RSM	San Marino
1:3 000 000	RUS	Rossija
1:1 000 000	S	Sverige
1:1 000 000	SK	Slovenská Republika
1:1 000 000	SLO	Slovenija

1:3 000 000	TR	Türkiye
1:3 000 000	UA	Ukraïna
1:140 000	V	Vaticano
1:1 000 000	YU	Jugoslavija

	Amsterdam	Athína	Barcelona	Bari	Basel	Belfast	Beograd	Bergen	Berlin	Bilbao	Birmingham	Bordeaux	Brest	Bruxelles/Brussel	Bucuresti	Budapest	Clermont-Ferrand	Dublin	Dubrovnik	Edinburgh	Firenze	Frankfurt am Main	Genève	Göteborg	Hamburg	Hannover	Helsinki	Istanbul	Kyïv	København	Köln	Lille	Lisboa	Liverpool
Athína	2836																																	
Barcelona	1564	3090																																
Bari	1924	2621	1745																															
Basel	699	2466	1019	1226																														
Belfast	1172	3874	2143	2709	1484																													
Beograd	1718	1118	1972	1503	1348	2756																												
Bergen	1506	4017	2816	3019	1863	336	2899																											
Berlin	668	2584	1853	1808	866	1744	1466	1320																										
Bilbao	1425	3422	613	2092	1201	1726	2304	2861	1977																									
Birmingham	681	3316	1651	2217	992	500	2198	352	1253	1198																								
Bordeaux	1084	3240	564	1893	859	963	2122	2520	1636	337	857																							
Brest	1002	3501	1179	2282	1065	381	2383	754	1575	959	397	618																						
Bruxelles/Brussel	209	2792	1360	1762	537	1010	1674	1623	776	1236	519	895	833																					
Bucuresti	2221	1238	2611	2142	1987	3259	639	3200	1711	2943	2701	2761	2886	2177																				
Budapest	1411	1510	1911	1431	1083	2381	392	2181	853	2258	1889	2065	2079	1366	828																			
Clermont-Ferrand	926	2752	628	1493	505	1524	1634	2270	1316	703	1032	362	805	736	2273	1601																		
Dublin	951	3586	1922	2488	1263	169	2468	463	1523	1136	279	795	212	789	2971	2160	1303																	
Dubrovnik	2024	1265	2049	1580	1425	2892	525	3204	1771	2381	2333	2199	2480	1970	1164	787	1711	2604																
Edinburgh	1094	3823	2064	2631	1406	220	2705	191	1666	1946	477	1605	865	932	3208	2302	1446	389	2840															
Firenze	1342	2115	1083	662	645	2127	997	2437	1226	1430	1636	1231	1688	1181	1636	930	891	1906	1074	2049														
Frankfurt am Main	432	2396	1319	1555	332	1402	1278	1536	539	1491	910	1151	1164	387	1781	973	781	1181	1583	1324	974													
Genève	918	2446	761	1197	258	1558	1328	2118	1075	1108	1066	680	1059	714	1967	1282	319	1337	1405	1480	602	587												
Göteborg	1040	3205	2350	2422	1385	585	2087	792	645	2396	291	2055	1992	1157	2388	1507	1802	580	2392	484	1840	1057	1640											
Hamburg	467	2780	1778	1971	815	1574	1662	1049	284	1823	1082	1483	1420	585	2026	1145	1230	1353	1967	1496	1390	488	1070	580										
Hannover	385	2637	1642	1825	669	1461	1519	1203	288	1695	970	1354	1292	493	2022	1034	1094	1240	1824	1383	1244	342	924	725	156									
Helsinki	1204	2540	2388	2346	1397	2441	1422	1186	505	2525	1883	2182	2199	1316	1858	1030	1846	2153	1893	2390	1766	1101	1656	662	776	823								
Istanbul	2665	1171	2919	2450	2295	3703	947	3846	2413	3251	3145	3069	3330	2621	692	1339	2581	3415	1326	3652	1944	2225	2275	3034	2609	2466	2369							
Kyïv	2017	2311	3114	2644	2187	3254	1336	2844	1383	3338	2696	2995	3012	2129	1073	1162	2636	2966	1861	3203	2138	1914	2339	2032	1670	1636	1146	489						
København	781	2938	2091	2162	1126	599	1820	1027	386	2137	1395	1796	1733	898	2121	1248	1543	1666	2125	498	1581	798	1381	238	321	466	795	2767	1765					
Köln	264	2579	1353	1716	493	1226	1461	1464	573	1413	734	1073	1010	212	1964	1155	805	1005	1766	1148	1135	177	706	997	425	290	1110	2408	1923	738				
Lille	281	2910	1267	1858	633	920	1792	1721	853	1149	428	808	723	119	2295	1477	649	699	2088	842	1276	498	682	1255	683	570	1384	2739	2197	996	323			
Lisboa	2284	4320	1240	2966	2240	2163	3202	3720	2836	899	2057	1203	1818	2094	3841	3132	1566	1994	3279	2803	2304	2349	1982	3253	2681	2553	3423	4149	4236	2994	2271	2006		
Liverpool	837	3504	1807	2374	1149	381	2386	298	1409	1366	165	1025	553	675	2889	2045	1189	167	2522	358	1792	1067	1222	447	1239	1126	2071	3333	2884	1552	891	585	2224	
London	477	3252	1447	2013	788	686	2134	477	1049	1328	194	987	428	315	2637	1685	828	465	2270	633	1432	706	862	141	878	766	1819	3081	2632	1191	530	224	2186	351
Luxembourg	381	2637	1153	1555	330	1226	1519	1655	756	1271	735	930	944	215	1993	1186	606	1006	1758	1148	975	236	508	1197	624	490	1302	2466	2115	937	200	310	2129	891
Lyon	932	2559	634	1301	409	1561	1441	2184	1220	982	1069	532	1016	728	2080	1433	171	1340	1518	1483	699	687	152	1718	1146	1010	1758	2388	2548	1459	721	685	1856	1226
Madrid	1776	3760	617	2343	1617	1656	2642	3212	2328	393	1550	696	1310	1586	3281	2509	1058	1487	2719	2296	1681	1841	1359	2746	2174	2045	2913	3589	3726	2487	1764	1498	621	1718
Málaga	2304	4086	962	2699	1973	2183	2968	3740	2807	920	2077	1223	1838	2114	3607	2865	1581	2015	3045	2823	2037	2273	1715	3274	2701	2573	3384	3915	4110	3014	2291	2026	619	2246
Marseille	1243	2621	504	1274	698	1873	1503	2496	1532	851	1381	651	1266	1039	2142	1439	477	1652	1580	1794	612	999	440	2029	1457	1321	2069	2450	2645	1770	1032	997	1725	1537
Milano	1043	2128	982	877	346	1828	1010	2162	1033	1329	1336	1130	1404	882	1649	945	638	1607	1087	1750	296	675	318	1684	1114	968	1575	1957	2151	1424	836	976	2203	1493
Moskva	2463	3169	3630	3306	2639	3700	2194	2313	1829	3784	3142	3441	3458	2575	1931	1918	3088	3412	2705	3649	2800	2360	2898	1789	2116	2082	1127	1347	858	2211	2369	2643	4682	3330
München	834	1621	1347	1218	393	1771	663	1833	586	1694	1280	1252	1422	730	860	657	911	1550	567	1693	636	397	592	1199	786	640	490	2380	638	940	580	824	2568	1436
Nantes	887	874	881	1994	854	639	710	859	1439	661	533	320	300	697	372	1865	461	470	1482	1012	1392	952	741	1856	1284	1156	1121	1585	1424	1597	874	609	1520	701
Napoli	1808	2443	1549	253	1111	2594	1102	2904	1693	1897	2102	1697	2154	1647	1603	1397	1357	2373	1675	2515	466	1440	1068	2306	1856	1710	1560	2583	1745	2047	1601	1742	2771	2258
Nice	1402	1877	662	1083	660	2031	454	2478	1349	1009	1539	810	1424	1198	931	1249	635	1810	1329	1953	421	989	461	2000	1431	1285	1135	1695	1401	1741	1150	1155	1883	1696
Nürnberg	667	1486	1426	1388	439	1637	719	1666	438	1673	1145	1332	1346	623	782	748	888	1416	419	1559	807	230	648	1051	618	472	323	2460	490	792	412	733	2531	1302
Oslo	1154	993	2464	2738	1511	767	1732	473	961	2510	607	2169	2107	1271	1509	1823	1916	938	1058	666	2156	1184	1766	320	697	851	1012	3434	890	554	1112	1369	3368	773
Palermo	1815	2449	1556	666	1118	2601	1109	2911	1700	1904	2109	1704	2161	1654	1610	1404	1364	2380	1682	2522	473	1447	1075	2313	1863	1717	1567	2590	1752	2054	1608	1749	2778	2265
Paris	500	946	1041	1727	501	1098	510	1936	1052	922	606	582	595	310	2297	1490	422	877	1097	1019	1132	576	503	1469	897	769	739	1847	1037	1210	487	222	1781	762
Porto	2077	2189	1133	2744	1853	1956	1693	3513	2629	692	1850	996	1611	1887	1561	2910	1359	1788	2671	2596	2082	2142	1760	3047	2474	2346	2316	848	2614	2787	2064	1799	305	2019
Praha	855	1753	1696	1601	709	1905	988	1662	339	1942	1413	1601	1615	890	1051	514	1157	1684	257	1827	1020	497	918	987	626	515	432	2729	441	728	680	1001	2800	1570
Roma	1609	2244	1350	413	912	2395	903	2705	1494	1698	1903	1498	1955	1448	1404	1198	1158	2174	1476	2316	267	1241	869	2107	1657	1511	1361	2384	1546	1848	1402	1543	2572	2060
Rovaniemi	2483	4683	3844	3910	2853	3778	3565	2824	2129	3862	3220	3519	3536	2635	3866	3038	3302	3490	3870	3727	3330	2530	3112	1528	2050	2193	837	4512	2557	1745	3288	2721	4760	3408
St. Peterburg	1637	2973	2821	2779	1830	2874	1855	1619	938	2958	2316	2615	2632	1749	2625	1463	2279	2588	2326	2823	2199	1534	2089	1095	1209	1256	433	2041	1552	1228	1543	1817	3856	2504
Salzburg	977	1777	1509	1171	532	1924	802	1977	729	1857	1432	1391	1575	882	1015	550	1050	1703	632	1846	629	540	731	1343	929	783	633	2543	781	1083	723	977	2731	1589
Sevilla	2306	2418	1009	2746	2020	2185	1696	3742	2854	922	2079	1225	1839	2116	1790	2911	1628	2016	2838	2825	2084	2320	1762	3275	2703	2575	2508	206	2843	3016	2293	2028	410	2248
Sofia	2104	818	2358	1889	1734	3142	386	3285	1852	2590	2584	2508	2769	2060	420	778	2020	2854	765	3091	1383	1664	1714	2473	2048	1905	1808	561	1493	2206	1847	2178	3588	2772
Stockholm	1394	1126	2705	2776	1740	1209	2058	1002	1000	2750	772	2410	2347	1512	1848	1861	2157	1061	1086	1108	2195	1412	1994	486	935	1080	1241	3675	929	593	1352	1610	3609	929
Strasbourg	605	1277	1119	1370	147	1428	473	1750	753	1406	936	1065	1079	426	516	1012	580	1207	734	1350	788	219	402	1271	702	556	406	2152	763	1012	359	521	2340	1093
Stuttgart	604	1409	1248	1361	227	1559	518	1706	632	1537	1068	1196	1210	518	647	874	710	1338	613	1481	780	191	447	1228	659	513	363	2281	684	969	352	612	2469	1224
Thessaloníki	2350	511	2604	2135	1980	3388	632	3531	2098	2936	2830	2754	3015	2306	727	1024	2266	3100	779	3337	1629	1910	1960	2719	2294	2151	2054	660	1800	2452	2093	2424	3834	3018
Torino	1103	1656	868	995	406	1805	250	2265	1131	1215	1313	863	1326	942	773	1076	502	1584	1109	1727	393	735	247	1787	1218	1072	922	1901	1183	1528	896	929	2089	1470
Toulouse	1202	1645	321	1647	921	1800	597	2638	1754	451	1308	247	861	1012	685	1812	372	1038	1740	1722	984	1221	663	2172	1599	1471	1408	1270	1765	1913	1189	924	1323	1465
Tromsø	3041	5241	4402	4468	3411	4336	4123	1893	2687	4420	3778	4077	4094	3193	4424	3596	3860	4048	4428	4285	3888	3088	3670	2570	2608	2751	1367	5070	3087	2303	3026	3279	5316	3966
Trondheim	1865	4065	3226	3292	2235	3160	2947	717	1511	3244	2602	2901	2918	2017	3238	2420	2684	2872	3252	3109	2712	1912	2494	1394	1432	1575	949	3894	2892	1127	1850	2103	4142	2790
Valencia	1899	2335	357	2093	1365	2487	1043	3164	2203	602	1995	796	1410	1711	1376	2257	973	2266	2185	2411	1430	1670	1107	2700	2124	1988	1857	688	2210	2437	1699	1612	973	2153
Venezia	1241	1928	1235	754	598	2081	643	2274	1063	1582	1589	1383	1665	1134	1112	693	899	1860	1043	2003	255	828	579	1676	1226	1080	930	2268	1115	1417	989	1229	2456	1746
Warszawa	1224	2149	2335	2001	1348	2300	1627	1910	591	2533	1808	2193	2130	1332	1631	671	1797	2079	605	2221	1500	1062	1557	951	874	843	948	3369	689	976	1129	1408	3392	1964
Wien	1151	1970	1792	1312	824	2122	1094	1945	622	2139	1630	1806	1819	1107	1256	247	1342	1901	540	2043	811	714	1023	1270	909	798	807	2825	724	1011	897	1217	3013	1786
Zagreb	1348	2166	1594	1115	888	2341	1000	2347	999	1942	1849	1742	1991	1304	1432	355	1258	2120	917	2262	614	911	939	1692	1299	1153	1004	2627	1131	1433	1093	1393	2815	2005
Zürich	784	1418	1046	1162	86	1569	356	1908	833	1393	1077	945	1151	622	597	988	604	1348	815	1491	581	393	285	1429	860	714	564	2079	885	1170	554	717	2267	1234

Distances   Entfernungen   Afstandstabel

Les distances sont comptées à partir du centre-ville et par la route la plus pratique, c'est-à-dire celle qui offre les meilleures conditions de roulage, mais qui n'est pas nécessairement la plus courte.

Distance are shown in kilometres and are calculated from town/city centres along the most practicable roads, although not necessarily taking the shortest route.

Die Entfernungen gelten ab Stadmitte unter Berücksichtigung der günstigsten, jedoch nicht immer kürzesten Strecke.

De afstanden zijn in km berekend van centrum tot centrum langs de geschicktste, dus niet noodzakelijkerwijze de kortste route.

Luxembourg - Warszawa 1289 km

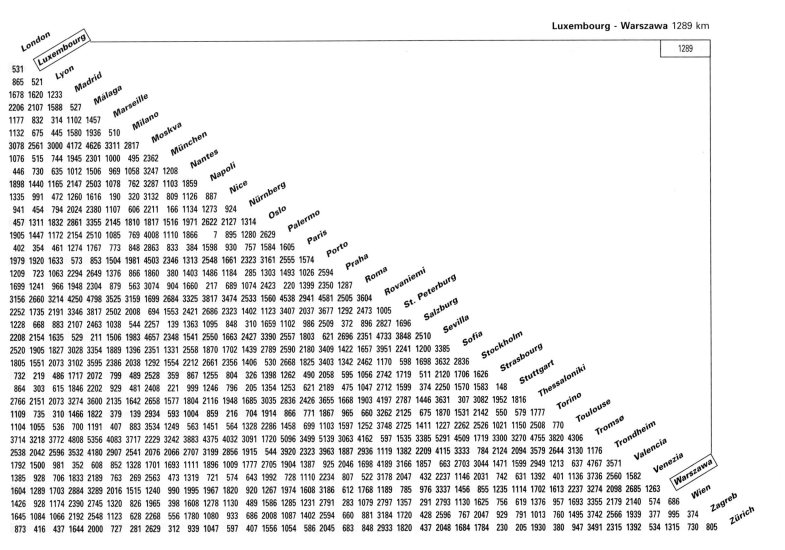

Conduire en Europe

Les tableaux d'information suivants indiquent les principaux règlements routiers communiqués au moment de la rédaction de cet atlas (01.07.97) ; la signification des symboles est indiquée ci-dessous, ainsi que quelques notes supplémentaires.

FIA **AIT** Organisations routières nationales :

Ces initiales désignent un membre des associations internationales de tourisme – Fédération Internationale de l'Automobile et Alliance Internationale de Tourisme.

Limitations de vitesse en kilomètres/heure s'appliquant aux :

autoroutes,

routes à une seule chaussée,

routes à chaussées séparées,

agglomérations urbaines

Péage sur les autoroutes ou toute autre partie du réseau routier

Jeu d'ampoules de rechange

Taux maximum d'alcool toléré dans le sang. On ne doit pas considérer ceci comme acceptable; il n'est JAMAIS raisonnable de boire et de conduire.

Age minimum du conducteur

Port de la ceinture de sécurité à l'avant

Port de la ceinture de sécurité à l'avant et à l'arrière

Âge minimum des enfants admis à l'avant.

Port du casque pour les motocyclistes

Triangle de présignalisation

Port du casque pour les motocyclistes et les passagers

Trousse de premiers secours

Allumage des codes jour et nuit

Extincteur

Pneus cloutés

Documents nécessaires obligatoires à tous les pays : certificat d'immatriculation du véhicule ou certificat de location, assurance responsabilité civile, plaque d'identification nationale.

Il est vivement conseillé de se renseigner auprès de l'Automobile Club.

Driving in Europe

The information panels which follow give the principal motoring regulations in force when this atlas was prepared for press (01/07/97). An explanation of the symbols is given below, together with some additional notes.

FIA **AIT** National motoring organisations:

These symbols indicate membership of the international touring associations Fédération Internationale de L'Automobile and Alliance Internationale de Tourisme.

Speed restrictions in kilometres per hour applying to:

motorways,

single carriageways,

dual carriageways,

urban areas

Whether tolls are payable on motorways and/or other parts of the road network.

Whether a spare bulb set must be carried

Maximum permitted level of alcohol in the bloodstream. This should not be taken as an acceptable level - it is NEVER sensible to drink and drive.

Minimum age for drivers

Whether seatbelts must be worn by the driver and front seat passenger

Whether seatbelts are compulsory for the driver and all passengers in both front and back seats

Minimum age for children to sit in the front passenger seat.

Whether crash helmets are compulsory for motorcyclists

Whether a warning triangle must be carried

Whether crash helmets are compulsory for both motorcyclists and their passengers

Whether a first aid kit must be carried

Whether headlights must be on at all times

Whether a fire extinguisher must be carried

Whether studded tyres are required

Documents required for all countries: vehicle registration document or vehicle on hire certificate, third party insurance cover, national vehicle identification plate.

You are strongly advised to contact the national Automobile Club for full details of local regulations.

Autofahren in Europa

Die nachfolgenden Tabellen geben Auskunft über die wichtigsten Verkehrsbestimmungen in den einzelnen Ländern dieses Atlasses; (Stand 01.07.97) die Erklärung der Symbole sowie einige ergänzende Anmerkungen finden Sie im Anschluß an diesen Text.

FIA **AIT** Nationale Automobilclubs :

Diese Abkürzungen verweisen auf die Mitgliedschaft bei den internationalen Touring-Organisationen, Fédération Internationale de l'Automobile und Alliance Internationale de Tourisme.

Geschwindigkeitsbegrenzungen in km/h bezogen auf :

Autobahnen,

Straßen mit einer Fahrbahn,

Schnellstraßen mit getrennten Fahrbahnen,

geschlossene Ortschaften

Autobahn-, Straßen- oder Brückenbenutzungsgebühren

Mitführen eines Satzes von Glühbirnen als Reserve

Promillegrenze : Es sei darauf hingewiesen, daß auch die kleinste Menge Alkohol am Steuer das Fahrvermögen beeinträchtigt.

Mindestalter für Kfz-Führer

Anschnallpflicht vorne

Mindestalter, ab welchem Kinder vorne sitzen dürfen.

Anschnallpflicht vorne und hinten

Mitführen eines Warndreiecks

Helmpflicht für Motorradfahrer

Mitführen eines Verbandkastens

Helmpflicht für Motorradfahrer und Beifahrer

Mitführen eines Feuerlöschers

Abblendlicht vorgeschrieben (Tag und Nacht)

Spikereifen

Notwendige und vorgeschriebene Dokumente in allen Staaten : Fahrzeugschein oder Mietwagenbescheinigun, Internationale grüne Versicherungskarte, Nationalitätskennzeichen.

Es empfiehlt sich, genauere Informationen bei den jeweiligen Automobilclubs einzuholen.

Autorijden in Europa

In de tabellen hierna staan de voornaamste verkeersregels medegedeeld bij het opstellen van deze Atlas (01-07-97); de betekenis van de symbolen is hieronder beschreven met enkele toelichtingen.

FIA **AIT** Nationale automobielclubs :

Deze initialen geven aan dat het om een lid van een internationale toeristische federatie gaat, nl. de Fédération Internationale de l'Automobile en de Alliance Internationale de Tourisme.

Snelheidsbeperkingen in km/uur op :

autosnelwegen,

wegen met één rijbaan,

wegen met gescheiden rijbanen,

binnen de bebouwde kom

Tol op de autosnelwegen of op een ander gedeelte van het wegennet

Reservelampen verplicht

Maximum toegestaan alcoholgehalte in het bloed. Dit dient niet beschouwd te worden als een aanvaardbaar gehalte; het is NOOIT verstandig om te rijden na gebruik van alcohol.

Minimumleeftijd bestuurder

Autogordel verplicht voor bestuurder en passagier voorin

Minimumleeftijd voor kinderen voorin het voertuig.

Autogordel, verplicht voor- en achterin

Gevarendriehoek verplicht

Valhelm verplicht voor motorrijders

EHBO-pakket verplicht

Valhelm verplicht voor motorrijders en passagiers

Brandblusapparaat

Dimlichten verplicht zowel 's nachts als overdag

Spijkerbanden

Vereiste documenten in alle landen : kentekenbewijs van het voertuig of huurcertificaat, verzekering burgerlijke aansprakelijkheid, plaat land van herkomst.

Het verdient aanbeveling informatie in te winnen bij de automobielclub.

	Motorway	Dual carriageway	Road	Town	Alcohol ‰	Belt (f)	Belt (r)	Child age	Triangle	First-aid	Extinguisher	Bulbs	Min. age	◐	◑	Lights	◀	Studded tyres
A ÖSTERREICH	90 110-130		100	50	0,08	●		12	●	●			18			●	●	
AL SHQIPËRIA ✳																		
AND ANDORRA	90	90	90	40	0,08			10	○	○		●	18			●		
B BELGIQUE, BELGIË	120	90-120	75-90	40-50	0,05		●	12	●	●	●		18	●		●		
BG BĂLQARIJA	120	80	80	60	0,00		●	12	●	●	●		18			●		
BIH BOSNA I HERCEGOVINA ✳																		
BY BELARUS' ✳																		
CH SCHWEIZ, SUISSE, SVIZZERA	120	100	80	50	0,08	●				●			18			●	●	
CZ ČESKÁ REPUBLIKA	110	110	90	60	0,00	●		12	●	●		●	18			●	●	
D DEUTSCHLAND	130	130	80	50	0,08	●		12	●	●			18			●	●	
DK DANMARK	110	80	80	50	0,08	●		✳	●	○	○		18			●	●	1/10-30/4
E ESPAÑA	120	120	90-100	50	0,08	●		12	●			●	18	●		●		
EST EESTI		90	90	50	0,00	●		12	●	●		○	18			●		
F FRANCE	110-130	110	90	50	0,05	●		10	○	○		○	18			●	●	
FIN SUOMI, FINLAND	100-120		80-100	50	0,05	●			●	○		○	18			●		
GB GREAT BRITAIN	112	112	96	48	0,08	●			○				17					
GR ELLÁDA	120	110	90	50	0,05		●	10	●	●	●		18	●		●		
H MAGYARORSZÁG	120	100	80	50	0,00	●		12	●	●		●	21			●		●
HR HRVATSKA		130	90-100	60	0,05	●		12	●	●		●	18			●		●
I ITALIA	130	110	90	50	0,08	●		12	●	○		●	18			●	●	
IRL IRELAND	112	96	64-80	48	0,08	●		12	○	○		○	17			●	●	1/11-30/4
IS ÍSLAND		80-90	80-90	35-50	0,05	●			●	○	○	○	17			●	●	15/11-30/4
L LUXEMBOURG	120	90	90	50	0,08	●		12	●	○			18			●		
LT LIETUVA		90	90	60	0,00		●	12	●	●	●		18			●		
LV LATVIJA		90	90	60	0,00		●	12					18			●		
MK MAKEDONIJA ✳																		
MOL MOLDOVA ✳																		
N NORGE	80-90	80-90	80-90	50	0,05	●			●	○		○	18-20			●	●	●
NL NEDERLAND	120	100	80	50	0,05	●		12					18			●		
P PORTUGAL	120	90	90	50	0,05	●		12	●	○		○	18	●		●		
PL POLSKA	110	90	90	60	0,02	●		10	●	○	●	○	17			●		●
RO ROMÂNIA	70-90	60-90	60-90	60	0,00	○		12	●	●		○	18			●		
RUS ROSSIJA	110	110	110	60	0,00		●	12	●	●	●	○	18			●		
S SVERIGE	90-110	70-110	70-110	50	0,02	●			●	○	○		18			●		
SK SLOVENSKÁ REPUBLIKA	110	90	90	50	0,00	●		12	●	●		●	18			●		
SLO SLOVENIJA	120	100	80	60	0,05	●		12	●	●	●	●	18	●		●		●
TR TÜRKIYE		90	90	50	0,05	●		12	●				18	●		●		●
UA UKRAÏNA ✳																		
YU JUGOSLAVIJA	120	100	80	60	0,05	●		12	●	●			18			●	●	

● Obligatoire / Compulsory / Vorgeschrieben / Verplicht
○ Recommandé / Recommended / Empfohlen / Aanbevolen
● Interdit / Prohibited / Verboten / Verboden
1/10-3/4 Période d'autorisation / Periode of regulation enforcement / Genehmigungsdauer / Toegelaten periode
✳ Renseignement non communiqué / No information currently available / Keine Auskunft erhalten / Informatie niet meegedeeld

Ⓐ Österreich

Österreichischer Automobil-, Motorrad- und Touring Club (ÖAMTC) ⒶⓉⓉ ⒻⒾⒶ Schubertring 1-3, 1010 Wien
✆ (43) 1 711990 Fax (43) 1 713 18 07
http: //www.oeamtc-co.at/oeamtc

ⒶⓃⒹ Andorra

Automobil Club d'Andorra ⒻⒾⒶ
Babot Camp 13, Andorra la Vella
✆ (376) 8-20-8-90 Fax (376) 82 25 60

Ⓑ Belgique, België

Royal Automobile Club de Belgique (RACB) ⒻⒾⒶ rue d'Arlon 53,
1040 Bruxelles
✆ (32) 2 287 09 11 Fax (32) 2 230 75 84
Touring Club Royal de Belgique (TBC) ⒶⓉⓉ rue de la Loi 44, 1040 Bruxelles
✆ (32) 2 233 22 11 Fax (32) 2 233 22 05
Vlaamse Automobilistenbond (VTB-VAB) Sint-Jakobs-Markt 45,
2000 Antwerpen ✆ (03) 220 34 34

ⒷⒼ Bălgarija

Union des Automobilistes Bulgares (UAB) ⒶⓉⓉ ⒻⒾⒶ
3 Place Positano, Sofia 1090
✆ (359) 2 86 151 Fax (359) 287 63 61

ⒷⒾⒽ Bosna Hercegovina

ACNAIT ✆ 0387 71 664 374

ⒷⓎ Belarus'

Fédération de l'Automobile de Byelorus P.O.B. 50, 22090 Minsk 90
✆ (375) 17 269 56 42 / 269 56 11
Fax (375) 17 227 43 88

ⒸⒽ Schweiz, Suisse, Svizzera

Automobile Club de Suisse (ACS) ⒻⒾⒶ
Wasserwerkgasse 39, 3000 bern 13
✆ (41) 31 328 31 11
Fax (41) 31 311 03 10
Touring Club Suisse (TCS) ⒶⓉⓉ
Chemin de Blandonnet 4
BP 820 1214 Vernier
✆ (41) 22 417 27 27
Fax (41) 22 417 20 20

ⒸⓏ Česká Republika

Ústredni Automotoklub CR (UAMK) ⒶⓉⓉ ⒻⒾⒶ Na rybničku 16, 120 76 Praha 2
✆ (42) 2 24 911 830
Fax (42) 2 24 22 37 11
Autoklub Ceské Republiky (ACR) ⒻⒾⒶ
Opletalova 29, 110 Praha 1
✆ (42) 2 24 21 02 66
Fax (42) 2 26 14 69

Ⓓ Deutschland

Allgemeiner Deutscher Automobil-Club (ADAC) ⒶⓉⓉ ⒻⒾⒶ
Am Westpark 8, 81373 München 70
✆ (49) 89 76760 Fax (49) 89 76762500
http : //www.adac.de
Automobil-Club von Deutschland (AvD) ⒶⓉⓉ Lyonerstraße 16,
60258 Frankfurt-am-Main
✆ (49) 69 66060 Fax (49) 69 66 06 210

ⒹⓀ Danmark

Forenede Danske Motorejere (FDM) ⒶⓉⓉ Firskovvej 32, 2800 Lyngby
✆ (45) 45 27 07 07 Fax (45) 45 27 09 93

Ⓔ España

Real Automóvil Club de España (RACE) ⒶⓉⓉ ⒻⒾⒶ José Abascal 10,
28003 Madrid ✆ (34) 1 447 3200
Fax (34) 1 447 79 48
http : //www.race.es

ⒺⓈⓉ Eesti

Estonian Auto Sport Union (EASU) ⒻⒾⒶ
1-5P Regati ave suite 306, 0019 Tallinn
✆ (372) 2 23 75 33 Fax 23 74 17

Ⓕ France

Automobile Club de France (ACF) ⒻⒾⒶ
6 Place de la Concorde, 75008 Paris
✆ (33) 1 43 12 43 12
Fax (33) 1 43 12 43 43

ⒻⒾⓃ Suomi, Finland

Autoliitto (Automobile and Touring Club of Finland) (ATCF) ⒶⓉⓉ ⒻⒾⒶ
Hämeentie 105, 00550 Helsinki 10
✆ (358) 0 774 761 / (358) 0 774 764 00
Fax (358) 0 774 76 444
http : //www.autoliitto.fi

ⒻⓁ Liechtenstein

Automobilclub des Fürstentums Liechtenstein (ACFL) ⒻⒾⒶ
Pflugstrasse 20, 9490 Vaduz
✆ (41) 75 232 67 67
Fax (41) 75 233 30 50

ⒼⒷ Great Britain

Automobile Association (AA) ⒶⓉⓉ ⒻⒾⒶ
Fanum House, Basingstoke,
Hampshire RG21 2EA
✆ (44) 1256 20123
Fax (44) 1256 493389
http://www.theaa.co.uk
Royal Automobile Club (RAC) ⒶⓉⓉ ⒻⒾⒶ
RAC House, Bartlett Street,
South Croydon CR2 6XW
✆ (44) 181 686 0088
Fax (44) 81 681 0182
http: //www.rac.co.uk

ⒼⓇ Elláda

Automobile et Touring Club de Grèce (ELPA) ⒶⓉⓉ ⒻⒾⒶ 2-4 Messogion
115 27 Athina ✆ (30) 1 748 8800
Fax (30) 1 778 6642
Touring Club Hellénique ⒶⓉⓉ
12 Politehniou, 104 33 Athina
✆ (30) 1 524 0854 Fax (30) 1 778 6642

Ⓗ Magyarország

Magyar Autóklub (MAK) ⒶⓉⓉ ⒻⒾⒶ
Rómer Flóris utca 4/a, 1024 Budapest
✆ (36) 1 212 29 38 Fax (36) 1 212 3890

ⒽⓇ Hrvatska

Hrvatski Auto-Klub (HAK) ⒶⓉⓉ ⒻⒾⒶ
Draskoviceva 25, 41000 Zagreb,
P.O.B. 0218 ✆ (385) 1 454 433
Fax (385) 1 448 630
Centre d'Information Derencinova 20,
41000 Zagreb ✆ (385) 1 415 800
Fax (385) 1 476 688

Ⓘ Italia

Automobile Club d'Italia (ACI) ⒶⓉⓉ ⒻⒾⒶ
Via Marsala 8, 00185 Roma
✆ (39) 6 49981 Fax (39) 6 499 82234
Touring-Club Italiano (TCI) ⒶⓉⓉ
Corso Italia 10, 20122 Milano
✆ (39) 2 85261 Fax (39) 2 8526 347
http://www.tci.iol.it
Federazione Italiana del Campeggio e del Caravanning ⒶⓉⓉ (FICC)
Federcampeggio via Vittorio Emanuele, 11 I 50041 Calenzano
✆ (39) 55 882 391 Fax (39) 55 882 5918

ⒾⓇⓁ Ireland

Automobile Association (AA) ⒶⓉⓉ
23 Rock Hill, Blackrock Co. Dublin
✆ (353) 1 283 355 Fax (353) 1 283 3660
Royal Automobile Club (RAC) ⒶⓉⓉ
34 Dawson Street, Dublin 2
✆ (353) 1 775 141 Fax (353) 1 710 793

ⒾⓈ Ísland

Félag Islenzkra Bifreidaeigenda (FIB), ⒶⓉⓉ ⒻⒾⒶ Borgartun 33, 105 Reykjavik
✆ (354) 5 62 99 99 Fax (354) 5 290 71
http: //www.itn.is/fib

Ⓛ Luxembourg

Automobile Club du Grand Duché de Luxembourg (ACL) ⒶⓉⓉ ⒻⒾⒶ
54 route de Longwy, 8007 Bertrange
✆ (352) 45 00 45 Fax (352) 45 04 55
http : //www.acl.lu

ⓁⓉ Lietuva

Lietuvos Automobilininku Sajunga (LAS) Gynéju 8, 2001 Vilnius
✆ (370) 2 250 556 Fax (370) 2 250 557

ⓁⓋ Latvija

Auto-moto Society of Latvia (LAMB) ⒶⓉⓉ 16b Raunas Str 1039 Riga
✆ (371) 256 62 22 Fax (371) 733 90 58

ⓂⓀ Makedonija

Auto-Moto Sojuz na Makedonija (AMSM)
ul. Ivo Ribar Lola 51
91000 Skopje Macidoine (FYROM)
✆ (389) 91 98 01

ⓂⓄⓁ Moldova

Asociatia de Autotransport International din Moldova (AITA)
Vlad Tepes Str. 3, BP 6964,
277028 Chisinău ✆ (373) 2 735 290
Fax (373) 2 729 527

Ⓝ Norge

Kongelig Norsk Automobiliklub (KNA) ⒻⒾⒶ Drammensveien 20c, 0201 Oslo 2
✆ (47) 22 56 19 00 Fax (47) 22 55 23 54
Norges Automobil-Forbund (NAF) ⒶⓉⓉ
Storgaten 2, 0155 Oslo 1
✆ (47) 22 34 14 00
Fax (47) 22 33 13 72/3

ⓃⓁ Nederland

Koninklijke Nederlandse Automobiel Club (KNAC)
Westvlieturg 118, Leidschendam
✆ (31) 70 399 74 51 Fax (31) 70 390 53 71
Koninklijke Nederlandse Automobiel Club (KNAC) ⒶⓉⓉ
Wassenaarseweg 220,
2596 EC Den Haag
✆ (31) 70 383 16 12 Fax (31) 70 383 19 06
Koninklijke Nederlandse Toeristenbond (ANWB) ⒶⓉⓉ
Wassenaarseweg 220,
2596 EC Den Haag
✆ (31) 70 314 71 47 Fax (31) 70 314 69 69
http: //www.anwb.nl
Nederlandse Toer Fiets Unie (NTFU) ⒻⒾⒶ
Landjuweel 11 3905 PE Veenendaal
✆ (31) 31 852 14 21 Fax (31) 31 855 01 55

Ⓟ Portugal

Automóvel Club de Portugal (ACP), ⒶⓉⓉ
✆ Rua Rosa Araújo 24, 1200 Lisboa
✆ (351) 1 356 3931 Fax (351) 1 574 732
http: //www.acp.pt

⒫ Polska

Polski Zwiazek Motorowy (PZM) ⒶⓉⓉ ⒻⒾⒶ
66 ul. Kazimierzowska,
02-518 Warszawa
✆ (48) 22 49 93 61 Fax (48) 22 48 19 51
http: //www.pzm.com.pl
Polskie Towarzystwo Turystyczno-Krajornawcze (PTTC) ⒶⓉⓉ
11 ul, Senatorska, 00-075 Warszawa
✆ (48) 22 265 735 Fax (48) 22 262 505
Auto Assistance P O Box 470,
17 ul, Sniadeckich, 00-950 Warszawa
✆ (48) 22 25 95 39 / 25 97 34 / 29 03 74
Fax (48) 22 25 97 33

ⓇⓄ România

Automobile-Club Roumain (ACR) ⒶⓉⓉ ⒻⒾⒶ Strada Take Ionescu 27,
70154 Bucuresti 22 ✆ (40) 1 659 39 10
Fax (40) 1 312 84 62

ⓇⓄⓈ Rossija

Intourist ⒶⓉⓉ ⒻⒾⒶ 13 Mokhovaya st.,
103009 Moscow ✆ (7) 095 292 3786
Fax (7) 095 230 2387 / (7) 095 200 0271
Federacia Automobilnozo Sporta (SSSR) BP 395, Moscow D-362
✆ (7) 095 491 8661
Fax telex : (7) 095 411 852 TANT/SU
Russian Automobile Society (RAS)
Leontjevskij per., 23 Moscow 103 009
✆ (7) 095 229 75 40
Fax : (7) 095 229 03 96
http: //www.autoclub.ru/assoc/voa/index.htm

Ⓢ Sverige

Kungl Automobil Klubben (KAK) ⒻⒾⒶ
Södra Balsieholmshamnen 16,
111 48 Stockholm
✆ (46) 8 678 00 51 Fax (46) 8 678 06 68
Motormännens Riksförbund (M) ⒶⓉⓉ
Sveavägen 159, 104 35 Stockholm
✆ (46) 8 690 38 00 Fax (46) 8 690 38 24
Sveriges Motorcyklisters Centralorganisation (SMC) ⒶⓉⓉ
Brudtallsvägen 14, Mora
✆ (46) 250 395 00 Fax (46) 250 395 18
http://www.algonet.sc/~smc
Svenska Turistföreningen (STF) ⒶⓉⓉ
Stureplan 4c, Stockholm
✆ (46) 8 463 21 00 Fax (46) 8 678 19 58
http://www.stfturist.sc

ⓈⓀ Slovenská Republika

Ústřední Automotoklub SR, ⒶⓉⓉ ⒻⒾⒶ
Wolkrova ul. C.4, 85101 Bratislava
✆ (42) 7 85 09 11 Fax (42) 7 85 09 10

ⓈⓁⓄ Slovenija

Auto-Moto Zveza Slovenije (AMZS)
Dunajska 128, 61 113 Ljubljana
✆ (386) 61 168 11 11
Fax (386) 61 34 23 78

ⓉⓇ Türkiye

Türkiye Turing ue Otomobil Kurumu (TTOK) ⒶⓉⓉ ⒻⒾⒶ
Oto Sanayi Sitesi Yani 4,
Levent, Istanbul
✆ (90) 212 282 8140
Fax (90) 212 282 8042

ⓊⒶ Ukraïna

Fédération Automobil d'Ukraine (FAU) 317 Schevtchenko str. Lviv,
Ukraine
✆ (380) 33 93 32 / 75 50 68
Fax (380) 76 15 85 / 34 03 23

ⓎⓊ Jugoslavija

Auto-Moto Saver Jugoslavije (AMSJ) ⒶⓉⓉ ⒻⒾⒶ Ruzveltova 18, 11000 Belgrade
✆ (381) 11 401 699
Fax (381) 11 402 520
http: //solair.eunet.yu/~amsj

Légende

Importance des itinéraires

Autoroute à chaussées séparées
Échangeurs : complet, demi-échangeur, partiel, sans précision
Numéro d'échangeur
Double chaussée de type autoroutier
Route de liaison internationale ou nationale
Route de liaison interrégionale ou de dégagement
Route de liaison régionale ou locale
Autoroute , route en construction
(le cas échéant : date prévisible de mise en service)

Largeur des routes - Obstacles

Chaussées séparées | 2 voies larges
4 voies | 2 voies
3 voies | 1 voie
Forte déclivité (montée dans le sens de la flèche) - péage sur route

Distances (totalisées et partielles)

sur autoroute : section à peage - section libre

GB et IRL 39 en kilomètres, 24 en miles

Numéros des routes

Autoroute, route européenne, autre route — A 6 E 10 N 51
Ville signalée en vert sur les grandes liaisons routières — YORK Wells

Administration - Ressources

Frontiere : Douane principale - Douane avec restriction
Capitale de division administrative — A L P
Localité ayant des ressources hôtelières
Refuge - Camping

Transport

Voie ferrée, train auto - Bac
Liaison maritime : Permanente - saisonnière
Aéroport

Principales curiosités isolées

Édifice religieux | Église en bois debout | Monastère
Château | Ruines | Site antique
Pierre runique | Gravure rupestre | Monument mégalithique
Grotte | Autres curiosités |
| Itinéraire agréable | Parc national

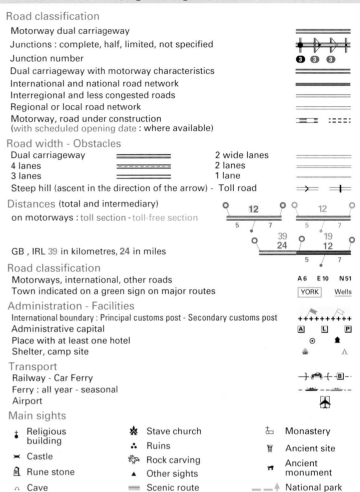

Key to symbols

Road classification

Motorway dual carriageway
Junctions : complete, half, limited, not specified
Junction number
Dual carriageway with motorway characteristics
International and national road network
Interregional and less congested roads
Regional or local road network
Motorway, road under construction
(with scheduled opening date : where available)

Road width - Obstacles

Dual carriageway | 2 wide lanes
4 lanes | 2 lanes
3 lanes | 1 lane
Steep hill (ascent in the direction of the arrow) - Toll road

Distances (total and intermediary)

on motorways : toll section - toll-free section

GB , IRL 39 in kilometres, 24 in miles

Road classification

Motorways, international, other roads — A 6 E 10 N 51
Town indicated on a green sign on major routes — YORK Wells

Administration - Facilities

International boundary : Principal customs post - Secondary customs post
Administrative capital — A L P
Place with at least one hotel
Shelter, camp site

Transport

Railway - Car Ferry
Ferry : all year - seasonal
Airport

Main sights

Religious building | Stave church | Monastery
Castle | Ruins | Ancient site
Rune stone | Rock carving | Ancient monument
Cave | Other sights |
| Scenic route | National park

Zeichenerklärung

Verkehrsbedeutung der Straßen

Autobahn: getrennte Fahrbahnen
Anschlußstellen: Autobahnein- und/oder -ausfahrt - ohne Angabe
Nummern der Anschlußstellen
Schnellstraße mit getrennten Fahrbahnen
Internationale bzw. nationale Hauptverkehrsstraße
Überregionale Verbindungsstraße oder Entlastungsstraße
Regionale oder lokale Verbindungsstraße
Autobahn, Straße im Bau
(ggf. voraussichtliches Datum der Verkehrsfreigabe)

Straßenbreite - Verkehrsbeschränkungen, Hindernisse

Getrennte Fahrbahnen | 2 breite Fahrspuren
4 Fahrspuren | 2 Fahrspuren
3 Fahrspuren | 1 Fahrspur
Starkes Gefälle (Steigung in Pfeilrichtung) - Gebührenpflichtige Straße

Entfernungen (Gesamt- und Teilentfernungen)

auf der Autobahn : gebührenpflichtiger Abschnitt
gebührenfreier Abschnitt

GB , IRL : 39 in Kilometern, 24 in Meilen

Straßennummern

Autobahn, Europastraße, sonstige Straße — A 6 E 10 N 51
Grün beschilderte Ortsdurchfahrt an Fernverkehrsstrecken — YORK Wells

Verwaltung - Unterkunft

Staatsgrenze : internationale Zollstation - Zollstation mit Einschränkungen
Verwaltungshauptstadt — A L P
Ort mit Übernachtungsmöglichkeiten
Schutzhütte, Campingplatz

Transport

Bahnlinie - Autozug, Bahnverladung - Fähre
Schiffsverbindung : ganzjährig - während der saison
Flughafen

Abgelegene, wichtige Sehenswürdigkeiten

Kirchliches Gebäude | Strabkirche | Kloster
Schloß, Burg | Ruine | antike Fundstätte
Runenstein | Felsenmalerei | Steindenkmal
Höhle | Sonstige Sehenswürdigkeit |
| reizvolle Strecke | Nationalpark

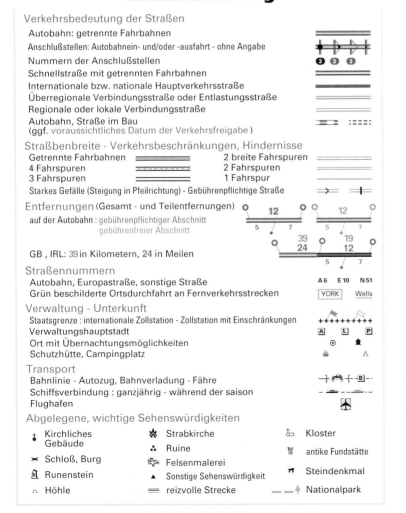

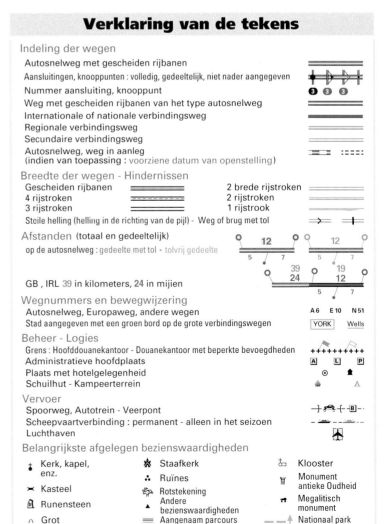

Verklaring van de tekens

Indeling der wegen

Autosnelweg met gescheiden rijbanen
Aansluitingen, knooppunten : volledig, gedeeltelijk, niet nader aangegeven
Nummer aansluiting, knooppunt
Weg met gescheiden rijbanen van het type autosnelweg
Internationale of nationale verbindingsweg
Regionale verbindingsweg
Secundaire verbindingsweg
Autosnelweg, weg in aanleg
(indien van toepassing : voorziene datum van openstelling)

Breedte der wegen - Hindernissen

Gescheiden rijbanen | 2 brede rijstroken
4 rijstroken | 2 rijstroken
3 rijstroken | 1 rijstrook
Steile helling (helling in de richting van de pijl) - Weg of brug met tol

Afstanden (totaal en gedeeltelijk)

op de autosnelweg : gedeelte met tol - tolvrij gedeelte

GB , IRL 39 in kilometers, 24 in mijlen

Wegnummers en bewegwijzering

Autosnelweg, Europaweg, andere wegen — A 6 E 10 N 51
Stad aangegeven met een groen bord op de grote verbindingswegen — YORK Wells

Beheer - Logies

Grens : Hoofddouanekantoor - Douanekantoor met beperkte bevoegdheden
Administratieve hoofdplaats — A L P
Plaats met hotelgelegenheid
Schuilhut - Kampeerterrein

Vervoer

Spoorweg, Autotrein - Veerpont
Scheepvaartverbinding : permanent - alleen in het seizoen
Luchthaven

Belangrijkste afgelegen bezienswaardigheden

Kerk, kapel, enz. | Staafkerk | Klooster
Kasteel | Ruïnes | Monument antieke Oudheid
Runensteen | Rotstekening | Megalitisch monument
Grot | Andere bezienswaardigheden |
| Aangenaam parcours | Nationaal park

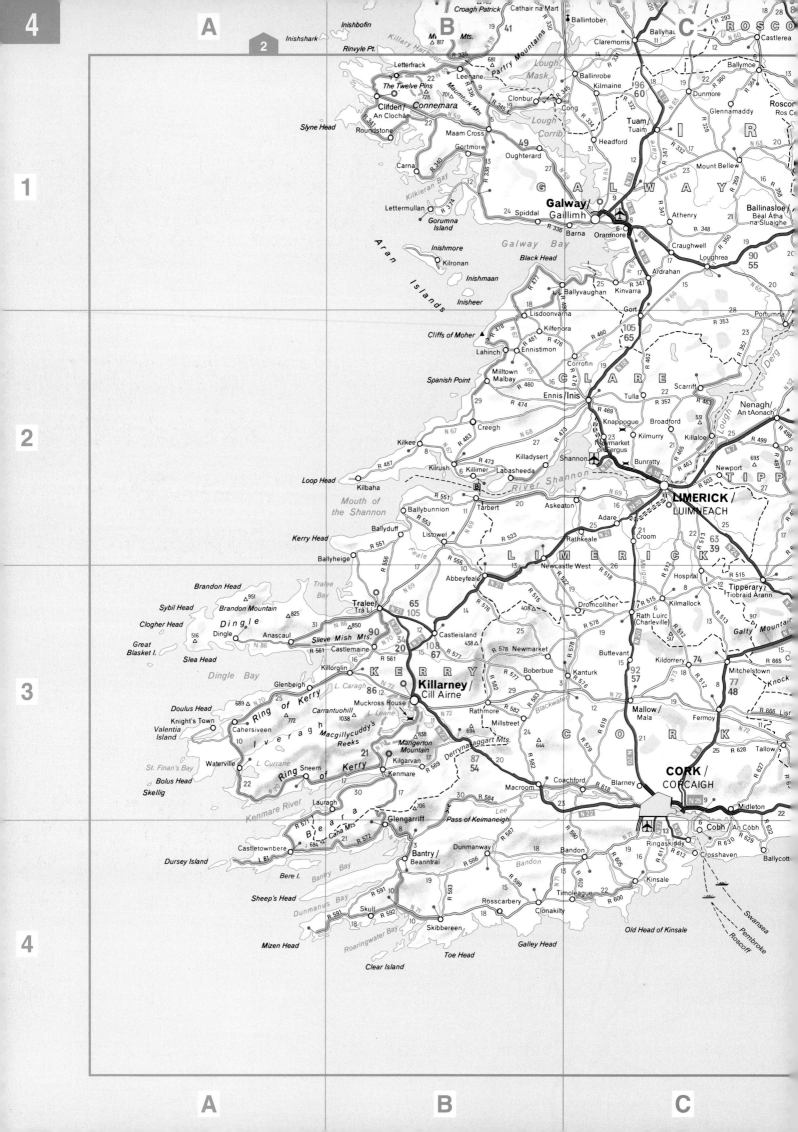

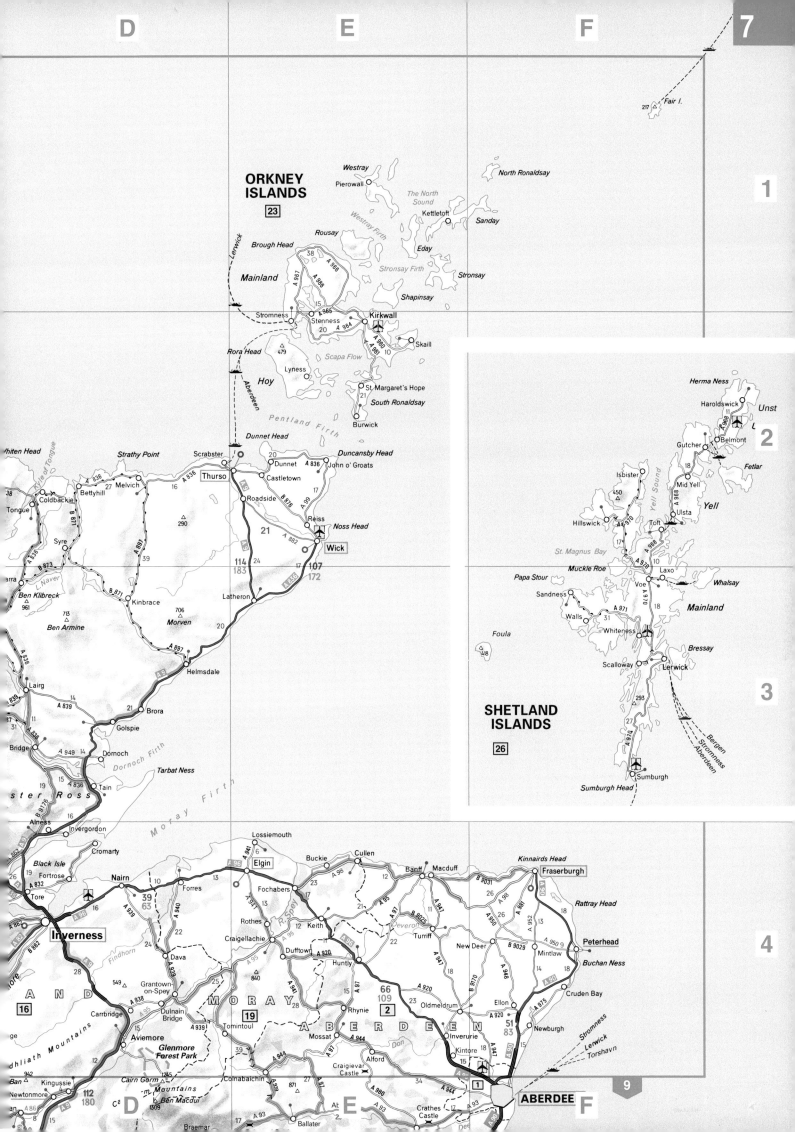

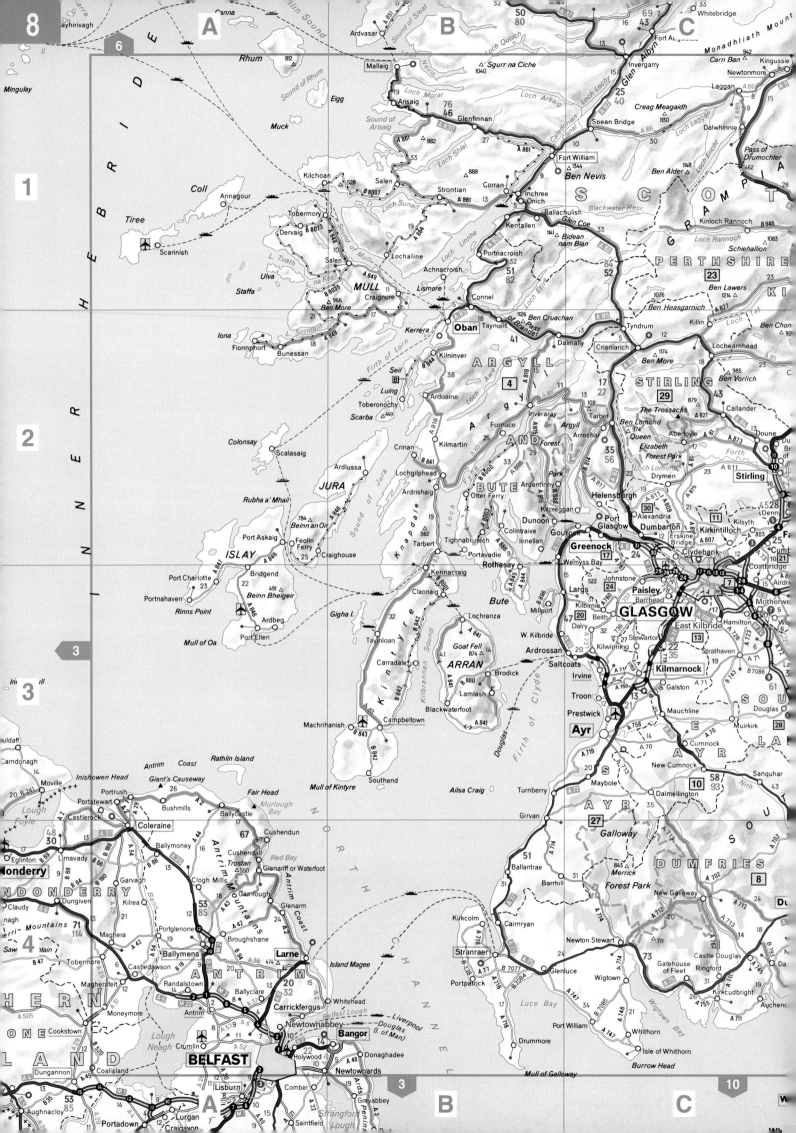

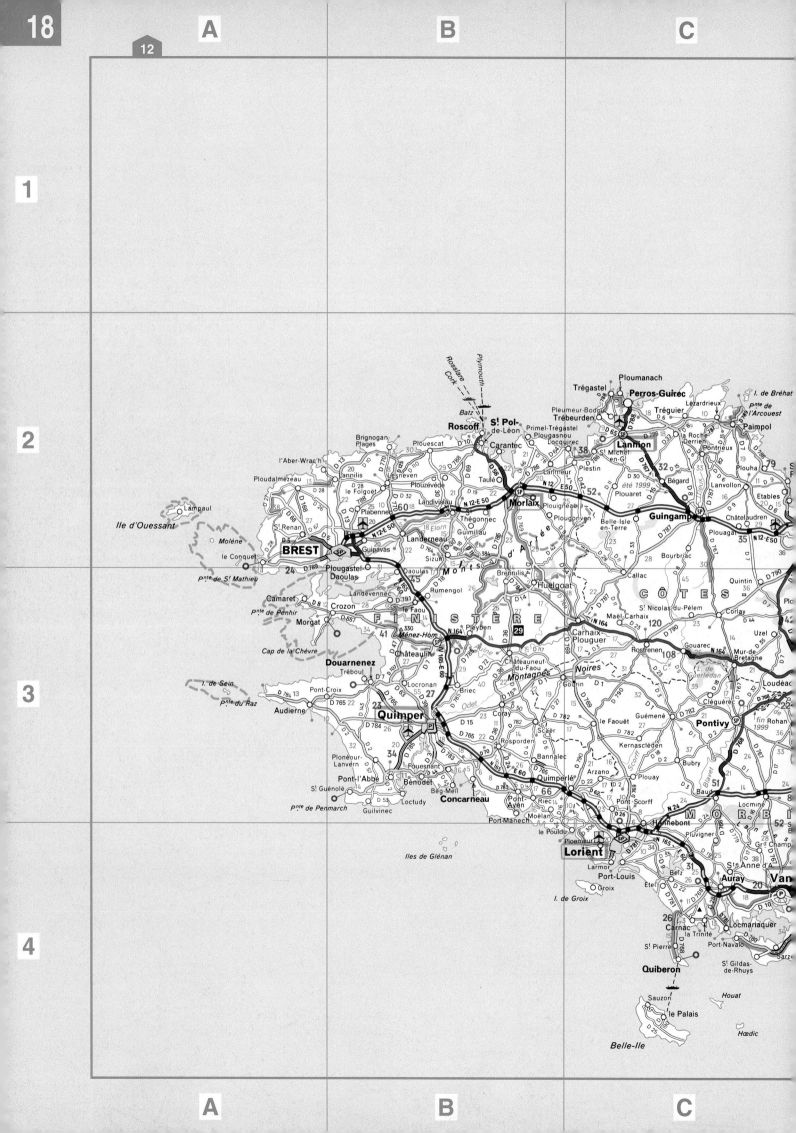

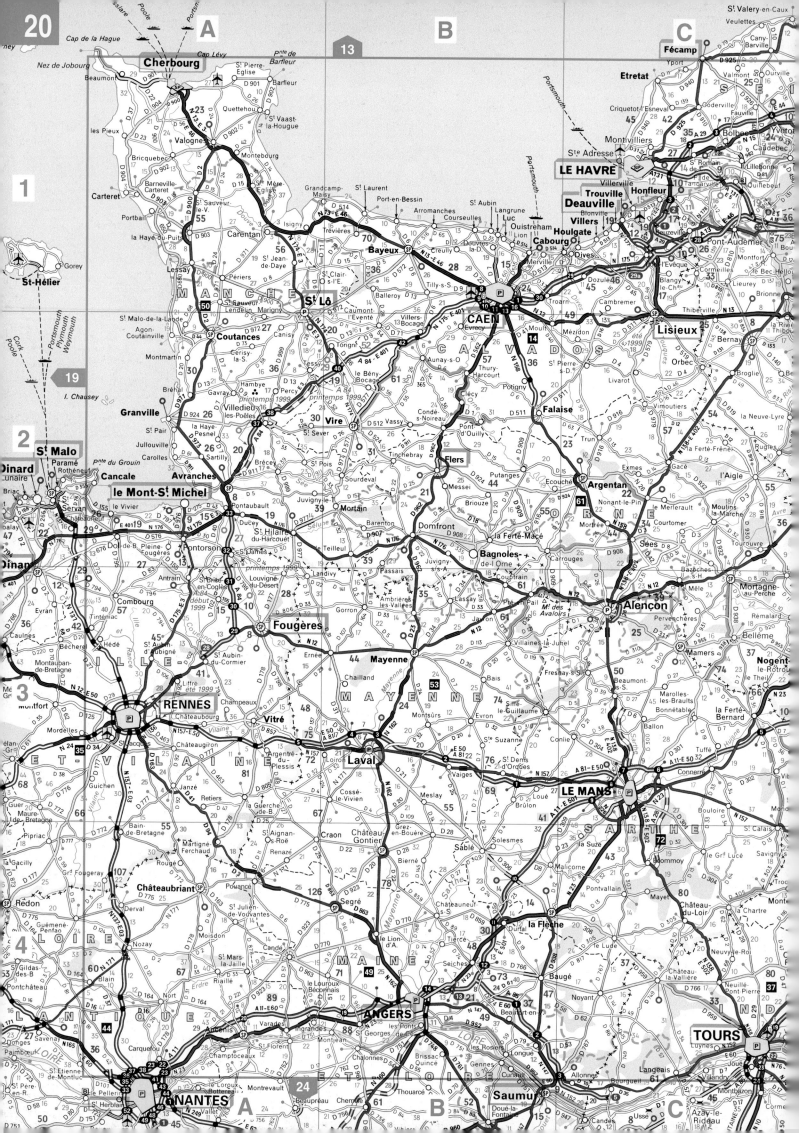

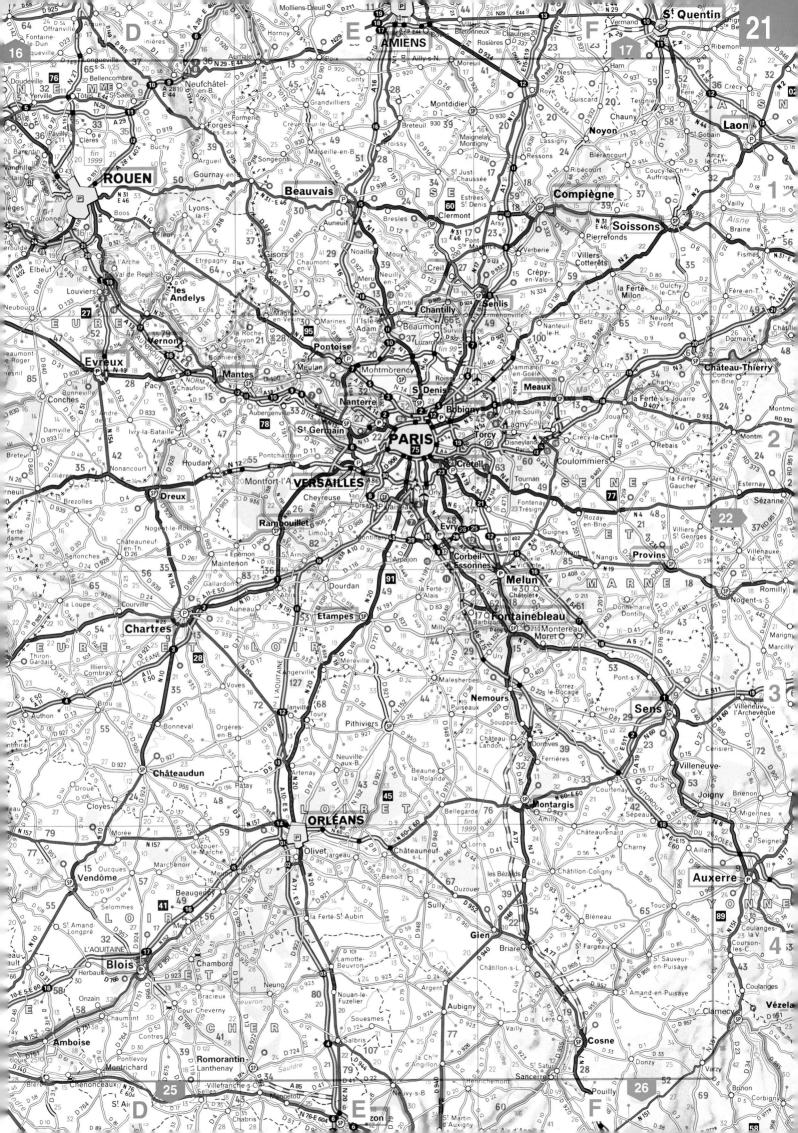

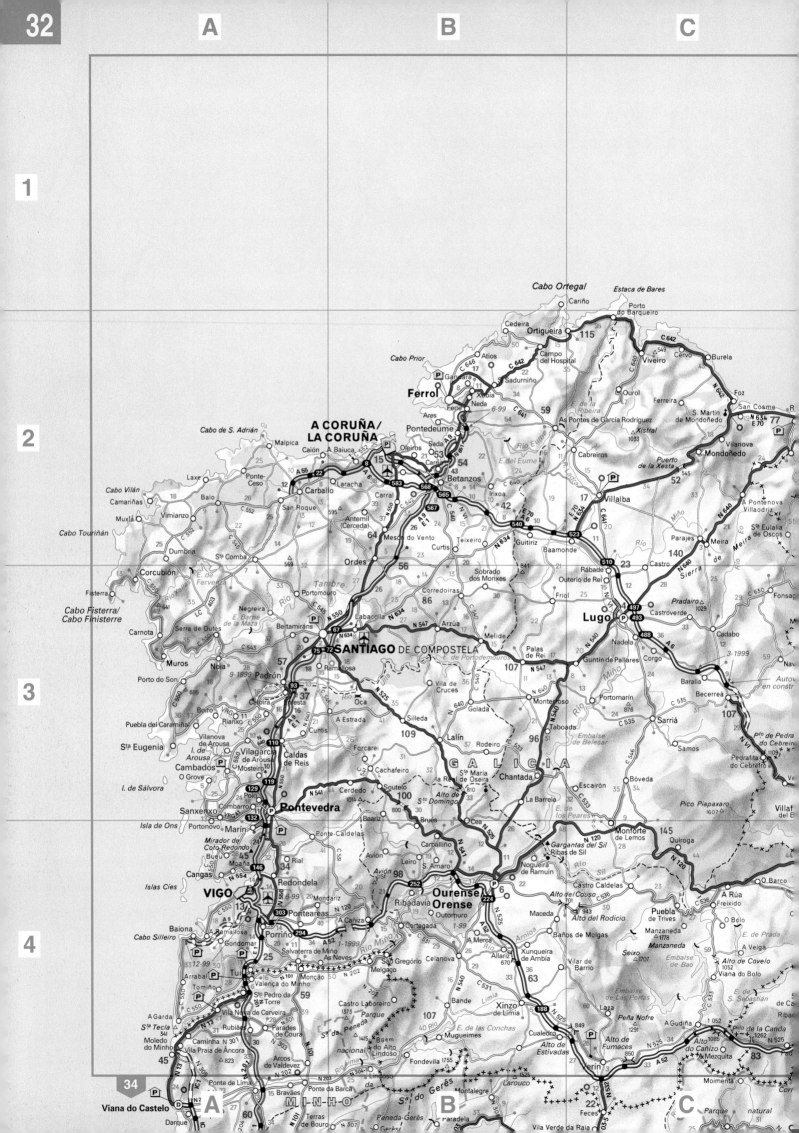

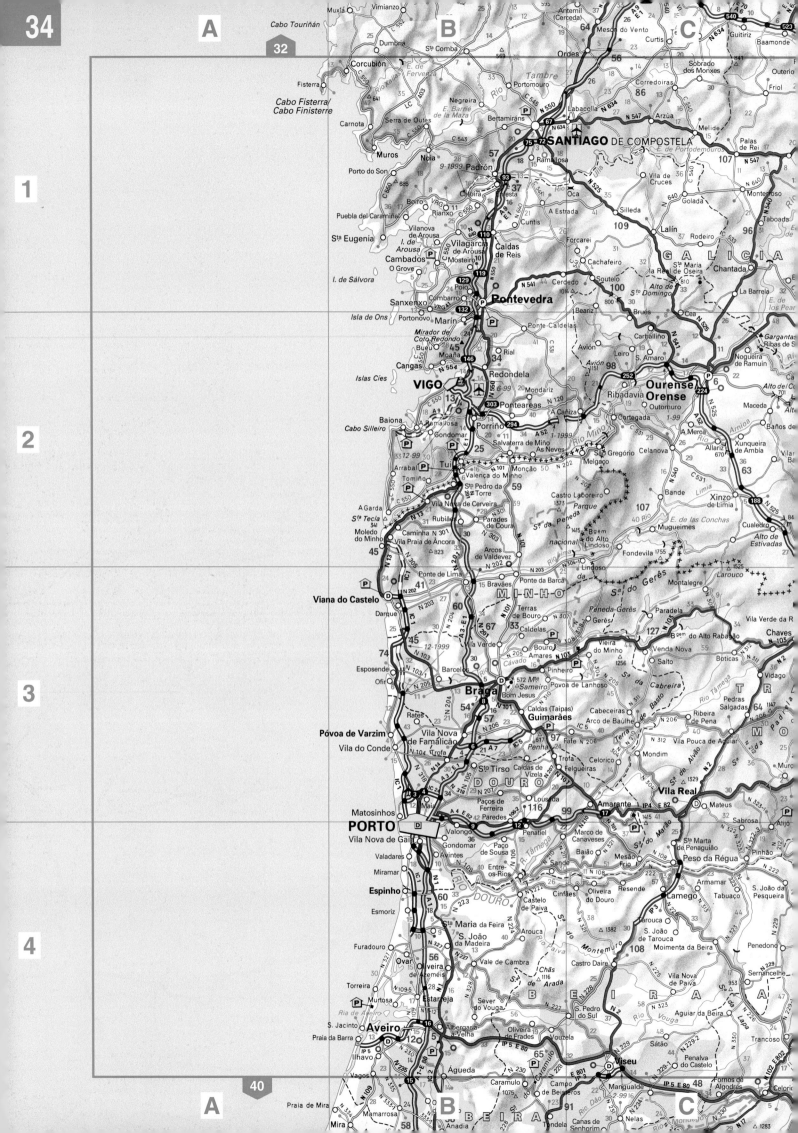

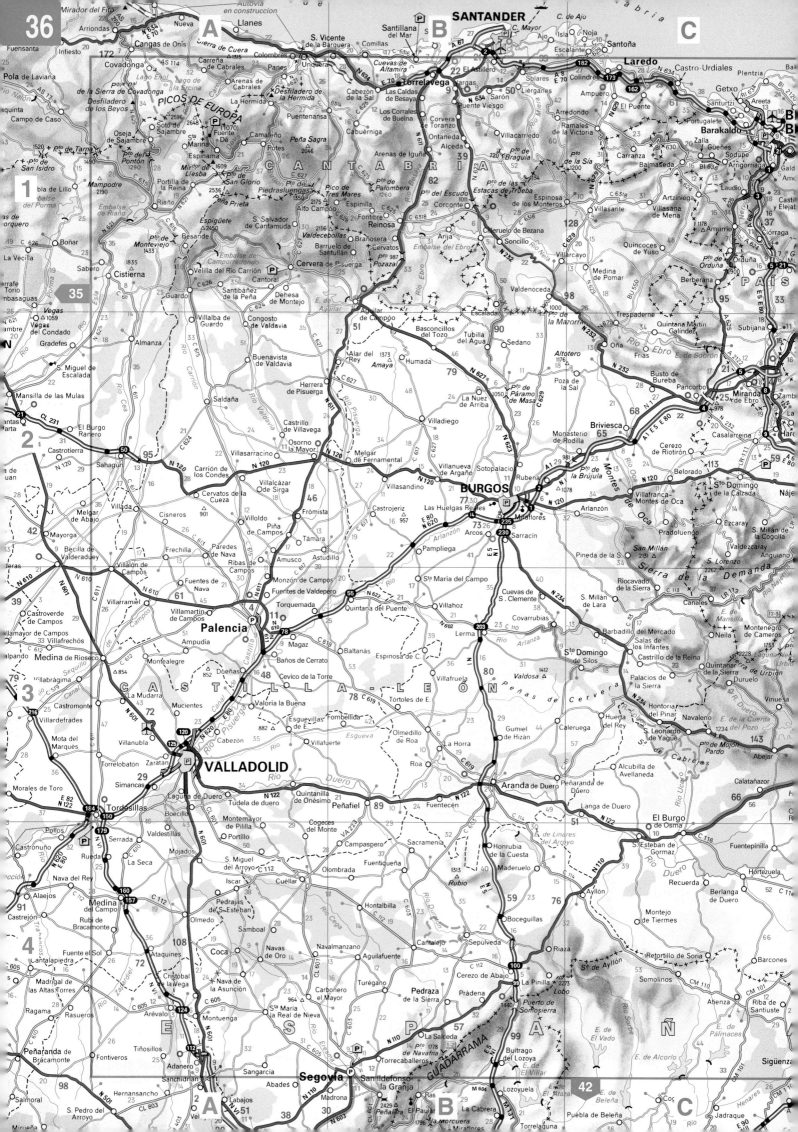

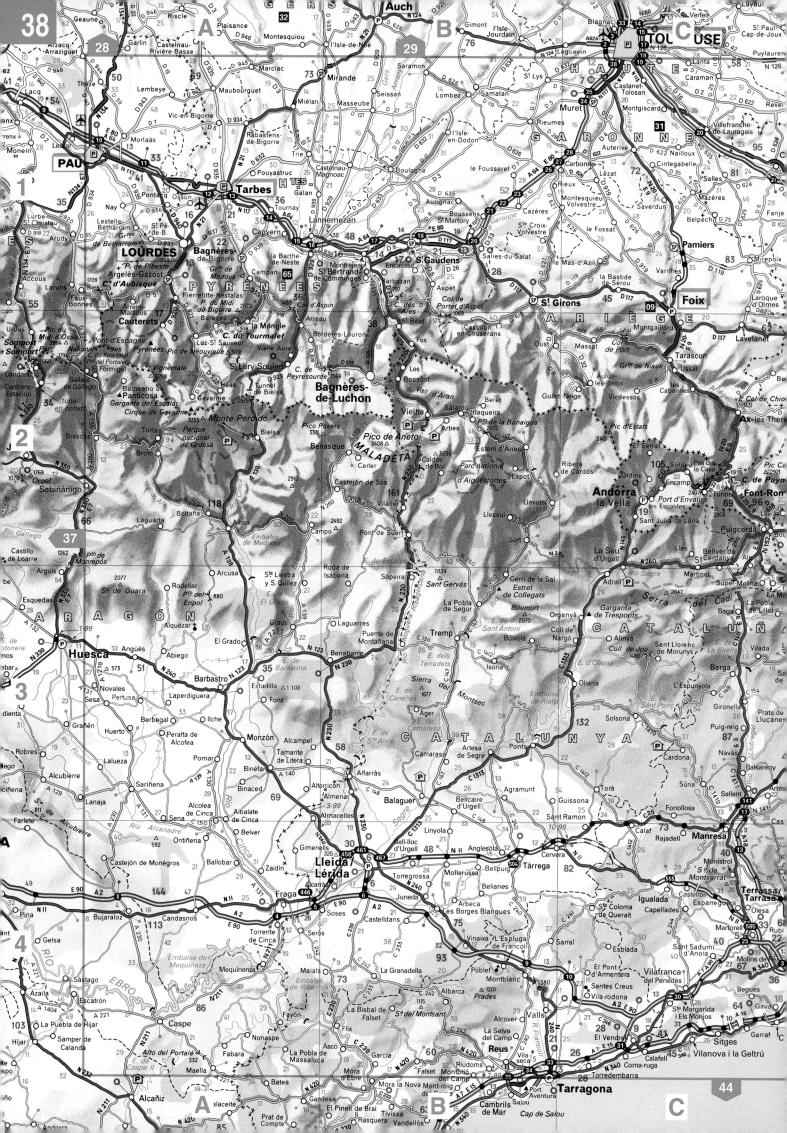

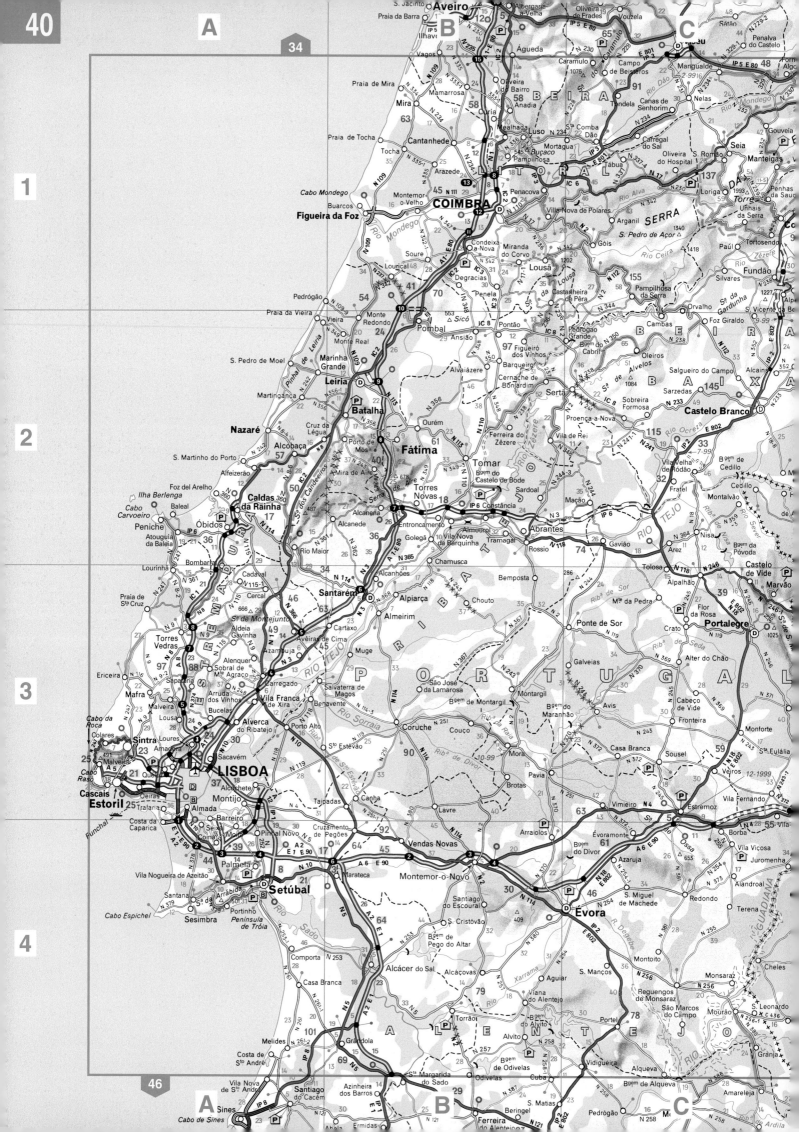

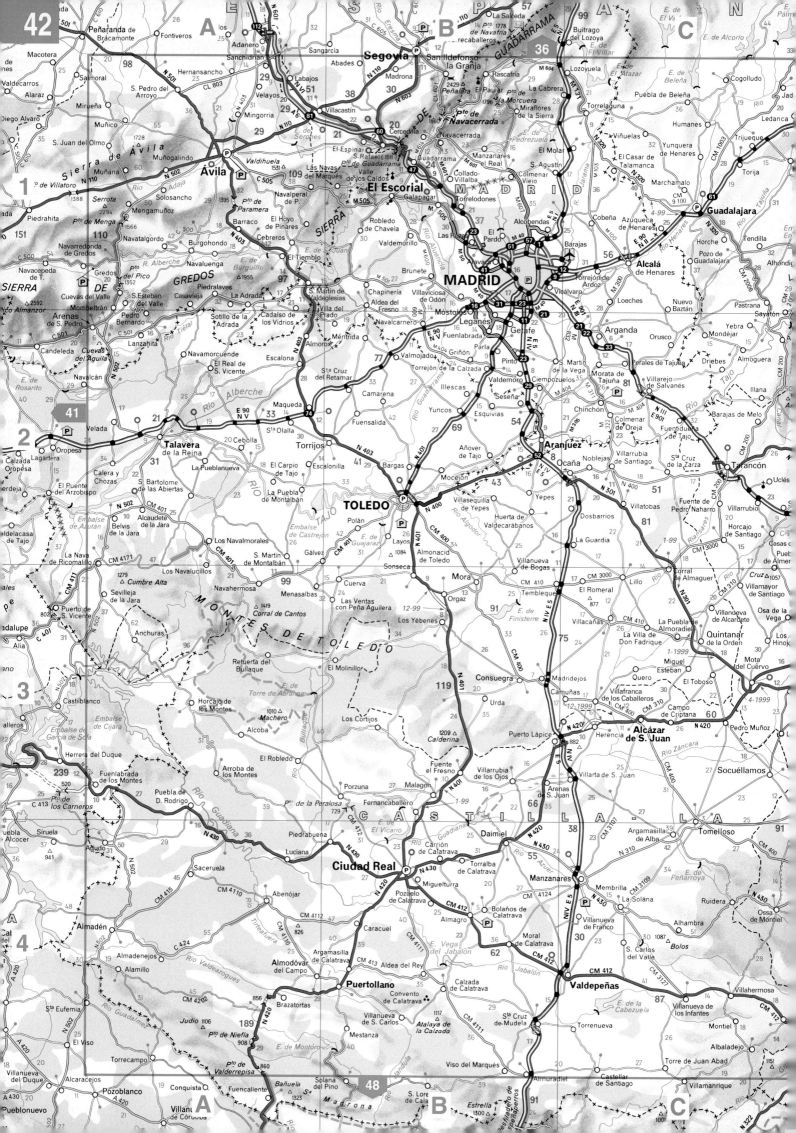

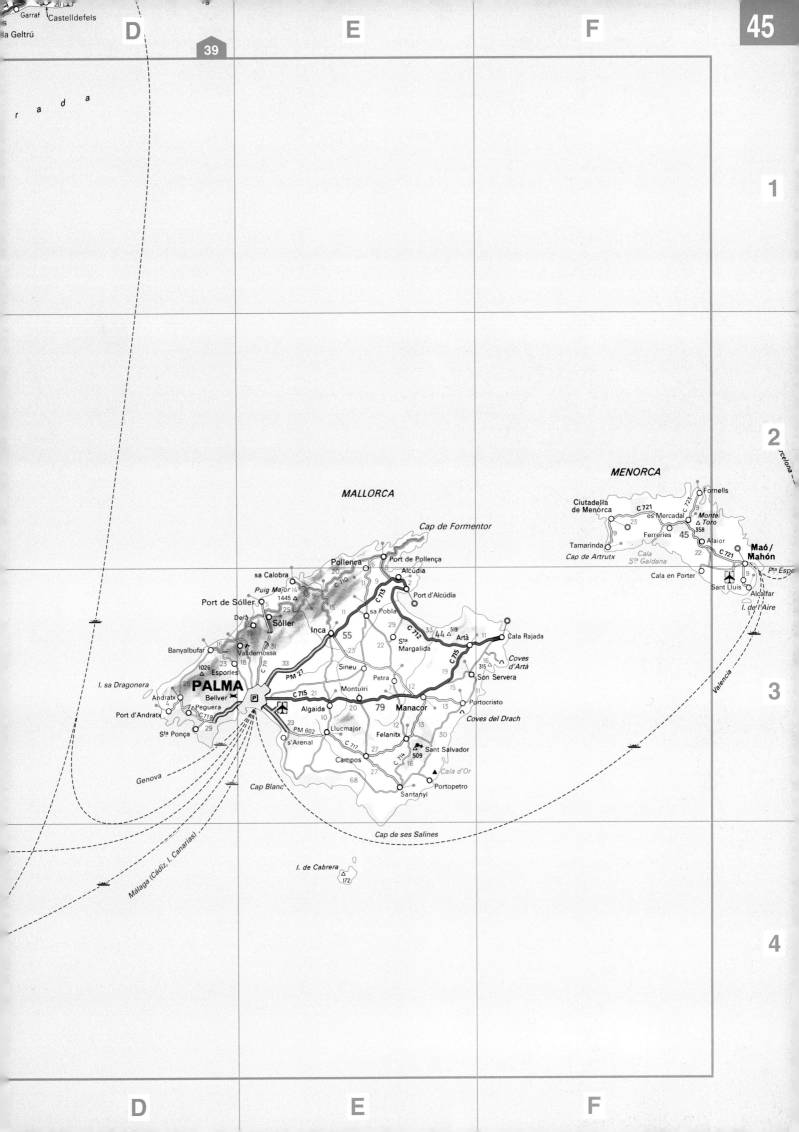

1

Garraf Castelldefels

la Geltrú

r a d a

2

MALLORCA

MENORCA

Cap de Formentor

Ciutadella
de Menorca   C 721   es Mercadal   *Monte*
△ *Toro*
358

Fornells

C 723

9

sa Calobra   Pollença   16   Port de Pollença
Alcúdia

Ferreries   45   Alaior

Tamarinda   9

Puig Major 14   c 710   20   11   9   2

Cap de Artrutx   *Cala*
Sta Galdana   22

C 721   **Maó /
Mahón**

1445 △   15   Port d'Alcúdia

Port de Sóller   5   23   sa Pobla

Cala en Porter   Sant Lluis

9   *Pta Espe*

Deià   *Sóller*   11   Alcalfar

19   Inca   55   29   C 712   33   44 △   519   Artà   11   Cala Rajada

I. de l'Aire

Banyalbufar   16   Valldemossa   31   Sta
Margalida   22   C 715   *Coves
d'Artà*

1026
△   Esporles   18   C 711   33   23   Sineu   315 △   Son Servera

23   PM 27   Petra   19

PALMA   21   C 715   21   Montuïri   7   12   15

I. sa Dragonera   Bellver   ✈   13   Portocristo

Andratx   10   Algaida   20   79   **Manacor**   13   *Coves del Drach*

Peguera   23   PM 602   Llucmajor   12   13

Port d'Andratx   C 719

Sta Ponça   29   s'Arenal   Felanitx   30

C 717   27   C 714   Sant Salvador

Genova   Campos   509

27   16   ▲ *Cala d'Or*

Cap Blanc   68   Santanyí   Portopetro

Cap de ses Salines

Málaga (Cádiz, I. Canarias)

I. de Cabrera

△ 172

Valencia

3

4

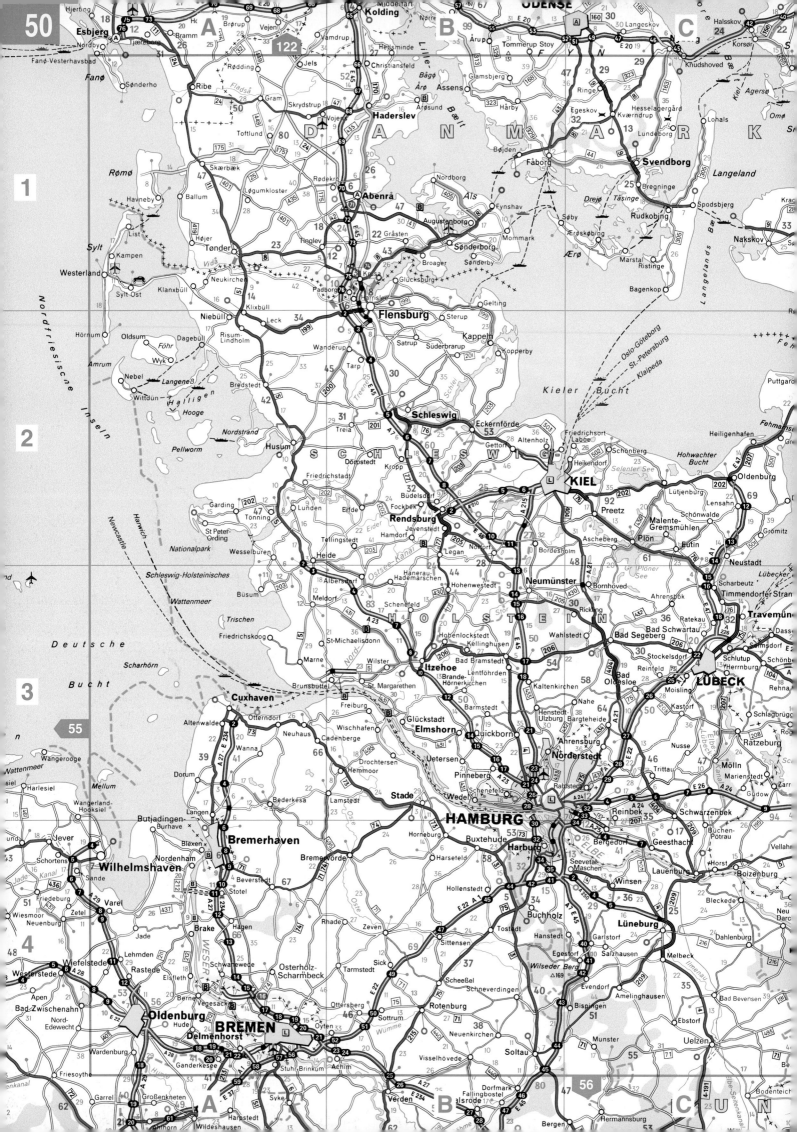

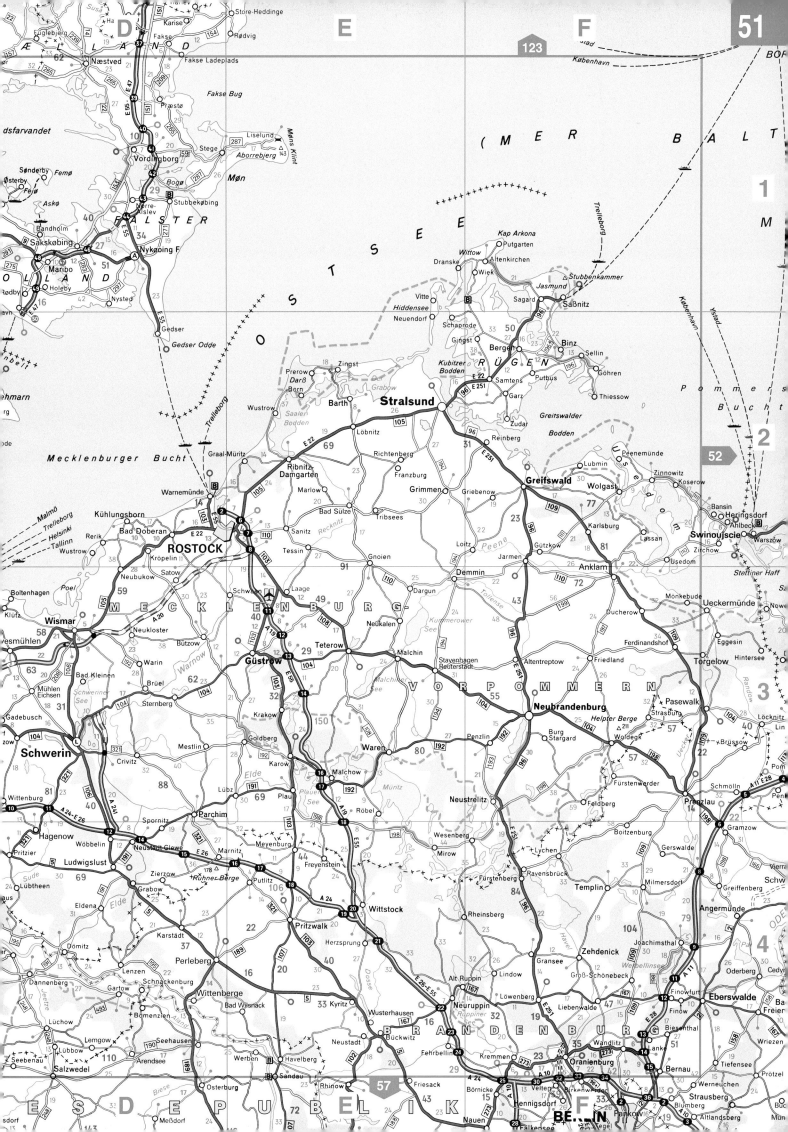

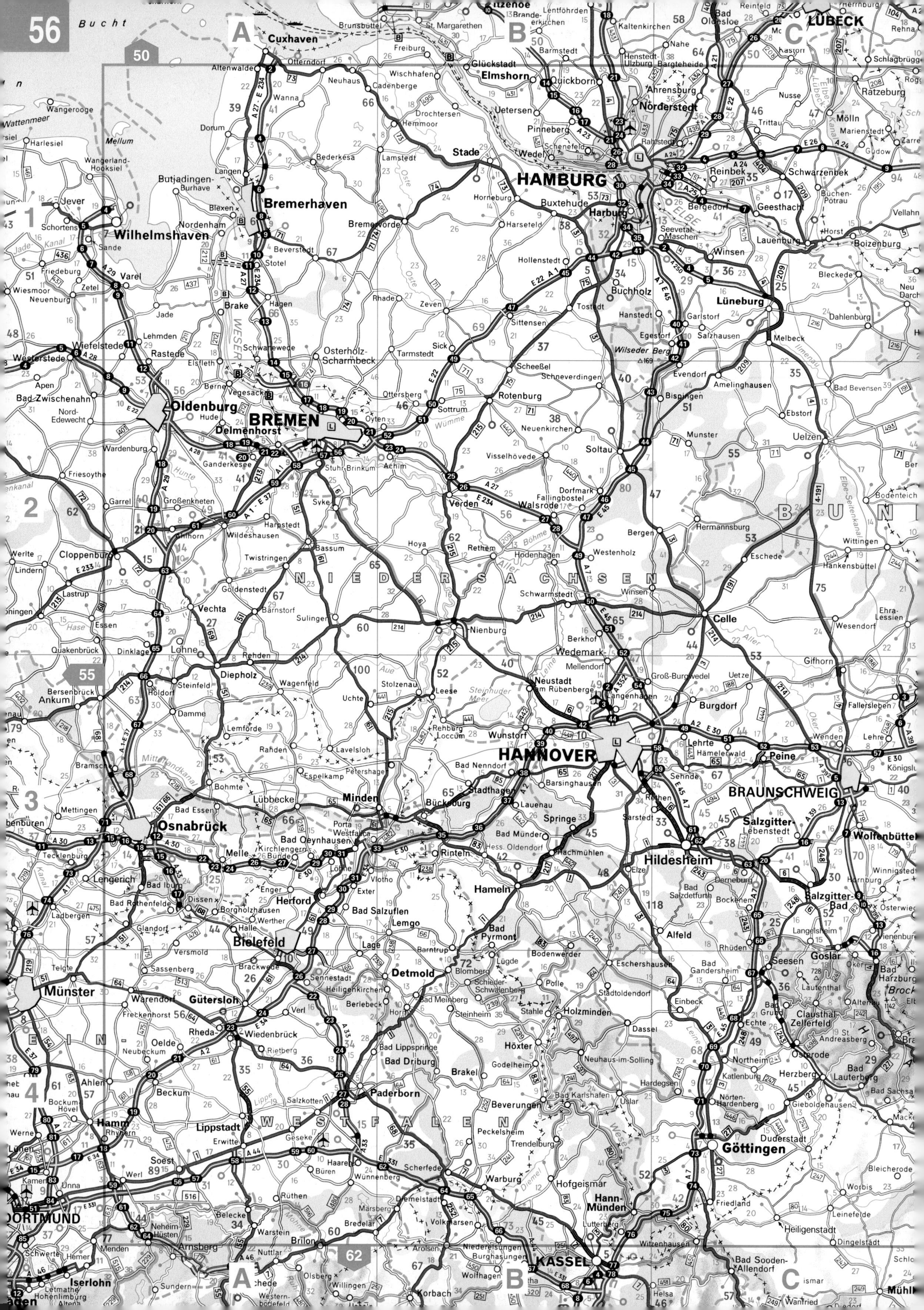

Bucht

50

55

62

Grid references: A | B | C | 1 | 2 | 3 | 4

Major cities and places:

LÜBECK, HAMBURG, BREMEN, HANNOVER, BRAUNSCHWEIG, KASSEL, DORTMUND, Münster, Osnabrück, Bielefeld, Oldenburg, Wilhelmshaven, Bremerhaven, Cuxhaven, Lüneburg, Celle, Hildesheim, Göttingen, Paderborn, Gütersloh, Detmold, Hameln, Goslar, Salzgitter, Wolfenbüttel, Peine

Other places:

Wangerooge, Harlesiel, Carolinensiel, Jever, Schortens, Sande, Varel, Zetel, Neuenburg, Wiesmoor, Friedeburg, Apen, Bad Zwischenahn, Nord-Edewecht, Westerstede, Wiefelstede, Rastede, Elsfleth, Berne, Vegesack, Delmenhorst, Ganderkesee, Wardenburg, Hude, Friesoythe, Garrel, Großenkneten, Wildeshausen, Harpstedt, Cloppenburg, Lindern, Lastrup, Essen, Quakenbrück, Dinklage, Löhne, Vechta, Barnstorf, Goldenstedt, Twistringen, Bassum, Syke, Sulingen, Rehden, Diepholz, Wagenfeld, Steinfeld, Damme, Holdorf, Lemförde, Rahden, Lavelsloh, Espelkamp, Bohmte, Lübbecke, Bramsche, Ankum, Bersenbrück, Mettingen, Tecklenburg, Lengerich, Ladbergen, Glandorf, Bad Iburg, Dissen, Borgholzhausen, Werther, Halle, Melle, Bünde, Bad Oeynhausen, Minden, Porta Westfalica, Bückeburg, Stadthagen, Bad Nenndorf, Barsinghausen, Springe, Bad Münder, Lauenau, Hachmühlen, Rinteln, Vlotho, Exter, Herford, Enger, Bad Salzuflen, Lemgo, Lage, Barntrup, Bad Pyrmont, Blomberg, Schieder-Schwalenberg, Bad Meinberg, Steinheim, Horn, Heiligenkirchen, Berlebeck, Sennestadt, Verl, Brackwede, Rietberg, Wiedenbrück, Rheda, Neubeckum, Oelde, Warendorf, Freckenhorst, Beckum, Ahlen, Hamm, Lippstadt, Erwitte, Geseke, Soest, Werl, Unna, Kamen, Bockum Hövel, Werne, Iserlohn, Hemer, Menden, Neheim-Hüsten, Arnsberg, Warstein, Belecke, Rüthen, Büren, Wünnenberg, Bad Lippspringe, Bad Driburg, Brakel, Godelheim, Höxter, Beverungen, Warburg, Hofgeismar, Hann.-Münden, Holzminden, Stadtoldendorf, Einbeck, Dassel, Northeim, Katlenburg, Nörten-Hardenberg, Uslar, Bodenwerder, Eschershausen, Bad Gandersheim, Seesen, Lautenthal, Clausthal-Zellerfeld, St. Andreasberg, Bad Grund, Osterode, Herzberg, Bad Lauterberg, Bad Sachsa, Bad Harzburg, Rhüden, Langelsheim, Alfeld, Bockenem, Derneburg, Bad Salzdetfurth, Elze, Sarstedt, Lehrte, Hämelerwald, Sehnde, Burgdorf, Groß-Burgwedel, Uetze, Wittingen, Fallersleben, Königslutter, Schöppenstedt, Winnigstedt, Salzgitter-Bad, Seesen

Northern places:

Cuxhaven, Altenwalde, Otterndorf, Wanna, Neuhaus, Cadenberge, Freiburg, St. Margarethen, Brunsbüttel, Glückstadt, Elmshorn, Wedel, Pinneberg, Uetersen, Quickborn, Norderstedt, Ahrensburg, Bargteheide, Bad Oldesloe, Kaltenkirchen, Reinfeld, Mölln, Ratzeburg, Schwarzenbek, Geesthacht, Lauenburg, Boizenburg, Bleckede, Dahlenburg, Bad Bevensen, Ebstorf, Uelzen, Bispingen, Munster, Soltau, Schneverdingen, Fallingbostel, Walsrode, Dorfmark, Bad Fallingbostel, Bergen, Hermannsburg, Faßberg, Eschede, Hankensbüttel, Gifhorn, Wesendorf, Wietzendorf, Dorum, Langen, Nordenham, Brake, Hagen, Jade, Lehmden, Blexen, Butjadingen-Burhave, Wangerland-Hooksiel, Schwanewede, Osterholz-Scharmbeck, Tarmstedt, Ottersberg, Oyten, Achim, Verden, Dörverden, Rethem, Hoya, Eystrup, Nienburg, Stolzenau, Leese, Loccum, Rehburg, Wunstorf, Neustadt am Rübenberge, Garbsen, Langenhagen, Wedemark, Mellendorf, Berkhof, Schwarmstedt, Hodenhagen, Westenholz, Winsen, Bergen, Hermannsburg

Stade, Buxtehude, Harsefeld, Horneburg, Bremervörde, Bederkesa, Lamstedt, Hemmoor, Drochtersen, Wischhafen, Hollenstedt, Buchholz, Tostedt, Sittensen, Zeven, Scheeßel, Rotenburg, Sottrum, Visselhövede, Neuenkirchen, Sick, Harburg, Seevetal-Maschen, Winsen, Garlstorf, Salzhausen, Egestorf, Amelinghausen, Evendorf, Bispingen, Melbeck

Hamburg area: Elmshorn, Pinneberg, Schenefeld, Rahlstedt, Reinbek, Bergedorf, Geesthacht, Harburg, Seevetal

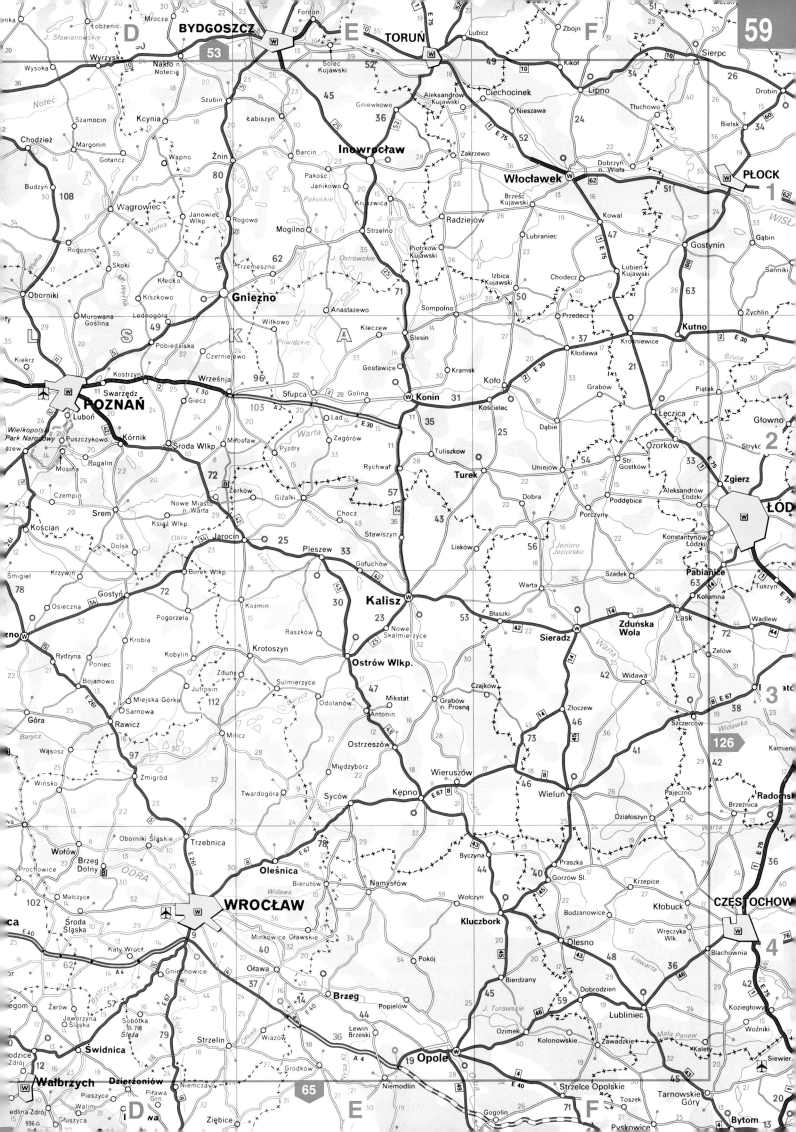

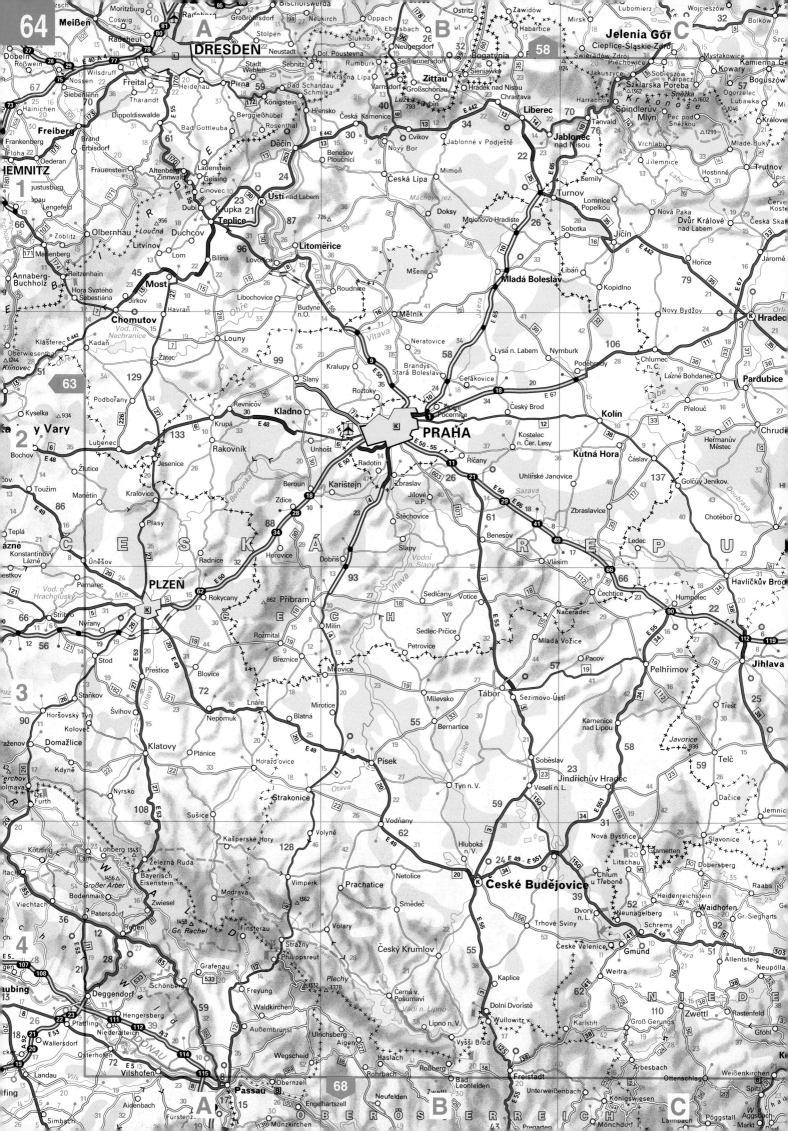

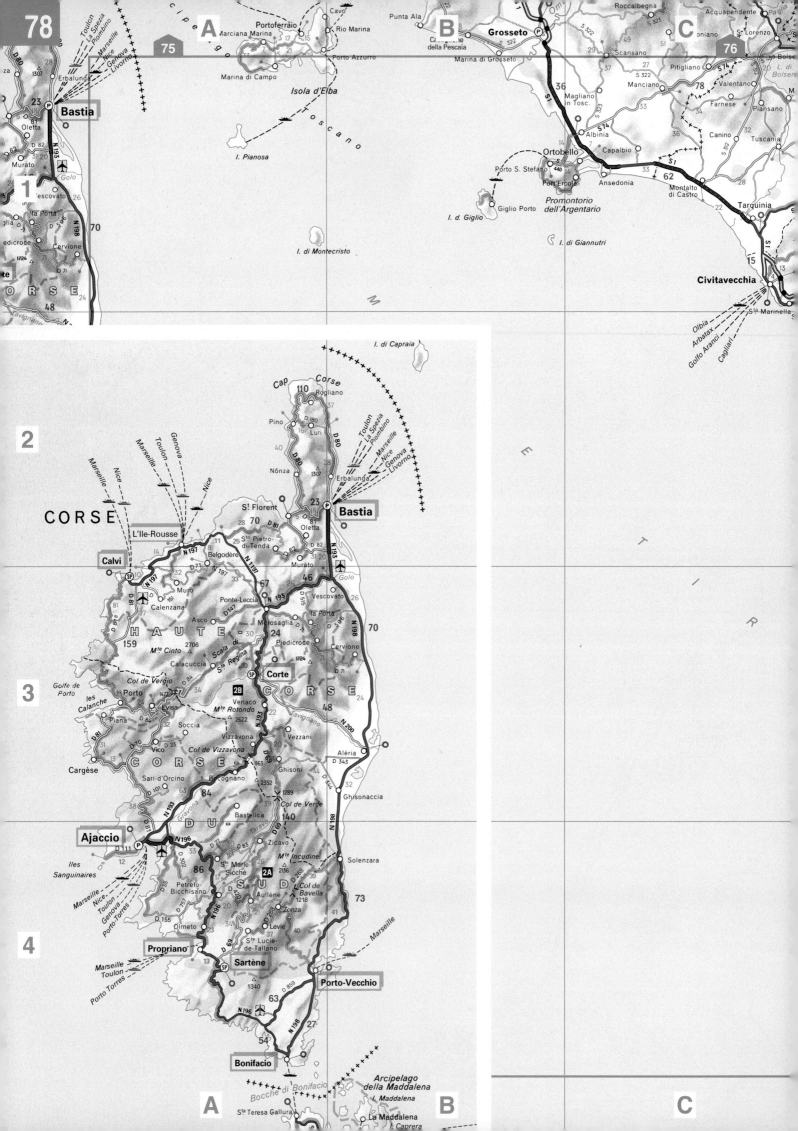

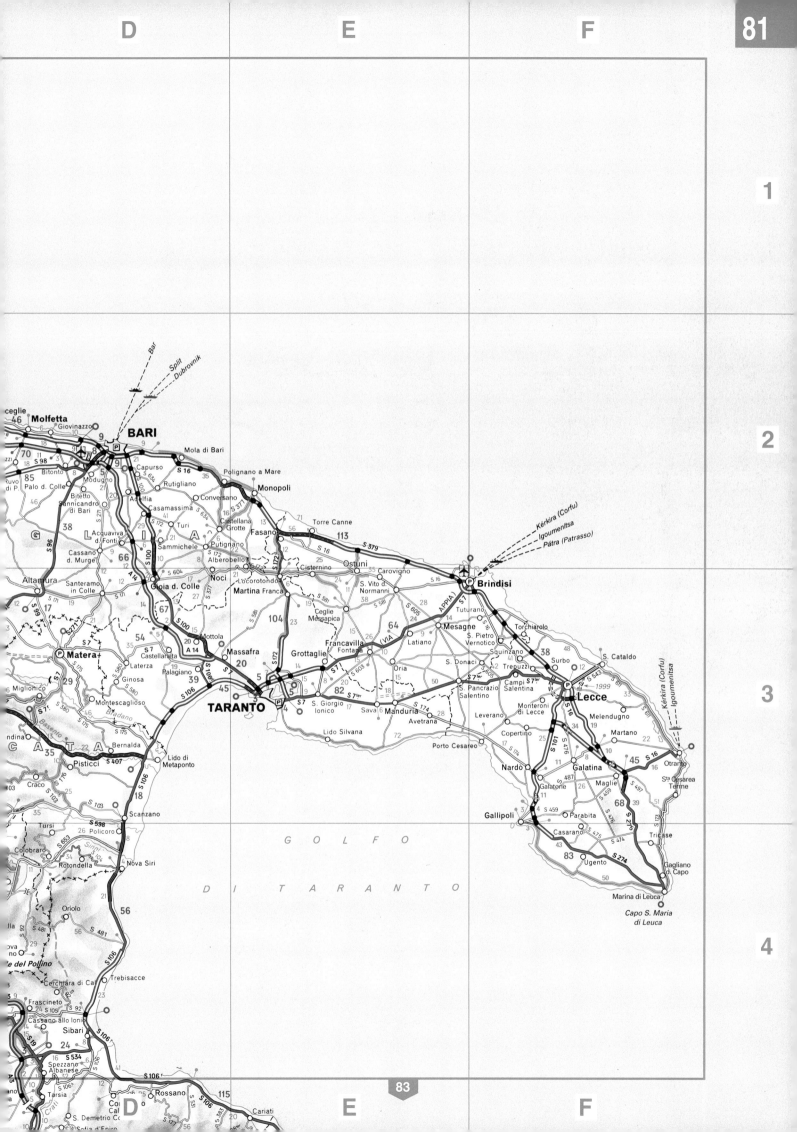

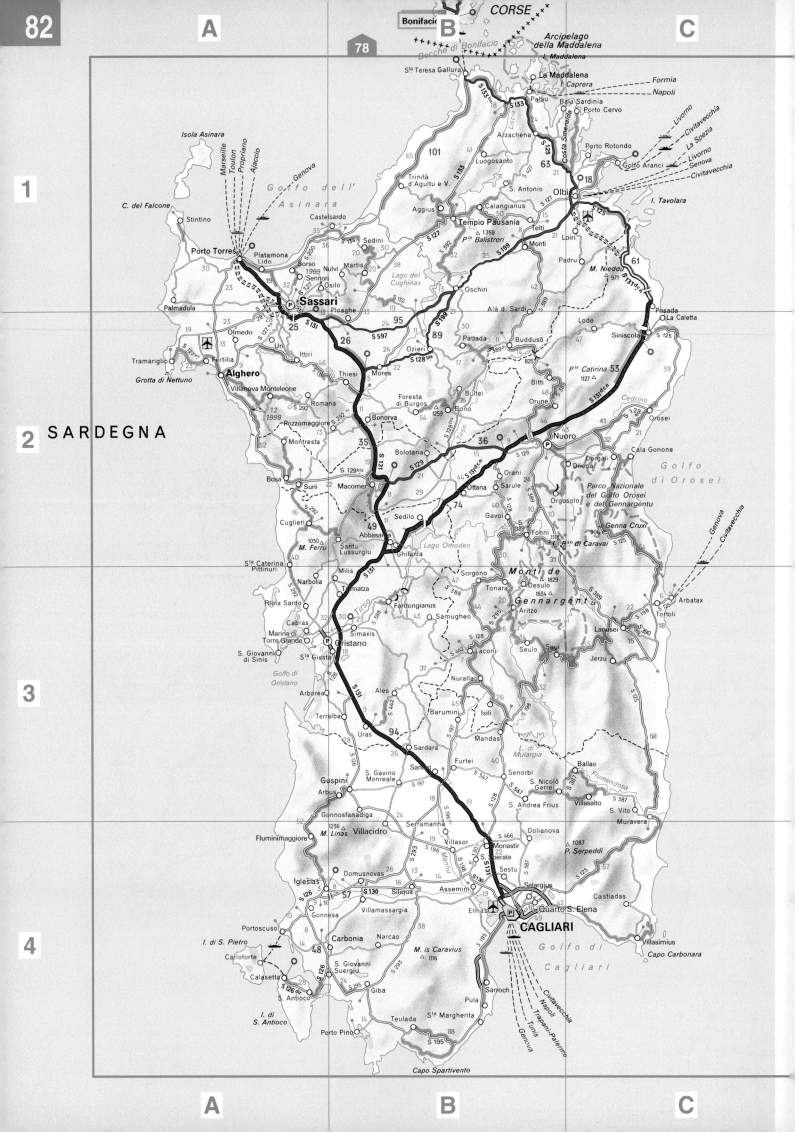

A   B   C

1

MARE   TIRRENO

I. di Ustica

SICILIA

Livorno
Genova
Cagliari

Napoli

2

Capo Gallo
Sferracavallo   Mondello
Punta Raisi   *M. Pellegrino*
6 30   A 29   24   606
S 113   Capaci   **PALERMO**
Cinisi   Carini   44   Solunto
Cagliari   S. Vito lo Capo   Torre d. Impiso   17   63   **Bagheria**   Casteldaccia
Golfo di   Monreale   44   Altavilla   20 S 113   54   Termini   S 113   Cefalù   S. Ste
Castellammare   29   S 186   8   Trabia   47   Imerese   19   di Cam
Castellammare   26   Partinico   31   Piana   14   S 121   26   S 113   24   98
d. Golfo   S 187   d. Albanesi   Villafrati   S 113   A 19   Collesano   Castelbuono
Erice   34   S 115   16   Marineo   S 121   Caccamo   Buonfornello   P.^ta Carbonara   C. de
Trapani   S 113   32   Alcamo   S. Cipirello   58   S 18   34   Montemaggiore   16   S 286   43   Petralia   Gang
Isole   I. Levanzo   Paceco   41   20   Fulgatore   12   S 119   24   Belsito   M   Caltavuturo   32   S 643   66
Egadi   Segesta   53   Calatafimi   R.^ca Busambra   Roccapalumba   S 285   34   Alia   38   126   S 120   56
I. Maréttimo   I. Favignana   42   A 29 dir   43   △ 1613   50   S 121   Lercara   23   Resultano   26   S 290
Birgi   50   18   155   Corleone   41   Friddi   126   S 121   14
Tunis   36   S 115   6   41 A 29   S 624   44   S 188   Prizzi   18   S. Caterina   S 122°   15   33
I. di Pantelleria   12   Salemi   4   S 119   28   Mussomeli   Villarosa   22
Marsala   38   57   S 188   Chiusa Sclafani   S 189   **Caltanissetta**   S 122
S 188   Sta Ninfa   Sta Margherita   S 188   Alessandria   S. Stefano   S. Cataldo   S 122
19   Partanna   di Belice   Sambuca   d. Rocca   Quisquina   62   Serradifalco
Castelvetrano   3   di Sicilia   31   S 386   Casteltermini   Montedoro   S 626
22 A 29   18   9f   17   33   Caltabellotta   S. Biagio Platani   58   Delia   28   Sommatino
Mazara d. Vallo   21   S 115   14   44   Ribera   83   Aragona   35   S 190   Pietr
Campobello   11   S 188   16   Platani   Raffadali   S 189   Canicattì   S 410   Riesi
di Mazara   22   Menfi   Sciacca   S 640   Naro   S 123   Ravanusa   22
Selinunte   20   **Agrigento**   Favara   S 576   Campobello   1999
Marinella   Porto Empedocle   6   S 115   di Licata   S 626   18
S 115   72   Palma   43   S 115   Salso
I. di Linosa   di Montechiaro

Licata

3

4

Trapani   *I. di Linosa*   Porto Empedocle

I s o l e

P e l a g i e

Pantelleria   Tracino
836
I. di Pantelleria   *I. di Lampedusa*   Lampedusa

A   B   C

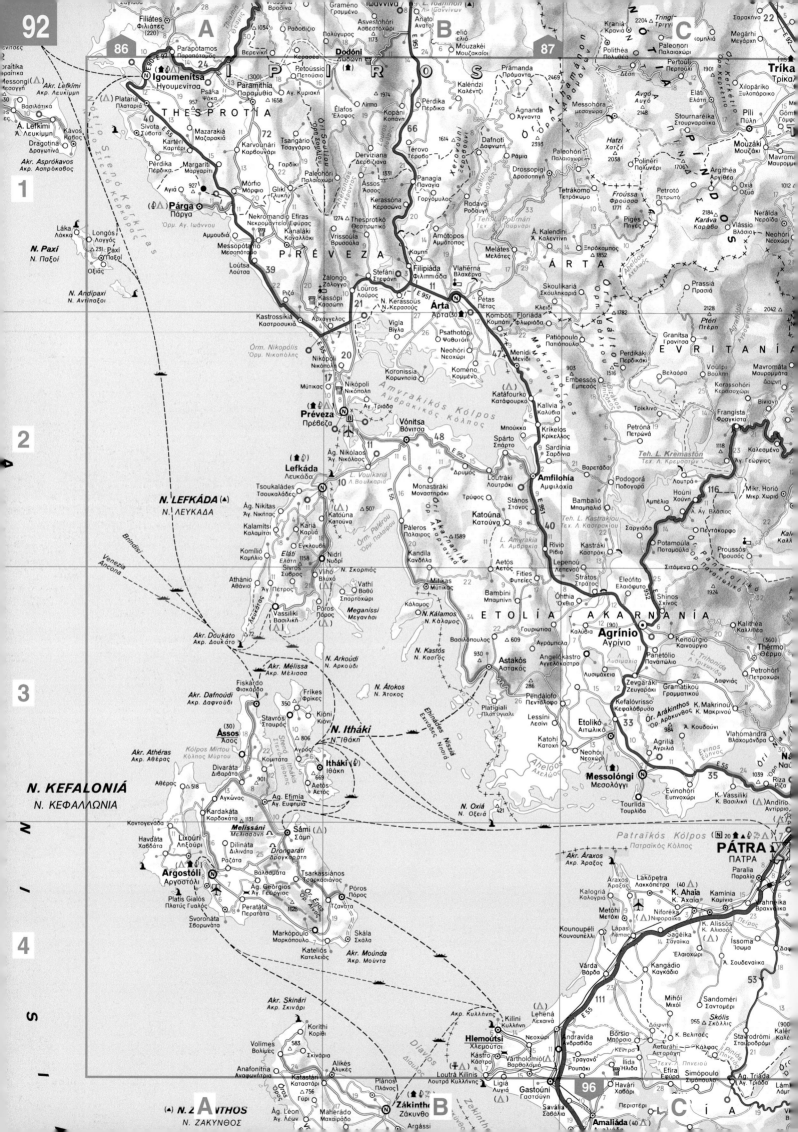

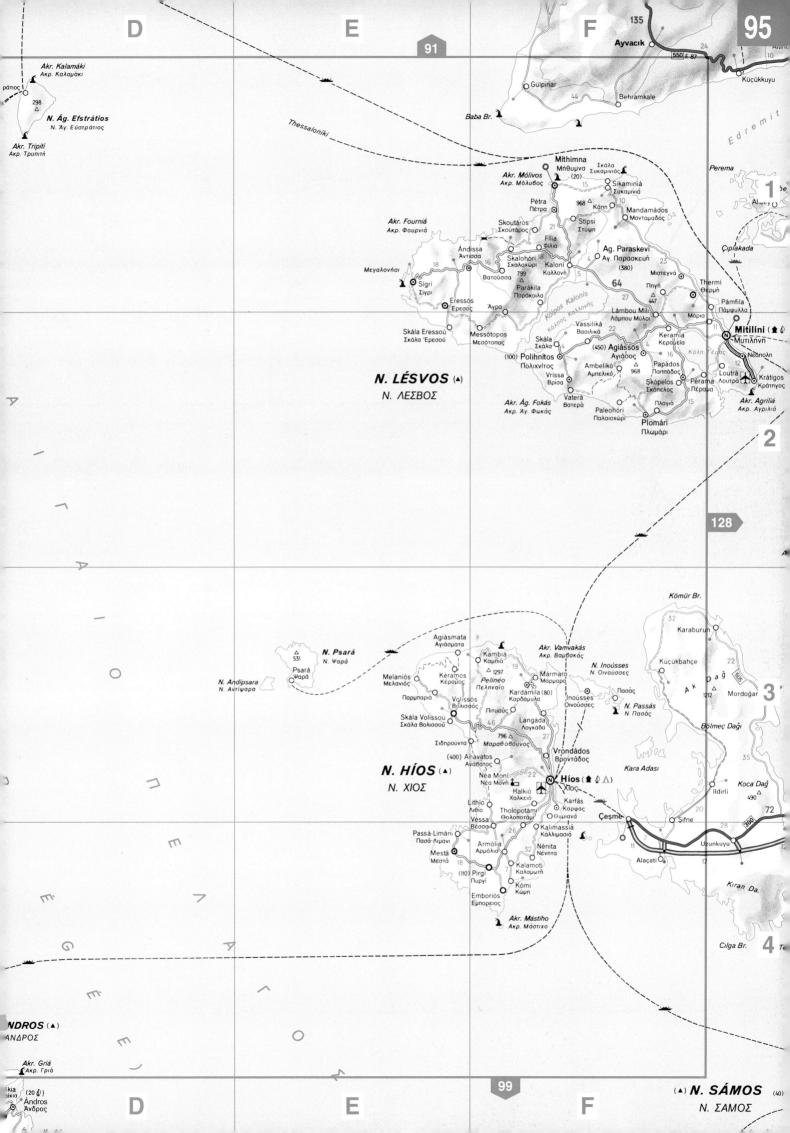

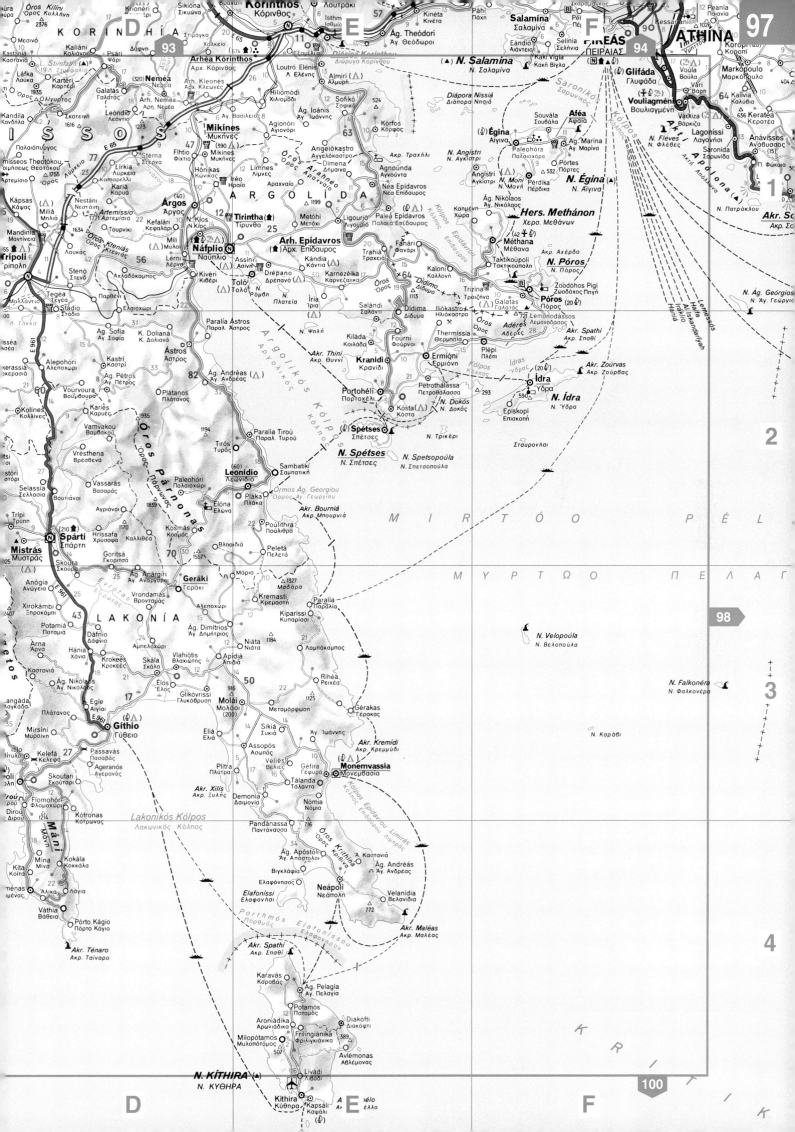

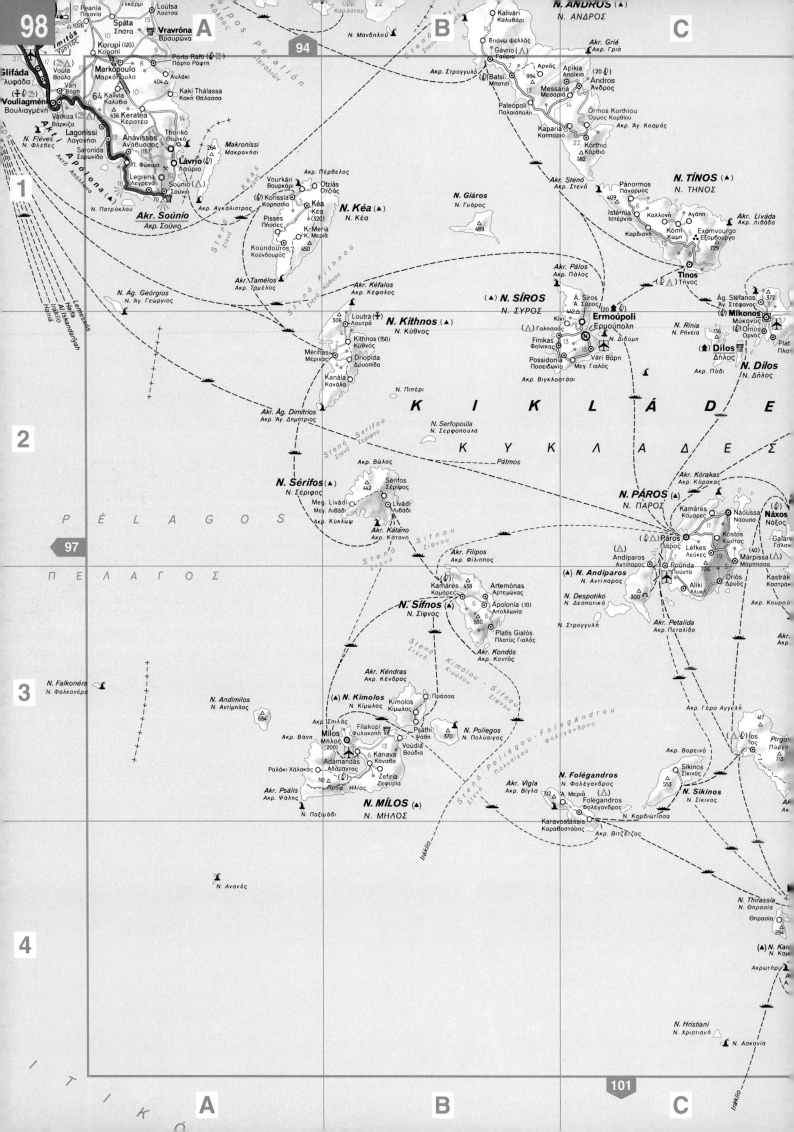

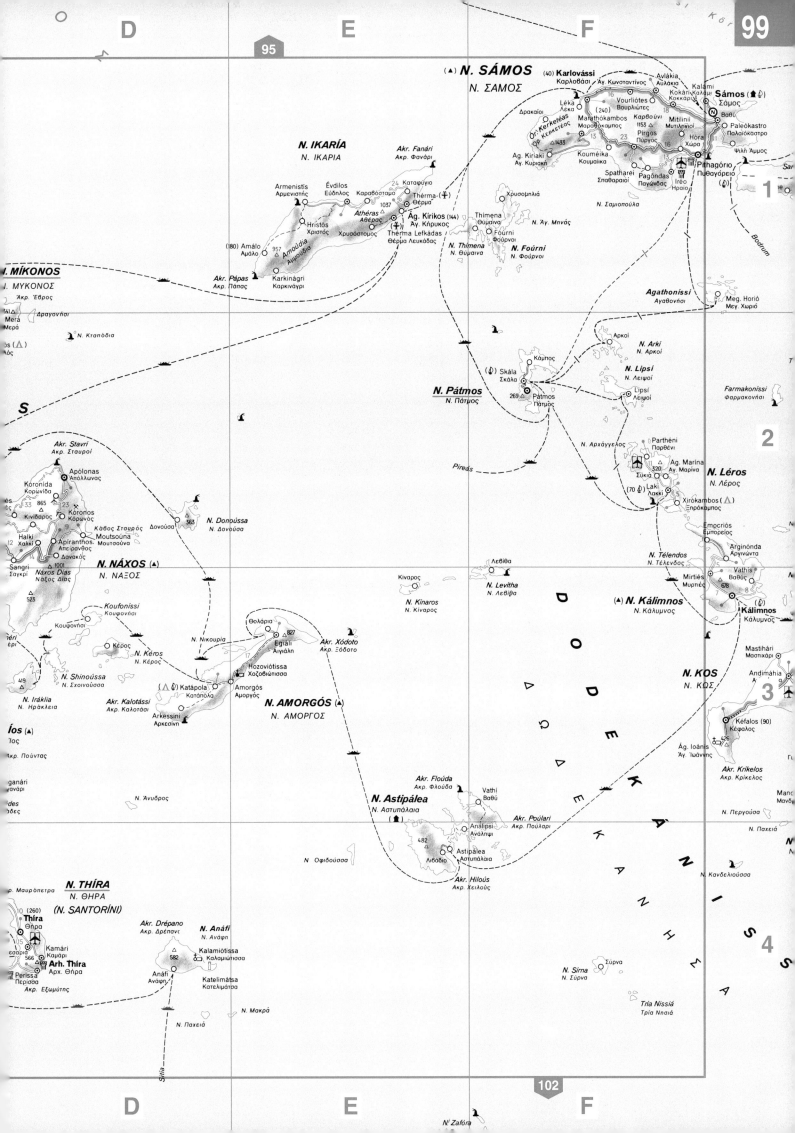

(▲) **N. SÁMOS**
Ν. ΣΑΜΟΣ

(40) **Karlovássi**
Καρλοβάσι

Karlovádai · Άγ. Κωνσταντίνος · Αυλάκια
Άγ. Κωνσταντίνος · Αυλάκια
Κοκκάρι Καλάμι
Κοκκάρι Κοκκάρι · **Sámos** (♠ ⚓)
Σάμος

Léka 16 Vourliótes
Léka (240) Βουρλιώτες 18 Mitilinii Βαθύ
Δρακαίοι Μαραθόκαμπος Mitilinií **N** Paleókastro
N. IKARÍA Όρ. Kerketéas Marathókambos 1153 Καρδούνι Μυτιληνιοί Παλαιόκαστρο
Ν. ΙΚΑΡΙΑ Κερκετέας Μαραθόκαμπος 13 23 Pirgos 16 Hóra Ψιλή Άμμος
Άκρ. Fanári Δ1433 Πύργος Χώρα
Άκρ. Φανάρι Koumeïka Pithagório

Armenistis Évdilos Καταφύγιο Ag. Kiriaki Κουμαίικα Spatharéi Pagóndas Πυθαγόρειο
Αρμενιστής Εύδηλος Καραβόσταμο 24 Άγ. Κυριακή Σπαθαραίοι Παγώνδας Ίρεο (♠)
Δράκαιοι Athéras Thérma (♨) Chrisomiliá Ηραίο
Hristós Αθέρας Αθέρας Θέρμα Χρυσομηλιά
Χριστός Χρυσόστομος 1037 Ág. Kirikos (144) Thimena
Αγ. Κήρικος Θύμαινα N. Samiopoúla
(180) Amálo 957 Thérma Lefkádas Foúrni Ν. Σαμιοπούλα
Αμάλο Αμούδια Θέρμα Λευκάδας N. Thimena Φούρνι N. Áy. Mnás
Ν. Θύμαινα **N. Foúrni**
Άκρ. Páras Karkinágri Ν. Φούρνι
Άκρ. Πάπας Καρκινάγρι

N. MÍKONOS
Ν. ΜΥΚΟΝΟΣ
Άκρ. Έβρος

Μερά

Δραγονήσι **Agathoníssi**
Αγαθονήσι Meg. Horió
Μεγ. Χωριό
os (▲)

N. Ктаπόδια Arkoí
Άρκοι N. Arkí
Ν. Αρκοί

Κάμπος **N. Lipsí**
(♦) Skála Ν. Λειψοί **Farmakoníssi**
Σκάλα Φαρμακονήσι

N. Pátmos 269 Lipsí
Ν. Πάτμος Πάτμος Λειψοί
Πάτμος

Partheni
N. Αρχάγγελος Parthéni
Parthéni
Pireás N. Αρχάγγελος 320 Ag. Marina **N. Léros**
Sikiá Άγ. Μαρίνα Ν. Λέρος
Σύκια (70)(♦) Laki
Lakkí Xirókambos (△)
Λακκί Ξηρόκαμπος

Emporiós
Εμπορειός

Arginónda
Αργινώντα
N. Télendos
Ν. Τέλενδος

Akr. Stavrí N. Donoússa Levitha 5 Vathis
Άκρ. Σταυροί 363 Λέβιθα Mirtiés Βαθύς
Apólonas Δονούσα Ν. Δονούσσα Μυρτιές 678
Απόλωνας N. Levitha **(▲) N. Kálimnos**
Koronída Ν. Λέβιθα Ν. Κάλυμνος 7 8
Κορωνίδα 865 Κίναρος Kínaros
33 23 Kóronos Κίναρος **Kálimnos**
Κίνδαρος 9 Kóronos N. Kínaros Mastihári Κάλυμνος
Κόρωνος Ν. Κίναρος Μαστιχάρι
Halki 14 Apíranthos **N. KOS**
Χαλκί Απείρανθος Κάθος Σταυρός Ν. ΚΩΣ
Δανακός Κάθος Σταυρός Andimáhia
Sangri △1001 Moutsoúna Αντιμάχια
Σαγκρί Náxos Dias Μουτσούνα Koufonissi
N. NÁXOS (▲) Νάξος Δίας Κουφονήσι Kéfalos (90)
523 Ν. ΝΑΞΟΣ Κέφαλος
Koufonái Ág. Ioánis Ακρ. Κρίκελος 426
419 Κουφονάι Tholária Άγ. Ιωάννης
N. Iráklia N. Shinoússa Θολάρια 827 **Akr. Krikelos**
Ν. Ηράκλεια Ν. Σχοινούσσα Akr. Chódoto Άκρ. Κρίκελος
Kéros N. Nikouriá Egiáli Άκρ. Ξόδοτο
Κέρος Ν. Νικουριά Αιγιάλη
N. Kéros 17 Hozoviótissa
Ν. Κέρος Χοζοβιώτισσα
Íos (▲) (△)(♦) Katápola Amorgós
Άκρ. Πούντας Κατάπολα Αμοργός
Arkessini **N. AMORGÓS** (▲)
Akr. Kalotássi Αρκεσίνη Ν. ΑΜΟΡΓΟΣ
Άκρ. Καλοτάσι

Akr. Floúda Vathí
Άκρ. Φλούδα Βαθύ
ganári N. Άνυδρος
ανάρι **N. Astipálea** Akr. Poúlari
Ν. Αστυπάλαια Άκρ. Πούλαρι
 des N. Οφιδούσσα Análipsi N. Περγούσα
(♠) Ανάλιψη N. Παχειά
482
Astipálea
N. THÍRA Λιβάδιο Αστυπάλαια N. Κανδελιούσσα
Ν. ΘΗΡΑ Akr. Hiloús
(N. SANTORÍNI) Άκρ. Χειλούς
Μαυρόπετρα
(260)
Thira Akr. Drépano **N. Anáfi** N. Σίρνα Σύρνα
Θήρα Άκρ. Δρέπανο Ν. Ανάφη N. Σύρνα
Kamári Σύρνα
Καμάρι Kalamiótissa
566 **Arh. Thíra** Kalamiótissa Καλαμιώτισσα
Perissa Αρχ. Θήρα 582 Καλαμιώτισσα
Περίσσα Anáfi **Tría Nissiá**
Άκρ. Εξωμύτης Ανάφη Katelimátsa Τρία Νησιά
Κατελιμάτσα

N. Makrá
Ν. Μακρά

Sitia N. Παχειά N' Zafóra

DODEKANISSA
ΔΩΔΕΚΑΝΗΣΑ

1

2

3

4

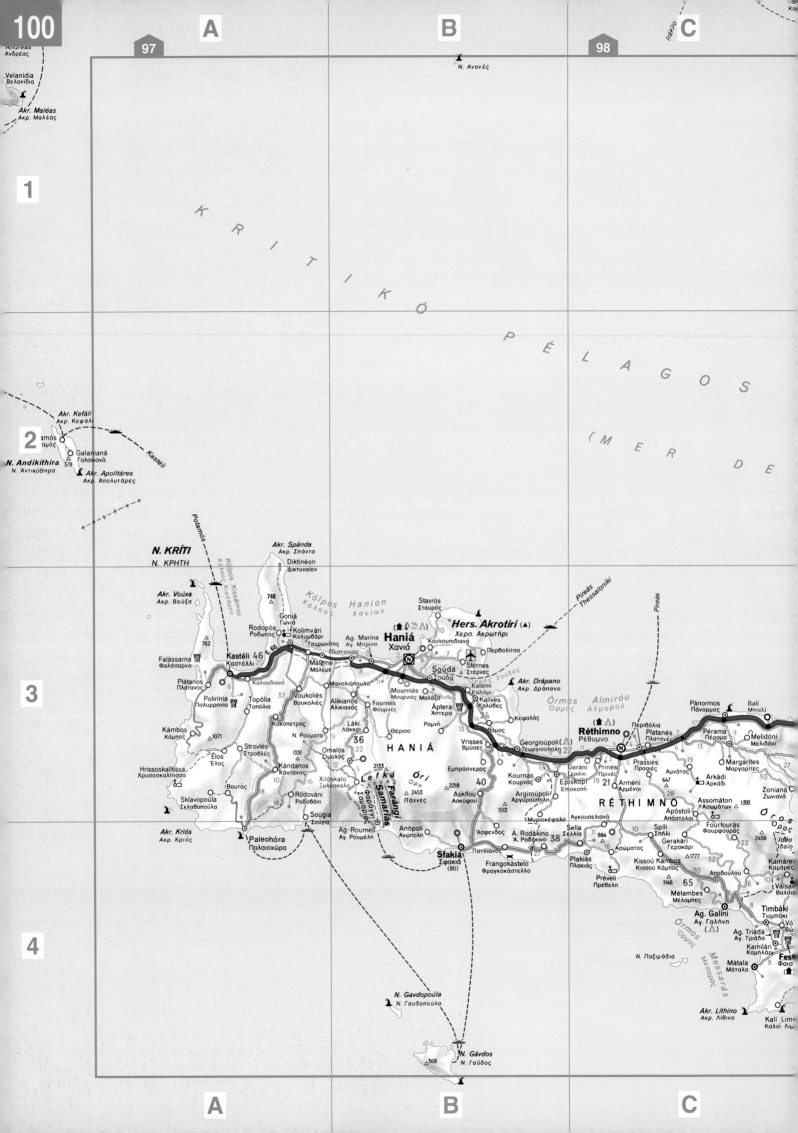

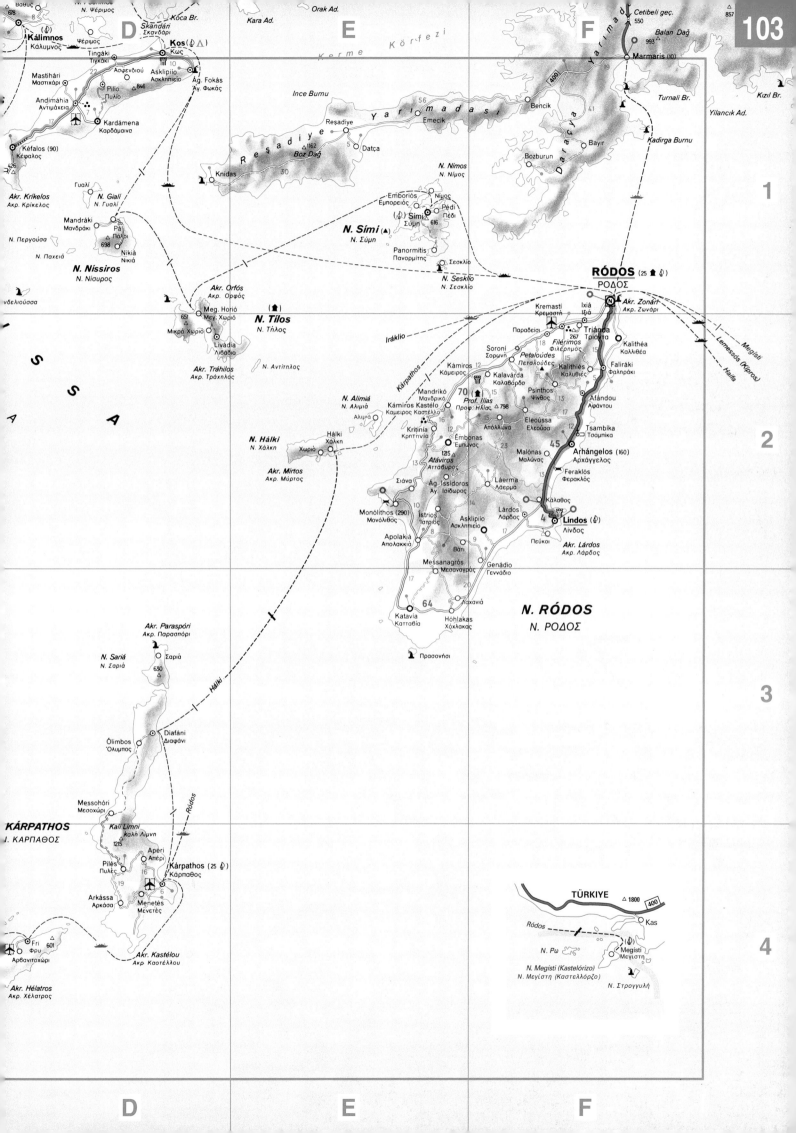

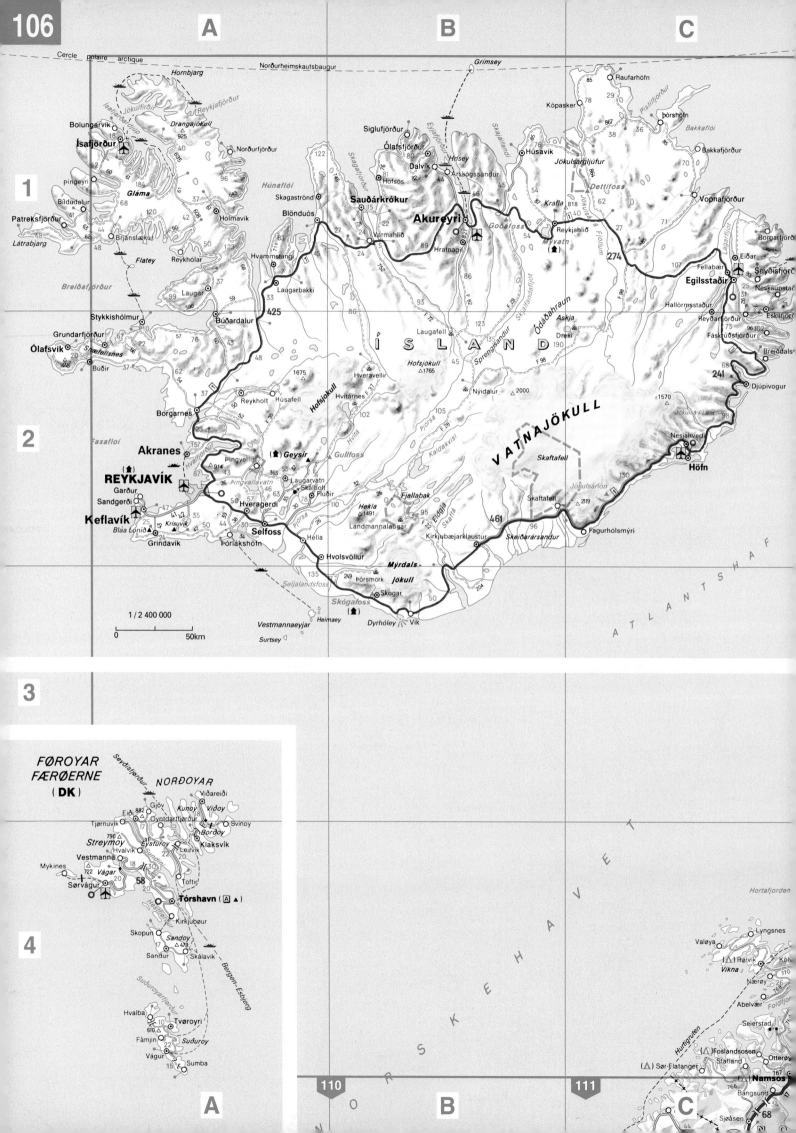

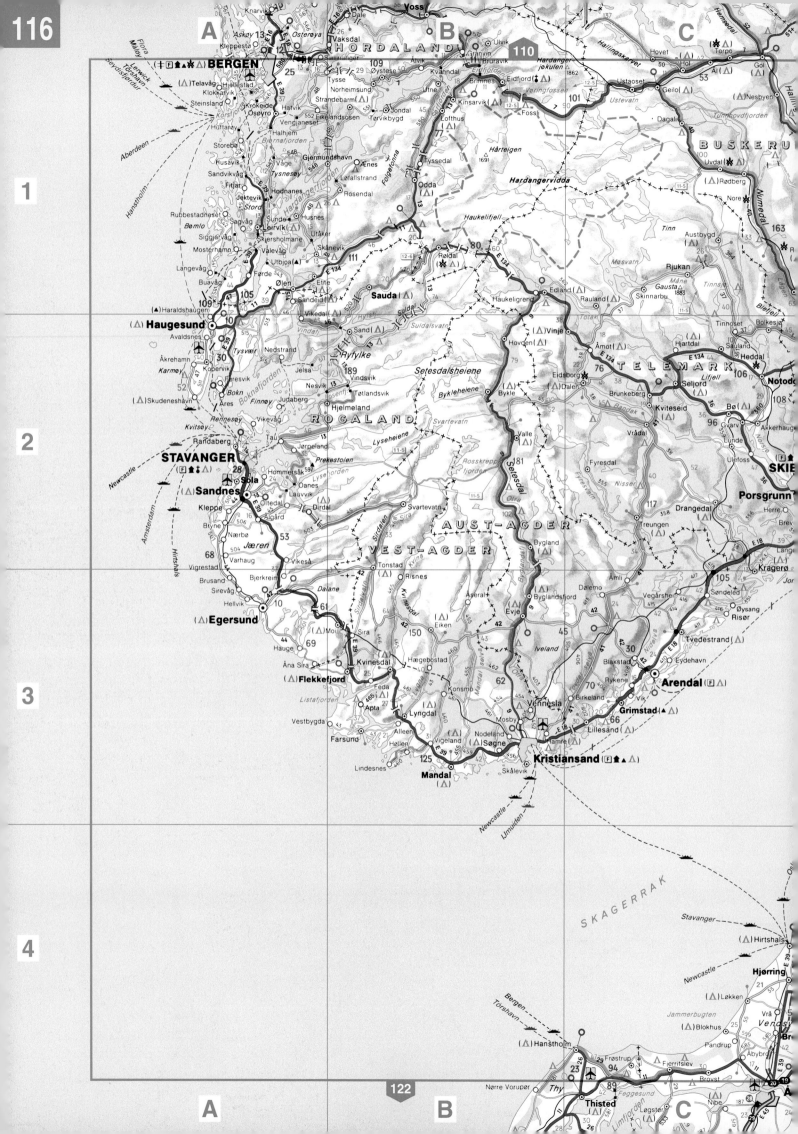

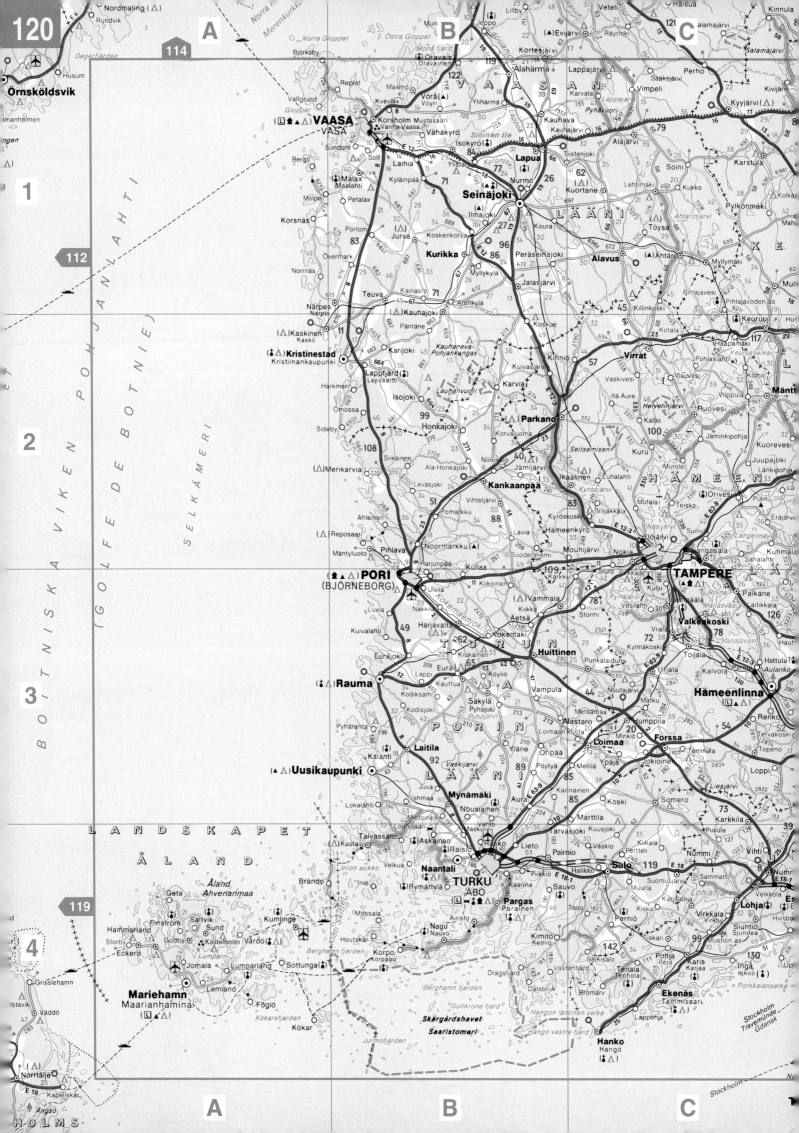

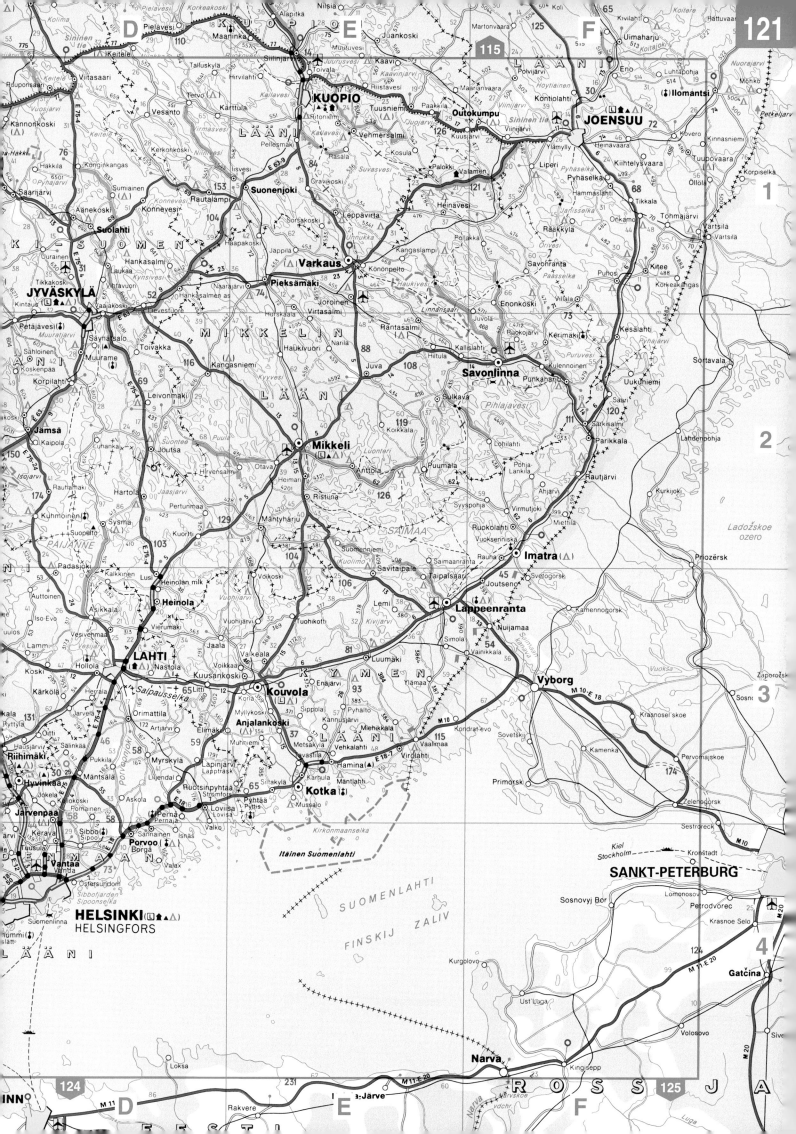

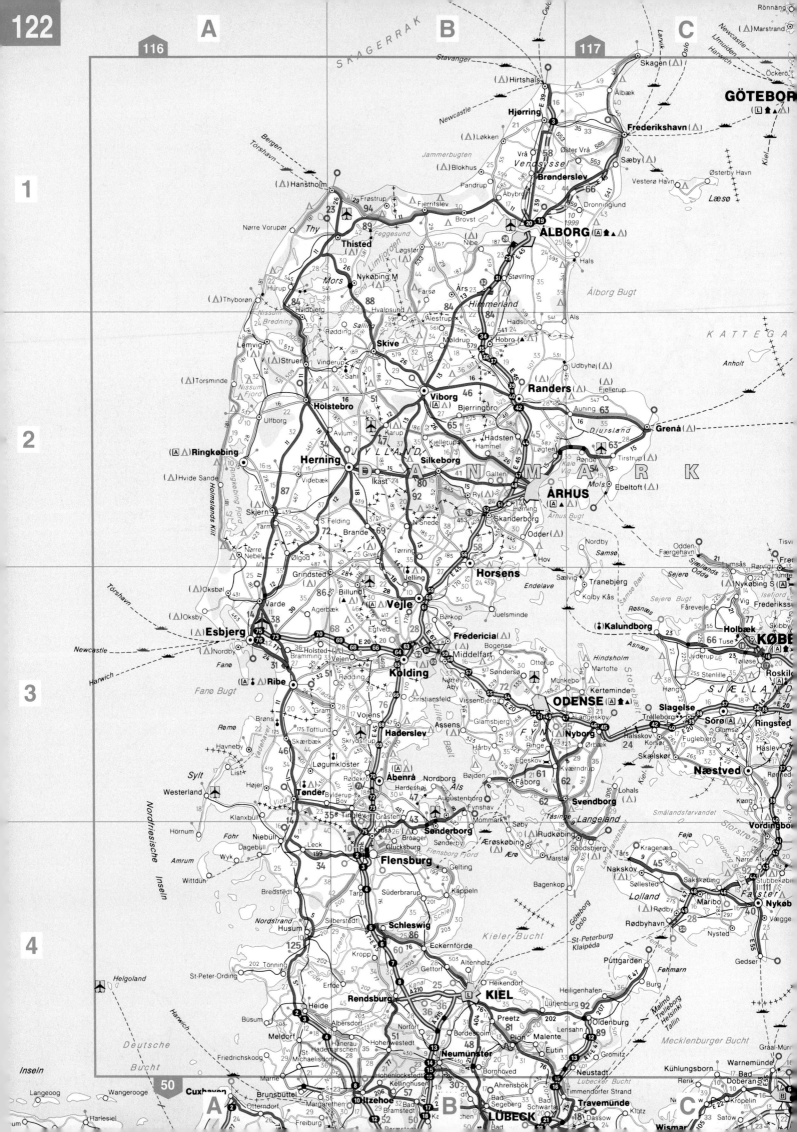

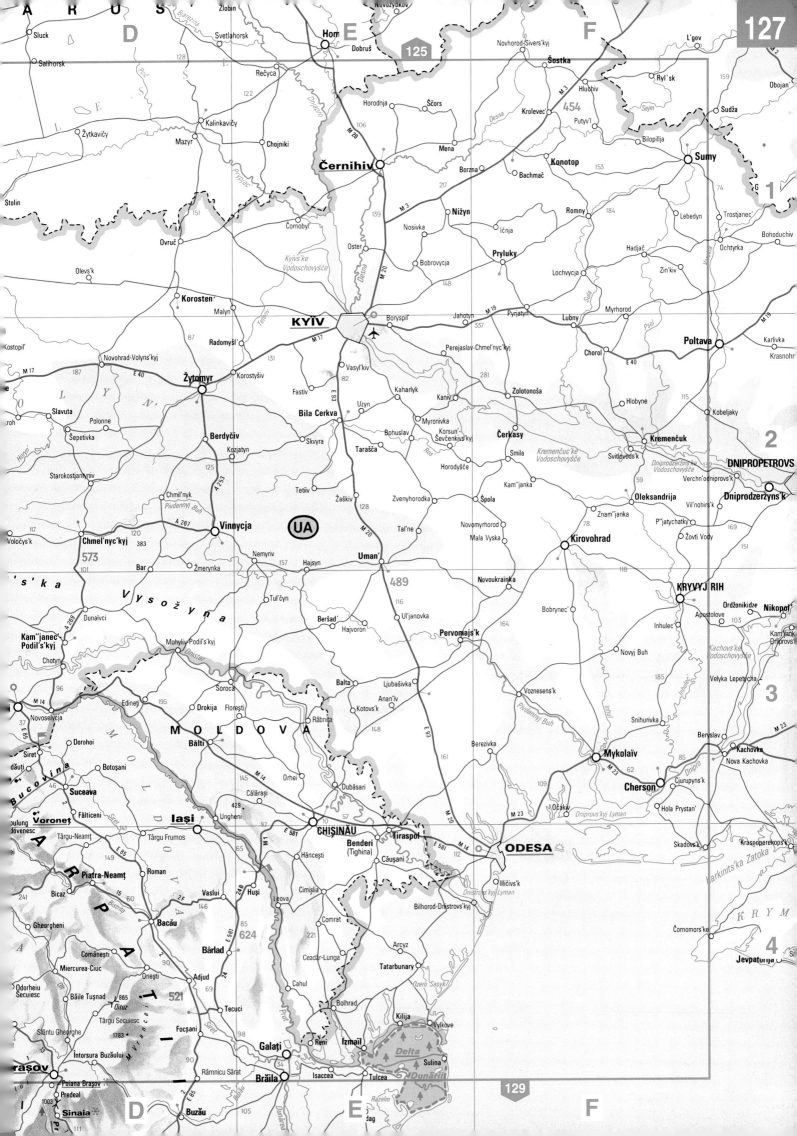

A, Å, Ä

A. Drossiní GR 91 D2
Á. Hóra GR 93 D3
Á. Kalendíni GR 92 B1
Á. Kaliníki GR 87 E1
Á. Kómi GR 87 F3
Á. Lefkími GR 92 A1
Á. Melás GR 87 E2
Á. Merá GR 98 C2
Á. Polidéndri GR 88 B4
A. Poróia GR 88 B1
Á. Rodákino GR 100 B4
Á. Sangrí GR 99 D2
Á. Síros GR 98 C2
Á. Viános GR 101 E4
Á. Vrondoú GR 88 C1
Á. Zervohóri GR 87 F2
Aachen D 61 E2
Aalen D 66 C1
Aalsmeer NL 54 B3
Aalst B 17 E2
Aalten NL 55 D4
Aalter B 15 F4
Äänekoski FIN 115 D3
Aapajärvi FIN 109 E1
Aarau CH 23 F4
Aarberg CH 27 F1
Aarburg CH 23 F4
Aarschot B 17 E1
Aavasaksa FIN 108 C2
Abades E 42 B1
Abadiño E 37 D1
Abanilla E 49 E1
Abano Terme I 72 A4
Abbadia S. Salvatore I 76 B4
Abbasanta I 82 B2
Abbeville F 16 B3
Abbey Town GB 9 D4
Abbeyfeale IRL 4 B3
Abbeyleix / Mainistir Laoise IRL 5 D2
Abbiategrasso I 71 D4
Abborrträsk S 108 A4
Abbots Bromley GB 11 D4
Abbotsbury GB 13 E3
Abcoude NL 54 B3
Abejar E 36 C3
Abejuela E 43 F2
Abela P 46 A1
Abelvær N 106 C4
Abenberg D 63 D4
Abenójar E 42 A4
Åbenrå DK 122 B3
Abensberg D 63 E4
L'Aber-Wrac'h F 18 A2
Aberaeron GB 10 A4
Aberdare / Aberdâr GB 13 D1
Aberdaron GB 10 A3
Aberdeen GB 9 E1
Aberdovey / Aberdyfi GB 10 B4
Aberfeldy GB 9 D1
Aberfoyle GB 8 C2
Abergavenny / Y-Fenni GB 13 D1
Abergele GB 10 B3
Aberlady GB 9 D2
Aberporth GB 12 C1
Abersoch GB 10 A3
Abertillery GB 13 D1
Aberystwyth GB 10 A4
Abetone I 75 F2
Abiego E 38 A3
Abingdon GB 13 F2
Abington GB 9 D3
Abisko S 104 B4
Abla E 48 C3
Ablis F 21 E3
Abondance F 27 E2
Abony H 126 A4
Aboyne GB 9 E1
Abrantes P 40 B2
Abreschviller F 23 E2
Les Abrets F 27 D3
Abriès F 27 F4
Abtenau A 68 A2
Åby S 119 D30
Åbybro DK 122 B1
Acceglio I 31 F1
Accettura I 80 C3
Acciaroli I 80 B4
Accous F 28 B4
Accrington GB 10 C2
Acebo E 41 D1
Acedo E 37 D2
Acehuche E 41 D2
Acerno I 80 B3
Acerra I 80 A3
Aceuchal E 41 D4
Achenkirch A 67 E2
Achern D 23 F2
Acheux-en-Amiénois F 16 C3
Achim D 50 B4
Achnacroish GB 8 B1
Achnasheen GB 6 C4
Aci Castello I 85 E3
Aci Trezza I 85 E3
Acıpayam TR 129 F4
Acireale I 85 E3
Acle GB 15 D1
Acqualagna I 76 C3
Acquapendente I 76 B4
Acquasanta Terme I 77 D4
Acquasparta I 76 C4
Acquaviva delle Fonti I 81 D2
Acqui Terme I 75 D2
Acri I 83 E2
Adak S 108 A4
Adámandas GR 98 B3
Adamclisi RO 129 E1
Adamuz E 47 F1
Adanero E 36 A4
Adapazarı TR 129 F3
Adare IRL 4 C2
Adelboden CH 27 F2
Adelfia I 81 D2
Adelsheim D 62 B4
Ademuz E 43 E2
Adenau D 61 F2
Ádendro GR 88 A2
Adjud RO 127 D4
Admont A 68 B2
Adolfsström S 107 F3
Adorf D 63 E2
Adra E 48 B3
Adrada (La) E 42 A1
Adradas E 37 D4
Adrall E 38 C3
Adrano I 85 D3
Adria I 76 B1
Ænes N 116 B1
Aerinó GR 93 E1
Ærøskøbing DK 122 B4
Aetópetra GR 86 C4
Aetoráhi GR 92 C4
Aetós GR 87 E2
Aetós GR 92 B2
Aetós GR 92 A3
Äetsä FIN 120 B3
Afándou GR 103 F2
Åfarnes N 110 C2
Aféa GR 97 F1
Affi I 71 F4
Afiónas GR 86 B4
Afissos GR 93 F1
Áfitos GR 88 C3
Afjord N 111 D1
Aflenz Kurort A 68 C2
Afráti GR 94 A3
Afyon TR 129 F4
Ag. Ána GR 94 A2
Ag. Ána GR 93 F4
Ag. Anárgiri GR 97 D3
Ag. Anárgiri GR 93 E1
Ag. Andónios GR 88 B3
Ag. Andréas GR 97 D2
Ag. Apóstoli GR 97 E4
Ag. Apóstoli GR 94 B3
Ag. Apóstoli GR 94 B4
Ag. Athanássios GR 89 D1
Ag. Athanássios GR 87 F2
Ag. Avgoustínos GR 96 C3
Ag. Déka GR 101 D4
Ag. Dimítrios GR 94 C4
Ag. Dimítrios GR 93 D3
Ag. Dimítrios GR 97 D3
Ag. Dimítrios GR 87 F3
Ag. Efimía GR 92 A3
Ag. Efstrátios (Nissí) GR 95 D1
Ag. Efthimía GR 93 E3
Ag. Fokás GR 103 D1
Ag. Fotiá GR 101 F4
Ag. Galíni GR 100 C4
Ag. Geórgios GR 92 A4
Ag. Geórgios GR 101 E4
Ag. Geórgios GR 93 F2
Ag. Geórgios GR 93 D2
Ag. Geórgios (Nissí) GR 98 A1
Ag. Germanós GR 87 E2
Ag. Górdis GR 86 B4
Ag. Harálambos GR 91 D2
Ag. Ioánis GR 97 A1
Ag. Ioánis GR 93 E2
Ag. Ioánis GR 93 F1
Ag. Ioánis GR 93 F4
Ag. Issídoros GR 103 E2
Ag. Kiriakí GR 96 B2
Ag. Kiriakí GR 87 D2
Ag. Kiriakí GR 99 F1
Ág. Kírikos GR 99 E1
Ág. Konstandínos GR 93 F2
Ág. Konstandínos GR 93 E1
Ág. Kosmás GR 89 E1
Ág. Kosmás GR 87 E3
Ág. Léon GR 96 A1
Ág. Loukás GR 94 B3
Ág. Mámas GR 88 C3
Ág. Marína GR 100 B3
Ág. Marína GR 94 B4
Ág. Marína GR 93 E2
Ág. Marína GR 99 F2
Ág. Marína GR 97 F1
Ág. Márkos GR 88 B1
Ág. Mathéos GR 86 B4
Ág. Míronas GR 101 D3
Ág. Nikítas GR 92 A2
Ág. Nikólaos GR 92 B2
Ág. Nikólaos GR 96 C3
Ág. Nikólaos GR 88 C3
Ág. Nikólaos GR 86 C4
Ág. Nikólaos GR 101 E4
Ág. Nikólaos GR 97 F1
Ág. Nikólaos GR 93 D3
Ág. Nikólaos GR 93 F2
Ág. Nikólaos GR 97 D3
Ág. Pandeleímonas GR 87 F2
Ag. Paraskeví GR 88 B1
Ag. Paraskeví GR 89 D1
Ag. Paraskeví GR 87 D3
Ag. Paraskeví GR 95 F1
Ag. Paraskiés GR 101 D4
Ag. Pávlos GR 88 B3
Ag. Pelagía GR 101 D3
Ag. Pelagía GR 97 E4
Ag. Pétros GR 97 D2
Ag. Pnévma GR 88 C1
Ag. Pródromos GR 88 C2
Ag. Rouméli GR 100 B3
Ag. Sofía GR 94 A3
Ag. Sofía GR 97 D2
Ag. Sóstis GR 93 D2
Ag. Sotíra GR 93 E1
Ag. Stéfanos GR 94 A4
Ag. Stéfanos GR 98 C1
Ag. Theódori GR 87 E4
Ag. Theódori GR 93 F4
Ag. Theódori GR 93 F2
Ag. Thomás GR 94 A4
Ag. Thomás GR 101 D4
Ag. Triáda GR 94 A4
Ag. Triáda GR 96 B1
Ag. Triáda GR 88 B2
Ag. Varvára GR 101 D4
Ag. Vassílios GR 88 B2
Ag. Vassílios GR 93 F4
Ag. Vissários GR 93 D1
Ágalos GR 87 F1
Agathoníssi GR 99 F1
Agay F 31 F3
Agazzano I 75 E1
Agde F 30 A3
Agen F 29 D2
Ager E 38 B3
Ageranós GR 97 D3
Agerbæk DK 122 A3
Aggius I 82 B1
Aggsbach A 68 C1
Agiá GR 88 A4
Agía Lávra GR 93 A4
Agía Triáda GR 100 C4
Agíasma GR 89 D1
Agiásmata GR 95 E2
Agiássos GR 95 F2
Ágio Óros GR 90 A4
Agiófilo GR 87 E4
Agiókambos GR 88 B4
Agiókambos GR 93 F2
Agionóri GR 97 E1
Agiopigí GR 93 D1
Agira I 85 D3
Ágnanda GR 92 B1
Agnanderó GR 93 D1
Ágnandi GR 93 F3
Agnóndas GR 94 A2
Agnone I 80 A1
Agoitz E 28 A4
Agon-Coutainville F 19 E2
Agorá GR 89 D1
Agordo I 67 F4
Agost E 49 F1
Agramunt E 38 B3
Agrate Brianza I 71 D4
Ágreda E 37 D3
Agreliá GR 87 F4
Agriá GR 93 E2
Agrigento I 84 C4
Agriliá GR 92 C3
Agrínio GR 92 C3
Agriovótano GR 93 F2
Agropoli I 80 B4
Ågskaret N 107 E2
Aguadulce E 48 C3
Aguadulce E 47 F2
Aguaviva E 44 A1
Agudo E 42 A4
Águeda P 40 B1
Aguiar P 40 B4
Aguiar da Beira P 34 C4
Aguilafuente E 36 B4
Aguilar E 47 F2
Aguilar de Campóo E 36 B1
Aguilar del Alfambra E 43 F1
Águilas E 49 D2
Aharnés GR 94 A4
Ahaus D 55 E3
Åheim N 110 B3
Ahendriás GR 101 D4
Ahigal E 41 E1
Ahilío GR 86 B4
Ahílio GR 93 E1
Ahinós GR 88 C1
Ahjärvi FIN 121 F2
Ahladerí GR 94 B3
Ahladohóri GR 88 C1
Ahlainen FIN 120 B2
Ahlbeck D 52 A2
Ahlen D 55 F4
Ahlhorn D 55 F2
Ahrensbök D 50 C3
Ahrensburg D 50 C3
Ähtäri FIN 114 C4
Ahtopol BG 136 E2
Ahun F 25 F3
Åhus S 123 E3
Ahvenselkä FIN 109 E2
Aichach D 67 E1
Aidenbach D 68 A1
Aidone I 85 D3
Aigen im Mühlkreis A 64 B4
L'Aigle F 20 C2
Aigle CH 27 E2
Aignan F 28 C2
Aignay-le-Duc F 22 B4
Aigre F 24 C3
Aigrefeuille-d'Aunis F 24 B2
Aigrefeuille-sur-Maine F 24 B1
Aigua Blava E 39 E3
Aiguebelette-le-Lac F 27 D3
Aiguebelle F 27 E3
Aigueperse F 26 A3
Aigues-Mortes F 30 B3
Aiguilles F 31 E1
Aiguillon F 29 D1
L'Aiguillon-sur-Mer F 24 B2
Aigurande F 25 E2
Ailefroide F 27 E4
Aillant-sur-Tholon F 21 F4
Ailly-le-Haut-Clocher F 16 B3
Ailly-sur-Noye F 16 C4
Aimargues F 30 B2
Aime F 27 E3
Ainhoa F 28 A3
Ainsa E 28 C4
Ainsdale GB 10 C2
Ainzón E 37 E3
Airaines F 16 B3
Airasca I 27 F4
Airdrie GB 8 C3
Aire-sur-la-Lys F 15 E4
Aire-sur-l'Adour F 28 C2
Airisto FIN 120 B4
Airolo CH 66 B4
Airvault F 24 C1
Aiterhofen D 63 F4
Aitrach D 66 C2
Aiud RO 126 C4
Les Aix-d'Angillon F 25 F1
Aix-en-Othe F 22 A3
Aix-en-Provence F 31 D3
Aix-les-Bains F 27 D3
Aixe-sur-Vienne F 25 E3
Aizenay F 24 A1
Aizkraukle LV 124 C3
Ajaccio F 78 A4
Ajaureforsen S 107 F3
Ajdovščina SLO 73 D3
Ajka H 69 F2
Ajo E 36 B1
Ajos FIN 109 D3
Ajtos BG 129 E2
Äkäsjokisuu FIN 108 C1
Äkäslompolo FIN 108 C1
Akçakoca TR 129 F2
Aken D 57 E3
Åkers styckebruk S 119 E2
Åkersberga S 119 F2
Akhisar TR 129 E4
Åkirkeby DK 123 E4
Akkerhaugen N 116 C2
Akranes IS 106 A2
Akráta GR 93 E4
Akréfnio GR 93 F3
Åkrehamn N 116 A2
Akrestrømmen N 111 E4
Akrítas GR 87 E2
Akrogiáli GR 88 C2
Akropótamos GR 89 D2
Akrotíri GR 99 D4
Akrotíri GR 99 D4
Akrotíri (Hers.) GR 100 B3
Akrovoúni GR 89 D1
Akujärvi FIN 105 F3
Akureyri IS 106 B1
Ål N 110 C4
Ala I 71 F4
Alà dei Sardi I 82 B2
Ala di Stura I 27 F4
Ala-Honkajoki FIN 120 B2
Ala-Vuokki FIN 115 E1
Alacant / Alicante E 49 F1
Alaejos E 35 F4
Alagí GR 96 C2
Alagna Valsesia I 70 C4
Alagón E 37 E3
Alagoniá GR 96 C2
Alahärmä FIN 114 B3
Alaior E 45 F2
Alakylä FIN 109 D1
Alalkomenés GR 93 F3
Alameda E 47 F3
Alamillo E 42 A4
Alanäs S 112 B1
Alandroal P 40 C4
Alange E 41 E4
Alanís E 47 E1
Alapitkä FIN 115 E3
Alaraz E 41 F1
Alarcón E 43 D3
Alar del Rey E 36 B2
Alaşehir TR 129 F4
Alassio I 74 C3
Alastaro FIN 120 B3
Alatoz E 43 E4
Alatri I 79 E2
Alavieska FIN 114 C2
Alavus / Alavo FIN 114 C4
Alba I 74 C2
Alba Adriatica I 77 D4
Albacete E 43 E4
Albacken S 112 B2
Alba de Tormes E 41 F1
Ålbæk DK 122 C1
Albaida E 43 F4
Alba Iulia RO 126 C4
Albaladejo E 42 C4
Albalate de Cinca E 38 A4
Albalate del Arzobispo E 37 F4
Albalate de las Nogueras E 43 D2
Alban F 29 F2
Albánchez E 49 D3
Albano di Lucania I 80 C3
Albano Laziale I 79 E2
Albarca E 38 B4
Albares de la Ribera E 33 D4
Albarracín E 43 E2
Albatana E 49 E1
Albatera E 49 E1
Albena BG 129 E1
Albenga I 74 C3
Albens F 27 D3
Alberca (La) E 41 E1
Alberca de Záncara (La) E 43 D3
Alberga S 119 D2
Albergaria-a-Velha P 34 B4
Alberguería de Argañán (La) E 41 D1
Alberic E 43 F4
Albernoa P 46 B1
Alberobello I 81 E2
Albersdorf D 50 B3
Albert F 16 C3
Albertville F 27 E3
Albestroff F 23 D2
Albi F 29 F2
Albiano d'Ivrea I 70 C4
Albinia I 78 C1
Albino I 71 E4
Albissola Marina I 75 D2
Albocàsser E 44 A2
Alboloduy E 48 C3
Albolote E 48 B3
Alborea E 43 E3
Ålborg DK 122 B1
Albox E 49 D2
Albstadt D 66 B2
Albuera (La) E 41 D4
Albufeira P 46 A2
Albujón E 49 E2
Albuñol E 48 B3
Alburquerque E 41 D3
Alby S 112 B3
Alby-sur-Chéran F 27 D3
Alcácer do Sal P 40 B4
Alcáçovas P 40 B4
Alcadozo E 43 D4
Alcafozes P 41 D2
Alcains P 40 C2
Alcalà de Xivert E 44 A2
Alcalá de Guadaira E 47 E2
Alcalá de Henares E 42 C1
Alcalá de la Selva E 43 F2
Alcalá de los Gazules E 47 E4
Alcalá del Río E 47 D2
Alcalá la Real E 48 A2
Alcalá del Júcar E 43 E4
Alcalfar E 45 F3
Alcamo I 84 B3
Alcampel E 38 A3
Alcanar E 44 B1
Alcanede P 40 A2
Alcanena P 40 B2
Alcanhes P 40 B3
Alcántara E 41 D2
Alcantarilha P 46 A2
Alcantarilla E 49 E2
Alcañices E 35 E3
Alcañiz E 44 A1
Alcaracejos E 47 F1
Alcaraz E 43 D4
Alcaria Ruiva P 46 B1
Alcarràs E 38 B4
Alcaudete E 48 A2
Alcaudete de la Jara E 42 A2
Alcázar de San Juan E 42 C3
Alcázares (Los) E 49 E2
Alceda E 36 B1
Alcester GB 13 F1
Alcobaça P 40 A2
Alcoba de los Montes E 42 A3
Alcobendas E 42 B1
Alcocer E 43 D1
Alcochete P 40 A3
Alcoi / Alcoy E 43 F4
Alcolea E 47 F1
Alcolea de Cinca E 38 A3
Alcolea del Pinar E 37 D4
Alcolea del Río E 47 E2
Alconchel E 41 D4
Alcora (L') E 44 A2
Alcorisa E 44 A1
Alcossebre E 44 A2
Alcoutim P 46 B2
Alcover E 38 B4
Alcoy / Alcoi E 43 F4
Alcubierre E 37 F3
Alcubilla de Avellaneda E 36 C3
Alcublas E 43 F3
Alcúdia de Crespins (L') E 43 F4
Alcúdia (L') E 43 F4
Alcúdia E 45 E3
Alcudia de Guadix E 48 B3
Alcuéscar E 41 E3
Aldea (L') E 44 B1
Aldeacentenera E 41 F3
Aldea del Cano E 41 E3
Aldea del Fresno E 42 B1
Aldea del Rey E 42 B4
Aldeanueva de Ebro E 37 E3
Aldeanueva de la Vera E 41 F2
Aldeanueva del Camino E 41 E1
Aldeburgh GB 15 D2
Aldeia da Ponte P 41 D1
Aldeia Gavinha P 40 A3
Aldershot GB 14 B3
Aledo E 49 D2
Aleksandrov RUS 125 F2
Aleksin RUS 125 F3
Aleksinac YU 128 B2
Alençon F 20 C3
Alenquer P 40 A3
Alepohóri GR 97 D2
Alepohóri GR 93 F4
Aléria F 78 B3
Alès F 30 B2
Ales I 82 B3
Aleşd RO 126 B4
Alessandria I 75 D1
Alessandria della Rocca I 84 B3
Ålestrup DK 122 B2
Ålesund N 110 B2
Alexándria GR 88 A2
Alexandria GB 8 C2
Alexandria RO 129 D1

Alexandroúpoli *GR* ... 91 D2	Alfeld *D* ... 56 C3	Algar (El) *E* ... 49 E2	Algorta *E* ... 36 C1	Alía *E* ... 41 F3	Alikianós *GR* ... 100 B3
Alf *D* ... 61 F3	Alfeld *D* ... 63 E3	Ålgård *N* ... 116 A2	Algoz *P* ... 46 A2	Aliaga *E* ... 43 F1	Alimiá (Nissí) *GR* ... 103 E2
Alfajarín *E* ... 37 F4	Alfiós *GR* ... 96 C1	Algarinejo *E* ... 48 A2	Alhama de Granada *E* 48 A3	Aliaguilla *E* ... 43 E3	Alingsås *S* ... 118 B4
Alfambra *P* ... 46 A2	Alfonsine *I* ... 76 B1	Algarrobo *E* ... 48 A3	Alhama de Almería *E* 48 C3	Alíartos *GR* ... 93 F3	Alinyà *E* ... 38 C3
Alfambra *E* ... 43 F1	Alford *GB* ... 7 E4	Algatocín *E* ... 47 E3	Alhama de Aragón *E* . 37 D4	Alibunar *YU* ... 128 B1	Alise-Ste-Reine *F* ... 22 B4
Alfândega da Fé *P* ... 35 D4	Alfreton *GB* ... 11 D3	Algeciras *E* ... 47 E4	Alhama de Murcia *E* . 49 E2	Alicante / Alacant *E* ... 49 F1	Aliseda *E* ... 41 D3
Alfaro *E* ... 37 E3	Alfta *S* ... 112 B4	Algemesí *E* ... 43 F3	Alhambra *E* ... 42 C4	Alicún de Ortega *E* ... 48 B2	Alistráti *GR* ... 89 D1
Alfarràs *E* ... 38 B3	Algaba (La) *E* ... 47 D2	Alghero *I* ... 82 A2	Alhaurín el Grande *E*. 47 E3	Alife *I* ... 80 A2	Alivéri *GR* ... 94 B3
Alfàs del Pi (L') *E* ... 49 F1	Algaida *E* ... 45 E3	Alginet *E* ... 43 F3	Alhóndiga *E* ... 42 C1	Alijó *P* ... 34 C4	Aljezur *P* ... 46 A2
Alfedena *I* ... 79 F2	Algar *E* ... 47 E3	Algodonales *E* ... 47 E3	Alì Terme *I* ... 83 D4	Alikés *GR* ... 92 B4	Aljucén *E* ... 41 E3
Alfeizerão *P* ... 40 A2	Algar de Palància *E* .. 44 A3	Algora *E* ... 43 D1	Alia *I* ... 84 C3	Alikí *GR* ... 98 C3	Aljustrel *P* ... 46 B1

Alkmaar NL — 54 B3
Allaire F — 19 D4
Allanche F — 26 A4
Alland A — 69 D1
Allariz E — 32 B4
Alleen N — 116 B3
Alleghe I — 67 F4
Allègre F — 26 A4
Allensbach D — 66 B2
Allentsteig A — 64 C4
Allepuz E — 43 F1
Allersberg D — 63 E4
Allershausen D — 67 E1
Alleuze F — 26 A4
Allevard F — 27 D4
Allinge Sandvig DK — 123 E3
Allo E — 28 A4
Alloa GB — 9 D2
Allonnes F — 24 C1
Alloza E — 43 F1
Allstedt D — 57 D4
Almacelles E — 38 A3
Almáchar E — 48 A3
Almada P — 40 A3
Almadén E — 42 A4
Almadén de la Plata E — 47 D1
Almadenejos E — 42 A4
Almagro E — 42 B4
Almajano E — 37 D3
Almancil P — 46 B2
Almansa E — 43 F4
Almanza E — 33 F4
Almaraz E — 41 F2
Almarcha (La) E — 43 D3
Almargen E — 47 F3
Almarza E — 37 D3
Almassora E — 44 A2
Almazán E — 37 D4
Almedinilla E — 48 A2
Almeida P — 35 D4
Almeida E — 35 E4
Almeirim P — 40 B3
Almeirim P — 40 B3
Almelo NL — 55 D3
Almenar E — 38 B3
Almenara E — 44 A2
Almenar de Soria E — 37 D3
Almendral E — 41 D4
Almendralejo E — 41 E4
Almendro (El) E — 46 C2
Almere-Stad NL — 54 C3
Almería E — 48 C3
Almerimar E — 48 C3
Almese I — 27 F4
Älmhult S — 123 E2
Almirí GR — 97 E1
Almiró GR — 96 C3
Almiropótamos GR — 94 B4
Almirós GR — 93 E1
Almodôvar P — 46 B2
Almodóvar del Campo E — 42 A4
Almodóvar del Pinar E — 43 E3
Almodóvar del Río E — 47 F1
Almogía E — 47 F3
Almoguera E — 42 C2
Almoharín E — 41 E3
Almonacid de Toledo E — 42 B2
Almonacid de Zorita E — 42 C2
Almonació de la Sierra E — 37 E4
Almonaster la Real E — 46 C1
Almonte E — 47 D2
Almoradí E — 49 E1
Almorox E — 42 A2
Almudévar E — 37 F3
Almunia de Doña Godina (La) E — 37 E4
Almuñécar E — 48 A3
Almuradiel E — 48 B1
Alness GB — 7 D4
Alnö S — 112 C3
Alnwick GB — 9 F3
Alónia GR — 88 A3
Alónissos GR — 94 A2
Alónissos (Nissí) GR — 94 B1
Álora E — 47 F3
Alosno E — 46 C2
Alozaina E — 47 F3
Alp E — 38 C2
Alpalhão P — 40 C3
Alpbach A — 67 F3
L'Alpe-d'Huez F — 27 D4
Alpedrinha P — 40 C1
Alpera E — 43 E4
Alphen aan den Rijn NL — 54 B3
Alpiarça P — 40 B3
Alpignano I — 27 F4
Alpirsbach D — 23 F3

Alpua FIN — 114 C2
Alqueva P — 40 C4
Alquián (El) E — 48 C3
Als DK — 122 B2
Alsdorf D — 61 E2
Alsen S — 112 A2
Alsfeld D — 62 B2
Alsleben D — 57 E4
Alstahaug N — 107 D3
Alston GB — 9 E4
Alt Ruppin D — 51 E4
Alta N — 105 D2
Altamura I — 81 D3
Altastenberg D — 62 A1
Altaussee A — 68 B2
Altavilla Milicia I — 84 B2
Altdöbern D — 58 A3
Altdorf CH — 66 B4
Altdorf b. Nürnberg D — 63 E4
Altea E — 49 F1
Altedo I — 76 A1
Altena D — 61 F1
Altenahr D — 61 F2
Altenau D — 56 C4
Altenberg D — 64 A1
Altenberge D — 55 E4
Altenburg D — 63 E1
Altenholz D — 50 B2
Altenhundem D — 62 A1
Altenkirchen D — 51 F1
Altenkirchen i. Westerwald D — 61 F2
Altenmarkt A — 68 A2
Altenmarkt bei St. Gallen A — 68 C2
Altenmarkt a. d. Alz D — 67 F2
Altenstadt D — 66 C2
Altensteig D — 23 F2
Altentreptow D — 51 F3
Altenwalde D — 50 A3
Alter do Chão P — 40 C3
Altglashütten D — 23 F3
Altheim A — 68 A1
Althofen A — 68 C3
Altkirch F — 23 E4
Altlandsberg D — 57 F2
Altlengbach A — 69 D1
Altmünster A — 68 B2
Altnaharra GB — 7 D3
Altötting D — 67 F1
Alton GB — 14 B4
Altopascio I — 75 F3
Altorricón E — 38 A3
Altrincham GB — 10 C3
Altsasu E — 37 D1
Altshausen D — 66 C2
Altstätten CH — 66 C3
Altura E — 43 F3
Altweilnau D — 62 A2
Alustante E — 43 E1
Alva GB — 9 D2
Alvaiázere P — 40 B2
Alvalade P — 46 A1
Alverca do Ribatejo P — 40 A3
Alvignac F — 29 E1
Älvik N — 116 B1
Alvito P — 40 B4
Älvkarleby S — 119 E1
Alvor P — 46 A2
Älvros S — 112 B3
Älvsbyn S — 108 B3
Alyth GB — 9 D1
Alytus LT — 124 B4
Alzenau D — 62 B3
Alzey D — 62 A3
Alzira E — 43 F4
Alzola E — 37 D1
Alzon F — 30 A2
Alzonne F — 29 F3
Åmål S — 118 B2
Amalfi I — 80 A3
Amaliáda GR — 96 B1
Amaliápoli GR — 93 F1
Amáló GR — 99 E1
Amance F — 23 D4
Amancey F — 27 D1
Amandola I — 77 D4
Amantea I — 83 E2
Amárandos GR — 93 D1
Amárandos GR — 87 D3
Amarante P — 34 C3
Amareleja P — 46 C1
Amares P — 34 B3
Amárinthos GR — 94 B3
Amatrice I — 77 D4
Amay B — 17 F2
Ambarès-et-Lagrave F — 24 C4
Ambasaguas E — 33 E3

Ambazac F — 25 E3
Ambelákia GR — 88 A4
Ambelákia GR — 91 E1
Ambelía GR — 93 E1
Ambelikó GR — 95 F2
Ambelióna GR — 96 C2
Ambelónas GR — 88 A4
Amberg D — 63 E3
Ambérieu-en-Bugey F — 27 D3
Ambert F — 26 B3
Ambès F — 24 C4
Ambierle F — 26 B2
Amble GB — 9 F4
Ambleside GB — 10 C1
Amboise F — 21 D4
Ambra I — 76 B3
Ambrières-les-Vallées F — 19 F3
Ameixial P — 46 B2
Amelia I — 79 D1
Amélie-les-Bains-Palalda F — 29 F4
Amelinghausen D — 50 C4
Amer E — 39 D3
Amerongen NL — 54 C4
Amersfoort NL — 54 C3
Amersham GB — 14 B3
Amesbury GB — 13 F2
Ametlla de Mar (L') E — 44 B1
Amfiaraío GR — 94 A4
Amfíklia GR — 93 E3
Amfilohía GR — 92 B2
Amfípoli GR — 88 C2
Ámfissa GR — 93 E3
Amiens F — 16 C3
Amigdaleónas GR — 89 D1
Amigdaliá GR — 93 D3
Amilly F — 21 F3
Amíndeo GR — 87 E2
Åmli N — 116 C2
Amlwch GB — 3 F4
Ammanford / Rhydaman GB — 12 C1
Ämmänsaari FIN — 115 E1
Ammarnäs S — 107 F3
Amohóri GR — 87 E2
Amoliani GR — 89 D3
Amoliani (Nissí) GR — 89 D3
Amorbach D — 62 B3
Amorebieta E — 37 D1
Amorgós GR — 99 D3
Amorgós (Nissí) GR — 99 D3
Amório GR — 91 E1
Åmot N — 116 C2
Åmot S — 112 C4
Åmot N — 117 D1
Åmotfors S — 118 B2
Amótopos GR — 92 B1
Amou F — 28 B3
Amoudára GR — 101 D4
Amoudára GR — 101 E4
Ampezzo I — 68 A4
Ampfing D — 67 F1
Amphion-les-Bains F — 27 E2
Amplepuis F — 26 B3
Ampolla (L') E — 44 B1
Amposta E — 44 B1
Ampthill GB — 14 B2
Ampudia E — 36 A3
Ampuero E — 36 C1
Amriswil CH — 66 C3
Amsele S — 113 D1
Amstelveen NL — 54 B3
Amsterdam NL — 54 B3
Amstetten A — 68 C1
Amurrio E — 36 C1
Amusco E — 33 F4
Åna Sira N — 116 A3
Anadia P — 40 B1
Anáfi GR — 99 D4
Anáfi (Nissí) GR — 99 D4
Anafonítria GR — 92 A4
Anagni I — 79 E2
Análipsi GR — 99 E4
Análipsi GR — 93 F3
Análipsis GR — 96 C2
Anan'ïv UA — 127 E3
Anaráhi GR — 87 E2
Anárgiri GR — 87 E2
Anascaul IRL — 4 A3
Anatolí GR — 88 A4
Anatolí GR — 87 D4
Anatolí GR — 101 E4
Anatolikó GR — 87 E2
Anávatos GR — 95 F3
Anávissos GR — 98 A1
Anávra GR — 93 D1
Anávra GR — 93 E2
Ancenis F — 19 E4
Ancerville F — 22 B2
Anchuras E — 42 A3

Ancona I — 77 D3
Ancy-le-Franc F — 22 A4
Anda N — 110 B3
Andalo I — 71 F3
Åndalsnes N — 110 C3
Andartikó GR — 87 E2
Andebu N — 117 D2
Andelot F — 22 C3
Les Andelys F — 16 B4
Andenes N — 104 A3
Andenne B — 17 F2
Anderlues B — 17 E2
Andermatt CH — 66 B4
Andernach D — 61 F2
Andernos-les-Bains F — 28 B1
Anderstorp S — 123 E1
Andígonos GR — 87 F2
Andikíra GR — 93 E3
Andikíthira (Nissí) GR — 100 A2
Andimáhia GR — 103 D1
Andímilos (Nissí) GR — 98 A3
Andíparos GR — 98 C3
Andíparos (Nissí) GR — 98 C3
Andípaxi (Nissí) GR — 92 A1
Andípsara (Nissí) GR — 95 E3
Andírio GR — 92 C3
Ándissa GR — 95 E1
Andoain E — 28 A3
Andorno Micca I — 70 C3
Andorra E — 44 A1
Andosilla E — 28 A4
Andover GB — 13 F2
Andratx E — 45 D3
Andravída GR — 92 B4
Andretta I — 80 B3
Anzio I — 79 E2
Andrézieux-Bouthéon F — 26 B3
Andria I — 80 C2
Andrijevica YU — 128 B3
Andrítsena GR — 96 C1
Ándros GR — 98 C1
Ándros (Nissí) GR — 94 C4
Androússa GR — 96 C2
Andselv N — 104 B3
Andújar E — 48 A1
Anduze F — 30 B2
Aneby S — 118 C4
Ånes N — 110 C2
Anet F — 21 D2
Angáli GR — 94 A2
Ånge S — 112 A2
Ånge S — 112 B3
Angeja P — 34 B1
Ängelholm S — 123 D2
Angeli FIN — 105 E3
Angelohóri GR — 87 F2
Angelókastro GR — 92 C3
Angelókastro GR — 97 E1
Anger A — 69 D2
Angera I — 71 D4
Angermünde D — 52 A4
Angern a. d. March A — 65 E4
Angers F — 19 F4
Angerville F — 21 E3
Anghiari I — 76 B3
Angístri (Nissí) GR — 97 F1
Ángistro GR — 88 C1
Anglès E — 39 D3
Anglès F — 29 F3
Angles-sur-l'Anglin F — 25 D2
Anglesola E — 38 B4
Anglet F — 28 A3
Anglure F — 22 A2
Angoulême F — 24 C3
Angri I — 80 A3
Angüés E — 38 A3
Anguiano E — 36 C2
Anguillara Veneta I — 72 B4
Aniane F — 30 B2
Aniche F — 17 D3
Ánixi GR — 87 E4
Anizy-le-Château F — 17 D4
Anjalankoski FIN — 121 D2
Anjum NL — 55 D1
Ankaran SLO — 73 D3
Ankarsrum S — 119 D4
Anklam D — 51 F3
Ankum D — 55 E3
Ånn S — 112 A2
Annaberg im Lammertal A — 68 C1
Annaberg-Buchholz D — 63 F1
Annaburg D — 57 F3
Annan GB — 9 D4
Anndalsvågen N — 107 D3
Annecy F — 27 D3
Annemasse F — 27 E2
Annevoie-Rouillon B — 17 F3
Annonay F — 26 C4
Annone Veneto I — 72 B3
Annot F — 31 E2

Annweiler D — 23 F1
Anógia GR — 101 D3
Anógia GR — 97 D3
Anópoli GR — 100 B3
Ansbach D — 63 D4
Anse F — 26 C3
Ansedonia I — 78 C1
Ansião P — 40 B2
Ansnes N — 111 D1
Ansó E — 28 B4
Anstruther GB — 9 E1
Antas E — 49 D3
Antegnate I — 71 E4
Antemil E — 36 B2
Antemil E — 32 B2
Antequera E — 47 F3
Anterselva di Mezzo / Antholz Mittertal I — 67 F4
Anthi GR — 88 C1
Ánthia GR — 91 D2
Anthíli GR — 93 E2
Anthótopos GR — 93 E1
Antibes F — 31 F2
Antilla (La) E — 46 C2
Antraigues-sur-Volane F — 30 B1
Antrain F — 19 E3
Antrim GB — 3 E2
Antrodoco I — 79 E1
Anttola FIN — 121 E2
Antwerpen B — 17 E1
Antwerpen-Deurne B — 17 E1
Anzano di Puglia I — 80 B2
Anzola d'Ossola I — 70 C3
Anzy-le-Duc F — 26 B2
Aosta / Aoste I — 27 F3
Apecchio I — 76 B3
Apel (Ter) NL — 55 E2
Apeldoorn NL — 54 C3
Apen D — 55 E2
Apéri GR — 103 D4
Aphrodisias TR — 129 F4
Apidiá GR — 97 D3
Apíkia GR — 98 C1
Apíranthos GR — 99 D2
Apolakiá GR — 103 E2
Apolda D — 63 E1
Apólonas GR — 99 D2
Apólonas GR — 98 B3
Apolonía GR — 88 C2
Apolonía GR — 98 C3
Apóstoli GR — 100 C3
Apostolove UA — 127 F3
Äppelbo S — 118 C1
Appenweier D — 23 F2
Appenzell CH — 66 C3
Appiano s. str. d. vino / Eppan I — 67 E4
Appingedam NL — 55 D1
Appleby GB — 10 C1
Aprica I — 71 E3
Apricena I — 80 B1
Aprília I — 79 E2
Apt F — 31 D2
Apta N — 116 B3
Áptera GR — 100 B3
Aquileia I — 72 C3
Arabba I — 67 F4
Aracena E — 47 D1
Arad RO — 126 B4
Aragona I — 84 C3
Arahal (El) E — 47 E2
Aráhova GR — 93 D3
Aráhova GR — 93 E3
Aramits F — 28 B3
Aranda de Duero E — 36 B3
Aranðelovac YU — 128 B1
Aranjuez E — 42 B2
Arantzazu E — 37 D1
Aras de Alpuente E — 43 F2
Arasluokta S — 107 F1
Áratos GR — 91 D2
Aravaca E — 42 B1
Aravissós GR — 88 A2
Áraxos GR — 92 C4
Arazede P — 40 B1
Arbatax I — 82 C3
Arbeca E — 38 B4
Arbesbach A — 64 C4
Arboga S — 119 D2
Arbois F — 27 D1
Arbon CH — 66 C3
Arborea (Località) I — 82 A3
Arborio I — 70 C4
Arbrå S — 112 B4
L'Arbresle F — 26 C3
Arbroath GB — 9 E1
Arbúcies E — 39 D3
Arbus I — 82 B3
Arc-en-Barrois F — 22 B3
Arcachon F — 28 B1

Arce I — 79 F2
Arcen NL — 61 E1
Arcevia I — 76 C3
Archena E — 49 E1
Archiac F — 24 C3
Archidona E — 48 A3
Arcidosso I — 76 B4
Arcis-sur-Aube F — 22 A3
Arco I — 71 F3
Arco de Baulhe P — 34 C3
Arcos E — 36 B2
Arcos (Los) E — 37 D2
Arcos de Jalón E — 37 D4
Arcos de la Frontera E — 47 E3
Arcos de Valdevez P — 32 A4
Les Arcs F — 27 E3
Les Arcs F — 31 E3
Arcusa E — 38 A3
Ardales E — 47 F3
Årdalstangen N — 110 C4
Ardánio GR — 91 E2
Ardara IRL — 2 C2
Ardberg D — 8 A3
Ardee / Baile Átha Fhirdhia IRL — 3 D3
Ardentes F — 25 E1
Ardentinny GB — 8 B2
Ardes F — 26 A4
Ardglass GB — 3 E3
Ardisa E — 37 F3
Ardlussa GB — 8 B2
Ardmore / Aird Mhór IRL — 5 D3
Ardrahan IRL — 2 B4
Ardres F — 15 E4
Ardrishaig GB — 8 B2
Ardrossan GB — 3 F1
Arduaine GB — 8 B2
Ardvasar GB — 6 B4
Åre S — 112 A2
Areeta E — 36 C1
Arenas de Cabrales E — 33 F3
Arenas de Iguiña E — 36 B1
Arenas de San Juan E — 42 B4
Arenas de San Pedro E — 41 F3
Arendal N — 116 C3
Arendonk B — 17 F1
Arendsee D — 51 D4
Arenys de Mar E — 39 D4
Arenzano I — 75 D2
Areópoli GR — 97 D3
Ares N — 116 A3
Arès F — 28 B1
Ares E — 32 B2
Aréthoussa GR — 88 C2
Areti GR — 88 B2
Arévalo E — 36 A4
Arez P — 40 C2
Arezzo I — 76 B3
Arfará GR — 96 C2
Argamasilla de Alba E — 42 C4
Argamasilla de Calatrava E — 42 B4
Arganda E — 42 C2
Arganil P — 40 C1
Argássi GR — 96 A1
Argelès-Gazost F — 28 C4
Argelès-sur-Mer F — 30 A4
Argenta I — 76 B1
Argentan F — 20 C2
Argentat F — 25 F4
Argente E — 43 F1
L'Argentière-la-Bessée F — 31 E1
Argenton-Château F — 24 C1
Argenton-sur-Creuse F — 25 E2
Argentona E — 39 D4
Argentré-du-Plessis F — 19 E3
Arginónda GR — 99 F2
Argirádes GR — 86 B4
Argiró GR — 94 B4
Argiropoúlio GR — 88 A4
Argiroúpoli GR — 100 B3
Argithéa GR — 93 D2
Árgos GR — 97 D1
Árgos Orestikó GR — 87 E2
Argostóli GR — 92 A4
Arguedas E — 37 E3
Argueil F — 16 B4
Arguellite E — 48 C1
Arguis E — 37 F3
Arh. Kleonés GR — 97 D1
Arh. Neméa GR — 97 D1

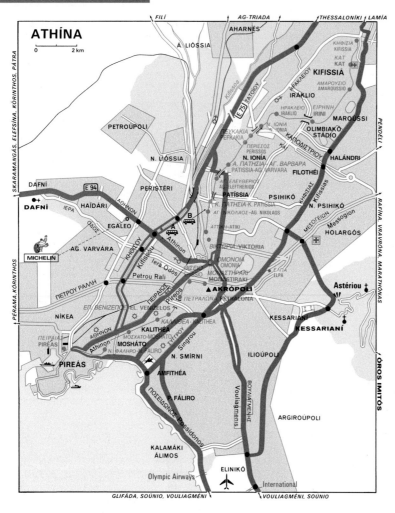

ATHÍNA

Arkássa *GR* 103 D4
Arkessíni *GR* 99 D3
Arkí (Nissí) *GR* 99 F2
Arkítsa *GR* 93 F2
Arklow / An tInbhear Mór *IRL* 5 E2
Arkoúdi (Nissí) *GR* 92 A3
Arlanc *F* 26 B4
Arlanda *S* 119 E2
Arlanzón *E* 36 C2
Arlempdes *F* 26 B4
Arles *F* 30 C2
Arles-sur-Tech *F* 29 F4
Arlesheim *CH* 23 E4
Arlon *B* 22 C1
Arma di Taggia *I* 74 C3
Armação de Pêra *P* 46 A2
Armadale *GB* 9 D2
Armagh *GB* 3 D3
Armamar *P* 34 C4
Arméni *GR* 100 C3
Armenistís *GR* 99 E1
Armentières *F* 15 F4
Armilla *E* 48 B3
Armólia *GR* 95 F4
Árna *GR* 97 D3
Arnac-Pompadour *F* 25 E4
Arnay-le-Duc *F* 26 B1
Arnéa *GR* 88 C2
Arneburg *D* 57 E2
Arnedillo *E* 37 D3
Arnedo *E* 37 D3
Arnés *E* 44 A1
Árnes *N* 117 D2
Arnhem *NL* 54 C4
Árni *GR* 75 F2
Árnissa *GR* 87 F2
Arnoldstein *A* 68 B4
Arnsberg *D* 62 A1
Arnstadt *D* 63 D1
Arnstein *D* 62 C3
Aroanía *GR* 93 D4
Aroche *E* 46 C1
Arogí *GR* 89 F1
Arolsen *D* 56 B4
Arona *I* 70 C4
Aroniádika *GR* 97 E4
Aronkylä *FIN* 114 B4
Áros *N* 117 D2
Arosa *CH* 66 C4

Arouca *P* 34 B4
Årøysund *N* 117 D2
Arpajon *F* 21 E2
Arpela *FIN* 109 D3
Arquata del Tronto *I* 77 D4
Arques *F* 15 E4
Arques-la-Bataille *F* 16 A3
Arquillos *E* 48 B1
Arrabal *E* 32 A4
Arracourt *F* 23 D2
Arraiolos *P* 40 B4
Arras *F* 16 C3
Arrasate / Mondragón *E* 37 D1
Arreau *F* 29 D4
Arredondo *E* 36 C1
Arrens-Marsous *F* 28 C4
Arrifana *P* 41 D3
Arrigorriaga *E* 36 C1
Arriondas *E* 33 F2
Arroba de los Montes *E* 42 A3
Arrochar *GB* 8 C2
Arromanches-les-Bains *F* 19 F1
Arronches *P* 40 C3
Arroyo de la Luz *E* 41 E4
Arroyo del Ojanco *E* 48 C1
Arroyo de San Serván *E* 41 D4
Arroyomolinos de Léon *E* 47 D1
Arroyomolinos de Montánchez *E* 41 E3
Arruda dos Vinhos *P* 40 A3
Års *DK* 122 B1
Ars-en-Ré *F* 24 A2
Ars-sur-Moselle *F* 22 C2
Arsié *I* 72 A3
Arsiero *I* 72 A3
Arskógssandur *IS* 106 B1
Årsunda *S* 119 E1
Arsy *F* 16 C4
Artà *E* 45 E3
Árta *GR* 92 A3
Arta Terme *I* 68 A4
Artajona *E* 28 A4
Artemissía *GR* 96 C2
Artemíssio *GR* 93 F2
Artemónas *GR* 98 B3
Artena *I* 79 E2

Artenay *F* 21 E3
Artern *D* 57 D4
Artés *E* 38 C3
Artesa de Segre *E* 38 B3
Artessianó *GR* 93 D1
Arth *CH* 66 B4
Arth *D* 67 F1
Arthurstown *IRL* 5 E3
Arties *E* 29 D4
Artjärvi *FIN* 121 D3
Artotína *GR* 93 D3
Artziniega *E* 36 C1
Arudy *F* 28 C3
Arundel *GB* 14 B4
Árvi *GR* 101 E4
Arvidsjaur *S* 108 A3
Árvik *N* 110 B3
Arvika *S* 118 C3
Årviksand *N* 104 C2
Arzachena *I* 78 A3
Arzacq-Arraziguet *F* 28 C3
Arzano *F* 18 C3
Arzberg *D* 63 E2
Arzignano *I* 72 A4
Árzos *GR* 91 E1
Arzúa *E* 32 B3
As *B* 17 F1
Åsa *S* 118 B4
Åsarna *S* 112 A3
Åsarp *S* 118 C4
Ascain *F* 28 A3
Ascha *D* 63 F4
Aschach an der Donau *A* 68 B1
Aschaffenburg *D* 62 B3
Aschau i. Chiemgau *D* 67 F2
Aschbach-Markt *A* 68 C1
Ascheberg *D* 50 C2
Ascheberg *D* 55 E4
Aschendorf (Ems) *D* 55 E2
Aschersleben *D* 57 D4
Asciano *I* 76 B4
Asco *F* 78 A3
Ascó *E* 38 B4
Ascoli Piceno *I* 77 D4
Ascoli Satriano *I* 80 B2
Ascona *CH* 71 D3
Åse *N* 104 A3
Åseda *S* 123 F1
Åsele *S* 112 A1

Åsen *N* 111 E1
Asenovgrad *BG* 129 D2
Åseral *N* 116 B3
Asfáka *GR* 87 D4
Asfeld *F* 17 E4
Åsgårdstrand *N* 117 D2
Ashbourne *GB* 11 D3
Ashbourne *IRL* 3 D4
Ashburton *GB* 13 D3
Ashby de la Zouch *GB* 11 D4
Ashford *GB* 15 D4
Ashington *GB* 9 F4
Ashton-under-Lyne *GB* 11 D3
Asiago *I* 72 A3
Asikkala *FIN* 121 D3
Asín *E* 37 F3
Asipovičy *BY* 125 D4
Ask *N* 117 D1
Askainen *FIN* 120 B4
Askeaton *IRL* 4 C2
Askersund *S* 119 D3
Askífou *GR* 100 B3
Asklipío *GR* 103 D1
Asklipío *GR* 103 F2
Askola *FIN* 121 D3
Askós *GR* 88 C2
Askvoll *N* 110 A3
Asmunti *FIN* 109 E3
Asola *I* 71 F4
Asolo *I* 72 A3
Aspang Markt *A* 69 D2
Aspatria *GB* 9 D4
Aspe *E* 49 F1
Asperg *D* 66 B1
Aspet *F* 29 D4
Aspra Spítia *GR* 93 E3
Aspres-lès-Corps *F* 31 D1
Áspro *GR* 87 F2
Asprópirgos *GR* 94 A4
Aspróvalta *GR* 88 C2
Asse *B* 17 E2
Assemini *I* 82 B4
Assen *NL* 55 D2
Assens *DK* 122 B3
Assergi *I* 79 E1
Assíni *GR* 97 E1
Assisi *I* 76 C4
Assmannshausen *D* 62 A3

Assopía *GR* 94 A4
Assopós *GR* 97 E3
Ássos *GR* 92 A3
Ássos *GR* 92 B1
Astaffort *F* 29 D2
Astakída (Nissí) *GR* 102 C3
Astakós *GR* 92 B3
Asten *A* 68 B1
Asti *I* 74 C1
Astillero (El) *E* 36 B1
Astipálea *GR* 99 E4
Astipálea (Nissí) *GR* 99 E4
Astorga *E* 33 D4
Ástorp *S* 123 D2
Ástros *GR* 97 D2
Astudillo *E* 36 B2
Asvestádes *GR* 91 E1
Asvestohóri *GR* 87 D4
Asvestópetra *GR* 87 E2
Atalándi *GR* 93 F3
Átali *GR* 94 A3
Ataquines *E* 36 A4
Atarfe *E* 48 A3
Ateca *E* 37 E4
Atella *I* 80 C3
Atessa *I* 80 A1
Ath *B* 17 D2
Atháni *GR* 92 A3
Athánio *GR* 92 A3
Athboy *IRL* 3 D4
Athenry / Baile Átha an Rí *IRL* 2 B4
Atherstone *GB* 11 D4
Athína *GR* 94 A4
Áthira *GR* 88 A2
Athlone / Baile Átha Luain *IRL* 2 C4
Áthos *GR* 89 D3
Athy / Baile Átha *IRL* 5 E2
Atienza *E* 36 C4
Atina *I* 79 F2
Atios *E* 32 B2
Átokos (Nissí) *GR* 92 B3
Atouguia da Baleia *P* 40 A2
Ätran *S* 123 D1
Atri *I* 77 E4
Atsikí *GR* 89 F4
Attendorn *D* 62 A1
Attersee *A* 68 A2
Attigliano *I* 79 D1
Attigny *F* 17 E4
Attleborough *GB* 15 D1
Attnang-Puchheim *A* 68 B1

Ault *F* 16 B3
Aulus-les-Bains *F* 29 E4
Auma *D* 63 E1
Aumale *F* 16 B4
Aumetz *F* 22 C1
Aumont-Aubrac *F* 30 A1
Aunay-sur-Odon *F* 19 F2
Auneau *F* 21 E3
Auneuil *F* 16 B4
Auning *DK* 122 C2
Aups *F* 31 E2
Aura *FIN* 120 B3
Auray *F* 18 C4
Aurdal *N* 111 D4
Aure *N* 110 C2
Aurec-sur-Loire *F* 26 B4
Aurich *D* 55 E1
Aurignac *F* 29 D3
Aurillac *F* 25 F4
Auritz *E* 28 A3
Auron *F* 31 F1
Auronzo di Cadore *I* 67 F4
Auros *F* 28 C1
Ausonia *I* 79 F2
Aussa-Corno *I* 72 C3
Außernbrünst *D* 64 A4
Austbygd *N* 116 C1
Auterive *F* 29 E3
Authon-du-Perche *F* 21 D3
Autol *E* 37 D3
Autrans *F* 27 D4
Autrey-lès-Gray *F* 22 C4
Autti *FIN* 109 E2
Auttoinen *FIN* 121 D3
Autun *F* 26 B1
Auvillar *F* 29 D2
Auxerre *F* 22 A4
Auxi-le-Château *F* 16 C3
Auxonne *F* 27 D1
Auzances *F* 25 F3
Auzon *F* 26 A4
Availles-Limouzine *F* 25 D2
Avaldsnes *N* 116 A2
Avallon *F* 22 A4
Ávas *GR* 91 D2
Avaviken *S* 108 A3
Avebury *GB* 13 F2
Aveiras de Cima *P* 40 A3
Aveiro *P* 34 B4
Avellino *I* 80 A1
Aversa *I* 80 A2
Avesnes-le-Comte *F* 16 C3
Avesnes-sur-Helpe *F* 17 E3
Avesta *S* 119 D1
Avetrana *I* 81 E3
Avezzano *I* 79 E1
Avgerinós *GR* 87 D3
Avía *GR* 96 C3
Aviano *I* 72 B3
Aviemore *GB* 7 D3
Avigliana *I* 27 F4
Avigliano *I* 80 C3
Avignon *F* 30 C2
Ávila *E* 42 A1
Avilés *E* 33 E2
Avintes *P* 34 B4
Avión *E* 32 B4
Avioth *F* 17 F4
Avis *P* 40 C3
Avize *F* 22 A2
Avlákia *GR* 99 F1
Avlémonas *GR* 97 E4
Avlés *GR* 87 F3
Avlí *GR* 89 D2
Avliótes *GR* 86 B4
Avlóna *GR* 94 A4
Avlum *DK* 122 B2
Avola *I* 85 E4
Avonmouth *GB* 13 E2
Avord *F* 25 F1
Avoriaz *F* 27 E2
Avranches *F* 19 E2
Ax-les-Thermes *F* 29 E4
Axams *A* 67 E3
Axat *F* 29 F4
Axiohóri *GR* 88 A2
Axioúpoli *GR* 88 A1
Axminster *GB* 13 D3
Axós *GR* 100 C3

Azambuja P 40 A3
Azaruja P 40 C4
Azay-le-Ferron F 25 E1
Azay-le-Rideau F 25 D1
Azinheira dos Barros P ... 46 A1
Azkoitia E 37 D1
Aznalcázar E 47 D2
Aznalcóllar E 47 D2
Azohía (La) E 49 E2
Azpeitia E 37 D1
Azuaga E 47 E1
Azuara E 37 F4
Azuel E 48 A1
Azuqueca de Henares E ... 42 C1
Azzano Decimo I 72 B3

B

Baad A 67 D3
Baal D 61 E1
Baamonde E 32 C2
Baarle-Nassau NL 17 F1
Baarn NL 54 C3
Babadag RO 129 E1
Babajevo RUS 125 E1
Babelsberg D 57 F2
Babenhausen D 62 B3
Babenhausen D 67 D2
Babrujsk BY 125 D4
Bacău RO 127 D4
Baccarat F 23 D1
Baceno I 70 C3
Bacharach D 62 A3
Bachmač UA 127 F1
Bäckaskog S 123 E2
Backe S 112 C1
Bäckebo S 123 F2
Bäckefors S 118 C3
Backnang D 62 C4
Bacoli I 80 A3
Bacqueville-en-Caux F 16 A3
Bad Aussee A 68 B2
Bad Brambach D 63 F2
Bad Deutsch Altenburg A 69 E1
Bad Doberan D 51 D2

Bad Elster D 63 E2
Bad Gleichenberg A 69 D3
Bad Goisern A 68 A2
Bad Hall A 68 B1
Bad Hofgastein A 68 A3
Bad Ischl A 68 A2
Bad Kleinen D 51 D3
Bad Kleinkirchheim A 68 B3
Bad Leonfelden A 64 B4
Bad Liebenstein D 62 C1
Bad Mitterndorf A 68 B2
Bad Radkersburg A 69 D3
Bad Salzungen D 62 C1
Bad St. Leonhard im Lavanttal A 68 C3
Bad Schallerbach A 68 B1
Bad Soden am Taunus D 62 A3
Bad Soden-Salmünster D 62 B2
Bad Sülze D 51 E2
Bad Tatzmannsdorf A 69 E2
Bad Vöslau A 69 D1
Bad Aibling D 67 F2
Badajoz E 41 D3
Badalona E 39 D4
Bad Bentheim D 55 E3
Bad Bergzabern D 23 F1
Bad Berka D 63 D1
Bad Berleburg D 62 A1
Bad Berneck D 63 E2
Bad Bertrich D 61 F3
Bad Bevensen D 50 C4
Bad Bibra D 63 E1
Bad Blankenburg D 63 D1
Bad Bramstedt D 50 B3
Bad Brückenau D 62 C2
Bad Buchau D 66 C2
Bad Camberg D 62 A2
Bad Driburg D 56 B4
Bad Düben D 57 F4
Bad Dürkheim D 23 F1
Bad Dürrenberg D 57 E4
Bad Dürrheim D 23 F3
Bad Ems D 62 A2
Baden A 69 D1
Baden CH 23 F4
Baden-Baden D 23 F2
Bad Endorf D 67 F2
Badenweiler D 23 E4

Bad Essen D 55 F3
Bad Frankenhausen D 57 D4
Bad Freienwalde D 52 A4
Bad Friedrichshall D 62 B4
Bad Gandersheim D 56 C4
Badgastein A 68 A3
Bad Godesberg D 61 F2
Bad Gottleuba D 64 A1
Bad Griesbach i. Rottal D 68 A1
Bad Grund D 56 C4
Bad Harzburg D 56 C4
Bad Herrenalb D 23 F2
Bad Hersfeld D 62 C1
Bad Hönningen D 61 F2
Bad Homburg D 62 A2
Bad Honnef D 61 F2
Badia Polesine I 76 A1
Badia Tedalda I 76 B3
Bad Iburg D 55 F3
Bad Karlshafen D 56 B4
Bad Kissingen D 62 C2
Bad König D 62 B3
Bad Königshofen D 62 C2
Bad Kösen D 63 E1
Bad Kreuznach D 62 A3
Bad Krozingen D 23 E3
Bad Laasphe D 62 A1
Bad Langensalza D 63 D1
Bad Lauchstädt D 57 E4
Bad Lausick D 57 F4
Bad Lauterberg D 56 C4
Bad Liebenwerda D 57 F4
Bad Liebenzell D 23 F2
Bad Lippspringe D 55 F4
Bad Mergentheim D 62 C4
Bad Münder D 56 B3
Bad Münster a. Stein D 62 A3
Bad Münstereifel D 61 E2
Bad Muskau D 58 B4
Bad Nauheim D 62 B2
Bad Nenndorf D 56 B3
Bad Neuenahr-Ahrweiler D 61 F2
Bad Neustadt D 62 C2
Bad Oeynhausen D 55 F3
Badolato I 83 E3
Badolatosa E 47 F2

Bad Oldesloe D 50 C3
Badonviller F 23 D2
Bad Orb D 62 B2
Bad Peterstal-Griesbach D 23 F2
Bad Pyrmont D 56 B3
Bad Rappenau D 62 B4
Bad Reichenhall D 68 A2
Bad Rothenfelde D 55 F3
Bad Saarow-Pieskow D 58 A2
Bad Sachsa D 56 C4
Bad Säckingen D 23 F4
Bad Salzdetfurth D 56 C3
Bad Salzschlirf D 62 B2
Bad Salzuflen D 55 F3
Bad Schandau D 64 A1
Bad Schmiedeberg D 57 F4
Bad Schönborn D 23 F1
Bad Schussenried D 66 C2
Bad Schwalbach D 62 A3
Bad Schwartau D 50 C3
Bad Segeberg D 50 C3
Bad Sooden-Allendorf D 62 C1
Bad Sulza D 63 E1
Bad Tennstedt D 63 D1
Bad Tölz D 67 E2
Bad Urach D 66 C1
Bad Vilbel D 62 B2
Bad Waldsee D 66 C2
Bad Wiessee D 67 E2
Bad Wildungen D 62 B1

Bad Wilsnack D 51 E4
Bad Wimpfen D 62 B4
Bad Windsheim D 63 D3
Bad Wörishofen D 67 D2
Bad Wurzach D 66 C2
Bad Zwischenahn D 55 E2
Baena E 48 A2
Bärnau D 63 F3
Baeza E 48 B1
Bâga E 38 C3
Bâgé-le-Châtel F 26 C2
Bagenalstown / Muine Bheag IRL ... 5 E2
Bagenkop DK 122 C4
Bagheria I 84 B3
Bagn N 111 D4
Bagnacavallo I 76 B2
Bagnara Calabra I 83 E4
Bagnères-de-Bigorre F 28 C3
Bagnères-de-Luchon F 29 D4
Bagni del Masino I 71 E3
Bagni di Lucca I 75 F2
Bagno a Ripoli I 76 A3
Bagno di Romagna I 76 B3
Bagnoles-de-l'Orne F 19 F2
Bagnoli del Trigno I 80 A2
Bagnolo Mella I 71 E4
Bagnols-les-Bains F 30 B1
Bagnols-sur-Cèze F 30 C2
Bagnoregio I 76 A4
Bagolino I 71 E3
Bagrationovsk RUS 124 A4

Baia Sardinia I 78 A3
Baia Mare RO 126 C4
Baiano I 80 A3
Baião P 34 C4
Baiersbronn D 23 F2
Baignes-Ste-Radegonde F ... 24 C3
Baigneux-les-Juifs F 22 B4
Băile Herculane RO 128 C1
Băile tuşnad RO 127 D4
Bailén E 48 A1
Bailieborough / Coill an Chollaigh IRL ... 3 D3
Bailleul F 15 F4
Bain-de-Bretagne F 19 E4
Bains-les-Bains F 23 D3
Baio E 32 A2
Baiona E 32 A4
Bais F 19 F3
Baiuca (A) E 32 B2
Baja H 128 A1
Bakewell GB 11 D3
Bakio E 37 D1
Bakkafjörður IS 106 C1
Bakvattnet S 112 A1
Bala GB 10 B3
Balaguer E 38 B3
Balanegra E 48 C3
Balaruc-les-Bains F 30 C2
Balassagyarmat H 126 A3
Balatonfüred H 126 A4
Balatonlelle H 126 A4
Balazote E 43 D4
Balbigny F 26 B3

Barcelona

E	POBLE ESPANYOL
M⁴	MUSEU D'ART DE CATALUNYA
M⁵	MUSEU ARQUEOLÒGIC
P¹	PALAU SANT JORDI
T¹	TEATRE GREC
W	FUNDACIÓ JOAN MIRÓ
Z	PAVELLÓ MIES VAN DER ROHE

Balbriggan /
  Baile Brigín *IRL* 3 E4
Balčik *BG* 129 E1
Balderschwang *D* 67 D3
Baldock *GB* 14 C2
Baleal *P* 40 A2
Baleizão *P* 46 B1
Balerma *E* 48 C3
Balestrand *N* 110 B4
Balí *GR* 100 C3
Balikesir *TR* 129 E3
Bälinge *S* 119 E2
Bälingen *D* 66 B2
Balivanich *GB* 6 A4
Ballachulish *GB* 8 B1
Ballaghaderreen /
  Bealach
  an Doirín *IRL* 2 B3
Ballangen *N* 104 A4
Ballantrae *GB* 3 F1
Ballao *I* 82 C3
Ballater *GB* 9 D1
Ballaugh *GB* 3 F3
Ballenstedt *D* 57 D4
Balleroy *F* 19 F1
Ballerup *DK* 123 D30
Ballina /
  Béal an Átha *IRL* 2 B3
Ballinamore / Béal an
  Átha Mhóir *IRL* 2 C3
Ballinasloe / Béal Átha
  na Sluaighe *IRL* 2 B4
Ballingarry *IRL* 5 D2
Ballinrobe / Baile an
  Róba *IRL* 2 B3
Ballintubber *IRL* 2 A3
Ballobar *E* 38 A4
Ballon *F* 20 C3
Ballstad *N* 107 E1
Ballybay *IRL* 3 D3
Ballybofey / Bealach
  Féich *IRL* 2 C2

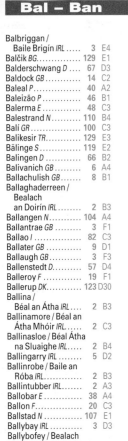
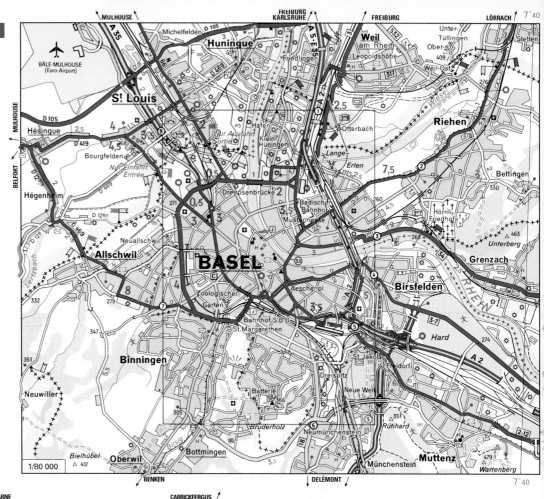

Ballybunnion *IRL* 4 B2
Ballycastle *GB* 3 E1
Ballycastle *IRL* 2 B2
Ballyclare *GB* 3 E2
Ballyconnell *IRL* 2 C3
Ballycotton *IRL* 4 C4
Ballycroy *IRL* 2 A3
Ballyduff *IRL* 4 B2
Ballyforan *IRL* 2 B4
Ballygawley *GB* 3 D2
Ballyhaunis / Béal Átha
  hAmhnais *IRL* 2 B3
Ballyheige *IRL* 4 B3
Ballyjamesduff *IRL* ... 3 D3
Ballymahon / Baile Uí
  Mhatháin *IRL* 2 C4
Ballymena *GB* 3 E2
Ballymoe *IRL* 2 B3
Ballymoney *GB* 3 D1
Ballymore *IRL* 2 C4
Ballymote / Baile an
  Mhóta *IRL* 2 B3
Ballynahinch *GB* 3 E3
Ballysadare *IRL* 2 B3
Ballyshannon / Béal Átha
  Seanaidh *IRL* 2 C2
Ballyvaughan *IRL* 2 A4
Balmaseda *E* 36 C1
Balme *I* 27 F4
Balneario
  de Panticosa *E* 28 C4
Balsareny *E* 38 C3
Balsicas *E* 49 E3
Balsorano *I* 79 F2
Bålsta *S* 119 E2
Balsthal *CH* 23 E4
Balta *UA* 127 E3
Baltanás *E* 36 B3
Baltar *E* 32 B4
Bălţi *MOL* 127 D4
Baltijsk *RUS* 124 A4
Baltinglass / Bealach
  Conglais *IRL* 5 D2
Baltrum *D* 55 E1
Bambalió *GR* 92 C2
Bamberg *D* 63 D3
Bambíni *GR* 92 B3
Bamburgh Castle *GB* . 9 F3
Bampton *GB* 13 D3
Banagher *IRL* 2 C4
Banbridge *GB* 3 E3
Banbury *GB* 13 F1
Banchory *GB* 9 E1
Bande *E* 32 B4
Bandırma *TR* 129 E3
Bandol *F* 31 D3

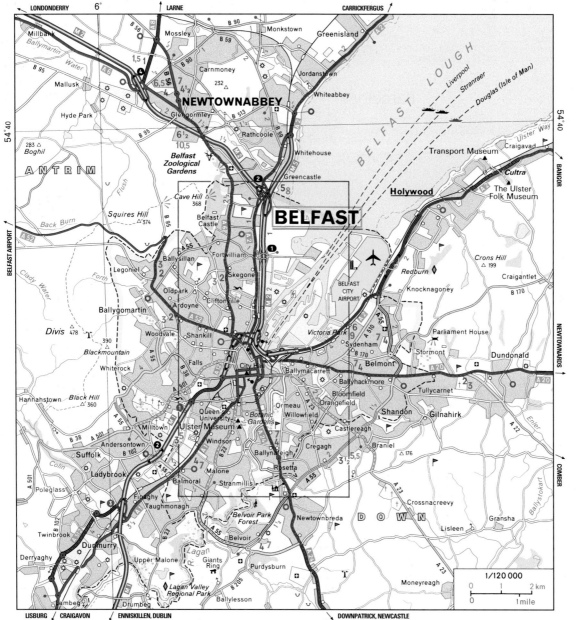

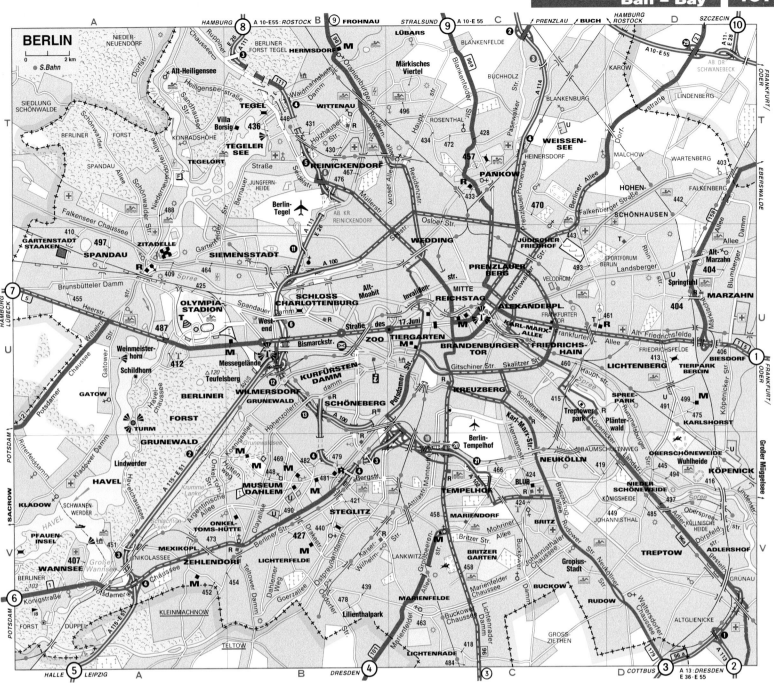

Bandon / Droichead na
  Bandan *IRL* 4 C4
Banff *GB* 7 E4
Bangor *GB* 10 B3
Bangor *GB* 3 E2
Bangor *IRL* 2 A3
Bangsund *N* 111 E1
Banja Luka *BIH* 128 A1
Bankeryd *S* 118 C4
Bannalec *F* 18 B3
Banon *F* 31 D2
Bansin *D* 52 A2
Banská Bystrica *SK* ... 126 A3
Banská Štiavnica *SK* ... 126 A3
Bantry / Beanntraí *IRL* ... 4 B4
Banyalbufar *E* 45 D3
Banyeres
  de Mariola *E* 43 F4
Banyoles *E* 39 F3
Banyuls-sur-Mer *F* 30 A4
Bañeza (La) *E* 33 E4
Bañón *E* 43 F1
Baños de Cerrato *E* ... 36 A3
Baños de la Encina *E* .. 48 B1
Baños
  de la Fuensanta *E* .. 49 D2
Baños de Molgas *E* 32 B4
Baños
  de Montemayor *E* ... 41 F1
Bapaume *F* 16 C3
Baqueira 1500 *E* 29 D4
Bar *YU* 128 A3
Bar *UA* 127 D2
Bar-le-Duc *F* 22 B3

Bar-sur-Aube *F* 22 B3
Le Bar-sur-Loup *F* 31 F2
Bar-sur-Seine *F* 22 B3
Barajas *E* 42 B1
Barajas de Melo *E* 42 C2
Barakaldo *E* 36 C1
Baralla *E* 32 C3
Baranavičy *BY* 124 C3
Baraona *E* 36 C4
Baraque-
  de-Fraiture *B* 61 D3
Baraque-Michel *B* 61 E2
Baraqueville *F* 29 F1
Barbadillo
  del Mercado *E* 36 C3
Barbarano
  Vicentino *I* 72 A4
Barbastro *E* 38 A3
Barbate *E* 47 D4
Barbazan *F* 29 D3
Barberino
  di Mugello *I* 76 A2
Barbezieux *F* 24 C3
Barbizon *F* 21 F3
Barbotan-
  les-Thermes *F* 28 C2
Barby *D* 57 E3
Barca de Alva *P* 35 D4
Barca
  de la Florida (La) *E* . 47 D3
Barcarrota *E* 41 D4
Barcellona Pozzo di
  Gotto *I* 83 D4
Barcelona *E* 39 D4

Barcelonnette *F* 31 E1
Barcelos *P* 34 B3
Barchfeld *D* 62 C1
Barcis *I* 72 B3
Barco (O) *E* 32 C4
Barco de Ávila (El) *E* . 41 F1
Barcones *E* 36 C4
Barcs *H* 128 A1
Bardal *N* 111 E1
Bardejov *SK* 126 B30
Bardi *I* 75 E2
Bardineto *I* 74 C2
Bardolino *I* 71 F4
Bardonecchia *I* 27 C4
Bardufoss *N* 104 B3
Barèges *F* 28 C4
Barentin *F* 16 A4
Barenton *F* 19 F2
Barfleur *F* 19 E1
Bargas *E* 42 B2
Bargoed *GB* 13 D1
Bargteheide *D* 50 C3
Bari *I* 81 D2
Barisciano *I* 79 F1
Barjac *F* 30 B1
Barjols *F* 31 E3
Bârlad *RO* 127 D4
Barlby *GB* 11 E2
Barletta *I* 80 C2
Barmouth /
  Abermaw *GB* 10 B4
Barmstedt *D* 50 B3
Barna / Bearna *IRL* ... 2 A4
Barnard Castle *GB* ... 11 D1

Barneveld *NL* 54 C3
Barneville-Carteret *F* . 19 E1
Barnsley *GB* 11 D2
Barnstaple *GB* 12 C2
Barnstorf *D* 55 F3
Barntrup *D* 56 B3
Barquero *P* 40 B2
Barr *F* 23 E2
Barracas *E* 43 F2
Barrachina *E* 43 F1
Barraco *E* 42 A1
Barrafranca *I* 84 C3
Barrancos *P* 46 C1
Barranco Velho *P* 46 B2
Barranda *E* 49 D1
Barrax *E* 43 D4
Barre-
  des-Cévennes *F* ... 30 A2
Barrea *I* 79 F2
Barreiro *P* 40 A4
Barrela (La) *E* 32 B3
Barrême *F* 31 E2
Barrhead *GB* 8 C3
Barrhill *GB* 3 F1
Barrière-
  de-Champlon *B* ... 17 F3
Barrios (Los) *E* 47 E4
Barrow-
  in-Furness *GB* 10 C1
Barruecopardo *E* 35 D4
Barruelo
  de Santullán *E* 36 B1
Barry / Barri *GB* 13 D2
Barsinghausen *D* 56 B3

Barth *D* 51 E2
La Barthe-de-Neste *F* . 29 D3
Barton-
  upon-Humber *GB* .. 11 E2
Barumini *I* 82 B3
Baruth *D* 57 F3
Barvas *GB* 6 B2
Barysaŭ *BY* 125 D4
Barzio *I* 71 E3
Bas-en-Basset *F* 26 B4
Bàscara *E* 39 E3
Baschi *I* 76 B4
Basconcillos
  del Tozo *E* 36 B2
Basel *CH* 23 E4
Baselga di Pinè *I* ... 72 A3
Basildon *GB* 14 C3
Basingstoke *GB* 13 F2
Baslow *GB* 11 D3
Basovizza *I* 73 D3
Bassano del Grappa *I* . 72 A3
La Bassée *F* 16 C2
Bassens *F* 24 C4
Bassum *D* 55 F2
Båstad *S* 123 D2
Bastelica *F* 78 A4
Bastia *I* 78 B2
La Bastide-
  Clairence *F* 28 B3
La Bastide-
  de-Sérou *F* 29 E4
Bastogne *B* 61 D3
Bastuträsk *S* 108 B4
Batak *BG* 129 D3

Batalha *P* 40 B2
Batea *E* 44 B1
Bath *GB* 13 E2
Bathgate *GB* 9 D2
La Bâtie-Neuve *F* 31 E1
Båtsfjord *N* 105 F1
Batsí *GR* 98 B1
Battaglia Terme *I* ... 72 A4
Battenberg *D* 62 A1
Battice *B* 61 D2
Battipaglia *I* 80 B3
Battle *GB* 14 C4
Batuecas
  (Monasterio Las) *E* . 41 E1
Batz-sur-Mer *F* 19 D4
Baud *F* 18 C3
Baugé *F* 19 F4
Baugy *F* 25 F1
La Baule *F* 19 D40
Baume-les-Dames *F* . 23 D4
Baumholder *D* 23 E1
Bauska *LV* 124 B3
Bautzen *D* 58 B4
Les Baux-
  de-Provence *F* 30 C2
Bavay *F* 17 D3
Bavella *F* 75 D3
Baveno *I* 70 C4
Bawtry *GB* 11 E3
Bayerisch
  Eisenstein *D* 64 A4
Bayeux *F* 19 F1
Bayhirivagh *GB* 6 A4
Bayındır *TR* 129 E4

Bayon F 23 D3
Bayonne F 28 A3
Bayreuth D 63 E3
Bayrischzell D 67 F2
Baza E 48 C2
Bazas F 28 C1
Bazoches-
sur-Hoëne F 20 C2
Bazzano I 76 A2
Beaconsfield GB 14 B3
Beaminster GB 13 E3
Beariz E 32 B3
Beas E 46 C2
Beasain F 37 D1
Beas de Segura E 48 C1
Beattock GB 9 D4
Beaucaire F 30 C2
Beaufort F 27 D2
Beaufort F 27 E3
Beaufort-en-Vallée F . 19 F4
Beaugency F 21 D4
Beaujeu F 26 C2
Beaulieu GB 13 F3
Beaulieu-
sur-Dordogne F ... 25 E4
Beaulieu-sur-Mer F . 31 F2
Beaumaris GB 10 B3
Beaumesnil F 20 C2
Beaumetz-
lès-Loges F 16 C3
Beaumont F 29 D1
Beaumont B 17 E3
Beaumont-
de-Lomagne F 29 D2
Beaumont-Hague F .. 19 E1
Beaumont-le-Roger F 21 D2
Beaumont-sur-Oise F 21 E2
Beaumont-
sur-Sarthe F 20 C3
Beaune F 26 C1
Beaune-la-Rolande F . 21 E3
Beaupréau F 24 B1
Beauraing B 17 F3
Beaurepaire F 26 C4
Beaurepaire-
en-Bresse F 27 D2
Le Beausset F 31 D3
Beauvais F 16 C4
Beauvoir-sur-Mer F .. 24 A1
Beauvoir-sur-Niort F. 24 C2
Bebington GB 10 C3
Bebra D 62 C1
Le Bec-Hellouin F 16 A4
Beccles GB 15 D1
Becedas E 41 F1
Beceite E 44 A1
Bečej YU 128 B1
Becerreá E 32 C3
Bécherel F 19 D3
Bechet RO 128 C2
Bechhofen D 63 D4
Becilla
de Valderaduey E .. 33 E4
Beckenried CH 66 B4
Beckington GB 13 E2
Beckum D 55 F4
Bedale GB 11 D1
Bédarieux F 30 A3
Beddgelert GB 10 B3
Bederkesa D 50 A3
Bedford GB 14 B2
Bedlington GB 9 F4
Bedmar E 48 B2
Bedonia I 75 E2
Bedum NL 55 D2
Bedwas GB 13 D2
Bedworth GB 11 D4
Beeford GB 11 E2
Beelitz D 57 F3
Beerfelden D 62 B3
Beeskow D 58 A3
Beesten D 55 E3
Beetzendorf D 57 D2
Beg-Meil F 18 B3
Bégard F 18 C2
La Bégude-
de-Mazenc F 30 C1
Begues E 38 C4
Begur E 39 E3
Behobia E 28 A3
Behringersmühle D .. 63 E3
Beiarn N 107 E2
Beilen NL 55 D2
Beilngries D 63 E4
Beisfjord N 104 B4
Beith GB 8 C3
Beitostølen N 110 C4
Beiuş RO 126 B4
Beja P 46 B1
Béjar E 41 F1
Békés H 126 B4
Békéscsaba H 126 B4
Bel E 44 A1

Bela Palanka YU 128 C2
Bélâbre F 25 E2
Belalcázar E 41 F4
Belcaire F 29 F4
Belchite E 37 F4
Belcoo GB 2 C3
Belecke D 55 F4
Belev RUS 125 F3
Belfast GB 3 E2
Belford GB 9 E3
Belfort F 23 D4
Belforte all'Isauro I .. 76 B3
Belgern D 57 F4
Belgodère F 78 A3
Belgodère F 75 D2
Beli Manastir HR 128 A1
Belianes E 38 B4
Belin-Béliet F 28 B1
Bell-lloc d'Urgell E .. 38 B4
Bellac F 25 D2
Bellagio I 71 D3
Bellano I 71 D3
Bellaria-Igea Marina I 76 B2
Bellcaire d'Urgell E .. 38 B4
Belle-Isle-en-Terre F.. 18 C2
Belleek GB 2 C2
Bellegarde F 30 C2
Bellegarde F 21 E3
Bellegarde-
en-Marche F 25 F3
Bellegarde-
sur-Valserine F 27 D2
Bellême F 20 C3
Bellencombre F 16 B4
Bellerive-sur-Allier F. 26 A2
Belleville F 26 C2
Belley F 27 D3
Bellinzona CH 71 D3
Bello E 43 E1
Bellpuig E 38 B4
Belluno I 72 B3
Bellver
de Cerdanya E 38 C2
Bélmez E 47 F1
Belmont GB 7 F2
Belmont-
de-la-Loire F 26 B2
Belmont-sur-Rance F 30 A2
Belmonte P 41 D1
Belmonte E 43 D3
Belmonte
de Miranda E 33 D2
Belmullet / Béal an
Mhuirthead IRL.. 2 A2
Bellil B 17 D2
Belogradčik BG 128 C2
Belorado E 36 C2

Belpech F 29 E3
Belper GB 11 D3
Belsay GB 9 E4
Beltinci SLO 73 F1
Belturbet /
Béal Tairbirt IRL.... 2 C3
Belvedere
Marittimo I 83 D2
Belver E 38 A4
Belvès F 29 D1
Belvís de la Jara E ... 42 A2
Belyj RUS 125 E2
Belz F 18 C4
Belzig D 57 E3
Bełchatów PL 59 F3
Bembibre E 33 D4
Bemposta P 40 B3
Benabarre E 38 B3
Benaguasil E 43 F3
Benahadux E 48 C3
Benalmádena-
Costa E 47 F4
Benalúa de Guadix E. 48 B2
Benalúa
de las Villas E 48 B2
Benamargosa E 48 A3
Benamaurel E 48 C2
Benameji E 47 F2
Benamocarra E 48 A3
Benaoján E 47 E3
Benasque E 29 D4
Benassal E 44 A2
Benavente P 40 A3
Benavente E 35 F3
Benavides E 33 E4
Benderi MOL 127 E4
Bendorf D 61 F2
Benediktbeuern D .. 67 E2
Bénévent-l'Abbaye F. 25 E2
Benevento I 80 A2
Benfeld F 23 E3
Benfleet GB 14 C3
Bengtsfors S 118 B2
Benicarló E 44 B2
Benicàssim /
Benicasim E 44 A2
Benidorm E 49 F1
Benifaió E 43 F3
Benissa E 44 A4
Benítses GR 86 B4
Benneckenstein D .. 57 D4
Bénodet F 18 B3
Benquerencia de la
Serena E 41 F4
Bensberg D 61 F1
Bensersiel D 55 E1
Bensheim D 62 B3

Bentley GB 11 E3
Le Bény-Bocage F ... 19 F2
Beograd YU 128 B1
Bera E 28 A3
Berane YU 128 B2
La Bérarde F 27 E4
Berat AL 128 B3
Berazino BY 125 D4
Berbegal E 38 A3
Berberana E 36 C1
Berceto I 75 E2
Berching D 63 E4
Berchtesgaden D 68 A2
Berck-Plage F 16 B2
Berdyčiv UA 127 D2
Berdyk'ov UA 127 F3
Bere Regis GB 13 E3
Berehove UA 126 B3
Berezivka UA 127 F3
Berg S 112 B2
Berg N 107 D4
Berg A 69 E1
Berga E 38 C3
Berga D 57 D4
Bergama TR 129 E3
Bergamo I 71 E4
Bergara E 37 D1
Bergby S 119 E1
Bergedorf
(Hamburg-) 50 C4
Bergen N 110 A4
Bergen D 51 F2
Bergen NL 54 B3
Bergen aan Zee NL .. 54 B3
Bergen (Dumme) D.. 51 D4
Bergen op Zoom NL. 17 E1
Bergerac F 29 D1
Berggießhübel D 64 A1
Bergheim D 61 E1
Bergisch Gladbach D. 61 F1
Bergnäset S 108 C3
Bergneustadt D 61 F1
Bergö FIN 114 A3
Bergsjö S 112 C3
Bergsviken S 108 C3
Bergues F 15 E4
Bergün /
Bravuogn CH 66 C4
Beringel P 46 B1
Beringen B 17 F1
Berja E 48 B3
Berka D 62 C1
Berkåk N 111 D2
Berkhamsted GB 14 B3

Berkheim D 66 C2
Berkhof D 56 B2
Berkovica BG 128 C2
Berlaimont F 17 D3
Berlanga E 47 E1
Berlanga de Duero E. 36 C4
Berlebeck D 56 B4
Berlevåg N 105 F1
Berlin D 57 F2
Bermeo E 37 D1
Bermillo de Sayago E 35 E4
Bern CH 27 F1
Bernalda I 81 D3
Bernau D 51 F4
Bernau D 23 F4
Bernau
a. Chiemsee D 67 F2
Bernaville F 16 C3
Bernay F 20 C3
Bernburg D 57 E4
Berndorf A 69 D1
Berne D 50 A4
Bernhardsthal A 65 F4
Bernkastel-Kues D... 61 F3
Bernsdorf D 58 A4
Bernstein A 69 E2
Beroun CZ 64 A2
Berra I 76 B1
Berre-l'Étang F 30 C3
Berrón (El) E 33 E2
Berşad' UA 127 E3
Bersenbrück D 55 E3
Bertamiráns E 32 A3
Bertinoro I 76 B2
Bertrix B 17 F3
Berwang A 67 D3
Berwick-
upon-Tweed GB 9 E3
Beryslav UA 127 F3
Berzocana E 41 F3
Besalú E 39 D3
Besançon F 27 D1
Besande E 33 F3
Besigheim D 62 B4
Besse-
en-Chandesse F .. 26 A3
Besse-sur-Issole F .. 31 E3
Bessèges F 30 B1
Bessines F 24 C2
Bessines-
sur-Gartempe F .. 25 E2
Betanzos E 32 B2
Betelu E 28 A3
Bétera E 43 F3
Beteta E 43 D1
Bethesda GB 10 B3

Bettna S 119 E3
Bettola I 75 E1
Bettolle I 76 B4
Bettyhill GB 7 D2
Betws-y-Coed GB ... 10 B3
Betz F 21 F2
Betzdorf D 62 A2
Beuil F 31 F2
Beura-Cardezza I 70 C3
Beuron D 66 B2
Beuzeville F 16 A4
Bevagna I 76 C4
Beveren B 17 E1
Beverley GB 11 E2
Beverstedt D 50 A4
Beverungen D 56 B4
Beverwijk NL 54 B3
Bewdley GB 10 C4
Bex CH 27 E2
Bexhill GB 14 C4
Beynac-et-Cazenac F. 29 E1
Beynat F 25 E4
Les Bézards F 21 F4
Bezas E 43 E2
Béznar E 48 B3
Bežeck RUS 125 F1
Béziers F 30 A4
Béznar E 48 B3
Białystok PL 126 A1
Biała Podlaska PL.... 126 B1
Białogard PL 52 B2
Biancavilla I 85 D3
Bianco I 83 E4
Biandrate I 70 C4
Biar E 49 F1
Biarritz F 28 A3
Biasca CH 71 D3
Biasteri E 37 D2
Bibbiena I 76 B3
Biberach a. d. Riß D. 66 C2
Biberach i. Kinzigtal D 23 F3
Bibione I 72 C3
Bibury GB 13 F1
Bicaz RO 127 D4
Bicester GB 13 F1
Bichl D 67 E2
Bidache F 28 B3
Bidart F 28 A3
Biddenden GB 14 C4
Bideford GB 12 C3
Biebelried D 62 C3
Biedenkopf D 62 A1
Biel / Bienne CH 27 F1
Bielefeld D 55 F3
Biella I 70 C4
Bielsa E 28 C4
Bielsk Podlaski PL ... 126 B1
Bielsko-Biała PL 126 A3

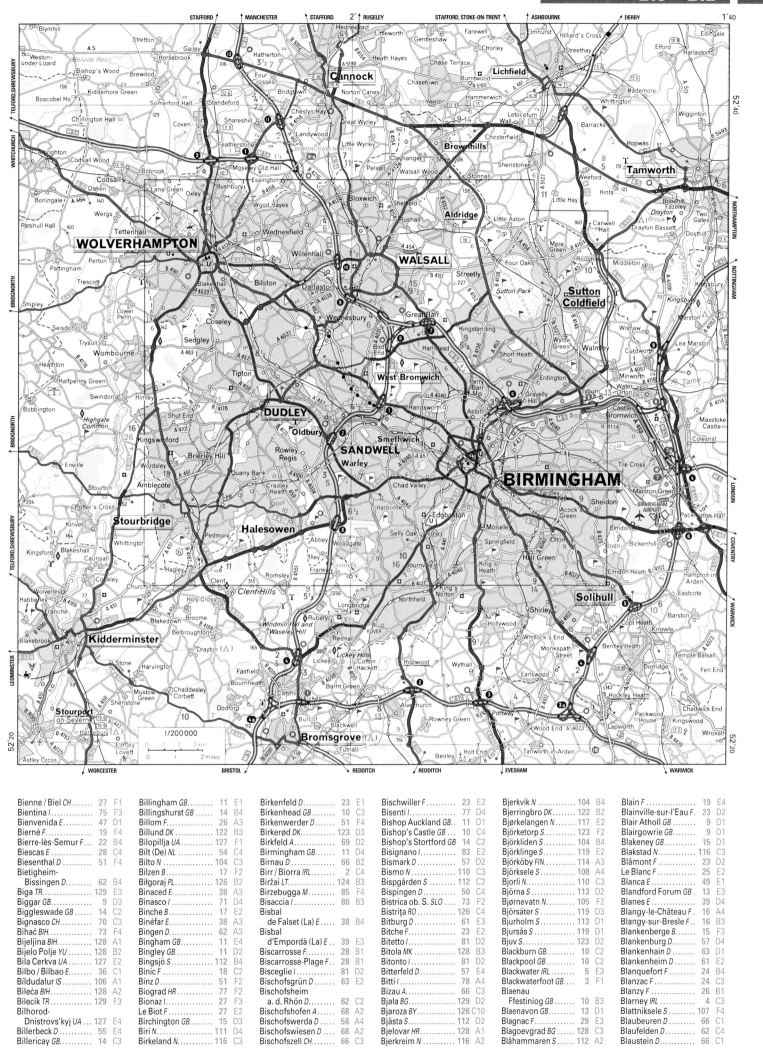

Bienne / Biel CH	27	F1	Billingham GB	11	E1	Birkenfeld D	23	E1	Bischwiller F	23	E2
Bientina I	75	F3	Billingshurst GB	14	B4	Birkenhead GB	10	C3	Bisenti I	77	D4
Bienvenida E	47	D1	Billom F	26	A3	Birkenwerder D	51	F4	Bishop Auckland GB	11	D1
Bierné F	19	F4	Billund DK	122	B3	Birkerød DK	123	D3	Bishop's Castle GB	10	C4
Bierre-lès-Semur F	22	B4	Bilopillja UA	127	F1	Birkfeld A	69	D2	Bishop's Stortford GB	14	C2
Biescas E	28	C4	Bilt (De) NL	54	C4	Birmingham GB	11	D4	Bisignano I	83	D2
Biesenthal D	51	F4	Bilto N	104	C3	Birnau D	66	B2	Bismark D	57	D2
Bietigheim-			Bilzen B	17	F2	Birr / Biorra IRL	2	C4	Bismo N	110	C3
Bissingen D	62	B4	Biłgoraj PL	126	B2	Birżai LT	124	B3	Bispgården S	112	C2
Biga TR	129	E3	Binaced E	38	A3	Birzebugga M	85	F4	Bispingen D	50	C4
Biggar GB	9	D3	Binasco I	71	D4	Bisaccia I	80	B3	Bistrica ob. S. SLO	73	F2
Biggleswade GB	14	C2	Binche B	17	E2	Bisbal			Bistrița RO	126	C4
Bignasco CH	70	C3	Binéfar E	38	A3	de Falset (La) E	38	B4	Bitburg D	61	E3
Bihać BIH	73	F4	Bingen D	62	A3	Bisbal			Bitche F	23	E2
Bijeljina BIH	128	A1	Bingham GB	11	E4	d'Empordà (La) E	39	E3	Bitetto I	81	D2
Bijelo Polje YU	128	B2	Bingley GB	11	D2	Biscarrosse F	28	B1	Bitola MK	128	B3
Bila Cerkva UA	127	E2	Bingsjö S	112	B4	Biscarrosse-Plage F	28	B1	Bitonto I	81	D2
Bilbo / Bilbao E	36	C1	Binic F	18	C2	Bisceglie I	81	D2	Bitterfeld D	57	E4
Bíldudalur IS	106	A1	Binz D	51	F2	Bischofsgrün D	63	E2	Bitti I	78	A4
Bileća BIH	128	A2	Biograd HR	77	D1	Bischofsheim			Bizau A	66	C3
Bilecik TR	129	F3	Bionaz I	27	F3	a. d. Rhön D	62	C2	Bjala BG	129	D2
Bilhorod-			Le Biot F	27	E2	Bischofshofen A	68	A3	Bjaroza BY	126	C10
Dnistrovs'kyj UA	127	E4	Birchington GB	15	D3	Bischofswerda D	58	A4	Bjästa S	112	D2
Billerbeck D	55	E4	Biri N	111	D4	Bischofswiesen D	68	A2	Bjelovar HR	128	A1
Billericay GB	14	C3	Birkeland N	116	C3	Bischofszell CH	66	C3	Bjerkreim N	116	A2
									Bjerkvik N	104	B4	Blain F	19	E4
									Bjerringbro DK	122	B2	Blainville-sur-l'Eau F	23	D2
									Bjørkelangen N	117	E2	Blair Atholl GB	9	D1
									Bjørketorp S	123	F2	Blairgowrie GB	9	D1
									Bjørkliden S	104	B4	Blakeney GB	15	D1
									Bjørklinge S	119	E2	Blakstad N	116	C3
									Bjørköby FIN	114	A3	Blâmont F	23	D2
									Bjørksele S	108	A4	Le Blanc F	25	E2
									Bjorli N	110	C3	Blanca E	49	E1
									Björna S	113	D2	Blandford Forum GB	13	E3
									Bjørnevatn N	105	F2	Blanes E	39	D4
									Björsäter S	119	D3	Blangy-le-Château F	16	A4
									Bjurholm S	113	D1	Blangy-sur-Bresle F	16	B3
									Bjursås S	119	D1	Blankenberge B	15	F3
									Bjuv S	123	D2	Blankenburg D	57	D4
									Blackburn GB	10	C2	Blankenhain D	63	D1
									Blackpool GB	10	C2	Blankenheim D	61	E2
									Blackwater IRL	5	E3	Blanquefort F	24	B4
									Blackwaterfoot GB	3	F1	Blanzac F	24	C3
									Blaenau			Blanzy F	26	B1
									Ffestiniog GB	10	B3	Blarney IRL	4	C3
									Blaenavon GB	13	D1	Blattniksele S	107	F1
									Blagnac F	29	E3	Blaubeuren D	66	C1
									Blagoevgrad BG	128	C3	Blaufelden D	62	C4
									Blåhammaren S	112	A2	Blaustein D	66	C1

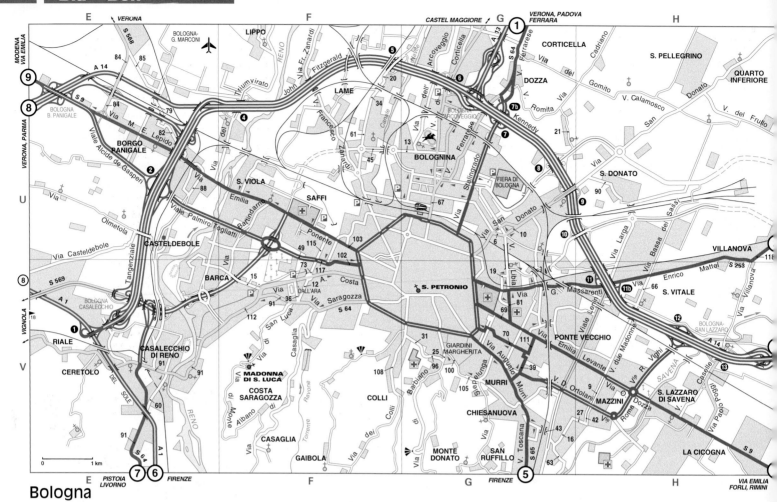

Bologna

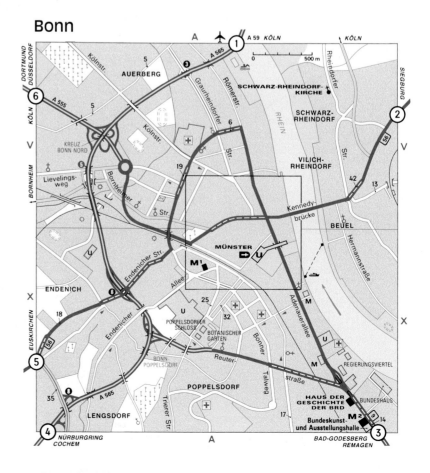

Bonn

Blaye F	24	B4	Bodenmais D	64	A4	Bolkesjø N	116	C2	Bolo (O) E	32	C4
Bleckede D	50	C4	Bodenteich D	56	C2	Bollebygd S	118	B4	Bolochovo RUS	125	F3
Bled SLO	73	D2	Bodenwerder D	56	B3	Bollène F	30	C1	Bologna I	76	A2
Bleiburg A	68	C4	Bodenwöhr D	63	F4	Bollnäs S	112	B4	Bologne F	22	B3
Bleicherode D	56	C4	Bodman D	66	B2	Bollstabruk S	112	C2	Bologoje RUS	125	E1
Bleik N	104	A3	Bodmin GB	12	C3	Bollullos			Bolotana I	82	B2
Bléneau F	21	F4	Bodø N	107	E2	de la Mitación E	47	D2	Bolsena I	76	B4
Blénod-lès-Pont-à-			Bodón (El) E	41	E1	Bollullos			Bolsward NL	54	C2
Mousson F	22	C2	Böblingen D	66	B1	del Condado E	47	D2	Boltaña E	28	C4
Blérancourt F	17	D4	Boecillo E	36	A3				Boltenhagen D	51	D3
Bléré F	21	D4	Böckstein A	68	A3				Bolton GB	10	C2
Blesle F	26	A4	Boëge F	27	E2	Bonassola I	75	E2
Bletchley GB	14	B2	Böhlen D	57	E4	Bolungarvik IS	106	A1	Bondeno I	76	A1
Bletterans F	27	D1	Böhmenkirch D	66	C1	Bolzano / Bozen I	67	E4	Bonefro I	80	A1
Blexen D	50	A4	Bömenzien D	51	D4	Bombarral P	40	A3	Bonete E	43	E4
Le Bleymard F	30	B1	Boën F	26	B3	Bom Jesus			Bonifacio F	78	A4
Blieskastel D	23	E1	Börger D	55	E2	do Monte P	34	B3	Bonillo (El) E	43	D4
Bligny-sur-Ouche F	26	C1	Börnicke D	57	F2	Bolsena I			Bonn D	61	F2
Bloemendaal NL	54	B3	Boeza E	33	D3	Bonar Bridge GB	7	D3	Bonnåsjøen N	107	F1
Blois F	21	D4	Boffalora			Bonares E	46	C2	Bonnat F	25	E2
Blokhus DK	122	B2	sopra Ticino I	71	D4						
Blomberg D	56	B4	Bogarra E	49	D1						
Blönduós IS	106	A1	Bogen N	104	A4						
Blonville-sur-Mer F	20	C1	Bogen D	63	F4						
Blosenberg D	63	E2	Bogense DK	122	B3						
Bloška polica SLO	73	D3	Bognanco I	70	C3						
Bludenz A	66	C3	Bognes N	107	F1						
Blumberg D	57	F2	Bognor Regis GB	14	B4						
Blumberg D	23	F3	Bohain-								
Blyth GB	9	F4	en-Vermandois F	17	D3						
Bo' Ness GB	9	D2	Boherboy IRL	4	B3						
Bø N	116	C2	Bohinjska								
Boal E	33	D2	Bistrica SLO	73	D2						
Boara Pisani I	76	A1	Bohmte D	55	F3						
Bobbio I	75	E1	Bohoduchiv UA	127	F1						
Bobbio Pellice I	27	F4	Böhönye H	69	F3						
Bobigny F	21	E2	Bohuslav UA	127	E2						
Bobingen D	67	D1	Boiro E	32	A3						
Boblitz D	58	A3	Bois-d'Amont F	27	D2						
Bobrovcja UA	127	E1	Boitzenburg D	51	E2						
Bobrynec' UA	127	F3	Böixols E	38	B3						
Bocairent E	43	F4	Boizenburg D	50	C4						
Boceguillas E	36	B4	Bojano I	80	A2						
Bocholt D	55	D4	Bøjden DK	122	B3						
Bochum D	55	E4	Bøla N	111	E1						
Bockenem D	56	C3	Bolaños								
Bockum-Hövel D	55	E4	de Calatrava E	42	B4						
Bocognano F	78	A3	Bolbec F	16	A4						
Boda S	112	B4	Bolchov RUS	125	F3						
Böda S	123	F1	Bolesławiec PL	58	C4						
Bodafors S	118	C4	Bolhrad UA	127	E4						
Bodegraven NL	54	B4	Boliden S	108	B4						
Boden S	108	B3	Boliqueime P	46	A2						

Bonndorf D	23	F3
Bonnétable F	20	C3
Bonneuil-Matours F	25	D2
Bonneval F	21	D3
Bonneville F	27	E2
La Bonneville-sur-Iton F	21	D2
Bonnières-sur-Seine F	21	D2
Bonnieux F	31	D2
Bono I	82	B2
Bonorva I	82	B2
Bønsnes N	117	D1
Boñar E	33	E3
Boo S	119	F2
Boom B	17	E1
Boos F	16	B4
Bootle GB	10	C2
Bopfingen D	63	D4
Boppard D	61	F2
Bor YU	128	C2
Borås S	118	B4
Borba P	40	C4
Borbona I	79	E1
Bordeaux F	28	C1
Bordères-Louron F	29	D4
Bordesholm D	50	B2
Bordighera I	74	C3
Bore I	75	E1
Borello I	76	B2
Borensberg S	119	D3
Le Boréon F	31	F2
Borgafjäll S	107	E4
Borgarfjörður IS	106	C1
Borgarnes IS	106	A2
Borger NL	55	D2
Borges Blanques (Les) E	38	B4
Borghetto I	79	D1
Borghetto Sto Spirito I	74	C3
Borgholm S	123	F2
Borgholzhausen D	55	F3
Borghorst D	55	E3
Borgia I	83	E3
Borgo S. Dalmazzo I	31	F1
Borgo S. Lorenzo I	76	A2
Borgo Tufico I	76	C3
Borgo Val di Taro I	75	E2
Borgo Valsugana I	72	A3
Borgomanero I	70	C4
Borgone Susa I	27	F4
Borgonovo Val Tidone I	75	E1
Borgorose I	79	E1
Borgosesia I	70	C4
Borgsjö S	112	B3
Borgund N	110	C4
Borgvattnet S	112	B2
Borja E	37	E3
Borken D	55	D4
Borkenes / Kvæfjord N	104	A3
Børkop DK	122	B3
Borkum D	55	D1
Borlänge S	119	D1
Bormes-les-Mimosas F	31	E3
Bormio I	67	D4
Born D	51	E2
Borna D	63	F1
Bornes P	35	D3
Bornhöved D	50	B4
Bornos E	47	B3
Boroughbridge GB	11	D2
Borovec BG	128	C2
Boroviči RUS	125	E1
Borovnica SLO	73	D3
Borovsk RUS	125	F2
Borre N	117	D2
Borriana / Burriana E	44	A2
Borriol E	44	A2
Borris IRL	5	D3
Borrisokane / Buiríos Uí Chéin IRL	4	C2
Borşa RO	126	C3
Børselv N	105	D2
Bórsio GR	92	C4
Bort-les-Orgues F	25	F4
Börtnan S	112	A2
Boryspil' UA	127	E2
Borzna UA	127	F1
Borzonasca I	75	E2
Bosa I	82	A2
Bosanska Dubica BIH	128	A1
Bosanska Krupa BIH	73	F4
Bosanski Novi BIH	128	A1
Bosanski Petrovac BIH	128	A1
Bosansko Grahovo BIH	128	A2
Bosco I	76	C4
Bosco Chiesanuova I	71	F4
Boscoreale I	80	A3
Bosjökloster S	123	D3
Boskoop NL	54	B4
Bosque (El) E	47	E3
Bossolasco I	74	C2
Bossòst E	29	D4
Boštanj SLO	73	E2
Boston GB	11	F3
Botevgrad BG	128	C2
Bothel GB	9	D4
Boticas P	34	C3
Botley GB	13	F3
Botngård N	111	D1
Botoşani RO	127	D3
Botsmark S	113	D1
Bottrop D	55	E4
Bouaye F	24	A1
Boucau F	28	A3
Bouchain F	17	D3
Les Bouchoux F	27	D2
Boudry CH	27	E1
Bouillon B	17	F3
Bouilly F	22	A3
Boúka GR	96	C2
Boulay-Moselle F	23	D1
Boulogne-sur-Gesse F	29	D3
Boulogne-sur-Mer F	15	D4
Bouloire F	20	C3
Le Boulou F	30	A4
Bourbon-Lancy F	26	B2
Bourbon-l'Archambault F	26	A2
Bourbonne-les-Bains F	22	C3
La Bourboule F	25	F3
Bourbourg F	15	E4
Bourbriac F	18	C2
Bourdeaux F	30	C1
Bourdeilles F	25	D4
Bourg F	24	C3
Bourg-Achard F	16	A4
Bourg-Argental F	26	C4
Bourg-de-Péage F	26	C4
Bourg-de-Visa F	29	D1
Le Bourg-d'Oisans F	27	D4
Bourg-en-Bresse F	26	C2
Bourg-Lastic F	25	F3
Bourg-Madame F	29	F4
Bourg-St-Andéol F	30	C1
Bourg-St-Maurice F	27	E3
Bourganeuf F	25	E3
Bourges F	25	F1
Le Bourget-du-Lac F	27	D3
Bourgneuf-en-Retz F	24	A1
Bourgoin-Jallieu F	26	C3
Bourgtheroulde-Infreville F	16	A4
Bourgueil F	25	D1
Bourmont F	22	C3
Bourne GB	11	E4
Bournemouth GB	13	F3
Le Bousquet-d'Orb F	30	A2
Boussac F	25	F2
Boussens F	29	D3
Bouxwiller F	23	E2
Bouzonville F	23	D1
Bova Marina I	83	E4
Bovalino Marina I	83	E4
Bovec SLO	72	C2
Bóveda E	32	C3
Bóveda de Toro (La) E	35	F4
Bøverdal N	110	C3
Boves F	16	C3
Boves I	31	F1
Bovey Tracey GB	13	D3
Bovolone I	72	A4
Bowes GB	11	D1
Bowness-on-Windermere GB	10	C1
Bowness-on-Solway GB	9	D4
Boxholm S	119	D4
Boxmeer NL	54	C4
Boxtel NL	54	C4
Boyle / Mainistir na Búille IRL	2	C3
Bozdoğan TR	129	F4
Bozel F	27	E3
Bozen / Bolzano I	67	E4
Bozouls F	29	F1
Bozüyük TR	129	F3

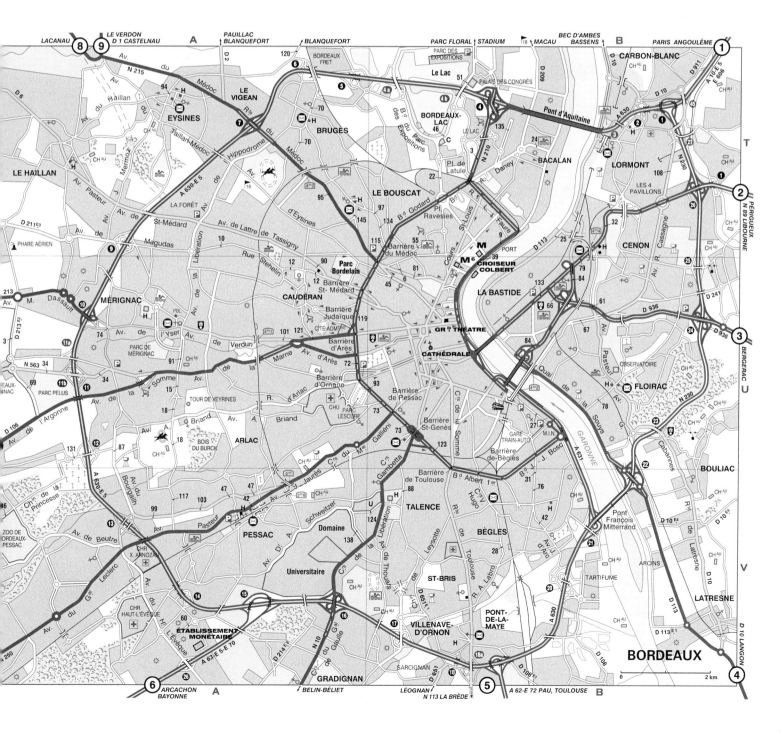

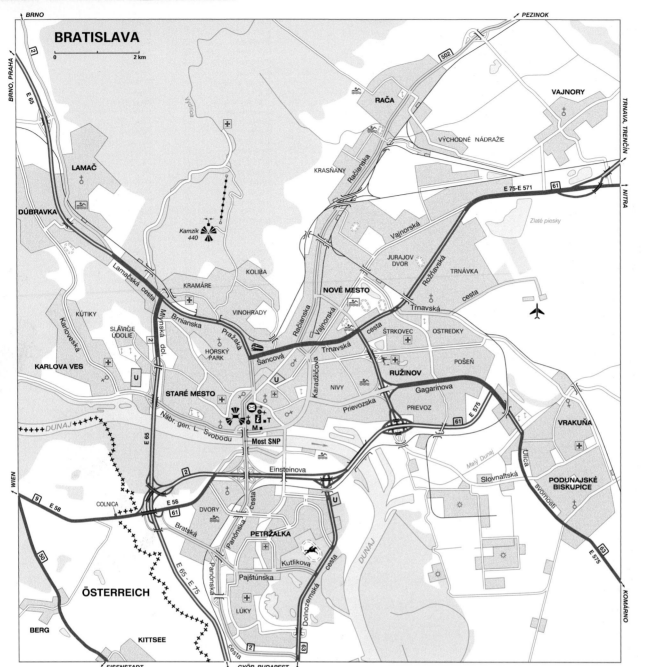

BRATISLAVA

0   2 km

Brazatortas E	42	A4
Brčko BIH	128	A1
Brea E	37	E4
Brécey F	19	E2
Brechin GB	9	E1
Brecht B	17	E1
Brecon / Aberhonddu GB	13	D1
Breda E	39	D3
Breda NL	17	E1
Bredbyn S	112	C2
La Brède F	28	C1
Bredelar D	56	B4
Bredstedt D	50	A2
Bree B	17	F1
Breganze I	72	A4
Bregenz A	66	C3
Bréhal F	19	E2
Brehna D	57	E4
Breiðdalsvik IS	106	C2
Breil-sur-Roya F	31	F2
Breisach D	23	E3
Breitengüßbach D	63	D3
Breitungen D	62	C1
Breivikbotn N	104	C1
Breivikeidet N	104	B2
Brekke N	110	A4
Brekken N	111	E2
Brekkvasselv N	107	D4
Brekstad N	111	D1
Bremen D	50	A4
Bremerhaven D	50	A4
Bremervörde D	50	B4
Bremsnes N	110	C2
Brenes E	47	E2
Brennilis F	18	B3
Breno I	71	F3
Brénod F	27	D2
Brentwood GB	14	C3
Brescia I	71	E4
Breskens NL	17	D1
Bresles F	16	C4
Bressanone / Brixen I	67	E4
La Bresse F	23	D3
Bressuire F	24	C1
Brest BY	126	B1
Brest F	18	B2
Brestanica SLO	73	F2
Bretenoux F	25	E4
Breteuil F	16	C4
Breteuil-sur-Iton F	21	D2
Bretten D	23	F1
Breuil Cervinia I	27	F3
Brevik N	116	C2
Brežice SLO	73	F3
Brezno SK	126	A3
Brézolles F	21	D2
Briançon F	27	E4
Briare F	21	F4
Bricquebec F	19	E1
Brides-les-Bains F	27	E3
Bridge of Allan GB	8	C2
Bridgend / Pen-y-bont GB	13	D2
Bridgend GB	8	A2

Bozzolo I	75	F1	Brand A	66	C3
Bra I	74	C2	Brandbu N	117	D1
Brač HR	128	A2	Brande DK	122	B2
Bracadale GB	6	B4	Brande-Hörnerkirchen D	50	B3
Bracciano I	79	D1	Brandenburg D	57	E2
Bracieux F	21	D4	Brandis D	57	F4
Bräcke S	112	B3	Brändö FIN	120	A4
Brackenheim D	62	B4	Brandon GB	11	F4
Brackley GB	13	F1	Braniewo PL	124	A4
Bracknell GB	14	B3	Branne F	28	C1
Brackwede D	55	F4	Br'ansk RUS	125	F4
Brad RO	126	C4	Brantôme F	25	D4
Bradford GB	11	D2	Braňosera E	36	B1
Bradford-on-Avon GB	13	E2	Braskereidfoss N	117	E1
Brading GB	13	F3	Braslaŭ BY	124	C3
Bradwell-on-Sea GB	15	D3	Brașov RO	127	D4
Braemar GB	9	D1	Brassac F	29	F3
Braga P	34	B3	Brassac-les-Mines F	26	A4
Bragança P	35	D3	Brasschaat B	17	E1
Brăila RO	127	E4	Bratislava SK	126	A3
Braine F	17	D4	Brattvåg N	110	B2
Braine-le-Comte B	17	E2	Braubach D	61	F2
Braintree GB	14	C2	Braunau A	68	A1
Brake (Unterweser) D	50	A4	Braunfels D	62	A2
Brakel D	56	B4	Braunlage D	56	C4
Bräkne-Hoby S	123	E2	Braunsbedra D	57	E4
Brallo di Pregola I	75	D1	Braunschweig D	56	C3
Brálos GR	93	E3	Braunton GB	12	C2
Bramming DK	122	A3	Bravães P	34	B3
Brampton GB	9	D4	Bray / Bré IRL	3	E4
Bramsche D	55	F3	Bray-Dunes F	15	F3
Brancaleone Marina I	83	E4	Bray-sur-Seine F	21	F3
Brancion F	26	C2	Bray-sur-Somme F	16	C3
Brand-Erbisdorf D	63	F1			

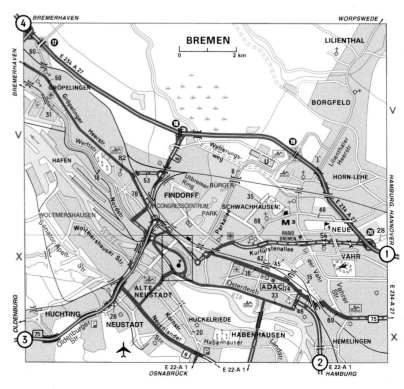

BREMEN

0   2 km

Brüssow D	52 A3	Buckie GB	7 E4	Bultei I	82 B2
Brugg CH	23 F4	Buckingham GB	14 B2	Bunclody IRL	5 E2
Brugge B	15 F3	Buckow D	58 A2	Buncrana / Bun Cranncha IRL	3 D1
Bruksvallarna S	112 A3	Bucureşti RO	129 D1	Bunde D	55 E2
Brûlon F	19 F3	Bud N	110 C2	Bundoran / Bun Dobhráin IRL	2 C2
Brumath F	23 E2	Budapest H	126 A4	Bunessan GB	8 A2
Brummen NL	55 D4	Búðardalur IS	106 A1	Bungay GB	15 D1
Brumunddal N	111 D4	Buddusò I	82 B2	Bunmahon IRL	5 D3
Brunete E	42 B1	Bude GB	12 C3	Buntingford GB	14 C2
Brunflo S	112 B2	Budleigh Salterton GB	13 D3	Buñuel E	37 E3
Brunico / Bruneck I	67 F4	Budrio I	76 A1	Buñol E	43 F3
Bruniquel F	29 E2	Budva YU	128 A3	Buonabitàcolo I	80 C4
Brunkeberg N	116 C2	Büchen D	50 C4	Buonalbergo I	80 B2
Brunnen CH	66 B4	Büchen-Pötrau D	50 C4	Buonconveto I	76 A4
Brunsbüttel D	50 B3	Bückeburg D	56 B3	Buonfornello I	84 C4
Brunssum NL	61 E1	Bückwitz D	51 E4	Burbach D	62 A2
Bruntál CZ	65 E2	Büdelsdorf D	50 B2	Burbáguena E	43 E1
Bruravik N	110 B4	Büdingen D	62 B2	Burdur TR	129 F4
Brusand N	116 A2	Bühl D	23 F2	Bureå S	108 B4
Brusasco I	74 C1	Buenache de Alarcón E	43 D3	Burela E	32 C2
Brusson F	27 F3	Buenavista de Valdavia E	33 F4	Buren NL	54 C1
Bruton GB	13 E2	Bünde D	55 F3	Burfjord N	104 C2
Bruxelles / Brussel B	17 E2	Buendia E	43 D2	Burford GB	13 F1
Bruxelles-Brussel-National B	17 E2	Büren D	55 F4	Burg D	57 D3
Bruyères F	23 D3	Bürgel D	63 E1	Burg a. Fehmarn D	51 D2
Bryne N	116 A2	Bürstadt D	62 A3	Burgas BG	129 E2
Brynmawr GB	13 D1	Büsum D	50 A3	Burgau D	67 D1
Brzeg PL	59 F4	Bueu E	32 A4	Burgbernheim D	62 C4
Břeclav CZ	65 E4	Bugeat F	25 F3	Burg (Den) NL	54 B2
Buarcos P	40 B1	Bugojno BIH	128 A2	Burgdorf D	56 C3
Buavåg N	116 A1	Bugøynes N	105 F2	Burgdorf CH	27 F1
Bubry F	18 C3	Le Bugue F	25 D4	Burgess Hill GB	14 C4
Bučač UA	126 C3	Builth Wells / Llanfairym-Muallt GB	13 D1	Burggrub D	63 D2
Buçaco P	40 B1	Buis-les-Baronnies F	31 D1	Burghasungen D	62 B1
Buccheri I	85 D4	Le Buisson-Cussac F	29 D1	Burghausen D	67 F1
Bucchianico I	79 F1	Buitrago del Lozoya E	36 B4	Burgjoß D	62 B2
Bucelas P	40 A3	Bujalance E	48 A1	Burgkunstadt D	63 D2
Buchen D	62 B4	Bujaraloz E	38 A4	Burglengenfeld D	63 E4
Buchenwald D	63 D1	Bülach CH	23 F4	Burgo (El) E	47 F3
Buchholz i. d. Nordheide D	50 B4	Buldan TR	129 F4	Burgo de Osma (El) E	36 C4
Buchloe D	67 D2	Bulgnéville F	22 C3	Burgohondo E	42 A1
Buchs CH	66 C3	Bullas E	49 D1	Burgo Ranero (El) E	33 E4
Buchy F	16 B4	Bulle CH	27 F2	Burgos E	36 B2
Bucine I	76 B3	Büllingen B	61 E2	Burgsinn D	62 C2
Buckfastleigh GB	13 D3	Bully-les-Mines F	16 C2	Burgstädt D	63 F1
Buckhaven GB	9 D2			Burg Stargard D	51 F3

Burgsvik S	119 F4
Burgui E	28 B4
Burguillos del Cerro E	41 D4
Burgum NL	54 C2
Burgwedel D	56 B3
Burhaniye TR	129 E4
Burhave D	50 A4
Burie F	24 C3
Burjassot E	44 A3
Burkau D	58 A4
Burnham-on-Crouch GB	15 D3
Burnham-on-Sea GB	13 D2
Burnley GB	10 C2
Burntisland GB	9 D2
Buronzo I	70 C4
Burrel AL	128 B3
Burry Port / Porth Tywyn GB	12 C1
Bursa TR	129 F3
Burscheid D	61 F1
Burton-upon-Trent GB	11 D4
Burträsk S	113 E1
Bury GB	10 C2
Bury St. Edmunds GB	15 D2
Busalla I	75 D2
Busca I	31 F1
Bushmills GB	3 E1
Busko-Zdrój PL	126 B2
Bussang F	23 D3
Busseto I	75 E1
Bussière-Badil F	25 D3
Bussolengo I	71 F4
Bussum NL	54 C3
Busto Arsizio I	71 D4
Busto de Bureba E	36 C2
Butera I	84 C4
Buttermere GB	10 C1
Buttevant IRL	4 C3
Buttstädt D	63 D1
Butzbach D	62 B2
Buxtehude D	50 B4
Buxton GB	11 D3
Buxy F	26 C1
Buzançais F	25 E1
Buzancy F	17 F4
Buzău RO	129 D1

Brugge

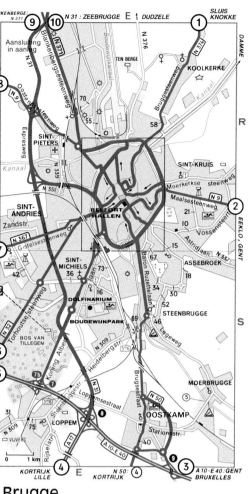

Budapest

Bridgnorth GB	10 C4			Brodnica PL	126 A1
Bridgwater GB	13 D2			Brody UA	126 C2
Bridlington GB	11 F2			Broglie F	20 C2
Bridport GB	13 E3			Brohl Lützing D	61 F2
Brie-Comte-Robert F	21 F2			Brolo I	85 D2
Briec F	18 B3			Bromarv FIN	120 C4
Brielle NL	54 B4			Brome D	57 D2
Brienne-le-Château F	22 B3			Bromölla S	123 D2
Brienon-sur-Armançon F	22 A3			Bromsgrove GB	11 D4
Brienz CH	66 A4			Bromyard GB	13 E1
Brienza I	80 C3			Bronchales E	43 E1
Briey F	22 C1			Brønderslev DK	122 B1
Brig CH	70 C3			Broni I	75 D1
Brigg GB	11 E3			Brønnøysund N	107 D3
Brighouse GB	11 D2			Brøns DK	122 A3
Brightlingsea GB	15 D3			Brösarp S	123 E3
Brighton GB	14 C4			Brossac F	24 C4
Brignogan-Plages F	18 B2			Brøstadbotn N	104 B3
Brignoles F	31 E2			Brotas P	40 B3
Brihuega E	42 C1			Broto E	28 C4
Briksdal N	110 B3			Brotton GB	11 E1
Brilon D	62 A1			Brøttum N	111 D4
Brimnes N	116 B1			Brou F	26 C2
Brinches P	46 B1			Brou F	21 D3
Brindisi I	81 E3			Brouage F	24 B3
Brinon-sur-Beuvron F	26 A1			Brough GB	10 C1
Brionne F	16 A4			Broughshane GB	3 E2
Brioude F	26 A4			Broughton-in-Furness GB	10 C1
Brioux-sur-Boutonne F	24 C2			Brovst DK	122 B1
Briouze F	19 F2			Brownhills GB	11 D4
Brisighella I	76 B2			Brozas E	41 D2
Brissac-Quincé F	19 F4			Bruay-la-Buissière F	16 C2
Brissago CH	71 D3			Bruay-sur-l'Escaut F	17 D2
Bristol GB	13 E2			Bruchsal D	23 F1
Brive-la-Gaillarde F	25 E4			Bruck i. d. Oberpfalz D	63 F4
Briviesca E	36 C2			Bruck an der Großglocknerstraße A	68 A3
Brixham GB	13 D3			Bruck an der Leitha A	69 E1
Brixlegg A	67 F3			Bruck an der Mur A	68 C2
Brjánslækur IS	106 A1			Brückl A	68 C3
Brno CZ	65 D3			Bruckmühl D	67 F2
Bro S	119 F4			Brück D	57 F3
Bro S	119 E2			Brüel D	51 D3
Broadford GB	6 B4			Brügge D	61 F1
Broadford IRL	4 C2			Brühl D	61 F2
Broadstairs GB	15 D3			Brués E	32 B4
Broadway GB	13 F1				
Broager DK	122 B4				
Broby S	123 E2				
Brodick GB	3 F1				

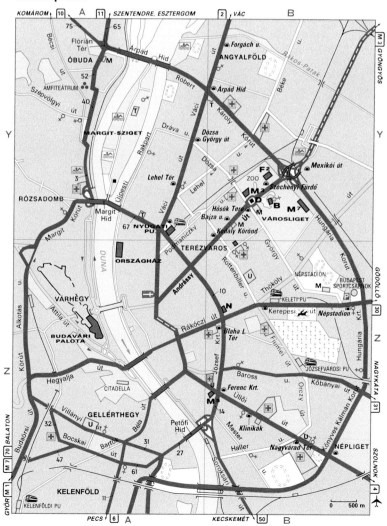

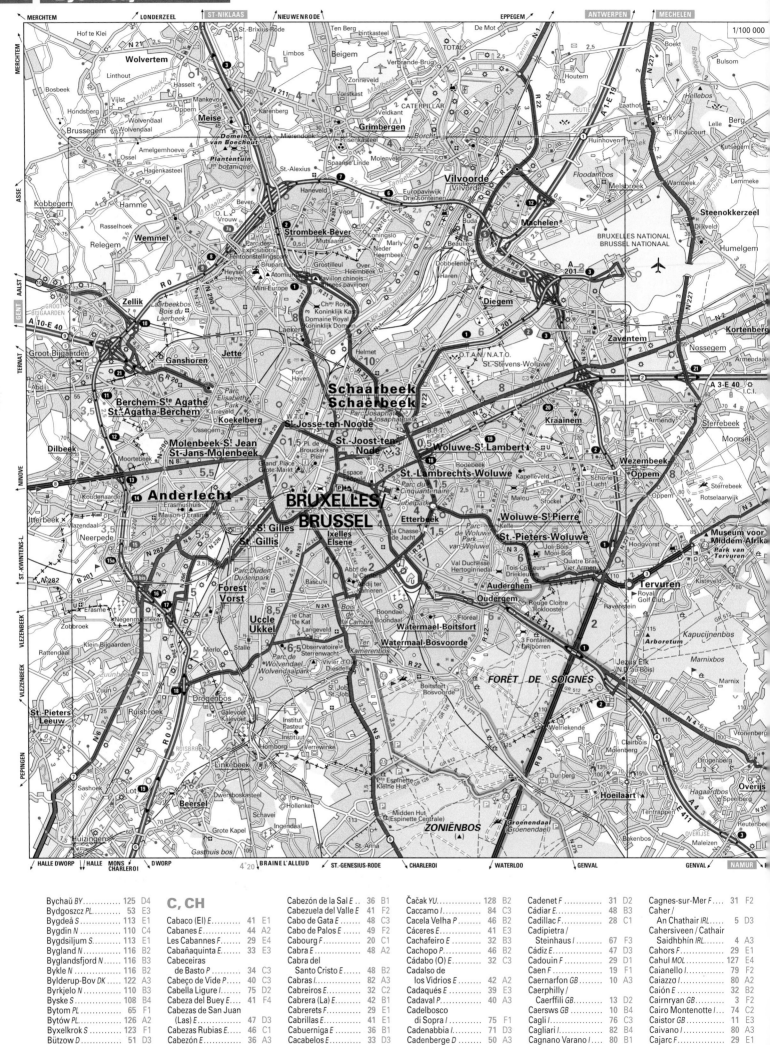

Bychaŭ *BY*	125 D4	**C, CH**	
Bydgoszcz *PL*	53 E3		
Bygdeå *S*	113 E1	Cabaco (El) *E*	41 E1
Bygdin *N*	110 C4	Cabanes *E*	44 A2
Bygdsiljum *S*	113 E1	Les Cabannes *F*	29 E4
Bygland *N*	116 B2	Cabañaquinta *E*	33 E3
Byglandsfjord *N*	116 B3	Cabeceiras	
Bykle *N*	116 B2	de Basto *P*	34 C3
Bylderup-Bov *DK*	122 A3	Cabeço de Vide *P*	40 C3
Byrkjelo *N*	110 B3	Cabella Ligure *I*	75 D2
Byske *S*	108 B4	Cabeza del Buey *E*	41 F4
Bytom *PL*	65 F1	Cabezas de San Juan	
Bytów *PL*	126 A2	(Las) *E*	47 D3
Byxelkrok *S*	123 F1	Cabezas Rubias *E*	46 C1
Bützow *D*	51 D3	Cabezón *E*	36 A3

Cabezón de la Sal *E*	36 B1	Čačak *YU*	128 B2
Cabezuela del Valle *E*	41 F2	Caccamo *I*	84 C3
Cabo de Gata *E*	48 C3	Cacela Velha *P*	46 B2
Cabo de Palos *E*	49 F2	Cáceres *E*	41 E3
Cabourg *F*	20 C1	Cachafeiro *E*	32 B3
Cabra *E*	48 A2	Cachopo *P*	46 B2
Cabra del		Cádabo (O) *E*	32 C3
Santo Cristo *E*	48 B2	Cadalso de	
Cabras *I*	82 A3	los Vidrios *E*	42 A2
Cabreiros *E*	32 C2	Cadaqués *E*	39 E3
Cabrera (La) *E*	42 B1	Cadaval *P*	40 A3
Cabrerets *F*	29 E1	Cadelbosco	
Cabrillas *E*	41 E1	di Sopra *I*	75 F1
Cabuerniga *E*	36 B1	Cadenabbia *I*	71 D3
Cacabelos *E*	33 D3	Cadenberge *D*	50 A3

Cadenet *F*	31 D2	Cagnes-sur-Mer *F*	31 F2
Cádiar *E*	48 B3	Caher /	
Cadillac *F*	28 C1	An Chathair *IRL*	5 D3
Cadipietra /		Cahersiveen / Cathair	
Steinhaus *I*	67 F3	Saidhbhín *IRL*	4 A3
Cádiz *E*	47 D3	Cahors *F*	29 E1
Cadouin *F*	29 D1	Cahul *MOL*	127 E4
Caen *F*	19 F1	Caianello *I*	79 F2
Caernarfon *GB*	10 A3	Caiazzo *I*	80 A2
Caerphilly /		Caión *E*	32 B2
Caerffili *GB*	13 D2	Cairnryan *GB*	3 F2
Caersws *GB*	10 B4	Cairo Montenotte *I*	74 C2
Cagli *I*	76 C3	Caistor *GB*	11 E3
Cagliari *I*	82 B4	Caivano *I*	80 A3
Cagnano Varano *I*	80 B1	Cajarc *F*	29 E1

Čakovec HR............ 73 F2
Çal TR............... 129 F4
Cala en Porter E...... 45 F3
Cala Gonone I......... 82 C2
Cala Rajada E......... 45 F3
Calabor E............. 35 D3
Calaceite E........... 44 A1
Calacuccia F.......... 78 A3
Calaf E............... 38 C4
Calafat RO........... 128 C2
Calafell E............ 38 C4
Calahonda E........... 48 B3
Calahorra E........... 37 E2
Calais F.............. 15 E4
Calamocha E........... 43 E1
Calanda E............. 44 A1
Calangianus I......... 82 B1
Calañas E............. 46 C2
Călăraşi RO.......... 129 E1
Calasetta I........... 82 A4
Calasparra E.......... 49 D1
Calatafimi I.......... 84 B3
Calatañazor E......... 36 C3
Calatayud E........... 37 E4
Calatorao E........... 37 E4
Calau D............... 58 A3
Calbe D............... 57 E3
Calcena E............. 37 E4
Caldaro s. str.
  d. vino / Kaltern I... 67 E4
Caldarola I........... 77 D3
Caldas da Rainha P.... 40 A2
Caldas
  de Besayas (Las) E... 36 B1
Caldas de Reis E...... 32 A3
Caldas de Vizela P.... 34 B3
Caldelas P............ 34 B3
Caldelas (Taipas) P... 34 B3
Caldes de Boi E....... 29 D4
Caldes de Malavella E. 39 D3
Caldes de Montbui E... 39 D4
Caldirola I........... 75 D1
Calella E............. 39 D4
Calella
  de Palafrugell E.... 39 E3
Calenzana F........... 78 A3
Calera de León E...... 47 D1
Calera y Chozas E..... 42 A2
Caleruega E........... 36 B3
Càlig E............... 44 B2
Călimăneşti RO....... 128 C1
Calitri I............. 80 B3
Calizzano I........... 74 C2
Callac F.............. 18 C3
Callan / Callainn IRL.. 5 D3
Callander GB.......... 8 C2
Callas F.............. 31 E2
Callington GB......... 12 C3
Callosa d'en Sarrià E. 49 F1
Callosa de Segura E... 49 E1
Calmazzo I............ 76 C3
Calmbach D............ 23 F2
Calne GB.............. 13 F2
Caló de Sant Agustí E 44 C4
Calolziocorte I....... 71 E4
Calonge E............. 39 E3
Calp / Calpe E........ 49 F1
Caltabellotta I....... 84 B3
Caltagirone I......... 85 D3
Caltanissetta I....... 84 C3
Caltavuturo I......... 84 C3
Caluso I.............. 74 C1
Calvi F............... 78 A3
Calvörde D............ 57 D3
Calw D................ 23 F2
Calzada
  de Calatrava E..... 42 B4
Calzada
  de Oropesa (La) E... 41 F2
Calzada
  de Valdunciel E.... 35 F4
Camaiore I............ 75 F3
Camaldoli
  (Convento) I........ 76 B3
Camaleño E............ 33 F3
Camarasa E............ 38 B3
Camarena E............ 42 B2
Camarès F............. 30 A2
Camaret-sur-Mer F..... 18 A3
Camarillas E.......... 43 F1
Camariñas E........... 32 A2
Camarzana de Tera E.. 35 E3
Camas E............... 47 D2
Cambas P.............. 40 C2
Camberley GB.......... 14 B3
Cambil E.............. 48 B2
Cambo-les-Bains F..... 28 A3
Camborne GB........... 12 B4
Cambrai F............. 17 D3
Cambre E.............. 32 B2
Cambremer F........... 20 C1

Cambridge GB......... 14 C2
Cambrils de Mar E... 44 B1
Camburg D............ 63 E1
Camelford GB......... 12 C3
Camerino I........... 76 C4
Camigliatello Silano I 83 E2
Caminha P............ 32 A4
Caminomorisco E...... 41 E1
Caminreal E.......... 43 E1
Camogli I............ 75 D2
Campagna I........... 80 B3
Campagne-
  lès-Hesdin F........ 16 B2
Campan F............. 28 C3
Campana I............ 83 E2
Campana (La) E....... 47 E2
Campanario E......... 41 F4
Campanas E........... 28 A4
Campaspero E......... 36 B4
Campbeltown GB...... 3 E1
Campello (El) E...... 49 F1
Campi Bisenzio I..... 76 A3
Campi Salentina I.... 81 F3
Campiglia
  Marittima I......... 75 F4
Campillo
  de Altobuey E....... 43 E3
Campillo de Aragón E 37 E4
Campillo de Arenas E 48 B2
Campillo de Llerena E 41 E4
Campillos E.......... 47 F3
Campitello Matese I... 80 A2
Campli I............. 77 D4
Campo di Giove I..... 79 F1
Campo E.............. 29 D4
Campo Ligure I....... 75 D2
Campo Tures / Sand in
  Taufers I........... 67 F3
Campobasso I......... 80 A2
Campobello
  di Licata I......... 84 C4
Campobello
  di Mazara I......... 84 A3
Campo
  de Beisteros P...... 40 C1
Campo de Caso E...... 33 E3
Campo de Criptana E 42 C3
Campo del Hospital E 32 B2
Campo
  de Peñaranda (El) E 35 F4
Campodonico I........ 76 C3
Campoformido I....... 72 C3
Campogalliano I...... 75 F1
Campo Maior P........ 41 D3
Campomanes E......... 33 E3
Campomarino I........ 80 A1
Campóo (Alto) E...... 36 B1
Campora
  S. Giovanni I....... 83 E3
Camporrobles E....... 43 E3
Campos E............. 45 E3
Camposampiero I...... 72 A4
Camprodon E.......... 39 D3
Camucia I............ 76 B3
Camuñas E............ 42 C3
Çanakkale TR........ 129 E3
Canal S. Bovo I...... 72 A3
Canales E............ 36 C3
Canals E............. 43 F4
Canas de Senhorim P 40 C1
Canazei I............ 67 F4
Cancale F............ 19 E2
Cancarix E........... 49 E1
Cancon F............. 29 D1
Candanchú E.......... 28 B4
Candás E............. 33 E2
Candasnos E.......... 38 A4
Candé F.............. 19 E4
Candela I............ 80 B2
Candelario E......... 41 F1
Candeleda E.......... 41 F2
Candes-St-Martin F... 24 C1
Canelli I............ 74 C2
Canero E............. 33 D2
Canet-Plage F........ 30 A4
Canet de Mar E....... 39 D4
Canfranc-Estación E. 28 B4
Cangas E............. 32 A4
Cangas del Narcea E. 33 D3
Cangas de Onís E..... 33 E3
Canha P.............. 40 B3
Canicattì I.......... 84 C3
Canicattini Bagni I.. 85 E4
Caniles E............ 48 C2
Canino I............. 78 C1
Canisy F............. 19 E2
Canjáyar E........... 48 C3
Cannero Riviera I.... 71 D3
Cannes F............. 31 F2
Canneto I............ 75 F4
Cannich GB........... 6 C4
Cannobio I........... 71 D3
Cannock GB........... 11 D4

Canonbie GB.......... 9 D4
Canosa di Puglia I... 80 C2
La Canourgue F....... 30 A1
Cansano I............ 79 F1
Cantalapiedra E...... 35 F4
Cantalejo E.......... 36 B4
Cantalpino E......... 35 F4
Cantanhede P......... 40 B1
Cantavieja E......... 44 A1
Canterbury GB........ 15 D3
Cantillana E......... 47 E2
Cantoira I........... 27 F4
Cantoral E........... 33 F3
Cantoria E........... 49 D3
Cantù I.............. 71 D4
Canvey Island GB..... 14 C3
Cany-Barville F...... 16 A3
Cañigral (El) E...... 43 E2
Cañada
  de Benatanduz E..... 43 F1
Cañamero E........... 41 F3
Cañaveral E.......... 41 E2
Cañaveral de Léon E. 47 D1
Cañaveras E.......... 43 D2
Cañete E............. 43 E2
Cañete
  de las Torres E..... 48 A1
Cañete la Real E..... 47 F3
Cañiza (A) E......... 32 A4
Cañizal E............ 35 F4
Caorle I............. 72 C4
Caorso I............. 75 E1
Le Cap-d'Agde F...... 30 A3
Cap-Ferret F......... 28 B1
Capaccio I........... 80 B4
Capaci I............. 84 B2
Capalbio I........... 78 C1
Caparroso E.......... 37 E2
Capbreton F.......... 28 A2
Capdenac-Gare F...... 29 F1
Capel Curig GB....... 10 B3
Capellades E......... 38 C4
La Capelle F......... 17 D3
Capendu F............ 29 F3
Capestang F.......... 30 A3
Capestrano I......... 79 F1
Capileira E.......... 48 B3
Capistrello I........ 79 E1
Capmany E............ 39 E2
Capo d'Orlando I..... 85 D2
Cappelle sul Tavo I.. 77 E4
Cappoquin / Ceapach
  Choinn IRL.......... 5 D3
Capracotta I......... 80 A1
Capri I.............. 80 A3
Capriati a Volturno I. 79 F2
Captieux F........... 28 C1
Capua I.............. 80 A3
Capurso I............ 81 D2
Capvern F............ 28 C3
Caracal RO.......... 128 C1
Caracuel
  de Calatrava E..... 42 B4
Caraman F............ 29 E3
Caramanico Terme I.. 79 F1
Caramulo P........... 40 C1
Caransebeş RO....... 128 B1
Carantec F........... 18 B2
Caravaca de la Cruz E 49 D1
Carbajales de Alba E. 35 E3
Carballiño E......... 32 B4
Carballo E........... 32 A2
Carbon-Blanc F....... 24 C4
Carboneras E......... 49 D3
Carboneras de
  Guadazaón E......... 43 E2
Carbonero el Mayor E 36 A4
Carbonia I........... 82 B4
Carbonin /
  Schluderbach I...... 67 F4
Carbonne F........... 29 E3
Carcaboso E.......... 41 E2
Carcabuey E.......... 48 A2
Carcaixent E......... 43 F4
Carcans F............ 24 B4
Carcans-Plage F...... 24 B4
Carcare I............ 74 C2
Carcastillo E........ 28 A4
Carcès F............. 31 E3
Çardak TR........... 129 F4
Cardedeu E........... 39 D4
Cardenete E.......... 43 E3
Cardeña E............ 48 A1
Cardiff /
  Caerdydd GB......... 13 D2
Cardigan /
  Aberteifi GB........ 12 C1
Cardona E............ 38 C3
Carei RO............ 126 B4
Carentan F........... 19 E1
Carevo BG........... 129 E2
Cargèse F............ 78 A3

Carhaix-Plouguer F .. 18 C3
Caria P.............. 41 D1
Cariati I............ 83 F2
Carignan F........... 17 F4
Carignano I.......... 27 F4
Carini I............. 84 B2
Carinola I........... 79 F2
Cariñena E........... 37 E4
Cariño E............. 32 C1
Carisio I............ 70 C4
Carlet E............. 43 F4
Carling F............ 23 D1
Carlingford IRL...... 3 E3
Carloforte I......... 82 A4
Carlota (La) E....... 47 F2
Carlow /
  Ceatharlach IRL..... 5 E2
Carloway GB.......... 6 B2
Carluke GB........... 8 C3
Carmagnola I......... 27 F4
Carmarthen /
  Caerfyrddin GB..... 12 C1
Carmaux F............ 29 F2
Carmona E............ 47 E2
Carna IRL............ 2 A4
Carnac F............. 18 C4
Carndonagh / Carn
  Domhnach IRL....... 3 D1
Carnew IRL........... 5 E2
Carnforth GB......... 10 C1
Carnia I............. 68 A4
Carnlough GB......... 3 E2
Carnon-Plage F....... 30 B3
Carnota E............ 32 A3
Carnoustie GB........ 9 E2
Carnwath GB.......... 9 D3
Carolei I............ 83 E2
Carolina (La) E...... 48 B1
Carolles F........... 19 E2
Carovigno I.......... 81 E3
Carpaneto
  Piacentino I........ 75 E1
Carpegna I........... 76 B3
Carpenedolo I........ 71 F4
Carpentras F......... 30 C2
Carpi I.............. 75 F1
Carpignano Sesia I... 70 C4
Carpineti I.......... 75 F2
Carpineto Romano I... 79 E2
Carpinone I.......... 80 A2
Carpio (El) E........ 47 F1
Carpio de Tajo (El) E. 42 A2
Carquefou F.......... 19 E4
Carqueiranne F....... 31 E3
Carracedelo E........ 33 D4
Carradale GB......... 3 F1
Carral E............. 32 B2
Carrapateira P....... 46 A2
Carrara I............ 75 F2
Carrascosa
  del Campo E......... 43 D2
Carrazeda
  de Ansiães P........ 35 D4
Carrazedo de
  Montenegro P........ 34 C3
Carrbridge GB........ 7 D4
Carregado P.......... 40 A3
Carregal do Sal P.... 40 C1
Carrenza E........... 36 C1
Carreña E............ 33 F3
Carrick-on-Shannon-
  Cora Droma
  Rúisc IRL........... 2 C3
Carrick-on-Suir /
  Carraig
  na Siúire IRL....... 5 D3
Carrickfergus GB..... 3 E2
Carrickmacross / Carraig
  Mhachaire Rois IRL. 3 D3
Carrigart /
  Carraig Airt IRL.... 2 C1
Carrió E............. 32 B2
Carrión
  de Calatrava E..... 42 B4
Carrión
  de los Condes E.... 33 F4
Carrizo E............ 33 E4
Carro F.............. 30 C3
Carrouges F.......... 19 F2
Carrù I.............. 74 C2
Carry-le-Rouet F..... 30 C3
Carsoli I............ 79 E1
Cartagena E.......... 49 E2
Cártama E............ 47 F3
Cartaxo P............ 40 A3
Cartaya E............ 46 C2
Carteret F........... 19 E1
Carviçais P.......... 35 D4
Carvin F............. 16 C2
Carvoeiro P.......... 46 A2
Casabermeja E........ 47 F3
Casa Branca P........ 40 C3
Casa Branca P........ 40 A4

Casacalenda I......... 80 A1
Casaio E............. 33 D4
Casal di Principe I.. 80 A3
Casalarreina E....... 36 C2
Casalbordino I....... 80 A1
Casalbuttano
  ed Uniti I.......... 75 E1
Casale Monferrato I.. 74 C1
Casale sul Sile I.... 72 B4
Casalecchio di Reno I 76 A3
Casalmaggiore I...... 75 F1
Casalpusterlengo I... 75 E1
Casamari
  (Abbazia di) I..... 79 F2
Casamassima I........ 81 D2
Casamicciola Terme I 79 F3
Casarabonela E....... 47 F3
Casarano I........... 81 F4
Casar de Cáceres E.. 41 E2
Casar
  de Talamanca (El) E 42 C1
Casares E............ 47 E4
Casares
  de las Hurdes E.... 41 E1
Casariche E.......... 47 F2
Casarsa della Delizia I 72 B3
Casas de Don Pedro E 41 F3
Casas de Fernando
  Alonso E........... 43 D3
Casas
  de Juan Núñez E.... 43 E4
Casas del Puerto E.. 49 E1
Casas de Luján E.... 42 C3
Casas de Miravete E. 41 F2
Casas Ibáñez E...... 43 E3
Casasimarro E........ 43 D3
Casas Nuevas E...... 49 E1
Casatejada E......... 41 F2
Casavieja E.......... 42 A1
Cascais P............ 40 A3
Cascante E........... 37 E3
Cascia I............. 76 C4
Casciana Terme I.... 75 F3
Cascina I............ 75 F3
Casei Gerola I....... 75 D1
Caselle in Pittari I. 80 C4
Caselle Torinese I... 27 F4
Caserta I............ 80 A3
Caserta Vecchia I... 80 A3
Casetas E............ 37 E3
Cashel / Caiseal IRL. 5 D3
Casicas
  del Río Segura E... 48 C1
Casillas de Coria E.. 41 D2
Casina I............. 75 F2
Casinos E............ 43 F3
Casola in Lunigiana I. 75 F2
Casoli I............. 79 F1
Casoria I............ 80 A3
Caspe E.............. 38 A4
Cassà de la Selva E. 39 E3
Cassagnes-
  Bégonhès F......... 29 F2
Cassano allo Ionio I.. 81 D4
Cassano
  delle Murge I...... 81 D2
Cassel F............. 15 E4
Cassino I............ 79 F2
Cassis F............. 31 D3
Castalla E........... 49 F1
Castanet-Tolosan F.. 29 E3
Castanheira
  de Pêra P.......... 40 B1
Castasegna CH........ 71 E3
Casteggio I.......... 75 D1
Castejón
  de Monegros E...... 38 A4
Castejón de Sos E... 29 D4
Castejón
  de Valdejasa E..... 37 F3
Castel del Monte I... 80 C2
Castel del Monte I... 79 F1
Castel del Rio I.... 76 A2
Castel di Sangro I... 79 F2
Castel Gandolfo I.... 79 E2
Castel Madama I..... 79 E2
Castel S. Giovanni I. 75 E1
Castel S. Lorenzo I... 80 B4
Castel
  S. Pietro Terme I.. 76 A2
Castel Volturno I.... 79 F3
Castelbuono I....... 84 C2
Casteldaccia I...... 84 B2
Casteldelfino I..... 31 F1
Castelfidardo I..... 77 D3
Castelfiorentino I... 76 A3
Castelfranco Emilia I. 76 A1
Castelfranco
  in Miscano I....... 80 B2
Castelfranco Veneto I 72 A4
Casteljaloux F...... 28 C1
Castellabate I...... 80 B4

Castellammare
  del Golfo I........ 84 B2
Castellammare
  di Stabia I........ 80 A3
Castellamonte I..... 27 F3
Castellana Grotte I.. 81 D2
Castellane F........ 31 E2
Castellaneta I...... 81 D3
Castellar
  de la Muela E...... 43 E1
Castellar del Vallès E. 39 D4
Castellar
  de Santiago E...... 42 C4
Castellar
  de Santisteban E... 48 B1
Castell'Arquato I... 75 E1
Castelldans E....... 38 B4
Castelldefels E..... 38 C4
Castell de Ferro E.. 48 B3
Castelleone I....... 71 E4
Castellfollit
  de la Roca E....... 39 D3
Castellina in Chianti I 76 A3
Castelló de Rugat E.. 44 A4
Castello di Lago I... 80 B3
Castello Tesino I... 72 A3
Castelló de la Plana /
  Castellón
  de la Plana E...... 44 A2
Castelló
  d'Empúries E....... 39 E3
Castellolí E........ 38 C4
Castellón de la Plana /
  Castelló
  de la Plana E...... 44 A2
Castellote E........ 44 A1
Castellterçol E..... 39 D3
Castelluccia I...... 77 D4
Castelmassa I....... 76 A1
Castelmauro I....... 80 A1
Castelmoron-
  sur-Lot F.......... 29 D1
Castelnau-
  de-Médoc F......... 24 B4
Castelnau-
  de-Montmiral F..... 29 E2
Castelnau-
  Magnoac F.......... 29 D3
Castelnau-
  Montratier F....... 29 E1
Castelnau-
  Rivière-Basse F.... 28 C3
Castelnaudary F..... 29 F3
Castelnovo
  ne' Monti I........ 75 F2
Castelnuovo
  Berardenga I....... 76 A3
Castelnuovo Bocca
  d'Adda I........... 75 E1
Castelnuovo della
  Daunia I........... 80 B2
Castelnuovo di
  Garfagnana I....... 75 F2
Castelnuovo
  di Porto I......... 79 D1
Castelnuovo Scrivia I 75 D1
Castelo Branco P.... 40 C2
Castelo de Paiva P... 34 B4
Castelo de Vide P... 40 C3
Castelraimondo I.... 76 C3
Castelrotto /
  Kastelruth I....... 67 E4
Castelsardo I....... 82 B1
Castelsarrasin F.... 29 E2
Castelserás E....... 44 A1
Casteltermini I..... 84 C3
Castelvecchio
  Subequo I.......... 79 F1
Castelvetrano I..... 84 A3
Castets F........... 28 B2
Castiadas I......... 82 C4
Castiglion
  Fiorentino I....... 76 B3
Castiglioncello I... 75 F3
Castiglione d'Adda I. 75 E1
Castiglione
  dei Pepoli I....... 76 A2
Castiglione del Lago I 76 B4
Castiglione
  della Pescaia I.... 76 A4
Castiglione
  delle Stiviere I... 71 F4
Castiglione
  in Teverina I...... 76 B4
Castiglione Messer
  Marino I........... 80 A1
Castiglione Olona I.. 71 D4
Castilblanco E...... 41 F3
Castilblanco de los
  Arroyos E.......... 47 D2
Castilleja
  del Campo E........ 47 D2
Castilléjar E....... 48 C2

Castillejo
de Martín Viejo E... 41 E1
Castillo de las
Guardas (El) E...... 47 D2
Castillo de Locubín E. 48 A2
Castillon-
en-Couserans F...... 29 D4
Castillon-la-Bataille F 24 C4
Castillonnès F......... 29 D1
Castillo
y Elejabeitia E...... 37 D1
Castilruiz E............ 37 D3
Castions di Strada I.. 72 C3
Castle Douglas GB... 8 C4
Castlebar / Caisleán an
Bharraigh IRL....... 2 A3
Castlebay GB......... 6 A4
Castlebellingham IRL. 3 D3
Castleblayney /
Baile na Lorgan IRL 3 D3
Castlecomer / Caisleán
an Chomair IRL..... 5 D2
Castledawson GB..... 3 D2
Castlederg GB........ 2 C2
Castledermot IRL..... 5 E2
Castleford GB........ 11 D2
Castleisland / Oileán
Ciarraí IRL.......... 4 B3
Castlemaine IRL....... 4 B3
Casltepollard IRL..... 2 C4
Castlerea / An Caisleán
Riabhach IRL........ 2 B3
Castlerock GB........ 3 D1
Castleton GB......... 11 D3
Castletown GB........ 7 E2
Castletown GB........ 3 F3
Castletownbere IRL... 4 A4
Castlewellan GB...... 3 E3
Castrejón E.......... 35 F4
Castres F............. 29 F3
Castries F............ 30 B2
Castril E............. 48 C2
Castrillo de la Reina E 36 C3
Castrillo
de Villavega E...... 33 F4
Castro Caldelas E..... 32 C4
Castro E............. 32 C3
Castrocalbón E....... 33 E4
Castrocaro Terme I... 76 B2
Castrocontrigo E..... 33 D4
Castro Daire P........ 34 C4
Castro del Río E...... 47 F2
Castrojeriz E......... 36 B2
Castro Laboreiro P... 32 B4
Castro Marim P....... 46 B2
Castromonte E........ 36 A3
Castronuevo E........ 35 F3
Castronuño E......... 35 F4
Castrop-Rauxel D..... 55 E4
Castropol E.......... 32 C2
Castroreale I......... 83 D4
Castroreale Terme I... 83 D4
Castrotierra E........ 33 E4
Castro-Urdiales E..... 36 C1
Castro Verde P....... 46 B1
Castroverde E........ 32 C3
Castroverde
de Campos E....... 35 F3
Castrovillari I......... 81 D4
Castuera E........... 41 F4
Catania I............. 85 E3
Catanzaro I.......... 83 E3
Catanzaro Lido I...... 83 E3
Catarroja E.......... 44 A3
Le Cateau-
Cambrésis F........ 17 D3
Le Catelet F.......... 17 D3
Catenanuova I........ 85 D3
Catez SLO........... 73 F3
Catignano I.......... 79 F1
Catoira E............ 32 A3
Catral E............. 49 F1
Cattenom F........... 23 D1
Cattolica I........... 76 C2
Catus F.............. 29 E1
Caudebec-en-Caux F. 16 A4
Caudete E............ 43 F4
Caudiel E............ 43 F2
Caudry F............. 17 D3
Caulnes F............ 19 D3
Caulonia I............ 83 E4
Caumont-l'Éventé F.. 19 F2
Caunes-Minervois F.. 29 F3
Căuşani MOL........ 127 E4
Caussade F........... 29 E2
Cauterets F.......... 28 C4
Cava de' Tirreni I.... 80 A3
Cava (La) I........... 44 B1
Cavaglià I............ 70 C4
Cavaillon F........... 30 C2
Cavalaire-sur-Mer F.. 31 E3
La Cavalerie F........ 30 A2
Cavalese I............ 72 A3

Cavalière F........... 31 E3
Cavan /
An Cabhán IRL...... 2 C3
Cavarzere I........... 72 B4
Cavazzo Carnico I.... 68 A4
Çavdarhisar TR...... 129 F4
Cavezzo I............ 76 A1
Cavo I............... 75 F4
Cavour I............. 27 F4
Cavtat HR........... 128 A2
Cayeux-sur-Mer F.... 16 B3
Le Caylar F........... 30 A2
Caylus F............. 29 E2
Cayres F............. 26 B4
Cazalla de la Sierra E. 47 E1
Cazals F............. 29 E1
Cazaubon F.......... 28 C2
Cazaux F............ 28 B1
Cazères F............ 29 D3
Cazorla E............ 48 C2
Cea E............... 32 B4
Ceadîr-Lunga MOL.. 127 E4
Ceanannus Mór
(Kells) /
Ceanannas IRL...... 3 D4
Cebolla E............ 42 A2
Cebreros E........... 42 A1
Ceccano I............ 79 E2
Cece H.............. 126 A4
Čechov RUS......... 125 F2
Cecina I.............. 75 F4
Ceclavín E........... 41 D2
Cedeira E............ 32 B2
Cedillo E............ 40 C2
Cedrillas E........... 43 F2
Cefalù I.............. 84 C2
Cegléd H............ 126 A4
Ceglie Messapia I.... 81 E3
Cehegín E............ 49 D1
Ceknica SLO......... 73 D3
Celano I............. 79 F1
Celanova E........... 32 B4
Celbridge E.......... 3 D4
Cella E............... 43 E2
Celle D.............. 56 C2
Celle Ligure I......... 75 D2
Celles-sur-Belle F.... 24 C2
Celorico da Beira P.. 41 D1
Celorico de Basto P.. 34 C3
Cencenighe
Agordino I.......... 67 F4
Cenicero E........... 37 D2
Centelles E.......... 39 D3
Centenillo (El) E...... 48 B1
Cento I.............. 76 A1
Centuripe I........... 85 D3
Cepagatti I........... 79 F1
Ceppo di Rocca Sta
Maria I............. 77 D4
Ceprano I............ 79 F2
Cerbère F............ 30 A4
Cercal P............. 40 A3
Cercal E............. 46 A1
Cercedilla E.......... 42 B1
Cerchiara
di Calabria I........ 81 D4
Cerdedo E........... 32 B3
Cerdeira P........... 41 D1
Cerea I.............. 72 A4
Čerepovec RUS...... 125 F1
Ceres I.............. 27 F4
Ceresole Reale I...... 27 F3
Céret F.............. 30 A4
Cerezo de Abajo E... 36 B4
Cerezo de Riotirón E. 36 C2
Cerignola I.......... 80 C2
Cérilly F............. 26 A2
Cerisiers F........... 22 A3
Cerisy-la-Salle F..... 19 E2
Cerizay F............ 24 C1
Čerkasy UA......... 127 F2
Cerknica SLO........ 73 D3
Cerkno SLO.......... 73 D3
Cerler E.............. 29 D4
Cernache
de Bonjardim P...... 40 B2
Čern'achovsk RUS... 124 B4
Cernavodă RO....... 129 E1
Cernay F............. 23 E4
Černihiv UA......... 127 E1
Černivci UA.......... 127 D3
Cernobbio I........... 71 D4
Cerreto Sannita I..... 80 A2
Cerrigydrudion GB... 10 B3
Cërrik AL........... 128 B3
Cerro
de Andévalo (El) E.. 46 C1
Certaldo I............ 76 A3
Cervatos E........... 36 B1
Cervatos
de la Cueza E....... 33 F4
Červen' BY.......... 125 D4
Cervera E............ 38 B4

Cervera
de la Cañada E..... 37 E4
Cervera
del Río Alhama E... 37 D3
Cervera
de Pisuerga E....... 33 F3
Cerveteri I........... 79 D1
Cervia I.............. 76 B2
Cervignano
del Friuli I.......... 72 C3
Cervinara I........... 80 A3
Cervione I............ 78 B3
Cervo E............. 32 C2
Červonohrad UA..... 126 C2
Cesana Torinese I.... 27 E4
Cesarò I............. 85 D2
Cesena I............. 76 B2
Cesenatico I......... 76 B2
Čl'elsis LV.......... 124 B2
Çeşme TR........... 129 E4
Çespedosa E......... 41 F1
Cessalto I............ 72 B3
Cetina E............. 37 D4
Cetinje YU.......... 128 A3
Cetraro I............. 83 D2
Ceuta E............. 47 E4
Ceutí E.............. 49 E1
Ceva I............... 74 C2
Cevico de la Torre E.. 36 A3
Ceyrat F............. 26 A3
Ceyzériat F........... 27 D2
Chabanais F.......... 25 D3
Chabeuil F........... 26 C4
Chablis F............ 22 A4
Chabris F............ 25 E1
Chagny F............ 26 C1
Chailland F........... 19 F3
Chaillé-les-Marais F.. 24 B2
La Chaise-Dieu F..... 26 B4
Chalabre F........... 29 F4
Chalais F............ 24 C4
Chalamont F......... 26 C3
Chalampé F.......... 23 E4
Chalindrey F......... 22 C4
Chalkis GR.......... 94 A3
Challans F........... 24 A1
Challes-les-Eaux F.... 27 D3
Chalon-sur-Saône F.. 26 C1
Chalonnes-
sur-Loire F.......... 19 F4
Châlons-
en-Champagne F... 22 B2
Châlus F............. 25 D3
Cham D............. 63 F4
Chambéry F.......... 27 D3
Chambley-
Bussières F......... 22 C2
Chambly F........... 21 E2
Le Chambon-
Feugerolles F....... 26 B4
Chambon-sur-Lac F.. 26 A3
Le Chambon-
sur-Lignon F........ 26 B4
Chambon-
sur-Voueize F....... 25 F2
Chambord F.......... 21 D4
La Chambre F........ 27 E4
Chamonix-
Mont-Blanc F....... 27 E3
Champagnac-
de-Belair F.......... 25 D4
Champagne-
Mouton F........... 25 D3
Champagnole F....... 27 D1
Champdeniers-
Saint-Denis F....... 24 C2
Champeaux F........ 19 E3
Champeix F.......... 26 A3
Champéry CH........ 27 E2
Champex CH......... 27 F2
Champlitte-
et-le-Prélot F....... 22 C4
Champoluc I......... 27 F3
Champorcher I....... 27 F3
Champs-
sur-Tarentaine F.... 25 F4
Champtoceaux F..... 19 E4
Chamrousse F........ 27 D4
Chamusca P......... 40 B2
Chanac F............ 30 A1
Chanas F............ 26 C4
Chantada E.......... 32 B3
Chantelle F........... 26 A2
Chantemerle F........ 27 E4
Chantilly F........... 16 C4
Chantonnay F........ 24 B1
Chaource F........... 22 A3
Chapel-
en-le-Frith GB....... 11 D3
La Chapelle-
d'Angillon F......... 21 D4
La Chapelle-
de-Guinchay F...... 26 C2

La Chapelle-en-
Valgaudémar F..... 27 E4
La Chapelle-
en-Vercors F........ 27 D4
Chapinería E......... 42 B1
Charbonnières-
les-Bains F.......... 26 C3
Chard GB............ 13 D3
Charenton-du-Cher F. 25 F1
La Charité-sur-Loire F 26 A1
Charleroi B.......... 17 E2
Charlestown IRL...... 2 B3
Charleville-
Mézières F.......... 17 E3
Charlieu F............ 26 B2
Charlottenberg S.... 118 B2
Charly F............. 21 F2
Charmes F........... 23 D3
Charny F............. 21 F4
Charny-sur-Meuse F.. 17 F4
Charolles F.......... 26 B2
Chârost F............ 25 F1
Charquemont F...... 27 E1
Charroux F........... 25 D2
La Chartre-
sur-le-Loir F........ 20 C4
Chassenueil-sur-
Bonnieure F........ 25 D3
La Châtaigneraie F... 24 B2
Château-Arnoux-St-
Auban F............ 31 D2
Château-Chinon F... 26 B1
Le Château-
d'Oléron F.......... 24 B3
Château-du-Loir F... 20 C4
Château-Gontier F... 19 F4
Château-la-Vallière F. 20 C4
Château-Landon F... 21 F3
Château-Porcien F... 17 E4
Château-Queyras F.. 31 E1
Château-Regnault F.. 17 E3
Château-Renault F... 21 D4
Château-Salins F..... 23 D2
Château-Thierry F... 21 F2
Châteaubourg F...... 19 E3
Châteaubriant F...... 19 E4
Château-d'Oex CH... 27 F2
Châteaudun F........ 21 D3
Châteaugiron F....... 19 E3
Châteaulin F......... 18 B3
Châteaumeillant F.... 25 F2
Châteauneuf-
de-Randon F........ 30 B1
Châteauneuf-d'Ille-et-
Vilaine F............ 19 D2
Châteauneuf-
du-Faou F........... 18 B3
Châteauneuf-
du-Pape F........... 30 C2
Châteauneuf-en-
Thymerais F........ 21 D2
Châteauneuf-
la-Forêt F........... 25 E3
Châteauneuf-
les-Bains F.......... 26 A3
Châteauneuf-sur-
Charente F.......... 24 C3
Châteauneuf-
sur-Cher F........... 25 F1
Châteauneuf-
sur-Loire F.......... 21 E4
Châteauneuf-
sur-Sarthe F........ 19 F4
Châteauponsac F.... 25 E2
Châteaurenard F..... 30 C2
Châteaurenard F..... 21 F4
Châteauroux F....... 25 E1
Châteauvillain F...... 22 B3
Châtel F............. 27 E2
Châtel-Montagne F.. 26 B2
Châtel-St. Denis CH... 27 E2
Châtel-sur-Moselle F. 23 D3
Châtelaillon-Plage F.. 24 B2
Le Châtelard F....... 27 D3
Châteaudren F....... 18 C2
Châteldon F.......... 26 A3
Châtelet B........... 17 E2
Le Châtelet F......... 25 F2
Le Châtelet-en-Brie F. 21 F3
Châtelguyon F....... 26 A3
Châtellerault F....... 25 D1
Châtres-Malvaleix F.. 25 F2
Châtenois F.......... 22 C3
Chatham GB......... 14 C3
Châtillon I........... 27 F3
Châtillon-Coligny F.. 21 F4
Châtillon-en-Bazois F 26 B1
Châtillon-en-Diois F.. 31 D1
Châtillon-sur-
Chalaronne F....... 26 C2
Châtillon-sur-Indre F. 25 E1
Châtillon-sur-Loire F. 21 F4

Châtillon-
sur-Marne F......... 22 A2
Châtillon-sur-Seine F 22 B4
La Châtre F.......... 25 F2
Chatteris GB......... 11 F4
Chaudes-Aigues F.... 30 A1
Chauffailles F........ 26 B2
Chaufour-
lès-Bonnières F..... 21 D2
Chaulnes F........... 16 C3
Chaumergy F........ 27 D1
Chaumont F.......... 22 B3
Chaumont-
en-Vexin F.......... 16 B4
Chaumont-
sur-Loire F.......... 21 D4
Chauny F............ 17 D4
Chaussin F........... 27 D1
Chauvigny F......... 25 D2
Chaux-de-Fonds
(La) CH............. 27 E1
Chaves P............ 34 C3
Chazelles-sur-Lyon F. 26 B3
Cheb CZ............. 63 F2
Chef-Boutonne F..... 24 C2
Cheles E............. 40 C4
Chelmsford GB....... 14 C3
Cheltenham GB...... 13 E1
Chelva E............. 43 F3
Chemillé F........... 24 B1
Chemin F............ 26 C1
Chemnitz D.......... 63 F1
Chénérailles F........ 25 F2
Chenonceaux F...... 21 D4
Chepstow /
Cas-Gwent GB..... 13 E2
Chera E............. 43 F3
Cherbourg F......... 19 E1
Chéroy F............ 21 F3
Cherson UA......... 127 F3
Cheshunt GB........ 14 C3
Le Chesne F......... 17 E4
Chester GB.......... 10 C3
Chester-le-Street GB. 9 F4
Chesterfield GB...... 11 D3
Chevagnes F......... 26 A2
Chevillon F.......... 22 B2
Chevreuse F......... 21 E2
Le Cheylard F........ 26 C4
La Chèze F.......... 19 D3
Chiampo I........... 72 A4
Chianciano Terme I.. 76 B4
Chiaramonte Gulfi I.. 85 D4
Chiaravalle I.......... 77 D3
Chiaravalle Centrale I 83 E3
Chiari I.............. 71 E4
Chiasso CH.......... 71 D4
Chiavari I............ 75 E2
Chiavenna I.......... 71 D3
Chichester GB....... 14 B4
Chiclana
de la Frontera E.... 47 D4
Chieming D.......... 67 F2
Chieri I.............. 74 C1
Chiesa
in Valmalenco I..... 71 E3
Chiesina Uzzanese I.. 75 F3
Chieti I.............. 79 F1
Chimay B........... 17 E3
Chinchilla de Monte
Aragón E........... 43 E4
Chinchón E.......... 42 C2
Chinon F............ 25 D1
Chioggia I........... 72 B4
Chipiona E.......... 47 D3
Chippenham GB..... 13 E2
Chipping
Campden GB...... 13 F1
Chipping Norton GB.. 13 F1
Chipping Sodbury GB 13 E2
Chirivel E............ 48 C3
Chişinău MOL....... 127 E3
Chişinău-Criş RO.... 126 B4
Chiusa di Pesio I..... 31 F1
Chiusa / Klausen I.... 67 E3
Chiusa Sclafani I..... 84 B3
Chiusaforte I......... 68 A4
Chiusi I.............. 76 B4
Chiva E............. 43 F3
Chivasso I........... 74 C1
Chmel'nyc'kyj UA... 127 D2
Chmil'nyk UA........ 127 D2
Chojnice PL......... 53 D2
Chojniki BY......... 127 E1
Cholet F............. 24 B1
Chollerford GB...... 9 E4
Cholm RUS......... 125 D2
Chomutov CZ........ 64 A1
Chorges F........... 31 E1
Chorley GB.......... 10 C2

Chorol UA........... 127 F2
Choszczno PL........ 52 B3
Chotyn UA.......... 127 D3
Chouto P............ 40 B3
Christchurch GB..... 13 F3
Christiansfeld DK.... 122 B3
Chur CH............ 66 C4
Church Stretton GB.. 10 C4
Chust UA........... 127 C3
Cicciano I........... 80 A3
Cidones E........... 37 D3
Ciechanów PL....... 126 A1
Ciechocinek PL...... 126 A1
Ciempozuelos E..... 42 B2
Cieszyn PL.......... 126 A3
Cieza E............. 49 E1
Cifuentes E.......... 43 D1
Cigliano I............ 74 C1
Cigüela E........... 36 B1
Cilavegna I.......... 75 D1
Cillas E.............. 43 E1
Cilleros E............ 41 D2
Cilleruelo
de Bezana E........ 36 B1
Cimişlia MOL........ 127 E4
Cîmpeni RO......... 126 C4
Cîmpina RO......... 129 D1
Cîmpulung RO....... 129 D1
Cîmpulung
Moldovenesc RO... 127 D3
Cinctorres E......... 44 A1
Ciney B............. 17 F3
Cinfães P............ 34 C4
Cingoli I............. 77 D3
Cinigiano I........... 76 A4
Cinisi I.............. 84 B2
Cintegabelle F........ 29 E3
Cintruénigo E........ 37 E3
Ciórraga E........... 36 C1
La Ciotat F.......... 31 D3
Cirencester GB...... 13 F1
Cirey-sur-Vezouze F. 23 D2
Ciria E.............. 37 D4
Cirié I............... 27 F4
Cirò I............... 83 F2
Cirò Marina I........ 83 F2
Čirpan BG........... 129 D2
Cisneros E........... 33 F4
Cisterna di Latina I... 79 E2
Cisternino I.......... 81 E3
Cistierna E.......... 33 F3
Città della Pieve I.... 76 B4
Città di Castello I.... 76 B3
Città S. Angelo I..... 77 E4
Cittadella I........... 72 A4
Cittaducale I......... 79 E1
Cittanova I........... 83 E4
Cittareale I........... 77 D4
Ciudad Real E....... 42 B4
Ciudad Rodrigo E.... 41 E1
Ciutadella
de Menorca E....... 45 F2
Cividale del Friuli I... 72 C3
Civita Castellana I.... 79 D1
Civitanova Marche I.. 77 D3
Civitavecchia I....... 78 C1
Civitella del Tranto I.. 77 D4
Civitella Roveto I..... 79 E1
Civray F............. 25 D2
Čivril TR........... 129 F4
Cjurupyns'k UA...... 127 F3
Clacton-on-Sea GB... 15 D3
Clairvaux-les-Lacs F.. 27 D2
Clamecy F........... 22 A4
Claonaig GB......... 8 B3
Clapham GB......... 10 C1
Clara / Clóirtheach IRL 2 C4
Clare GB............ 14 C2
Claremorris /
Clár Chlainne
Mhuiris IRL......... 2 B3
Claudy GB.......... 3 D2
Clausthal-
Zellerfeld D......... 56 C4
Claut I.............. 68 A4
Clavière I............ 27 E4
Clay Cross GB....... 11 D3
Claye-Souilly F....... 21 F2
La Clayette F........ 26 B2
Clécy F............. 19 F2
Cleethorpes GB...... 11 F3
Clefmont F.......... 22 C3
Cléguérec F......... 18 C2
Clelles F............. 31 D1
Clères F............. 16 A4
Clermont F.......... 16 C4
Clermont-
en-Argonne F....... 22 B2
Clermont-Ferrand F.. 26 A3
Clermont-l'Hérault F. 30 A3
Clerval F............ 23 D4
Clervaux L.......... 61 E3
Cléry-St-André F..... 21 E4
Cles I............... 67 E4

Clevedon GB 13 E2
Cleveleys GB 10 C2
Clifden /
  An Clochán IRL 2 A4
Clisson F............. 24 B1
Clitheroe GB.......... 10 C2
Clogh Mills GB 3 E1
Cloghan IRL 2 C4
Clogheen IRL 4 C3
Clogherhead IRL 3 E3
Clonakilty / Cloich na
  Coillte IRL 4 B4
Clonbur /
  An Fhairche IRL..... 2 A4
Clondalkin IRL........ 3 D4
Clones /
  Cluain Eois IRL...... 3 D3
Clonmel /
  Cluain Meala IRL ... 5 D3
Cloppenburg D 55 F2
Clovelly GB 12 C2
Cloyes-sur-le-Loir F.. 21 D3
Cluj-Napoca RO... 126 C4
Clun GB 10 C4
Cluny F 26 C2
La Clusaz F 27 E3
Cluses F 27 E2
Clusone I 71 E3
Clydebank GB 8 C2
Coachford IRL........ 4 C3
Coalisland GB 3 D2
Coalville GB 11 D4
Coaña E.............. 33 D2
Coatbridge GB 8 C3
Cobeña E............ 42 C1
Cobh / An Cóbh IRL... 4 C4
Coburg D 63 D2
Coca E 36 A4
Cocconato I 74 C1
Cocentaina E......... 43 F4
Cochem D 61 F3
Cockburnspath GB .. 9 E3
Cockermouth GB 9 D4
Codevigo I 72 B4
Codigoro I............ 76 B1
Codogno I 75 E1
Codos E.............. 37 E4
Codosera (La) E...... 41 D3
Codroipo I 72 C3
Cölbe D 62 B1
Coesfeld D........... 55 E4
Coevorden NL 55 D3
Cofrentes E 43 F4
Cognac F 24 C3
Cogne I 27 F3
Cogolin F 31 E3
Cogolludo E.......... 42 C1
Coimbra P 40 B1
Coín E 47 F3
Coina P 40 A4
Col SLO.............. 73 D3
Colares E 40 A3
Colchester GB........ 15 D2
Coldbackie GB 7 D2
Colditz D............. 57 F4
Coldstream GB....... 9 E3
Coleford GB 13 E1
Coleraine GB 3 D1
Colfiorito I........... 76 C4
Colico I 71 D3
Coligny F 27 D2
Colinas E 47 D2
Colindres E 36 C1
Colintraive GB........ 8 B2
Coll de Nargó E 38 C3
Colle di Val d'Elsa I.. 76 A3
Colle Isarco /
  Gossensaß I........ 67 E3
Colle Sannita I 80 A2
Collecchio I 75 F1
Colleferro I 79 E2
Collesalvetti I 75 F3
Collesano I........... 84 C2
Colli a Volturno I...... 79 F2
Collinée F............ 19 D3
Collio I 71 F4
Collioure F 30 A4
Collobrières F........ 31 E3
Collodi I 75 F3
Collonges F 27 D2
Collonges-la-Rouge F 25 E4
Colmar F............. 23 E3
Colmars F 31 E2
Colmenar E........... 48 A3
Colmenar de Oreja E. 42 C2
Colmenar Viejo E..... 42 B1
Colnabaichin GB..... 7 E4
Colne GB............. 11 D2
Cologna Veneta I 72 A4
Cologne F 29 D2
Colombey-
  les-Belles F 22 C2

Colombey-les-Deux-
  Églises F 22 B3
Colombres E 33 F2
Colomera E........... 48 A3
Colorno I............. 75 F1
Colosimi I 83 E2
Colunga E 33 F2
Colwyn Bay /
  Bae Colwyn GB 10 B3
Comacchio I 76 B1
Comăneşti RO....... 127 D4
Coma-ruga E......... 38 C4
Combarro E........... 32 A3
Combeaufontaine F... 22 C4
Combe Martin GB 12 C2
Comber GB........... 3 E2
Combloux F 27 E3
Combourg F 19 E3
Combronde F......... 26 A3
Comeglians I.......... 68 A4
Comillas E............ 33 F2
Comines B............ 15 F4
Comines F............ 15 F4
Comiso I.............. 85 D4
Commentry F......... 25 F2
Commercy F 22 C2
Como I............... 71 D4
Cómpeta E 48 A3
Compiègne F......... 16 C4
Comporta P 40 A4
Comps-sur-Artuby F.. 31 E2
Comrat MOL........ 127 E4
Comunanza I......... 77 D4
Concarneau F......... 18 B3
Conches-en-Ouche F. 21 D2
Concordia
  sulla Secchia I...... 76 A1
Condat F............. 26 A4
Condé-en-Brie F...... 22 A2
Condé-
  sur-l'Escaut F....... 17 D2
Condé-
  sur-Noireau F....... 19 F2
Condeixa-a-Nova P .. 40 B1
Condom F 29 C2
Condrieu F 26 C4
Conegliano I.......... 72 B3
Conflans-
  en-Jarnisy F 22 C1
Confolens F 25 D3
Cong / Conga IRL..... 2 A4
Conga / Cong IRL..... 2 A4
Congleton GB 10 C3
Congosto
  de Valdavia E 33 F4
Congresbury GB...... 13 E2
Conil
  de la Frontera E 47 D4
Conisbrough GB...... 11 D3
Coniston GB.......... 10 C1
Conlie F.............. 20 C3
Conliège F 27 D2
Connel GB 8 B1
Connerré F 20 C3
Conques F............ 29 F1
Le Conquet F......... 18 A2
Conquista E 48 A1
Conselice I 76 B1
Conselve I............ 72 B4
Consett GB 9 E4
Constância P.......... 40 B2
Constanţa RO....... 129 E1
Constantina E........ 47 E1
Consuegra E 42 B3
Consuma I 76 A3
Les Contamines-
  Montjoie F.......... 27 E3
Contarina I........... 76 B1
Conthey CH.......... 27 F2
Contigliano I......... 79 E1
Contin GB 6 C1
Contres F 21 D4
Contrexéville F....... 22 C3
Contursi Terme I...... 80 B3
Conty F 16 C4
Conversano I 81 D2
Conwy GB 10 B3
Cookstown GB 3 D2
Cootehill /
  Muinchille IRL 3 D3
Čop UA............. 126 B3
Cope E 49 E2
Copertino I........... 81 F3
Copparo I............ 76 B1
Corabia RO......... 128 C2
Corato I.............. 80 C2
Coray F 18 B3
Corbeil-Essonnes F .. 21 E2
Corbie F 16 C3
Corbigny F 26 B1
Corbola I............. 76 B1
Corbridge GB......... 9 E4
Corby GB 11 E4

Corcieux F............ 23 D3
Corconte E 36 B1
Corcubión E.......... 32 A3
Cordes-sur-Ciel F.... 29 F2
Córdoba E............ 47 F1
Cordobilla
  de Lácara E 41 E3
Corduente E.......... 43 E1
Corella E............. 37 E3
Coreses E............ 35 F3
Corfe Castle GB 13 E3
Corgo E.............. 32 C3
Cori I................ 79 E2
Coria E.............. 41 E2
Coria del Río E....... 47 D2
Corias E.............. 33 D3
Corigliano Calabro I.. 83 E2
Corinaldo I........... 76 C3
Coripe E 47 E3
Cork / Corcaigh IRL .. 4 C3
Corlay F.............. 18 C3
Corleone I............ 84 B3
Corleto Perticara I.... 80 C3
Çorlu TR............ 129 E3
Cormatin F........... 26 C2
Cormeilles F 16 A4
Cormery F 25 D1
Cormons I............ 72 C3
Cornago E............ 37 D3
Cornellana E 33 E2
Corniglio I........... 75 F2
Cornimont F.......... 23 D3
Čornobyl' UA........ 127 E1
Čornomors'ke UA ... 127 F4
Cornuda I............ 72 B3
Cornus F............. 30 A2
Coronada (La) E 41 F4
Coronil (El) E......... 47 E3
Corps F.............. 31 D1
Corral
  de Almaguer E 42 C2
Corrales
  de Buelna (Los) E .. 36 B1
Corrales del Vino E... 35 F4
Corran GB 8 B1
Corredoiras E 32 B3
Correggio I........... 75 F1
Corrèze F 25 E4
Corridonia I 77 D3
Corrofin IRL.......... 4 C2
Corsham GB.......... 13 E2
Corte F 78 A3
Corte de Peleas E 41 E4
Cortegada E.......... 32 B4
Cortegana E.......... 46 C1
Cortemaggiore I...... 75 E1
Cortemilia I.......... 74 C2
Corteolona I.......... 75 E1
Cortes de Aragón E .. 43 F1
Cortes de Baza E..... 48 C2
Cortes E.............. 37 E3
Cortes
  de la Frontera E 47 E3
Cortijos de Abajo
  (Los) E............. 42 B3
Cortijos Nuevos E.... 48 C1
Cortina d'Ampezzo I.. 67 F4
Čortkiv UA.......... 126 C3
Cortona I............. 76 B3
Coruche P 40 B3
Coruña (A) /
  La Coruña E........ 32 B2
Corvara in Badia I 67 F4
Corvera E............ 49 E2
Corvera
  de Toranzo E........ 36 B1
Corwen GB 10 B3
Cosenza I............ 83 E2
Cosham GB.......... 13 F3
Cosne-d'Allier F...... 26 A2
Cosne-sur-Loire F 21 F4
Cossato I............. 70 C4
Cossé-le-Vivien F..... 19 F3
Cossonay CH......... 27 E2
Costa de Caparica P.. 40 A4
Costa
  de Santo André P... 40 A4
Costigliole d'Asti I.... 74 C1
Coswig D 58 A4
Coswig D 57 E3
La Côte-St-André F... 26 C4
Cotignac F........... 31 E3
Cottbus D............ 58 A3
Couches F 26 C1
Couço P.............. 40 B3
Coucy-le-Château-
  Auffrique F......... 17 D4
Couhé F.............. 24 C2
Couilly-
  Pont-aux-Dames F.. 21 F2
Couiza F 29 F4
Coulanges-
  la-Vineuse F 22 A4

Coulanges-
  sur-Yonne F......... 22 A4
Coulommiers F 21 F2
Coulon F............. 24 C2
Coulonges-
  sur-l'Autize F........ 24 C2
Coupar Angus GB ... 9 D1
Couptrain F 19 F3
Cour-Cheverny F 21 D4
Courçon F............ 24 B2
Courmayeur F........ 27 F3
Cournon-
  d'Auvergne F....... 26 A3
La Couronne F 24 C3
Courpière F 26 A3
Cours F 26 B2
Coursan F 30 A3
Coursegoules F 31 F2
Courseulles-
  sur-Mer F........... 19 F1
Courson-
  les-Carrières F...... 22 A4
Courtenay F.......... 21 F3
Courthézon F......... 30 C2
La Courtine F......... 25 F3
Courtomer F 20 C2
Courtown IRL......... 5 E2
Courville-sur-Eure F.. 21 D3
Coussey F 22 C3
Coutances F.......... 19 E2
Coutras F............ 24 C4
La Couvertoirade F... 30 A2
Couvin F............. 17 E3
Cova da Iria P........ 40 B2
Covadonga E......... 33 F3
Covarrubias E........ 36 B3
Coventry GB.......... 11 D4
Coves de Vonromà
  (Les) E............. 44 A2
Covilhã P............ 40 C1
Cowbridge /
  Bont-faen GB 13 D2
Cowdenbeath GB 9 D2
Cowes GB............ 13 F3
Cowfold GB.......... 14 B4
Cozes F.............. 24 B3
Craco I.............. 81 D3
Craigavon GB 3 E2
Craigellachie GB..... 7 E4
Craighouse GB....... 8 A2
Craignure GB........ 8 B1
Crail GB 9 E2
Crailsheim D 62 C4
Craiova RO......... 128 C1
Cranborne GB........ 13 F3
Cranwinkel D........ 63 D1
Crawley GB.......... 14 C4
Creagorry GB......... 6 A4
Crécy-en-Ponthieu F. 16 B3
Crécy-la-Chapelle F.. 21 F2
Crécy-sur-Serre F..... 17 D4
Crediton GB 13 D3
Creegh IRL........... 4 B2
Creeslough IRL....... 2 C1
Creglingen D......... 62 C4
Creil F............... 16 C4
Crema I.............. 71 E4
Crémieu F 26 C3
Cremona I............ 75 E1
Créon F.............. 28 C1
Crépy-en-Valois F 16 C4
Cres HR.............. 77 E1
Cres HR.............. 73 E4
Crescentino I......... 74 C1
Crespino I............ 76 B1
Crest F.............. 30 C1
Cresta CH............ 66 C4
Créteil F............. 21 E2
Creully F............. 19 F1
Creußen D........... 63 E3
Creutzwald F......... 23 D1
Creuzburg D.......... 62 C1
Crevacuore I 70 C4
Crevalcore I 76 A1
Crèvecœur-
  le-Grand F.......... 16 C4
Crevillent E 49 E1
Crewe GB............ 10 C3
Crewkerne GB........ 13 E3
Crianlarich GB 8 C2
Criccieth GB.......... 10 A3
Crickhowell GB....... 13 D1
Cricklade GB.......... 13 F2

Crieff GB 9 D2
Criel-sur-Mer F....... 16 B3
Crikvenica HR 73 E4
Crimmitschau D 63 E1
Crinan GB 8 B2
Criquetot-l'Esneval F. 16 A4
Crissolo I 31 F1
Crivitz D............. 51 D3
Čmošnjice SLO....... 73 E3
Črna SLO............. 73 E2
Crni Vrh SLO......... 73 D3
Crnomelj SLO 73 E3
Crocq F.............. 25 F3
Le Croisic F 19 D4
La Croix-Valmer F 31 E3
Crolly / Croithlí IRL.... 2 C1
Cromarty GB......... 7 D4
Cromer GB........... 15 D1
Crook GB............. 11 D1
Croom IRL 4 C2
Cross Hands GB...... 12 C1
Crosshaven IRL....... 4 C4
Crossmaglen GB...... 3 D3
Crossmolina / Crois
  Mhaoilíona IRL 2 B3
Crotone I............. 83 F2
Le Crotoy F 16 B3
Crowborough GB..... 14 C4
Crowland GB 11 F4
Crowle GB 11 E3
Croyde GB 12 C2
Croydon GB 14 C3
Crozant F 25 E2
Crozon F............. 18 B3
Cruden Bay GB....... 7 F4
Crudgington GB 10 C4
Crumlin GB 3 E2
Cruseilles F........... 27 D3
Cruz da Légua P 40 A2
Cruzamento
  de Pegões P........ 40 B4
Cuacos de Yuste E.... 41 F4
Cualedro E 32 B4
Cuba P 46 B1
Cubel E 37 E4
Cubillo (El) E 43 E2
Cubo de
  Don Sancho (El) E.. 35 E4
Cubo de Tierra
  del Vino (El) E...... 35 F4
Cuckfield GB......... 14 C4
Cudillero E 33 E2
Čudovo RUS......... 125 D1
Cuéllar E 36 A4
Cuenca E 43 D2
Cuers F 31 E3
Cuerva E............. 42 B3
Cuervo (El) E 47 D3
Cuevas
  del Almanzora E ... 49 D3
Cuevas
  del Becerro E 47 F3
Cuevas
  del Campo E........ 48 C2
Cuevas del Valle E ... 42 A1
Cuevas
  de San Clemente E. 36 B3
Cuevas
  de San Marcos E ... 48 A2
Cuglieri I............. 82 A2
Cuijk NL 54 C4
Cuiseaux F 27 D2
Cuisery F 26 C2
Cúllar Baza E 48 C2
Cullen GB 7 E4
Cullera E............. 44 A4
Cullompton GB 13 D3
Culross GB 9 D2
Cumbernauld GB 8 C2
Cumbre (La) E........ 41 E3
Cumbres Mayores E . 47 D1
Cumiana I 27 F4
Cumnock GB 8 C3
Cunault F............ 19 F4
Cuneo I.............. 31 F1
Cunlhat F 26 A3
Cupar GB 9 D2
Cupello I............. 80 A1
Cupramontana I...... 76 C3
Ćuprija YU.......... 128 C2
La Cure F 27 D2
Curia P.............. 40 B1
Curtea de Argeş RO.. 128 C1
Curtis E.............. 32 B2
Cusano Mutri I....... 80 A2
Cushendall GB 3 E1

Cushendun GB........ 3 E1
Cusset F 26 A2
Cutro I............... 83 F2
Cuxhaven D 50 A3
Cwmbrân GB......... 13 D1
Cysoing F............ 17 D2
Czarnków PL 52 C4
Czersk PL 53 D2
Częstochowa PL 126 A2
Człuchów PL......... 53 D2
Čadca SK 126 A3
České Budějovice CZ. 64 B4
Český Krumlov CZ.... 64 B4
Csongrád H 126 B4

D

D. Logatec SLO....... 73 D3
D. Miholjac HR...... 128 A1
Dabo F............... 23 E2
Dachau D 67 E1
Dadiá GR............ 91 E2
Dáfnes GR 93 D4
Dafni GR 94 A4
Dáfni GR 96 C1
Dáfni GR 93 D3
Dáfni GR 89 D3
Dáfni GR 89 F3
Dáfnio GR............ 97 D3
Dafnónas GR 93 D3
Dafnónas GR 89 E1
Dafnotí GR 92 B1
Dagali N 116 C1
Dagebüll D 50 A2
Dagenham GB 14 C3
Dahlen D............. 57 F4
Dahlenburg D........ 50 C4
Dahme D 50 C2
Dahme D 57 F3
Dahn D.............. 23 E1
Daimiel E 42 B4
Daimús E............ 44 A4
Đakovica YU........ 128 B3
Đakovo HR.......... 128 A1
Dal N 117 E1
Dalbeattie GB 8 C4
Dalby S 123 D3
Dale N............... 110 A3
Dale N............... 110 B4
Dalen N............. 116 C2
Dalhem S............ 119 F4
Dalías E 48 C3
Daliburgh GB......... 6 A4
Dalkeith GB 9 D3
Dalkey IRL 3 E4
Dalmally GB.......... 8 B2
Dalmellington GB..... 8 C3
Dalmine I 71 E4
Dalry GB 8 C3
Dals Långed S 118 B3
Dalsbruk FIN......... 120 B4
Dalsjöfors S 118 B4
Dalton in Furness GB. 10 C1
Dalvík IS 106 B1
Dalwhinnie GB 8 C1
Damaskiniá GR 87 E3
Damássi GR 87 F4
Damazan F 28 C1
Damelevières F....... 23 D2
Damgan F 19 D4
Damianó GR.......... 88 A2
Dammartin-
  en-Goële F 21 F2
Damme D............. 55 F3
Dampierre F.......... 27 D1
Dampierre-
  sur-Salon F......... 22 C4
Damville F............ 21 D2
Damvillers F 17 F4
Dangé-St-Romain F.. 25 D1
Danilov RUS......... 125 F1
Dannemarie F 23 E4
Dannenberg (Elbe) D. 51 D4
Daoulas F 18 B3
Dardesheim D........ 57 D3
Darfo-Boario Terme I 71 E3
Dargun D 51 E3
Darlington GB........ 11 D1
Darłowo PL 52 C1
Darmstadt D 62 B3
Darney F 22 C3
Daroca E............. 37 E4
Darque P............. 34 B3
Dartford GB.......... 14 C3
Dartmouth GB........ 13 D4
Daruvar HR......... 128 A1
Darwen GB 10 C2
Dasburg D 61 D3
Dasing D 67 D1
Dassel D............. 56 B4
Dassohóri GR 89 E1
Dassow D............ 50 C3

Dijon

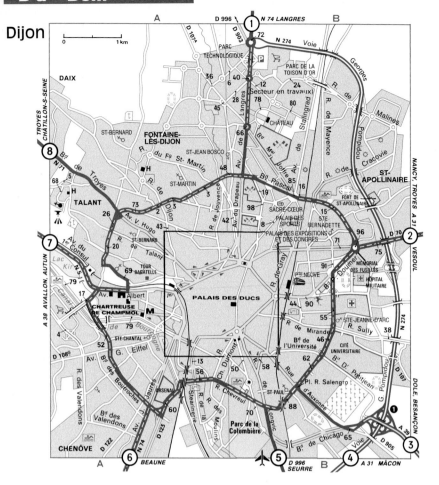

Dietmannsried D	67	D2	Divoúnia (Nissí) GR...	102	C3
Dieulefit F	30	C1	Dívri GR	93	E2
Dieulouard F	22	C2	Djúpivogur IS	106	C2
Dieuze F	23	D2	Djupvik N	104	C2
Diez D	62	A2	Djurås S	119	D1
Diezma E	48	B2	Dmitrov RUS	125	F2
Differdange L	22	C1	Dniprodzeržyns'k UA	127	F2
Digermulen N	104	A4	Dnipropetrovs'k UA	127	F2
Dignano I	72	C3	Dno RUS	125	D2
Digne-les-Bains F	31	E2	Dobbiaco / Toblach I	67	F4
Digoin F	26	B2	Dobel D	23	F2
Dijon F	22	B4	Dobele LV	124	C3
Dikanäs S	107	F4	Doberlug-Kirchhain D	58	C4
Díkea GR	91	E1	Dobersberg A	64	C4
Díkela GR	91	D2	Doboj BIH	128	A1
Diksmuide B	15	F4	Döbriach A	68	B3
Diktéo Ándro GR	101	E4	Dobrič BG	129	E1
Dílessi GR	94	A3	Dobrna SLO	73	E2
Dilináta GR	92	A4	Dobrovnik SLO	73	F1
Dillenburg D	62	A2	Dobruš BY	125	E4
Dillingen D	23	E1	Docksta S	113	C2
Dillingen D	67	D1	Dodóni GR	92	B1
Dílofos GR	91	E1	Döbeln D	57	F4
Dílos (Nissí) GR	98	C2	Döbern D	58	B3
Dímena GR	97	E1	Dörpstedt D	50	B2
Dimitra GR	88	A4	Dörzbach D	62	C4
Dimitrítsi GR	88	C1	Doesburg NL	55	D4
Dimitrovgrad YU	128	C2	Doetinchem NL	55	D4
Dimitrovgrad BG	129	D2	Dogliani I	74	C2
Dimitsána GR	96	C1	Doïráni GR	88	B1
Dinali M	85	F4	Dokka N	111	D4
Dinami I	83	E3	Dokkum NL	54	C1
Dinan F	19	D3	Dokós (Nissí) GR	97	E2
Dinant B	17	F3	Dol-de-Bretagne F	19	E2
Dinar TR	129	F4	Dole F	27	D1
Dinard F	19	D2	Dølemo N	116	C3
Dingelstädt D	56	C4	Dolenjavas SLO	73	E3
Dingle / An Daingean IRL	4	A3	Dolenjske Toplice SLO	73	E3
Dingle S	118	B3	Dolgas Vas SLO	73	F1
Dingolfing D	67	F1	Dolgellau GB	10	B4
Dingwall GB	7	D2	Doliana GR	86	C4
Dinkelsbühl D	63	D4	Dolianova I	82	B4
Dinklage D	55	F2	Dolíhi GR	87	F3
Dinslaken D	55	D4	Dolla IRL	4	C2
Dío GR	88	A3	Döllach A	68	A3
Diónissos GR	94	B4	Dollar GB	9	D2
Dipótama GR	90	B1	Dolle D	57	D3
Dippoldiswalde D	64	A1	Dolo I	72	B4
Diráhio GR	96	C2	Dolores E	49	F1
Dirdal N	116	A2	Dolores (Los) E	49	E2
Diroú (Spílea) GR	97	D3	Dolyna UA	126	C3
Disentis / Mustér CH	66	B4	Domart-en-Ponthieu F	16	C3
Dispílio GR	87	E2	Domažlice CZ	63	F3
Diss GB	15	D2	Dombås N	111	D3
Dissen D	55	F3	Dombasle-sur-Meurthe F	23	D2
Distomo GR	93	E3	Dombóvár H	126	A4
Distos GR	94	B3	Domburg NL	15	F3
Ditzingen D	66	B1	Domène F	27	D4
Divača SLO	73	D3	Doméniko GR	87	F4
Divaráta GR	92	A3	Domèvre-en-Haye F	22	C2
Dives-sur-Mer F	20	C1	Domfront F	19	F2
Divonne-les-Bains F	27	D2			

D'at'kovo RUS	125	F4	Demmin D	51	E3
Datteln D	55	E4	Demonía GR	97	E3
Daugavpils LV	124	C3	Denain F	17	D3
Daun D	61	F3	Denbigh / Dinbych GB	10	B3
Dava GB	7	D4	Dendermonde B	17	D1
Daventry GB	13	F1	Dendrohóri GR	87	D2
Daviá GR	96	C1	Denekamp NL	55	D3
Dávlia GR	93	E3	Dénia E	44	A4
Davos CH	66	C4	Denizli TR	129	F4
Dawlish GB	13	D3	Denkendorf D	63	E4
Dax F	28	B2	Dennington GB	15	D2
Deal GB	15	D3	Denny GB	8	C2
Deauville F	20	C1	Derby GB	11	D4
Deba E	37	D1	Dereköy TR	129	E2
Debar MK	128	C3	Derenburg D	57	D4
Debrecen H	126	B4	Dermbach D	62	C1
Decazeville F	29	F1	Derneburg D	56	C3
Decize F	26	A1	Deruta I	76	C4
Děčín CZ	64	A1	Dervaig GB	8	A1
Dedemsvaart NL	55	D3	Derval F	19	E4
Degaña E	33	D3	Dervéni GR	93	E4
Degerfors S	118	C2	Derventa BIH	128	A1
Degerndorf a. Inn D	67	F2	Dervíziana GR	92	B1
Deggendorf D	64	A4	Desborough GB	11	E4
Dego I	74	C2	Descartes F	25	D1
Degracias P	40	B1	Desenzano del Garda I	71	F4
Dehesa de Montejo E	33	F3	Desfína GR	93	E3
Deià E	45	E3	Desio I	71	D4
Deidesheim D	23	F1	Deskáti GR	87	F4
Deinze B	17	D2	Despotikó (Nissí) GR	98	C3
Deiva Marina I	75	E2	Dessau D	57	E3
Dej RO	126	C4	Destriana E	33	D4
Deje S	118	C2	Desulo I	82	B3
Delčevo MK	128	C3	Desvres F	15	E4
Delden NL	55	D3	Deta RO	128	B1
Deleitosa E	41	F2	Detmold D	56	B4
Delémont CH	23	E4	Dettelbach D	62	C3
Deléria GR	88	A4	Deurne NL	17	F1
Delfi GR	93	E3	Deutschkreutz A	69	E2
Delft NL	54	B4	Deutschlandsberg A	69	D3
Delfzijl NL	55	D1	Deutsch Wagram A	65	E4
Delia I	84	C3	Les Deux-Alpes F	27	E4
Delianuova I	83	E4	Deva RO	126	C4
Deliceto I	80	B2	Deventer NL	55	D3
Delitzsch D	57	E4	Devil's Bridge / Pontarfynach GB	10	B4
Delle F	23	E4	Devizes GB	13	F2
Delme F	23	D2	Devnja BG	129	E2
Delmenhorst D	50	A4	Dewsbury GB	11	D2
Delnice HR	73	E4	Deza E	37	D4
Delsbo S	112	C4	Dezzo I	71	E3
Deltebre E	44	B1	Dębica PL	126	B2
Delvin IRL	3	D4	Dęblin PL	126	B1
Delvináki GR	86	C4	Día (Nissí) GR	101	D3
Demidov RUS	125	E3			
Demirci TR	129	F4			

Diablerets (Les) CH	27	F2	Diego Alvaro E	41	F1
Diafáni GR	103	D3	Diekirch L	61	E3
Diakófti GR	97	E4	Diemelstadt D	56	B4
Diakoftó GR	93	D4	Diepholz D	55	F3
Diamante I	83	D2	Dieppe F	16	A3
Diano Marina I	74	C3	Dierdorf D	61	F2
Diápora Nissiá GR	97	E1	Dieren NL	55	D4
Diavolítsi GR	96	C2	Diesdorf D	56	C2
Dibbersen D	50	B4	Dießen a. Ammersee D	67	E2
Dicomano I	76	A3	Diest B	17	F1
Didima GR	97	E2	Dietenheim D	66	C2
Didimótiho GR	91	E1	Dietfurt a. d. Altmühl D	63	E4
Die F	31	D1	Dietikon CH	23	F4
Dieburg D	62	B3			
Diedorf D	62	C1			

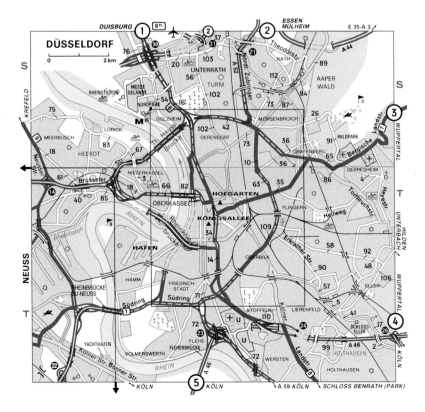

Domme F	29	E1
Dommitzsch D	57	F4
Domnísta GR	93	D2
Domodedovo RUS	125	F2
Domodossola I	70	C3
Domokós GR	93	E2
Dompaire F	23	D3
Dompierre-sur-Besbre F	26	B2
Domrémy-la-Pucelle F	22	C3
Domusnovas I	82	B4
Domžale SLO	73	E2
Donaghadee GB	3	E2
Donaueschingen D	23	F3
Donauwörth D	67	D1
Donawitz A	68	C2
Don Benito E	41	E4
Doncaster GB	11	E3
Donegal / Dún na nGall IRL	2	C2
Doneztebe E	28	A3
Dongen NL	54	B4
Donges F	19	D4
Donington GB	11	F4
Donji Vakuf BIH	128	A2
Le Donjon F	26	B2
Donnemarie-Dontilly F	21	F3
Donnersbachwald A	68	B2
Dønnes N	107	D3
Donostia / San Sebastián E	28	A3
Donoússa (Nissí) GR	99	D2
Donzenac F	25	E4
Donzère F	30	C1
Donzy F	21	F4
Doña María Ocaña E	48	C3
Doña Mencía E	48	A2
Doorn NL	54	C4
Le Dorat F	25	E2
Dorchester GB	13	E1
Dordives F	21	F3
Dordrecht NL	54	B4
Dorfen D	67	F1
Dorfmark D	56	B2
Dorgali I	82	C2
Dóri GR	96	C2
Dorkáda GR	88	B2
Dorking GB	14	B3
Dormagen D	61	E1
Dormans F	22	A2
Dornbirn A	66	C3
Dornburg D	63	E1
Dorndorf D	62	C1
Dornes F	26	A2
Dornie GB	6	B4
Dornoch GB	7	D3
Dornstetten D	23	F2
Dornum D	55	E3
Dorog H	126	A4
Dorogobuž RUS	125	E3
Dorohoi RO	127	D3
Dorotea S	112	C1
Dorsten D	55	E4
Dortan F	27	D2
Dortmund D	55	E4
Dorum D	50	A3
Dosbarrios E	42	C2
Dos Hermanas E	47	D3
Doucier F	27	D2
Doudeville F	16	A4
Doué-la-Fontaine F	24	C1
Douglas GB	8	C3
Douglas GB	3	E1
Doulaincourt F	22	B3
Doulevant-le-Château F	22	B3
Doullens F	16	C3
Doune GB	8	C2
Dourdan F	21	E3
Dourgne F	29	F3
Doŭsk BY	125	E4
Douvaine F	27	E2
Douvres-la-Délivrande F	19	F1
Dover GB	15	D4
Dovre N	111	D3
Downham Market GB	11	F4
Downpatrick GB	3	E3
Dowra IRL	2	C3
Doxarás GR	93	E3
Doxáto GR	89	D1
Dozulé F	20	C1
Drachten NL	55	D3
Drag N	107	F1
Drăgăşani RO	128	C1
Dragoman BG	128	C2
Dragoni I	80	A2
Dragør DK	123	D3
Dragotiná GR	92	A1
Dragsfjärd FIN	120	B4
Dragsvik N	110	B4
Draguignan F	31	E3
Dráma GR	89	D1
Drammen N	117	D2
Drangedal N	116	C2
Dranske D	51	E1
Drasenhofen A	65	E4
Dravograd SLO	73	E2
Drawsko Pomorskie PL	52	B3
Drebkau D	58	A3
Dreki IS	106	B1
Drépano GR	97	E1
Drépano GR	87	F3
Dresden D	58	A4
Dreux F	21	D2
Driebergen-Rijsenburg NL	54	C4
Driebes E	42	C2
Driméa GR	93	E3
Drimós GR	88	B2
Driopída GR	98	B2
Driós GR	98	C3
Drnovo SLO	73	F3
Drøbak N	117	D2
Drobeta-Turnu Severin RO	128	C1
Drochtersen D	50	B3
Drogheda / Droichead Átha IRL	3	D4
Drohobyč UA	126	C2
Droitwich GB	13	E1
Drokija MOL	127	D3
Dromcolliher IRL	4	C3
Dromore GB	3	E2
Dromore GB	2	C2
Dronero I	31	F1
Dronfield GB	11	D3
Drongaráti GR	92	A4
Dronninglund DK	122	C1
Dronten NL	54	C3
Drosendorf Stadt A	64	C4
Drossáto GR	88	B1
Drosseró GR	88	A2
Drossiá GR	94	A3
Drossohóri GR	93	E3
Drossopigí GR	92	B1
Drossopigí GR	87	E2
Drossopigí GR	87	D3
Drottningholm S	119	D2
Droué F	21	D3
Drulingen F	23	E2
Drumkeeran IRL	2	C3
Drummore GB	3	F2
Drumnadrochit GB	6	C4
Drumshanbo IRL	2	C3
Drusenheim F	23	F2
Druskininkai LT	124	B4
Druten NL	54	C4
Drvar BIH	128	A2
Dryburgh Abbey GB	9	E3
Drymen GB	8	C2
Dubăsari MOL	127	E3
Duben D	58	A3
Dublin / Baile Átha Cliath IRL	3	D4
Dubna RUS	125	F2
Dubno UA	126	C2
Dubrovnik HR	128	A3
Ducey F	19	E2
Ducherow D	51	F3
Duchovščina RUS	125	E3
Duclair F	16	A4
Dudelange L	22	C1
Duderstadt D	56	C4
Dudley GB	11	D4
Dudweiler D	23	D1
Dülken D	61	E1
Dülmen D	55	E4
Dueñas E	36	A3
Düren D	61	E2
Dürnkrut A	65	E4
Dürnstein A	68	C1
Düsseldorf D	61	E1
Duesund N	110	A4
Dufftown GB	7	E4
Dugi otok HR	77	E2
Duingt F	27	E2
Duino-Aurisina I	72	C3
Duisburg D	61	E1
Duleek IRL	3	D4
Dulnain Bridge GB	7	D4
Dulovo BG	129	E1
Dumbarton GB	8	C2
Dumbría E	32	A2
Dumfries GB	9	D4
Dun Laoghaire IRL	3	E4
Dun-le-Palestel F	25	E2
Dun-sur-Auron F	25	F1
Dunaföldvár H	126	A4
Dunaïvci UA	127	D3
Dunaújváros H	126	A4
Dunbar GB	9	E2
Dunblane GB	8	C2
Dundalk / Dún Dealgan IRL	3	D3
Dundee GB	9	D2
Dundonnell GB	6	C3
Dunfanaghy IRL	2	C1
Dunfermline GB	9	D2
Dungannon GB	3	D2
Dungarvan / Dún Garbhán IRL	5	D3
Dungiven GB	3	D2
Dunglow / An Clochán Liath IRL	2	C1
Dunkeld GB	9	D1
Dunkerque F	15	E4
Dunmanway / Dún Mánmhaí IRL	4	B4
Dunmore / Dún Mór IRL	2	B4
Dunmore East IRL	5	D3
Dunnamanagh GB	3	D2
Dunnet GB	7	E2
Dunoon GB	8	B2
Duns GB	9	E3
Dunshaughlin IRL	3	D4
Dunstable GB	14	B2
Dunster GB	13	D2
Dunvegan GB	6	B4
Dupnica BG	128	C2
Durango E	37	D1
Duras F	28	C1
Durban-Corbières F	30	A4
Durbuy B	17	F3
Dúrcal E	48	B3
Đurđevac HR	128	A1
Durham GB	9	F4
Durlach D	23	F2
Durness GB	6	C2
Durrës AL	128	B3
Durrow IRL	5	D2
Dursley GB	13	E1

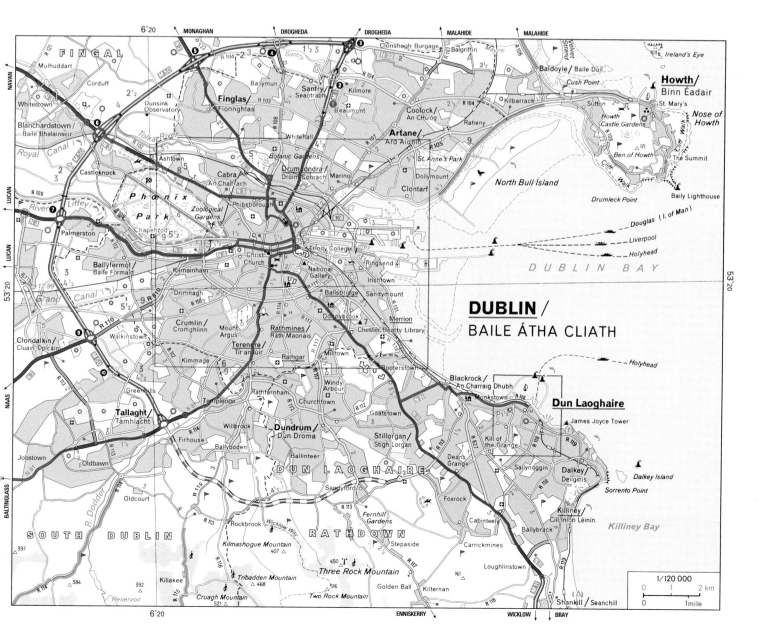

DUBLIN / BAILE ÁTHA CLIATH

Durtal F ... 19 F4
Duruelo E ... 36 C3
Duved S ... 112 A2
Düzce TR ... 129 F3
Dverberg N ... 104 A3
Dyrnes N ... 110 C1
Dzermiádo GR ... 101 E4
Dzierżoniów PL ... 65 D1
Dzjarżynsk BY ... 124 C4
Dömitz D ... 51 D4

E
Eaglescliffe GB ... 11 D1
Eándio GR ... 94 A4
Eaní GR ... 87 F3
Earith GB ... 14 C2
Earlston GB ... 9 E3
Easingwold GB ... 11 E2
Easky IRL ... 2 B2
East Dereham GB ... 15 D1
East Grinstead GB ... 14 C4
East Kilbride GB ... 8 C3
East Linton GB ... 9 E2
Eastbourne GB ... 14 C4
Eastleigh GB ... 13 F3
Eaux-Bonnes F ... 28 C4
Eauze F ... 28 C2
Ebbw Vale /
  Glyn Ebwy GB ... 13 D1
Ebeleben D ... 57 D4
Ebeltoft DK ... 122 C2
Eben im Pongau A ... 68 A2
Ebenfurth A ... 69 E1
Ebensee A ... 68 B2
Eberbach D ... 62 B4
Ebermannstadt D ... 63 D3
Ebern D ... 63 D2
Eberndorf A ... 68 C4
Ebersbach D ... 58 B4
Ebersberg D ... 67 F2
Eberstein A ... 68 C3
Eberswalde D ... 52 A4
Ebmath D ... 63 E2
Eboli I ... 80 B3
Ebrach D ... 63 D3
Ebreichsdorf A ... 69 E1
Ébreuil F ... 26 A2
Ebstorf D ... 50 C4
Eccleshall GB ... 10 C4
Eceabat TR ... 129 E3
Echallens CH ... 27 E1
Les Écharmeaux F ... 26 B2
Les Échelles F ... 27 D4

Echt NL ... 61 D1
Echte D ... 56 C4
Echternach L ... 61 E3
Écija E ... 47 F2
Eckartsberga D ... 63 E1
Eckernförde D ... 50 B2
Eckerö FIN ... 120 A4
Écommoy F ... 20 C4
Écos F ... 21 D2
Écouché F ... 19 F2
Écueillé F ... 25 E1
Ed S ... 118 B3
Eda glasbruk S ... 118 B2
Edam NL ... 54 B3
Edane S ... 118 B2
Ede NL ... 54 C4
Edelény H ... 126 B3
Édenderry /
  Éadan Doire IRL ... 3 D4
Edenkoben D ... 23 F1
Édessa GR ... 87 F2
Edinburgh GB ... 9 D2
Edineţi MOL ... 127 D3
Edipsós GR ... 93 F2
Edirne TR ... 129 E3
Edland N ... 116 B1
Edolo I ... 71 F3
Edremit TR ... 129 E4
Edsåsdalen S ... 112 A2
Edsbro S ... 119 F2
Edsbyn S ... 112 B4
Edsele S ... 112 C2
Eeklo B ... 17 D1
Eelde NL ... 55 D2
Eemshaven NL ... 55 D1
Eferding A ... 68 B1
Efes TR ... 129 E4
Efíra GR ... 96 B1
Efkarpía GR ... 88 B1
Efkarpía GR ... 88 C2
Eforie RO ... 129 E1
Efxinoúpoli GR ... 93 E1
Egeln D ... 57 D3
Eger H ... 126 B4
Egersund N ... 116 A3
Egeskov DK ... 122 B3
Egestorf D ... 50 C4
Egg A ... 66 C3
Eggenburg A ... 65 D3
Eggenfelden D ... 67 F1
Eggesin D ... 52 A3
Eggum N ... 107 D2
Eghezée B ... 17 F2
Egiáli GR ... 99 E3
Egié GR ... 97 D3

Egilsstaðir IS ... 106 C1
Égina GR ... 97 F1
Égina (Nissí) GR ... 97 F1
Egínio GR ... 88 A2
Égio GR ... 93 D4
Égira GR ... 93 E4
Égletons F ... 25 F4
Eglinton GB ... 3 D1
Egloffstein D ... 63 D3
Egmond aan Zee NL ... 54 B3
Egósthena GR ... 93 F4
Egremont GB ... 10 B1
Egtved DK ... 122 B3
Egüés E ... 28 A4
Éguzon F ... 25 E2
Ehinádes Nissiá GR ... 92 B3
Ehingen D ... 66 C1
Ehínos GR ... 89 F1
Ehra-Lessien D ... 56 C2
Ehrang D ... 61 E3
Ehrenberg D ... 62 C2
Ehrenhausen A ... 69 D3
Ehrwald A ... 67 E3
Eibar E ... 37 D1
Eibenstock D ... 63 F2
Eibiswald A ... 69 D3
Eichstätt D ... 63 E4
Eiðar IS ... 106 C1
Eide N ... 110 C2
Eidfjord N ... 116 B1
Eidi DK ... 106 A3
Eidkjosen N ... 104 B2
Eidsborg N ... 116 C2
Eidsbugarden N ... 110 C4
Eidsdal N ... 110 C3
Eidsfoss N ... 117 D2
Eidsvåg N ... 110 C2
Eidsvoll N ... 117 E1
Eikelandsosen N ... 116 A1
Eiken N ... 116 B3
Eikesdal N ... 110 C2
Eilenburg D ... 57 F4
Eilsleben D ... 57 D3
Einbeck D ... 56 C4
Eindhoven NL ... 17 F1
Eindhoven NL ... 17 F1
Einsiedeln CH ... 66 B3
Eisenach D ... 62 C1
Eisenberg D ... 63 E1
Eisenerz A ... 68 C2
Eisenhüttenstadt D ... 58 B3
Eisenkappel A ... 68 C3
Eisenstadt A ... 69 E1
Eisfeld D ... 63 D2
Eišiškės LT ... 124 C4

Eisleben
  Lutherstadt D ... 57 D4
Eislingen D ... 66 C1
Eitorf D ... 61 F2
Eivissa / Ibiza E ... 44 C4
Ejea
  de los Caballeros E ... 37 E3
Ejido (El) E ... 48 C3
Ejulve E ... 43 F1
Ekára GR ... 93 D1
Ekenäs /
  Tammisaari FIN ... 120 C4
Ekshärad S ... 118 C1
Eksjö S ... 118 C3
Elafohóri GR ... 91 E1
Elafoníssi GR ... 97 E4
Élafos GR ... 92 B2
Elassóna GR ... 87 F4
Eláti GR ... 92 C1
Elátia GR ... 93 E3
Elatohóri GR ... 88 A3
Elatoú GR ... 93 D3
Elatóvrissi GR ... 93 D3
Elbasan AL ... 128 B3
Elbeuf F ... 16 A4
Elbigenalp A ... 67 D3
Elbingerode D ... 57 D4
Elbląg PL ... 124 A4
Elburg NL ... 54 C3
Elche / Elx E ... 49 F1
Elche de la Sierra E ... 49 D1
Elda E ... 49 F1
Eldena D ... 51 D4
Elefsína GR ... 94 A4
Eleftherés GR ... 94 A4
Eleftherés GR ... 89 D2
Eleftherés GR ... 93 E1
Eléfthero GR ... 87 D3
Eleftherohóri GR ... 87 E3
Eleftheroúpoli GR ... 89 D1
Elena BG ... 128 D2
Eleófito GR ... 92 C3
Eleohóri GR ... 89 D2
Eleohória GR ... 88 B3
Eleónas GR ... 93 E3
Eleoússa GR ... 103 F2
Elgå N ... 111 E3
Elgin GB ... 7 E4
Elgoibar E ... 37 D1
Elgol GB ... 6 B1
Elhovo BG ... 129 D2
Eliá GR ... 97 D3
Elie GB ... 9 E2
Elimäki FIN ... 121 D3
Elinikó GR ... 96 C1

Elinohóri GR ... 91 E1
Elizondo E ... 28 A3
Ellesmere GB ... 10 C3
Ellesmere Port GB ... 10 C3
Ellingen D ... 63 D4
Ellon GB ... 7 F4
Ellös S ... 118 A3
Ellrich D ... 56 C4
Ellwangen D ... 62 C4
Elm CH ... 66 B3
Elmas I ... 82 B4
Elmshorn D ... 50 B3
Elne F ... 30 A4
Elóna GR ... 97 D2
Elopía GR ... 93 F4
Elorrio E ... 37 D1
Élos GR ... 100 A3
Élos GR ... 97 D3
Eloúnda GR ... 101 E3
Éloyes F ... 23 D3
Elphin IRL ... 2 C3
Elsdorf D ... 61 E1
Elsendorf D ... 67 E1
Elsfleth D ... 50 A4
Elsterberg D ... 63 E1
Elsterwerda D ... 58 A4
Eltisley GB ... 14 C2
Elvanfoot GB ... 9 D3
Elvas P ... 41 D3
Elven F ... 19 D4
Elverum N ... 111 E4
Elvekrok N ... 110 C3
Elx / Elche E ... 49 F1
Ely GB ... 11 F4
Elzach D ... 23 F3
Elze D ... 56 B3
Ełk PL ... 124 B4
Em. Papás GR ... 88 C1
Embessós GR ... 92 C3
Embid E ... 43 E1
Embid de Ariza E ... 37 D4
Émbonas GR ... 103 E2
Emboriós GR ... 103 E1
Emboriós GR ... 99 F2
Emboriós GR ... 95 F4
Embrun F ... 31 E1
Emden D ... 55 D1
Emet TR ... 129 F4
Emlichheim D ... 55 D3
Emmaboda S ... 123 F2
Emmeloord NL ... 54 C3
Emmen NL ... 55 D2
Emmendingen D ... 23 F3
Emmerich D ... 55 D4
Empoli I ... 76 A3
Emsdetten D ... 55 E3
Emskirchen D ... 63 D3
Enafors S ... 112 A2
Enäjärvi FIN ... 121 E3
Encausse-
  les-Thermes F ... 29 D3
Encinas de Abajo E ... 35 F4
Encinasola E ... 46 C1
Encinedo E ... 33 D4
Endrinal E ... 41 F1
Enego I ... 72 A3
Enfesta E ... 32 B3
Eng A ... 67 E3
Engarés GR ... 99 D2
Engelberg CH ... 66 B4
Engelhartszell A ... 68 A1
Engelsdorf D ... 57 E4
Engelskirchen D ... 61 F1
Engen D ... 66 B2
Enger D ... 55 F3
Engerdal N ... 111 E3
Enghien B ... 17 E2
Engstingen D ... 66 B1
Enguera E ... 43 F4
Enguídanos E ... 43 E3
Enkhuizen NL ... 54 C3
Enköping S ... 119 E2
Enna I ... 85 D3
Ennepetal D ... 61 F1
Ennezat F ... 26 A3
Ennis / Inis IRL ... 4 C2
Enniscorthy / Inis
  Córthaidh IRL ... 5 E3
Enniskerry IRL ... 3 D4
Enniskillen GB ... 2 C2
Ennistimon / Inis
  Díomáin IRL ... 4 B2
Enns A ... 68 B1
Eno FIN ... 115 F3
Enonkoski FIN ... 115 F4
Enontekiö FIN ... 105 D4
Enschede NL ... 55 D3
Ensisheim F ... 23 E3
Entlebuch CH ... 66 A4
Entraygues-
  sur-Truyère F ... 29 F1
Entre-os-Rios P ... 34 B4
Entrevaux F ... 31 E2
Entrèves I ... 27 E3

Entroncamento P ... 40 B2
Envermeu F ... 16 B3
Enviken S ... 119 D1
Enzklösterle D ... 23 F2
Epanomí GR ... 88 B3
Epe NL ... 54 C3
Épernay F ... 22 A2
Épernon F ... 21 D2
Épila E ... 37 E4
Épinac F ... 26 C1
Épinal F ... 23 D3
L'Épine F ... 22 B2
Episkopí GR ... 100 B3
Episkopí GR ... 101 D3
Episkopí GR ... 87 F2
Episkopí GR ... 97 F2
Epitálio GR ... 96 B1
Epping GB ... 14 C3
Eppingen D ... 62 B4
Eptahóri GR ... 87 D3
Eptálofos GR ... 93 E3
Epworth GB ... 11 E3
Eraclea I ... 72 B4
Eraclea Mare I ... 72 B4
Eräjärvi FIN ... 120 C2
Eratiní GR ... 93 D3
Eratinó GR ... 89 E1
Erátira GR ... 87 E3
Erba I ... 71 D4
Erbach i. Odenwald D ... 62 B3
Erbalunga F ... 78 B2
Erbendorf D ... 63 E3
Ercolano I ... 80 A3
Érd H ... 126 A4
Erdek TR ... 129 E3
Erding D ... 67 E1
Ereğli TR ... 129 F2
Eresfjord N ... 110 C2
Eressós GR ... 95 E1
Erétria GR ... 94 A3
Erezée B ... 17 F3
Erfde D ... 50 B2
Erftstadt D ... 61 E2
Erfurt D ... 63 D1
Ergoldsbach D ... 67 F1
Erice I ... 84 A3
Ericeira P ... 40 A3
Erikoússa (Nissí) GR ... 86 B4
Eriksberg S ... 119 E3
Eriksmåle S ... 123 F2
Erithrés GR ... 93 F4
Erkelenz D ... 61 E1
Erkner D ... 58 A2
Erla E ... 37 F3
Erlangen D ... 63 D3
Erlsbach A ... 67 F3
Ermenonville F ... 21 F2
Ermidas-Aldeia P ... 46 A1
Ermióni GR ... 97 E2
Ermoúpoli GR ... 98 C2
Ermsleben D ... 57 D4
Erndtebrück D ... 62 A1
Ernée F ... 19 F3
Ernstbrunn A ... 65 D4
Erquy F ... 19 D2
Erratzu E ... 28 A3
Erstein F ... 23 E3
Ervidel P ... 46 B1
Ervy-le-Châtel F ... 22 A3
Erwitte D ... 55 F4
Erzberg A ... 68 C2
Esbjerg DK ... 122 A3
Esblada E ... 38 C4
Escairón E ... 32 C2
Escala (L') /
  La Escala E ... 39 E3
Escalada E ... 36 B1
Escalante E ... 36 C1
Escalona E ... 42 A2
Escalonilla E ... 42 A2
Escalos de Cima E ... 40 C2
L'Escarène F ... 31 F2
Escároz E ... 28 B4
Escatrón E ... 38 A3
Esch-sur-Alzette L ... 22 C1
Esch-sur-Sûre L ... 61 E3
Esch (Waldems-) D ... 62 A2
Eschede D ... 56 B2
Eschenbach i. d.
  Oberpfalz D ... 63 E3
Eschershausen D ... 56 B4
Eschwege D ... 62 C1
Eschweiler D ... 61 E2
Escombreras E ... 49 E2
Escorial (El) E ... 42 B1
Escorihuela E ... 43 F1
Escullar E ... 48 C3
Escurial E ... 41 E3
Esens D ... 55 E1
Esguevillas
  de Esgueva E ... 36 A3
Esher GB ... 14 B3

EDINBURGH

1/100000 — 0 1 2 km / 0 1 mile

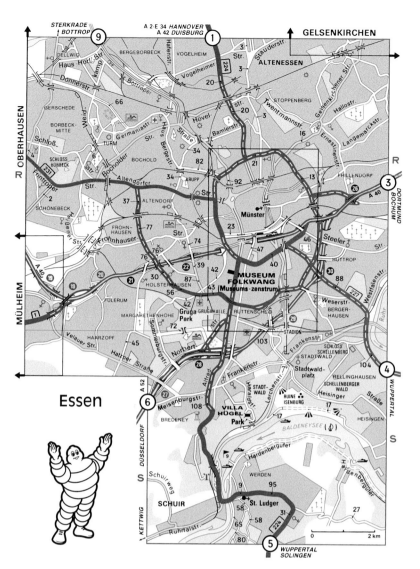

Essen

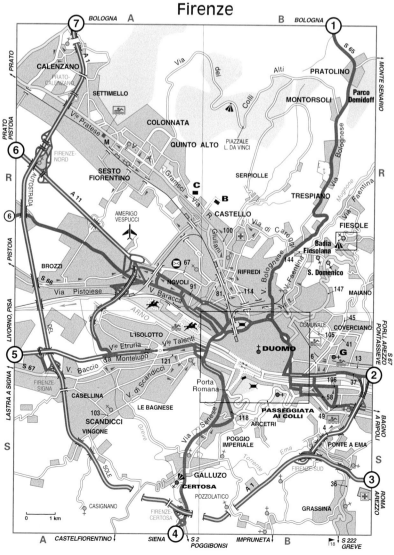

Firenze

F

Faak A	68	B4
Fabara E	38	A4
Fåberg N	111	D4
Fabero E	33	D3
Fåborg DK	122	B4
Fabriano I	76	C3
Fábricas de Ríopar E	48	C1
Fabro I	76	B4
Facinas E	47	E4
Facture F	28	B1
Faenza I	76	B2
Faeto I	80	B2
Fafe P	34	C3
Făgăraş RO	126	C4
Fågelfors S	123	F1
Fagernes N	104	B3
Fagernes N	110	C4
Fagersta S	119	D2
Fagurhólsmýri IS	106	C1
Fairford GB	13	C1
Fakenham GB	15	D1
Fakse DK	123	D3
Fakse Ladeplads DK	123	D3
Falaise F	19	F2
Falássarna GR	100	A3
Falcade I	67	F4
Falces E	28	A4
Falconara Marittima I	77	D3
Falcone I	83	D4
Falerna I	83	E3
Faliráki GR	103	F2
Falkenberg S	123	F1
Falkenberg D	57	F4
Falkensee D	57	F4
Falkenstein D	63	F2
Falkirk GB	9	D2
Falkland GB	9	D2
Falkonéra (Nissí) GR	98	A3
Falköping S	118	C3
Fallersleben D	56	C3
Fällfors S	108	B4
Fallingbostel D	56	B2
Falmouth GB	12	B4
Falset E	38	B4
Fälticeni RO	127	D3
Falun S	119	D1
Famjin DK	106	A4

Fanári GR	96	C1
Fanári GR	93	D1
Fanári GR	97	E1
Fanári GR	89	F1
Fanefjord DK	123	D4
Fanjeaux F	29	F3
Fano I	76	C2
Fanós GR	88	A1
Le Faou F	18	B3
Le Faouët F	18	C3
Fara Novarese I	70	C4
Fårbo S	123	F1
Fareham GB	13	F3
Fårevejle DK	122	C3
Färgelanda S	118	B3
Färila S	112	B4
Farindola I	79	F1
Faringdon GB	13	F2
Farini I	75	E1
Färjestaden S	123	F2
Farkadóna GR	87	F4
Farlete E	37	F4
Farmakoníssi GR	99	F2
Farnborough GB	14	B3
Farnese I	78	C1
Farnham GB	14	B3
Faro P	46	B2
Fårösund S	119	F4
Farra d'Alpago I	72	B3
Fársala GR	93	E1
Farsø DK	122	B1
Farsund N	116	B3
Farum DK	123	D3
Fasano I	81	E2
Fáskrúðsfjörður IS	106	C1
Fastiv UA	127	E2
Fatež RUS	125	F4
Fátima P	40	B2
Fatmomakke S	107	E4
Faucogney-et-la-Mer F	23	D4
Faulquemont F	23	D2
Fauquembergues F	15	E4
Fauske N	107	E2
Fauville-en-Caux F	16	A4
Fåvang N	111	D4
Favara E	44	A4
Favara I	84	C4
Faverges F	27	E3

Eskifjörður IS	106	C1
Eskilstuna S	119	D2
Eskişehir TR	129	F3
Eskoriatza E	37	D1
Eslarn D	63	F3
Eslohe D	62	A1
Eslöv S	123	D3
Esmoriz P	34	B4
Espa N	117	E1
Espadañedo E	33	D4
Espalion F	30	A1
Esparreguera E	38	C4
Espedal N	111	D4
Espejo E	47	F2
Espelette F	28	A3
Espelkamp D	55	F3
Espenschied D	62	A3
Espera E	47	E3
Espiel E	47	F1
Espina (La) E	33	D2
Espinama E	33	F3
Espinar (El) E	42	B1
Espinho P	34	B4
Espinilla E	36	B1
Espinosa de Cerrato E	36	B3
Espinosa de los Monteros E	36	C1
Espluga de Francolí (L') E	38	B4
Espoo / Esbo FIN	121	D4
Esporles E	45	D3
Esposende P	34	B3
Espot E	29	D4
Espunyola (L') E	38	C3
Esquedas E	37	F3
Esquivias E	42	B2
Les Essarts F	24	B1
Esse FIN	114	B3
Essen D	55	E2
Essen D	61	F1
Essenbach D	67	F1
Essími GR	91	D2
Esslingen D	66	B1
Essoyes F	22	B3
Estación de Salinas E	48	A3
Estadilla E	38	A3
Estagel F	29	F4
Estaing F	29	F1

Estaires F	15	F4
Estarreja P	34	B4
Estartit (L') E	39	E3
Estavayer-le-Lac CH	27	E1
Este I	72	A4
Estepa E	47	F2
Estepona E	47	E4
Esteras de Medinaceli E	37	D4
Esternay F	22	A2
Esterri d'Àneu F	29	D4
Estissac F	22	A3
Estói P	46	B2
Estoril P	40	A3
Estrada (A) E	32	B3
Estrées-St-Denis F	16	C4
Estremoz P	40	C3
Esztergom H	126	A4
Étables-sur-Mer F	18	C2
Étain F	17	F4
Étampes F	21	E3
Étang-sur-Arroux F	26	B1
Étaples F	16	B2
Étel F	18	C4
Etelhem S	119	F4
Etne N	116	A1
Etolikó GR	92	C3
Etrépagny F	16	B4
Étretat F	20	C1
Ettelbruck L	61	E3
Ettenheim D	23	E3
Etten-Leur NL	17	E1
Ettington GB	13	F1
Ettlingen D	23	F2
Ettlingenweier D	23	F2
Etxarri-Aranatz E	28	A3
Eu F	16	B3
Eugénie-les-Bains F	28	C2
Eupen B	61	E2
Eura FIN	120	B3
Eurajoki FIN	120	B3
Euratsfeld A	68	C1
Europoort NL	54	B4
Euskirchen D	61	E2
Eußenhausen D	62	C2
Eutin D	50	C2
Evangelismós GR	88	A4
Evangelístria GR	93	F3
Évaux-les-Bains F	25	F2

Évdilos GR	99	E1
Evendorf D	50	C4
Evenes N	104	A4
Evenskjær / Skånland N	104	A4
Evergem B	17	D1
Everöd S	123	E3
Evertsberg S	112	A4
Evesham GB	13	F1
Évia (Nissí) GR	94	A2
Évian-les-Bains F	27	E2
Evijärvi FIN	114	C3
Evinohóri GR	92	C3
Évisa F	78	A3
Evje N	116	B3
Evlalo GR	89	E1
Evolène CH	27	F2
Évora P	40	B4
Évoramonte P	40	C4
Évran F	19	D3
Évrecy F	19	F2
Évreux F	21	D2
Évron F	19	F3
Evropós GR	88	A1
Evrostína GR	93	E4
Évry F	21	E2
Évzoni GR	88	A1
Exaplátanos GR	87	F1
Éxarhos GR	93	F3
Excideuil F	25	D4
Exeter GB	13	D3
Exmes F	20	C2
Exmouth GB	13	D3
Exohí GR	87	D3
Exohí GR	88	C1
Exohí GR	88	A3
Exómvourgo GR	98	C1
Exter D	55	F3
Eydehavn N	116	C3
Eye GB	11	F4
Eyemouth GB	9	E3
Eyguières F	30	C2
Eygurande F	25	F3
Eymet F	29	D1
Eymoutiers F	25	E3
Les Eyzies-de-Tayac F	25	D4
Ezcaray E	36	C2
Èze F	31	F2
Ezine TR	129	E4

Faverney F 23 D4
Faversham GB 15 D3
Fawley GB 13 F3
Fay-sur-Lignon F 26 B4
Fayence F 31 E2
Fayl-Billot F 22 C4
Fayón E 38 A4
Fécamp F 16 A4
Feces de Abaixo P..... 35 D3
La Féclaz F 27 D3
Feda N 116 B3
Fehmarn D 50 C2
Fehrbellin D 51 E4
Fehring A 69 D3
Felanitx E 45 E3
Feldafing D 67 E2
Feld am See A......... 68 B3
Feldbach A 69 D3
Feldberg D 23 F3
Feldberg D 51 F3
Feldkirch A 66 C3
Feldkirchen
  in Kärnten A 68 B3
Felgueiras P.......... 34 B3
Felgueras E........... 33 E3
Felixstowe GB......... 15 D2
Fellabær IS........... 106 C1
Fellbach D 66 B1
Felletin F............ 25 F3
Fellingsbro S.......... 119 D2
Felton GB 9 F4
Feltre I 72 A3
Fene E 32 B2
Fener I 72 A3
Fenestrelle I......... 27 F4
Fénétrange F.......... 23 D2
Feolin Ferry GB 8 A2
Feraklós GR........... 103 F2
Ferbane IRL 2 C4
Ferdinandshof D....... 51 F3
La Fère F 17 D4
Fère-Champenoise F. 22 A2
Fère-en-Tardenois F.. 17 D4
Ferentino I 79 E2
Féres GR 91 E2
Feria E 41 D4
Ferlach A 68 C4
Fermo I 77 D3
Fermoselle E.......... 35 E4
Fermoy / Mainistir
  Fhear Maí IRL 4 C3
Fernancaballero E..... 42 B3
Fernán Núñez E........ 47 F2
Ferney-Voltaire F..... 27 D2
Ferrandina I.......... 81 D3
Ferrara I 76 A1
Ferreira E 32 C2
Ferreira
  do Alentejo P....... 46 B1
Ferreira do Zêzere P.. 40 B2
Ferreiras P........... 46 A2
Ferreras de Abajo E .. 35 E3
Ferreries F........... 45 F2
Ferreruela
  de Huerva E......... 43 F1
Ferrette F............ 23 E4
Ferriere I............ 75 E2
Ferrières F........... 21 F3
Ferrol E 32 B2
La Ferté-Alais F 21 E3
La Ferté-Bernard F ... 20 C3
La Ferté-Frênel F..... 20 C2
La Ferté-Gaucher F ... 21 F2
La Ferté-Macé F....... 19 F2
La Ferté-Milon F...... 17 D4
La Ferté-St-Aubin F .. 21 E4
La Ferté-
  sous-Jouarre F..... 21 F2
La Ferté-Vidame F..... 21 D2
Fertília I............ 82 A2
Festós GR............. 100 C4
Festvåg N............. 107 E1
Fethard /
  Fiodh Ard IRL 5 D3
Fetsund N 117 D1
Feucht D 63 D4
Feuchtwangen D 63 D4
Feurs F 26 B3
Feyzin F 26 B3
Ffestiniog GB......... 10 B3
Fiamignano I.......... 79 E1
Fiano Romano I........ 79 D1
Fiastra I 77 D4
Ficarolo I 76 A1
Fidenza I 75 E1
Fieberbrunn A 67 F2
Fier AL 128 B3
Fiera di Primiero I .. 72 A3
Fiesole I 76 A3
Figaró (El) E 39 D4
Figeac F 29 F1
Figline Valdarno I.... 76 A3
Figueira da Foz P..... 40 B1

Figueira de Castelo
  Rodrigo P........... 35 D4
Figueiró dos Vinhos P 40 B2
Figueras / Figueres E. 39 E3
Figueres / Figueras E. 39 E3
Figueruela
  de Arriba E 35 E3
Fíhtio GR............. 97 D1
Filadélfi GR.......... 88 C2
Filadelfia I.......... 83 E3
Fíláki GR............. 93 E1
Filákio GR............ 91 E1
Filakopí GR........... 98 B3
Filérimos GR.......... 103 F2
Filey GB 11 E1
Filí GR............... 94 A4
Fília GR.............. 96 C1
Fília GR.............. 95 F1
Filiátes GR........... 86 C4
Filiatrá GR........... 96 B3
Filípi GR............. 89 D1
Filipiáda GR.......... 92 B1
Filipstad S........... 118 C2
Filíra GR............. 91 D2
Fillan N 111 D1
Fílo GR............... 93 D1
Filótas GR............ 87 F2
Filottrano I.......... 77 D3
Finale Emilia I....... 76 A1
Finale Ligure I....... 74 C2
Finchingfield GB...... 14 C2
Finikas GR............ 98 B2
Finikoúndas GR........ 96 B3
Finja S 123 E2
Finneidfjord N 107 E3

Finnentrop D.......... 62 A1
Finnsnes / Lenvik N... 104 B3
Finow D............... 51 F4
Finowfurt D 51 F4
Finspång S 119 C3
Finsterau D........... 64 A4
Finsterwalde D........ 58 A4
Finström FIN.......... 120 A4
Fintona GB............ 3 D2
Fintown /
  Baile na Finne IRL .. 2 C2
Fiñana E 48 C3
Fionnphort GB 8 A2
Fiorenzuola d'Arda I.. 75 E1
Firenze I 76 A3
Firenzuola I.......... 76 A2
Firminy F............. 26 B4
Firmo I............... 81 D4
Fischamend Markt A. 69 E1
Fischbach D 63 D3
Fischbeck D 57 E2
Fischen i. Allgäu D.... 67 D3
Fishbourne GB........ 13 F3
Fishguard /
  Abergwaun GB...... 12 C1
Fiskárdo GR........... 92 A3
Fiskari FIN........... 120 C4
Fiskebøl N............ 104 A4
Fismes F.............. 17 D4
Fissíni GR............ 89 F4
Fisterra E 32 A3
Fitero E 37 E3
Fitíes GR............. 92 B3
Fitjar N.............. 116 A1
Fiuggi I 79 E2

Fiumicino I........... 79 D2
Fivemiletown GB 3 D2
Fivizzano I........... 75 F2
Fjærland N 110 B3
Fjällåsen S........... 108 B1
Fjällbacka S 118 A3
Fjällnäs S............ 112 A3
Fjärdhundra S 119 E2
Fjätervålen S......... 112 A3
Fjelie S.............. 123 D3
Fjellerup DK.......... 122 C2
Fjerritslev DK........ 122 B1
Flå N................. 117 D1
Fladungen D 62 C2
Flaine F.............. 27 E2
Flakk N............... 111 D2
Flåm N................ 110 B4
Flambourári GR........ 87 D4
Flámbouro GR.......... 88 C1
Flámbouro GR.......... 87 F2
Flamouriá GR.......... 87 F2
Flattnitz A........... 68 B3
Flatval N............. 111 D1
La Flèche F 19 F4
Fleetwood GB 10 C1
Flekkefjord N......... 116 B3
Flen S 119 E3
Flensburg D 50 B1
Flers F............... 19 F2
Flesberg N............ 116 C1
Flesnes N............. 104 A3
Fleurance F........... 29 D2
Fleurier CH........... 27 E1
Fleurus B 17 E2
Fleury-en-Bière F..... 21 E3

Fleury-sur-Andelle F. 16 B4
Fléves (Nissí) GR..... 97 F1
Flims-Waldhaus CH .. 66 C4
Flint / Fflint GB....... 10 C3
Flintsbach D.......... 67 F2
Flisa N 117 E1
Flix E 38 B4
Flixecourt F 16 C3
Flize F............... 17 E4
Floda S 119 D1
Flöha D 63 F1
Flörsheim-
  Dalsheim D 62 A3
Flogny-la-Chapelle F. 22 A3
Flomohóri GR.......... 97 D3
Florac F.............. 30 B1
Flor da Rosa P........ 40 C3
Florennes B 17 E3
Florensac F........... 30 A3
Florenville B......... 17 F4
Florešti MOL.......... 127 D3
Floriáda GR........... 92 B2
Floridia I............ 85 E4
Flórina GR............ 87 E2
Flötningen S 112 A3
Fluðir IS............. 106 A2
Flüelen CH............ 66 B4
Flühli CH............. 66 A4
Flumet F.............. 27 E3
Fluminimaggiore I..... 82 A4
Flums CH.............. 66 C3
Foča BIH.............. 128 A2
Foça TR 129 E4
Foce Verde I.......... 79 E2
Fochabers GB 7 E4

Fockbek D 50 B2
Focşani RO 127 D4
Fódele GR............. 101 D3
Förderstedt D......... 57 D3
Foggia I.............. 80 B2
Föglö FIN............. 120 A4
Fohnsdorf A........... 68 C3
Foiano della Chiana I 76 B4
Foix F 29 E4
Foldereid N........... 107 D4
Foleá GR.............. 89 D2
Folégandros GR....... 98 C3
Folégandros
  (Nissí) GR 98 C3
Folgaria I............ 72 A3
Le Folgoët F.......... 18 B2
Folgoso
  de la Ribera E...... 33 D3
Foligno I............. 76 C4
Folkestad N 110 B3
Folkestone GB......... 15 D4
Follafoss N 111 E1
Folldal N............. 111 D3
Follina I............. 72 B3
Föllinge S............ 112 B1
Follonica I........... 76 A4
Fombellida E.......... 36 B3
Fondevila E........... 32 B4
Fondi I 79 F2
Fondo I 67 E4
Fondó de les Neus
  (El) E 49 E1
Fonfría E 43 F1
Fonn N 110 B3

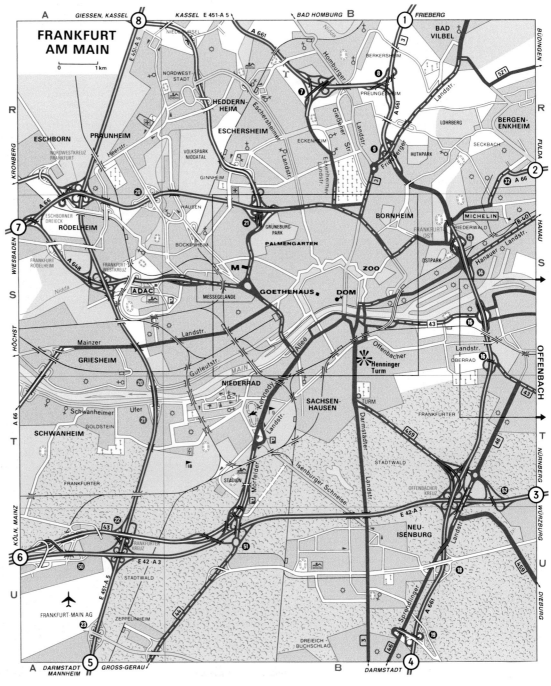

Fonni I 82 B2
Fonollosa E 38 C3
Fonsagrada E 32 C3
Font de la Figuera (La) E 43 F4
Font-Romeu-Odeillo-Via F 29 F4
Fontaine F 23 E4
Fontaine-de-Vaucluse F 30 C2
Fontaine-Française F 22 C4
Fontaine-Henry F 19 F1
Fontaine-le-Dun F 16 A3
Fontainebleau F 21 F3
Fontanigorda I 75 E2
Fontenay-le-Comte F .. 24 B2
Fontenay-Trésigny F .. 21 F2
Fontevraud-l'Abbaye F 24 C1
Fontgombault F 25 D2
Fontibre E 36 B1
Fontiveros E 35 F4
Fontoy F 22 C1
Fontvieille F 30 C2
Fonz E 38 A3
Fonzaso I 72 A3
Foppolo I 71 E3
Forbach F 23 D1
Forcall E 44 A1
Forcalquier F 31 D2
Forcarei E 32 B3
Forchheim D 63 D3
Førde N 116 A1
Førde N 110 B3
Fordingbridge GB 13 F3
Fordongianus I 82 B3
Forenza I 80 C3
Foresta di Burgos I .. 82 B2
Føresvik N 116 A2
Forfar GB 9 D1
Forges-les-Eaux F 16 B4
Forio I 79 F3
Forlì I 76 B2
Forlì del Sannio I ... 79 F2
Forlimpopoli I 76 B2
Formazza I 70 C3
Formby Point GB 10 C2
Formentor (Cap de) E . 45 E2
Formerie F 16 B4
Formia I 79 F2
Formigal (El) E 28 C4
Formigine I 75 F1
Fornaci di Barga I ... 75 F2
Fornells E 45 F2
Forni Avoltri I 68 A4
Forni di Sopra I 68 A4
Forno di Zoldo I 67 F4
Fornos de Algodres P . 40 C1
Fornovo di Taro I 75 E1
Forøy N 107 E2
Forres GB 7 D4
Forsa S 112 C4
Forserum S 118 C4
Forshaga S 118 C2
Forsnes N 110 C1
Forssa FIN 120 C3
Forst D 58 B3
Fort Augustus GB 6 C4
Fort-Mahon-Plage F ... 16 B3
Fort William GB 8 B1
Forte dei Marmi I 75 F3
Forth D 63 D3
Fortrose GB 7 D4
Fortuna E 49 E1
Forvik N 107 E2
Fos F 29 D4
Fos-sur-Mer F 30 C3
Foslandsosen N 106 C4
Fosnavåg N 110 B2
Fossacesia I 80 A1
Fossano I 74 C2
Fossanova (Abbazia di) I 79 E2
Le Fossat F 29 E3
Fossbakken N 104 B3
Fosses-la-Ville B 17 E2
Fossli N 116 B1
Fossombrone I 76 C3
Fotiná GR 88 A3
Fotolívos GR 89 D1
Fouesnant F 18 B3
Foug F 22 C2
Fougères F 19 E3
Fougerolles F 23 D3
Fouras F 24 B3
Fourchambault F 26 A1
Fourfourás GR 100 C4
Fourmies F 17 E3
Fourná GR 93 D2
Fournels GR 30 A1
Foúrni GR 97 E2
Fourní GR 101 E3

Foúrni GR 99 F1
Foúrni (Nissí) GR 99 F1
Fours F 26 B1
Le Fousseret F 29 D3
Foústani GR 87 F1
Fowey GB 12 C3
Foxford IRL 2 B1
Foyers GB 6 C4
Foz E 32 C2
Foz do Arelho P 40 A2
Foz Giraldo P 40 C2
Frabosa Soprana I 74 C2
Fraddon GB 12 B3
Fraga E 38 A4
Frailes E 48 A3
Fraize F 23 E3
Fram SLO 73 F2
Frammersbach D 62 B3
Franca (La) E 33 F2
Francavilla al Mare I . 77 E3
Francavilla di Sicilia I 85 E2
Francavilla Fontana I . 81 E3
Francavilla in Sinni I . 80 C4
Francofonte I 85 D3
Francorchamps B 61 E2
Frändefors S 118 B3
Franeker NL 54 C2
Frangádes GR 87 D4
Frangísta GR 92 C2
Frangokástelo GR 100 B4
Frangy F 27 D3
Frankenberg D 62 B1
Frankenberg D 63 F1
Frankenburg A 68 A1
Frankenmarkt A 68 A2
Frankenstein D 23 E1
Frankenthal D 23 F1
Frankfurt a. Main D .. 62 B3
Frankfurt an der Oder D .. 58 A2
Františkovy Lázně CZ . 63 F2
Franzburg D 51 E2
Franz Josephs-Höhe A 68 A3
Frascati I 79 E2
Frascineto I 81 D4
Fraserburgh GB 7 F4
Fratel P 40 C2
Fratta Polesine I 76 A1
Frauenfeld CH 66 B3
Frauenkirchen A 69 E1
Frauenstein D 64 A1
Frechen D 61 E1
Frechilla E 33 F4
Freckenhorst D 55 F4
Fredensborg DK 123 D3
Fredericia DK 122 B3
Frederikshavn DK 122 C1
Frederikssund DK 123 D3
Frederiksværk DK 123 D3
Fredrika S 113 D1
Fredriksberg S 118 C1
Fredrikstad N 117 D2
Fregenal de la Sierra E .. 47 D1
Fregene I 79 D2
Fregeneda (La) E 35 D4
Freiberg D 63 F1
Freiburg D 50 B3
Freiburg i. Breisgau D . 23 F3
Freienhufen D 58 A4
Freihung D 63 E3
Freilassing D 68 A2
Freilingen D 62 A2
Freising D 67 E1
Freistadt A 64 B4
Freital D 64 A1
Freiwalde D 58 A3
Freixedas P 41 D1
Freixido E 32 C4
Freixo de Espada a Cinta P 35 D4
Fréjus F 31 E3
Frenchpark IRL 2 B3
Freren D 55 E3
Freshford IRL 5 D2
Freshwater GB 13 F3
Fresnay-sur-Sarthe F . 20 C3
Fresne-St-Mamès F 22 C4
Fresnes-en-Woëvre F .. 22 C2
Fresno Alhándiga E ... 41 F1
Freudenberg D 62 A1
Freudenberg D 62 B3
Freudenstadt D 23 F2
Frévent F 16 C3
Freyburg D 57 E4
Freyenstein D 51 E4
Freyming-Merlebach F . 23 D1
Freyung D 64 A4

Fri GR 103 D4
Frías E 36 C2
Frías de Albarracín E . 43 E2
Fribourg CH 27 F1
Fridingen D 66 B2
Friedberg D 62 B2
Friedberg A 69 D2
Friedberg D 67 D1
Friedeburg D 55 E1
Friedersdorf D 58 A2
Friedland D 56 C4
Friedland D 51 F3
Friedrichroda D 63 D1
Friedrichshafen D 66 C3
Friedrichskoog D 50 A3
Friedrichsort D 50 B2
Friedrichstadt D 50 A2
Friedrichsthal D 23 E1
Friesach A 68 C3
Friesack D 57 E2
Friesoythe D 55 E2
Frigiliana E 48 A3
Frihetsli N 104 B3
Fríkes GR 92 A3
Frilingiánika GR 97 E4
Frinton-on-Sea GB 15 D2
Friol E 32 B3
Fristad S 118 B4
Fritsla S 118 B4
Fritzlar D 62 B1
Frizington GB 10 B1
Frodsham GB 10 C3
Frogner N 117 D1
Frohburg D 63 F1
Frohnleiten A 69 D2
Froissy F 16 C4
Froitzheim D 61 E2
Frome GB 13 E2
Fromentine F 24 A1
Frómista E 33 F4
Fronfría E 35 F3
Fronteira P 40 C3
Frontenay-Rohan-Rohan F 24 C2

Frontenhausen D 67 F1
Frontera (La) E 43 D2
Frontignan F 30 B3
Fronton F 29 E2
Frosinone I 79 E2
Frosolone I 80 A2
Frösön S 112 B2
Frosta N 111 E1
Frøstrup DK 122 B1
Frouard F 23 D2
Frövi S 119 D2
Frøyfjorden N 116 B1
Fruges F 16 C2
Frutigen CH 27 F2
Frýdek-Místek CZ 65 F2
Fteliá GR 89 D1
Ftéri GR 93 D4
Ftéri GR 87 F3
Fucecchio I 75 F3
Fügen A 67 F3
Fuencaliente E 48 A1
Fuendejalón E 37 E3
Fuendetodos E 37 F4
Fuengirola E 48 A3
Fuenlabrada E 42 B2
Fuenlabrada de los Montes E 42 A3
Fuenmayor E 37 D2
Fuensalida E 42 B2
Fuensanta E 33 E2
Fuensanta de Martos E 48 A2
Fuente Álamo E 43 E4
Fuente Álamo E 49 E2
Fuentecén E 36 B3
Fuente Dé E 33 F3
Fuente de Cantos E ... 47 D1
Fuente del Maestre E 41 D4
Fuente de Pedro Naharro E 42 C2
Fuente de Piedra E ... 47 F3
Fuente de San Esteban (La) E 35 E4
Fuente el Fresno E ... 42 B3
Fuenteguinaldo E 41 D1

Fuentelapeña E 35 F4
Fuente Obejuna E 47 E1
Fuente Palmera E 47 F2
Fuentepinilla E 36 C4
Fuentes de Oñoro E ... 41 D1
Fuentes de Ropel E ... 35 F3
Fuentesaúco E 35 F4
Fuentes de Andalucía E 47 E2
Fuentes de Ayódar E .. 44 A2
Fuentes de Ebro E 37 F4
Fuentes de León E 47 D1
Fuentes de Nava E 36 A3
Fuentes de Valdepero E 36 A3
Fuentidueña E 36 B4
Fuentidueña de Tajo E 42 C2
Fürstenau D 55 E3
Fürstenberg D 51 F4
Fürstenfeld A 69 D3
Fürstenfeldbruck D ... 67 E1
Fürstenwalde D 58 A2
Fürstenwerder D 51 F3
Fürstenzell D 68 A1
Fürth D 63 D3
Füssen D 67 D3
Fuglebjerg DK 122 C3
Fulda D 62 C2
Fulgatore I 84 A3
Fulpmes A 67 E3
Fumay F 17 E3
Fumel F 29 D1
Funäsdalen S 112 A3
Fundão P 40 C1
Funes / Villnöß I 67 F4
Furadouro P 34 B4
Furci I 80 A1
Furnace GB 8 B2
Furtei I 82 B3
Furth i. Wald D 63 F3
Furtwangen D 23 F3
Furudal S 112 B4

Furuflaten N 104 C3
Fuscaldo I 83 E2
Fusch a. d. Großglockner-straße A 68 A3
Fuschl A 68 A2
Fusignano I 76 B2
Fustiñana E 37 E3
Fuzeta P 46 B2
Fynshav DK 122 B3

G

G. Straža SLO 73 E3
Gaaldorf A 68 C2
Gabarret F 28 C2
Gabia la Grande E 48 B3
Gabicce Mare I 76 B2
Gabrovka SLO 73 E3
Gabrovo BG 129 D2
Gacé F 20 C2
La Gacilly F 19 D4
Gäddede S 112 A1
Gadebusch D 51 D3
Gádor E 48 C3
Gaður IS 106 A2
Găeşti RO 129 D1
Gaeta I 79 F3
Gagarin RUS 125 F2
Gaggenau D 23 F2
Gagliano del Capo I .. 81 F4
Gagnef S 119 D1
Gaildorf D 62 C4
Gailey GB 11 D4
Gaillac F 29 E2
Gaillon F 21 D2
Gainsborough GB 11 E3
Gairloch GB 6 B3
Galan F 29 D3
Galanádo GR 99 D2
Galanianá GR 100 A2
Galanta SK 126 A3
Galapagar E 42 B1
Galarinós GR 88 B3
Galaroza E 47 D1

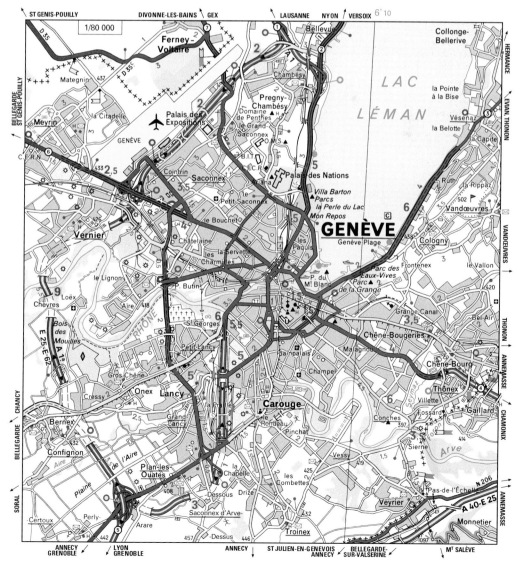

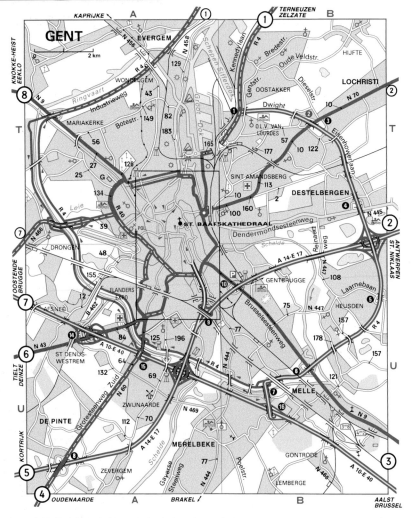

Gallsbach A	68	B1	Garípa GR	101	D4
Gallur E	37	E3	Garlasco I	75	D1
Galston GB	8	C3	Garlin F	28	C3
Galten DK	122	B2	Garlstorf D	50	C4
Galtür A	67	D4	Garmisch-		
Galveias P	40	C3	Partenkirchen D	67	E3
Gálvez E	42	A2	Garpenberg S	119	D1
Galway / Gaillimh IRL	2	B4	Garraf E	38	C4
Gamaches F	16	B3	Garrafe de Torío E	33	E3
Gambarie I	83	F4	Garray E	37	D3
Gaming A	68	C1	Garrel D	55	F2
Gamleby S	119	D1	Garriga (La) E	39	D4
Gammelstaden S	108	C3	Garrovillas E	41	E2
Gammertingen D	66	B2	Garrucha E	49	D3
Gams CH	66	C3	Gars am Kamp A	65	D4
Gamvik N	105	F1	Gartow D	51	D4
Ganacker D	63	F4	Gartz D	52	A3
Gándara E	32	B2	Garvagh GB	3	D1
Ganderkesee D	50	A4	Garvão P	46	A1
Gandesa E	44	B1	Garve GB	6	C4
Gandia E	44	A4	Garynahine GB	6	B2
Gandino I	71	E4	Garz D	51	F2
Gandria CH	71	D3	Gaschurn A	67	D4
Gangáles GR	101	D4	Gassino Torinese I	74	C1
Ganges F	30	B2	Gasteiz / Vitoria E	37	D2
Gangi I	84	C3	Gastoúni GR	96	A1
Gangkofen D	67	F1	Gata E	41	E1
Gannat F	26	A2	Gata de Gorgos E	44	A4
Gänserndorf A	65	E4	Gatčina RUS	125	D1
Gañuelas E	49	E2	Gatehouse		
Gap F	31	E1	of Fleet GB	8	C4
Garching a. d. Alz D	67	F1	Gateshead GB	9	C4
Garcia E	38	B4	Gattinara I	70	C4
Garciaz E	41	F3	Gattorna I	75	D2
Garda (A) E	32	A4	Gaucín E	47	E4
Garda I	71	F4	Gaulstad N	111	E1
Gardanne F	31	D3	Gauteguiz		
Gårdby S	123	F2	de Arteaga E	37	D1
Garde S	119	F4	Gauting D	67	E2
La Garde-Freinet F	31	E3	Gavà E	38	C4
Gardelegen D	57	D2	Gavardo I	71	F4
Gardermoen N	117	D1	Gavarnie F	28	C4
Gardíki GR	93	D2	Gavdopoúla		
Garding D	50	A2	(Nissí) GR	100	B4
Gardjönäs S	107	F4	Gávdos (Nissí) GR	100	B4
Gärdnäs S	112	B1	Gavi I	75	D2
Gardone Riviera I	71	F4	Gavião P	40	C2
Gardone			Gavirate I	71	D4
Val Trompia I	71	E4	Gävle S	119	E1
Gärdslösa S	123	F2	Gavoi I	82	B2
Garessio I	74	C2	Gavray F	19	E2
Garforth GB	11	D2	Gavrilov-Jam RUS	125	F1
Gargaliáni GR	96	B2	Gávrio GR	98	B1
Garganta la Olla E	41	F2	Gåvsta S	119	E2
Gargellen A	66	C4	Gäxsjö S	112	B1
Gargilesse-			Gazzuolo I	75	F1
Dampierre F	25	E2	Gdańsk PL	124	A4
Gargnano I	71	F4	Gdov RUS	125	C1
Gargnäs S	108	A4	Gdynia PL	53	E1

Galashiels GB	9	D3	Galátista GR	88	B2	Galipsós GR	89	D2	Gallargues-		
Galatádes GR	88	A2	Galatone I	81	F3	Galisteo E	41	E2	le-Montueux F	30	B2
Galatás GR	97	F1	Galaxídi GR	93	E3	Gallarate I	71	D4	Galliate I	71	D4
Galatás GR	97	D1	Galdakao E	36	C1	Gallardon F	21	E3	Gallipoli I	81	F3
Galați RO	127	E4	Galeata I	76	B2	Gallardos			Gällivare S	108	B2
Galatina I	81	F3	Galende E	33	D4	(Los) E	49	D3	Gallneukirchen A	68	B1
Galatiní GR	87	E3	Galera E	48	C2	Gallareto I	74	C1	Gällö S	112	B2

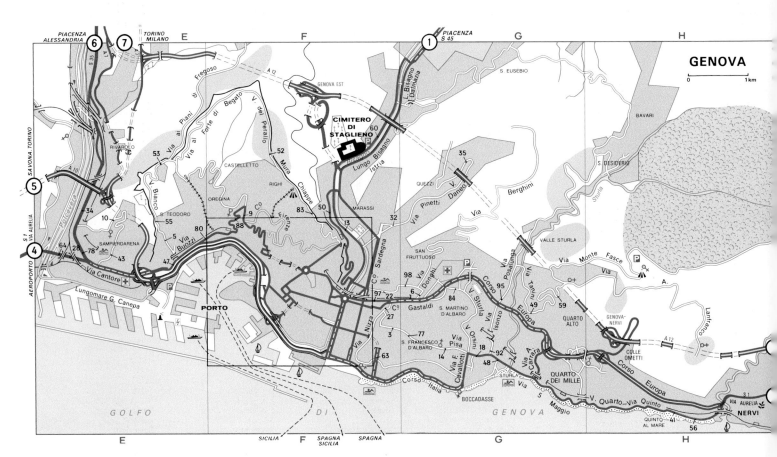

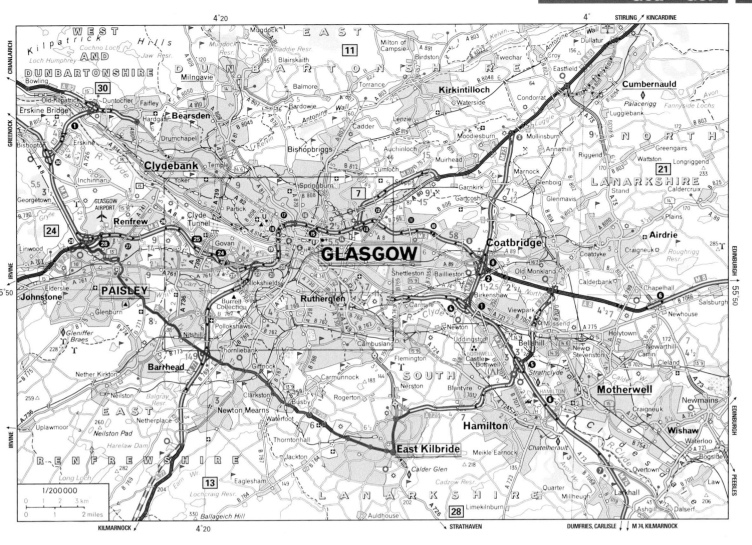

Geaune F	28	C2	Gemünden (Wohra) D	62	B1	Gernsheim D	62	A3	Gieboldehausen D	56	C4	Gizéla GR	89	E1	Glomfjord N	107	E2
Gebesee D	63	D1	Gemünden a. Main D	62	B1	Gerola Alta I	71	E3	Gien F	21	F4	Giżycko PL	124	B4	Glommersträsk S	108	A4
Gebze TR	129	F3	Genádio GR	103	F2	Geroliménas GR	97	D4	Giengen D	67	D3	Gjendesheim N	110	C4	Glossop GB	11	D3
Gedern D	62	B2	Gençay F	25	D2	Gerolstein D	61	E3	Giens F	31	E3	Gjermundshavn N	116	A1	Gloucester GB	13	E1
Gediz TR	129	F4	General-Toševo BG	129	E1	Gerolzhofen D	62	C3	Gießen D	62	B2	Gjesvær N	105	E1	Glücksburg D	50	B1
Gedser DK	122	C4	Genève CH	27	D2	Gerona / Girona E	39	D3	Giethoorn NL	55	D2	Gjirokastër AL	128	B4	Glückstadt D	50	B3
Geel B	17	F1	Genisséa GR	89	F1	Geroplátanos GR	88	C2	Gifhorn D	56	C3	Gjøra N	111	D2	Glumsø DK	122	C3
Geertruiden-			Genk B	17	F2	Gerri de la Sal E	38	B3	Giglio Porto I	78	B1	Gjøv DK	106	A3	Głogów PL	58	C3
berg NL	54	B4	Genlis F	26	C1	Gersau CH	66	B4	Gignac F	30	A2	Gjøvik N	111	D4	Głogów PL	58	C3
Geesthacht D	50	C4	Gennep NL	55	D4	Gersfeld D	62	C2	Gijón E	33	E2	Gla GR	93	F3	Głubczyce PL	65	E1
Gefell D	63	E2	Gennes F	19	F4	Gerstetten D	66	C1	Gilching D	67	E2	Gladbeck D	55	E4	Głuchołazy PL	65	E1
Géfira GR	88	A2	Génolhac F	30	B1	Gersthofen D	67	D1	Gilford GB	3	E3	Gladenbach D	62	A2	Gmund D	67	E2
Géfira GR	97	E3	Genova I	75	D2	Gerswalde D	51	F4	Gilleleje DK	123	D2	Gladstad N	107	D3	Gmünd A	68	B3
Gefíria GR	93	D1	Gent B	17	D1	Gescher D	55	E4	Gillhov S	112	B3	Glamis GB	9	D1	Gmünd A	64	C4
Gefrees D	63	E2	Genthin D	57	E2	Geseke D	55	F4	Gillingham GB	13	E3	Glamsbjerg DK	122	B3	Gmunden A	68	B2
Gehren D	63	D1	Genzano di Lucania I	80	C3	Gesualdo I	80	B3	Gillingham GB	14	C3	Glan-Münchweiler D	23	E1	Gnarp S	112	C3
Geilenkirchen D	61	E2	Genzano di Roma I	79	E2	Geta FIN	120	A4	Gilze NL	17	F1	Glandorf D	55	F3	Gnesta S	119	E3
Geilo N	116	C1	Georgianí GR	87	F2	Getafe E	42	B2	Gimenells E	38	A4	Glanshammar S	119	D2	Gniezno PL	53	D4
Geiranger N	110	C3	Georgioúpoli GR	100	B3	Les Gets F	27	E2	Gimnó GR	94	B3	Glarus CH	66	B4	Gnjilane YU	128	B2
Geisa D	62	C1	Georgítsi GR	96	C2	Gettorf D	50	B2	Gimo S	119	E1	Glasgow GB	8	C3	Gnoien D	51	E2
Geiselhöring D	63	F3	Georgsmarienhütte D	55	F3	Getxo E	36	C1	Gimont F	29	D3	Glastonbury GB	13	E2	Gnosjö S	123	E1
Geisenfeld D	67	E1	Gera D	63	E1	Gevelsberg D	61	F1	Gineta (La) E	43	D4	Glauchau D	63	F1	Goce Delčev BG	128	C3
Geisenhausen D	67	F1	Geraardsbergen B	17	D2	Gevgelija MK	128	C3	Gingst D	51	F2	Gleisdorf A	69	D3	Goch D	55	D4
Geising D	64	A1	Gerabronn D	62	C4	Gevrey-Chambertin F	26	C1	Ginosa I	81	D3	Glenamoy / Gleann			Godalming GB	14	B3
Geisingen D	23	F3	Gerace I	83	E4	Gex F	27	D2	Ginzling A	67	F3	na Muaidhe IRL	2	A2	Godby FIN	120	A4
Geislingen a. d.			Gerakári GR	88	B1	Geyve TR	129	F3	Gioia del Colle I	81	D3	Glenarm GB	3	E2	Godelheim D	56	B4
Steige D	66	C1	Gerakári GR	100	C4	Gföhl A	64	C4	Gioia Tauro I	83	E4	Glenariff			Goderville F	16	A4
Geismar D	62	C1	Gerakaroú GR	88	B2	Ghedi I	71	F4	Gioúra (Nissí) GR	94	B1	or Waterfoot GB	3	E1	Godmanchester GB	14	C2
Geisnes N	107	D4	Gérakas GR	97	E3	Gheorgheni RO	127	D4	Giovinazzo I	81	D2	Glenarm GB	3	E2	Godovič SLO	73	D3
Geithain D	63	F1	Geráki GR	97	D3	Ghilarza I	82	B2	Girifalco I	83	E3	Glenbeigh IRL	4	A3	Göggingen D	67	D1
Gela I	85	D4	Gerakiní GR	88	C3	Ghisonaccia F	78	B3	Giromagny F	23	D4	Glencolumbkille / Gleann			Göhren D	51	F2
Geldern D	55	D4	Geráni GR	100	C3	Ghisoni F	78	A3	Girona / Gerona E	39	D3	Cholm Cille IRL	2	B2	Göllersdorf A	65	D4
Geldrop NL	17	F1	Gérardmer F	23	D3	Gialí (Nissí) GR	103	D1	Gironella E	38	C3	Glendalough IRL	5	E2	Göppingen D	66	C1
Geleen NL	61	D1	Geras A	65	D4	Giálova GR	96	B3	Girvan GB	3	F1	Glenelg GB	6	B4	Görzke D	57	E3
Gelibolu TR	129	E3	Gerbéviller F	23	D2	Giáltra GR	93	F2	Gisburn GB	10	C2	Glenfinnan GB	8	B1	Goes NL	17	D1
Gelnhausen D	62	B2	Gerbini I	85	D3	Gianitsá GR	88	A2	Gislaved S	123	E1	Glengarriff / An Gleann			Gößnitz D	63	E1
Gelsa E	37	F4	Gerbstedt D	57	D4	Gianítsi GR	94	C4	Gisors F	16	B4	Garbh IRL	4	B4	Gößweinstein D	63	E3
Gelsdorf D	61	F2	Gerena E	47	D2	Giannádes GR	86	B4	Gistel B	15	F4	Glenluce GB	3	F2	Göstling A	68	C2
Gelsenkirchen D	55	E4	Gerês P	34	C3	Gianoúli GR	91	E2	Githio GR	97	D3	Glennamaddy IRL	2	B4	Göttingen D	56	C4
Gelting D	50	B1	Geretsried D	67	E2	Giardini-Naxos I	85	E2	Gittun S	108	A3	Glenrothes GB	9	D2	Götzis A	66	C3
Gembloux B	17	E2	Gérgal E	48	C3	Giáros (Nissí) GR	98	B1	Giugliano			Glenties IRL	2	C2	Goirle NL	17	F1
Gemeaux F	22	B4	Gergioúpoli GR	100	B3	Giarratana I	85	D4	in Campania I	80	A3	Glifa GR	93	F2	Góis P	40	C1
Gémenos F	31	D3	Geringswalde D	63	F1	Giarre I	85	E3	Giulianova Lido I	77	E4	Glifáda GR	93	D3	Goito I	71	F4
Gemert NL	17	F1	Gerlos A	67	F3	Giat F	25	F3	Giurgiu RO	129	D1	Glifáda GR	97	F1	Gol N	110	C4
Gemlik TR	129	F3	Gérmas GR	87	E2	Giaveno I	27	F4	Give DK	122	B2	Gliki GR	92	A1	Golada E	32	B3
Gemona del Friuli I	68	A4	Germering D	67	E2	Giba I	82	B4	Givet F	17	E3	Glikóvrissi GR	97	D3	Goldbach D	62	B3
Gémozac F	24	B3	Germersheim D	23	F1	Gibostad N	104	B3	Givors F	26	C3	Glina HR	73	F3	Goldberg D	51	E3
Gemünd (Eifel) D	61	E2	Gernika-Lumo E	37	D1	Gibraleón E	46	C2	Givry F	26	C1	Gliwice PL	126	A2	Goldenstedt D	55	F2
Gemünden D	61	F3	Gernrode D	57	D4	Gideå S	113	D2	Givry-en-Argonne F	22	B2	Gloggnitz A	69	D2	Golegã P	40	B2
												Goleniów PL	52	A3

Golfe-Juan F.......... 31 F2
Golfo Aranci I......... 78 A3
Golling A 68 A2
Golnik SLO........... 73 D2
Golpejas E............ 35 E4
Golspie GB 7 D3
Golßen D............. 58 A3
Golzow D............. 57 E3
Gómara E............. 37 D4
Gomáti GR............ 88 C3
Gombrèn E............ 39 D3
Gomecello E........... 35 F4
Gómfi GR 92 C1
Gommern D............ 57 E3
Goncelin F............ 27 D4
Gondomar E 32 A4
Gondomar P 34 B4
Gondrecourt-
   le-Château F.......... 22 C2
Gönen TR............. 129 E3
Góni GR............... 88 A4
Goniá GR 100 A3
Goniés GR 101 D3
Gonnesa I 82 A4
Gonnosfanadiga I...... 82 B3
Goole GB 11 E2
Goor NL 55 D3
Goppenstein CH 27 F2
Gördalen S 112 A4
Gordes F.............. 30 C2
Gorenja Vas SLO 73 D3
Gorey / Guaire IRL 5 E2
Gorgonzola I.......... 71 E4
Gorgopótamos GR 87 D3
Gorinchem NL 54 B4
Goritsá GR............ 97 D2
Gorizia I 72 C3
Gorlice PL............. 126 B3
Görlitz D.............. 58 B4
Gorna Orjahovica BG. 129 D2
Gornja Radgona SLO.. 73 F1
Gornji Grad SLO....... 73 E2
Gornji Petrovci SLO... 73 F1
Goro I................ 76 B1
Gorredijk NL........... 54 C2
Gorron F.............. 19 F3
Gorsleston-
   on-Sea GB........... 15 E1
Gort / An Gort IRL 2 B4
Gorteen IRL........... 2 B3
Gortin GB 3 D2
Górtis GR 101 D4
Gortmore /
   An Gort Mór IRL 2 A4
Gorzów
   Wielkopolski PL..... 52 B4
Gosaldo I............. 72 A3
Gosau A 68 A2
Göschenen CH........ 66 B4
Gosforth GB 10 B1
Goslar D.............. 56 C3
Gospić HR 77 F1
Gosport GB 13 F3
Gossau CH............ 66 C3
Gosselies B............ 17 E2
Gostyń PL............. 59 D3
Göteborg S........... 118 B4
Götene S 118 C3
Gotha D............... 63 D1
Gothem S 119 F4
Gouarec F............. 18 C3
Gouda NL............. 54 B4
Gouménissa GR 88 A1
Goumois F 23 E4
Goúra GR 93 E4
Gourdon F............ 29 E1
Gourin F.............. 18 C3
Gournay-en-Bray F... 16 B4
Goúrnes GR 101 D3
Gourniá E............. 101 E4
Gourock GB 8 C2
Gouveia P 40 C1
Goúves GR 101 D3
Gouviá GR 86 B4
Gouzon F............. 25 F2
Göynük TR............ 129 F3
Gozd SLO 73 D2
Gozzano I............. 70 C4
Gödöllő H 126 A4
Graal-Müritz D........ 51 E2
Graben-Neudorf D 23 F1
Grabenstätt D......... 67 F2
Grabow D 51 D4
Graçay F.............. 25 E1
Grächen CH........... 27 F2
Gradara I............. 76 C2
Gradefes E 33 F4
Gradisca d'Isonzo I... 72 C3
Grado I 72 C3
Grado E............... 33 E4
Grado (El) E........... 38 A3
Gräfelfing D........... 67 E2
Gräfenberg D 63 D3

Gräfenhainichen D ... 57 E4
Grafenau D........... 64 A4
Grafenwöhr D......... 63 E3
Grafing D............. 67 F2
Gragnano I............ 80 A3
Grahovo SLO.......... 73 D2
Graiguenamanagh /
   Graig
   na Manach IRL..... 5 E3
Grain GB 14 C3
Grainau D 67 E3
Grajewo PL........... 124 B4
Grajvoron RUS....... 127 F1
Gram DK............. 122 B3
Gramat F 29 E1
Gramatikó GR......... 93 D1
Gramatikoú GR 92 C3
Graméni GR 89 D1
Graméno GR 87 D4
Gramenten A 64 C4
Grammichele I......... 85 D3
Gramzow D 52 A4
Gran N 117 D1
Granada E 48 B3
Granadella (La) E 38 B4
Gránard / Granard IRL 2 C3
Grancey-le-Château F 22 B4
Grand-Champ F 18 C4
La Grand-Combe F... 30 B2
Le Grand-Bornand F . 27 D4
Le Grand-Bourg F ... 25 E2
Grand-Champ F 18 C4
La Grand-Combe F... 30 B2
Grand-Couronne F... 16 A4
La Grand-Croix F 26 C3
Grand-Fougeray F.... 19 E4
Le Grand-Lemps F... 27 D4
Le Grand-Lucé F..... 20 C4
Le Grand-Pressigny F 25 D1
Le Grand-Serre F 26 C4
Grandas de Salime E.. 33 D2
Grandcamp-Maisy F.. 19 F1
La Grande-Motte F... 30 B3
Grândola P 40 B4
Grandpré F 17 F4
Grandrieu F 30 B1
Grandvilliers F........ 16 B4
Grängärde S 119 D1
Grange-
   over-Sands GB 10 C1
Granges-
   sur-Vologne F 23 D3
Grängesberg S 119 D1
Granítis GR 89 D1
Granja P.............. 40 C4
Granja
   de Torrehermosa E 47 E1
Granjuela (La) E 47 E1
Gränna S 118 C4
Granollers E........... 39 D4
Granön S 113 D1
Gransee D............ 51 F4
Grantham GB 11 E4
Grantown-
   on-Spey GB 7 D4
Granville F 19 E2
Granvin N 110 B4
Grañén F 37 F3
Grasleben D........... 57 D3
Grasmere GB......... 10 C1
Grassano I 80 C3
Grasse F.............. 31 F2
Gråsten DK 122 B3
Grästorp S 118 B3
Gratangen N 104 B4
Gratiní GR 91 D2
Gratkorn A 69 D3
Grau de Castelló E.... 44 A2
Grau de València
   (El) E.............. 44 A3
Le Grau-du-Roi F 30 B3
Graulhet F............ 29 F2
Graus E............... 38 A3
Grávalos E 37 D3
Gravdal N 107 E1
Grave NL 54 C4
La Grave F............ 27 E4
Gravedona I.......... 71 D3
Gravellona Toce I..... 70 C4
Gravelines F 15 E4
Gravendeel ('s-) NL... 54 B4
Gravesend GB........ 14 C3
Graviá GR............. 93 E3
Gravina in Puglia I.... 81 D3
Gravoúna GR......... 89 E1
Gray F................ 22 C4
Grays Thurrock GB ... 14 C3
Graz A................ 69 D3
Graz A................ 69 D3
Grazalema E 47 E3
Grazzanise I.......... 80 A3
Great Driffield GB..... 11 E2
Great Dunmow GB ... 14 C2

Great Grimsby GB.... 11 F3
Great Malvern GB 13 E1
Great Torrington GB.. 12 C3
Great Yarmouth GB... 15 E1
Grebbestad S 118 A3
Greccio I.............. 79 D1
Greding D............. 63 E4
Greenhead GB 9 E4
Greenlaw GB 9 E3
Greenock GB 8 C2
Greenodd GB 10 C1
Greggio I............. 70 C4
Gregolímano GR...... 93 F2
Greifenburg A 68 A4
Greiffenberg D........ 52 A4
Greifswald D.......... 51 F2
Grein A 68 C1
Greiz D............... 63 E1
Grená DK 122 C2
Grenade F............. 29 E2
Grenade-
   sur-l'Adour F....... 28 C2
Grenchen CH......... 27 F1
Grenoble F 27 D4
Grense Jakobselv N.. 105 F2
Gréoux-les-Bains F... 31 D2
Gresse-en-Vercors F . 27 D4
Gressoney-la Trinité I 27 F3
Gressoney-St. Jean I. 27 F3
Gresten A............. 68 C1
Grésy-sur-Isère F..... 27 E3
Greußen D 63 D1
Greve in Chianti I..... 76 A3
Greve Strand DK...... 123 D3
Greven D............. 55 E3
Grevená GR 87 E3
Grevenbroich D....... 61 E1
Grevenbrück D........ 62 A1
Grevenítio GR........ 87 D4
Grevenmacher L...... 23 D1
Grevesmühlen D 51 D3
Greyabbey GB 3 E2
Greystones / Na Clocha
   Liatha IRL.......... 5 F2
Grez-en-Bouère F..... 19 F4
Grezzana I............ 71 F4
Griebenow D.......... 51 F2
Gries am Brenner A .. 67 E3
Gries im Sellrain A 67 E3
Grieskirchen A 68 B1
Griffen A.............. 68 C3
Grignan F............. 30 C1
Grigno I 72 A3
Grignols F............. 28 C1
Grimaldi I 83 E2
Grimaud F............ 31 E3
Grimma D............. 57 F4
Grimmen D........... 51 F2
Grimsbu N 111 D3
Grimstad N........... 116 C3
Grindaheim N......... 110 C4
Grindavík IS 106 A1
Grindelwald CH....... 66 A4
Grindsted DK......... 122 B3
Griñón E 42 B2

Gripsholm S 119 E2
Grisignano di Zocco I 72 A4
Grisolles F............. 29 E2
Grisslehamn S........ 119 F1
Gríva GR 88 A1
Grizáno GR 87 F4
Grøa N 110 C2
Gröbming A........... 68 B2
Gröditz D 57 F4
Grönenbach D 67 D2
Gröningen D 57 D3
Groenlo NL 55 D4
Groitzsch D........... 63 E1
Groix F 18 C4
Gronau (Westfalen) D 55 E3
Grong N 111 F1
Grönhögen S 123 F2
Groningen NL......... 55 D2
Grönskåra S........... 123 F1
Gropello Cairoli I...... 75 D1
Groscavallo I.......... 27 F4
Grosio I............... 71 E3
Groß Schönebeck D.. 51 F4
Großbreitenbach D .. 63 D2
Großenbrode D....... 50 C2
Großenhain D......... 58 A4
Großenkneten D...... 55 F2
Großenzersdorf A 69 E1
Grosseto I............ 76 A4
Groß-Gerau D........ 62 A3
Groß Gerungs A...... 64 C4
Großhabersdorf D.... 63 D4
Großheubach D 62 B3
Großpetersdorf A 69 E2
Großraming A......... 68 B1
Großraschen D........ 58 A4
Großreken D 55 E4
Großröhrsdorf D 58 A4
Großschönau D....... 64 B1
Groß-Siegharts A 64 C4
Groß-Umstadt D...... 62 B3
Großweil D............ 67 E3
Großwitzeetze D...... 51 D4
Grostenquin F 23 D2
Grosuplje SLO........ 73 E3
Grötlingbo S 119 F4
Grottaglie I........... 81 E3
Grottaminarda I...... 80 B2
Grottammare I........ 77 D4
Grotteria I 83 E4
Grove (O) E........... 32 A3
Grövelsjön S.......... 112 A3
Grovfjord N 104 A3
Grudziądz PL 126 A1
Grünberg D 62 B2
Grünstadt D 23 F1
Grünwald D 67 E2
Gruissan F............ 30 A3
Grums S 118 B3
Grünau im Almtal A.. 68 B2
Grundarfjörður IS 106 A1
Grundforsen S 112 A4
Grundlsee A 68 B2
Grundsund S......... 118 A3

Grundtjärn S.......... 112 C2
Gruyères CH.......... 27 F2
Grycksbo S........... 119 D1
Gryfice PL............. 52 B2
Gryllefjord /
   Torsken N 104 A3
Grythyttan S 118 C2
Gstaad CH 27 F2
Gstadt D.............. 67 F2
Guadahortuna E...... 48 B2
Guadalajara E......... 42 C1
Guadalaviar E......... 43 E2
Guadalcanal E........ 47 E1
Guadalest E........... 44 A4
Guadalupe E.......... 41 F3
Guadarrama E 42 B1
Guadassuar E......... 43 F4
Guadiaro E............ 47 E4
Guadix E.............. 48 B3
Gualdo Tadino I....... 76 C3
Guarda P 41 D1
Guardamar
   del Segura E........ 49 F1
Guardia (La) E......... 42 C2
Guardia
   Sanframondi I...... 80 A2
Guardia
   de Jaén (La) E 48 B2
Guardiagrele I 79 F1
Guardias Viejas E..... 48 C4
Guardo E 33 F3
Guareña E 41 E4
Guarromán E 48 B1
Guastalla I............ 75 F1
Gubbio I.............. 76 C3
Guben D.............. 58 B3
Gudhjem DK 123 E3
Gudiña (A) E 32 C4
Gudow D.............. 50 C3
Gudvangen N......... 110 B4
Guebwiller F 23 E3
Güglingen D 62 B4
Guémené-Penfao F .. 19 D4
Guémené-
   sur-Scorff F 18 C3
Günzburg D 67 D1
Güeñes E 36 C1
Guer F 19 D3
Guérande F 19 D4
La Guerche-
   de-Bretagne F 19 E3
La Guerche-
   sur-l'Aubois F 26 A1
Guéret F.............. 25 E2
Guérigny F 26 A1
Güssing A 69 E2
Güsten D 57 D4
Güstrow D............ 51 E3
Gütersloh D 55 F4
Guéthary F 28 A3
Gueugnon F 26 B2
Guglionesi I 80 A1
La Guerche-
   de-Bretagne F 19 E3
Guidonia I 79 E1
Guignes F 21 F2

Guijo de Granadilla E 41 E1
Guijuelo E 41 F1
Guillaumes F.......... 31 F2
Guillena E 47 D2
Guillestre F 31 E1
Guillon F.............. 22 A4
Guildford GB 14 B3
Guilvinec F............ 18 B3
Guimarães P 34 B3
Guimiliau F............ 18 B2
Guînes F.............. 15 E4
Guingamp F 18 C2
Guipavas F............ 18 B2
Guisborough GB...... 11 E1
Guiscard F 17 D4
Guise F 17 D3
Guissona E 38 C3
Guist GB 15 D1
Guitiriz E 32 B2
Guîtres F.............. 24 C4
Gujan-Mestras F...... 28 B1
Gulbene LV 124 C2
Gullspång S 118 C3
Gumiel de Hizán E.... 36 B3
Gummersbach D 61 F1
Gundelfingen a.d.
   Donau D............ 67 D1
Gundelsheim D....... 62 B4
Gunnarn S............ 107 F4
Gunnarsbyn S 108 B3
Gunnarskog S 118 B2
Gunten D............. 27 F1
Guntín de Pallares E . 32 C3
Gunzenhausen D..... 63 D4
Gurk A 68 B3
Gurrea de Gállego E . 37 F3
Gusev RUS........... 124 B4
Guspini I.............. 82 B3
Gutcher GB 7 F2
Gutenstein A 69 D1
Guyhirn GB 11 F4
Guzet-Neige F........ 29 E4
Gvardejsk RUS....... 124 B4
Gvarv N 116 C2
Gy F 22 C4
Győr H 69 F1
Gysinge S 119 E1
Gyula H 126 B4
Gyöngyös H.......... 126 B4
Günterode D.......... 56 C4
Gützkow D............ 51 F2

H

Haag A............... 68 B3
Haag am Hausruck A. 68 A1
Haag (Den)=
   's-Gravenhage NL.. 54 B4
Haag i. Oberbayern D 67 F1
Haaksbergen NL...... 55 D3
Haamstede NL........ 54 A4
Haan (D)= 15 F3
Haapajärvi FIN 114 C2
Haapakoski FIN....... 115 E4

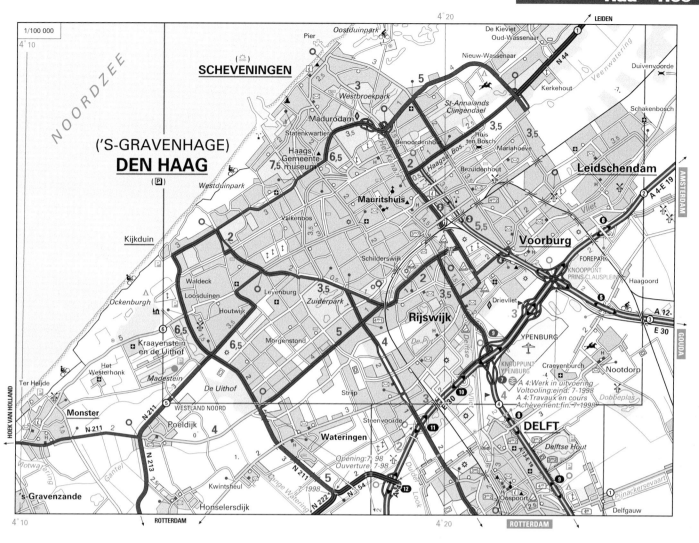

Haapamäki FIN	120	C2	Hakarp S	118	C4	Halsua FIN	114	C3	Hanstedt D	50	C4	Harsvik N	111	D1	Hautajärvi FIN	109	F2

Haapamäki FIN........ 120 C2
Haapamäki FIN........ 115 D2
Haapavesi FIN......... 114 C2
Haapsalu EST.......... 124 B1
Haar D 67 E2
Haaren D 55 F4
Haarlem NL............ 54 B3
Habay-la-Neuve B..... 17 F4
Habo S................. 118 C4
Habsheim F 23 E4
Håbu N................. 117 D2
Hachenburg D 62 A2
Hachmühlen D......... 56 B3
Hackås S............... 112 B2
Hadamar D............. 62 A2
Haddington GB 9 E2
Hadersdorf
  am Kamp A......... 65 D4
Haderslev DK.......... 122 B3
Hadjač UA............. 127 F1
Hadleigh GB........... 15 D2
Hadmersleben D 57 D3
Hadsten DK............ 122 B2
Hadsund DK............ 122 B2
Hægebostad N......... 116 B3
Hämelerwald D........ 56 C3
Hagen D 61 F1
Hagen
  i. Bremischen D 50 A4
Hagenow D............. 51 D4
Hagetmau F............ 28 B2
Hagfors S.............. 118 C1
Häggdånger S 112 C3
Haggenås S 112 B2
Hagondange F......... 23 D1
Haguenau F............ 23 E2
Hahnbach D............ 63 E3
Haigerloch D.......... 66 B1
Hailsham GB 14 C4
Hailuoto FIN........... 114 C1
Hainburg a. d.
  Donau A............ 69 E1
Hainfeld A............. 69 D1
Hainichen D............ 63 F1
Hajdúböszörmény H. 126 B4
Hajdúszoboszló H 126 B4
Hajnówka PL.......... 124 B2
Hajsyn UA 127 E2
Hajvoron UA 127 E3

Hakkas S.............. 108 B2
Häkkilä FIN............ 115 D3
Halandrítsa GR........ 93 D4
Halbe D................. 58 A3
Halberstadt D 57 D3
Halden N 117 D2
Haldensleben D....... 57 D3
Halesowen GB 11 D4
Halesworth GB....... 15 D2
Halhjem N............. 116 A1
Halifax GB 11 D2
Halikko FIN............ 120 C4
Halkeró GR........... 89 E1
Hálki GR............... 99 D2
Hálki GR............... 93 E1
Hálki GR............... 103 E2
Hálki (Nissi) GR 103 E2
Halkiádes GR 93 E1
Halkidóna GR......... 88 A2
Halkió GR 95 F3
Halle D................. 57 E4
Halle D................. 55 F3
Halle B................. 17 E2
Halle-Neustadt D..... 57 E4
Hällefors S............ 118 C2
Hälleforsnäs S 119 D2
Hallein A.............. 68 A2
Hällekis S............. 118 C3
Hallenberg D 62 A1
Hallencourt F.......... 16 B3
Hällesjö S.............. 112 C2
Hällevadsholm S 118 B3
Hall in Tirol A......... 67 E3
Hällnäs S 113 D1
Hallörmsstaður IS.... 106 C1
Hallsberg S........... 119 D3
Hallstadt D 63 D3
Hallstahammar S..... 119 D2
Hallstatt A 68 B2
Hallstavik S........... 119 F2
Halluin F............... 15 F4
Halmstad S............ 123 D2
Hals DK............... 122 C1
Halsa N 110 C2
Hälsingtuna S......... 112 C4
Halsskov DK.......... 122 C3
Halstead GB 14 C4
Halsteren NL 17 E1

Halsua FIN............. 114 C3
Haltdålen N 111 E2
Haltern D 55 E4
Halver D 61 F1
Ham F.................. 17 D4
Hamar N............... 111 D4
Hamarøy N............ 104 F3
Hamburg D............ 50 B3
Hamdorf D............ 50 B2
Hämeenkyrö FIN...... 120 C2
Hämeenlinna FIN 120 C30
Hameln D.............. 56 B3
Hamersleben D....... 57 D3
Hamili (Nissi) GR.... 102 B3
Hamilton GB.......... 8 C3
Hamina FIN............ 121 E3
Hamm (Westfalen) D. 55 E4
Hammarland FIN...... 120 A4
Hammarstrand S..... 112 C2
Hammaslahti FIN 115 F3
Hammel DK............ 122 B2
Hammelburg D....... 62 C2
Hammerdal S......... 112 B2
Hammerfest N........ 105 D1
Hammershus DK..... 123 E3
Hamningberg N 105 F1
Hamoir B 17 F2
Hamra S 112 B4
Hamre N............... 116 B3
Han-sur-Lesse B 17 F3
Hanákia GR........... 96 B1
Hanau D 62 B3
Hăncești MOL......... 127 E4
Handrás GR........... 101 F4
Hanerau-
  Hademarschen D .. 50 B3
Haniá GR............. 100 B3
Hánia GR.............. 97 D3
Hánia GR.............. 93 F1
Haniótis GR........... 88 C4
Hankamäki FIN....... 115 E2
Hankasalmen as FIN. 115 D4
Hankasalmi FIN 115 D4
Hankensbüttel D..... 56 C2
Hanko / Hangö FIN... 120 C4
Hann. Münden D 56 B4
Hannover D............ 56 B3
Hannut B 17 F2
Hansnes N............. 104 B2

Hanstedt D 50 C4
Hanstholm DK........ 122 B1
Haparanda S.......... 108 C3
Haradok BY........... 125 D3
Harads S............... 108 B3
Haraldshaugen N..... 116 A1
Haravgí GR 87 F3
Harburg D............. 67 D1
Harburg D............. 50 B4
Hårby DK.............. 122 B3
Hardbakke N.......... 110 A4
Hardegg A............. 65 D4
Hardegsen D.......... 56 C4
Hardelot-Plage F...... 15 D4
Hardenberg NL........ 55 D3
Harderwijk NL........ 54 C3
Hardeshøj DK........ 122 B3
Hardheim D 62 C3
Hareid N............... 110 B2
Harelbeke B 15 F4
Haren D................ 55 E2
Haren NL............... 55 D2
Harewood GB 11 D2
Haritoméni GR 89 D1
Harjavalta FIN........ 120 B3
Harjunpää FIN........ 120 B2
Härkmeri FIN......... 120 B2
Harlech GB 10 B3
Harlesiel D............ 55 E1
Harleston GB.......... 15 D2
Harlingen NL.......... 54 C2
Harlow GB............. 14 C3
Harmånger S 112 C3
Harmanli BG.......... 129 D2
Härnösand S.......... 112 C3
Haro E................. 36 C2
Harokopió GR......... 96 C3
Haroldswick GB...... 7 F2
Haroué F............... 23 D3
Harøysund N.......... 110 C2
Harpenden GB 14 B2
Harplinge S........... 123 D2
Harpstedt D........... 55 F2
Harrislee D............ 50 B1
Harrogate GB......... 11 D2
Härryda S.............. 118 B3
Harsefeld D............ 50 B4
Harsprånget S 108 A2
Harstad N.............. 104 A3

Harsvik N.............. 111 D1
Hartberg A 69 D2
Hartha D............... 63 F1
Hartlepool GB 11 E1
Hartmannsdorf D..... 63 F1
Hartola FIN............ 121 D2
Harwich GB............ 15 D3
Harzgerode D 57 D4
Haselünne D 55 E2
Haskovo BG 129 D2
Haslach
  an der Mühl A 64 B4
Haslach
  i. Kinzingtal D...... 23 F3
Hasle DK.............. 123 E3
Haslemere GB........ 14 B4
Haslev DK............. 122 C3
Hasparren F.......... 28 B3
Hassela S............. 112 C3
Hasselfelde D 57 D4
Hasselt B 17 F2
Haßfurt D.............. 63 D3
Hässleholm S........ 123 E2
Hastière-Lavaux B.... 17 F3
Hastings GB 14 C4
Hatherleigh GB........ 12 C3
Hattem NL............. 55 D3
Hattfjelldal N......... 107 E3
Hattingen D 61 F1
Hattula FIN............ 120 C3
Hattuvaara FIN....... 115 F2
Hattuvaara FIN....... 115 F3
Hatvan H............... 126 A4
Hatvik N............... 116 A1
Haubourdin F.......... 15 F4
Hauge N 116 A3
Haugesund N......... 116 A1
Hauho FIN............. 120 C3
Haukeligrend N....... 116 B1
Haukipudas FIN...... 114 C1
Haukivuori FIN....... 121 E2
Haunstetten D 67 D1
Haus A................. 68 B2
Hausach D............. 23 F3
Hausham D............ 67 E2
Hausjärvi FIN......... 121 D3

Hautajärvi FIN........ 109 F2
Hautefort F............ 25 E4
Hauteville-
  Lompnes F.......... 27 D3
Hautmont F 17 E3
Havant GB 14 B4
Havári GR.............. 96 B1
Havdáta GR........... 92 A4
Havelange B 17 F2
Havelberg D........... 51 E4
Haverfordwest /
  Hwlffordd GB 12 B1
Haverhill GB........... 14 C2
Haverö S............... 112 B2
Havneby DK 122 A3
Havøysund N 105 D1
Le Havre F............ 20 C1
Hawes GB............. 11 D1
Hawick GB............. 9 D3
Hawkhurst GB........ 14 C4
Hay-on-Wye GB...... 13 D1
Hayange F............. 22 C1
La Haye-du-Puits F... 19 E2
La Haye-Pesnel F.... 19 E2
Hayle GB............... 12 B4
Haywards Heath GB.. 14 C4
Hazebrouck F 15 E4
Headford /
  Áth Cinn IRL........ 2 B4
Heanor GB............. 11 D3
Héas F 28 C4
Heathfield GB 14 C4
Heby S................. 119 E3
Hechingen D 66 B1
Hecho E............... 28 B4
Hechtel B 17 F1
Hecklingen D.......... 57 D3
Hedal N................ 117 D1
Heddal N............... 116 C2
Hede S................. 112 A3
Hédé F 19 E3
Hedemora S........... 119 D1
Hedenäset S 108 C3
Hedeviken S........... 112 A3
Hedon GB.............. 11 F2
Heemstede NL........ 54 B3
Heerde NL............. 55 D3
Heerenberg ('s-) NL.. 55 D4
Heerenveen NL....... 54 C2

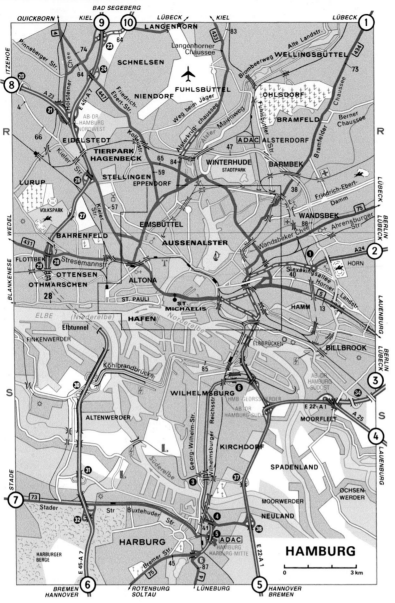

HAMBURG

0   3 km

Heerlen *NL*	61	E1
Heeze *NL*	17	F1
Hegge *N*	110	C4
Hegra *N*	111	E2
Heia *N*	104	B3
Heide *D*	50	A2
Heidelberg *D*	23	F1
Heidenau *D*	64	A1
Heidenheim a. d. Brenz *D*	66	C1
Heidenreichstein *A*	64	C4
Heikendorf *D*	50	C2
Heikkilä *FIN*	109	F3
Heilbronn *D*	62	B4
Heiligenberg *D*	66	C2
Heiligenblut *A*	68	A3
Heiligenhafen *D*	50	C2
Heiligenkirchen *D*	56	B4
Heiligenkreuz im Lafnitztal *A*	69	E3
Heiligenstadt *D*	56	C4
Heilsbronn *D*	63	D4
Heimari *FIN*	121	E2
Heimdal *N*	111	D2
Heimertingen *D*	67	D2
Heinävaara *FIN*	115	F3
Heinävesi *FIN*	115	E3
Heinola *FIN*	121	D3
Heinolan mlk *FIN*	121	D3
Heinsberg *D*	61	E1
Heist *B*	15	F3
Heist-op-den-Berg *B*	17	E1
Hejde *S*	119	F4
Heldburg *D*	63	D2
Helder (Den) *NL*	54	B2
Heldrungen *D*	57	D4
Helechal *E*	41	F4
Helensburgh *GB*	8	C2
Hella *IS*	106	A2
Hella *N*	110	B4
Hellendoorn *NL*	55	D3
Hellesylt *N*	110	B3

Hellevoetsluis *NL*	54	B4
Hellín *E*	49	D1
Hellvik *N*	116	A3
Helmbrechts *D*	63	E2
Helmond *NL*	17	F1
Helmsdale *GB*	7	D3
Helmsley *GB*	11	E1
Helmstadt *D*	62	C3
Helmstedt *D*	57	D3
Helsa *D*	62	B1
Helsingborg *S*	123	D2
Helsinge *DK*	123	D2
Helsingør *DK*	123	D2
Helsinki / Helsingfors *FIN*	121	D4
Helston *GB*	12	B4
Hemau *D*	63	E3
Hemavan *S*	107	E3
Hemel Hempstead *GB*	14	B3
Hemer *D*	61	F1
Hemnes *N*	117	E2
Hemnesberget *N*	107	E3
Hemsedal *FIN*	110	C4
Hendaye *F*	28	A3
Hengelo *NL*	55	D3
Hengersberg *D*	64	A4
Hénin-Beaumont *F*	16	C2
Henley *GB*	14	A2
Henley-on-Thames *GB*	14	B3
Henneberg *D*	62	C2
Hennebont *F*	18	C4
Hennef *D*	61	F2
Hennigsdorf *D*	57	F2
Henrichemont *F*	25	F1
Henstedt-Ulzburg *D*	50	B3
Henstridge *GB*	13	E3
Heppenheim a. d. Weise *D*	23	F1
Herbault *F*	21	D4
Herbertingen *D*	66	C2
Les Herbiers *F*	24	B1

Herbignac *F*	19	D4
Herbolzheim *D*	23	E3
Herborn *D*	62	A2
Herbrechtingen *D*	66	C1
Herbstein *D*	62	B2
Hercegnovi *YU*	128	A3
Hereford *GB*	13	E1
Herencia *E*	42	C3
Herentals *B*	17	E1
Herford *D*	55	F3
Héricourt *F*	23	D4
Heringsdorf *D*	52	A2
Herisau *CH*	66	C3
Hérisson *F*	25	F2
Herk-de-Stad *B*	17	F2
Herleshausen *D*	62	C1
Hermagor *A*	68	A4
Hermannsburg *D*	56	C2
Hermansverk *N*	110	B4
L'Hermenault *F*	24	B2
Herment *F*	25	F3
Hermeskeil *D*	23	D1
Hermida (La) *E*	33	F3
Hermsdorf *D*	63	E1
Hernani *E*	28	A3
Hernansancho *E*	42	A1
Herne *D*	55	E4
Herne Bay *GB*	15	D3
Herning *DK*	122	B2
Heroldsberg *D*	63	D3
Herónia *GR*	93	F3
Herradura (La) *E*	48	A3
Herrala *FIN*	121	D3
Herre *N*	116	C2
Herrenberg *D*	66	B1
Herrera *E*	47	F2
Herrera de Alcántara *E*	40	C2
Herrera del Duque *E*	41	F3
Herrera de los Navarros *E*	37	E4
Herrera de Pisuerga *E*	36	B2

Herreruela *E*	41	D3
Herrestad *S*	118	B3
Herrieden *D*	63	D4
Herrljunga *S*	118	B4
Herrnburg *D*	50	C3
Herrnhut *D*	58	B4
Herrsching *D*	67	E2
Herrskog *S*	112	C2
Herselt *B*	17	E1
Hersbruck *D*	63	E3
Hérso *GR*	88	B1
Herstal *B*	17	F2
Herten *D*	55	E4
Hertford *GB*	14	C3
Hertogenbosch ('s-) *NL*	54	C4
Hervás *E*	41	F1
Herzberg *D*	56	C4
Herzberg *D*	57	F4
Herzogenaurach *D*	63	D3
Herzogenburg *A*	69	D1
Herzsprung *D*	51	E4
Hesdin *F*	16	B3
Hesel *D*	55	E1
Hesseng *N*	105	F2
Hessisch Lichtenau *D*	62	C1
Hessisch Oldendorf *D*	56	B3
Hetekylä *FIN*	115	D1
Hettange-Grande *F*	22	C1
Hettstedt *D*	57	D4
Heubach *D*	66	C1
Heuchin *F*	16	C2
Hexham *GB*	9	E4
Heyrieux *F*	26	C3
Heysham *GB*	10	C2
Hiddensee *D*	51	E1
Hieflau *A*	68	C2
Hiersac *F*	24	C3
Hietaniemi *FIN*	109	F1
High Wycombe *GB*	14	B3
Higham Ferrers *GB*	14	B2

Higuera de Arjona *E*	48	A1
Higuera de la Serena *E*	41	E4
Higuera de la Sierra *E*	47	D1
Higuera de Vargas *E*	41	D4
Higuera la Real *E*	47	D1
Higueruela *E*	43	E4
Hiiumaa *EST*	124	B1
Híjar *E*	37	F4
Hilchenbach *D*	62	A1
Hildburghausen *D*	63	D2
Hilden *D*	61	F1
Hilders *D*	62	C2
Hildesheim *D*	56	C3
Hiliomódi *GR*	97	E1
Hillegom *NL*	54	B3
Hillerød *DK*	123	D3
Hillesøy *N*	104	B2
Hillswick *GB*	7	F2
Hilpoltstein *D*	63	D4
Hiltula *FIN*	121	E2
Hilvarenbeek *NL*	17	F1
Hilversum *NL*	54	C3
Himanka *FIN*	114	C2
Hímaros *GR*	88	B1
Hinckley *GB*	11	D4
Hindelang *D*	67	D3
Hindhead *GB*	14	B4
Hinojares *E*	48	C2
Hinojosa de Duero *E*	35	D4
Hinojosa del Duque *E*	41	F4
Hinojosos (Los) *E*	42	C3
Hintersee *D*	52	A3
Hinterstoder *A*	68	B2
Hintertux *A*	67	E3
Hinterweidenthal *D*	23	E1
Híos *GR*	95	F3
Híos (Nissí) *GR*	95	E1
Hirschau *D*	63	E3
Hirschberg *D*	63	E2
Hirschegg *A*	67	D3
Hirsingue *F*	23	E4
Hirson *F*	17	E3
Hirtshals *DK*	122	B1
Hirvasvaara *FIN*	109	E2
Hirvensalmi *FIN*	121	E2
Hirvilahti *FIN*	115	E3
Hirwaun *GB*	13	D1
Hisarja *BG*	129	D2
Histria *RO*	129	E1
Hitchin *GB*	14	B2
Hitzacker *D*	51	D4
Hjartdal *N*	116	C2
Hjellestad *N*	112	A1
Hjelmeland *N*	116	A2
Hjo *S*	118	C3
Hjørring *DK*	122	B1
Hlemoútsi *GR*	92	B4
Hlobyne *UA*	127	F2
Hluboká *CZ*	64	B4
Hluchiv *UA*	127	F1
Hlybokae *BY*	124	C3
Hobro *DK*	122	B2
Hochdorf *CH*	66	B3
Hochfelden *F*	23	E2
Hochosterwitz *A*	68	C3
Hochspeyer *D*	23	E1
Hockenheim *D*	23	F1
Hoddesdon *GB*	14	C3
Hodenhagen *D*	56	B2
Hódmezővásárhely *H*	126	B4
Hodnanes *N*	116	A1
Hodnet *GB*	10	C4
Hodoš *SLO*	73	E2
Höchberg *D*	62	C3
Höchst i. Odenwald *D*	62	B3
Höchstadt a. d. Aisch *D*	63	D3
Höchstädt a. d. Donau *D*	67	D1
Hoedekenskerke *NL*	17	D1
Hoek van Holland *NL*	54	B4
Hoemsbu *N*	110	C2
Hönebach *D*	62	C1
Hörnum *D*	50	A2
Hösbach *D*	62	B3
Höxter *D*	56	B4
Hof *D*	63	E2
Hofgeismar *D*	56	B4
Hofheim *D*	63	D2
Hofles *N*	107	D4
Höfn *IS*	106	C2
Hofolding *D*	67	E2
Hofors *S*	119	D1
Hofsós *IS*	106	B1
Höganäs *S*	123	D2
Høgebru *N*	110	B30
Höglekardalen *S*	112	A2
Högsäter *S*	118	B3
Högsby *S*	123	F1
Hohenau *D*	65	A4
Hohenberg *D*	69	D3
Hohenems *A*	66	C3

Hohengandern *D*	56	C4
Hohenlimburg *D*	61	F1
Hohenlinden *D*	67	F1
Hohenlockstedt *D*	50	B3
Hohenmölsen *D*	63	E1
Hohenpeißenberg *D*	67	E2
Hohenseeden *D*	57	E3
Hohenstein *D*	63	F1
Hohentauern *A*	68	C2
Hohenwestedt *D*	50	B3
Hóhlakas *GR*	103	E3
Le Hohwald *F*	23	E3
Højer *DK*	122	A3
Hokksund *N*	117	D2
Hokstad *N*	111	E1
Hol *N*	116	C1
Hola Prystan' *UA*	127	F3
Holbæk *DK*	122	C3
Holbeach *GB*	11	F4
Holdorf *D*	55	F3
Höljäkkä *FIN*	115	F2
Höljes *S*	118	B1
Hollabrunn *A*	65	D4
Høllen *N*	116	B3
Hollenstedt *D*	50	B4
Hollfeld *D*	63	D3
Hollingsholm *N*	110	C2
Hollola *FIN*	121	D3
Hollum *NL*	54	C1
Hollywood *IRL*	5	E2
Holm *S*	112	C3
Holm *N*	107	D4
Hólmavík *IS*	106	A1
Holmec *SLO*	73	E2
Holmen *N*	117	D1
Holmestrand *N*	117	D2
Holmfirth *GB*	11	D2
Holmön *S*	113	E1
Holmsund *S*	113	E1
Holstebro *DK*	122	A2
Holsted *DK*	122	A3
Holsworthy *GB*	12	C3
Holt *GB*	15	D1
Holwerd *NL*	54	C1
Holy Cross *IRL*	5	D2
Holyhead / Caergybi *GB*	3	F4
Holywell / Treffynnon *GB*	10	B3
Holywood *GB*	3	E2
Holzappel *D*	62	A2
Holzgau *A*	67	D3
Holzkirchen *D*	67	E2
Holzminden *D*	56	B4
Homberg (Efze) *D*	62	B1
Homberg (Niederrhein) *D*	61	E1
Homberg (Ohm) *D*	62	B2
Homburg *D*	23	E1
Homel' *BY*	125	E4
Hommelstø *N*	107	D4
Hommelvik *N*	111	E2
Hommersåk *N*	116	A2
Hondarribia / Fuenterrabía *E*	28	A3
Hondschoote *F*	15	E4
Hønefoss *N*	117	D1
Honfleur *F*	20	C1
Høng *DK*	122	C3
Hónikas *GR*	97	D1
Honiton *GB*	13	D3
Honkajoki *FIN*	120	B2
Honningsvåg *N*	105	E1
Honrubia *E*	43	D3
Honrubia de la Cuesta *E*	36	B4
Hontalbilla *E*	36	B4
Hontoria del Pinar *E*	36	C3
Hoogeveen *NL*	55	D2
Hoogezand Sappemeer *NL*	55	D2
Hoogstraten *B*	17	E1
Höör *S*	123	D3
Hoorn *NL*	54	B3
Hopfgarten *A*	67	F3
Hopperstad *N*	110	B4
Hóra *GR*	96	B2
Hóra *GR*	99	F1
Horb *D*	23	F2
Hörby *S*	123	D3
Horcajada (La) *E*	41	F1
Horcajo de los Montes *E*	42	A3
Horcajo de Santiago *E*	42	C2
Horcajo Medianero *E*	41	F1
Horche *E*	42	C1
Horden *GB*	11	E1
Horeftó *GR*	93	F1
Horezu *RO*	128	C2
Horgen *CH*	23	F4
Horki *BY*	125	E3
Horley *GB*	14	C4

Hranice CZ	65	F2
Hrastnik SLO	73	E2
Hrastovlje SLO	73	D4
Hríssafa GR	97	D2
Hrissi (Nissí) GR	101	E4
Hrissó GR	88	C1
Hrissoúpoli GR	89	E1
Hrissovítsi GR	96	C1
Hristianí GR	96	B2
Hristianí (Nissí) GR	98	C4
Hristós GR	99	E1
Hrodna BY	124	B4
Hrómio GR	87	F3
Hucknall GB	11	D3
Hucqueliers F	16	B2
Huddersfield GB	11	D2
Hude D	50	A4
Hudiksvall S	112	C4
Hückeswagen D	61	F1
Huedin RO	126	C4
Hüfingen D	23	F3
Huélago E	48	B2
Huélamo E	43	E2
Huelgas (Real Monasterio de las) E	36	B2
Huelgoat F	18	B3
Huelma E	48	B2
Huelva E	46	C2
Hünfeld D	62	C2
Huércal Overa E	49	D2
Huérguina E	43	E2
Huerta del Rey E	36	C3
Huerta de Valdecarábanos E	42	B2
Huertahernando E	43	D1
Hürth D	61	F1
Huerto E	38	A3
Huesa E	48	B2
Huesca E	37	F3
Huéscar E	48	C2
Huete E	43	D2
Huétor Santillán E	48	B3
Huétor Tájar E	48	A3
Huftarøy N	116	A1
Huittinen FIN	120	B3
Huizen NL	54	C3
Hulst NL	17	E1
Hultsfred S	119	F1
Humada E	36	B2
Humanes E	42	C1
Humenné SK	126	B3

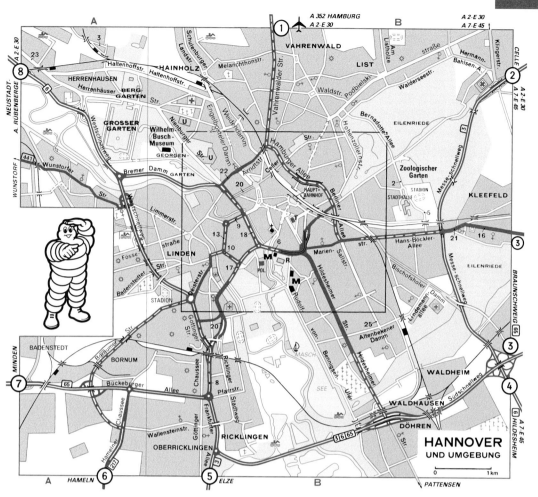

HANNOVER UND UMGEBUNG

0   1 km

Horn D	66	B3
Horn N	107	D3
Horn A	65	D4
Horn-Bad Meinberg D	56	B4
Hornachos E	41	E4
Hornachuelos E	47	E1
Hornberg D	23	F3
Hornburg D	56	C3
Horncastle GB	11	F3
Horndal S	119	D1
Horneburg D	50	B4
Hörnefors S	113	D2
Hornindal N	110	B3
Hørning DK	122	B2
Hornos E	48	C1
Hornoy F	16	B3
Hornsea GB	11	F2
Horodnja UA	127	E1
Horodok UA	126	C2
Horodyšče UA	127	E2
Horra (La) E	36	B3
Horsens DK	122	B2
Horsham GB	14	B4
Hørsholm DK	123	D3
Horst D	50	C4
Horstmar D	55	B3
Horten N	117	D2
Hortezuela E	36	C4
Hortiátis GR	88	B2
Hospental CH	66	B4
Hospital IRL	4	C3
Hospital de Órbigo E	33	E4
Hospitalet de l'Infant (L') E	44	B1
Hossa FIN	109	F3
Hossegor F	28	A2
Hostalric E	39	D3
Hotagen S	112	A1
Hoting S	112	C1
Hotton B	17	F3
Les Houches F	27	E3
Houdain F	16	C2
Houdan F	21	D2
Houeillès F	28	C2
Houffalize B	61	D3
Houghton-le-Spring GB	9	F4
Houlgate F	20	C1
Houmnikó GR	88	C2
Houni GR	92	C2
Hourtin F	24	B4
Houtskär FIN	120	B4
Hov DK	122	B2
Hovden N	116	B2
Hove GB	14	C4
Hovet N	110	C4
Hovmantorp S	123	F2
Høvringen N	111	D3
Howden GB	11	E2
Howth / Binn Éadair IRL	3	E4
Hoya D	56	B2
Høyanger N	110	B4
Hoyerswerda D	58	A4
Hoylake GB	10	C3
Høylandet N	107	D4
Hoym D	57	D4
Hoyo de Pinares (El) E	42	A1
Hoyos E	41	D1
Hozoviótissa GR	99	E3
Hradec Králové CZ	64	C2
Hrafnagil IS	106	B1

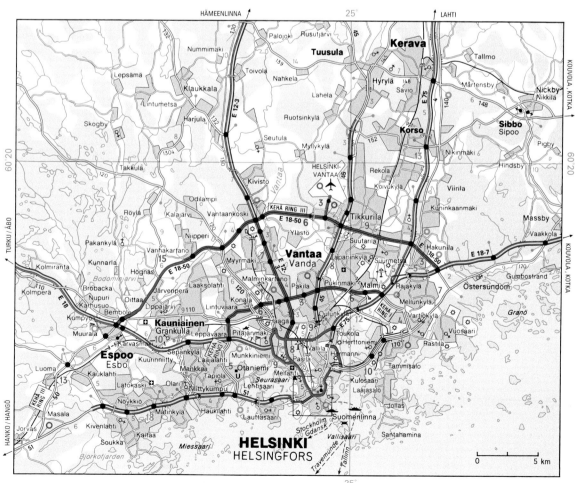

HELSINKI
HELSINGFORS

0   5 km

Humppila FIN..........120 C3
Hundested DK........122 C3
Hundorp N............111 D4
Hunedoara RO........128 C1
Hungerford GB.......13 F2
Hunnebostrand S.....118 A3
Hunspach F...........23 F2
Hunstanton GB.......11 F4
Huntingdon GB.......14 C2
Huntly GB............7 E4
Hurdal N.............117 D1
Huriel F.............25 F2
Hurort
  Semmering A......69 D2
Hurskaala FIN.......115 E4
Hurum N.............110 C4
Hurup DK............122 A1
Húsafell IS.........106 A2
Husavik N...........116 A1
Húsavík IS..........106 B1
Husbands
  Bosworth GB......11 E4
Hushinish GB........6 A3
Huşi RO.............127 E4
Huskvarna S.........118 C4
Husnes N............116 A1
Husum S.............113 D2
Husum D.............50 A2
Hüttenberg A........68 C3
Hüttschlag A........68 A3
Huttula FIN.........120 C2
Huttwil CH..........27 F1
Huy B...............17 F2
Hvalba DK...........106 A4
Hvalpsund DK........122 B2
Hvalvik DK..........106 A3
Hvammstangi IS......106 A1
Hvar HR.............128 A2
Hvar HR.............128 A2
Hveragerði IS.......106 A2
Hveravellir IS......106 B2
Hvidbjerg DK........122 A2
Hvide
  Sande DK.........122 A2
Hvítárnes IS........106 B2
Hvittingfoss N......117 D2
Hvitträsk FIN.......120 C4
Hvolsvöllur IS......106 A2
Hyaler N............117 D2
Hyde GB.............11 D3
Hyen N..............110 B3
Hyères F............31 E3
Hyltebruk S.........123 D1
Hyrynsalmi FIN......115 E1
Hythe GB............15 D4
Hyvinkää FIN........121 D3
Hyypiö FIN..........109 E2

I

Ía GR...............98 C4
Iaşi RO.............127 D3
Íasmos GR...........89 F1
Ibbenbüren D........55 E3
Ibestad N...........104 A3
Ibi E...............49 F1
Ibiza / Eivissa E...44 C4
Ičnja UA............127 F1
Idanha-a-Nova P.....41 D2
Idar-Oberstein D....61 F3
Idéo Ándro GR.......100 C4
Idoméni GR..........88 A1
Ídra GR.............97 F2
Ídra (Nissí) GR.....97 F2
Idre S..............112 A3
Idrija SLO..........73 D3
Idro I..............71 F4
Idstein D...........62 A2
Ieper B.............15 F4
Ierápetra GR........101 F4
Ierissós GR.........89 D3
Ieropigí GR.........87 D2
Ifestía GR..........89 F4
Ifjord N............105 E1
Ifta D..............62 C1
Ig SLO..............73 D3
Iga vas SLO.........73 D3
Iggesund S..........112 C4
Iglesias I..........82 A4
Iglesuela
  del Cid (La) E...44 A2
Igls A..............67 E3
Igoumenítsa GR......92 A1
Igualada E..........38 C4
Ihtiman BG..........128 C2
Ii FIN..............114 C1
Iisalmi FIN.........115 D2
Iisvesi FIN.........115 E3
Iitti FIN...........121 D3
IJmuiden NL.........54 B3
IJsselmuiden NL.....54 C3
IJzendijke NL.......17 D1
Ikaalinen FIN.......120 C2
Ikaría (Nissí) GR...99 E1
Ikast DK............122 B2
Ilanz D.............66 C4
Ilche E.............38 A3
Ilchester GB........13 E3
L'Île-Bouchard F....25 D1
L'Île-Rousse F......78 A2
Ilfracombe GB.......12 C2
Ílhavo P............34 B4
Ilia GR.............93 F2
Ílida GR............92 C4
Ilíki GR............93 F3

Iliókastro GR.......97 E2
Ilirska Bistrica SLO...73 D3
Ilkeston GB.........11 D3
Ilkley GB...........11 D2
Illana E............42 C2
Illano E............33 D2
Illar E.............48 C3
Ille-sur-Têt F......29 F4
Illertissen D.......66 C2
Illescas E..........42 B2
Illhaeusern F.......23 E3
Illičivs'k UA.......127 F4
Illiers-Combray F...21 D3
Illingen D..........62 B4
Illmitz A...........69 E1
Illora E............48 A2
Illueca E...........37 E4
Ilmajoki FIN........114 B4
Ilmenau D...........63 D1
Ilminster GB........13 D3
Ilomantsi FIN.......115 F3
Ilsenburg D.........56 C4
Ilsfeld D...........62 B4
Iława PL............124 A4
Imatra FIN..........121 F2
Ímeros GR...........89 F1
Imitós GR...........94 A4
Immenstaad D........66 C3
Immenstadt D........67 D3
Immingham GB........11 F2
Immingham
  Dock GB..........11 F2
Imola I.............76 A2
Imotski HR..........128 A2
Imperia I...........74 C3
Imphy F.............26 A1
Impruneta I.........76 A3
Imst A..............67 D3
Inari FIN...........105 E3
Inca E..............45 E3
Inchnadamph GB......6 C3
Inchree GB..........8 B1
Incisa
  in Val d'Arno I..76 A3
Indal S.............112 C3
Infiesto E..........33 E2
Ingå / Inkoo FIN....120 C40
Ingelmunster B......15 F4
Ingleton GB.........10 C1
Ingolstadt D........67 E1
Ingrandes F.........19 F4
Ingwiller F.........23 E2
Inhulec' UA.........127 F3
Iniesta E...........43 E3
Iniö FIN............120 B4
Inishcrone IRL......2 B2
Inkee FIN...........109 F3

Innbygda N..........111 E4
Inndyr N............107 E2
Innellan GB.........8 B2
Innerleithen GB.....9 D3
Innfield IRL........3 D3
Innhavet N..........107 F1
Inning
  a. Ammersee D....67 E2
Innsbruck A.........67 E3
Innsbruck A.........67 E3
Innset N............104 B4
Innvik N............110 B3
Inói GR.............94 A4
Inói GR.............96 B1
Inoússes GR.........95 F3
Inoússes (Nissí) GR.95 F3
Inowrocław PL.......126 A1
Ins CH..............27 F1
Interlaken CH.......27 F1
Întorsura
  Buzăului RO......127 D4
Inveraray GB........8 B2
Inverbervie GB......9 E1
Invergarry GB.......6 C4
Invergordon GB......7 D4
Inverkeithing GB....9 D2
Invermoriston GB....6 C4
Inverness GB........7 D4
Inverurie GB........7 E4
Inzell D............67 F2
Ioánina GR..........87 D4
Ioannínon (L.) GR...87 D4
Ionía GR............88 B2
Íos GR..............98 C3
Íos (Nissí) GR......98 C3
Ipáti GR............93 D2
Ipéria GR...........93 E1
Iphofen D...........62 C3
Ipsala TR...........129 E3
Ipsilí Ráhi GR......89 D1
Ípsos GR............86 B4
Ipsoúnda GR.........96 C1
Ipswich GB..........15 D2
Iráklia GR..........88 B1
Iráklia GR..........93 E2
Iráklia (Nissí) GR..99 D3
Iráklio GR..........101 D3
Irdning A...........68 B2
Iréo GR.............97 D1
Iréo GR.............99 F1
Iréo (Akr.) GR......93 F4
Íria GR.............97 E1
Irixoa E............32 B2
Iron-Bridge GB......10 C4
Irschenberg D.......67 F2
Irsina I............80 C3
Irún E..............28 A3

Iruñea /
  Pamplona E.......28 A4
Irurtzun E..........28 A4
Irvine GB...........3 F1
Irvinestown GB......2 C2
Irxleben D..........57 D3
Is-sur-Tille F......22 B4
Isaba E.............28 B4
Isaccea RO..........127 E4
Ísafjörður IS.......106 A1
Isane N.............110 B3
Isbister GB.........7 F2
Iscar E.............36 A4
Ischgl A............67 D3
Ischia I............79 F3
Ise N...............117 D2
Iselle I............70 C3
Iselsberg A.........68 A3
Iseo I..............71 E4
Iserlohn D..........61 F1
Isernia I...........80 A2
Isfjorden N.........110 C2
Isili I.............82 B3
Isla E..............36 C1
Isla Cristina E.....46 C2
L'Isle-Adam F.......21 E2
L'Isle-d'Abeau F....26 C3
L'Isle-de-Noé F.....29 D3
L'Isle-en-Dodon F...29 D3
L'Isle-Jourdain F...25 D2
L'Isle-Jourdain F...29 D1
L'Isle-sur-la-Sorgue F.30 C2
L'Isle-sur-le-Doubs F.23 D4
L'Isle-sur-Serein F.22 A4
Isle of Whithorn GB...3 E2
Isleornsay GB.......6 B4
Ismaning D..........67 E1
Isnäs FIN...........121 D4
Isny D..............66 C2
Iso-Evo FIN.........121 D3
Isojoki FIN.........120 B2
Isokylä FIN.........109 E2
Isokyrö FIN.........114 B3
Isola 2000 F........31 F1
Isola del Gran Sasso
  d'Italia I.......77 D4
Isola del Liri I....79 F2
Isola della Scala I.71 E4
Isola di Capo Rizzuto I.83 F2
Isona E.............38 B3
Isorella I..........71 F4
Ispica I............85 E4
Les Issambres F.....31 E3
Issigeac F..........29 D1
Issoire F...........26 A3
Íssoma GR...........92 C4
Issoudun F..........25 F1
Issóva (M) GR.......96 C1
Issy-l'Évêque F.....26 B1
Istán E.............47 F4
Istanbul TR.........129 F3
Istérnia GR.........98 C1
Istha D.............62 B1
Isthmía GR..........93 F4
Istiéa GR...........93 F2
Istres F............30 C3
Ístrios GR..........103 E2
Itä-Aure FIN........120 C2
Itéa GR.............87 E2
Itéa GR.............93 E3
Itéa GR.............87 E3
Itéa GR.............93 D1
Itháki GR...........92 A3
Itháki (Nissí) GR...92 A3
Ithómi GR...........96 C2
Íti GR..............93 E2
Ítilo GR............97 D3
Itri I..............79 F2
Ittiri I............82 A2
Itzehoe D...........50 B3
Ivacevičy BY........126 C1
Ivajlovgrad BG......129 D3
Ivalo FIN...........105 E3
Ivančna gorica SLO..73 E3
Ivanjica YU.........128 B2
Ivano-
  Frankivs'k UA....126 C3
Ívira GR............88 C1
Ivrea I.............70 C4
Ivry-la-Bataille F..21 D2
Ixiá GR.............103 F2
Izeda P.............35 D3
Izegem B............15 F4
Izernore F..........27 D2
Izlake SLO..........73 E2
Izmaïl UA...........127 E4
Izmir TR............129 E40
Izmit (Kocaeli) TR..129 F3
Iznájar E...........48 A2
Iznalloz E..........48 B2
Iznik TR............129 F3
Izola SLO...........73 D4

J

Jaala FIN...........121 D3
Jabbeke B...........15 F4
Jablanac HR.........77 E1
Jablanica BIH.......128 A2
Jablonec
  nad Nisou CZ.....64 B1
Jabugo E............46 C1
Jaca E..............28 B4
Jäder S.............119 E2
Jaderberg D.........50 A4
Jadraque E..........42 C1
Jaén E..............48 A2
Jävenitz D..........57 D2
Jagsthausen D.......62 C4
Jahotyn UA..........127 E2
Jajce BIH...........128 A2
Jäkkvik S...........107 F3
Jakobstad /
  Pietarsaari FIN..114 B2
Jalasjärvi FIN......114 B4
Jaligny-sur-Besbre F.26 A2
Jambol BG...........129 D2
Jämijärvi FIN.......120 B2
Jäminkipohja FIN....120 C2
Jämjö S.............123 F2
Jämsä FIN...........121 D2
Jämsänkoski FIN.....121 D2
Jana (La) E.........44 A1
Janakkala FIN.......120 C3
Janville F..........21 E3
Janzé F.............19 E3
Jaraba E............37 D4
Jarafuel E..........43 F4
Jaraicejo E.........41 E2
Jaraiz de la Vera E.41 F2
Jarandilla
  de la Vera E.....41 F2
Järbo S.............119 E1
Jarcevo RUS.........125 E30
Jard-sur-Mer F......24 A2
Jaren N.............117 D1
Jargeau F...........21 E4
Jarmen D............51 F2
Järna S.............119 D1
Järna S.............119 E2
Jarnac F............24 C3
Jarnages F..........25 F2
Jarny F.............22 C1
Jarocin PL..........59 E2
Jaroslavl' RUS......125 F1
Jarosław PL.........126 B2
Järpen S............112 A2
Jarrow GB...........9 F4
Järvelä FIN.........121 D3
Järvenpää FIN.......121 D3
Järvsö S............112 B4
Jasło PL............126 B2
Jastrowie PL........52 C3
Jászberény H........126 A4
Jaunay-Clan F.......25 D2
Jausiers F..........31 E1
Jávea : Xàbia E.....44 A4
La Javie F..........31 E2
Javoriv UA..........126 C2
Jävre S.............108 B4
Javron F............19 F3
Jedburgh GB.........9 E3
Jeesiö FIN..........109 D1
Jegun F.............29 D2
Jēlkabpils LV.......124 C3
Jektevik N..........116 A1
Jektvik N...........107 E2
Jelenia Góra PL.....58 C4
Jelgava LV..........124 B3
Jelling DK..........122 B3
Jel'n'a RUS.........125 E3
Jelsa N.............116 A2
Jelsi I.............80 A2
Jena D..............63 E1
Jenbach A...........67 E3
Jennersdorf A.......69 E3
Jeppo FIN...........114 B3
Jerez de la Frontera E.47 D3
Jerez
  de los Caballeros E.41 D4
Jérica E............43 F2
Jerichow D..........57 E2
Jerte E.............41 F1
Jerxheim D..........57 D3
Jerzu I.............82 C3
Jesenice SLO........73 D2
Jeseník CZ..........65 E1
Jesi I..............77 D3
Jesolo I............72 B4
Jessen D............57 F3
Jessheim N..........117 D1
Jeßnitz D...........57 E4
Jetzelsdorf A.......65 D4
Jeumont F...........17 E3
Jevenstedt D........50 B2
Jever D.............55 E1

KILYOS · SARIYER · BEYKOZ
E 80 · Kavákcik · Kanlica
Kágithane · Bebek · Anadólu Hisari
Alibeköy · Siáhdaraǧa
MECIDIYEKÖY · Ortaköy · Arnavutköy · Kandilli · Vaniköy · Çengelköy
Halidioǧtu · Taksim · BEŞIKTAŞ
EYÜP · Hasköy · BEYOĞLU · Dolmabahçe · BEYLERBEYI
Atikali · Galata Kulesi · KUZGUNCUK
FATIH · Süleymaniye Camii · SALACAK · ÜMRANIYE · ÜSKÜDAR
Kapan Çarşi · Topkapı Sarayı · Sehremini · Ayasofya · Validebagi · Harem · HAYDARPASA
Sultanahmet Camii · Fikirtepe
İSTANBUL · KADIKÖY · Kiziltoprak
FENERBAHÇE · Göztepe · ERENKÖY
MARMARA DENIZI
EDIRNE · KEŞAN · SARAY · ŞILE · İZMIT

1 / 150 000

Jevnaker N ... 117 D1
Jevpatorija UA ... 127 F4
Jezersko SLO ... 73 D2
Jędrzejów PL ... 126 A2
Jičín CZ ... 64 C1
Jihlava CZ ... 64 C3
Jimbolia RO ... 128 B1
Jimena E ... 48 B2
Jimena
  de la Frontera E ... 47 E4
Jindřichův
  Hradec CZ ... 64 C3
Joachimsthal D ... 51 F4
Jockfall S ... 108 C2
Jódar E ... 48 B2
Jodoigne B ... 17 F2
Joensuu FIN ... 115 F3
Jgeva EST ... 124 C1
Johanngeorgen-
  stadt D ... 63 F2
John o' Groats GB ... 7 E2
Johnstone GB ... 8 C3
Joigny F ... 21 F3
Joinville F ... 22 B3
Jokela FIN ... 121 D3
Jokijärvi FIN ... 109 F3
Jokikylä FIN ... 115 E1
Jokioinen FIN ... 120 C3
Jokkmokk S ... 108 A2
Joloskylä FIN ... 115 D1
Jomala FIN ... 120 A4
Jönåker S ... 119 E3
Joniškis LT ... 124 B3
Jönköping S ... 118 C4
Jonquera (La) E ... 39 E2
Jonzac F ... 24 C4
Jordbro S ... 119 E3
Jormlien S ... 107 E4
Jörn S ... 108 B4
Joroinen FIN ... 115 E4
Jørpeland N ... 116 A2
Jørstadmoen N ... 111 D4
Josselin F ... 19 D3
Jouarre F ... 21 F2
Joué-lès-Tours F ... 20 C4
Jougne F ... 27 E1
Joukokylä FIN ... 115 E1
Joutsa FIN ... 121 D2
Joutseno FIN ... 121 F3
Joutsijärvi FIN ... 109 E2
Joyeuse F ... 30 B1
Juan-les-Pins F ... 31 F2
Juankoski FIN ... 115 E3
Juchnov RUS ... 125 F3
Judaberg N ... 116 A2
Judenau A ... 69 D1
Judenburg A ... 68 C3
Jüchen D ... 61 E1
Jülich D ... 61 E1
Juelsminde DK ... 122 B3
Jüterbog D ... 57 F3
Jugon-les-Lacs F ... 19 D3
Jugorje SLO ... 73 E3
Juillac F ... 25 E4
Juist D ... 55 D1
Jukkasjärvi S ... 108 B3
Jullouville F ... 19 E2
Jumaliskylä FIN ... 115 E1
Jumeaux F ... 26 A4
Jumièges F ... 16 A4
Jumilhac-
  le-Grand F ... 25 D3
Jumilla E ... 49 E1
Juminen FIN ... 115 E2
Jumisko FIN ... 109 E2
Juneda E ... 38 B4
Juniville F ... 17 E4
Junosuando S ... 108 C1
Junsele S ... 112 C1
Juntusranta FIN ... 109 F3
Juoksenki FIN ... 108 C2
Juorkuna FIN ... 115 D1
Jurbarkas LT ... 124 B4
Jūrmala LV ... 124 B3
Jurmu FIN ... 109 E3
Juromenha P ... 40 C4
Jurva FIN ... 114 B4
Jussey F ... 22 C4
Justel E ... 33 D4
Juuka FIN ... 115 E3
Juuma FIN ... 109 F2
Juupajoki FIN ... 120 C2
Juva FIN ... 120 B3
Juva FIN ... 121 E2
Juvigny-
  le-Tertre F ... 19 E2
Juvigny-
  sous-Andaine F ... 19 F2
Juvola FIN ... 115 F4
Jyderup DK ... 122 C3
Jyrkkä FIN ... 115 E2
Jyväskylä FIN ... 115 D4

K

K. Ahaïa GR ... 92 C4
K. Alissós GR ... 92 C4
K. Asséa GR ... 96 C2
K. Doliána GR ... 97 D2
K. Figália GR ... 96 B1
K. Gadzéa GR ... 93 F1
K. Kamíla GR ... 88 C1
K. Klinés GR ... 87 E2
K. Makrinoú GR ... 92 C3
K. Meriá GR ... 98 A1
K. Nevrokópi GR ... 90 A4
K. Tithoréa GR ... 93 E3
K. Vassilikí GR ... 92 C3
K. Vérga GR ... 96 C3
K. Vérmio GR ... 87 F2
K. Vlassiá GR ... 93 D4
K. Zahloroú GR ... 93 D4
Kaakamo FIN ... 109 D3
Kaamanen FIN ... 105 F3
Kaaresuvanto FIN ... 105 D4
Kaarina FIN ... 120 B4
Kaatsheuvel NL ... 54 C4
Kaavi FIN ... 115 E3
Kåbdalis S ... 108 B3
Kachovka UA ... 127 F3
Kåfjord N ... 105 E1
Kaga S ... 119 D3
Kåge S ... 108 B4
Kaharlyk UA ... 127 E2
Kahla D ... 63 E1
Kaiáfas GR ... 96 B1
Kailbach D ... 62 B4
Kainasto FIN ... 114 B4
Kaindorf A ... 69 D2
Kaipola FIN ... 121 D2
Kairala FIN ... 109 E1
Kaiserslautern D ... 23 E1
Kaisheim D ... 67 D1
Kajaani FIN ... 115 E2
Kaki Thálassa GR ... 98 A1
Kakí Vígla GR ... 94 A4
Kakslauttanen FIN ... 105 F4
Kalá Nerá GR ... 93 F1
Kalá Nissiá GR ... 93 F4
Kalak N ... 105 E1
Kalamáki GR ... 93 E1
Kalamáki GR ... 93 F1
Kalamáta GR ... 96 C2
Kalambáka GR ... 87 E4
Kalambáki GR ... 89 D1
Kalámi GR ... 100 B3
Kalámi GR ... 99 F1
Kalamítsi GR ... 92 A2
Kalamítsi GR ... 89 D4
Kálamos (Nissí) GR ... 92 B3
Kalamotí GR ... 95 F4
Kalándra GR ... 88 C4
Kalanti FIN ... 120 B3
Kalapódi GR ... 93 F3
Kälarne S ... 112 B2
Kalavárda GR ... 103 F2
Kalávrita GR ... 93 D4
Kal'azin RUS ... 125 F1
Kalbe D ... 57 D2
Kalce SLO ... 73 D3
Kaléndzi GR ... 92 B1
Kaléndzi GR ... 93 D4
Kalérgo GR ... 94 C4
Kalí Liménes GR ... 100 C4
Kaliáni GR ... 93 E4
Kalífitos GR ... 89 D1
Kalimassiá GR ... 95 F4
Kálimnos GR ... 99 F3
Kálimnos (Nissí) GR ... 99 F3
Kaliningrad RUS ... 124 A4
Kalinkavičy BY ... 127 D1
Kalipéfki GR ... 88 A4
Kaliráhi GR ... 87 E3
Kalisz PL ... 126 A2
Kalithéa GR ... 92 C3
Kalithéa GR ... 88 C3
Kalithéa GR ... 89 D1
Kalithéa GR ... 103 F2
Kalithéa GR ... 96 C1
Kalithiés GR ... 103 F2
Kalíthiro GR ... 93 D1
Kalivári GR ... 94 C4
Kalíves GR ... 100 B3
Kalívia GR ... 98 A1
Kalívia GR ... 92 B2
Kalívia GR ... 96 C1
Kalívia GR ... 93 D4
Kalívia Varikoú GR ... 88 A3
Kalix S ... 108 C3
Kaljord N ... 104 A4
Kalkar D ... 55 D4
Kalkkinen FIN ... 121 D3

Kall S ... 112 A2
Källby FIN ... 114 B3
Källby S ... 118 C3
Kallinge S ... 123 F2
Kallio FIN ... 120 C2
Kalliojoki FIN ... 115 F1
Kallislahti FIN ... 121 E2
Kallmünz D ... 63 E4
Kalmar S ... 123 F2
Kaló Horió GR ... 101 E4
Kaló Neró GR ... 96 B2
Kalocsa H ... 126 A4
Kalogriá GR ... 92 C4
Kalohóri GR ... 87 F4
Kalókastro GR ... 88 C1
Kaloní GR ... 97 E1
Kaloní GR ... 95 F1
Kaloskopí GR ... 93 E3
Kalpáki GR ... 86 C4
Kals A ... 68 A3
Kalsdorf A ... 69 D3
Kaltbrunn CH ... 66 C3
Kaltenkirchen D ... 50 B3
Kaltennordheim D ... 62 C2
Kaltezés GR ... 97 D2
Kaluga RUS ... 125 F3
Kalundborg DK ... 122 C3
Kaluš UA ... 126 C3
Kalvåg N ... 110 A3
Kalvehave DK ... 122 C4
Kälviä FIN ... 114 C2
Kalvola FIN ... 120 C3
Kalvträsk S ... 108 B4
Kamáres GR ... 100 C4
Kamáres GR ... 93 D4
Kamáres GR ... 98 C2
Kamáres GR ... 98 B3
Kamári GR ... 99 D4
Kamariótissa GR ... 91 D3
Kambánis GR ... 88 B1
Kambiá GR ... 95 F3
Kambohóri GR ... 88 A2
Kámbos GR ... 100 A3
Kámbos GR ... 96 C3
Kámbos GR ... 93 D1
Kamen D ... 55 E4
Kaména Voúrla GR ... 93 E2
Kaméni (Nissí) GR ... 99 D4
Kamenz D ... 58 A4
Kamień Pomorski PL ... 52 A2
Kamilári GR ... 100 C4
Kamínia GR ... 92 C4
Kaminiá GR ... 87 D3
Kamínia GR ... 89 F4
Kámiros GR ... 103 F2
Kámiros Kastélo GR ... 103 E2
Kam"janec'-
  Podil's'kyj UA ... 127 D3
Kam"janka UA ... 127 F2
Kam"janka
  Dniprovs'ka UA ... 127 F3
Kamnik SLO ... 73 E2
Kamp Bornhofen D ... 61 F2
Kampen NL ... 54 C3
Kampen (Sylt) D ... 50 A1
Kamp-Lintfort D ... 55 D4
Kanal SLO ... 72 C3
Kanála GR ... 98 B2
Kanáli GR ... 92 A3
Kanália GR ... 93 D1
Kanália GR ... 93 F1
Kanatádika GR ... 93 F2
Kánava GR ... 98 B3
Kándanos GR ... 100 A3
Kandel D ... 23 F1
Kandern D ... 23 E4
Kandersteg CH ... 27 F2
Kándia GR ... 97 E1
Kandíla GR ... 92 B2
Kandíla GR ... 97 D1
Kandıra TR ... 129 F3
Kandrše SLO ... 73 E2
Kanestraum N ... 110 C2
Kangádio GR ... 92 C4
Kangasala FIN ... 120 C2
Kangaslampi FIN ... 115 E4
Kangasniemi FIN ... 121 D2
Kangosjärvi FIN ... 108 C1
Kaniv UA ... 127 E2
Kanjiža YU ... 128 C2
Kankaanpää FIN ... 120 B2
Kannonkoski FIN ... 115 D3
Kannus FIN ... 114 C2
Kannusjärvi FIN ... 121 E3
Kanturk /
  Ceann Toirc IRL ... 4 B3
Kapandríti GR ... 94 A4
Kaparéli GR ... 93 F2
Kapariá GR ... 98 C1
Kapellskär S ... 119 F2
Kapfenberg A ... 68 C2
Kaposvár H ... 126 A4
Kapp N ... 117 D1

Kappel D ... 61 F3
Kappeln D ... 50 B2
Kaprun A ... 68 A3
Kapsáli GR ... 97 E4
Kápsas GR ... 97 D1
Kapsoúri GR ... 94 C4
Kapuvár H ... 69 E1
Karabiga TR ... 129 E3
Karaburun TR ... 129 E3
Karačev RUS ... 125 F4
Karasjok N ... 105 E2
Karasu TR ... 129 F2
Karats S ... 108 A2
Karavás GR ... 97 E4
Karavómilos GR ... 93 E2
Karavónissia
  (Nissiá) GR ... 102 C3
Karavostássis GR ... 98 C4
Kárböle S ... 112 B3
Karcag H ... 126 B4
Kardakáta GR ... 92 A3
Kardámena GR ... 103 D1
Kardámila GR ... 95 F3
Kardamíli GR ... 96 C3
Kardiá GR ... 88 B2
Kardítsa GR ... 93 D1
Kärdla EST ... 124 B1
Karesuando S ... 105 D4
Karfás GR ... 95 F3
Karhukangas FIN ... 114 C2
Karhula FIN ... 121 E3
Kariá GR ... 92 A2
Kariá GR ... 88 A4
Kariá GR ... 97 D1
Kariá GR ... 93 E2
Kariani GR ... 89 D2
Kariés GR ... 97 D2
Kariés GR ... 89 D3
Kariés GR ... 93 E2
Karigasniemi FIN ... 105 E3
Karijoki FIN ... 120 B2
Karinainen FIN ... 120 B3
Kariótissa GR ... 88 A2
Karis / Karjaa FIN ... 120 C4
Káristos GR ... 94 C4
Karitena GR ... 96 C1
Karjalohja FIN ... 120 C4
Karkaloú GR ... 96 C1
Karkinágri GR ... 99 E1
Karkkila FIN ... 121 C3
Karkku FIN ... 120 C3
Kärkölä FIN ... 121 D3
Karlevi S ... 123 F2
Karlobag HR ... 77 E1
Karlovac HR ... 73 F3
Karlovássi GR ... 99 F1
Karlovo BG ... 129 D2
Karlovy Vary CZ ... 63 F2
Karlsborg S ... 118 C3
Karlsburg D ... 51 F2
Karlsfeld D ... 67 E1
Karlshamn S ... 123 E2
Karlshuld D ... 67 E1
Karlskoga S ... 118 C2
Karlskrona S ... 123 F2
Karlsruhe D ... 23 F2
Karlstadt D ... 62 C3
Karlstift A ... 64 C4
Karlštejn CZ ... 64 B2
Karnezéika GR ... 97 E1
Karnobat BG ... 129 E2
Karow D ... 51 E3
Kärpänkylä FIN ... 109 F3
Kárpathos GR ... 103 D4
Kárpathos (Nissí) GR ... 103 D4
Karpeníssi GR ... 93 D2
Karperí GR ... 88 C1
Karperó GR ... 87 E4
Kärsämäki FIN ... 115 D2
Kärsava LV ... 124 C2
Karstädt D ... 51 D4
Karstula FIN ... 114 C3
Kartal TR ... 129 F3
Kartéri GR ... 92 A1
Kartéri GR ... 97 D1
Karterós GR ... 101 D3
Karttula FIN ... 115 D3
Kartuzy PL ... 53 D1
Karungi S ... 108 C3
Karup DK ... 122 B2
Karvala FIN ... 114 C3
Kärväskylä FIN ... 115 D3
Karvia FIN ... 120 B2
Karviná CZ ... 65 F2
Karvoskylä FIN ... 114 C2
Karvounári GR ... 92 A1
Kašin RUS ... 125 F1
Kašira RUS ... 125 F3

Káspakas GR ... 89 F4
Kassándra GR ... 88 C4
Kassándria GR ... 88 C3
Kassel D ... 62 B1
Kassiópi GR ... 86 B4
Kassópi GR ... 91 A1
Kássos (Nissí) GR ... 103 D4
Kastaniá GR ... 93 D1
Kastaniá GR ... 97 D1
Kastaniá GR ... 87 F3
Kastaniá GR ... 87 E4
Kastaniés GR ... 91 E1
Kastaniótissa GR ... 93 F2
Kastéla GR ... 94 A3
Kastelholm FIN ... 120 A4
Kastéli GR ... 100 A3
Kastéli GR ... 101 D3
Kastellaun D ... 61 F3
Kasterlee B ... 17 F1
Kastl D ... 63 E3
Kastorf D ... 50 C3
Kastóri GR ... 96 C2
Kastoriá GR ... 87 E2
Kastós (Nissí) GR ... 92 B3
Kastráki GR ... 92 C2
Kastráki GR ... 98 C3
Kastráki GR ... 87 E4
Kastrí GR ... 88 A4
Kastrí GR ... 93 D2
Kastrí GR ... 97 D2
Kástro GR ... 94 A1
Kástro GR ... 92 B4
Kástro GR ... 92 F3
Kastrossikiá GR ... 92 A2
Katáfigio GR ... 87 F3
Katáfito GR ... 88 C1
Katáfourko GR ... 92 B2
Katáhas GR ... 88 A2
Katákolo GR ... 96 B1
Katálako GR ... 89 F4
Katápola GR ... 99 D3
Katastári GR ... 96 A1
Katavía GR ... 103 E3
Kateliós GR ... 92 B4
Kateríni GR ... 88 A3
Katharó GR ... 101 E4
Kathení GR ... 94 A3
Kätkäsuvanto FIN ... 108 C1
Katlenburg-Lindau D ... 56 C4
Káto Zákros GR ... 101 F4
Katohí GR ... 92 C3
Katoúna GR ... 92 B2
Katoúna GR ... 92 B3
Katowice PL ... 126 A2
Katrineholm S ... 119 D3
Katwijk aan Zee NL ... 54 B3
Kaub D ... 23 E1
Kaufbeuren D ... 67 D2
Kauhajärvi FIN ... 114 C3
Kauhajoki FIN ... 114 B3
Kauhava FIN ... 114 C3
Kaukonen FIN ... 109 D1
Kaunas LT ... 124 B4
Kaupanger N ... 110 B3
Kaustinen FIN ... 114 C3
Kautokeino N ... 105 D3
Kauttua FIN ... 120 B3
Kavajë AL ... 128 B3
Kavála GR ... 89 E1
Kavarna BG ... 129 E2
Kavíli GR ... 91 E1
Kavírio-Hlói GR ... 89 F4
Kävlinge S ... 123 D3
Kávos GR ... 92 A1
Kavoússi GR ... 101 E4
Käyla FIN ... 109 F2
Kaysersberg F ... 23 E3
Kazanlãk BG ... 129 D2
Kazárma GR ... 96 C3
Kazimierz Dolny PL ... 126 B2
Kazincbarcika H ... 126 B3
Kéa GR ... 98 A1
Kéa (Nissí) GR ... 98 A1
Keadew IRL ... 2 C3
Keady GB ... 3 D2
Kebnekaise S ... 108 A1
Kecskemét H ... 126 A4
Kédainiai LT ... 124 B3
Kédros GR ... 93 D1
Keel IRL ... 2 A3
Keerbergen B ... 17 E1
Kefalári GR ... 97 D1
Kefaloniá (Nissí) GR ... 92 A3
Kéfalos GR ... 103 D1
Kefalóvrisso GR ... 96 B2
Kefalóvrisso GR ... 92 C3
Kefalóvrisso GR ... 87 F4
Kehl D ... 23 E2
Kehrókambos GR ... 89 E1
Kéhros GR ... 91 D2

Keighley GB ... 11 D2
Keitele FIN ... 115 D3
Keith GB ... 7 E4
Kéla GR ... 87 F2
Kelankylä FIN ... 109 E3
Kelberg D ... 61 E3
Kelbra D ... 57 D4
Këlcyrë AL ... 128 B4
Kelefá GR ... 97 D3
Kelheim D ... 63 E4
Kellinghusen D ... 50 B3
Kellokoski FIN ... 121 D3
Kelso GB ... 9 E3
Kelujärvi FIN ... 109 E1
Kemberg D ... 57 F3
Kembs F ... 23 E4
Kemi FIN ... 109 D3
Kemijärvi FIN ... 109 E2
Keminmaa FIN ... 109 D3
Kemnath D ... 63 E3
Kempele FIN ... 114 C1
Kempen D ... 61 E1
Kempenich D ... 61 E3
Kempten D ... 67 D2
Kendal GB ... 10 C1
Kendrikó GR ... 88 B1
Kenilworth GB ... 11 D4
Kenmare / Neidín IRL ... 4 B3
Kennacraig GB ... 8 B3
Kenoúrgio GR ... 92 C3
Kentallen GB ... 8 B1
Kenzingen D ... 23 E3
Kepi i Gjuhezës AL ... 128 B4
Keramía GR ... 95 F2
Keramídi GR ... 93 F1
Keramítsa GR ... 86 C4
Kéramos GR ... 95 E3
Keramotí GR ... 89 E2
Kerassiá GR ... 93 F2
Kerassiá GR ... 93 F1
Kerassiés GR ... 87 F2
Kerassohóri GR ... 92 C2
Kerassóna GR ... 92 B1
Keratéa GR ... 98 A1
Kerava FIN ... 121 D1
Kerí GR ... 96 A1
Kerimäki FIN ... 121 F2
Kerken D ... 61 E1
Kérkira GR ... 86 B4
Kérkira (Nissí) GR ... 86 B4
Kerkonkoski FIN ... 115 D3
Kerkrade NL ... 61 E2
Kernascléden F ... 18 C3
Kéros (Nissí) GR ... 99 D3
Kerpen D ... 61 E1
Kerteminde DK ... 122 C3
Kértezi GR ... 93 D4
Kerzers CH ... 27 F1
Kesälahti FIN ... 121 F2
Keşan TR ... 129 E3
Kesh GB ... 2 C2
Kessariáni GR ... 94 A4
Kestilä FIN ... 115 D2
Keswick GB ... 10 C1
Keszthely H ... 69 F3
Kettering GB ... 11 E4
Kettletoft GB ... 7 E1
Kettwig D ... 61 F1
Ketzin D ... 57 F2
Keuruu FIN ... 120 C2
Kevelaer D ... 55 D4
Kevo FIN ... 105 E2
Keynsham GB ... 13 E2
Kežmarok SK ... 126 B3
Kętrzyn PL ... 124 A4
Kiani GR ... 91 E1
Kiáto GR ... 93 E4
Kiberg N ... 105 F1
Kičevo MK ... 128 C3
Kidderminster GB ... 10 C4
Kidlington GB ... 13 F1
Kidsgrove GB ... 10 C3
Kidwelly / Cydweli GB ... 12 C1
Kiefersfelden D ... 67 F2
Kiekinkoski FIN ... 115 F2
Kiel D ... 50 B2
Kielce PL ... 126 A2
Kiental CH ... 27 F2
Kierinki FIN ... 109 D1
Kietz D ... 58 A2
Kifissiá GR ... 94 A4
Kifjord N ... 105 E1
Kihlanki FIN ... 108 C1
Kihniö FIN ... 120 C2
Kiihtelysvaara FIN ... 115 F3
Kiikala FIN ... 120 C4
Kiikka FIN ... 120 B3
Kiikoinen FIN ... 120 B3
Kiiminki FIN ... 115 D1
Kiiskilä FIN ... 114 C2
Kiistala FIN ... 109 D1
Kikinda YU ... 128 B1
Kil S ... 118 C2

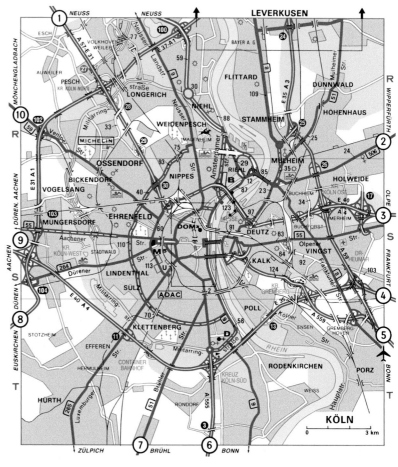

Kíla GR.............. 87 F3
Kiláda GR............ 97 E2
Kiláda GR............ 87 F3
Kilafors S............. 112 C4
Kilbaha IRL........... 4 B2
Kilbeggan IRL......... 2 C4
Kilbirnie GB.......... 8 C3
Kilboghamn N......... 107 D2
Kilbotn N............ 104 A3
Kilchoan GB.......... 8 A1
Kilcock IRL........... 3 D4
Kilcormac IRL........ 2 C4
Kilcreggan GB........ 8 C2
Kilcullen IRL.......... 5 E2
Kildare / Cill Dara IRL . 3 D4
Kildorrery IRL......... 4 C3
Kilfenora IRL.......... 2 A4
Kilgarvan IRL......... 4 B3
Kilija UA.............. 127 E4
Kilingi-Nmme EST..... 124 B2
Kilíni GR............. 92 B4
Kilkee / Cill Chaoi IRL . 4 B2
Kilkeel GB............ 3 E3
Kilkenny / Cill Chainnigh
  IRL 5 D2
Kilkhampton GB...... 12 C3
Kilkís GR 88 B1
Killadysert IRL........ 4 B2
Killaloe /
  Cill Dalua IRL....... 4 C2
Killarney /
  Cill Airne IRL....... 4 B3
Killashandra IRL...... 2 C3
Killenaule IRL......... 5 D2
Killimer IRL........... 4 B2
Killin GB............. 8 C2
Killinkoski FIN........ 114 C4
Killorglin /
  Cill Orglan IRL...... 4 B3
Killybegs / Na Cealla
  Beaga IRL 2 C2
Killyleagh GB......... 3 E3
Kilmaine IRL.......... 2 B4
Kilmallock / Cill
  Mocheallóg IRL..... 4 C3
Kilmarnock GB........ 8 C3
Kilmartin GB.......... 8 B2
Kilmore Quay IRL..... 5 E3
Kilmurry IRL.......... 4 C2
Kilninver GB.......... 8 B2
Kilnsea GB............ 11 F2
Kilpisjärvi FIN........ 104 C3
Kilrea GB............. 3 D2
Kilronan /
  Cill Rónáin IRL...... 2 A4
Kilrush / Cill Rois IRL.. 4 B2
Kilsyth GB............ 8 C2
Kiltealy IRL........... 5 E3
Kiltimagh IRL......... 2 B3
Kilwinning GB........ 3 F1
Kılyos TR............. 129 F3
Kimássi GR........... 94 A3
Kiméria GR........... 89 E1
Kími GR.............. 94 B3
Kímina GR............ 88 A2
Kimísseos
  Theotókou GR...... 97 D1
Kimito / Kemiö FIN... 120 B4
Kímolos GR........... 98 B3
Kímolos (Nissí) GR ... 98 B3
Kimry RUS........... 125 F2
Kimstad S 119 D3
Kínaros (Nissí) GR 99 E3
Kinbrace GB.......... 7 D3
Kincardine GB........ 9 D2
Kindberg A........... 69 D2
Kindelbrück D........ 57 D4
Kinéta GR............ 93 F4
King's Lynn GB....... 11 F4
Kingisepp RUS....... 125 C1
Kingsbridge GB....... 12 C4
Kingscourt IRL 3 D3
Kingston-
  upon-Hull GB...... 11 E2
Kingston-
  upon-Thames GB .. 14 B3
Kingswear GB........ 13 D1
Kington GB........... 13 E1
Kingussie GB......... 7 D4
Kínira GR............ 89 E2
Kinloch Rannoch GB . 8 C1
Kinlochbervie GB..... 6 C2
Kinlochewe GB....... 6 C4
Kinna S 118 B4
Kinnasniemi FIN...... 115 E1
Kinnegad IRL......... 3 D4
Kinnitty IRL.......... 2 C4
Kinnula FIN.......... 114 C3
Kinross GB........... 9 D2
Kinsale /
  Cionn tSáile IRL.... 4 C4
Kinsarvik N.......... 116 B10
Kintaus FIN 115 D4

Kintore GB............ 7 E4
Kinvarra IRL 2 B4
Kióni GR 92 A3
Kíos (Nissí) GR 97 D1
Kiparíssi GR 97 E3
Kiparissía GR 96 B2
Kipárissos GR 93 E1
Kípi GR 87 D4
Kípi GR 91 E2
Kipinä FIN............ 115 D1
Kipourío GR 87 E4
Kipséli GR............ 93 E1
Kirá Panagiá
  (Nissí) GR 94 B1
Kirchbach
  in Steiemark A...... 69 D3
Kirchberg D 63 F1
Kirchberg A 67 F3
Kirchberg
  (Hunsrück) D 61 F3
Kirchberg
  am Wagram A...... 65 D4
Kirchberg
  an der Pielach A.... 68 C1
Kirchdorf
  an der Krems A..... 68 B2
Kirchenlamitz D....... 63 E3
Kirchenthumbach D.. 63 E3
Kirchhain D........... 62 B1
Kirchheim D.......... 62 B1
Kirchheim a. Neckar D 62 B4
Kirchheimbolanden D 62 A3
Kirchhundem D....... 62 A1
Kirchlengern D........ 55 F3
Kirchmöser D 57 E2
Kirchschlag in der
  Bucklingen Welt A . 69 E2
Kiriaki GR 91 E1
Kiriáki GR 93 E3
Kiriši RUS 125 D1
Kırkağaç TR........... 129 E4
Kirkby Lonsdale GB .. 10 C1
Kirkby Stephen GB ... 10 C1
Kirkcaldy GB.......... 9 D2
Kirkcolm GB.......... 3 F2
Kirkcudbright GB 8 C4
Kirkenær N........... 117 E1
Kirkenes N........... 105 F2
Kirkham GB.......... 10 C2
Kírki GR 91 D2
Kirkintilloch GB 8 C2
Kirkjubæjar-
  klaustur IS 106 B2
Kirkjubøur DK........ 106 A3
Kirkkonummi /
  Kyrkslätt FIN....... 120 C4
Kirklareli TR.......... 129 E2
Kirkwall GB.......... 7 E2
Kirov RUS........... 125 F3
Kirovohrad UA....... 127 F2
Kirovsk RUS......... 125 D1
Kirriemuir GB 9 D1
Kirtorf D 62 B1
Kiruna S 108 B1
Kiržač RUS 125 F2
Kisa S 119 D4
Kisko FIN............ 120 C4
Kiskőrös H........... 126 A4
Kiskunfélegyháza H.. 126 A4
Kiskunhalas H........ 126 A4
Kißlegg D............ 66 C2
Kissoú Kámbos GR... 100 C4
Kisújszállás H........ 126 B4
Kisvárda H........... 126 B3
Kíta GR.............. 97 D4
Kitee FIN............ 115 F4
Kíthira GR........... 97 E4
Kíthira (Nissí) GR 97 E4
Kíthnos GR.......... 98 B2
Kíthnos (Nissí) GR ... 98 B2
Kitka FIN............ 109 F2
Kittilä FIN........... 109 D1
Kitzbühel A........... 67 F3
Kitzingen D.......... 62 C3
Kiukainen FIN........ 120 B3
Kiuruvesi FIN........ 115 D2
Kivéri GR 97 D1
Kivijärvi FIN......... 114 C3
Kivitaipale FIN....... 109 D2
Kivotós GR.......... 87 E3
Kizário GR 91 D2
Kjellerup DK......... 122 B2
Kjerringøy N 107 E1
Kjerringvåg N........ 111 D1
Kjøllefjord N 105 E1
Kjøpsvik N........... 107 F1
Kjustendil BG......... 128 C2
Kladanj BIH.......... 128 A2
Kladno CZ 64 A2
Kladovo YU......... 128 C1
Klæbu N............ 111 D2

Klagenfurt A 68 C4
Klagenfurt A 68 C4
Klaipėda LT........... 124 A3
Klaksvik DK.......... 106 A3
Klanxbüll D........... 50 A1
Klässbol S 118 B2
Klatovy CZ........... 64 A3
Klaukkala FIN........ 121 D4
Klazienaveen NL...... 55 D2
Kleinhaugsdorf A..... 65 D4
Kleppe N............. 116 A2
Kleppestø N.......... 110 A4
Kleve D 55 D4
Klimavičy BY......... 125 E4
Klimpfjäll S........... 107 E4
Klin RUS............. 125 F2
Klincy RUS........... 125 E4
Klingenbach A........ 69 E1
Klingenthal D 63 F2
Klintehamn S 119 F4
Klippan S............ 123 D2
Klippen S 107 E3
Klissoúra GR 87 E2
Klitoría GR 93 D4
Klitten D 58 B4
Klixbüll D............ 50 A1
Ključ BIH............ 128 A1
Klösterle A 67 D3
Kløfta N............ 117 D1
Klokkarvik N......... 116 A1
Klosterneuburg A 69 D1
Klosters CH.......... 66 C4
Kloten CH 23 F4
Klöverträsk S........ 108 B3
Klövsjö S 112 A3
Kluczbork PL 126 A2
Kłodzko PL.......... 65 D1
Klötze D............. 57 D2
Klütz D 51 D3
Knäred S............ 123 D2
Knaresborough GB... 11 D2
Knarvik N........... 110 A4
Kneža BG 128 C2
Knežak SLO 73 D3
Knídi GR 87 E3
Knighton /
  Trefyclawdd GB ... 10 C4
Knight's Town IRL ... 4 A3
Knin HR 128 A2
Knittelfeld A.......... 68 C3
Knivsta S 119 E2
Knjaževac YU........ 128 C2
Knokke-Heist B...... 15 F3
Knossós GR......... 101 D3
Knutsford GB........ 10 C3
Kobarid SLO......... 72 C2

Kobeljaky UA......... 127 F2
København DK...... 123 D3
Kobern-Gondorf D ... 61 F2
Koblenz D 61 F2
Kobryn BY.......... 126 C1
Kočevje SLO 73 E3
Kochel a. See D....... 67 D2
Kodiksami FIN........ 120 B3
Kodisjoki FIN........ 120 B3
Kölleda D 63 D1
Köln D............... 61 F1
Köngernheim D....... 62 A3
Königs
  Wusterhausen D ... 57 F2
Königsbrück D........ 58 A4
Königsbrunn D 67 D1
Königsee D........... 63 D1
Königsfeld i.
  Schwarzwald D 23 F3
Königslutter D........ 57 D3
Königssee D.......... 68 A20
Königstein D......... 64 A1
Königstein D 62 A2
Königswinter D....... 61 F2
Könnern D........... 57 E4
Köpenick D.......... 57 F2
Kössen D 67 F2
Köthen D 57 E4
Kötzting D........... 64 A2
Köflach A............ 68 C3
Køge DK............ 123 D3
Kohtla-Järve EST 124 C1
Koikkala FIN......... 121 E2
Koirakoski FIN....... 115 E2
Koivu FIN........... 109 D3
Kokála GR........... 97 D4
Kökar FIN........... 120 A4
Kokári GR........... 99 F1
Kokemäki FIN........ 120 B3
Kókino Neró GR...... 88 B4
Kokkola / Karleby FIN. 114 C2
Kokotí GR 93 E2
Koksijde-Bad B 15 F4
Koláka GR 93 F3
Kolari FIN........... 108 C1
Kolåsen S............ 112 A1
Kolbäck S........... 119 D2
Kolbermoor D........ 67 E2
Kolby Kås DK........ 122 C3
Kolding DK.......... 122 B3
Kolho FIN........... 120 C2
Koli FIN............. 115 F3
Kolimvári GR........ 100 A3
Kolín CZ............ 64 C2
Kolindrós GR........ 88 A2
Kolínes GR.......... 97 D2

Kolka LV.............. 124 B2
Kolkanlahti FIN....... 115 D3
Kolkasrags LV........ 124 B2
Kołobrzeg PL........ 52 B2
Kolomyja UA......... 126 C3
Kolpino RUS......... 125 D1
Kolsva S 119 D2
Kolvereid N.......... 107 D4
Koło PL............. 126 A1
Komagfjord N........ 105 D2
Kómanos GR......... 87 F2
Kómara GR.......... 91 E1
Komárno SK......... 126 A4
Kombóti GR 92 B2
Koménó GR 92 B2
Kómi GR............ 98 C1
Kómi GR............ 95 F4
Komílio GR 92 A2
Komló H............ 128 A1
Komniná GR......... 89 E1
Komniná GR......... 87 F2
Komninádes GR 87 D2
Komotiní GR......... 89 F1
Konakovo RUS 125 F2
Kondiás GR.......... 89 F4
Kondopóuli GR 89 F4
Kondovázena GR 96 C1
Königswiesen A 68 C1
Konin PL............ 126 A1
Koniskós GR......... 87 F4
Konístres GR......... 94 B3
Kónitsa GR........... 87 D3
Konjic BIH........... 128 A2
Konnevesi FIN........ 115 D3
Könönpelto FIN...... 115 E4
Konotop UA......... 127 F1
Konsmo N........... 116 B3
Konstanz D.......... 66 B3
Kontich B............ 17 E1
Kontiolahti FIN....... 115 F3
Kontiomäki FIN....... 115 E1
Konttajärvi FIN....... 109 D2
Konz D 23 D1
Koog (De) NL........ 54 B2
Kopáni GR 92 B1
Kopanós GR 87 F2
Kóparnes N 110 B3
Kópasker IS 106 B1
Koper SLO 73 D4

Kopervik N 116 A2
Köping S............. 119 D2
Köpingsvik S......... 123 F2
Köpmanholmen S.... 113 D2
Koppang N 111 E4
Kopparberg S......... 119 D2
Kopperby D 50 B2
Koprivnica HR........ 128 A1
Korbach D........... 62 B1
Korçë AL............ 128 B3
Korčula HR.......... 128 A2
Korčula HR.......... 128 A2
Kórfos GR............ 97 E1
Korgen N 107 E3
Koria FIN............ 121 E3
Korifássi GR 96 B3
Koríkio Ándro GR ... 93 E3
Kórimvos GR 91 E1
Koríni GR 93 F4
Korinós GR 88 A3
Korínthio
  (Dióriga) GR........ 93 F4
Kórinthos GR......... 93 F4
Korissía GR 98 A1
Korissós GR 87 E2
Koríthi GR........... 92 A4
Korkeakangas FIN 115 F4
Körmend H.......... 69 E3
Korneuburg A........ 65 D4
Kornofoléa GR 91 E2
Kornwestheim D 66 B1
Koróna GR 88 A1
Koróni GR 96 C3
Korónia GR 93 F1
Koronída GR.......... 99 D2
Koronissía GR 92 B2
Kóronos GR.......... 99 D2
Koronoúda GR 88 B1
Koropí GR............ 94 A4
Korosten' UA......... 127 D1
Korostyšiv UA........ 127 D2
Korouoma FIN 114 C3
Korpilahti FIN........ 115 D3
Korpilombolo S....... 108 C2
Korpo / Korppoo FIN. 120 B4
Korsberga S.......... 123 F1
Korsholm /
  Mustasaari FIN 114 B3
Korsnäs FIN.......... 114 A3
Korsør DK........... 136 C3
Korsun'-
  Ševčenkivs'kyj UA . 127 D2
Korsvoll N 110 C2
Kortesjärvi FIN 114 B3
Kórthio GR........... 98 C1
Kortrijk B 15 F4

Kournás GR............ 100 B3
Kouroúta GR........ 96 B1
Koutselió GR........ 87 D4
Koutsó GR............ 89 F1
Koutsóhero GR...... 87 F4
Kouvola FIN........ 121 E3
Kovel' UA.......... 126 D4
Kovero FIN........ 115 F3
Köyliö FIN........ 120 B3
Kozáni GR.......... 87 F3
Kozel'sk RUS...... 125 F3
Kozina SLO........ 73 D3
Kozjatyn UA........ 127 D2
Kragenæs DK...... 122 C4
Kragerø N.......... 116 C2
Kragujevac YU...... 128 B2
Krakhella N........ 110 A4
Kraków PL.......... 126 A2
Kraljevo YU........ 128 B2
Kramfors S........ 112 C2
Kranenburg D...... 55 D4
Kraniá GR.......... 87 E4
Kraniá GR.......... 87 E4
Kraniá Elassónas GR. 87 F4
Kranichfeld D...... 63 D1
Kranídi GR.......... 97 E2
Kranj SLO.......... 73 D2
Kranjska Gora SLO... 73 D2
Kráslava LV........ 124 C2
Krasnohrad UA...... 127 F2
Krasnoperekops'k UA 127 F4
Krasnyj Cholm RUS... 125 F1
Krasnystaw PL...... 126 B2
Kraśnik PL.......... 126 B2
Kráthio GR.......... 93 E4
Krátigos GR........ 95 F2
Krauchenwies D..... 66 C2
Krautheim D........ 62 C4
Krefeld D.......... 61 E1
Kremastí GR........ 97 E3
Kremastí GR........ 103 F2
Kremastón
  (Teh. L.) GR........ 92 C2
Kremenčuk UA...... 127 F2
Kremenec' UA...... 126 C2
Kremmen D.......... 51 F4
Kremnica SK........ 126 A3
Krems a. d. Donau A.. 65 D4
Kremsmünster A..... 68 B1
Krestcy RUS........ 125 E1
Kréstena GR........ 96 B1
Kreuth D.......... 67 E2
Kreuzlingen CH...... 66 B3
Kreuztal D.......... 62 A1
Kría Vríssi GR...... 88 A2
Kría Vríssi GR...... 94 A3
Krieglach A........ 69 D2
Kriens CH.......... 66 B4
Kríkelo GR.......... 93 D2
Kríkelos GR........ 92 B2
Krimml A.......... 67 F3
Krimpen
  aan den IJssel NL .. 54 B4
Krinídes GR........ 89 D1
Krionéri GR........ 96 B2
Krionéri GR........ 88 B2
Krionéri GR........ 93 E2
Kriopigí GR........ 88 C4
Kristalopigí GR...... 87 D2
Kristdala S........ 123 F1
Kristiansand N...... 116 B3
Kristianstad S...... 123 E3
Kristiansund N...... 110 C1
Kristineberg S...... 108 A4
Kristinehamn S...... 118 C2
Kristinehov S...... 123 E3
Kristinestad /
  Kristiinan-
  kaupunki FIN........ 120 B2
Krithéa GR.......... 88 B2
Kríti (Nissí) GR 100 A2
Kritinía GR........ 103 E2
Kritsá GR.......... 101 E4
Kriva Palanka MK... 128 C3
Krk HR............ 73 E4
Krka SLO.......... 73 E3
Krnov CZ.......... 65 E1
Krokeés GR........ 97 D3
Krokeide N........ 116 A1
Krokek S.......... 119 D3
Krokílio GR........ 93 D3
Krokom S.......... 112 B2
Krókos GR.......... 87 F3
Kroksjö S.......... 112 C1
Krolevec' UA...... 127 F1
Kroměříž CZ........ 65 E3
Kronach D.......... 63 D2
Kronoby /
  Kruunupyy FIN...... 114 B3
Kronshagen D...... 50 B2
Kronštadt RUS...... 124 C1
Kropp D............ 50 B2

Kroppenstedt D...... 57 D3
Krosno PL.......... 126 B2
Krosno Odrzańskie PL 58 B3
Krotoszyn PL........ 59 E3
Kroussónas GR...... 101 D4
Krško SLO.......... 73 F3
Krün D............ 67 E3
Kruiningen NL...... 17 E1
Krujë AL.......... 128 B3
Krumbach
  (Schwaben) D 67 D1
Krumpendorf A...... 68 B4
Kruså DK.......... 122 B4
Kruševac YU........ 128 B2
Kryčaǔ BY.......... 125 E4
Krynica PL.......... 126 B3
Kryvyj Rih UA...... 127 F3
Kröpelin D.......... 51 D2
Ktísmata GR........ 86 C4
Kuchl A............ 68 A2
Kudowa-Zdrój PL... 65 D1
Külsheim D........ 62 C3
Künzelsau D........ 62 C4
Kufstein A........ 67 F2
Kuhmalahti FIN...... 120 C2
Kuhmo FIN........ 115 F2
Kuhmoinen FIN...... 121 D2
Kuivajärvi FIN...... 115 F1
Kuivalahti FIN...... 120 B3
Kuivaniemi FIN...... 109 D3
Kuivasjärvi FIN...... 120 B2
Kukës AL.......... 128 B3
Kukko FIN.......... 114 C3
Kula BG.......... 128 C2
Kula TR............ 129 F4
Kuldīga LV........ 124 A3
Kulennoinen FIN.... 121 F2
Kulju FIN.......... 120 C3
Kullaa FIN........ 120 B3
Kulm CH............ 23 F4
Kulmbach D........ 63 E2
Kuloharju FIN...... 109 E2
Kultakero FIN...... 109 E2
Kumanovo MK...... 128 B3
Kumla S.......... 119 D3
Kumlinge FIN...... 120 A4
Kummavuopio S..... 104 C3
Kumrovec SLO...... 73 F2
Kungälv S.......... 118 B4
Kungsbacka S...... 118 B4
Kungshamn S...... 118 A3
Kungsör S.......... 119 D2
Kunrau D.......... 57 D2
Kunszentmárton H.. 126 B4
Kuolio FIN........ 109 F3
Kuopio FIN........ 115 E3
Kuoresvesi FIN...... 120 C2
Kuortane FIN...... 114 C3
Kuortti FIN........ 121 D2
Kupferzell D........ 62 C4
Kuressaare EST...... 124 B2
Kurikka FIN........ 114 B4
Kuršėnai LT........ 124 B3
Kursk RUS.......... 125 F4
Kursu FIN.......... 109 E2
Kurtakko FIN...... 108 C1
Kuru FIN.......... 120 C2
Kuşadası TR........ 129 E4
Kusel D............ 23 E1
Küsnacht CH........ 23 F4
Küssnacht CH...... 66 B3
Kustavi FIN........ 120 B4
Kütahya TR........ 129 F3
Kutina HR.......... 128 A1
Kutná Hora CZ...... 64 C2
Kutno PL.......... 126 A1
Kuttanen FIN...... 105 D4
Kuttura FIN........ 105 E2
Kuumu FIN........ 115 E1
Kuusamo FIN...... 109 F3
Kuusankoski FIN... 121 E3
Kuusjärvi FIN...... 75 E3
Kuusjoki FIN........ 120 C4
Kuvšinovo RUS...... 125 E2
Kuzma SLO.......... 73 F1
Kvænangsbotn N... 104 C2
Kværndrup DK...... 122 B3
Kvalsund N........ 105 D1
Kvalvåg N.......... 110 C2
Kvam N............ 111 D3
Kvanndal N........ 116 B1
Kvanne N.......... 110 C2
Kvernes N.......... 110 C2
Kvevlax N.......... 114 B3
Kvikkjokk S........ 108 A2
Kvikne N.......... 111 D2
Kvinesdal N........ 116 B3
Kviteseid N........ 116 C2
Kwidzyn PL........ 124 A4
Kyïv UA.......... 127 E2
Kyläinpää FIN...... 114 B3
Kylänlahti FIN...... 115 F2

Kyleakin GB.......... 6 B4
Kylerhea GB.......... 6 B4
Kylestrome GB...... 6 C3
Kyllburg D.......... 61 E3
Kylmäkoski FIN...... 120 C3
Kylmälä FIN........ 115 D1
Kyritz D.......... 51 E4
Kyrksæterøra /
  Hemme N.......... 111 D2
Kyröskoski FIN...... 120 C3
Kyyjärvi FIN........ 114 C3

L, LL

La Caletta I.......... 78 A4
La Maddalena I...... 78 A3
La Spezia I.......... 75 E2
La Sterza I.......... 75 F3
La Verna I.......... 76 B3
La Villa / Stern I.... 67 F4
Laa an der Thaya A.. 65 D4
Laage D............ 51 E3
Labacolla E........ 32 B3
Labajos E.......... 42 A1
Labasheeda IRL.... 4 B2
Labastida E........ 36 C2
Labastide-Murat F.... 29 E1
Labastide-
  Rouairoux F 29 F3
Laboe D............ 50 C2
Labouheyre F........ 28 B2
Labrit F............ 28 B2
Labruguière F...... 29 F3
Lacalahorra E...... 48 B3
Lacanau F.......... 24 B4
Lacanau-Océan F.... 24 B4
Lacapelle-Marival F.. 29 E1
Lacaune F.......... 29 F2
Lacco Ameno I...... 79 F3
Lacedonia I........ 80 B2
Läckö S.......... 118 C3
Laconi I.......... 82 B3
Lacq F............ 28 B3
Ladbergen D........ 55 E3
Ládi GR............ 91 E1
Ladispoli I........ 79 D2
Ladoeiro P........ 41 D2
Lærdalsøyri N...... 110 C4
Lærma GR.......... 103 F2
Laferté-sur-Amance F 22 C4
Laffrey F.......... 27 D4
Láfka GR.......... 97 D1
Láfkos GR.......... 93 F2
Lafrançaise F...... 29 E2
Lagan S.......... 123 B4
Laganás GR........ 96 A1
Lagartera E........ 41 F2
Lage D............ 55 F4
Laggan GB.......... 8 C1
Laginá GR.......... 88 B2

Laginá GR.......... 91 E2
Lagnieu F.......... 27 D3
Lagny-sur-Marne F... 21 F2
Lago I............ 83 E2
Lagoa I............ 46 A2
Lagoaça P........ 35 D4
Lagonegro I........ 80 C4
Lagoníssi GR........ 98 A1
Lagos P............ 46 A2
Lágos GR.......... 89 F1
Lagrasse F........ 29 F3
Laguarres E........ 38 A3
Laguarta E........ 28 C4
Laguépie F........ 29 F2
Laguiole F........ 30 A1
Laguna de Duero E... 36 A3
Lahanás GR........ 88 B1
Lahinch /
  An Leacht IRL...... 4 B2
Lahnstein D........ 61 F2
Laholm S.......... 123 D2
Lahr D............ 23 F3
Lahti FIN.......... 121 D3
Laichingen D........ 66 C1
Laignes F.......... 22 B4
Laigueglia I........ 74 C3
Laihia FIN.......... 114 B3
Laïliás GR.......... 88 C1
Laimbach A........ 68 C1
Laimoluokta S...... 104 C4
Lainate I.......... 71 D4
Lairg GB.......... 7 D3
Laissac F.......... 30 A1
Laïsta GR.......... 87 D4
Laisvall S........ 107 F3
Laitikkala FIN...... 120 C3
Laitila FIN........ 120 B3
Láka GR.......... 92 A1
Láki GR.......... 100 B3
Lakí GR.......... 99 F2
Lákoma GR........ 91 D3
Lákones GR........ 86 B4
Lakópetra GR...... 92 C4
Lakselv N.......... 105 D2
Lálas GR.......... 96 B1
Lalbenque F........ 29 E1
Lalín E.......... 32 B3
Lalinde F.......... 29 D1
Laliótis GR........ 93 E4
Lalm N............ 111 D3
Lalouvesc F........ 26 C4
Lalueza E.......... 38 A3
Lam D............ 64 A4
Lama dei Peligni I.. 79 F1
Lamalou-les-Bains F. 30 A1
Lamarche F........ 22 C3
Lamarque F........ 24 B4
Lamastre F........ 26 C4
Lambach A........ 68 B1
Lamballe F........ 19 D2
Lambesc F........ 31 D2
Lámbia GR........ 96 C1

Lambíri GR........ 93 D3
Lámbou Míli GR.... 95 F2
Lambrecht D........ 23 F1
Lamego P.......... 34 C4
Lamia GR.......... 93 E2
Lamlash GB.......... 3 F1
Lammhult S........ 123 E1
Lammi FIN........ 121 D3
Lamotte-Beuvron F .. 21 E4
Lampaul F.......... 18 A2
Lampedusa I........ 84 A4
Lampertheim D...... 23 F1
Lampeter / Llanbedr Pont
  Steffan GB........ 12 C1
Lamstedt D........ 50 B3
Lamure-
  sur-Azergues F..... 26 C3
Lana I............ 67 E4
Lanaja E.......... 37 F3
Lanaken B........ 17 F2
Lanark GB.......... 9 D3
Lancaster GB...... 10 C2
Lanchester GB...... 9 E4
Lanciano I........ 80 A1
Landau i. d. Pfalz D... 23 F1
Landau a. d. Isar D.... 67 F1
Landeck A........ 67 D3
Landerneau F...... 18 B2
Landete E.......... 43 E2
Landévennec F...... 18 B3
Landivisiau F...... 18 B2
Landivy F.......... 19 E2
Landmannalauger IS. 106 B2
Landquart CH...... 66 C4
Landrecies F........ 17 D3
Landriano I........ 71 D4
Landsberg D........ 57 E4
Landsberg a. Lech D. 67 D2
Landshut D........ 67 F1
Landskrona S...... 123 D3
Landstuhl D........ 23 E1
Landverk S........ 112 A2
Lanersbach A...... 67 E3
Lanesborough IRL .. 2 C4
Langáda GR........ 97 D3
Langáda GR........ 95 F3
Langadás GR...... 88 B2
Langa de Duero E .. 36 C3
Langádia GR........ 96 C1
Langadíkia GR...... 88 B3
Langangen N........ 117 D2
Langeais F........ 20 C4
Längelmäki FIN.... 120 C2
Langelsheim D...... 56 C3
Langen D.......... 62 B3
Langen D.......... 50 A3
Langenargen D...... 66 C2
Langenau D........ 66 C1
Langenberg D...... 63 E1
Langenbruck D...... 67 E1
Langenburg D...... 62 C4
Langenfeld D........ 61 F1

Langenhagen D.... 56 B3
Langenhahn D...... 62 A2
Langenlois A........ 65 D4
Langenthal CH...... 23 F4
Langenwang A...... 69 D2
Langenzenn D...... 63 D3
Langeoog D........ 55 E1
Långeserud S...... 118 B2
Langeskov DK...... 122 C3
Langesund N........ 117 D2
Langevåg N........ 116 A1
Langevåg N........ 110 B2
Langfjord N........ 104 C20
Langhirano I........ 75 F1
Langholm GB........ 9 D4
Langnau
  im Emmental CH ... 27 F1
Langogne F........ 30 B1
Langon F.......... 28 C1
Langres F.......... 22 C4
Langrune-sur-Mer F.. 19 F1
Långsele S........ 112 C2
Långshyttan S...... 119 D1
Långträsk S........ 108 B4
Lanjarón E........ 48 B3
Lanke D.......... 51 F4
Länkipohja FIN...... 120 C2
Lanmeur F.......... 18 B2
Lannemezan F...... 29 D3
Lannilis F.......... 18 B2
Lannion F.......... 18 C2
Lanouaille F........ 25 E4
Lans-en-Vercors F.. 27 D4
Lanslebourg-
  Mont-Cenis F...... 27 E4
Lanta F............ 29 E3
Lantejuela (La) E.... 47 E2
Lantosque F........ 31 F2
Lanusei I.......... 82 C3
Lanvollon F........ 18 C2
Lanzahita E........ 42 A2
Lanzo Torinese I.... 27 F4
Laon F............ 17 D4
Lapalisse F........ 26 B2
Lápas GR.......... 92 C4
Laperdiguera E.... 38 A3
Lapinjärvi /
  Lappträsk FIN.... 121 D3
Lapinlahti FIN...... 115 E3
Lapleau F.......... 25 F4
Laplume F.......... 29 D2
Lapoutroie F...... 23 E3
Lappajärvi FIN...... 114 C3
Lappalaisten-
  Kesätuvat FIN.... 105 D3
Lappea FIN........ 108 C2
Lappeenranta FIN.. 121 E3
Lappfjärd /
  Lapväärtti FIN.... 120 B3
Lappfors FIN...... 114 B3
Lappi FIN.......... 120 B3
Lappohja FIN...... 120 C4

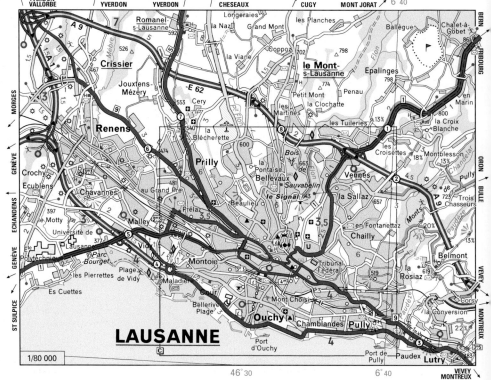

LAUSANNE

1/80 000

Lappträsk *S* 108 C3	Laruns *F* 28 C4	Laudio/Llodio *E*....... 36 C1	Lautenthal *D* 56 C4	Lavinio-Lido di Enea *I* .. 79 D2	Leciñena *E*.............. 37 F3
Lapua *FIN* 114 B3	Larv *S* 118 B3	Lauenau *D*............ 56 B3	Lauterbach *D*.......... 62 B2	Lavis *I*.................... 71 F3	Leck *D*.................. 50 A2
L'Aquila *I* 79 E1	Larvik *N*............... 117 D2	Lauenburg *D* 50 C4	Lauterbourg *F*........ 23 F2	Lavit-de-Lomagne *F*.. 29 D2	Les Lecques *F*........ 31 D3
Laracha *E*............. 32 B2	Lasalle *F* 30 B2	Lauenstein *CH*....... 27 E1	Lauterbrunnen *CH* 27 F1	Låvong *N*............... 107 D3	Lectoure *F*.............. 29 D2
Laragh *IRL* 5 E2	Lasarte *E*.............. 28 A3	Lauf a. d. Pegnitz *D* ... 63 E1	Lauterecken *D* 23 E1	Lavoûte-Chilhac *F*.... 26 A4	Ledanca *E* 42 C1
Laragne-Montéglin *F* .. 31 D1	Laško *SLO*............ 73 E2	Laufen *D*.............. 68 A2	Lautrec *F* 29 F2	Lavre *P*................. 40 B3	Ledaña *E*................ 43 E3
Lärbro *S* 119 F4	Lassan *D*.............. 51 F2	Laufen *CH*............ 23 E4	Lauvstad *N*.......... 110 B3	Lávrio *GR* 98 A3	Ledbury *GB*............ 13 E1
Larche *F* 31 E1	Lassay-les-Châteaux *F* .. 19 F3	Laufenburg *D* 23 F4	Lauvvik *N*........... 116 A2	Laxå *S*................. 118 C3	Ledesma *E* 35 E4
Larche *F* 25 E4	Lassigny *F*............ 16 C4	Laufenburg *CH* 23 F4	Lauzerte *F*............ 29 D2	Laxe *E*.................. 32 A2	Lédignan *F* 30 B2
Larderello *I*............ 76 A4	Lassíthi *GR* 101 E4	Lauffen a. Neckar *D* .. 62 B4	Le Lauzet-Ubaye *F*.... 31 E1	Laxford Bridge *GB*.... 6 C2	Ledmore *GB*............ 6 C3
Lárdos *GR* 103 F2	Lastovo *HR* 128 A2	Laugafell *IS*.......... 106 B1	Lauzun *F*............... 29 D1	Laxo *GB* 7 F3	Leeds *GB*.............. 11 D2
Laredo *E*............... 36 C1	Laugar *IS* 106 A1	Laugar *IS*............ 106 A1	Lavagna *I*............... 75 E2	Layos *E* 42 B2	Leek *GB* 11 D3
Laren *NL* 54 C3	Lastra a Signa *I* 76 A3	Laugarbakki *IS*...... 106 A1	Laval *F*................ 19 F3	Laza *E*.................. 32 C4	Leenane *IRL* 2 A3
Largentière *F*........ 30 B1	Lastres *E*.............. 33 F2	Laugarvatn *IS*....... 106 A2	Lavamünd *A* 68 C3	Lazise *I*................. 71 F4	Leer *D*.................. 55 E2
Largs *GB* 8 B3	Lastrup *D*............. 55 F2	Lauingen *D*.......... 67 D1	Lavangen *N*......... 104 B3	Leadenham *GB* 11 E3	Leerdam *NL* 54 C4
Lárimna *GR* 93 F3	Latarza *I*.............. 81 D3	Laujar de Andarax *E* .. 48 C3	Lávara *GR*............ 91 E1	Lebach *D* 23 D1	Leese *D* 56 B3
Larino *I*................ 80 A1	Lathen *D*.............. 55 E2	Laukaa *FIN*........... 115 D4	Lavardac *F* 29 D2	Lebedyn *UA* 127 F1	Leeuwarden *NL* 54 C2
Lárissa *GR* 88 A4	Latheron *GB*.......... 7 E3	Lauksundskaret *N* ... 104 C2	Lavaur *F*.............. 29 E2	Lebenstedt *D*......... 56 C3	Lefkáda *GR* 92 A2
Larmor-Plage *F* 18 C4	Latiano *I*.............. 81 E3	Launceston *GB*....... 12 C3	Lavelanet *F* 29 E4	Lebesby *N*............ 105 E1	Lefkáda (Nissí) *GR* ... 92 A2
Larne *GB*............... 3 E2	Latikberg *S*.......... 107 F4	Laupheim *D*.......... 66 C2	Lavello *I*.............. 80 C2	Lebrija *E* 47 D3	Lefkádia *GR*........... 87 F2
Lárnaka *GR* 93 F3	Latina *I*............... 79 E2	Lauragh *IRL* 4 A3	Lavelsloh *D*........... 55 F3	Lebus *D*................ 58 A2	Lefkadíti *GR* 93 D3
Larino *I*................ 80 A1	Latisana *I*............ 72 C3	Laureana di Borrello *I* .. 83 E3	Lavenham *GB* 15 D2	Lecce *I* 81 F3	Lefkandí *GR* 94 A3
Laroche-d'Olmes *F*... 29 E4	Lató *GR* 101 E4	Laurencekirk *GB* 9 E1	Laveno Monbello *I* ... 71 D4	Lecco *I* 71 D4	Léfkara *GR* 87 F3
Laroque-Timbaut *F*... 29 D1	Latour-de-France *F*.... 29 F4	Laurenzana *I*......... 80 C3	Lavéra *F* 30 C3	Lécera *E* 37 F4	Léfkes *GR* 98 C2
Laroquebrou *F*....... 25 F4	Latronico *I*........... 80 C4	Lauria *I*............... 80 C4	Lavia *FIN* 120 B2	Lech *A* 67 D3	Lefkími *GR* 91 E2
Larraga *E* 28 A4	Latronquière *F*....... 29 F1	Laurière *F* 25 E3	Laviano *I* 80 B3	La Léchère *F*.......... 27 E2	Lefkógia *GR* 90 A4
Larseng *N* 104 B3	Lauchhammer *D*...... 58 A4	Lausanne *CH* 27 E2	Lavik *N*................ 110 A4	Lechlade *GB* 13 F1	Lefkopigí *GR*.......... 87 F3
Larsmo / Luoto *FIN* ... 114 B3	Lauder *GB* 9 E1	Lauta *D* 58 A4			Léfktra *GR* 93 F4

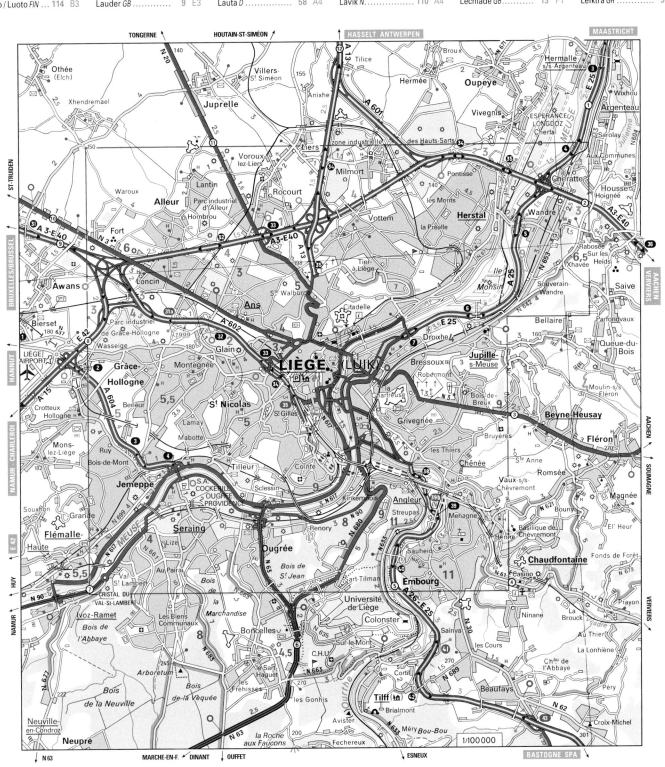

Legan D.	50	B2	Leirpollskogen N	105	F1	Lempdes-sur-Alagnon F	26	A4	Léoncel F	26	C4	Lesina I	80	B1	Leuze-en-Hainaut B	17	D2

Legan D. 50 B2
Leganés E 42 B2
Legé F. 24 A1
Legnago I 72 A4
Legnano I 71 D4
Legnica PL 58 C4
Legrená GR 98 A1
Léguevin F 29 E3
Legutiano / Villarreal E 37 D1
Lehená GR 92 B4
Lehmden D 50 A4
Lehnin D 57 F3
Léhovo GR 87 E2
Lehrberg D 63 D4
Lehre D 56 C3
Lehrte D 56 C3
Lehtimäki FIN 114 C3
Lehtovaara FIN 109 D1
Leibnitz A 69 D3
Leicester GB 11 E4
Leiden NL 54 B3
Leighton Buzzard GB . 14 B2
Leikanger N 110 B4
Leiknes N 104 A4
Leinefelde D 56 C4
Leinì I 27 F4
Leipheim D 67 D1
Leipzig D 57 E4
Leira N 110 C2
Leira N 111 D4
Leirbotn N 105 D2
Leiria P. 40 B2
Leiro E 32 B4

Leirpollskogen N 105 F1
Leirvåg N 110 A4
Leirvik DK 106 A3
Leirvik N 107 E3
Leirvik N 116 A1
Leirvik N 110 A4
Leisnig D 57 F4
Léndas GR 101 D4
Lendava SLO 73 F1
Lendinara I 76 A1
Lengefeld D 63 F1
Lengenfeld D 63 E1
Lengerich D 55 E3
Lenggries D 67 E2
Lenhovda S 123 F2
Lenk CH 27 F2
Lennestadt D 62 A1
Lens F 16 C2
Lensahn D 50 C2
Lentföhrden D 50 B3
Lenti H 69 E3
Lenting D 63 E4
Lentini I 85 E3
Lenzburg CH 23 F4
Lenzen D 51 D4
Lenzerheide / Lai CH . 66 C4
Lenzkirch D 23 F3
Lemgo D 56 B3
Lemland FIN 120 A4
Lemmenjoki FIN 115 E1
Lemmer NL 54 C2
Lemonodássos GR 97 F1
Lempäälä FIN 120 C3

Lempdes-sur-Alagnon F 26 A4
Lemvig DK 122 A2
Lenart SLO 73 F1
Lencloître F 25 D1
Lend A 68 A3
Léndas GR 101 D4
Leoncel F 26 C4
Leondári GR 96 C2
Leondári GR 93 D1
Leóndio GR 97 D1
Leonessa I 76 C4
Leonforte I 85 D3
Leonídio GR 97 E2
Leopoldsburg B 17 F1
Leopoldsdorf im Marchfelde A 69 E1
Leova MOL 127 E4
Lepe E 46 C2
Lepel' BY 125 D3
Lepenoú GR 92 C2
Lépoura GR 94 B3
Leppäjärvi FIN 105 D4
Leppävirta FIN 115 E3
Leptokariá GR 88 A3
Leptokariá GR 91 D2
Lercara Friddi I 84 C3
Léré F 21 F4
Lerici I 75 E2
Lérida / Lleida E 38 B4
Lerín E 28 A4
Lerma E 36 B3
Lermoos A 67 D3
Lérni GR 97 D1
Léros (Nissí) GR 99 F2
Lerum S 118 B4
Lerwick GB 7 F3
Les E 29 D4
Lescar F 28 C3
Lesce SLO 73 D2
Lescun F 28 B4

Lesina I 80 B1
Lesja N 110 C3
Lesjöfors S 118 C2
Leskovac YU 128 C2
Lesneven F 18 B2
Lesparre-Médoc F 24 B4
Lessay F 19 E1
Lessebo S 123 F2
Lessines B 17 D2
Lessíni GR 92 B3
Lestelle-Bétharram F . 28 C3
Lestijärvi FIN 114 C3
Lésvos (Nissí) GR 95 F1
Letchworth GB 14 C2
Letenye H 69 E3
Letino I 80 A2
Letmathe D 61 F1
Letterfrack IRL 2 A3
Letterkenny / Leitir Ceanainn IRL 2 C1
Lettermullan / Leitir Mealláin IRL 2 A4
Letur E 49 D1
Letus SLO 73 E2
Letzlingen D 57 D3
Leuchars GB 9 D2
Leukerbad CH 27 F2
Leuna D 57 E4
Leutenberg D 63 D3
Leutershausen D 63 D4
Leutkirch D 66 C2
Leutschach A 69 D3
Leuven B 17 E2

Leuze-en-Hainaut B .. 17 D2
Levajok N 105 E2
Levanger N 111 E1
Levanto I 75 C2
Leväsjoki FIN 120 B2
Leven GB 11 E2
Leven GB 9 D2
Levene S 118 B3
Levens F 31 F2
Leverano I 81 F3
Leverburgh GB 6 A3
Leverkusen D 61 F2
Levet F 25 F1
Levice SK 126 A3
Levico Terme I 72 A3
Levídi GR 96 C1
Levie F 78 A4
Levier F 27 D1
Levítha (Nissí) GR ... 99 F3
Levoča SK 126 B3
Levroux F 25 E1
Lewes GB 14 C4
Leyburn GB 11 D1
Leyland GB 10 C2
Leysdown-on-Sea GB ... 15 D3
Leysin CH 27 E2
Lézardrieux F 18 C2
Lézat-sur-Lèze F 29 E3
Lezay F 24 C2
Lezhë AL 128 B3
Lézignan-Corbières F . 30 A3
Lezoux F 26 A3
Lezuza E 43 D4
Lębork PL 53 D1

Lille

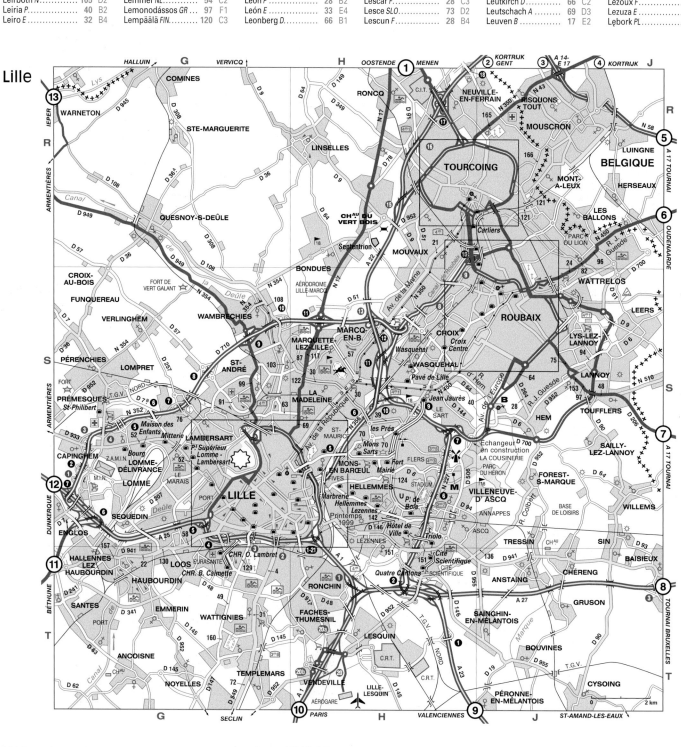

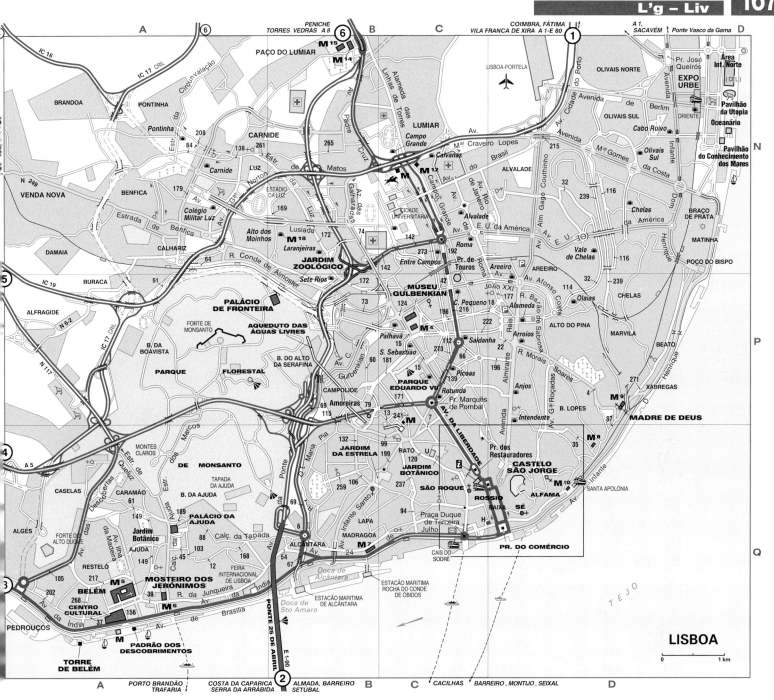

LISBOA

0 — 1 km

L'gov RUS............ 125 F2
Liabygda N........... 110 C3
Lianokládi GR........ 93 E2
Liberec CZ........... 64 B1
Libourne F........... 24 C4
Librilla E........... 49 E2
Licata I............. 84 C4
Licciana Nardi I..... 75 E2
Lich D............... 62 B2
Lichfield GB......... 11 D4
Lichoslavl' RUS...... 125 D2
Lichtenberg D........ 63 E2
Lichtenfels D........ 63 D2
Lichtenstein D....... 63 F1
Lichtenvoorde NL..... 55 D4
Lida BY.............. 124 C4
Liden S.............. 112 C1
Lidhult S............ 123 D2
Lidingö S............ 119 E2
Lidköping S.......... 118 B3
Lido degli Estensi I. 76 B1
Lido delle Nazioni I. 76 B1
Lido di Camaiore I... 75 F3
Lido di Classe I..... 76 B2
Lido di Jesolo I..... 72 B4
Lido
 di Metaponto I..... 81 D3
Lido di Ostia I...... 79 D2
Lido di Savio I...... 76 B2
Lido di Spina I...... 76 B1
Lido di Torre Mileto I. 80 B1
Lido di Venezia I.... 72 B4
Lido Silvana I....... 81 E3
Lidoríki GR.......... 93 D3

Lidzbark
 Warmiński PL....... 124 A4
Liebenwalde D........ 51 F4
Lieberose D.......... 58 A3
Lieksa FIN........... 115 F2
Liège B.............. 17 F2
Liège-Bierset B...... 17 F2
Lienen D............. 17 E1
Lienz A.............. 68 A3
Liepāja LV........... 124 A3
Liérganes E.......... 36 B1
Liernais F........... 26 B1
Liestal CH........... 23 E4
Lieto FIN............ 120 B4
Liétor E............. 49 D1
Lieurey F............ 16 A4
Lievestuore FIN...... 115 D4
Liévin F............. 16 C2
Liezen A............. 68 B2
Liffol-le-Grand F.... 22 C3
Lifford IRL.......... 2 C2
Liffré F............. 19 E3
Ligiá GR............. 92 B4
Lignano Pineta I..... 72 C3
Lignano Sabbiadoro I. 72 C3
Lignières F.......... 25 F1
Ligny-en-Barrois F... 22 C2
Ligny-le-Châtel F.... 22 A4
Ligourió GR.......... 97 E1
Ligueil F............ 25 D1
Liháda GR............ 93 F2
Liikasenvaara FIN.... 109 F2
Likenäs S............ 118 C1
Likófos GR........... 91 E2

Likoporiá GR......... 93 E4
Likórahi GR.......... 87 D3
Likóstomo GR......... 89 E1
Likouría GR.......... 96 C1
Liland N............. 104 A4
Lilea GR............. 93 E3
Lilienfeld A......... 69 D1
Liljendal FIN........ 121 D3
Lilla Edet S......... 118 B3
Lillby FIN........... 114 B3
Lille F.............. 15 F4
Lillebonne F......... 16 A4
Lillehammer N........ 111 D4
Lillerød DK.......... 123 D3
Lillers F............ 16 C2
Lillesand N.......... 116 C3
Lillestrøm N......... 117 D1
Lillhärdal S......... 112 A3
Lillholmsjön S....... 112 B1
Lillögda S........... 112 C1
Lima S............... 112 A4
Limáni
 Hersoníssou GR.... 101 E3
Limáni Litohórou GR.. 88 A3
Limavady GB.......... 3 D1
Limbach D............ 63 F1
Limburg a. d. Lahn D. 62 A2
Limenária GR......... 89 E2
Limerick /
 Luimneach IRL..... 4 C2
Limingen N........... 107 E4
Liminka FIN.......... 114 C1
Liminpuro FIN........ 115 D1

Límnes GR............ 97 E1
Límni GR............. 93 F2
Limniá GR............ 89 D1
Limnítsa GR.......... 93 D3
Límnos GR............ 89 F4
Limoges F............ 25 E3
Limogne-
 en-Quercy F....... 29 E1
Limone Piemonte I.... 31 F1
Limonest F........... 26 C3
Limours-
 en-Hurepoix F..... 21 E2
Limoux F............. 29 F3
Linares E............ 48 B1
Linares de Mora E.... 43 F2
Linares de Riofrío E. 41 E1
Linariá GR........... 94 C2
Lincoln GB........... 11 E3
Lindås N............. 110 A4
Lindau
 i. Bodensee D..... 66 C3
Linden D............. 63 D2
Lindenberg
 i. Allgäu D....... 66 C3
Lindern D............ 55 E2
Lindesberg S......... 119 D2
Lindesnes N.......... 116 B3
Lindö S.............. 119 D3
Líndos GR............ 103 F2
Lindoso P............ 32 B4
Lindow D............. 51 F4
Lindsdal S........... 123 F2
Línea de la
 Concepción (La) E. 47 E4

Lingbo S............. 112 C4
Linge N.............. 110 C3
Lingen D............. 55 E3
Linghem S............ 119 D3
Linken D............. 52 A3
Linköping S.......... 119 D2
Linlithgow GB........ 9 D2
Linsell S............ 112 A3
Linslade GB.......... 14 B2
Linthal CH........... 66 C3
Linyola E............ 38 B4
Linz D............... 68 B1
Linz A............... 68 B1
Linz a. Rhein D...... 61 F2
Le Lion-d'Angers F... 19 F4
Lion-sur-Mer F....... 19 F1
Lioni I.............. 80 B3
Lióprasso GR......... 87 F4
Le Lioran F.......... 25 F4
Liperi FIN........... 115 F3
Lipica SLO........... 73 D3
Lippstadt D.......... 55 F4
Lipsí GR............. 99 F2
Lipsí (Nissí) GR..... 99 F2
Liptovský Mikuláš SK. 126 A3
Lírkia GR............ 97 D1
Lisboa P............. 40 A3
Lisburn GB........... 3 E2
Lisdoonvarna /
 Lios Dúin
 Bhearna IRL....... 2 A4
Lisieux F............ 20 C2
Liskeard GB.......... 12 C3

Lisle-sur-Tarn F..... 29 E2
Lismore /
 Lios Mór IRL...... 4 C3
Lisnaskea GB......... 2 C3
Lisse NL............. 54 B3
List D............... 50 A1
Listowel /
 Lios Tuathail IRL. 4 B2
Lit S................ 112 B2
Lit-et-Mixe F........ 28 B2
Lithakiá GR.......... 96 A1
Lithines GR.......... 101 F4
Lithío GR............ 95 F3
Lití GR.............. 88 B2
Litija SLO........... 73 E2
Litóhoro GR.......... 88 A3
Litóhoro GR.......... 88 A3
Litoměřice CZ........ 64 A1
Litomyšl CZ.......... 65 D2
Litschau A........... 64 C4
Littlehampton GB..... 14 B4
Littleport GB........ 11 F4
Livaderó GR.......... 89 D1
Livaderó GR.......... 87 F3
Livádi GR............ 88 B2
Livádi GR............ 98 B2
Livádi GR............ 97 E4
Livádia GR........... 103 D2
Livadiá GR........... 93 F3
Livádítis GR......... 89 E1
Livadohóri GR........ 89 F4
Livanátes GR......... 93 F3
Livarot F............ 20 C2
Liverá GR............ 87 E3

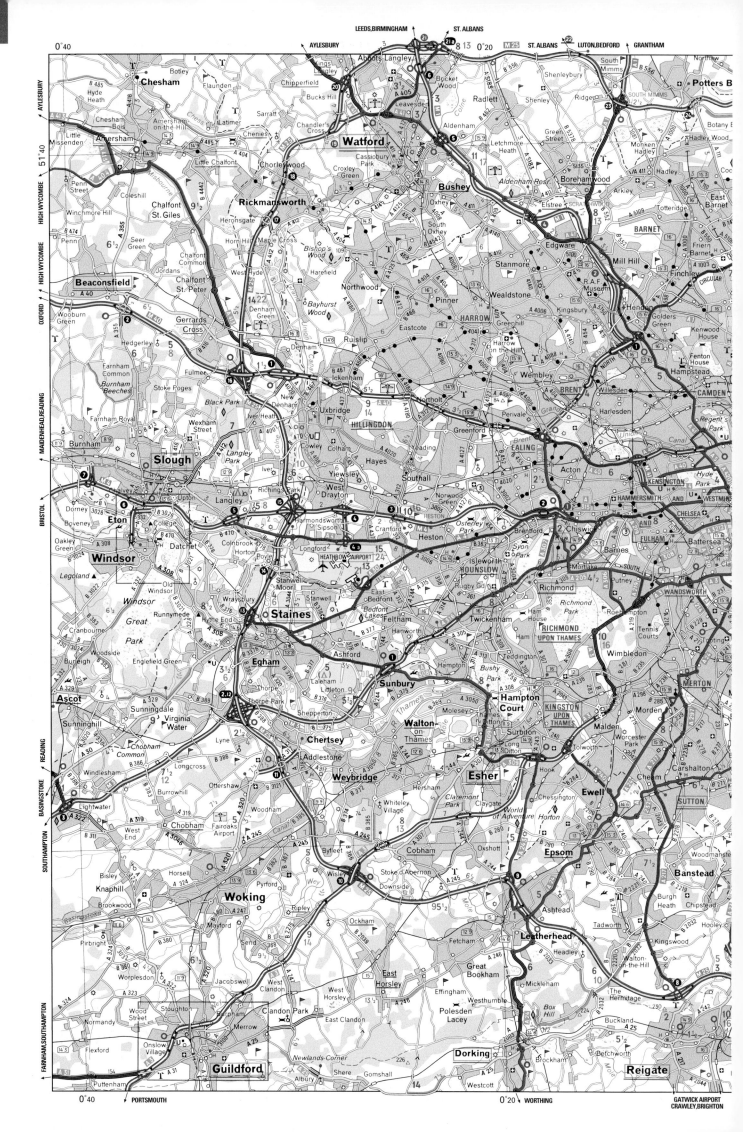

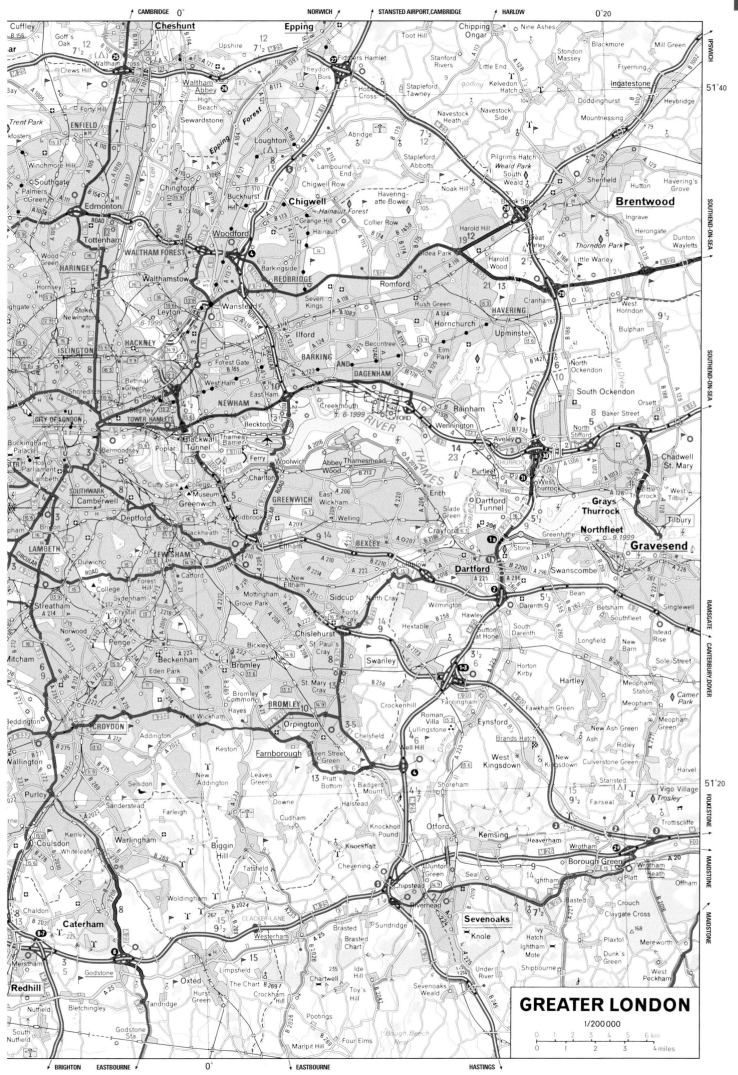

GREATER LONDON

1/200 000

0 1 2 3 4 5 6 km

0   1   2   3   4 miles

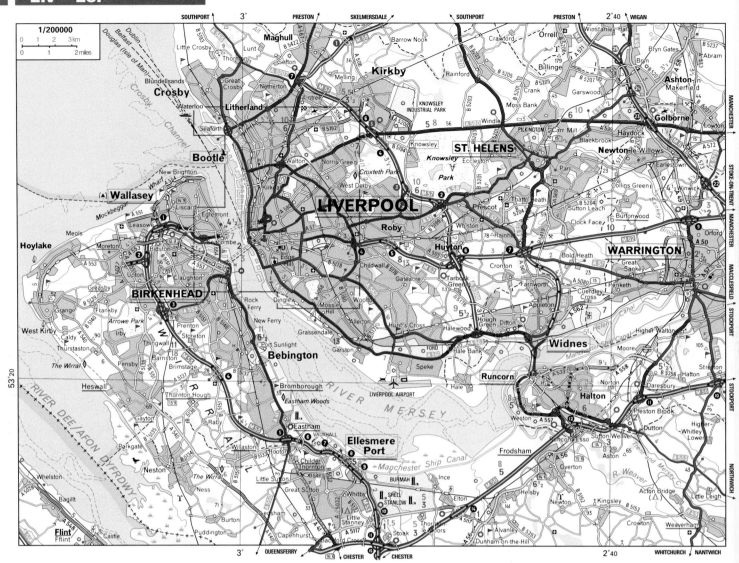

Liverdun *F*	22	C2	Llangefni *GB*	10	A3	Locquirec *F*	18	C2		
Livernon *F*	29	E1	Llangollen *GB*	10	B3	Locri *I*	83	E4		
Liverpool *GB*	10	C3	Llangurig *GB*	10	B4	Locronan *F*	18	B3		
Livigno *I*	67	D4	Llanidloes *GB*	10	B4	Loctudy *F*	18	B3		
Livingston *GB*	9	D3	Llanrhystud *GB*	10	A4	Lodè *I*	78	A4		
Livo *FIN*	109	E3	Llanrwst *GB*	10	B3	Lodève *F*	30	A2		
Livold *SLO*	73	E3	Llanwrtyd			Lodi *I*	71	E4		
Livorno *I*	75	F3	Wells *GB*	13	D1	Løding *N*	107	E2		
Livorno Ferraris *I*	74	C1	Llavorsí *E*	29	E4	Lødingen *N*	104	A4		
Livron-sur-Drôme *F*	30	C1	Lleida / Lérida *E*	38	B4	Lodosa *E*	37	D2		
Lixoúri *GR*	92	A4	Llera *E*	41	E4	Łódź *PL*	126	A1		
Lizard *GB*	12	B4	Llerena *E*	47	E1	Löbau *D*	58	B4		
Lizarra / Estella *E*	28	A4	Lles *E*	38	C2	Löbejün *D*	57	F3		
Lizy *F*	17	D4	Llessui *E*	29	D4	Löbnitz *D*	51	E2		
Lizzano			Llíria *E*	43	F3	Loeches *E*	42	C1		
in Belvedere *I*	76	A2	Lloret de Mar *E*	39	E3	Löcknitz *D*	52	A3		
Ljubašivka *UA*	127	E3	Llosses (Les) *E*	39	D3	Löffingen *D*	23	F3		
Ljubljana *SLO*	73	D3	Llucena *E*	44	A2	Löhne *D*	55	F3		
Ljubno *SLO*	73	E2	Llucmajor *E*	45	E3	Loen *N*	110	B3		
Ljuboml' *UA*	126	C2	Llynclys *GB*	10	C4	Löningen *D*	55	E2		
Ljugarn *S*	119	F4	Loanhead *GB*	9	D3	Lörrach *D*	23	E4		
Ljungby *S*	123	E2	Loano *I*	74	C2	Lößnitz *D*	63	F1		
Ljungbyhed *S*	123	D2	Lobenstein *D*	63	E1	Löwenberg *D*	51	F4		
Ljungdalen *S*	112	A2	Lobón *E*	41	D4	Løfallstrand *N*	116	B1		
Ljungsbro *S*	119	D3	Lobos (Los) *E*	49	D3	Lofário *GR*	91	D2		
Ljungskile *S*	118	B3	Loburg *D*	57	F3	Lofer *A*	67	F2		
Ljusdal *S*	112	B4	Locana *I*	27	F3	Lofsdalen *S*	112	A3		
Ljusne *S*	112	C4	Locarno *CH*	71	D3	Lofthus *N*	116	B1		
Ljutomer *SLO*	73	F2	Lochaline *GB*	8	B1	Loftus *GB*	11	E1		
Llagostera *E*	39	E3	Lochcarron *GB*	6	C4	Log *SLO*	72	C2		
Llanberis *GB*	10	B3	Lochearnhead *GB*	8	C2	Logarska dolina *SLO*	73	D2		
Llançà *E*	39	E2	Lochem *NL*	55	D3	Logroño *E*	37	D2		
Llandeilo *GB*	12	C1	Loches *F*	25	D2	Logrosán *E*	41	F3		
Llandovery /			Lochgelly *GB*	9	D2	Løgstør *DK*	122	B1		
Llanymddyfri *GB*	13	D1	Lochgilphead *GB*	8	B2	Løgten *DK*	122	B2		
Llandrindod			Lochinver *GB*	6	C3	Løgumkloster *DK*	122	A3		
Wells *GB*	13	D1	Lochmaben *GB*	9	D4	Lohals *DK*	122	C3		
Llandudno *GB*	10	B3	Lochmaddy *GB*	6	A3	Lohberg *D*	64	A4		
Llandysul *GB*	12	C1	Lochranza *GB*	8	B3	Lohilahti *FIN*	121	F2		
Llanelli *GB*	12	C1	Lochvycja *UA*	127	F1	Lohiniva *FIN*	109	D2		
Llanerchymedd *GB*	3	F4	Lockenhaus *A*	69	E2	Lohja *FIN*	120	C4		
Llanes *E*	33	F2	Lockerbie *GB*	9	D4	Lohne				
Llanfairfechan *GB*	10	B3	Locle (Le) *CH*	27	E1	(Oldenburg) *D*	55	F2		
Llanfyllin *GB*	10	B4	Locmariaquer *F*	18	C4	Lohr a. Main *D*	62	C3		
Llangadog *GB*	13	D1	Locminé *F*	18	C3	Lohtaja *FIN*	114	C2		
			Locorotondo *I*	81	E3	Loiano *I*	76	A2		

Luxembourg

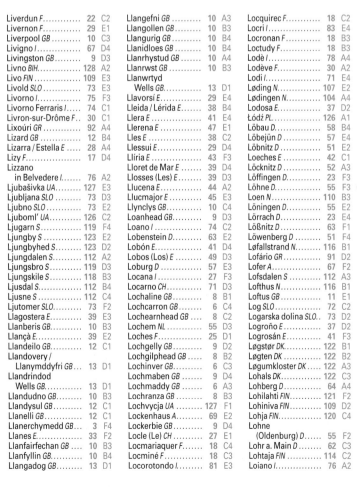

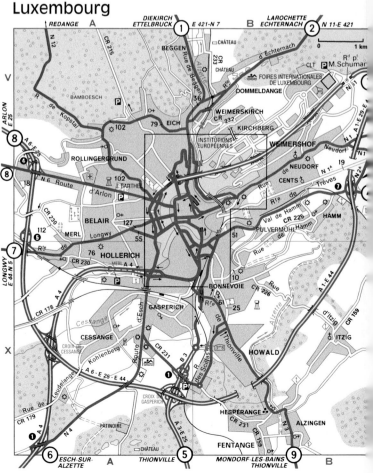

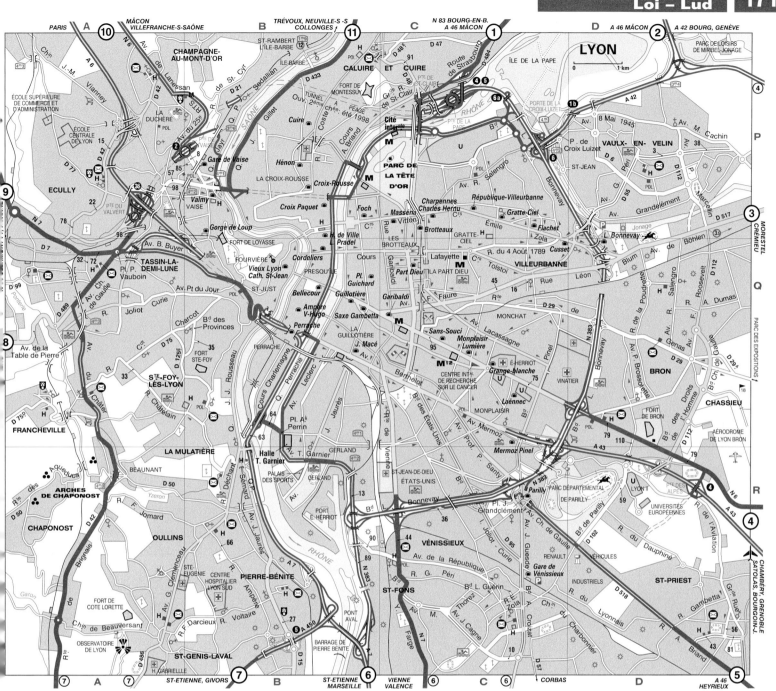

LYON

Loimaa FIN	120	C3
Loimaan kunta FIN	120	C3
Loiri I	78	A4
Loiron F	19	F3
Loitz D	51	F2
Loja E	48	A3
Lojsta S	119	F4
Lokalahti FIN	120	B3
Løken N	117	E2
Lokeren B	17	E1
Lokka FIN	109	E1
Løkken DK	122	B1
Løkken N	111	D2
Lokn'a RUS	125	D2
Lokve SLO	73	D3
Lom BG	128	C2
Lom N	110	C3
Lomazzo I	71	D4
Lombez F	29	D3
Lomello I	75	D1
Lomen N	110	C4
Lomma S	123	D3
Lommatzsch D	57	F4
Lommel B	17	F1
Lomonosov RUS	124	C1
Lompolo FIN	109	D1
Łomża PL	126	A1
Lonato I	71	E4
Londinières F	16	B3
London GB	14	C3
Londonderry GB	3	D1
Long Eaton GB	11	D4
Long Preston GB	10	C2
Long Sutton GB	11	F4

Longá GR	96	C3
Longádes GR	87	D4
Longaníkos GR	96	C3
Longares E	37	E4
Longarone I	67	F4
Longeau F	22	C4
Longford /		
An Longfort IRL	2	C3
Longny-au-Perche F	20	C3
Longobucco I	83	E2
Longós GR	92	A1
Longtown GB	9	D4
Longué F	19	F4
Longueville-		
sur-Scie F	16	A3
Longuyon F	17	F4
Longwy F	22	C1
Lonigo I	72	A4
Lons-le-Saunier F	27	D1
Lönsboda S	123	E2
Lønsdal N	107	F2
Loosdorf A	68	C1
Lopcombe Corner GB	13	F2
Lopera E	48	A1
Loppa N	104	C2
Loppi FIN	120	C3
Lora N	110	C3
Lora del Río E	47	E2
Lorca E	49	D2
Lorcé B	17	F2
Lorch D	62	A3
Lorch D	66	C1
Loreo I	76	B1
Loreto I	77	D3

Loreto Aprutino I	77	E4
Lorgues F	31	E3
Lorica I	83	E2
Lorient F	18	C4
Loriga P	40	C1
Loriol-sur-Drôme F	30	C1
Lormes F	26	B1
Loro Ciuffenna I	76	B3
Le Loroux-		
Bottereau F	24	B1
Lorquin F	23	D2
Lorrez-le-Bocage F	21	F3
Lorris F	21	E4
Los S	112	B4
Losa (La) E	48	C1
Losar de la Vera E	41	F2
Losenstein A	68	B1
Losheim D	23	D1
Lošinj HR	77	E1
Loßburg D	23	F2
Lossiemouth GB	7	E4
Lostwithiel GB	12	C3
Lote N	110	B3
Løten N	111	E4
Löttorp S	123	F1
Loudéac F	18	C3
Loudes F	26	B4
Loudías GR	88	A2
Loudun F	24	C1
Loué F	19	F3
Loughborough GB	11	D4
Loughrea /		
Baile Locha		
Riach IRL	2	B4

Louhans F	26	C2
Louhisaari FIN	120	B3
Louisburgh IRL	2	A3
Loukíssia GR	94	A3
Loulay F	24	C3
Loulé P	46	B2
Louny CZ	64	A2
La Loupe F	21	D3
Lourdes F	28	C3
Loures P	40	A3
Louriçal P	40	B1
Lourinhã P	40	A3
Loúros GR	92	B1
Le Louroux-		
Béconnais F	19	F4
Lousa P	40	A3
Lousã P	40	B1
Lousada P	34	B3
Louth GB	11	F3
Loutrá GR	98	B2
Loutrá GR	96	C1
Loutrá GR	88	C4
Loutrá GR	95	F2
Loutrá Aridéas GR	87	F2
Loutrá Edipsoú GR	93	F2
Loutrá Eleftherón GR	89	D2
Loutrá Ipátis GR	93	D2
Loutrá Kaïtsas GR	93	D2
Loutrá Kilínis GR	92	B4
Loutrá Langadá GR	88	C2
Loutrá Smokóvou GR	93	D2
Loutrá Vólvis GR	88	C2
Loutráki GR	94	A2
Loutráki GR	92	B2

Loutráki GR	93	F4
Loutró Elénis GR	97	E1
Loutropigí GR	93	D2
Loutrópirgos GR	94	A4
Loutrós GR	91	D2
Loútsa GR	92	A1
Loútsa GR	94	B4
Louvain-la-Neuve B	17	E2
Louviére (La) B	17	E2
Louviers F	16	B4
Louvigné-		
du-Désert F	19	E3
Lövänger S	113	E1
Lövberga S	112	B1
Loveč BG	129	D2
Lovere I	71	E4
Loviisa / Lovisa FIN	121	D3
Lovrenc na P. SLO	73	E2
Lövstabruk S	119	E10
Lovund N	107	D2
Low Street GB	15	D1
Lowestoft GB	15	E1
Łowicz PL	126	A1
Loznica YU	128	A1
Lozoyuela E	42	B1
Luanco E	33	E2
Luarca E	33	D2
Lubań PL	58	B4
L'ubercy RUS	125	F2
Lubersac F	25	E2
L'ubim RUS	125	F1
Lubin PL	58	C4
Lublin PL	126	B2

Lubliniec PL	126	A2
Lubmin D	51	F2
Lubny UA	127	F2
Lubrín E	49	D3
Lübtheen D	51	A4
Le Luc F	31	E3
Luc-en-Diois F	31	D1
Luc-sur-Mer F	19	F1
Lucainena		
de las Torres E	48	C3
Lucan IRL	3	D4
Lucca I	75	F3
Luče SLO	73	E2
Lucena E	47	F2
Lucenay-		
l'Évêque F	26	B1
Luceni E	37	E3
Lucera I	80	B2
Luciana E	42	A4
Lucito I	80	A1
Luc'k UA	126	C1
Lucka D	63	E1
Luckau D	58	A3
Luckenwalde D	57	F3
Luçon F	24	B2
Lučenec SK	126	A3
Le Lude F	20	C4
Ludiente E	44	A4
Ludlow GB	10	C4
Ludvika S	119	D1
Ludwigsburg D	66	B1
Ludwigsfelde D	57	F3
Ludwigshafen D	66	B2

Ludwigshafen D 23 F1
Ludwigslust D 51 D4
Ludwigsstadt D 63 D2
Lübars D 57 E3
Lübbecke D 55 F3
Lübben D 58 A3
Lübbenau D 58 A3
Lübbow D 51 D4
Lübeck D 50 C3
Lübz D 51 E3
Lüchow D 51 D4
Lüdenscheid D 61 F1
Lüding-
  hausen D 55 E4
Lügde D 56 B4
Lüneburg D 50 E4
Lünen D 55 E4
Lütjenburg D 50 C2
Lützen D 57 E4
Luga RUS 125 D1
Lugagnano
  Val d'Arda I 75 E1
Lugano CH 71 D3
Lugau D 63 F1
Lugnano
  in Teverina I 79 D1
Lugo E 32 C3
Lugo I 76 B2
Lugoj RO 128 B1
Lugones E 33 E2
Luhačovice CZ 65 F3
Luhalahti FIN 120 C20
Luhanka FIN 121 D2
Luhtapohja FIN 115 F3

Luino I 71 D3
Luisiana (La) E 47 E2
Lukavac BIH 128 A1
Lukovica SLO 73 E2
Lukovit BG 128 C2
Luleå S 108 C3
Lüleburgaz TR 129 E3
Lumbier E 28 A4
Lumbrales E 35 D4
Lumbres F 15 E4
Lumezzane I 71 E4
Lumijoki FIN 114 C1
Lumparland FIN 120 A4
Lumsås DK 122 C3
Lumsheden S 119 D1
Luna E 37 F3
Lunas F 30 A2
Lund S 123 D3
Lünd N 107 D4
Lunde N 110 B3
Lunde N 116 C20
Lunden D 50 A2
Lunel F 30 B2
Lunéville F 23 D2
Lungern CH 66 A4
Lungro I 80 C4
Lunz A 68 C1
Luninec BY 126 C1
Luogosanto I 82 B1
Luopioinen FIN 120 C3
Luosto FIN 109 E1
Luque E 48 A2
Lurbe-
  St-Christau F 28 B3

Lurcy-
  Lévis F 26 A1
Lure F 23 D4
Lurgan GB 3 D2
Luri F 78 B2
Lurisia I 74 C2
Lury-
  sur-Arnon F 25 F1
Lusigny-
  sur-Barse F 22 A3
Lusk IRL 3 E4
Luso P 40 B1
Lussac F 24 C4
Lussac-
  les-Châteaux F 25 D2
Lussan F 30 B2
Lustenau A 66 C3
Luster N 110 C4
Luton GB 14 B2
Lutterberg D 56 B4
Lutterworth GB 11 D4
Lutzelbourg F 23 E2
Lutzerath D 61 F3
Lutzmanns-
  burg A 69 D2
Lützow D 51 D3
Lützow D 51 D3
Lüumäki FIN 121 E3
Luupuvesi FIN 115 D3
Luusua FIN 109 E2
Luvia FIN 120 B3
Luxembourg L 22 C1

Luxeuil-
  les-Bains F 23 D4
Luynes F 20 C4
Luz-
  St-Sauveur F 28 C4
Luzarches F 21 E2
Luzech F 29 E1
Luzern CH 66 B4
Luzy F 26 B1
Luzzara F 75 F1
Luzzi I 83 E2
L'viv UA 126 C2
Lychen D 51 F4
Lycksele S 113 D1
Lydd GB 15 D4
Lydney GB 13 E1
Lye S 119 F4
Lyme
  Regis GB 13 D3
Lymington GB 13 F3
Lyndhurst GB 13 F3
Lyngdal N 116 B3
Lyngseidet N 104 C3
Lyngsnes N 106 C4
Lynmouth GB 13 D1
Lynton GB 13 D2
Lyon F 26 C3
Lyons-
  la-Forêt F 16 B4
Lysekil S 118 A3
Lyss CH 27 F1
Lysvik S 118 C1
Lytham
  St. Anne's GB 10 C2

M

M. Doukáto GR 89 F1
Maam Cross /
  An Teach Dóite IRL . 2 A4
Maaninka FIN 115 E3
Maaninkavaara FIN 109 E2
Maanselkä FIN 115 E2
Maarianvaara FIN 115 E3
Maaseik B 61 D1
Maasmechelen B 17 F1
Maassluis NL 54 B4
Maastricht NL 17 F2
Maastricht NL 61 D1
Määttälänvaara FIN ... 109 F2
Mablethorpe GB 11 F3
Macael E 48 C3
Mação P 40 C2
Macclesfield GB. 11 D3
Macduff GB 7 E4
Maceda E 32 B4
Macedo
  de Cavaleiros P. ... 35 D3
Macerata I 77 D3
Macerata Feltria I. .. 76 B3
Machault F 17 E4
Machecoul F 24 A1
La Machine F. 26 A1
Machrihanish GB 3 E1
Machynlleth GB. 10 B4
Mackenrode D 56 C4
Mačkovci SLO 73 F1
Macomer I 82 B2
Mâcon F 26 C2

Macotera E 41 F1
Macroom / Maigh
  Chromtha IRL 4 B3
Macugnaga I 70 C4
Maddaloni I 80 A3
Maderuelo E 36 B4
Madesimo I 71 D3
Madona LV 124 C2
Madonna
  di Campiglio I 71 F3
Madrid E 42 B1
Madridejos E 42 B3
Madrigal de las Altas
  Torres E 35 F4
Madrigal de la Vera E. 41 F2
Madrigalejo E 41 F3
Madrona E 42 B1
Madroñera E 41 E3
Madroño (El) E. 47 D2
Mähring D 63 F3
Maël-Carhaix F 18 C3
Maella E 38 A4
Mære N 111 E1
Märkisch Buchholz D. . 58 A3
Maesteg GB 13 D1
Mafra P 40 A3
Magacela E 41 E4
Magallón E 37 E3
Magaña E 37 D3
Magaz E 36 A3
Magdalena (La) E. 33 E3
Magdeburg D 57 D3
Magenta I 71 D4
Maghera GB 3 D2

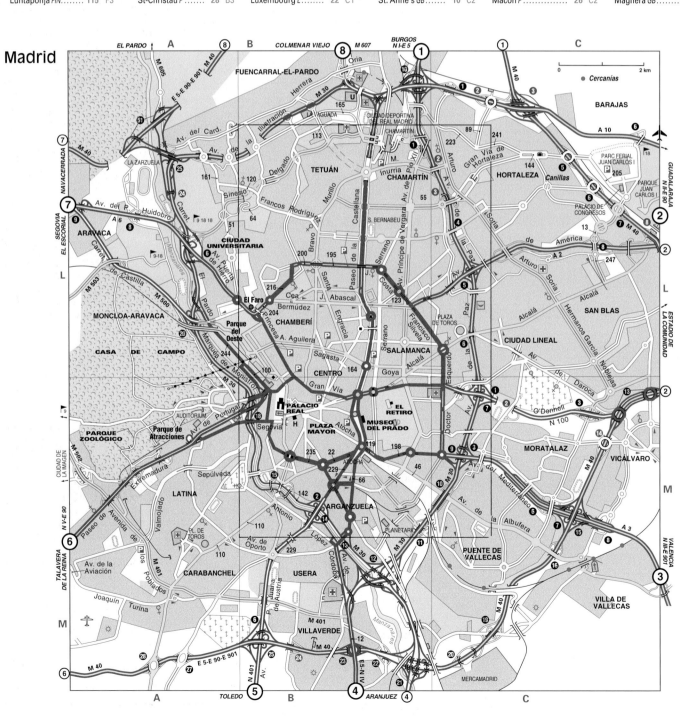

Madrid

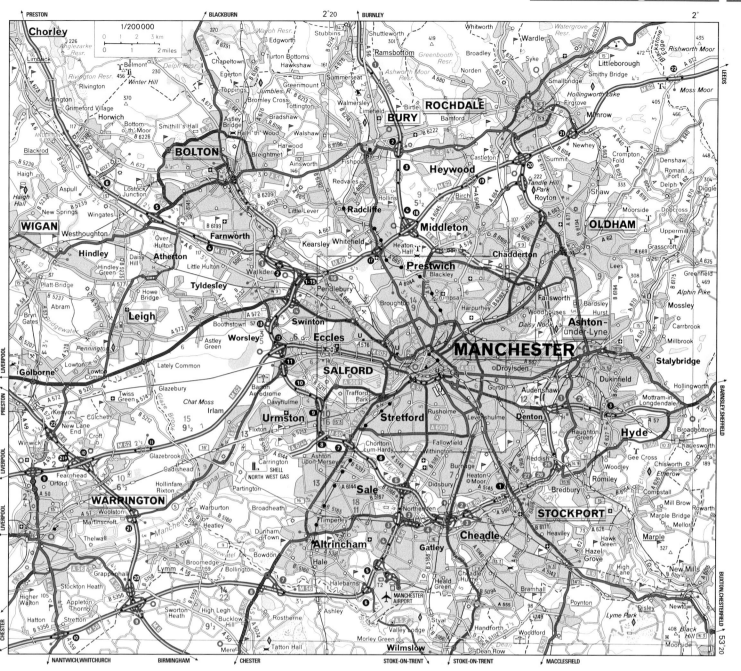

Magherafelt GB	3	D2	Mairena del Alcor E	47	E2	Malax / Maalahti FIN	114	B3	Malmédy B	61	E2
Magione I	76	B4	Maisach D	67	E1	Malbork PL	124	A4	Malmesbury GB	13	E2
Maglaj BIH	128	A1	Maison-Neuve F	22	B3	Malbuisson F	27	E1	Malmköping S	119	E3
Magliano de' Marsi I	79	E1	Maissau A	65	D4	Malcesine I	71	F4	Malmö S	123	D3
Magliano			Maizières-lès-Metz F	22	C1	Malchin D	51	E3	Malmslätt S	119	D3
in Toscana I	78	C1	Majdanpek YU	128	B1	Malchow D	51	E3	Malo I	72	A4
Magliano Sabina I	79	D1	Majšperk SLO	73	F2	Maldegem B	15	D3	Malo-les-Bains F	15	E4
Maglie I	81	F3	Makarska HR	128	A2	Maldon GB	14	C3	Maloarchangel'sk
Magnac-Laval F	25	E2	Makó H	126	B4	Malé I	67	E4	RUS	125	F4
Magnor N	117	E1	Makrahómi GR	93	D2	Máleme GR	100	A3	Maloja CH	71	E3
Magny-en-Vexin F	21	E2	Mákri GR	91	D2	La Malène F	30	A1	Malojaroslavec RUS	125	F3
Magoúla GR	96	B1	Makríamos GR	89	E2	Malente D	50	C2	Malónas GR	103	F2
Maherádo GR	96	A1	Makrígialos GR	88	A3	Máles GR	101	E4	Måløy N	110	A3
Mahilëü BY	125	D4	Makrigialós GR	101	E3	Malesherbes F	21	E3	Malpartida
Mahlu FIN	114	C3	Makrihóri GR	88	A4	Malessína GR	93	F3	de Cáceres E	41	E3
Mahón / Maó E	45	F3	Makrihóri GR	89	E1	Malestroit F	19	D4	Malpartida
Mahora E	43	E4	Makrinítsa GR	93	F1	Malgrat de Mar E	39	D4	de Plasencia E	41	E2
Maia P	34	B3	Makriplágio GR	89	D1	Mali Lošinj HR	77	E1	Malpica
Maials E	38	B3	Makriráhi GR	93	D2	Mália GR	101	E3	de Bergantiños E	32	A2
Maîche F	23	D4	Makrohóri GR	88	A2	Mália GR	101	E3	Malpica do Tejo P	40	C2
Maida I	83	E3	Makroníssi (Nissí) GR	98	A1	Malicorne-			Malsch D	23	E1
Maidenhead GB	14	B3	Maksniemi FIN	109	D3	sur-Sarthe F	19	F4	Malsta S	112	C4
Maidstone GB	14	C3	Malå S	108	A4	Maliskylä FIN	114	C2	Malta A	68	B3
Maienfeld CH	66	C4	Mala Vyska UA	127	E3	Malko Tïarnovo BG	129	E2	Maltby GB	11	E3
Maignelay-			Maladzečna BY	124	C4	Mallaig GB	6	B4	Malton GB	11	E2
Montigny F	16	C4	Málaga E	47	F3	Mallén E	37	E3	Maluenda E	37	E4
Maijanen FIN	109	D2	Malagón E	42	B3	Mallersdorf D	63	F4	Malung S	118	C1
Maillezais F	24	B2	Malahide /			Malles Venosta /			Malungsfors S	118	C1
Mailly-le-Camp F	22	A2	Mullach de IRL	3	E4	Mals I	67	D4	Malveira P	40	A3
Mainar E	37	E4	Malaja Višera RUS	125	D1	Mallnitz A	68	A3	Malveira P	40	A3
Mainburg D	67	E1	Malalbergo I	76	A1	Mallow / Mala IRL	4	C3	Malvik N	111	E2
Maintenon F	21	D2	Malámata GR	93	D3	Mallwyd GB	10	B4	Malyn UA	127	D1
Mainz D	62	A3	Malandríno GR	93	D3	Malm N	111	E1	Le Malzieu-Ville F	30	A1
Maiori I	80	A3	Malaucène F	30	C2	Malmberget S	108	B2	Mamaia RO	129	E1

Mamarrosa P	40	B1	Maniago I	72	B3
Mamers F	20	C3	Manilva E	47	E4
Mammola I	83	E4	Manisa TR	129	E4
Mamonovo RUS	125	A4	Manises E	43	F3
Manacor E	45	E3	Mank A	68	C1
Manacore I	80	C1	Månkarbo S	119	E1
Manamansalo FIN	115	D1	Manlleu E	39	D3
Mancha Real E	48	B2	Mannersdorf am
Manching D	67	E1	Leithagebirge A	69	E1
Manciano I	78	C1	Mannheim D	23	F1
Mandal N	116	B3	Manoppello I	79	F1
Mandamádos GR	95	F1	Manorhamilton /
Mandas I	82	B3	Cluainín IRL	2	C2
Mandela I	79	E1	Manosque F	31	D2
Mandelieu-			Manresa E	38	C4
la-Napoule F	31	F3	Le Mans F	20	C3
Manderscheid D	61	F3	Manschnow D	58	A2
Mandínia GR	97	D1	Mansfeld D	57	D4
Mandoúdi GR	94	A2	Mansfield GB	11	D3
Mándra GR	94	A4	Mansilla
Mándra GR	97	E1	de las Mulas E	33	E4
Mandráki GR	103	D1	Mansle F	24	C3
Mandrikó GR	103	E2	Manteigas P	40	C1
Manduria I	81	E3	Mantes-la-Jolie F	21	E2
Manerbio I	71	E4	Mantiel E	43	D1
Manfredonia I	80	C1	Mäntlahti FIN	121	E3
Mangalia RO	129	E1	Mantorp S	119	D3
Mángana GR	89	E1	Mantova I	75	F1
Manganári GR	98	C3	Mäntsälä FIN	121	D3
Manger N	110	A4	Mänttä FIN	120	C2
Mangualde P	40	C1	Mäntyharju FIN	121	E2
Máni GR	97	D4	Mäntyjärvi FIN	109	E3
Máni GR	91	E1	Mäntyluoto FIN	120	B2
			Manzanares E	42	C4

Manzanares el Real E ... 42 B1
Manzaneda E ... 32 C4
Manzanera E ... 43 F2
Manzat F. ... 26 A3
Manziana I ... 79 D1
Maó / Mahón E. ... 45 F3
Maqueda E ... 42 A2
Maranchón E. ... 37 D4
Maranello I. ... 75 F2
Marano di Napoli I. ... 80 A3
Marano Lagunare I. ... 72 C3
Marans F ... 24 B2
Marássia GR. ... 91 E1
Maratea I ... 80 C4
Marateca P ... 40 A4
Marathéa GR ... 93 D1
Marathiás GR. ... 93 D3
Marathókambos GR. ... 99 F1
Marathónas GR ... 94 B4
Marathópoli GR ... 96 B2
Márathos GR ... 93 F1
Marbach a. Neckar D. ... 62 B4
Mårbacka S ... 118 C2
Marbella E ... 47 F4
Marburg D. ... 62 B1
Marby S ... 112 A2
March GB ... 11 F4
Marchamalo E ... 42 C1
Marchaux F ... 23 D4
Marche-
en-Famenne B ... 17 F3
Marchegg A ... 65 E4
Marchena E ... 47 E2
Marchenoir F ... 21 D4
Marchiennes F. ... 17 D2
Marciac F ... 28 C3
Marcianise I. ... 80 A3
Marcigny F ... 26 B2
Marcilla E ... 37 E2
Marcillac-Vallon F ... 29 F1
Marcillat-
en-Combraille F. ... 25 F2
Marcilly-le-Hayer F ... 22 A3
Marckolsheim F ... 23 E3
Marco
de Canaveses P ... 34 B4
Marcoule F ... 30 C2
Marene I ... 74 C2
Marennes F ... 24 B3
Marentes E ... 33 D3
Mareuil F ... 25 D4
Mareuil-sur-Lay F ... 24 B2
Margarites GR. ... 100 C3
Margaríti GR. ... 92 A1
Margate GB. ... 15 D3
Margherita
di Savoia I ... 80 C2
Marguerittes F ... 30 C2
María E ... 49 D2
Maria Saal A ... 68 C3
Maria Taferl A ... 68 C1
Mariánské Lázně CZ. ... 63 F2
Mariazell A ... 68 C2
Maribo DK ... 122 C4
Maribor SLO. ... 73 F2
Mariborsko
Pohorje SLO. ... 73 F2
Mariefred S ... 119 E2
Mariehamn /
Maarrian-
hamina FIN. ... 120 A4
Marienberg D. ... 63 F1
Marienborn D. ... 57 D3
Marienstedt D. ... 50 C3
Mariestad S ... 118 C3
Marignane F ... 31 D3
Marigny F ... 19 E2
Marigny-le-Châtel F. ... 22 A3
Marijampolė LT ... 124 B4
Marín E ... 32 A4
Marina di Camerota I ... 80 B4
Marina di Campo I ... 78 A1
Marina di Carrara I ... 75 F2
Marina di Castagneto-
Marina di
Donoratico I. ... 75 F4
Marina
di Gioiosa Ionica I.. 83 E4
Marina di Grosseto I... 76 A4
Marina di Leuca I. ... 81 F4
Marina di Massa I ... 75 F3
Marina
di Pietrasanta I. ... 75 F3
Marina di Pisa I. ... 75 F3
Marina di Ragusa I... 85 D4
Marina di Ravenna I.. 76 B1
Marina
di Torre Grande I... 82 A3
Mar"ina Horka BY ... 125 D4
Marinella I. ... 84 B3
Marineo I. ... 84 B3
Marines F. ... 21 E2
Maringues F. ... 26 A3

Marinha Grande P.... 40 A2
Marinkainen FIN ... 114 C2
Marino I ... 79 E2
Marjaniemi FIN. ... 114 C1
Markaryd S. ... 123 E2
Markdorf D ... 66 C2
Market Drayton GB ... 10 C3
Market
Harborough GB ... 11 E4
Markethill GB. ... 3 C3
Market Rasen GB ... 11 E3
Market
Weighton GB ... 11 E3
Markgröningen D ... 66 B1
Markina E. ... 37 D1
Markkleeberg D. ... 57 E4
Markneukirchen D.... 63 F2
Markópoulo GR. ... 98 A1
Markópoulo GR. ... 92 A4
Markópoulo GR. ... 94 A4
Markranstädt D. ... 57 E4
Le Markstein F. ... 23 E3
Marktbreit D. ... 62 C3
Markt Erlbach D. ... 63 D3
Marktheidenfeld D. ... 62 C3
Markt Indersdorf D. ... 67 E1
Marktl D. ... 67 F1
Marktoberdorf D. ... 67 D2
Marktredwitz D. ... 63 E2
Markt St. Florian A ... 68 B1
Marl D. ... 55 E4
Marlborough GB. ... 13 F2
Marle F. ... 17 D4
Marlow GB. ... 14 B3

Marlow D. ... 51 E2
Marmande F ... 28 C1
Marmári GR ... 94 B4
Mármaro GR. ... 95 F3
Marmolejo E ... 48 A1
Marmoutier F. ... 23 E2
Marnay F. ... 22 C4
Marne D. ... 50 A3
Marnitz D. ... 51 D4
Marolles-
les-Braults F. ... 20 C3
Marónia GR. ... 91 D2
Marostica I. ... 72 A3
Marotta I. ... 76 C2
Marquartstein D. ... 67 F2
Marquion F. ... 17 D3
Marquise F. ... 15 E4
Marradi I. ... 76 A2
Marraskoski FIN. ... 109 D2
Mars-la-Tour F. ... 22 C4
Marsaglia I. ... 75 E1
Marsala I. ... 84 A3
Marsberg D ... 56 B4
Marsciano I. ... 76 C4
Marseillan F. ... 30 A3
Marseille F. ... 31 D3
Marseille-
en-Beauvaisis F. ... 16 B4
Marsico Nuovo I. ... 80 C3
Marske-
by-the-Sea GB ... 11 E1
Märsta S. ... 119 E2
Marstal DK. ... 122 B4

Marstrand S. ... 118 A4
Marta I. ... 78 C1
Martano I. ... 81 F3
Martel F. ... 25 E4
Martelange B ... 61 D3
Marthon F. ... 25 D3
Martignacco I. ... 72 C3
Martigné-Ferchaud F ... 19 E4
Martigny CH. ... 27 F2
Martigny-les-Bains F. ... 22 C3
Martigues F. ... 30 C3
Martim Longo P. ... 46 B2
Martin SK. ... 126 A3
Martina CH. ... 67 D4
Martina Franca I. ... 81 E3
Martín de la Jara E ... 47 E3
Martín de Yeltes E ... 41 E1
Martinengo I. ... 71 E4
Martinet E. ... 38 C2
Martiniemi FIN. ... 114 C1
Martíno GR. ... 93 F3
Martis I. ... 82 B1
Martjanci SLO ... 73 F1
Martofte DK. ... 122 C3
Martonvaara FIN. ... 115 F3
Martorell E. ... 38 C4
Martos E. ... 48 A2
Martti FIN. ... 109 E1
Marttila FIN. ... 120 C3
Marvão P. ... 40 C3
Marvejols F. ... 30 A1
Marykirk GB. ... 9 E1
Maryport GB. ... 9 D4

Mas-Cabardès F. ... 29 F3
Le Mas-d'Agenais F.. 28 C1
Le Mas-d'Azil F ... 29 E3
Mas de Barberáns E.. 44 B1
Mas de las Matas E... 44 A1
Masegoso
de Tajuña E ... 43 D1
Masevaux F. ... 23 E4
Masi N ... 105 D3
Masku FIN. ... 120 B4
Masnou (El) E ... 39 D4
Massa I ... 75 F2
Massa Fiscaglia I. ... 76 B1
Massa Marittima I. ... 76 A4
Massa Martana I. ... 76 C4
Massafra I. ... 81 D3
Massamagrell E ... 44 A3
Massarosa I. ... 75 F3
Massat F. ... 29 E4
Le Massegros F. ... 30 A1
Masseube F. ... 29 D3
Massiac F. ... 26 A4
Mastihári GR ... 103 D1
Masty BY ... 124 C4
Masueco E ... 35 D4
Mátala GR ... 100 C3
Matalascañas E ... 47 D3
Matalebreras E ... 37 D3
Matallana de Torío E. ... 33 E3
Mataránga GR. ... 93 D1
Mataró E ... 39 D4
Matelica I. ... 76 C3
Les Matelles F. ... 30 B2
Matera I ... 81 D3

Matészalka H. ... 126 B3
Mateus P ... 34 C3
Matfors S. ... 112 C3
Matha F. ... 24 C3
Mathráki (Nissí) GR. ... 86 A4
Máti GR. ... 94 B4
Matignon F. ... 19 D2
Matku FIN. ... 120 C3
Matlock GB ... 11 D3
Matosinhos P. ... 34 B3
Matour F. ... 26 C2
Matrei am Brenner A. ... 67 E3
Matrei in Osttirol A... 67 F3
Mattersburg A ... 69 E1
Mattighofen A ... 68 A1
Mattinata I. ... 80 C1
Mattmar S. ... 112 A2
Mattsee A ... 68 A2
Mattsmyra S ... 112 B4
Maubeuge F. ... 17 E3
Maubourguet F. ... 28 C3
Mauchline GB. ... 8 C3
Mauerkirchen A ... 68 A1
Mauguio F. ... 30 B3
Maula FIN. ... 109 D3
Maulbronn D. ... 23 F2
Mauléon F. ... 24 C1
Mauléon-Licharre F. ... 28 B3
Maure-de-Bretagne F ... 19 D3
Mauriac F. ... 25 F4
Mauron F. ... 19 D3
Maurs F. ... 29 F1
Mautern A. ... 68 C2
Mauterndorf A. ... 68 B3

Marseille

Mauthausen A	68	B1	Mazères F	29	E3	Meg. Horió GR	103	D2	Meitingen D	67	D1	Melissourgós GR	88	C2	Menat F	26	A2
Mauthen A	68	A4	Mázi GR	87	D3	Meg. Horió GR	99	F1	Mel I	72	B3	Melíti GR	87	E2	Mendavia E	37	D2
Mauvezin F	29	D2	Mazières-en-Gâtine F	24	C2	Meg. Livádi GR	98	B2	Melalahti FIN	115	E1	Melito Porto Salvo I	83	E4	Mende F	30	A1
Mauzé-sur-le-Mignon F	24	B2	Mazyr BY	127	D1	Meg. Monastíri GR	93	E1	Mélambes GR	100	C4	Melívia GR	90	B1	Menden (Sauerland) D	55	E4
Mavrohóri GR	87	E2	Mazzarino I	84	C3	Meg. Panagía GR	88	C3	Melaniós GR	95	E3	Melívia GR	88	B4	Mendenítsa GR	93	E2
Mavroklíssio GR	91	E1	Mazzarò I	85	E2	Meg. Vólvi GR	88	C2	Melánthio GR	87	D3	Melk A	68	C1	Mendig D	61	F2
Mavroléfki GR	89	D1	Mcensk RUS	125	F3	Méga Dério GR	91	D2	Melátes GR	92	B1	Melksham GB	13	E2	Mendrisio CH	71	D4
Mavromáta GR	92	C2	Mealhada P	40	B1	Méga Spiléo GR	93	D4	Melbeck D	50	C4	Mellansel S	113	D2	Menen B	15	F4
Mavromáti GR	92	C1	Meaux F	21	F2	Megáli Préspa GR	87	D1	Melbu N	104	A4	Melle F	24	C2	Menesjärvi FIN	105	E3
Mavroúda GR	88	C2	Mechelen B	17	E1	Megalohóri GR	93	D1	Meldal N	111	D2	Melle D	55	F3	Menetés GR	103	E4
Mavrovoúni GR	93	E1	Meckenbeuren D	66	C2	Megalópoli GR	96	C3	Meldola I	76	B2	Mellendorf D	56	B3	Ménez-Hom F	18	B3
Mavrovoúni GR	87	F2	Mêda P	35	D4	Meganíssi GR	92	B3	Meldorf D	50	A3	Mellerud S	118	B3	Menfi I	84	B3
Maxhütte-Haidhof D	63	E4	Mede I	75	D1	Megaplátanos GR	93	F3	Le Mêle-sur-Sarthe F	20	C3	Mellieha M	85	F4	Mengamuñoz E	42	A1
Maxmo FIN	114	B3	Medebach D	62	A1	Mégara GR	93	E4	Melegnano I	71	D4	Mellilä FIN	120	C3	Mengara I	76	C3
Maybole GB	3	F1	Medelim P	41	D2	Megárhi GR	87	E4	Melendugno I	81	F3	Mellin D	57	D2	Mengen D	66	C2
Mayen D	61	F2	Medellín E	41	E3	Megève F	27	E3	Melfi I	80	B2	Mellingen D	63	D1	Mengeš SLO	73	D2
Mayenne F	19	F3	Medemblik NL	54	C2	Megísti GR	103	F4	Melgaço P	32	B4	Mellrichstadt D	62	C2	Mengíbar E	48	A1
Mayerling A	69	D1	Mediaş RO	126	C4	Megísti (Kastelórizo) (Nissí) GR	103	F4	Melgar de Abajo E	33	F4	Mělník CZ	64	D3	Menídi GR	92	B2
Mayet F	20	C4	Medicina I	76	A2	Mehamn N	105	E1	Melgar de Fernamental E	36	B2	Melpers D	62	C2	Mennetou-sur-Cher F	25	E1
Le Mayet-de-Montagne F	26	B3	Medina Azahara E	47	F1	Mehedeby S	119	E1	Melhus N	111	D2	Melrose GB	9	E3	Mens F	31	D1
Maynooth / Maigh Nuad IRL	3	D4	Medina del Campo E	36	A4	Mehun-sur-Yèvre F	25	F1	Melía GR	93	E1	Melsungen D	62	B1	Mentana I	79	D1
Mayorga E	33	E4	Medina de Pomar E	36	C1	Meigle GB	9	D1	Melide E	32	B3	Meltaus FIN	109	D2	Menthon-St-Bernard F	27	E3
Mayrhofen A	67	F3	Medina de Rioseco E	36	A3	Meijel NL	61	D1	Melides P	40	A4	Melton Mowbray GB	11	E4	Menton F	31	F2
Mazagón E	46	C2	Medina-Sidonia E	47	D4	Meilen CH	66	B3	Melidóni GR	100	C3	Meltosjärvi FIN	109	D2	Méntrida E	42	B2
Mazagran F	17	E4	Médoussa GR	90	C1	Meillant F	25	F1	Meligalás GR	96	C2	Melun F	21	F3	Les Menuires F	27	E4
Mazamet F	29	F3	Meduno I	68	A4	Meimoa P	41	D1	Melíki GR	88	A2	Melvich GB	7	D2	Meppel NL	55	D3
Mazara del Vallo I	84	A3	Medvode SLO	73	D2	Meina I	70	D4	Melilli I	85	E4	Membrilla E	42	C4	Meppen D	55	E2
Mazarakiá GR	92	A1	Medyn' RUS	125	F3	Meinerzhagen D	61	F1	Mélisey F	23	D4	Membrío E	41	D3	Mequinenza E	38	A4
Mazarete E	43	D1	Meerane D	63	F1	Meiningen D	62	C2	Mélissa GR	89	E1	Memmingen D	67	D2	Mer F	21	D4
Mazarrón E	49	E2	Meersburg D	66	C2	Meira E	32	C1	Melissáni GR	92	A4	Mena UA	127	E1	Meráker N	111	E2
Mažeikiai LT	124	B3	Les Mées F	31	D2	Meiringen CH	66	A4	Melíssi GR	93	E4	Menaggio I	71	D3	Meran / Merano I	67	E4
			Mefjordbotn N	104	B3	Meisenheim D	62	A3	Melissohóri GR	93	F4	Menai Bridge / Porthaethwy GB	10	A3			
			Mefjordvær N	104	B3	Meißen D	58	A4	Melissópetra GR	86	C3	Menasalbas E	42	A3			
			Meg. Horió GR	92	C3												

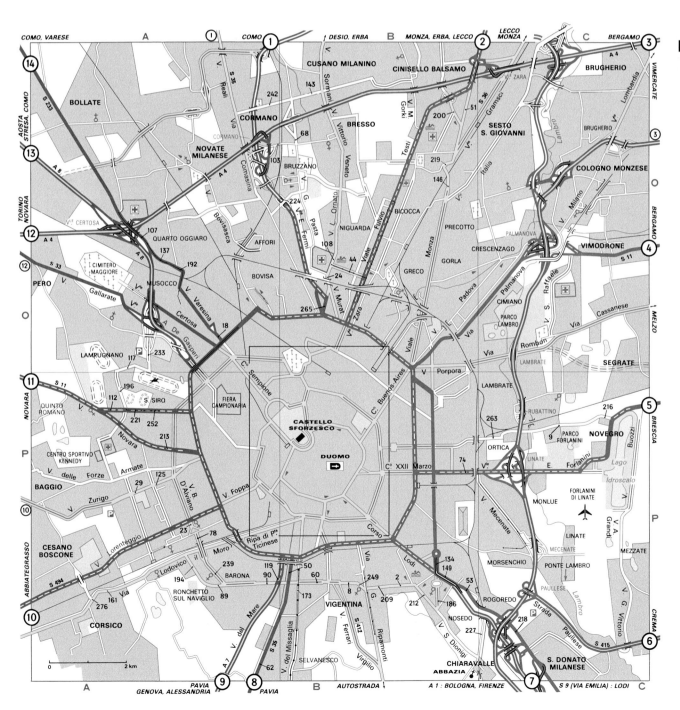

Milano

Merano / Meran I 67 E4
Merate I 71 E4
Merca (A) E. 32 B4
Mercadal (es) E 45 F2
Mercatale I. 76 C3
Mercatale I. 76 B3
Mercatino Conca I.... 76 C2
Mercato S. Severino I 80 A3
Mercato Saraceno I.. 76 B2
Merclur F 25 F4
Merdrignac F. 19 D3
Méréville F 21 E3
Mere GB 13 E2
Mergozzo I 70 C3
Méribel F 27 E4
Mérida E. 41 E4
Mérignac F 24 B4
Mérihas GR. 98 B2
Merijärvi FIN. 114 C2
Merikarvia FIN. 120 B2
Mering D. 67 D1
Merkendorf D. 63 D4
Merklingen D 66 C1
Le Merlerault F. 20 C2
Mers-les-Bains F. 16 B3
Mersch L 61 E2
Merseburg D. 57 E4
Merthyr Tydfil GB. 13 D1
Mértola P. 46 B1
Méru F. 16 C4
Merville F. 15 F4
Merville-Franceville-
  Plage F 19 F1
Méry-sur-Seine F..... 22 A3
Merzig D 23 D1
Mesagne I. 81 E3
Mesão Frio P. 34 C4
Mesa Roldán (La) E.. 49 D3
Mesas (Las) E 42 C3
Meschede D. 62 A1
Mescherin D 52 A3
Meschers-
  sur-Gironde F 24 B3
Meslay-du-Maine F .. 19 F3
Mesocco CH 71 D3
Mesola I. 76 B1
Mesón do Vento E ... 32 B2
Mesoraca I 83 F2
Mespelbrunn D 62 B3
Messanagrós GR 103 E3
Messariá GR. 98 C1
Messei F. 19 F2
Méssi GR. 89 F1
Messiméri GR. 88 B3
Messimvría GR. 91 D2
Messina I. 83 D4
Messíni GR 96 A1
Meßkirch D. 66 B2
Messlingen S 112 A3
Messohóra GR. 92 C1
Messohóri GR 103 D3
Messohóri GR. 87 F4
Messolonghi GR 92 C3
Messongí GR. 86 B4
Messopótamo GR ... 92 A1
Messótopos GR. 95 F2
Meßstetten D 66 B2
Mestá GR 95 E4
Mestanza E. 42 B4
Mésti GR. 91 D2
Mestlin D. 51 D3
Mestre I. 72 B4
Mesvres F. 26 B1
Metalikó GR. 88 B1
Metalío GR. 93 E2
Metamórfossi GR. 88 C3
Metamórfossi GR. 88 A1
Metangítsi GR. 88 C3
Metaxádes GR 91 E1
Metéora GR. 87 E4
Méthana GR. 97 F1
Methil GB. 9 D2
Methóni GR. 88 A3
Methóni GR. 96 B3
Metlika SLO. 73 E3
Metnitz A 68 B3
Metóhi GR. 94 B3
Metóhi GR. 92 C4
Metóhi GR. 97 E1
Metóhi GR. 93 F1
Metsäkylä FIN 121 E3
Metsäkyla FIN 109 E3
Metsämaa FIN. 120 C3
Métsovo GR. 87 E4
Mettingen D. 55 F3
Mettlach D. 23 D1
Mettmann D. 61 F1
Metz F. 23 D1
Metzervisse F. 23 D1
Metzingen D 66 B1
Meulan F. 21 E2
Meung-sur-Loire F ... 21 E4
Meursault F. 26 C1

Meuselwitz D 63 E1
Mevagissey GB 12 B4
Meximieux F. 26 C3
Meyenburg D 51 E3
Meymac F. 25 F3
Meyrueis F 30 A2
Meyzieu F. 26 C3
Mèze F. 30 B3
Mézel F. 31 E2
Mézières-
  en-Brenne F 25 E1
Mézières-
  sur-Issoire F 25 D2
Mézin F. 28 C2
Mezőberény H 126 B4
Mezőkövesd H 126 B4
Mezőtúr H 126 B4
Mezquita (A) E 32 C4
Mezquita de Jarque E 43 F1
Mezzano I. 72 A3
Mezzolombardo I..... 71 F3
Meßdorf D. 57 D2
Mgarr M 85 F4
Miajadas E 41 E3
Miastko PL. 52 C2
Micheldorf A 68 B2
Michelstadt D. 62 B3
Michendorf D 57 F3
Mid Yell GB 7 F2
Middelburg NL........ 17 D1
Middelfart DK 122 B3
Middelharnis NL 54 B4
Middelkerke-Bad B... 15 F4
Middlesbrough GB ... 11 E1
Middleton-
  in-Teesdale GB ... 11 D1
Middlewich GB....... 10 C3
Midhurst GB. 14 B4
Midleton / Mainistir
  na Corann IRL...... 4 C3
Midsund N 110 B2
Miedes E. 37 E4
Miehikkälä FIN 121 E3
Miélan F 28 C3
Mielec PL 126 B2
Mieluskylä FIN 114 C2
Miercurea-Ciuc RO . 127 D4
Mieres E. 33 E3
Miesbach D 67 E3
Mietoinen FIN 120 B3
Miettila FIN 121 F2
Międzychód PL....... 52 C4
Międzylesie PL 65 D1
Międzyrzec
  Podlaski PL 126 B1
Migennes F 22 A3
Migliarino I. 76 B1
Miglionico I. 81 D3
Miguel Esteban E.... 42 C3
Miguelturra E 42 B4
Míhas GR 93 D4
Mihói GR. 92 C4
Michalovce SK 126 B3
Mijas E. 47 F4
Mijoux F. 27 D2
Míki GR. 89 E1
Mikínes GR 97 D1
Mikínes GR 97 D1
Mikkelbostad N...... 104 B3
Mikkeli FIN 121 E3
Mikkelvik N.......... 104 B2
Míkonos GR 98 C2
Míkonos (Nissí) GR ... 98 C2
Mikr. Dério GR....... 91 E1
Mikr.
  Eleftherohóri GR ... 87 F4
Mikr. Horió GR....... 92 C2
Mikrí Mandínia GR.... 96 C3
Mikrí Préspa GR 87 D2
Mikrókambos GR 88 B3
Mikroklissoúra GR ... 90 A1
Mikrolímni GR........ 87 D2
Mikromiliá GR. 90 A1
Mikrópoli GR. 88 C1
Mikulov CZ 65 E4
Milagro E. 37 E3
Milano I. 71 D4
Milano Marittima I... 76 B2
Mílatos GR. 101 E3
Milazzo I. 83 D4
Milestone IRL. 4 C2
Mileto I. 83 E3
Milford GB. 14 B4
Milford Haven /
  Aberdaugleddau GB 5 F4
Milhão P. 35 E3
Míli GR. 97 D1
Miliá GR. 97 D1
Miliá GR. 91 E1
Miliá GR. 87 E3

Miliés GR 93 F1
Milína GR 93 F1
Milis I. 82 B3
Militello in Val
  di Catania I. 85 D3
Millares E. 43 F4
Millas F. 29 F4
Millau F. 30 A2
Millesimo I. 74 C2
Millford IRL 2 C1
Millom GB 10 C1
Millport GB 8 B3
Millstatt A 68 A3
Millstreet IRL 4 B3
Milltown Malbay /
  Sráid na
  Cathrach IRL 4 B2
Milly-la-Forêt F 21 E3
Milmarcos E. 37 D4
Milmersdorf D. 51 F4
Milopótamos GR. 97 E4
Mílos GR. 98 B3
Milos (Nissí) GR. 98 B2
Miltach D 63 F4
Miltenberg D. 62 B3
Milton Keynes GB ... 14 B2
Mimizan F. 28 B2
Mimizan-Plage F..... 28 B1
Mína GR. 97 D4
Mina
  de São Domingos P
  .... 46 B1
Minas (Las) E. 49 D1
Minas de Riotinto E. 47 D1
Minaya E 43 D3
Mindelheim D. 67 D2
Minden D. 56 B3
Mindin F. 19 D4
Minehead GB. 13 D2
Minerbe I. 72 A4
Minerbio I. 76 A1
Minervino Murge I... 80 C2
Minglanilla E. 43 E3
Mingorría E 42 A1
Minkiö FIN 120 C3
Minsk BY. 125 D4
Minsterley GB........ 10 C4

Mintlaw GB........... 7 F4
Mińsk Mazowiecki PL 126 A1
Mionnay F. 26 C3
Mira P. 40 B1
Mira I. 72 B4
Mira E. 43 E3
Mirabella Imbaccari I 85 D3
Mira de Aire P. 40 B2
Miraflores E. 36 B2
Miraflores
  de la Sierra E 42 B1
Miramar P. 34 B4
Miramar F. 31 F3
Miramare I. 76 C2
Miramas F. 30 C3
Mirambeau F. 24 C4
Miramont-
  de-Guyenne F...... 29 D1
Miranda de Ebro E.. 36 C2
Miranda
  del Castañar E. 41 E1
Miranda do Corvo P.. 40 B1
Miranda do Douro P.. 35 E3
Mirande F 29 D3
Mirandela P. 35 D3
Mirandola I. 76 A1
Mirano I. 72 B4
Mirebeau F. 25 D1
Mirebeau-sur-Bèze F. 22 C4
Mirecourt F. 23 D3
Mirepoix F. 29 E3
Míres GR. 101 D4
Miribel F. 26 C3
Mírina GR 89 F4
Mirna SLO 73 E3
Mirow D 51 E4
Mirsini GR. 97 D3
Mirtiés GR. 99 F3
Mírtos GR. 101 E4
Miruéna de los
  Infanzones E. 42 A1
Misi FIN 109 E2
Misilmeri I. 84 B2
Miskolc H 126 B3
Mislinja SLO 73 E2
Mistelbach A 65 E4
Misterbianco I 85 E3

Mistretta I 85 D2
Místros GR. 94 A3
Misurina I 67 F4
Misvær N 107 E2
Mitchelstown / Baile
  Mhistéala IRL 4 C3
Míthimna GR. 95 F1
Mítikas GR 92 B3
Mitilíni GR. 95 F2
Mitilinií GR. 99 F1
Mitrópoli GR. 93 D1
Mitrovica YU 128 B2
Mittelberg A. 67 D3
Mittersill A 67 F3
Mittelberg A. 67 D3
Mittenwald D 67 E3
Mittenwalde D. 57 F3
Mittersill A 67 F3
Mitterteich D. 63 E2
Mittweida D. 63 F1

Moelv N 111 D4
Moen / Målselv N .. 104 B3
Moena I 67 F4
Mönchengladbach D. 61 E1
Mönkebude D. 51 F3
Moers D 61 E1
Mössingen D. 66 B1
Moffat GB. 9 D3
Mogadouro P 35 D4
Moglia I 75 F1
Mogliano Veneto I... 72 B4
Mogón E. 48 C1
Moguer E 46 C2
Mohács H. 128 A1
Mohill / Maothail IRL . 2 C3
Möhkö FIN 115 F3
Móhlos GR. 101 F4
Moholm S 118 C3
Mohyliv-
  Podil's'kyj UA 127 D3
Moi N 116 B3
Moià E 39 D3
Moie I 76 C3
Moimenta I 75 D3
Moimenta da Beira P. 34 C4
Moirans F 27 D4
Moirans-
  en-Montagne F..... 27 D2
Moisdon-la-Rivière F. 19 E4
Moisiovaara FIN 115 E1
Moisling D. 50 C3
Moissac F 29 D2
Moita P. 40 A4
Moixent E 43 F4
Mojácar E 49 D3
Mojados E. 36 A4
Mojstrada SLO 73 D2
Mokronog SLO 73 E3
Mol B. 17 F1
Mola di Bari I. 81 D2
Moláï GR 97 E3
Molar (El) E. 42 C1
Mold /
  Yr Wyddgrug GB .. 10 C3
Molde N 110 C2
Moldova Nouă RO .. 128 B1
Møldrup DK 122 B2

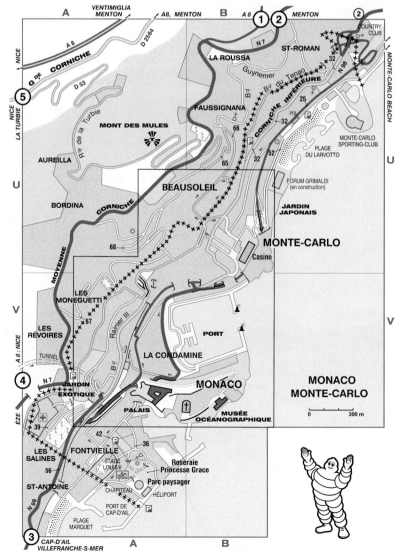

MONACO
MONTE-CARLO

0 ———— 300 m

Molfetta I	81	D2	Monastir I	82	B4	Monestiés F	29	F2	Mons B	17	E2
Molières F	29	E2	Monastiráki GR	92	B2	Le Monêtier-			Monsanto P	41	D2
Molina (La) E	38	C3	Monastiráki GR	91	E2	les-Bains F	27	E4	Monsaraz P	40	C4
Molina de Aragón E	43	E1	Monbazillac F	29	D1	Moneygall IRL	5	D2	Monschau D	61	C2
Molina de Segura E	49	E1	Moncalieri I	27	F4	Moneymore GB	3	D2	Monségur F	28	C1
Molinella I	76	A1	Moncalvo I	74	C1	Monfalcone I	72	C3	Monselice I	72	A4
Molinicos E	49	D1	Monção P	32	A4	Monflanquin F	29	D1	Monsols F	26	C2
Molinillo (El) E	42	B3	Moncarapacho P	46	B2	Monforte P	40	C4	Mönsterås S	123	F1
Molinos E	44	A1	Mönchdorf A	68	C1	Monforte de Lemos E	32	C4	Monsummano		
Molins de Rei E	38	C4	Monchique F	46	A2	Monfortinho P	41	D2	Terme I	75	F3
Moliterno I	80	C4	Monclar-de-Quercy F	29	E2	Monguelfo /			Mont-de-Marsan F	28	C2
Molitg-les-Bains F	29	F4	Moncofa E	44	A3	Welsberg I	67	F4	Le Mont-Dore F	26	A3
Molkom S	118	C2	Moncontour F	24	C1	Monheim D	63	D4	Mont-Louis F	29	F4
Mollerussa I	38	B4	Moncontour F	19	D3	Moní (Nissí) GR	97	F1	Mont-roig		
Molliens-Dreuil F	16	B3	Moncoutant F	24	C1	Monifieth GB	9	E2	del Camp E	44	B1
Mollina E	47	F3	Monda E	47	F3	Monistrol-d'Allier F	26	B4	Le Mont-St-Michel F	19	E2
Mollösund S	118	A4	Mondariz E	32	A4	Monistrol-sur-Loire F	26	B4	Mont-St-Vincent F	26	C2
Mólos GR	93	E2	Mondavio I	76	C3	Monistrol			Mont-sous-Vaudrey F	27	D1
Molpe FIN	114	A3	Mondéjar E	42	C2	de Montserrat E	38	C4	Montagnac F	30	A3
Molsheim F	23	E2	Mondello I	84	B2	Monmouth /			Montagnana I	72	A4
Molveno I	71	F3	Mondim de Basto P	34	C3	Trefynwy GB	13	E1	Montagrier F	25	D4
Mombeltrán E	42	A2	Mondolfo I	76	C3	Monnickendam NL	54	B3	Montaigu F	24	B1
Mombuey E	33	D4	Mondoñedo E	32	C4	Monodéndri GR	87	D4	Montaigu-		
Mommark DK	122	B4	Mondorf-les-Bains L	23	D1	Monódrio GR	94	B3	de-Quercy F	29	D1
Momo I	71	D4	Mondoubleau F	21	D3	Monólithos GR	103	E2	Montaigut F	26	A2
Mon Idée F	17	E3	Mondovì I	74	C2	Monopoli I	81	E2	Montaigut F	26	A2
Monaco MC	31	F2	Mondragon F	30	C1	Monor H	126	A4	Montaione I	76	A3
Monaghan /			Mondragone I	79	F3	Monòver E	49	E1	Montalbán E	43	F1
Muineachán IRL	3	D3	Mondsee A	68	A2	Monpazier F	29	D1	Montalbo E	43	D2
Monasterace			Monein F	28	B3	Monreal D	61	E2	Montalcino I	76	A4
Marina I	83	F3	Monemvassía GR	97	E3	Monreal del Campo E	43	E1	Montalegre P	34	C3
Monasterevin IRL	3	D4	Mónesi di Triora I	74	C3	Monreale I	84	B2	Montalieu-Vercieu F	27	D3
Monasterio			Monesterio E	47	D1	Monroy E	41	E2	Montalivet-		
de Rodilla E	36	C2	Monestier-			Monroyo E	44	A1	les-Bains F	24	B4
Le Monastier F	30	A1	de-Clermont F	27	D4				Montalto di Castro I	78	C1

Montalto			Monte		
di Marche I	77	D4	S. Angelo I	80	C1
Montalto Uffugo I	83	E2	Monte S. Savino I	76	B3
Montalvão P	40	C2	Monteagudo de las		
Montamarta E	35	D4	Vicarías E	37	D4
Montana BG	128	C2	Montealegre E	36	A3
Montana CH	27	F2	Montealegre		
Montánchez E	41	E3	del Castillo E	43	E4
Montanejos E	43	F2	Montebello Ionico I	83	E4
Montaña E	37	E4	Montebello		
Montargil P	40	B3	Vicentino I	72	A4
Montargis F	21	F3	Montebelluna I	72	B3
Montastruc-la-			Montebourg F	19	E1
Conseillère F	29	E2	Montecarotto I	76	C3
Montauban F	29	E2	Montecassino		
Montauban-			(Abbazia di) I	79	F2
de-Bretagne F	19	D3	Montecatini Terme I	75	F3
Montbard F	22	B4	Montecchio I	76	C2
Montbazens F	29	F1	Montecchio		
Montbazon F	25	D1	Maggiore I	72	A4
Montbéliard F	23	D4	Montech F	29	E2
Montbenoît F	27	E1	Montecorvino		
Montblanc E	38	B4	Rovella I	80	B3
Montbozon F	23	D4	Monte da Pedra P	40	C3
Montbrió			Montedoro I	84	C3
del Camp E	44	B1	Montefalco I	76	C4
Montbrison F	26	B3	Montefalcone di Val		
Montbron F	25	D3	Fortore I	80	B2
Montceau-			Montefalcone		
les-Mines F	26	B2	nel Sannio I	80	A1
Montcenis F	26	B1	Montefiascone I	79	D1
Montchanin F	26	B1	Montefiore dell'Aso I	77	D4
Montcornet F	17	E4	Montefiorino I	75	F2
Montcuq F	29	E1	Montefrío E	48	A2
Montdidier F	16	C4	Montegallo I	77	D4

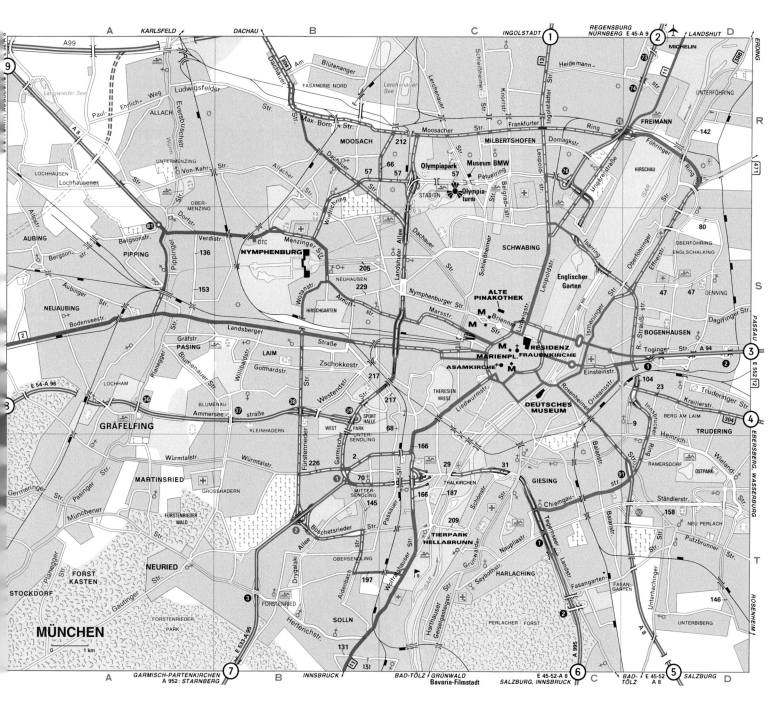

Montegiorgio I......... 77 D3
Montegranaro I...... 77 D3
Montegrotto Terme I. 72 A4
Montehermoso E..... 41 E2
Montejicar E......... 48 B2
Montejo de Tiermes E 36 C4
Monteleone
di Spoleto I......... 76 C4
Montélimar F......... 30 C1
Montella I............ 80 B3
Montellano E.......... 47 E3
Montelupo
Fiorentino I......... 76 A3
Montemaggiore
Belsito I............ 84 C3
Montemagno I....... 74 C1
Montemayor E........ 47 F2
Montemayor
de Pililla E......... 36 A4
Montemor-o-Novo P. 40 B4
Montemor-o-Velho P 40 B3
Montendre F.......... 24 C4
Montenegro
de Cameros E....... 36 C3
Montenero
di Bisaccia I........ 80 A1
Montenero Sabino I.. 79 E1
Montepulciano I...... 76 B4
Monte Real P......... 40 B2
Montereale I.......... 77 D4
Montereale
Valcellina I......... 72 B3
Montereau-
Fault-Yonne F...... 21 F3
Monte Redondo P.... 40 B2
Monterenzio I........ 76 A2
Monteriggioni I....... 76 A3
Monteroni di Lecce I. 81 F3
Monterosso al Mare I. 75 E2
Monterotondo I....... 79 D1
Monterotondo
Marittimo I........ 76 A4
Monterroso E........ 32 B3
Monterrubio de la
Serena E........... 41 F4
Monterubbiano I..... 77 D3
Montesano sulla
Marcellana I........ 80 C4
Montesarchio I....... 80 A3
Montescaglioso I..... 81 D3
Montesilvano
Marina I........... 77 E4
Montesquieu-
Volvestre F......... 29 E3
Montesquiou F....... 29 D3
Le Montet F......... 26 A2
Montevarchi I........ 76 A3
Montfaucon F........ 24 B1
Montfaucon-
d'Argonne F........ 17 F4
Montfaucon-
en-Velay F......... 26 B4
Montfort-
en-Chalosse F...... 28 B2
Montfort-l'Amaury F. 21 E2
Montfort-sur-Meu F.. 18 C3
Montfort-sur-Risle F. 16 A4
Montgaillard F....... 29 E4
Montgenèvre F....... 27 E4
Montgiscard F....... 29 E3
Montgomery /
Trefaldwyn GB..... 10 B4
Montguyon F........ 24 C4
Monthermé F........ 17 E3
Monthey CH.......... 27 E2
Monthois F........... 17 E4
Monthureux-
sur-Saône F........ 22 C3
Monti I.............. 82 B1
Montichiari I.......... 71 F4

Monticiano I......... 76 A4
Montiel E............ 42 C4
Montier-en-Der F.... 22 B3
Montignac F......... 25 E4
Montigny-le-Roi F... 22 C3
Montigny-sur-Aube F 22 B3
Montijo P............ 40 A3
Montijo E............ 41 D4
Montilla E............ 47 F2
Montioni I........... 76 A4
Montivilliers F........ 20 C1
Montjean-sur-Loire F 19 F4
Montlhéry F.......... 21 E2
Montlieu-la-Garde F . 24 C4
Montlouis-sur-Loire F 21 D4
Montluçon F.......... 25 F2
Montluel F........... 26 C3
Montmarault F....... 26 A2
Montmartin-
sur-Mer F......... 19 E2
Montmédy F......... 17 F4
Montmélian F........ 27 E3
Montmirail F......... 22 A2
Montmirail F......... 20 C3
Montmirey-
le-Château F....... 27 D1
Montmoreau-
St-Cybard F....... 24 C4
Montmorency F...... 21 E2
Montmorillon F...... 25 D2
Montmort F.......... 22 A2
Montoggio I.......... 75 D2
Montoire-
sur-le-Loir F...... 21 D4
Montoito P.......... 40 C4
Montorio al Vomano I 77 D4
Montoro E........... 48 A1
Montpellier F........ 30 B3
Montpezat-
de-Quercy F....... 29 E2
Montpezat-
sous-Bauzon F..... 30 B1
Montpon-
Ménestérol F...... 24 C4
Montpont-
en-Bresse F....... 26 C2
Montréal F 28 C2
Montréal F 29 F3
Montréal-la-Cluse F . 27 D2
Montredon-
Labessonnié F...... 29 F2
Montréjeau F........ 29 D3
Montrésor F......... 25 E1
Montresta I.......... 82 A2
Montret F........... 26 C2
Montreuil F.......... 16 B2
Montreuil-Bellay F ... 24 C1
Montreux CH........ 27 E2
Montrevault F........ 24 B1
Montrevel-
en-Bresse F....... 26 C2
Montrichard F....... 21 D4
Montrond-les-Bains F 26 B3
Montrose GB......... 9 E1
Monts-sur-Guesnes F 25 D1
Montsalvy F......... 29 F1
Montsauche-
les-Settons F...... 26 B1
Montseny E.......... 39 D3
Montserrat E........ 43 F3
Montserrat
(Monestir) E....... 38 C4
Montsûrs F.......... 19 F3
Montuenga E........ 36 A4
Montuïri E.......... 45 E3
Monza I............. 71 D4
Monzón E........... 38 A3
Monzón de Campos E 36 A3
Moordorf D.......... 55 E1
Moosburg a. d. Isar D 67 E1

Mór H................ 126 A4
Mora S.............. 112 A4
Mora P.............. 40 B3
Mora E.............. 42 B3
Móra d'Ebre E....... 44 B1
Mora de Rubielos E .. 43 F2
Morais P............ 35 D3
Moraítika GR........ 86 B4
Moraleda
de Zafayona E...... 48 A3
Moraleja E.......... 41 D1
Moraleja del Vino E .. 35 F3
Moraleja de Sayago E 35 E4
Morales de Rey E.... 33 E4
Morales de Toro E... 35 F3
Morano Calabro I.... 80 C4
Mörarp S............ 123 D2
Morata de Jalón E... 37 E4
Morata de Tajuña E.. 42 C2
Moratalla E.......... 49 D1
Moravce SLO........ 73 E2
Moravci SLO........ 73 F2
Moravske Toplice SLO 73 F1
Morbach D........... 61 F3
Morbegno I 71 E3
Mörbisch A.......... 69 E1
Mörbylånga S........ 123 F2
Morcenx F........... 28 B2
Morciano
di Romagna I....... 76 C2
Morcone I........... 80 A2
Morcote CH.......... 71 D4
Mordelles F.......... 19 D3
Morecambe GB 10 C1
Moreda E........... 48 B2
Morée F............. 21 D4
Morella E........... 44 A1
Mores I............. 82 B2
Morestel F.......... 27 D3
Moreton-in-Marsh GB 13 F1
Moreton-
hampstead GB..... 13 D3
Moreuil F........... 16 C4
Morez F............ 27 D2
Morfasso I.......... 75 E1
Mórfio GR........... 92 A1
Morgat F........... 18 B3
Morges CH.......... 27 E2
Morgex I........... 27 F3
Morhange F......... 23 D2
Mori I.............. 71 F3
Moritzburg D........ 58 A4
Morjärv S........... 108 C3
Morlaàs F........... 28 C3
Morlaix F........... 18 B2
Mormanno I......... 80 C4
Mormant F.......... 21 F2
Mormoiron F........ 30 C2
Mornant F.......... 26 C3
Morón
de Almazán E...... 37 D4
Morón
de la Frontera E ... 47 E3
Morosaglia F........ 78 A3
Morpeth GB......... 9 F4
Mörrum S 123 E2
Morsbach D......... 61 F1
Mörsil S........... 112 A2
Morsleben D........ 57 D3
Mortagne-
au-Perche F....... 20 C1
Mortagne-
sur-Gironde F..... 24 B3
Mortagne-
sur-Sèvre F....... 24 B1

Mortain F............ 19 F2
Mortara I............ 75 D1
Morteau F........... 27 E1
Mortrée F............ 20 C2
Morzine F............ 27 E2
Mosbach D........... 62 B4
Mosby N............. 116 B3
Moschendorf A....... 69 E2
Moshokariá GR....... 93 D2
Moshopótamos GR... 88 A3
Mosjøen N........... 107 D3
Moskosel S.......... 108 A3
Moskva RUS......... 125 F2
Mosonmagyaróvár H 69 F1
Mosqueruela E....... 44 A2
Moss N .... 116 D
Mossala FIN......... 120 B4
Mossat GB........... 7 E4
Most CZ............. 64 A1
Most na Soči SLO.... 73 D3
Mosta M............ 85 F4
Mostar BIH.......... 128 A2
Mosteiro E.......... 32 A3
Mosterhamn N....... 116 A1
Móstoles E.......... 42 B2
Mostrim IRL......... 2 C4
Mostys'ka UA........ 126 B2
Mosvik N........... 111 E1
Mota del Cuervo E.... 42 C3
Mota del Marqués E.. 35 F3
Motala S............ 119 D3
La Mothe-Achard F... 24 A2
La Mothe-St-Héray F. 24 C2
Motherwell GB....... 8 C3
Motilla del Palancar E 43 E3
Motril E............. 48 B3
Motta di Livenza I ... 72 B4
Motta S. Anastasia I.. 85 D3
Motta Visconti I....... 75 D1
La Motte-
Chalancon F....... 31 D1
La Motte-du-Caire F.. 31 D1
Mottola I............ 81 D3
Mouchard F......... 27 D1
Moudon CH.......... 27 E1
Moúdros GR......... 89 F4
Mougins F.......... 31 F2
Mouhijärvi FIN....... 120 C2
Mouilleron-
en-Pareds F....... 24 B1
Moulins F........... 26 A2
Moulins-Engilbert F.. 26 B1
Moulins-la-Marche F. 20 C2
Moult F............. 19 F2
Mount Bellew / An
Creagán IRL....... 2 B4
Mountain Ash /
Aberpennar GB.... 13 D1
Mountmellick/
Móinteach Mílic IRL 5 D2
Mountrath IRL....... 5 D2
Moura P............ 46 C1
Mourão P........... 40 C4
Mourenx F.......... 28 B3
Mouríki GR.......... 94 A3
Mourmelon-
le-Grand F........ 22 B2
Mourniés GR........ 100 B3
Mourujärvi FIN...... 109 E2
Mouscron B......... 15 F4
Moustiers-
Ste-Marie F....... 31 E2
Mouthe F........... 27 D1
Mouthier-
Haute-Pierre F.... 27 E1
Mouthoumet F...... 29 F4
Moutier CH......... 23 E4
Moûtiers F.......... 27 E3
Moutiers-
les-Mauxfaits F.... 24 B2

Moutsoúna GR....... 99 D2
Mouy F............. 16 C4
Mouzáki GR......... 87 D4
Mouzáki GR......... 92 C1
Mouzon F........... 17 F4
Moville / Bun
an Phobail IRL..... 3 D1
Moyenneville F...... 16 B3
Moyuela E.......... 37 F4
Možajsk RUS........ 125 F2
Mozirje SLO......... 73 E2
Mrągowo PL........ 124 A4
Mscislaŭ BY......... 125 E4
Muccia I............ 76 C4
Much D............. 61 F1
Much Wenlock GB... 10 C4
Mucientes E........ 36 A3
Mudanya TR......... 129 F3
Mudau D............ 62 B4
Mudurnu TR......... 129 F3
Mudurra (La) E...... 36 A3
Mügeln D........... 57 F4
Mühlacker D........ 62 B4
Mühlberg D......... 57 F4
Mühldorf D.......... 67 F1
Mühlhausen D....... 62 C1
Muel E............. 37 E4
Muela (La) E........ 37 E4
Muelas del Pan E 35 E3
Mülheim a. d. Ruhr D 61 E1
Müllheim D.......... 23 E4
Müllrose D.......... 58 A2
Münchberg D........ 63 E2
Müncheberg D....... 58 A2
München D.......... 67 E2
Münchhausen D..... 62 B1
Münnerstadt D...... 62 C2
Münsingen D........ 66 C1
Münster
(Westfalen) D...... 55 E4
Münstertal D........ 23 E4
Münzenberg D...... 62 B2
Muff IRL............ 3 D1
Muge P............ 40 B3
Muggia I............ 73 D2
Mugron F........... 28 B2
Mugueimes E....... 32 B4
Mühlbach
am Hochkönig A.... 68 A3
Mühltroff D......... 63 E2
Muhniemi FIN....... 121 E3
Muhos FIN.......... 115 D3
Muhu EST.......... 124 B2
Muir of Ord GB...... 7 D4
Muirkirk GB......... 8 C3
Mukačeve UA....... 126 B3
Mula E............. 49 E1
Mulhouse F......... 23 E4
Mullingar /
An Muileann
gCearr IRL........ 2 C4
Mullsjö S........... 118 C4
Mulrany / An Mhala
Raithní IRL....... 2 A3
Multia FIN.......... 114 C4
Mumbles (The) GB .. 12 C4
Mundesley GB...... 15 D1
Mundford GB....... 11 F4
Munera E........... 43 D4
Mungia E.......... 36 C1
Muniesa E.......... 43 F1
Munkebo DK........ 122 C4
Munkedal S......... 118 B3
Munkfors S......... 118 C2
Munsala FIN........ 114 B3
Münsingen CH...... 27 F1
Münster CH......... 70 C3
Munster D.......... 50 C4
Munster F.......... 23 E3

Münzkirchen A....... 68 A1
Muñana E........... 42 A1
Muñico E........... 42 A1
Muñogalindo E...... 42 A1
Muodoslompolo S... 108 C1
Muonio FIN......... 108 C1
Mur-de-Barrez F..... 29 F1
Mur-de-Bretagne F.. 18 C3
Murano I........... 72 B4
Murat F............ 26 A4
Murat-sur-Vèbre F.. 30 A2
Murato F........... 78 A3
Murau A............ 68 B3
Muravera I.......... 82 C3
Murcia E........... 49 E2
Murça P............ 34 C3
Murchante E........ 37 E3
La Mure F.......... 27 D4
Mureck A........... 69 D3
Muret F............ 29 E3
Murguía E.......... 36 C1
Muri CH............ 23 F4
Murias de Paredes E. 33 D3
Murjek S........... 108 B2
Murnau D........... 67 E2
Muro F............. 78 A3
Muro d'Alcoi E...... 43 F4
Muro Lucano I...... 80 B3
Murol I............ 26 A3
Murole FIN.......... 120 C20
Muros E............ 32 A3
Mürren CH.......... 27 F2
Murrhardt D......... 62 C4
Murska Sobota SLO .. 73 F1
Murten CH.......... 27 F1
Murtosa P.......... 34 B4
Murtovaara FIN...... 109 F3
Murviel-lès-Béziers F 30 A2
Mürzsteg A......... 69 D2
Mürzzuschlag A 69 D2
Mussalo FIN......... 121 E3
Musselburgh GB..... 9 D2
Musselkanaal NL 55 D2
Mussidan F.......... 25 D4
Mussomeli I......... 84 C3
Mussy-sur-Seine F .. 22 B3
Müstair CH.......... 67 D4
Mustion as FIN...... 120 C4
Mustvee EST........ 124 C1
Muta SLO........... 73 E2
Mutala FIN.......... 120 C2
Mutterstadt D....... 23 F1
Mutzschen D........ 57 F4
Muurame FIN....... 121 D2
Muurasjärvi FIN..... 114 C2
Muurla FIN.......... 120 C4
Muurola FIN........ 109 D2
Muuruvesi FIN...... 115 E3
Muxia E............ 32 A2
Le Muy F........... 31 E3
Muzillac F.......... 19 D4
Muzzana
del Turgnano I..... 72 C3
Myckelgensjö S...... 112 C2
Mykines DK......... 106 A3
Mykolaïv UA........ 126 C2
Mykolaïv UA......... 127 F3
Myllykoski FIN...... 121 E3
Myllykylä FIN....... 114 B4
Myllymäki FIN...... 114 C4
Mynämäki FIN...... 120 B3
Myre / Øksnes N.... 104 A3
Myrhorod UA....... 127 F2
Myronivka UA....... 127 E2
Myrskylä FIN........ 121 D3
Myrviken S......... 112 A2
Mysen N............ 117 D2
Myślibórz PL........ 52 B4
Mytišči RUS......... 125 F2
Mühlen Eichsen D.... 51 D3

N

N. Agathoúpoli GR ... 88 A3
N. Alikarnassós GR ... 101 D3
N. Anhíalos GR ... 93 F1
N. Artáki GR ... 94 A3
N. Éfessos GR ... 88 A3
N. Erásmio GR ... 89 E1
N. Fókea GR ... 88 C3
N. Hilí GR ... 91 D2
N. Iraklítsa GR ... 89 D2
N. Kalikrátia GR ... 88 B3
N. Kariá GR ... 89 E1
N. Karváli GR ... 89 E1
N. Kerassoús GR ... 92 B1
N. Kerdília GR ... 88 C2
N. Kíos GR ... 97 D4
N. Mákri GR ... 94 B4
N. Marmarás GR ... 88 C3
N. Messángala GR ... 88 A4
N. Mihanióna GR ... 88 B2
N. Monastíri GR ... 93 E1
N. Moudaniá GR ... 88 B3
N. Pagassés GR ... 93 F1
N. Péla GR ... 88 A2
N. Péramos GR ... 94 A4
N. Péramos GR ... 89 D2
N. Perivóli GR ... 93 E1
N. Petrítsi GR ... 88 B1
N. Potídea GR ... 88 B3
N. Róda GR ... 89 D3
N. Sánda GR ... 88 B2
N. Sánda GR ... 91 D2
N. Sílata GR ... 88 B3

N. Skióni GR ... 88 C4
N. Skopós GR ... 88 C1
N. Stíra GR ... 94 B4
N. Tríglia GR ... 88 B3
N. Víssa GR ... 91 E1
N. Zíhni GR ... 88 C1
N. Zoí GR ... 87 F2
Na Logu SLO ... 72 A2
Naamijoki FIN ... 108 C2
Naantali FIN ... 120 B4
Naarajärvi FIN ... 115 E4
Naarva FIN ... 115 F3
Naas / An Nás IRL ... 3 D4
Nabburg D ... 63 F3
Naddvik N ... 110 C4
Nadela E ... 32 C3
Nădlac RO ... 126 B4
Nadur M ... 85 F4
Nadvirna UA ... 126 C3
Nærbø N ... 116 A2
Nærøy N ... 106 C4
Næstved DK ... 122 C3
Näfels CH ... 66 B3
Náfpaktos GR ... 93 D3
Náfplio GR ... 97 D1
Naggen S ... 112 B3
Nagold D ... 23 F2
Nagu / Nauvo FIN ... 120 B4
Nagyatád H ... 69 F4
Nagykanizsa H ... 69 F3
Nagykálló H ... 126 B3
Nagykőrös H ... 126 A4
Nahe D ... 50 C3
Náchod CZ ... 65 D1
Naila D ... 63 E2

Nailloux F ... 29 E3
Nailsworth GB ... 13 E1
Nairn GB ... 7 D4
Najac F ... 29 F2
Nájera E ... 36 C2
Nakkila FIN ... 120 B3
Nakło n. Notecią PL ... 53 D3
Nakskov DK ... 122 C4
Näljänkä FIN ... 109 F3
Naltijärvi FIN ... 105 E3
Namdalseid N ... 111 E1
Namsos N ... 106 C4
Namsskogan N ... 107 D4
Namur B ... 17 F2
Nancy F ... 23 D2
Nangis F ... 21 F2
Nannestad N ... 117 D1
Nant F ... 30 A2
Nanterre F ... 21 E2
Nantes F ... 24 B1
Nanteuil-
le-Haudouin F ... 21 F2
Nantiat F ... 25 E3
Nantua F ... 27 D2
Nantwich GB ... 10 C3
Náoussa GR ... 98 C2
Náoussa GR ... 87 F2
Napoli I ... 80 A3
La Napoule F ... 31 F2
Narberth / Arberth GB ... 12 C1
Narbolia I ... 82 A3
Narbonne F ... 30 A3
Narbonne-Plage F ... 30 A3
Narcao I ... 82 B4
Nardo I ... 81 F3

Narila FIN ... 121 E2
Narkaus FIN ... 109 D2
Narni I ... 79 D1
Naro I ... 84 C4
Naro-Fominsk RUS ... 125 F2
Narthaíki GR ... 93 E1
Narva EST ... 124 C1
Narvik N ... 104 B4
Nås S ... 118 C1
Näsåker S ... 112 C2
Năsăud RO ... 126 C4
Nasbinals F ... 30 A1
Našice HR ... 128 A1
Naso I ... 85 D2
Nasereith A ... 67 D3
Nässjo S ... 118 C4
Nastola FIN ... 121 D3
Nattavaara S ... 108 B2
Nättraby S ... 123 F2
Nauceile F ... 29 F2
Nauders A ... 67 D4
Nauen D ... 57 F2
Naul IRL ... 3 D4
Naumburg D ... 63 E1
Naunhof D ... 57 F4
Naustdal N ... 110 B3
Nava E ... 33 D2
Navacepeda
de Tormes E ... 41 F1
Navacerrada E ... 42 B1
Navaconcejo E ... 41 F2
Nava
de la Asunción E ... 36 A4

Nava del Rey E ... 35 F4
Nava de Ricomalillo
(La) E ... 42 A2
Nava de Santiago
(La) E ... 41 D3
Navahermosa E ... 42 A3
Navahrudak BY ... 124 C4
Navalcán E ... 41 F2
Navalcarnero E ... 42 B2
Navaleno E ... 36 C3
Navalmanzano E ... 36 A4
Navalmoral
de la Mata E ... 41 F2
Navalmorales (Los) E ... 42 A2
Navalperal
de Pinares E ... 42 A1
Navalucillos (Los) E ... 42 A3
Navaluenga E ... 42 A1
Navalvillar de Pela E ... 41 F3
Navamorcuende E ... 42 A2
Navan / An Uaimh IRL ... 3 D4
Navarredonda
de Gredos E ... 41 F1
Navarrenx F ... 28 B3
Navarrés E ... 43 F4
Navarrete E ... 37 D2
Navàs E ... 38 C3
Navascués E ... 37 E3
Navas de la Concepción
(Las) E ... 47 E1
Navas del Madroño E ... 41 D2
Navas del Marqués
(Las) E ... 42 B1
Navas de Oro E ... 36 A4
Navas de San Juan E ... 48 B1

Navasfrias E ... 41 D1
Navatalgordo E ... 42 A1
Nave I ... 71 F4
Nävekvarn S ... 119 E3
Navelli I ... 79 F4
Nave Redonda P ... 46 A2
Naveros E ... 47 D4
Navia E ... 33 D2
Navia de Suarna E ... 32 C3
Navl'a RUS ... 125 F4
Náxos GR ... 98 C2
Náxos (Nissí) GR ... 99 D2
Nay F ... 28 C3
Nazaré P ... 40 A2
Nazilli TR ... 129 F4
Néa Epídavros GR ... 97 E1
Néa Koróni GR ... 96 C3
Néa Moní GR ... 95 F3
Neápoli GR ... 87 D3
Neápoli GR ... 101 E3
Neápoli GR ... 97 E4
Neath /
Castell-nedd GB ... 13 D1
Nebel D ... 50 A2
Nebra D ... 57 E4
Neckarelz D ... 62 B4
Neckargemünd D ... 23 F1
Neckarsteinach D ... 23 F1
Neckarsulm D ... 62 B4
Neda E ... 32 B2
Nedervetil FIN ... 114 B2
Nedstrand N ... 116 A2
Neede NL ... 55 D3
Neermoor D ... 55 E1
Nefyn GB ... 10 A3

NANTES

0 1 km

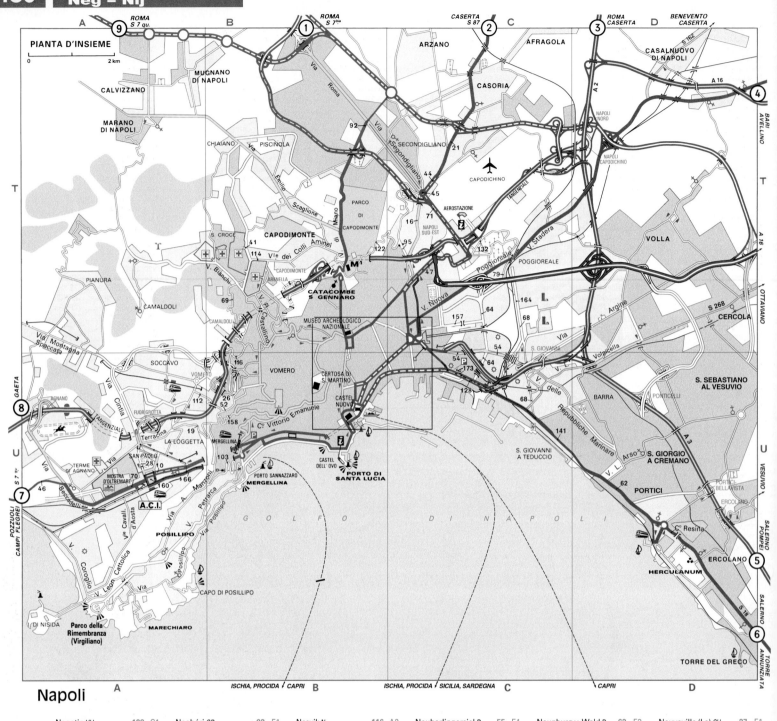

Napoli

Negotin *YU* 128 C1	Neohóri *GR* 93 F1	Nesvik *N* 116 A2	Neuharlingersiel *D* ... 55 E1	Neunburg v. Wald *D* .. 63 F3	Neuveville (La) *CH* 27 F1
Negra (La) *E* 49 D3	Neohóri *GR* 87 F4	Nettetal *D* 61 E1	Neuhaus *D* 50 C4	Neung-sur-Beuvron *F* 21 E4	Neuvic *F* 25 D4
Negrar *I* 71 F4	Nérac *F* 29 D2	Nettuno *I* 79 E2	Neuhaus *D* 63 D2	Neunkirchen *A* 69 D1	Neuvic *F* 25 F4
Negreira *E* 32 A3	Neráida *GR* 92 C1	Neuastenberg *D* 62 A1	Neuhaus (Oste) *D* 50 A3	Neunkirchen (Saar) *D* 23 E1	Neuville-aux-Bois *F* .. 21 E3
Nègrepelisse *F* 29 E2	Nerdvika *N* 110 C1	Neubeckum *D* 55 F4	Neuhaus i. Solling *D* . 56 B4	Neuötting *D* 67 F1	Neuville-de-Poitou *F*. 25 D2
Negru Vodă *RO* 129 E1	Neresheim *D* 67 D1	Le Neubourg *F* 21 D2	Neuhaus-	Neupölla *A* 64 C4	Neuville-
Neheim-Hüsten *D* 55 F4	Nereto *I* 77 D4	Neubrandenburg *D* ... 51 F3	Schierschnitz *D* ... 63 D2	Neuruppin *D* 51 E4	sur-Saône *F* 26 C3
Neiden *N* 105 F2	Néris-les-Bains *F* ... 25 F2	Neubukow *D* 51 D2	Neuhausen *CH* 23 F4	Neusiedl am See *A* ... 69 E1	Neuvy-le-Roi *F* 20 C4
Neila *E* 36 C3	Nerja *E* 48 A3	Neuburg	Neuhofen	Neuss *D* 61 E1	Neuvy-
Nekromandío	Néronde *F* 26 B3	a. d. Donau *D* 67 E1	an der Krems *A* ... 68 B1	Neustadt *D* 58 A4	St-Sépulchre *F* 25 E2
Efíras *GR* 92 A1	Nérondes *F* 26 A1	Neuchâtel *CH* 27 E1	Neuillé-Pont-Pierre *F*. 20 C4	Neustadt *D* 63 E1	Neuvy-
Neksø *DK* 123 E4	Nerotriviá *GR* 94 A3	Neu Darchau *D* 50 C4	Neuilly-en-Thelle *F* .. 16 C4	Neustadt *D* 51 E4	sur-Barangeon *F*... 25 E1
Nelas *P* 40 C1	Nerpio *E* 48 C1	Neuenbürg *D* 23 F2	Neuilly-le-Réal *F* 26 A2	Neustadt (Hessen) *D*. 62 B1	Neuwied *D* 61 F2
Nelidovo *RUS* 125 E2	Nerva *E* 47 D1	Neuendorf *D* 51 E2	Neuilly-l'Évêque *F*.... 22 C3	Neustadt a. d.	Névache *F* 27 E4
Nellim *FIN* 105 F3	Nervesa d. Battaglia *I* 72 B3	Neuendorf *D* 51 E20	Neuilly-St-Front *F* 17 D4	Weinstraße *D* 23 F1	Nevel *RUS* 125 D3
Nelson *GB* 11 D2	Nervi *I* 75 D2	Neuenhaus *D* 55 D3	Neu-Isenburg *D* 62 B3	Neustadt	Nevers *F* 26 A1
Neman *RUS* 124 B4	Nes *N* 117 D1	Neuenkirchen *D* 50 B4	Neukalen *D* 51 E3	a. Rübenberge *D*... 56 B3	Neves (As) *E* 32 A4
Neméa *GR* 97 D1	Nes *N* 117 E1	Neukirch *D* 58 A4	Neustadt-Glewe *D*.... 51 D4	Nevlunghavn *N*........ 117 D3
Nemours *F* 21 F3	Nes *NL* 54 C1	Neuenstadt *D* 62 B4	Neukirchen *D* 50 A1	Neustadt i. Holstein *D* 50 C2	New Abbey *GB*........ 9 D4
Nemyriv *UA* 127 E2	Nesbyen *N* 116 C1	Neuenstein *D* 62 B1	Neukirchen am	Neustadt	New Alresford *GB* 13 F2
Nenagh /	Nesebăr *BG* 129 E2	Neuerburg *D* 61 E3	Großvenediger *A* .. 67 F3	a. d. Aisch *D* 63 D3	New Cumnock *GB*..... 8 C1
An tAonach *IRL* 4 C2	Nesjahverfi *IS* 106 C2	Neuf-Brisach *F* 23 E3	Neukloster *D* 51 D3	Neustadt	New Deer *GB* 7 F4
Nénita *GR* 95 F4	Neskaupstaður *IS* ... 106 C1	Neufahrn *D* 63 F4	Neuleugbach *A* 69 D1	a. d. Donau *D* 63 E4	New Galloway *GB* 8 C1
Nenzing *A* 66 C3	Nesle *F* 16 C2	Neufchâteau *F* 22 C3	Neu Lübbenau *D* 58 A3	Neustadt	New Quay /
Neohoráki *GR* 94 A4	Nesna *N* 107 D3	Neufchâteau *B* 17 F3	Neumarkt *A* 68 A2	a. d. Waldnaab *D*... 63 E3	Ceinewydd *GB*...... 10 A4
Neohóri *GR* 91 E1	Nesoddtangen *N* 117 D2	Neufchâtel-en-Bray *F* 16 B4	Neumarkt	Neustadt b. Coburg *D* 63 D2	New Romney *GB* 15 D3
Neohóri *GR* 92 B2	Nesseby *N* 105 F2	Neufchâtel-	i. d. Oberpfalz *D* ... 63 E4	Neustift	New Ross / Ros Mhic
Neohóri *GR* 92 C3	Nesselwang *D* 67 D2	sur-Aisne *F*- 17 E4	Neumarkt	im Stubaital *A* 67 E3	Thriúin *IRL* 5 E3
Neohóri *GR* 94 B3	Nestáni *GR* 97 D1	Neufelden *A* 68 B1	in Steiermark *A*.... 68 C3	Neustrelitz *D* 51 F3	Newark-on-Trent *GB* . 11 E3
Neohóri *GR* 93 D2	Nestório *GR* 87 D3	Neuffen *D* 66 C1	Neumarkt-St. Veit *D*.. 67 F1	Neu Ulm *D* 66 C1	Newbiggin-
Neohóri *GR* 96 B1	Néstoros	Neugersdorf *D* 58 B4	Neumünster *D* 50 B3	La Neuve-Lyre *F* 20 C2	by-the-Sea *GB* 9 F4
Neohóri *GR* 92 C1	(Anáktora) *GR* 96 B2	Neuhardenberg *D* 58 A2	Neunagelberg *A*....... 64 C4	Neuves-Maisons *F* ... 22 C2	Newborough *GB*....... 10 A3

Name	Page	Grid
Newbridge / An Droichead Nua IRL	3	D4
Newburgh GB	7	F4
Newburgh GB	9	D2
Newbury GB	13	F2
Newcastle GB	3	E3
Newcastle Emlyn / Castell Newydd Emlyn GB	12	C1
Newcastle-under-Lyme GB	10	C3
Newcastle-upon-Tyne GB	9	F4
Newcastle West / An Caisleán Nua IRL	4	B2
Newhaven GB	14	C4
Newmarket IRL	4	B3
Newmarket GB	14	C2
Newmarket on Fergus IRL	4	C2
Newnham GB	13	E1
Newport / Casnewydd GB	13	D2
Newport GB	12	C1
Newport GB	13	F3
Newport / Baile Uí Fhiacháin IRL	2	A3
Newport GB	10	C4
Newport IRL	4	C2
Newport-on-Tay GB	9	D2
Newport Pagnell GB	14	B2
Newquay GB	12	B3
Newry GB	3	E3
Newton Abbot GB	13	D3
Newton-Aycliffe GB	11	D1
Newton Ferrers GB	12	C4
Newton Stewart GB	3	F2
Newtonmore GB	8	C1
Newtown GB	13	E1
Newtown / Drenewydd GB	10	B4
Newtownabbey GB	3	E2
Newtownards GB	3	E2
Newtownbutler GB	2	C3
Newtown-hamilton GB	3	D3
Newtown St. Boswells GB	9	E3
Newtown-stewart GB	3	D2
Nexon F	25	E3
Neyland GB	12	C1
Niáta GR	97	E3
Nibe DK	122	B1
Nicastro I	83	E3
Nice F	31	F2
Nickelsdorf A	69	E1
Nicolosi I	85	E3
Nicosia I	85	D3
Nicotera I	83	E3
Nidderau D	62	B2
Nideggen D	61	E2
Nidrí GR	92	A2
Niebla E	46	C2
Niebüll D	50	A2
Niederalteich D	64	A4
Niederaula D	62	B1
Niederbronn-les-Bains F	23	E2
Niederelsungen D	56	B4
Niederjossa D	62	B1
Niederkrüchten D	61	E1
Niederstetten D	62	C4
Niederstotzingen D	67	D1
Niegripp D	57	E3
Niemegk D	57	F3
Niemisel S	108	B3
Nienburg D	56	B2
Nienburg D	57	E3
Nierstein D	62	A3
Niesky D	58	B4
Nieul F	25	E3
Nieuweschans NL	55	E2
Nieuwpoort-Bad B	15	F4
Niforéka GR	92	C4
Nigríta GR	88	C1
Niinisalo FIN	120	B2
Nijar E	48	C3
Nijkerk NL	54	C3
Nijmegen NL	54	C4
Nijverdal NL	55	D3
Níkea GR	93	E1
Niki GR	87	E1
Nikiá GR	103	D1
Nikifóros GR	89	D1
Nikissiani GR	89	D1
Nikitas GR	88	C3
Nikkaluokta S	108	A1
Nikoléika GR	93	D4
Nikopol BG	129	D2
Nikopol' UA	127	F3
Nikópoli GR	92	B2
Nikópoli GR	92	B2
Nikšić YU	128	A2
Nilivaara S	108	B2
Nilsiä FIN	115	E3
Nîmes F	30	B2
Nimféa GR	89	F1
Nimféo GR	87	E2
Nímos (Nissí) GR	103	E1
Ninove F	17	E1
Niort F	24	C2
Nípsa GR	91	D2
Niš YU	128	B2
Nisa P	40	C2
Niscemi I	85	D4
Nissáki GR	86	B4
Nissilä FIN	115	D2
Níssiros (Nissí) GR	103	D1
Niton GB	13	F3
Nitra SK	126	A3
Nitry F	22	A4
Nittedal N	117	D1
Nittenau D	63	F4
Nittendorf D	63	E4
Nivala FIN	114	C2
Nivelles B	17	E2
Nižyn UA	127	E1
Nizza Monferrato I	74	C1
Njasviž BY	124	C4
Njurundabommen S	112	C3
Noailles F	16	C4
Noáin E	28	A4
Noblejas E	42	C2
Nocera Inferiore I	80	A3
Nocera Terinese I	83	E3
Nocera Umbra I	76	C4
Noceto I	75	F1
Noci I	81	D3
Nodeland N	116	B3
Nördlingen D	63	D4
Nörten-Hardenberg D	56	C4
Nlux-les-Mines F	16	C2
Nogara I	72	A4
Nogaro F	28	C2
Nogent F	22	C3
Nogent-le-Roi F	21	D2
Nogent-le-Rotrou F	21	D3
Nogent-sur-Seine F	22	A4
Noginsk RUS	125	F2
Nogueira de Ramuín E	32	B4
Noguera E	43	E1
Nohfelden D	23	E1
Noia E	32	A3
Noirétable F	26	B3
Noirmoutier-en-l'Ile F	24	A1
Noja E	36	C1
Nokia FIN	120	C2
Nola I	80	A3
Nolay F	26	C1
Noli I	75	D2
Nomeny F	23	D2
Nomexy F	23	D2
Nómia GR	97	E3
Nonancourt F	21	D2
Nonant-le-Pin F	20	C2
Nonaspe E	38	A4
None I	27	F4
Nonio I	70	C4
Nontron F	25	D3
Nonza F	78	A2
Noordwijk aan Zee NL	54	B3
Noormarkku FIN	120	B2
Nora S	119	D2
Norberg S	119	D1
Norcia I	76	C4
Nord-Lenangen N	104	C2
Nordborg DK	122	B3
Nordby DK	122	A3
Nordby DK	122	C2
Norddeich D	55	E1
Nord Edewecht D	55	E2
Nordeide N	110	B4
Norden D	55	E1
Nordenau D	62	A1
Nordenham D	50	A4
Norderney D	55	E1
Norderstedt D	50	B3
Nordfjordeid N	110	B3
Nordfold N	107	E1
Nordhalben D	63	E2
Nordhausen D	57	D4
Nordhorn D	55	E3
Nordingrå S	112	D2
Nordkjosbotn N	104	B3
Nordli N	111	F1
Nordmaling S	113	D2
Nordmark S	118	C2
Nordseter N	111	D4
Norðurfjörður IS	106	A1
Nore N	116	C1
Noresund N	117	D1
Norg NL	55	D2
Norheimsund N	116	B1
Norra Bergnäs S	108	A3
Norra Råda S	118	C1
Norråker S	112	B1
Norrby S	108	A4
Nørre Åby DK	122	B3
Nørre Alslev DK	122	C4
Nørre Nebel DK	122	A2
Nørre Snede DK	122	B2
Nørre Vorupør DK	122	A1
Norrent-Fontes F	16	C2
Norrköping S	119	D3
Norrnäs FIN	114	A4
Norrsunda S	119	E2
Norrsundet S	119	E1
Norrtälje S	119	F2
Norrviken S	123	D2
Norsjö S	108	A4
Nort-sur-Erdre F	19	E4
North Berwick GB	9	E2
North Walsham GB	15	D1
Northallerton GB	11	D1
Northam GB	12	C3
Northampton GB	14	B2
Northeim D	56	C4
Northleach GB	13	F1
Northwich GB	10	C3
Norton GB	11	E2
Nortorf D	50	B2
Norwich GB	15	D1
Nosivka UA	127	E1
Nossebro S	118	B3
Nossen D	63	F1
Nótia GR	87	F1
Noto I	85	E4
Notodden N	116	C1
Notre-Dame-de-Bellecombe F	27	E3
Nottingham GB	11	E3
Nouan-le-Fuzelier F	21	E4
Nova Zagora BG	129	D2
Novafeltria I	76	B2
Novales E	38	A3
Novara I	71	D4
Novara di Sicilia I	83	D4
Nové Mĕs to nad Váhom SK	126	A3
Nové Zámky SK	126	A4
Novelda E	49	F1
Novellara I	75	F1
Noventa Vicentina I	72	A4
Noves F	30	C2
Novgorod RUS	125	D1
Novhorod-Sivers'kyj UA	127	D1
Novi di Modena I	75	F1
Novi Ligure I	75	D1
Novi Pazar YU	128	B2
Novi Pazar BG	129	E2
Novi Sad YU	128	B1
Novion-Porcien F	17	E4
Novo mesto SLO	73	E3
Novohrad-Volyns'kyj UA	127	D2
Novomyrhorod UA	127	E2
Novoržev RUS	125	D2
Novoselycja UA	127	D3
Novosil' RUS	125	F4
Novoukraïnka UA	127	F3
Novovolyns'k UA	126	C2
Novozybkov RUS	125	D4
Novska HR	128	A1
Nový Jičín CZ	65	F2
Nousiainen FIN	120	B3
Nouvion-en-Ponthieu F	16	B3
Le Nouvion-en-Thiérache F	17	D3
Nouzonville F	17	E3
Nova Gorica SLO	72	C3
Nova Gradiška HR	128	A1
Nova Kachovka UA	127	F3
Nova Levante / Welschnofen I	67	E4
Nova Siri Stazione I	81	D4
Nova Vas SLO	73	E3
Novyj Buh UA	127	F2
Nowa Sól PL	58	C3
Nowogard PL	52	B3
Nowy Targ PL	126	A3
Nowy Sącz PL	126	A4
Noyant F	20	C4
Noyers F	22	A4
Noyers-sur-Jabron F	31	D2
Noyon F	17	D4
Nozay F	19	E4
Nürburg D	61	F2
Nürnberg D	63	D3
Nürnberg D	63	D3

NICE

Nürtingen D........... 66 C1
Nueva E............... 33 F2
Nueva Carteya E...... 47 F2
Nuévalos E............ 37 E4
Nuevo Baztán E....... 42 C2
Nuez de Arriba (La) E. 36 B2
Nuijamaa FIN......... 121 E3
Nuits-St-Georges F... 26 C1
Nules E............... 44 A3
Nulvi I............... 82 B1
Numana I.............. 77 D3
Numancia E............ 37 D3
Nummela FIN.......... 120 C4
Nummi FIN............ 120 C4
Nuneaton GB.......... 11 E4
Nunnanen FIN......... 105 E4
Nunspeet NL.......... 54 C3
Nuñomoral E.......... 41 E1
Nuorgam FIN.......... 105 F2
Nuoro I.............. 82 B2
Nuoro I.............. 50 B3
Nurallao I............ 82 B3
Núria E.............. 39 D2
Nurmes FIN........... 115 E3
Nurmijärvi FIN....... 121 D4
Nurmijärvi FIN....... 115 F2
Nurmo FIN............ 114 B3
Nus I................ 27 F3
Nusse D.............. 50 C3
Nuttlar D............ 62 A1
Nuttupera FIN........ 115 D2
Nyåker S............. 113 D1
Nybergsund N......... 111 E4
Nyborg DK............ 122 C3
Nybro S.............. 123 F2
Nýidalur IS.......... 106 B2
Nyíregyháza H........ 126 B3
Nykarleby /
  Uusikaarlepyy FIN . 114 B3
Nykøbing F DK........ 122 C4
Nykøbing M DK........ 122 B1
Nykøbing S DK........ 122 C3
Nyköping S........... 119 E3
Nykvarn S............ 119 E3
Nynäshamn S.......... 119 E3
Nyon CH.............. 27 E2
Nyons F.............. 30 C1
Nyrud N.............. 105 F3
Nysa PL.............. 65 E1
Nysäter S............ 118 B2
Nyseter N............ 110 C3
Nysted DK............ 122 C4
Nyvoll N............. 105 D2
Nyírbátor H.......... 126 B3

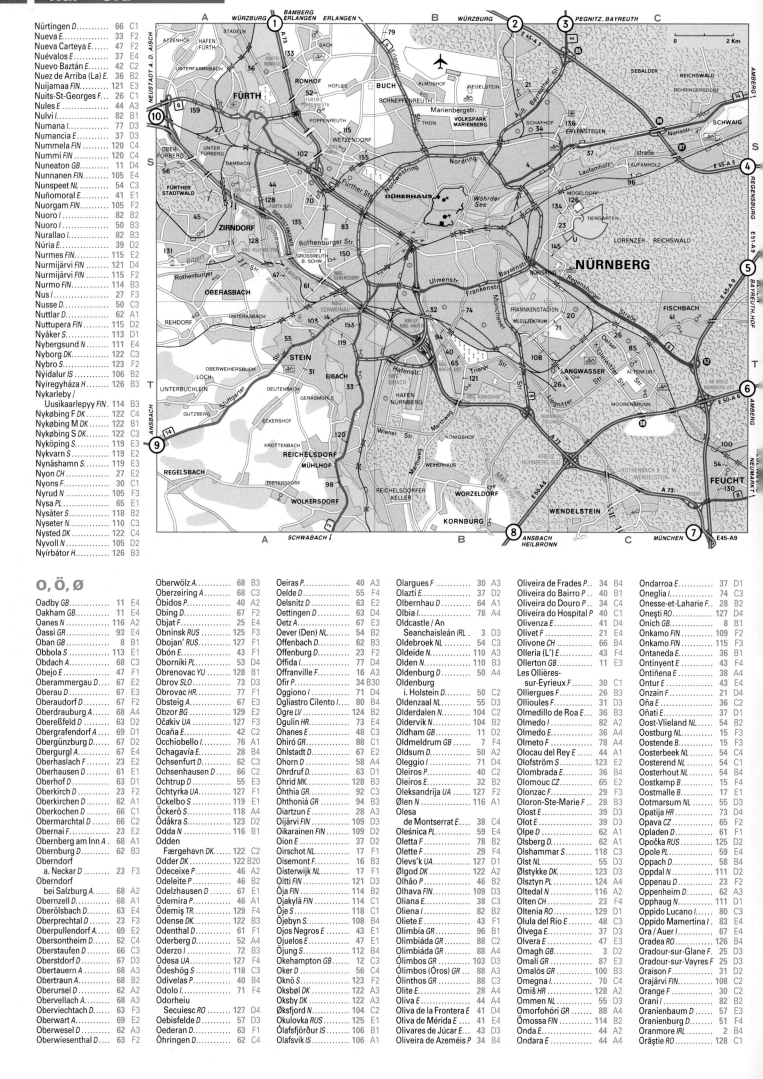

O, Ö, Ø

Oadby GB............. 11 E4
Oakham GB............ 11 E4
Oanes N.............. 116 A2
Óassi GR............. 93 E4
Oban GB.............. 8 B1
Obbola S............. 113 E1
Obdach A............. 68 C3
Obejo E.............. 47 F1
Oberammergau D....... 67 E2
Oberau D............. 67 E3
Oberaudorf D......... 67 F2
Oberdrauburg A....... 68 A4
Obereßfeld D......... 63 D2
Obergrafendorf A..... 69 D1
Obergünzburg D....... 67 D2
Obergurgl A.......... 67 E4
Oberhaslach F........ 23 E2
Oberhausen D......... 61 E1
Oberhof D............ 63 D1
Oberkirch D.......... 23 F2
Oberkirchen D........ 62 A1
Oberkochen D......... 66 C1
Obermarchtal D....... 66 C2
Obernai F............ 23 E2
Obernberg am Inn A . 68 A1
Obernburg D.......... 62 B3
Oberndorf
  a. Neckar D........ 23 F3
Oberndorf
  bei Salzburg A..... 68 A2
Obernzell D.......... 68 A1
Oberölsbach D........ 63 E4
Oberprechtal D....... 23 F3
Oberpullendorf A..... 69 E2
Obersontheim D....... 62 C4
Oberstaufen D........ 66 C3
Oberstdorf D......... 67 D3
Obertauern A......... 68 A3
Obertraun A.......... 68 B2
Oberursel D.......... 62 A4
Obervellach A........ 68 A3
Oberviechtach D...... 63 F3
Oberwart A........... 69 E2
Oberwesel D.......... 62 A3
Oberwiesenthal D..... 63 F2

Oberwölz A........... 68 B3
Oberzeiring A........ 68 C3
Óbidos P............. 40 A2
Obing D.............. 67 F2
Objat F.............. 25 E4
Obninsk RUS.......... 125 F3
Obojan' RUS.......... 127 F1
Obón E............... 43 F1
Oborniki PL.......... 53 D4
Obrenovac YU......... 128 B3
Obrov SLO............ 73 D3
Obrovac HR........... 77 F1
Obzor BG............. 129 E2
Očakiv UA............ 127 F3
Ocaña E.............. 42 C2
Occhiobello I........ 76 A1
Ochagavía E.......... 28 B4
Ochsenfurt D......... 62 C3
Ochsenhausen D....... 66 C2
Ochtrup D............ 55 E3
Ochtyrka UA.......... 127 F1
Öckerö S............. 118 A4
Ödåkra S............. 123 D2
Odden
  Færgehavn DK...... 122 C2
Odder DK............. 122 B20
Odeceixe P........... 46 A2
Odeleite P........... 46 B2
Odelzhausen D........ 67 E1
Odemira P............ 46 A1
Ödemiş TR............ 129 F4
Odense DK............ 122 B3
Odenthal D........... 61 F1
Oderberg D........... 52 A4
Oderzo I............. 72 B3
Odesa UA............. 127 F4
Ödeshög S............ 118 C3
Odivelas P........... 40 B4
Odolo I.............. 71 D4
Odorheiu
  Secuiesc RO....... 127 D4
Oebisfelde D......... 57 D3
Oederan D............ 63 F1
Öhringen D........... 62 C4

Oeiras P............. 40 A3
Oelde D.............. 55 F4
Oelsnitz D........... 63 E2
Oettingen D.......... 63 D4
Oetz A............... 67 E3
Oever (Den) NL....... 54 B2
Offenbach D.......... 62 B3
Offenburg D.......... 23 F2
Offida I............. 77 D4
Offranville F........ 16 A3
Ofir P............... 34 B30
Oggiono I............ 71 D4
Ogliastro Cilento I... 80 B3
Ogre LV.............. 124 B2
Ogulin HR............ 73 E4
Ohanes E............. 48 C3
Ohiró GR............. 88 C1
Ohlstadt D........... 67 E2
Ohorn D.............. 58 A4
Ohrdruf D............ 63 D1
Ohrid MK............. 128 B3
Óthia GR............. 92 C3
Othoniá GR........... 94 B3
Oiartzun E........... 28 A3
Oijärvi FIN.......... 109 D3
Oikarainen FIN....... 109 D2
Oion E............... 37 D2
Oirschot NL.......... 17 F1
Oisemont F........... 16 B3
Oisterwijk NL........ 17 F1
Oitti FIN............ 121 D3
Öja FIN.............. 114 B2
Öje S................ 118 C1
Öjebyn S............. 108 B4
Ojos Negros E........ 43 E1
Ojuelos E............ 47 D3
Öjung S.............. 112 B4
Okehampton GB........ 12 C3
Oker D............... 56 C4
Oknö S............... 123 F2
Oksby DK............. 122 A3
Øksfjord N........... 104 C2
Øksnes N............. 107 D1
Okulovka RUS......... 125 E1
Ólafsfjörður IS...... 106 B1
Olafsvík IS.......... 106 A1

Olargues F........... 30 A3
Olazti E............. 37 D2
Olbernhau D.......... 64 A1
Olbia I.............. 78 A4
Oldcastle / An
  Seanchaisleán IRL . 3 D3
Oldebroek NL......... 54 C3
Oldeide N............ 110 A3
Olden N.............. 110 B3
Oldenburg D.......... 50 A4
Oldenburg
  i. Holstein D...... 50 C2
Oldenzaal NL......... 55 D3
Olderdalen N......... 104 C2
Oldervik N........... 104 B2
Oldham GB............ 11 D2
Oldmeldrum GB........ 7 F4
Oldsum D............. 50 A2
Oleggio I............ 71 D4
Oleiros P............ 40 C2
Oleiros E............ 32 B3
Oleksandrija UA...... 127 F2
Ølen N............... 116 A1
Olesa
  de Montserrat E... 38 C4
Oleśnica PL.......... 59 E4
Oletta F............. 78 B2
Olette F............. 29 F4
Olevs'k UA........... 127 D1
Ølgod DK............. 122 A2
Olhão P.............. 46 B2
Olhava FIN........... 109 D3
Oliana E............. 38 C3
Oliena I............. 82 B2
Oliete E............. 43 F1
Olimbía GR........... 96 B1
Olimbiáda GR......... 88 C2
Olimbiáda GR......... 88 A4
Ólimbos GR........... 103 D3
Ólimbos (Óros) GR... 88 A3
Òlinthos GR.......... 88 C3
Olite E.............. 28 A4
Oliva E.............. 44 A4
Oliva de la Frontera E 41 D4
Oliva de Mérida E ... 41 E4
Olivares de Júcar E.. 43 D3
Oliveira de Azeméis P 34 B4

Oliveira de Frades P.. 34 B4
Oliveira do Bairro P .. 40 B1
Oliveira do Douro P .. 34 C4
Oliveira do Hospital P 40 C1
Olivenza E........... 41 D4
Olivet F............. 21 E4
Olivone CH........... 66 B4
Olleria (L') E....... 43 F4
Ollerton GB.......... 11 E3
Les Ollières-
  sur-Eyrieux F..... 30 C1
Olliergues F......... 26 B3
Ollioules F.......... 31 D3
Olmedillo de Roa E .. 36 B3
Olmedo I............. 82 A2
Olmedo E............. 36 A4
Olmeto F............. 78 A4
Olocau del Rey E..... 44 A1
Olofström S.......... 123 E2
Olombrada E.......... 36 B4
Olomouc CZ........... 65 E2
Olonzac F............ 29 F3
Oloron-Ste-Marie F . 28 B3
Olost E.............. 39 D3
Olot E............... 39 D3
Olpe D............... 62 A1
Olsberg D............ 62 A1
Olshammar S.......... 118 C3
Olst NL.............. 55 D3
Ølstykke DK.......... 123 D3
Olsztyn PL........... 124 A4
Oltedal N............ 116 A2
Olten CH............. 23 F4
Oltenia RO........... 129 D1
Olula del Río E...... 48 C3
Ólvega E............. 37 D3
Olvera E............. 47 E3
Omagh GB............. 3 D2
Omalí GR............. 87 E3
Omalós GR............ 100 B3
Omegna I............. 70 C4
Omiš HR.............. 128 A2
Ommen NL............. 55 D3
Omorfohóri GR........ 88 A4
Ómossa FIN........... 114 B2
Onda E............... 44 A2
Ondara E............. 44 A4

Ondarroa E........... 37 D1
Oneglia I............ 74 C3
Onesse-et-Laharie F.. 28 B2
Oneşti RO............ 127 D4
Onich GB............. 8 B1
Onkamo FIN........... 109 F2
Onkamo FIN........... 115 F3
Ontaneda E........... 36 B1
Ontinyent E.......... 43 F4
Ontiñena E........... 38 A4
Ontur E.............. 43 E4
Onzain F............. 21 D4
Oña E................ 36 C2
Oñati E.............. 37 D1
Oost-Vlieland NL..... 54 B2
Oostburg NL.......... 15 E3
Oostende B........... 15 F3
Oosterbeek NL........ 54 C4
Oosterend NL......... 54 C1
Oosterhout NL........ 54 B4
Oostkamp B........... 15 F4
Oostmalle B.......... 17 E1
Oostmarsum NL........ 55 D3
Opatija HR........... 73 D4
Opava CZ............. 65 F2
Opladen D............ 61 F1
Opočka RUS........... 125 D2
Opole PL............. 59 E4
Oppach D............. 58 B4
Oppau D.............. 23 F2
Oppenau D............ 23 F2
Oppenheim D.......... 62 A3
Opphaug N............ 111 D1
Oppido Lucano I...... 80 C3
Oppido Mamertina I .. 83 E4
Ora / Auer I......... 67 D4
Oradea RO............ 126 B4
Oradour-sur-Glane F . 25 D3
Oradour-sur-Vayres F 25 D3
Oraison F............ 31 D2
Orajärvi FIN......... 108 C2
Orange F............. 30 C2
Orani I.............. 82 B2
Oranienbaum D........ 57 E3
Oranienburg D........ 51 F4
Oranmore IRL......... 2 B4
Orăştie RO........... 128 C1

Oravais /			Oria *I*	81	E3	Orreaga /			Osimo *I*	77	D3
Oravainen *FIN*	114	B3	Oria *E*	48	C2	Roncesvalles *E*	28	A3	Oskarshamn *S*	123	F1
Oravikoski *FIN*	115	E3	Origny-Ste-Benoite *F*	17	D3	Orrefors *S*	123	F2	Oskarström *S*	123	D2
Oraviţa *RO*	128	B1	Orihuela *E*	49	E1	Orsa *S*	112	B4	Oslo *N*	117	D1
Ørbæk *DK*	122	C3	Orihuela			Orša *BY*	125	C4	Ösmo *S*	119	E3
Orbassano *I*	27	F4	del Tremedal *E*	43	E1	Orsay *F*	21	E2	Osnabrück *D*	55	F3
Orbe *CH*	27	E1	Orimattila *FIN*	121	D3	Orsières *CH*	27	F2	Osoppo *I*	68	A4
Orbec *F*	20	C2	Oriní *GR*	88	C1	Orsogna *I*	79	F4	Osorno la Mayor *E*	36	A2
Orbetello *I*	78	C1	Oriolo *I*	81	D4	Orşova *RO*	128	C1	Osøyro *N*	116	A1
Orbey *F*	23	E4	Oripää *FIN*	120	B3	Ørsta *N*	110	B3	Ospedaletti *I*	74	C3
Orce *E*	48	C2	Orissaare *EST*	124	B2	Örsundsbro *S*	119	E2	Ospitaletto *I*	71	E4
Orcera *E*	48	C1	Oristano *I*	82	A3	Orta Nova *I*	80	B2	Oss *NL*	54	C4
Orchies *F*	17	D2	Orivesi *FIN*	120	C2	Orta S. Giulio *I*	70	C4	Óssa *GR*	88	B2
Orcières *F*	31	E1	Orjahovo *BG*	128	C2	Orte *I*	79	D1	Ossa de Montiel *E*	42	C4
Orcival *F*	26	A3	Ørje *N*	117	E2	Orth *A*	69	E1	Ossiach *A*	68	B4
Ordes *E*	32	B2	Orkanger *N*	111	D2	Orthez *F*	28	B3	Óssios Loukás *GR*	63	E3
Ordizia *E*	37	D1	Örkelljunga *S*	123	D3	Ortigueira *E*	32	C2	Ossun *F*	28	C3
Orduña *E*	36	C2	Orléans *F*	21	E4	Ortisei /			Ostaškov *RUS*	125	E2
Ordžonikidze *UA*	127	F3	Orly *F*	21	E2	St. Ulrich *I*	67	F4	Østby *N*	111	E4
Ore *S*	112	B4	Orménio *GR*	91	E1	Ortnevik *N*	110	B4	Oster *UA*	127	E1
Orea *E*	43	E1	Ormilia *GR*	88	C3	Orton *GB*	10	C1	Øster Vrå *DK*	122	C1
Örebro *S*	119	D2	Órmos *GR*	88	B3	Ortona *I*	80	A4	Osterburg *D*	57	D2
Orechovo-			Órmos Korthíou *GR*	98	C1	Ortrand *D*	58	A4	Osterburken *D*	62	B4
Zujevo *RUS*	125	F2	Órmos			Örträsk *S*	113	D1	Østerbø *DK*	122	C1
Öregrund *S*	119	F1	Panagías *GR*	88	C3	Orune *I*	78	A4	Østerbybruk *S*	119	E1
Oreí *GR*	93	F2	Órmos Prínou *GR*	89	E2	Orusco *E*	42	C2	Österbymo *S*	119	D4
Orellana			Ormož *SLO*	73	F2	Orvalho *P*	40	C2	Österfärnebo *S*	119	E1
de la Sierra *E*	41	F3	Ormsjö *S*	112	B1	Orvieto *I*	76	B4	Osterfeld *D*	63	E1
Orellana la Vieja *E*	41	F3	Ormskirk *GB*	10	C2	Orvinio *I*	79	E1	Osterhofen *D*	64	A4
Orense / Ourense *E*	32	B4	Ornans *F*	27	D1	Orzinuovi *I*	71	E4	Osterholz-		
Oréo *E*	89	C1	Ørnes *N*	107	E2	Os *N*	111	E3	Scharmbeck *D*	50	A4
Oreókastro *GR*	88	B2	Orníós *GR*	98	C2	Osa			Osteria del Gatto *I*	76	C3
Orestiáda *GR*	91	E1	Örnsköldsvik *S*	113	D2	de la Vega *E*	42	C3	Osterode *D*	56	C4
Orgáni *GR*	91	D1	Or'ol *RUS*	125	F4	Osby *S*	123	E2	Östersund *S*	112	B2
Organyà *E*	38	C3	Oron-la-Ville *CH*	27	E2	Oschatz *D*	57	F4	Östersundom *FIN*	121	D4
Orgaz *E*	42	B3	Oropa *I*	70	C4	Oschersleben *D*	57	D3	Östervåla *S*	119	E1
Orgelet *F*	27	D2	Oropesa *E*	41	F2	Oschiri *I*	82	B1	Osterwieck *D*	56	C3
Orgères-en-Beauce *F*	21	E3	Orosei *I*	78	A4	Oseja			Östhammar *S*	119	F1
Orgiva *E*	48	B3	Orosháza *H*	126	B4	de Sajambre *E*	33	F3	Ostheim v. d. Rhön *D*	62	C2
Orgon *F*	30	C2	Orpesa / Oropesa del			Osen *N*	111	E1	Ostia Antica *I*	79	D2
Orgosolo *I*	82	B2	Mar *E*	44	A2	Osera *E*	37	F4	Ostiglia *I*	76	A1
Orhei *MOL*	127	E3	Orpierre *F*	31	D1	Osijek *HR*	128	A1	Östmark *S*	118	B1
Orhomenós *GR*	93	F3	Orpington *GB*	14	C3	Osilo *I*	82	A1	Ostra *I*	76	C3
									Ostrach *D*	66	C2
									Ostrava *CZ*	65	F2
									Ostritz *D*	58	B4
									Ostroh *UA*	127	D2
									Ostrołęka *PL*	126	B1
									Ostrov *RUS*	125	C2
									Ostrov *RO*	129	E1
									Ostrowiec-		
									Świętokrzyski *PL*	126	B2
									Ostrów		
									Wielkopolski *PL*	59	E3
									Ostróda *PL*	124	A4
									Ostrów		
									Mazowiecka *PL*	126	B1
									Ostuni *I*	81	E3
									Osuna *E*	47	F2
									Oswestry *GB*	10	C3
									Oświęcim *PL*	126	A2
									Otanmäki *FIN*	115	D2
									Otava *FIN*	121	E2
									Oteren *N*	104	C3
									Othem *S*	119	F4
									Othery *GB*	13	E2
									Othoní (Nissí) *GR*	86	A4
									Otívar *E*	48	A3
									Otley *GB*	11	D2
									Otnes *N*	111	E3
									Otocac *HR*	73	F4
									Otranto *I*	81	F3
									Otta *N*	111	D3
									Ottana *I*	82	B2
									Ottaviano *I*	80	A3
									Uttenschlag *A*	68	C1
									Ottensheim *A*	68	B1
									Otter Ferry *GB*	8	C2
									Otterburn *GB*	9	E4
									Otterlo *NL*	54	C4
									Otterndorf *D*	50	A3
									Otterøy *N*	106	C3
									Ottersberg *D*	50	B4
									Otterup *DK*	122	B3
									Ottery St. Mary *GB*	13	D3
									Ottmarsheim *F*	23	E4
									Ottnang *A*	68	A1
									Ottobeuren *D*	67	D2
									Ottobrunn *D*	67	E2
									Ottsjö *S*	112	A2
									Ottweiler *D*	23	E1
									Otwock *PL*	126	B1
									Otziás *GR*	98	A1
									Ouchy *CH*	27	E2
									Oucques *F*	21	D4
									Oud-Beijerland *NL*	54	B4
									Ouddorp *NL*	54	A4
									Oude Pekela *NL*	55	D2
									Oudenaarde *B*	17	D2
									Oudenbosch *NL*	17	E1
									Oughterard /		
									Uachtar Ard *IRL*	2	A4
									Oulainen *FIN*	114	C2
									Oulchy-le-Château *F*	17	D4
									Oulu (Uleåborg) *FIN*	114	C1
									Oulunsalo *FIN*	114	C1
									Oulx *I*	27	E4
									Oundle *GB*	11	E4
									Ouranópoli *GR*	89	D3
									Ourém *P*	40	B2
									Ourense / Orense *E*	32	B4
									Ourique *P*	46	A1
									Ourol *E*	32	C2
									Ourville-		
									en-Caux *F*	16	A4
									Oust *F*	29	E4
									Outeiro de Rei *E*	32	C3
									Outokumpu *FIN*	115	F3
									Outomuro *E*	32	B4
									Outwell *GB*	11	F4
									Ouzouer-		
									le-Marché *F*	21	D4
									Ouzouer-		
									sur-Loire *F*	21	E4
									Ovada *I*	75	D2
									Ovanåker *S*	112	B4
									Ovar *P*	34	B4
									Ovedskloster *S*	123	E3

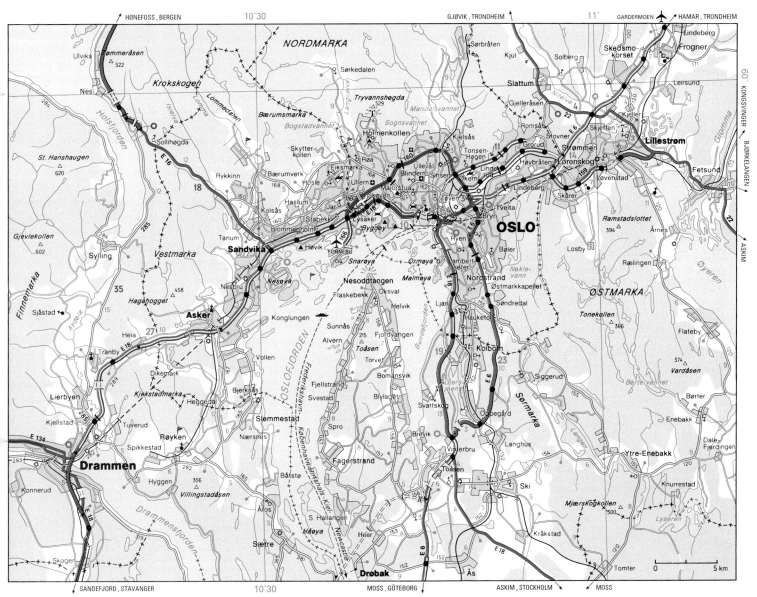

Overath D 61 F1
Øverbygd N 104 B3
Overhalla N 107 D4
Överhörnäs S 113 D2
Overijse B 17 E2
Överkalix S 108 C3
Övermark FIN 114 B4
Övertorneå S 108 C2
Överum S 119 D4
Oviedo E 33 E2
Ovindoli I 79 F1
Øvre Årdal N 110 C4
Övre Soppero S 108 B1
Ovruč UA 127 D1
Oxelösund S 119 E3
Oxford GB 13 F1
Oxiá E 92 C1
Oxiá (Nissí) GR 92 B3
Oxie S 123 D3
Oxilithos GR 94 B3
Oybin D 64 B1
Øye N 110 C4
Øyer N 111 D4
Oy-Mittelberg D 67 D2
Oyntdartfjørdur DK ... 106 A3
Øysang N 116 C3
Oyonnax F 27 D2
Øystese N 116 B1
Oyten D 50 B4
Ožbalt SLO 73 E2
Ózd H 126 B3
Ozieri I 82 B2

P
Paakkila FIN 115 E3
Paalasmaa FIN 115 F2
Paavola FIN 114 C1
Pabianice PL 126 A2
Paca (La) E 49 D2
La Pacaudière F 26 B2
Paceco I 84 A3
Pachino I 85 E4
Paço de Sousa P 34 B4
Paços de Ferreira P ... 34 B3
Pacy-sur-Eure F 21 D2
Padasjoki FIN 121 D3
Paderborn D 55 F4
Paderne P 46 A2
Padiham GB 10 C2
Padornelo E 32 C4
Padova I 72 A4
Padrón E 32 A3
Padru I 78 A4
Padstow GB 12 B3
Padul E 48 B3
Paesana I 31 F1
Paestum I 80 B4
Paestum Antica I 80 B4
Pag HR 77 E1
Paganico I 76 A4
Pagny-sur-Moselle F ... 22 C2
Pagóndas GR 94 A3
Pagóndas GR 99 F1

Pagoúria GR 89 F1
Páhi GR 94 A4
Pahiá Ámos GR 101 E4
Paide EST 124 B1
Paignton GB 13 D3
Paimbluf F 19 D4
Paimio FIN 120 B4
Paimpol F 18 C2
Painswick GB 13 E1
Paisley GB 8 C3
Pajala S 108 C2
Pajanosas (Las) E 47 D2
Paks H 126 A4
Pal. Kavála GR 89 E1
Pal. Krovíli GR 91 D2
Palacios de la Sierra E 36 C3
Palacios del Sil E 33 D3
Palacios de Sanabria E 33 D4
Palacios y Villafranca (Los) E 47 D2
Paládio GR 89 F1
Paladru F 27 D3
Palafrugell E 39 E3
Palagía GR 91 D2
Palagiano I 81 D3
Palagonía I 85 D3
Palaia I 75 F3
Le Palais F 18 C4
Palaiseau F 21 E2
Palamás GR 93 D1

Palamós E 39 E3
Palanga LT 124 A3
Palas de Rei E 32 B3
Palata I 80 A1
Palatítsa GR 88 A2
Palau I 82 B1
Palavas-les-Flots F ... 30 B3
Palazzo del Pero I 76 B3
Palazzo S. Gervasio I. 80 C3
Palazzolo Acreide I... 85 E4
Palazzolo sull'Oglio I. 71 E4
Palazzuolo sul Senio I 76 A2
Paldiski EST 124 B1
Paleá Epídavros GR .. 97 E1
Palékastro GR 101 E4
Palena I 79 F1
Palencia E 36 A3
Paleohóra GR 100 A4
Paleohóra GR 97 F1
Paleohóri GR 88 C2
Paleohóri GR 97 D2
Paleohóri GR 95 F2
Paleohóri GR 92 C1
Paleohóri GR 87 E3
Paleohóri GR 92 B1
Paleohóri GR 87 E4
Paleokastrítsa GR 86 B4
Paleókastro GR 93 D2
Paleókastro GR 87 E3
Paleókastro GR 99 F1
Paleókastro GR 88 C3
Paleókastro GR 88 C1
Paleokómi GR 89 D2
Paleópirgos GR 88 A4
Paleópirgos GR 93 D3
Paleópoli GR 98 B1
Paleópoli GR 91 D3
Palermo I 84 B2
Páleros GR 92 C3
Palestrina I 79 E2
Páli GR 103 D1
Paliano I 79 E2
Palidoro I 79 D2
Palinges F 26 B2
Palinuro I 80 B4
Palioúri GR 88 C4
Paliouriá GR 87 F4
Paliseul B 17 F3
Pälkäne FIN 120 C3
Pálkem S 108 B3
La Pallice F 24 B2
Palluau I 24 A1
Palma E 45 E3
Palma di Montechiaro I 84 C4
Palma del Condado (La) E 47 D2
Palma del Río E 47 E2
Palmadula I 82 A1
Palmanova I 72 A4
Palmela P 40 A4
Palmi I 83 E4
Palo del Colle I 81 D2
Palojoensuu FIN 105 D4
Palokki FIN 115 E3
Palomäki FIN 115 E2
Palomares del Campo E 43 D2
Palomas E 41 E4
Palombara Sabina I .. 79 E1
Palos de la Frontera E 46 C2
Pals E 39 E3
Pålsboda S 119 E3
Paltamo FIN 115 E1
Paltaniemi FIN 115 E2
Paluzza I 68 A4
Pámfila GR 95 F1
Pamhagen A 69 E1
Pamiers F 29 E3
Pampilhosa P 40 B1
Pampilhosa da Serra P 40 C1
Pampliega E 36 B2
Pamplona / Iruñea E.. 28 A4
Pamporovo BG 129 D3
Panagía GR 92 B1
Panagía GR 87 F4
Panagía GR 89 E2
Panagía GR 89 F4
Panagía GR 87 E3
Panagjurište BG 128 C2
Pancalieri I 27 F4
Pančevo YU 128 B1
Pancorbo E 36 C2
Pandánassa GR 97 E4
Pandeleimónas GR 88 A4
Pandino I 71 E4
Pandrup DK 122 B1
Panes E 33 F3
Panetólio GR 92 C3
Panevėžys LT 124 A3
Pangbourne GB 13 D3
Pankakoski FIN 115 F2

Pankow D 57 F2
Panne (De) B 15 F4
Panórama GR 88 C1
Panórama GR 88 B2
Panormítis GR 103 E1
Pánormos GR 98 C1
Pánormos GR 100 C3
Päntäne FIN 120 B2
Pantelleria I 84 A4
Paola I 83 E2
Pápa H 69 F20
Papádes GR 94 A2
Papádos GR 95 F2
Páparis GR 96 C2
Papasídero I 80 C4
Papenburg D 55 E2
Pápingo GR 87 D4
Pappenheim D 63 D4
Parabita I 81 F3
Paracuellos de Jiloca E 37 E4
Paradas E 47 E2
Paradela P 34 C3
Paradissiá GR 96 C2
Parádissos GR 89 E1
Parajes E 32 C2
Parakálamos GR 86 C4
Parákila GR 95 F1
Paralía GR 88 A3
Paralía GR 92 C4
Paralía GR 97 E3
Paralía GR 93 F4
Paralía Akrátas GR ... 93 E4
Paralía Ástros GR 97 D2
Paralía Kímis GR 94 A2
Paralía Kotsikiás GR . 94 A2
Paralía Skotínas GR .. 88 A3
Paralía Tiroú GR 97 E2
Paramé F 19 D2
Paramithía GR 92 A1
Páramo del Sil E 33 D3
Parapésti GR 89 E1
Parapótamos GR 86 C4
Paray-le-Monial F 26 B2
Parchim D 51 D3
Pardo (El) E 42 B1
Pardubice CZ 64 C2
Pareja E 43 D1
Parentis-en-Born F ... 28 B1
Párga GR 92 A1
Pargas / Parainen FIN. 120 B4
Parikkala FIN 121 F2
Paris F 21 E2
Parkalompolo S 108 C1
Parkano FIN 120 B2
Parla E 42 B2
Parlavà E 39 E3
Parma I 75 F1
Parnassós (Óros) GR . 93 E3
Parndorf A 69 E1
Párnitha (Óros) GR .. 94 A4
Pärnu EST 124 B2
Parola FIN 120 C3
Parsberg D 63 E4
Parsdorf D 67 E1
Partakko FIN 105 F3
Partanna I 84 B3
Partenen A 67 D4
Parthenay F 24 C2
Parthéni GR 99 F2
Partille S 118 B4
Partinico I 84 B2
Partney GB 11 F3
Pas-en-Artois F 16 C3
Pasaia / Pasajes E.... 28 A3
Pasewalk D 52 A3
Pashalítsa GR 93 D1
Passá-Limáni GR 95 E4
Passais F 19 F2
Passás (Nissí) GR 95 F3
Passau D 68 A1
Passavás GR 97 D3
Passignano sul Trasimeno I 76 B4
Pastavy BY 124 C3
Pastrana E 42 C1
Pásztó H 126 A4
Patay F 21 E3
Pateley Bridge GB 11 D2
Pateniemi FIN 114 C1
Paterna de Rivera E .. 47 D3
Paternò I 85 D3
Paternopoli I 80 B3
Patersdorf D 64 A4
Patiópoulo GR 92 C2
Patitíri GR 94 A2
Pátmos GR 99 F2

Pátmos (Nissí) GR 99 F2
Patras GR 92 C4
Patreksfjörður IS..... 106 A1
Patrington GB 11 F2
Pattada I 82 B2
Patterdale GB 10 C1
Patti I 85 D2
Pattijoki FIN 114 C1
Pau F 28 C3
Pauillac F 24 B4
Paul P 40 C1
Paular (El) E 42 A1
Paularo I 68 A4
Paulhaguet F 26 A4
Paullo I 71 E4
Pavia P 40 B3
Pavia I 75 D1
Pavia (Certosa di) I . 75 D1
Pavilly F 16 A4
Pávliani GR 93 E2
Pávlos GR 93 F3
Pavlovskij Posad RUS 125 F2
Pavullo nel Frignano I 75 F2
Paxí GR 92 A1
Paxí (Nissí) GR 86 A1
Payerne CH 27 E1
Paymogo E 46 C1
Payrac F 29 E1
Pazardžik BG 129 D2
Pazin HR 73 D4
Le Péage-de-Roussillon F 26 C4
Peal de Becerro E 48 B2
Peanía GR 94 A4
Peç YU 128 A2
Peccioli I 75 F3
Peckelsheim D 56 B4
Pécs H 128 A1
Pedaso I 77 D3
Pedernoso (El) E 42 C3
Pedersker DK 123 E4
Pedersöre / Pedersören K. FIN 114 B3
Pédi GR 103 E1
Pedrafita do Cebreiro E 32 C3
Pedrajas de San Esteban E 36 A4
Pedralba E 43 F3
Pedralba de la Pradería E 33 D4
Pedras Salgadas P ... 34 C3
Pedraza de la Sierra E 36 B4
Pedrera E 47 F2
Pedro Abad E 48 A1
Pedro Bernardo E 42 A2
Pedrógão P 46 B1
Pedrógão P 40 A1
Pedrógão Grande P .. 40 B2
Pedrola E 37 E3
Pedro Muñoz E 42 C3
Pedroñeras (Las) E .. 43 D3
Pedrosas (Las) E 37 F3
Pedroso (El) E 47 E1
Peebles GB 9 D3
Peel GB 3 F3
Peenemünde D 51 F2
Pefkári GR 89 E2
Pefkí GR 93 F2
Péfkos GR 87 D3
Pega P 41 D1
Pegalajar E 48 B2
Pegau D 63 E1
Pegli I 75 D2
Pegnitz D 63 E3
Pego E 44 A4
Pegognaga I 75 F1
Pegolotte I 72 B4
Peguera E 45 D3
Peine D 56 C3
Peio I 67 D4
Peíra-Cava F 31 F2
Peißenberg D 67 E2
Peiting D 67 E2
Peitz D 58 A3
Péla GR 88 A2
Pelasgía GR 93 E2
Pelekános GR 87 E3
Pélekas GR 86 B4
Peletá GR 97 E2
Pelhřimov CZ 64 C3
Peljašac HR 128 A2
Pelkosenniemi FIN ... 109 E1
Pellegrino Parmense I 75 E1
Pellegrue F 28 C1
Le Pellerin F 24 A1
Pellesmäki FIN 115 E3
Pello FIN 108 C2
Peltosalmi FIN 115 D2
Peltovuoma FIN 105 D4
Pélussin F 26 C4

PALERMO

0 — 1 km

MONDELLO · Pza Valdesi · V. Lorenzo Iandolino di Scalea · PARTANNA · V. Partanna Castelforte · PUNTA DI PRIOLA · GOLFO DI PALERMO · MONTE PELLEGRINO · SANTUARIO DI STA ROSALIA · VERGINE MARIA · PALLAVICINO · PATTI · PARCO DELLA FAVORITA · S. LORENZO · RESUTTANA · CRUILLAS · UDITORE · BOCCADIFALCO · ALTARELLO · CATACOMBE DEI CAPPUCCINI · Pal. della Zisa · PAL. DEI NORMANNI · ARENELLA · ACQUASANTA · PORTO · FIERA DEL MEDITERRANEO · CASTELLO UTVEGGIO · CIMITERO DEI ROTOLI · ROMAGNOLO · A.C.I. · PARTINICO · Lungomare

A 29: AEROPORTO, TRAPANI · TRAPANI / MONREALE · SCIACCA S 624 · AGRIGENTO · A 19: CATANIA, MESSINA · LIVORNO, GENOVA · NAPOLI, CAGLIARI · USTICA · S 113 · S 121 · S 186

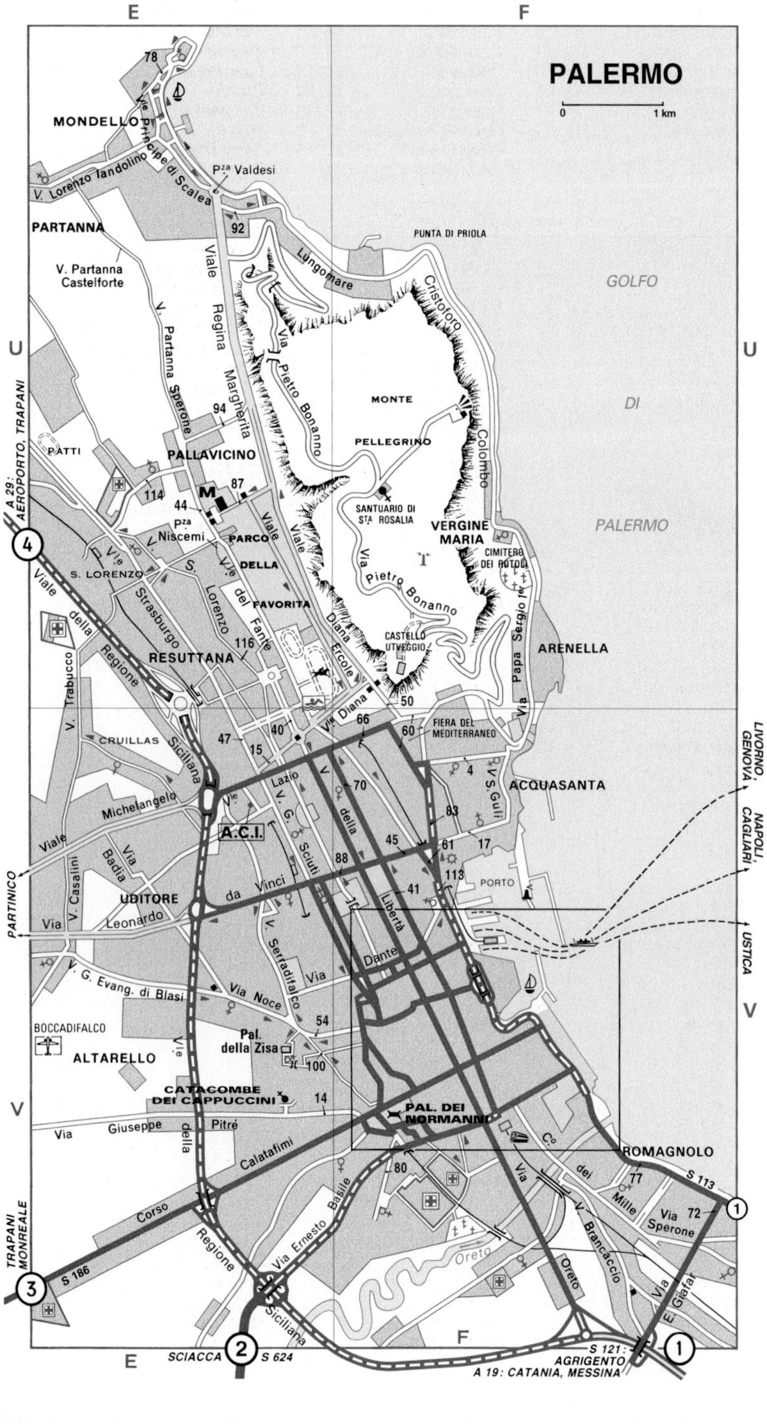

Pembroke Dock / Doc Penfro GB...... 12 C1
Pembroke / Penfro GB 12 C1
Penacova P............ 40 B1
Penafiel P............. 34 B4
Penalva do Castelo P. 34 C4
Penamacor P......... 41 D1
Penarth GB 13 D2
Pendagíi GR.......... 93 D3
Pendálofo GR......... 92 C3
Pendálofos GR........ 87 D3
Pénde Vrísses GR..... 88 B2
Pendéli GR........... 94 A4
Pendeória GR 93 E3
Pendine GB 12 C1
Penedono P........... 34 C4
Penela P............. 40 B1
Pénestin F............ 19 D4
Penhas da Saúde P... 40 C1
Penhas Juntas P..... 35 D3
Peniche P............ 40 A2
Penicuik GB.......... 9 D3
Penig D 63 F1
Peníscola / Peñíscola E 44 B2
Penkun D 52 A3
Penmaenmawr GB... 10 B3
Penna (Punta di) I 80 A1
Pennabilli I........... 76 B3
Penne I 77 E4
Penne-d'Agenais F.... 29 D1
Penrhyndeu- draeth GB 10 B3
Penrith GB 10 C1
Penryn GB 12 B4
Pentrofoelas GB 10 B3
Penzance GB 12 B4
Penzberg D........... 67 E2
Penzlin D 51 F3
Peñafiel E........... 36 B3
Peñaflor E 47 E2
Peñaranda de Bracamonte E 35 F4
Peñaranda de Duero E 36 B3
Peñarroya- Pueblonuevo E...... 47 F1
Peñascosa E.......... 43 D4
Peñas de San Pedro E 43 D4
Peñausende E........ 35 E4
Perä-Posio FIN 109 E2
Perahóra GR.......... 93 F4
Peraleda del Zaucejo E 41 F4
Peralejos de las Truchas E.... 43 E1
Perales del Alfambra E 43 F1
Perales del Puerto E.. 41 D1
Perales de Tajuña E .. 42 C2
Peralta E............ 37 E2
Peralta de Alcofea E.. 38 A3
Peralva P............ 46 B2
Pérama GR 94 A4
Pérama GR 86 B4
Pérama GR 100 C3
Pérama GR 95 F2
Pérama GR 87 D4
Pérama GR 87 D4
Peranka FIN 109 F3
Peräseinäjoki FIN .. 114 B4
Peratáta GR.......... 92 A4
Percy F.............. 19 E2
Pérdika GR........... 97 F1
Pérdika GR........... 92 B1
Pérdika GR........... 92 A1
Perdikáki GR......... 92 C2
Perdíkas GR.......... 87 F2
Peréa GR............ 88 B2
Peréa GR............ 87 F2
Perejaslav- Chmel'nyc'kyj UA .. 127 E2
Perelló (El) E 44 B1
Perelló (El) E 44 A3
Pereruela E........... 35 E4
Pereslavl'- Zalesskij RUS 125 F1
Perg A............... 68 B1
Pergine Valsugana I.. 72 A3
Pergola I............. 76 C3
Perho FIN 114 C2
Periana E............ 48 A3
Périers F............ 19 E1
Périgueux F 25 D4
Periklia GR........... 88 A1
Perino I 75 E1
Períssa GR........... 99 D4
Perísta GR........... 93 D3
Peristerá GR.......... 88 B2
Peristéria (Tímvos) GR 96 B2
Perithório GR......... 88 C1
Perívlepto GR 93 E1
Perivóli GR........... 87 D4

Perivólio GR.......... 93 D2
Perleberg D 51 D4
Përmet AL 128 B4
Pernå / Pernaja FIN . 121 D3
Pernes- les-Fontaines F.... 30 C2
Pernik BG 128 C2
Perniö FIN 120 C4
Pernitz A............ 69 D1
Péronne F 16 C3
Perosa Argentina I ... 27 F4
Pérouges F........... 26 C3
Perpignan F.......... 30 A4
Perrero I............ 27 F4
Perreux F............ 26 B3
Perros-Guirec F....... 18 C2
Persenbeug A......... 68 C1
Pershore GB.......... 13 E1
Persistéra (Nissí) GR.. 94 B1
Perstorp S........... 123 D2
Perth GB 9 D2
Le Perthus F.......... 30 A4
Pertisau A 67 E3
Pertoča SLO 73 F1
Pertoúli GR 92 C1
Pertteli FIN.......... 120 C4
Pertuis F............ 31 D2
Pertunmaa FIN 121 D2
Pertusa E............ 38 A3
Perugia I............. 76 C4
Péruwelz B 17 D2
Pervenchères F....... 20 C3
Pervomajs'k UA 127 E3
Pesaro I.............. 76 C2
Pescara I............. 77 E4
Pescasseroli I......... 79 F2
Peschici I............ 80 C1
Peschiera del Garda I. 71 F4
Pescia I............. 75 F3
Pescina I............ 79 F1
Pescocostanzo I....... 79 F1
Pescolanciano I....... 80 A2
Pescopagano I........ 80 B3
Pescorocchiano I...... 79 E1
Peshkopi AL 128 B3
Pesiökylä FIN 115 E1
Pesmes F............ 27 D1
Peso da Régua P..... 34 C4
Pesoz E.............. 33 D2
Pessáni GR 91 E2
Pestovo RUS........ 125 E1
Petäjäskoski FIN.... 109 D3
Petäjävesi FIN 121 D2
Petalax FIN......... 114 B3
Petalídi GR........... 96 C3
Petalii (Nissiá) GR.... 94 B4
Petaloúdes GR........ 96 B2
Pétange L............ 22 C1
Pétas GR............ 92 B1
Peterborough GB 11 E4
Peterhead GB 7 F3
Peterlee GB 9 F4
Petersfield GB........ 14 B4
Petershagen D....... 56 B3
Pethelinós GR........ 88 C1
Petilia Policastro I..... 83 F2
Petina I 80 B3
La Petite-Pierre F 23 E2
Petite-Rosselle F..... 23 D1
Petkula FIN......... 109 D1
Petoússio GR........ 92 A1
Pétra GR 88 A3
Pétra E.............. 45 E3
Pétra E.............. 95 F1
Petralia Sottana I..... 84 C3
Petrálona GR......... 88 B3
Petraná GR 87 F3
Petrer E............ 49 F1
Pétres GR........... 87 E2
Petreto-Bicchisano F.. 78 A4
Petrič BG 128 C3
Petrína GR........... 96 C3
Petrodvorec RUS..... 125 D1
Petrohóri GR 92 C3
Pétrola E............ 43 E4
Petróna GR........... 92 C2
Petroşani RO 128 C1
Petrotá GR........... 91 F1
Petrothálassa GR..... 97 E2
Petroússa GR......... 89 D1
Petrovac YU 128 B1
Pettenbach A........ 68 B1
Pettigoe IRL 2 C2
Petworth GB.......... 14 B4
Peuerbach A 68 A1
Peura FIN 109 D3
Pewsey GB 13 F2
Peyrat-le-Château F .. 25 E3
Peyrehorade F........ 28 B3
Peyriac-Minervois F.. 29 F3
Peyrolles- en-Provence F...... 31 D2

Peyruis F 31 D2
Pézenas F............ 30 A3
Pezinok SK......... 126 A3
Pezoúla GR 89 F1
Pfaffenhofen a. d. Ilm D 67 E1
Pfäffikon CH 66 B3
Pfalzgrafenweiler D .. 23 F2
Pfarrkirchen D 68 A1
Pfeffenhausen D...... 67 E1
Pforzheim D 23 F2
Pfreimd D............ 63 F3
Pfronten D........... 67 D3
Pfullendorf D......... 66 C2
Pfullingen D.......... 66 B1
Pfunds A............. 67 D4
Pfungstadt D......... 62 B3
Phalsbourg F......... 23 E2
Philippeville B 17 E3
Philippsreut D........ 64 A4
Piacenza I 75 E1
Piadena I............ 75 F1
Pian del Voglio I 76 A2
Piana F.............. 78 A3
Piana degli Albanesi I 84 B2
Piancastagnaio I...... 76 B4
Piancavallo I......... 72 B3
Piandelagotti I........ 75 F2
Pianella I............ 79 F1
Pianello I............ 76 C3
Piano del Cansiglio I.. 72 B3
Pianoro I............ 76 A2
Piansano I........... 78 C1
Piatra-Neamţ RO.... 127 D4
Piazza al Serchio I.... 75 F2
Piazza Armerina I..... 85 D3
Piazza Brembana I.... 71 E3
Piazzola sul Brenta I.. 72 A4
Piber A.............. 68 C3
Picassent E.......... 43 F3
Picazo (El) E 43 D3
Picerno I............ 80 C3
Pickering GB......... 11 E1
Pico I 79 F2
Picquigny F 16 C3
Piedicavallo I 70 C4
Piedicroce F.......... 78 A1
Piedicroce F.......... 78 B3
Piediluco I........... 79 D1
Piedimonte Matese I. 80 A2
Piedra (Monasterio de) E.. 37 E4
Piedrabuena E 42 B4
Piedrafita de Babia E. 33 D3
Piedrahita E 41 F1
Piedralaves E 42 A1
Piedras Albas E 41 D2
Piedratajada E 37 F3
Pieksämäki FIN 115 E3
Pielavesi FIN........ 115 D3
Piennes F............ 22 C1
Pienza I 76 B4
Pierowall GB 7 E1
Pierre-Buffière F...... 25 E3
Pierre-de-Bresse F.... 26 C1
Pierrefitte-Nestalas F. 28 C4
Pierrefitte-sur-Aire F. 22 C2
Pierrefonds F......... 17 D4
Pierrefontaine-les- Varans F........... 27 E1
Pierrefort F........... 26 A4
Pierrelatte F.......... 30 C1
Pieštany SK......... 126 A3
Pietra Ligure I 74 C3
Pietralunga I 76 C3
Pietraperzia I......... 84 C3
Pietrasanta I 75 F3
Les Pieux F........... 19 E1
Pieve di Cadore I 67 F4
Pieve di Bono I....... 71 F3
Pieve di Soligo I 72 B3
Pieve di Teco I........ 74 C3
Pieve Sto Stefano I... 76 B3
Pievepelago I......... 75 F2
Pigádi GR 93 F2
Pigés GR............ 92 C1
Pigí GR.............. 93 D3
Pigna I.............. 74 C3
Pihlajaveden as FIN.. 114 C2
Pihlajavesi FIN 114 C4
Pihlava FIN......... 120 B2
Piikkiö FIN.......... 120 B4
Piippola FIN......... 115 D2
Piispajärvi FIN...... 109 F3
Pikal'ovo RUS...... 125 E1
Pikérmi GR 94 B4
Piła PL............. 52 C3
Pilas E.............. 47 D3
Pilat-Plage F......... 28 B1
Piléa GR 91 E2
Piles E.............. 44 A4

Pilés GR............ 103 D4
Píli GR............. 94 A4
Píli GR............. 92 C1
Píli GR............. 87 D2
Pílio GR............ 94 A2
Pílio GR............ 103 D1
Pílio (Óros) GR 93 F1
Pilorí GR............ 87 E3
Pílos GR............ 96 B3
Pilštanj SLO......... 73 F2
Pina de Ebro E 37 F4
Pineda de la Sierra E 36 C2
Pineda de Mar E 39 D4
Pinell de Brai (El) E .. 44 B1
Pinerolo I 27 F4
Piney F............. 22 B3
Pinhal Novo P....... 40 A4
Pinhão P............ 34 C4
Pinheiro P........... 34 B3
Pinhel P............ 35 D4
Pinilla (La) E......... 36 B4
Pinkafeld A 69 D2
Pinneberg D.......... 50 B3
Pino F.............. 78 A2
Pinofranqueado E.... 41 E1
Pinols F............ 26 A4
Pinos Puente E....... 48 A3
Pinsk BY 126 C1
Pintamo FIN 109 E3
Pinto E 42 B2
Pinzano al Tagliamento I.... 68 A4
Pinzolo I 71 F3
Piña de Campos E 33 F4
Piobbico I........... 76 C3
Piombino I 75 F4
Pione I............. 75 E2
Pionsat F 25 F2
Piotrków Trybunalski PL ... 126 A2
Piove di Sacco I...... 72 B4
Piovene Rocchette I.. 72 A3
Pipéri (Nissí) GR 94 B1
Pipriac F............ 19 D4
Piran SLO 72 C4
Píreás GR 94 A4
Pirgadíkia GR........ 88 C3
Pirgetós GR.......... 88 A4
Pirgí GR............ 86 B4
Pírgí GR............ 89 D1
Pirgí GR............ 87 F2
Pírgí GR............ 95 F4
Pírgos GR........... 88 A2
Pírgos GR........... 96 B1
Pírgos GR........... 101 D4
Pírgos GR........... 99 F1
Pírgos GR........... 93 F3
Pírgos Diroú GR...... 97 D3
Piriac-sur-Mer F 19 D4
Pirkkala FIN 120 C2
Pirmasens D 23 E1
Pirna D............. 64 A1
Pirot YU 128 C2
Pirsógiani GR 87 D3
Pirttikoski FIN...... 109 E2
Pisa I 75 F3
Pisciotta I........... 80 B4
Písek CZ............ 64 B3
Pisogne I............ 71 E4
Písses GR........... 98 A1
Pissodéri GR......... 87 E2
Pissónas GR 94 A3
Pissos F............ 28 B1
Pisticci I............ 81 D3
Pistoia I 76 A3
Piteå S 108 B4
Piteşti RO 129 D1
Pithagório GR........ 99 F1
Píthio GR............ 91 F1
Píthio GR............ 87 F3
Pitigliano I.......... 78 C1
Pitlochry GB 9 D1
Pittenween GB 9 E2
Pivka SLO 73 D3
Pizarra E............ 47 F3
Pizzighettone I 75 E1
Pizzo I.............. 83 E3
Pizzoli I............ 79 E1

Pláka Litohórou GR... 88 A3
Plakiás GR 100 C4
Pláki GR............ 92 C2
Pláki GR............ 87 D2
Planina SLO.......... 73 D2
Planina SLO.......... 73 D3
Planina SLO.......... 73 E2
Plános GR........... 96 A1
Plasencia E.......... 41 E2
Platamona Lido I 82 A1
Platamónas GR 88 A4
Platamónas GR 89 E1
Platanákia GR........ 88 B1
Platanés GR......... 100 C3
Platánia GR.......... 96 C2
Plataniá GR.......... 89 E1
Plataniá GR.......... 93 F2
Platanistós GR 94 C4
Platanítis GR......... 93 D3
Plátanos GR........ 100 A3
Plátanos GR......... 97 D2
Plátanos GR......... 93 E2
Platariá GR.......... 92 A1
Plateau-d'Assy F..... 27 E3
Plateés GR.......... 93 F4
Pláti GR............ 91 E1
Platiána GR.......... 96 B1
Platígiali GR......... 92 B3
Platíkambos GR...... 88 A4
Platís Gialós GR...... 92 A4
Platís Gialós GR...... 98 C2
Platís Gialós GR...... 98 B3
Platístomo GR........ 93 D2
Platja de Sant Joan E. 49 F1
Platja i Grau de Gandia E........ 44 A4
Platja d'Aro (La) E ... 39 E3
Plattling D........... 63 F4
Plau D.............. 51 E3
Plaue D............. 57 E2
Plauen D............ 63 E2
Plavsk RUS......... 125 F3
Plaza (La) E 33 E3
Pleaux F............ 25 F4
Pleine-Fougères F.... 19 E2
Pleinfeld D........... 63 D4
Plélan-le-Grand F.... 19 D3
Plélan-le-Petit F...... 19 D3
Pléneuf-Val-André F.. 19 D2
Plentzia E........... 36 C1
Plépi GR............ 97 F2
Plestin-les-Grèves F.. 18 C2
Plettenberg D 62 A1
Pleumartin F 25 D1
Pleumeur-Bodou F... 18 C2
Pleven BG 129 D2
Pleyben F............ 18 B3
Pliego E............. 49 E2
Plítra GR............ 97 D3
Plitvice HR 73 F4
Pljevlja YU 128 A2
Ploaghe I........... 82 B2
Plochingen D......... 66 C1
Płock PL........... 126 A1
Ploemeur F.......... 18 C4
Plön D.............. 50 C3
Ploërmel F........... 19 D3
Ploieşti RO 129 D1
Plomári GR 95 F2
Plombières- les-Bains F........ 23 D3
Plomin HR 73 D3
Plonéour-Lanvern F.. 18 B3
Plouagat F........... 18 C2
Plouaret F........... 18 C2
Plouay F............ 18 C3
Ploubalay F 19 D2
Ploudalmézeau F..... 18 A2
Plouescat F.......... 18 B2
Plougasnou F 18 B2
Plougastel-Daoulas F 18 B2
Plougonven F........ 18 B2
Plouguenast F 19 D3
Plouha F............ 18 C2
Plouigneau F......... 18 B2
Ploumanac'h F 18 C2
Plouzévédé F......... 18 B2
Plovdiv BG.......... 129 D2
Plumbridge GB......... 3 D2
Plunge LT 124 B3
Pl'ussa RUS......... 125 D1
Pluvigner F.......... 18 C4
Plymouth GB 12 C4
Plympton GB 12 C3
Plymstock GB 12 C3
Plzeň CZ 64 A3
Płońsk PL 126 A1
Pobla de Benifassà (La) E 44 A1
Pobla de Lillet (La) E. 38 C3

Pobla de Massaluca (La) E 38 A4
Pobla de Segur (La) E 38 B3
Pobla de Vallbona (La) E 43 F3
Pobla Llarga (La) E .. 43 F4
Pobo de Dueñas (El) E 43 E1
Počep RUS........... 125 F4
Pöchlarn A 68 C1
Počinok RUS........ 125 E4
Pocking D........... 68 A1
Podčetrtek SLO...... 73 F2
Podensac F.......... 28 C1
Podersdorf am See A 69 D1
Podgorica YU 128 A3
Podgrad SLO 73 D3
Podkoren SLO 72 C2
Podogorá GR......... 92 C2
Podohóri GR 89 D2
Podol'sk RUS....... 125 F2
Podpec SLO......... 73 D3
Podsreda SLO 73 F2
Pörnbach D.......... 67 E1
Pößneck D........... 63 E1
Pöttmes D 67 D1
Poggibonsi I 76 A3
Poggio Imperiale I.... 80 B1
Poggio Mirteto I...... 79 D3
Poggio Renatico I 76 A1
Poggio Rusco I....... 76 A1
Pöggstall A 68 C1
Pogoniani GR 86 C3
Pogradec AL........ 128 B3
Pohja / Pojo FIN 120 C4
Pohja-Lankila FIN ... 121 D3
Pohjaslahti FIN 120 C2
Pohjaslahti FIN 109 E2
Poiana Braşov RO .. 129 D1
Poio E.............. 32 A3
Le Poiré-sur-Vie F ... 24 B1
Poirino I 74 C1
Poissons F........... 22 C3
Poitiers F............ 25 D2
Poix-de-Picardie F.... 16 B4
Poix-Terron F........ 17 E4
Pokka FIN.......... 105 E4
Polack BY 125 D3
Pola de Allande E.... 33 D2
Pola de Gordón (La) E 33 E3
Pola de Laviana E.... 33 E3
Pola de Lena E 33 E3
Pola de Siero E 33 E2
Polán E............. 42 B2
Polčane SLO 73 F2
Polcenigo I.......... 72 B3
Połczyn Zdrój PL 52 C2
Polegate GB 14 C4
Polesella I........... 76 A1
Polessk RUS........ 124 A4
Polhov Gradec SLO... 73 D3
Policastro Bussentino I......... 80 C4
Policoro I........... 81 D4
Polidéndri GR........ 94 A4
Polídrossos GR....... 93 E3
Poliégos (Nissí) GR .. 98 B3
Polígiros GR 88 C3
Polignano a Mare I... 81 D2
Poligny F............ 27 D1
Polihnítos GR........ 95 F2
Polikárpi GR......... 87 F1
Polikástano GR....... 87 D3
Polikastro GR 88 A1
Polímilos GR 87 F3
Polinéri GR.......... 92 C1
Polinéri GR.......... 87 E3
Polióhni GR.......... 89 F4
Polipótamo GR....... 87 E2
Polipótamos GR 94 B4
Políraho GR.......... 87 F3
Polirínia GR......... 100 A3
Políssito GR 89 F1
Polistena I........... 83 E4
Polithéa GR 87 E4
Politiká GR.......... 94 A3
Poljana SLO......... 73 E2
Polla I 80 B3
Pöllau A............ 69 D2
Polle D............. 56 B4
Pollença E 45 E3
Pollfoss N 110 C3
Pollos E............ 35 F4
Polmak N 105 F2
Polonne UA......... 127 D2
Polperro GB 12 C4
Poltava UA.......... 127 F2
Pîltsamaa EST...... 124 C1
Pîlva EST........... 124 C2
Polvijärvi FIN....... 115 F3
Polzela SLO......... 73 E2
Pomar E 38 A3

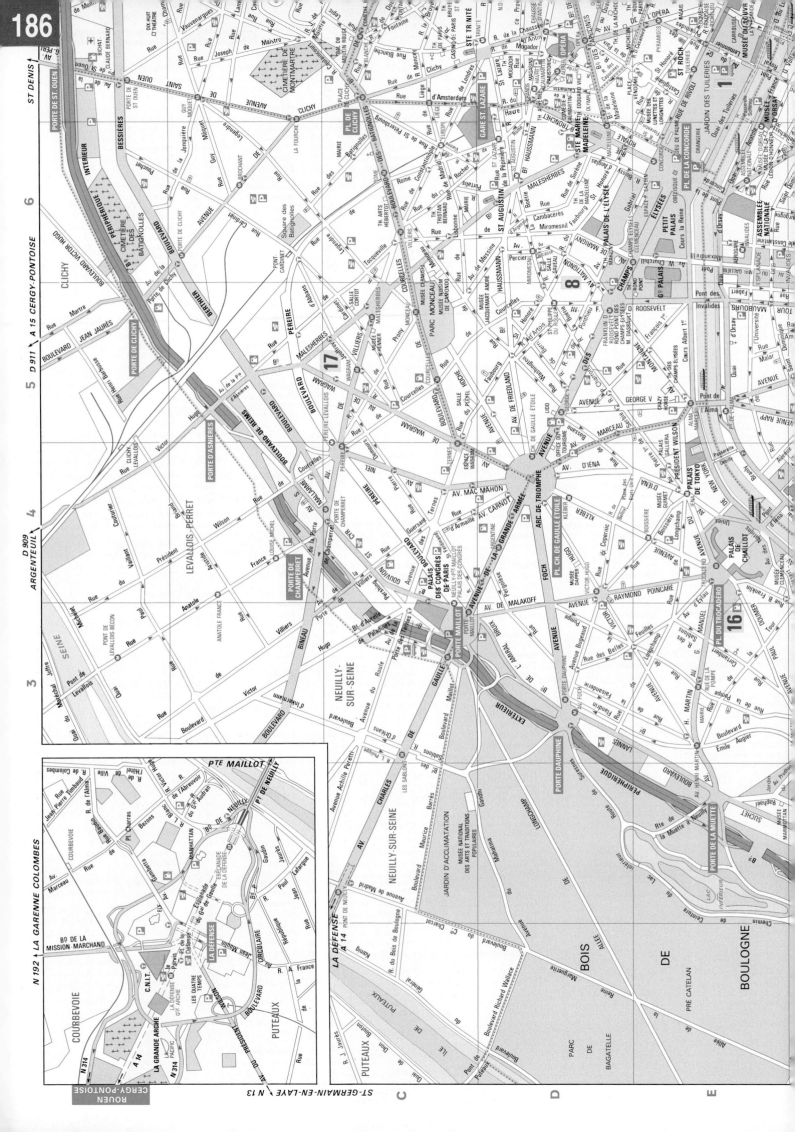

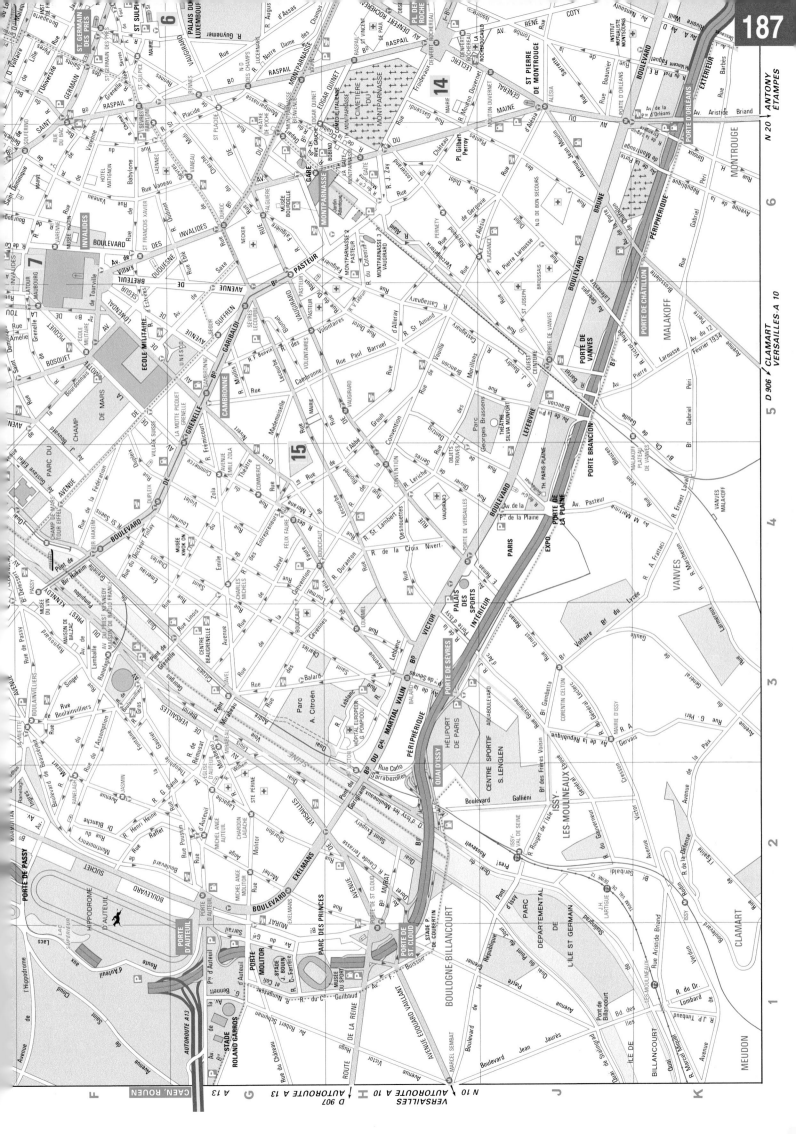

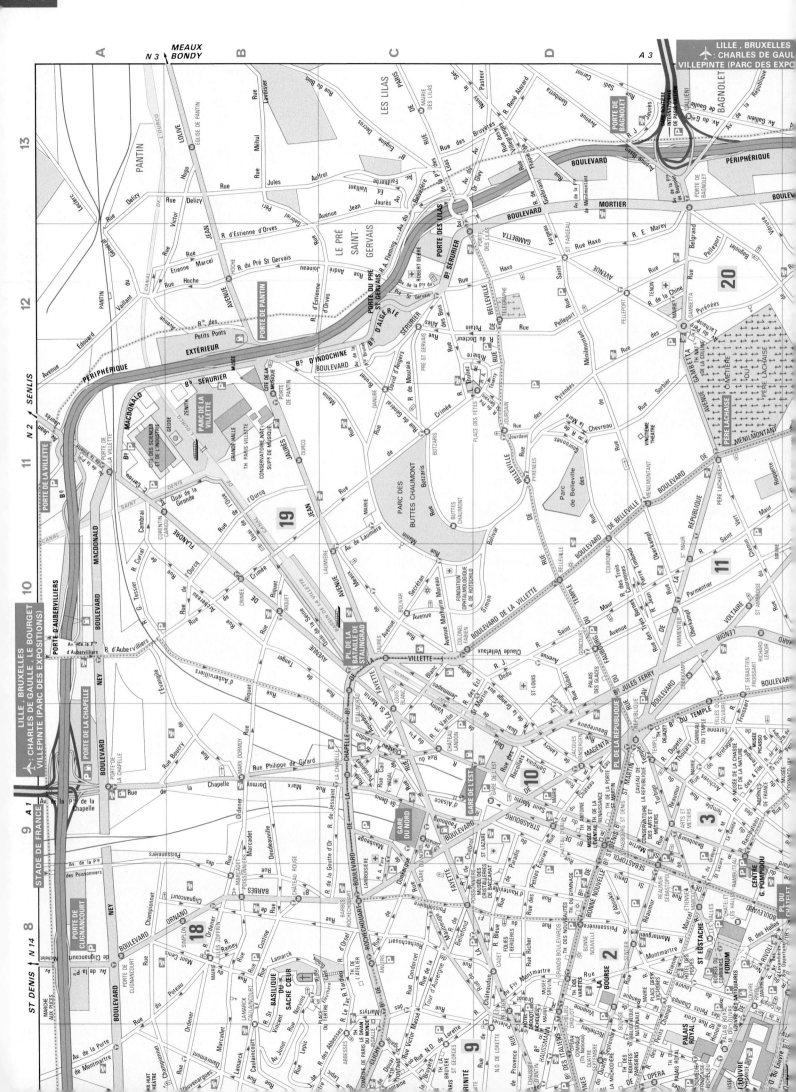

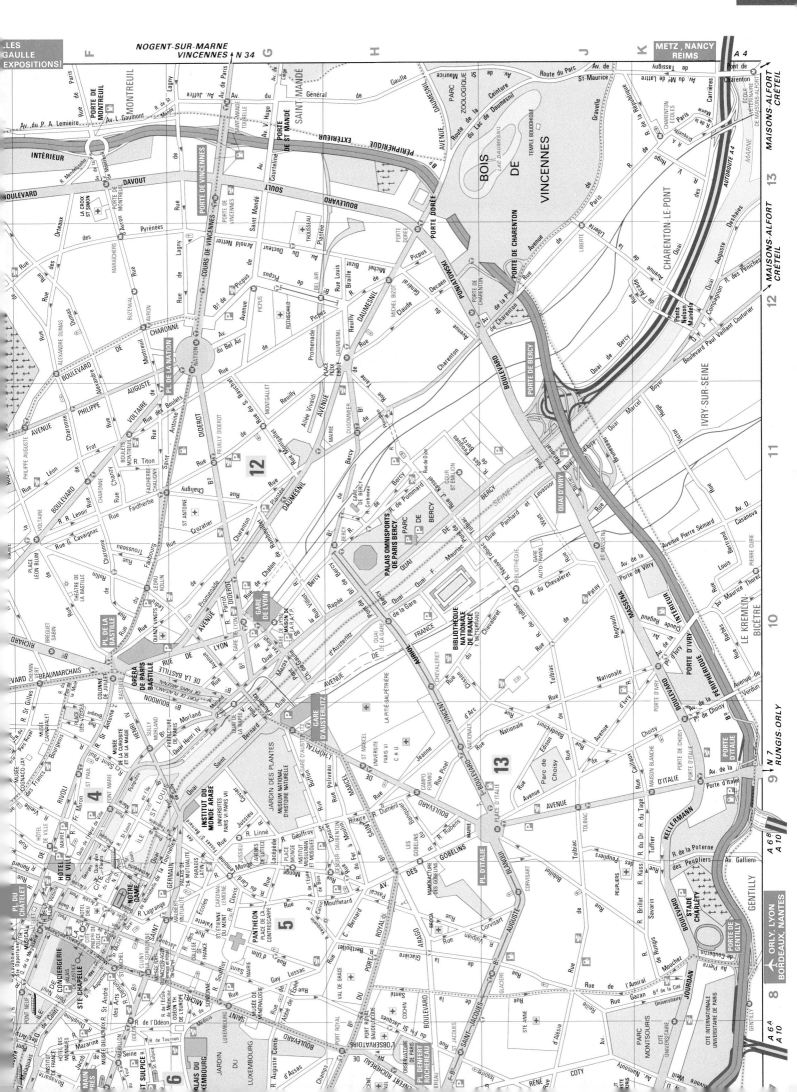

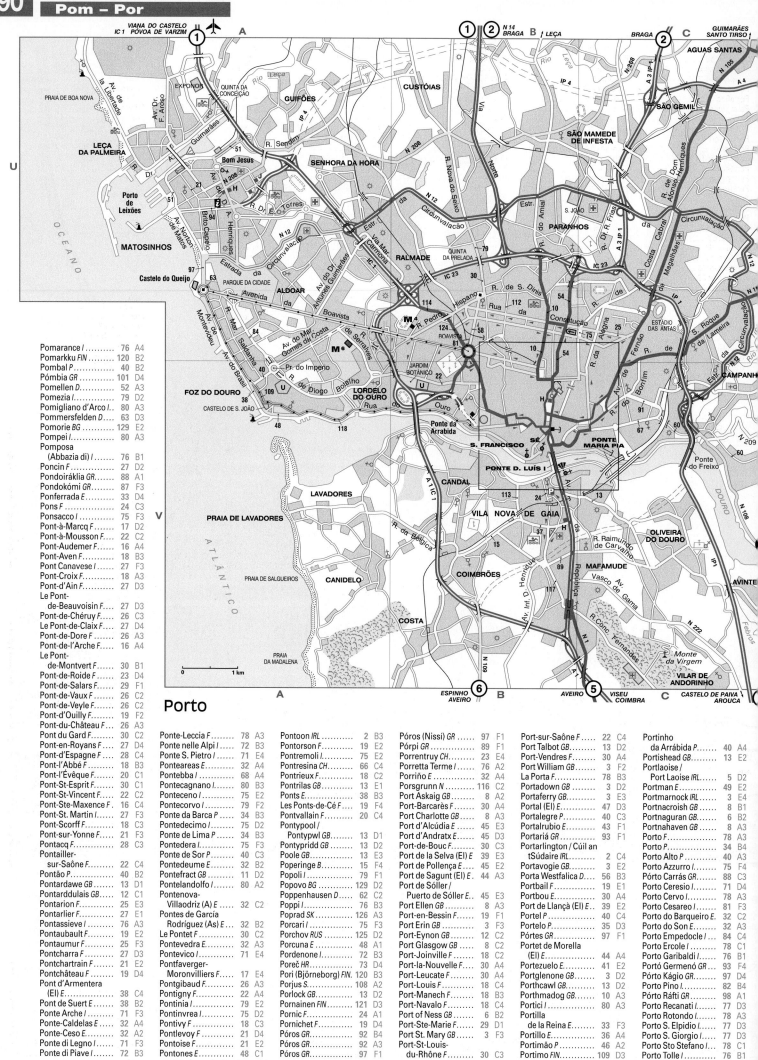

Porto

Pomarance I 76 A4
Pomarkku FIN 120 B2
Pombal P 40 B2
Pómbia GR 101 D4
Pomellen D 52 A3
Pomezia I 79 D2
Pomigliano d'Arco I... 80 A3
Pommersfelden D..... 63 D3
Pomorie BG 129 E2
Pompei I 80 A3
Pomposa
 (Abbazia di) I 76 B1
Poncin F 27 D2
Pondoiráklia GR...... 88 A1
Pondokómi GR....... 87 F3
Ponferrada E 33 D4
Pons F 24 C3
Ponsacco I 75 F3
Pont-à-Marcq F....... 17 D2
Pont-à-Mousson F.... 22 C2
Pont-Audemer F...... 16 A4
Pont-Aven F 18 B3
Pont Canavese I 27 F3
Pont-Croix F 18 A3
Pont-d'Ain F.......... 27 D3
Le Pont-
 de-Beauvoisin F..... 27 D3
Pont-de-Chéruy F.... 26 C3
Le Pont-de-Claix F... 27 D4
Pont-de-Dore F 26 A3
Pont-de-l'Arche F..... 16 A4
Le Pont-
 de-Montvert F....... 30 B1
Pont-de-Roide F...... 23 D4
Pont-de-Salars F...... 29 F1
Pont-de-Vaux F....... 26 C2
Pont-de-Veyle F....... 26 C2
Pont-d'Ouilly F........ 19 F2
Pont-du-Château F ... 26 A3
Pont du Gard F........ 30 C2
Pont-en-Royans F..... 27 D4
Pont-d'Espagne F 28 C4
Pont-l'Abbé F 18 B3
Pont-l'Évêque F....... 20 C1
Pont-St-Esprit F....... 30 C1
Pont-St-Vincent F..... 22 C2
Pont-Ste-Maxence F.. 16 C4
Pont-St. Martin I...... 27 F3
Pont-Scorff F 18 C3
Pont-sur-Yonne F..... 21 F3
Pontacq F............. 28 C3
Pontailler-
 sur-Saône F......... 22 C4
Pontão P.............. 40 B2
Pontardawe GB 13 D1
Pontarddulais GB..... 12 C1
Pontarion F........... 25 E3
Pontarlier F........... 27 E1
Pontassieve I 76 A3
Pontaubault F......... 19 E2
Pontaumur F.......... 25 F3
Pontcharra F.......... 27 D3
Pontchartrain F....... 21 E2
Pontchâteau F 19 D4
Pont d'Armentera
 (El) E................ 38 C4
Pont de Suert E 38 B2
Ponte Arche I 71 F3
Ponte-Caldelas E..... 32 A4
Ponte-Ceso E......... 32 A2
Ponte di Legno I 71 F3
Ponte di Piave I 72 B3

Ponte-Leccia F........ 78 A3
Ponte nelle Alpi I 72 B3
Ponte S. Pietro I 71 E4
Ponteareas E......... 32 A4
Pontebba I 68 A4
Pontecagnano I....... 80 B3
Ponteceno I 75 E2
Pontecorvo I 79 F2
Pontedecimo I........ 75 D2
Ponte de Lima P 34 B3
Pontedera I........... 75 F3
Ponte de Sor P 40 C3
Pontedeume E........ 32 B2
Pontefract GB 11 D2
Pontelandolfo I....... 80 A2
Pontenova-
 Villaodriz (A) E 32 C2
Pontes de García
 Rodríguez (As) E ... 32 B2
Le Pontet F 30 C2
Pontevedra E......... 32 A3
Pontevico I 71 E4
Pontfaverger-
 Moronvilliers F..... 17 E4
Pontgibaud F.......... 26 A3
Pontigny F............ 22 A4
Pontinia I 79 E2
Pontinvrea I 75 D2
Pontivy F 18 C3
Pontlevoy F........... 21 D4
Pontoise F 21 E2
Pontones E 48 C1

Pontoon IRL 2 B3
Pontorson F 19 E2
Pontremoli I........... 75 E2
Pontresina CH........ 66 C4
Pontrieux F........... 18 C2
Pontrilas GB 13 E1
Ponts E 38 B3
Les Ponts-de-Cé F ... 19 F4
Pontvallain F.......... 20 C4
Pontypool /
 Pontypwl GB........ 13 D1
Pontypridd GB 13 D2
Poole GB 13 E3
Poperinge B 15 F4
Popoli I 79 F1
Popovo BG 129 D2
Poppenhausen D..... 62 C2
Poppi I 76 B3
Poprad SK 126 A3
Porcari I 75 F3
Porchov RUS 125 D2
Porcuna E 48 A1
Pordenone I 72 B3
Poreč HR 73 D4
Pori (Björneborg) FIN . 120 B3
Porjus S. 108 A2
Porlock GB 13 D2
Pornainen FIN 121 D3
Pornic F 24 A1
Pornichet F 19 D4
Póros GR 92 A3
Póros GR 92 A3
Póros GR 97 F1

Póros (Nissí) GR 97 F1
Pórpi GR 89 F1
Porrentruy CH........ 23 E4
Porretta Terme I 76 A2
Porriño E 32 A4
Porsgrunn N 116 C2
Port Askaig GB 8 A2
Port-Barcarès F....... 30 A4
Port Charlotte GB 8 A3
Port d'Alcúdia E 45 E3
Port d'Andratx E..... 45 D3
Port-de-Bouc F....... 30 C3
Port de la Selva (El) E . 39 E3
Port de Pollença E... 45 E2
Port de Sagunt (El) E . 44 A3
Port de Sóller /
 Puerto de Sóller E.. 45 E3
Port Ellen GB 8 A3
Port-en-Bessin F...... 19 F1
Port Erin GB 3 F3
Port-Eynon GB 12 C2
Port Glasgow GB 8 C2
Port-Joinville F........ 18 C2
Port-la-Nouvelle F.... 30 A4
Port-Leucate F........ 30 A4
Port-Louis F 18 C4
Port-Manech F........ 18 B3
Port-Navalo F......... 18 C4
Port of Ness GB 6 B2
Port-Ste-Marie F...... 29 D1
Port St. Mary GB 3 F3
Port-St-Louis-
 du-Rhône F......... 30 C3

Port-sur-Saône F 22 C4
Port Talbot GB........ 13 D2
Port-Vendres F........ 30 A4
Port William GB 3 F2
La Porta F............. 78 B3
Portadown N 3 D2
Portaferry GB......... 3 E3
Portal (El) E........... 47 D3
Portalegre P 40 C3
Portalrubio E 43 F1
Portariá GR 93 F1
Portarlington / Cúil an
 tSúdaire IRL......... 2 C4
Portavogie GB........ 3 E2
Porta Westfalica D.... 56 B3
Portbail F 19 E1
Portbou E............. 30 A4
Port de Llançà (El) E.. 39 E3
Portel P 40 C4
Portelo P............. 35 D3
Pórtes GR 97 F1
Portet de Morella
 (El) E................ 44 A4
Portezuelo E.......... 41 E2
Portglenone GB 3 D2
Porthcawl GB 13 D2
Porthmadog GB....... 10 A3
Portici I 80 A3
Portilla
 de la Reina E 33 F3
Portillo E 36 A4
Portimão P 46 A2
Portimo FIN........... 109 D3

Portinho
 da Arrábida P....... 40 A4
Portishead GB........ 13 E2
Portlaoise /
 Port Laoise IRL...... 5 D2
Portman E 49 E2
Portmarnock IRL 3 E1
Portnacroish GB 8 B1
Portnaguran GB...... 6 B2
Portnahaven GB 8 A3
Porto I 78 A3
Porto P 34 B4
Porto Alto P 40 A3
Porto Azzurro I....... 75 F4
Pórto Carrás GR...... 88 C3
Porto Ceresio I 71 D4
Porto Cervo I 78 A3
Porto Cesareo I 81 F3
Porto do Barqueiro E. 32 C2
Porto do Son E....... 32 A3
Porto Empedocle I ... 84 C4
Porto Ercole I 78 C1
Porto Garibaldi I..... 76 B1
Portó Germenó GR ... 93 F4
Pórto Kágio GR....... 97 D4
Porto Pino I 82 B4
Pórto Ráfti GR 98 A1
Porto Recanati I 77 D3
Porto Rotondo I....... 78 A3
Porto S. Elpidio I..... 77 D3
Porto S. Giorgio I 77 D3
Porto Sto Stefano I... 78 C1
Porto Tolle I 76 B1

Porto Torres I	82	A1	Pošechonje-			Poussu FIN	109	F3	Prades F	29	F4	Pravdinsk RUS	124	A4	Preuilly-sur-Claise F	25	D1
Porto-Vecchio F	78	B4	Volodarsk RUS	125	F1	Pouyastruc F	28	C3	Prado del Rey E	47	E3	Pravia E	33	E2	Préveza GR	92	B2
Portocristo E	45	E3	Posio FIN	109	E2	Pouzauges F	24	B1	Pradoluengo E	36	C2	Pré-en-Pail F	19	F3	Priego E	43	D1
Porto de Lagos P	46	A2	Positano I	80	A3	Le Pouzin F	30	C1	Præstø DK	122	C3	Pré-St. Didier I	27	F3	Priego de Córdoba E	48	A2
Porto de Mós P	40	B2	Possídi GR	88	C4	Považská Bystrica SK	126	A3	Prägraten A	67	F3	Prebold SLO	73	E2	Prien D	67	F2
Portoferraio I	75	F4	Possidonía GR	98	C2	Poveda de la Sierra E	43	D1	Praha CZ	64	B2	Précy-sous-Thil F	22	B4	Prienai LT	124	B4
Portofino I	75	D2	Posta I	77	D4	Póvoa de Lanhoso P	34	B3	Prahecq F	24	C2	Predappio I	76	B2	Prievidza SK	126	A3
Portogruaro I	72	C3	Postojna SLO	73	D3	Póvoa de Varzim P	34	B3	Prachatice CZ	64	B4	Predazzo I	67	E4	Prijedor BIH	128	A1
Portohéli GR	97	E2	Potamí GR	90	A1	Poysdorf A	65	E4	Praia a Mare I	80	C4	Preddvor SLO	73	D2	Prijepolje YU	128	B2
Pörtom FIN	114	B4	Potamiá GR	97	D3	Pöytyä FIN	120	A3	Praia da Tocha P	40	B1	Predeal RO	129	D1	Prilep MK	128	B3
Portomaggiore I	76	B1	Potamiés GR	101	E2	Poza de la Sal E	36	C2	Praia da Barra P	34	B4	Predel SLO	72	C4	La Primaube F	29	F1
Portomarín E	32	C3	Potamós GR	100	A2	Požarevac YU	128	B1	Praia da Rocha P	46	A2	Predoi / Prettau I	67	F3	Primel-Trégastel F	18	B2
Portomouro E	32	A3	Potamós GR	97	E4	Požega HR	128	A1	Praia da Vieira P	40	A2	Predol I	72	A3	Primolano I	72	A3
Portonovo E	32	A4	Potamoúla GR	92	C2	Poznań PL	53	D4	Praia de Mira P	40	B1	Pregarten A	68	B1	Primorsk RUS	124	C1
Portopetro E	45	E3	Potenza I	80	A3	Pozo Alcón E	48	C2	Praia de Santa Cruz P	40	A3	Prémery F	26	A1	Primstal D	23	D1
Portorož SLO	72	C4	Potenza Picena I	77	D3	Pozoblanco E	47	F1	Prali I	27	F4	Premià de Mar E	39	D4	Princetown GB	12	C3
Portoscuso I	82	A4	Potes E	33	F3	Pozo Cañada E	43	E4	Pralognan-			Premilcuore I	76	B2	Prinés GR	100	C3
Portovenere I	75	E2	Potigny F	19	F2	Pozo			la-Vanoise F	27	E4	Premnitz D	57	E2	Prínos GR	89	E2
Portpatrick GB	3	F2	Potós GR	89	E2	de Guadalajara E	42	C1	Prámanda GR	92	B1	Prenzlau D	51	F3	Priština YU	128	B2
Portree GB	6	B4	Potsdam D	57	F2	Pozo Higuera E	49	D2	Prangío GR	91	E1	Prerow D	51	E2	Pritzerbe D	57	E2
Portrush GB	3	D1	Pottenstein A	69	D1	Pozohondo E	43	E4	Prassiá GR	92	C1	Préspa GR	87	D2	Pritzier D	51	D4
Portsalon IRL	2	C1	Potters Bar GB	14	C3	Pozondón E	43	E1	Prassiés GR	100	C3	Pressath D	63	E3	Pritzwalk D	51	E4
Pörtschach A	68	B4	Potton GB	14	C2	Pozuelo E	43	D4	Prat del Comte E	44	B1	Pressbaum A	69	D1	Privas F	30	C1
Portsmouth GB	13	F3	Pouancé F	19	E4	Pozuelo			Prat			Prestatyn GB	10	B3	Priverno I	79	E2
Portstewart GB	3	D1	Pougues-les-Eaux F	26	A1	de Calatrava E	42	B4	de Llobregat (El) E	39	D4	Presteigne GB	10	C4	Prizren YU	128	B3
Portugalete E	36	C1	Pouilly-en-Auxois F	26	C1	Pozuelo de Zarzón E	41	E2	Pratella I	80	A2	Prestfoss N	117	B2	Prizzi I	84	B3
Portumna /			Pouilly-			Pozzallo I	85	E4	Prati di Tivo I	77	D4	Preston GB	10	C2	Proaza E	33	E3
Port Omna IRL	2	B4	sous-Charlieu F	26	B2	Pozzomaggiore I	50	A3	Prato I	76	A3	Prestonpans GB	9	D2	Probstzella D	63	D2
Porvoo /			Pouilly-sur-Loire F	26	A1	Pozzomaggiore I	82	B2	Prato I	76	B4	Prestwick GB	3	F1	Procida I	79	F3
Borgå FIN	121	D4	Le Pouldu F	18	C4	Pozzuoli I	80	A3	Pratola Peligna I	79	F1	Pretoro I	79	F1	Pródromos GR	93	F4
Porzuna E	42	B3	Le Pouliguen F	19	D4	Pozzuolo del Friuli I	72	C3	Prats-de-Mollo-			Prettin D	57	F3	Proença-a-Nova P	40	C2
Posada I	78	A4	Poúlithra GR	97	E2	Pra-Loup F	31	E2	la-Preste F	39	D2	Pretzsch D	57	F4	Prötzel D	52	A4
Posadas E	47	F1	Poúnda GR	98	C3	Pradelles F	30	B1	Prats de Lluçanès E	38	C3	Pretoro I	79	F1	Profítis Ilías GR	103	F2
Poschiavo CH	71	E3	Pournári GR	93	E1	Prádena E	36	B4	Prauthoy F	22	C4	Pretzsch D	57	F4	Profondeville B	17	F2

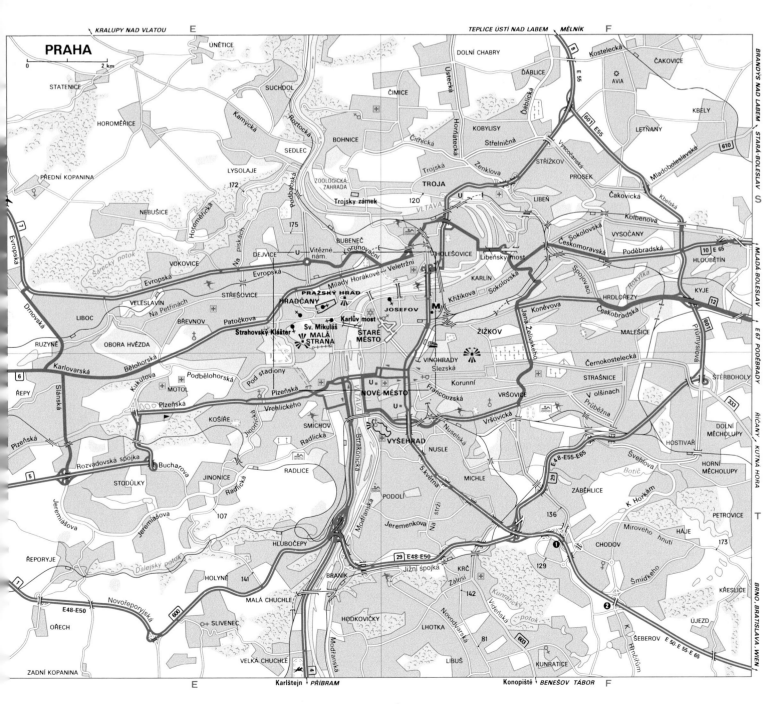

Próhoma *GR* 88 A2
Prokópi *GR* 94 A3
Prokuplje *YU* 128 B2
Prómahi *GR* 87 F1
Promahónas *GR* 88 C1
Promíri *GR* 93 F1
Pronsfeld *D* 61 E3
Propriano *F* 78 A4
Proskinás *GR* 93 F3
Prossedi *I* 79 E2
Prossílio *GR* 89 E1
Prossotsáni *GR* 89 D1
Prostějov *CZ* 65 E2
Próti *GR* 89 D1
Próti (Nissí) *GR* 96 B2
Protoklíssio *GR* 91 E1
Proussós *GR* 92 C2
Provatónas *GR* 91 E2
Provenchères-sur-Fave *F* 23 E3
Provencio (El) *E* 43 D3
Provins *F* 21 F2
Prudhoe *GB* 9 E4
Prüm *D* 61 E3
Pruna *E* 47 E3
Prunetta *I* 75 F2
Pružany *BY* 126 C1
Pryluky *UA* 127 F1
Przasnysz *PL* 126 A1
Przemyśl *PL* 126 B2
Přerov *CZ* 65 E2
Příbram *CZ* 64 A3
Psahná *GR* 94 A3
Psáka *GR* 92 A1
Psará *GR* 95 E3
Psará (Nissí) *GR* 95 E3
Psarádes *GR* 87 D2
Psári *GR* 96 C2
Psári *GR* 97 D1
Psáthi *GR* 98 B3
Psathópirgos *GR* 93 D3
Psathotópi *GR* 92 B2
Psérimos (Nissí) *GR* 103 D1
Psihikó *GR* 93 E1
Psihró *GR* 101 E4
Psínthos *GR* 103 F2
Pskov *RUS* 125 C2
Pteléa *GR* 89 E1
Ptolemaïda *GR* 87 E2
Ptuj *SLO* 73 F2
Puchberg am Schneeberg *A* 69 D1
Puckeridge *GB* 14 C2
Puçol *E* 44 A3
Pudasjärvi / Kurenalus *FIN* 109 E3
Puebla de Alcocer *E* 41 F4
Puebla de Almenara *E* 42 C2
Puebla de Almoradiel (La) *E* 42 C3
Puebla de Beleña *E* 42 C1
Puebla de Cazalla (La) *E* 47 E2
Puebla de Don Fadrique *E* 48 C1
Puebla de Don Rodrigo *E* 42 A3
Puebla de Guzmán *E* 46 C2
Puebla de Híjar (La) *E* 37 F4
Puebla de la Calzada *E* 41 D4
Puebla de la Reina *E* 41 E4
Puebla del Caramiñal *E* 32 A3
Puebla de Lillo *E* 33 F3
Puebla de los Infantes (La) *E* 47 E1
Puebla del Río (La) *E* 47 D2
Puebla de Montalbán (La) *E* 42 A2
Puebla de Obando *E* 41 D3
Puebla de Sanabria *E* 33 D4
Puebla de Trives *E* 32 C4
Puebla de Valverde (La) *E* 43 F2
Pueblanueva (La) *E* 42 A2
Pueblica de Valverde *E* 35 E3
Puente (El) *E* 36 C1
Puente de Domingo Flórez *E* 33 D4
Puente de Génave *E* 48 C1
Puente del Arzobispo (El) *E* 41 F2
Puente de los Fierros *E* 33 E3
Puente de Montañana *E* 38 B3
Puente-Genil *E* 47 F2
Puente la Reina *E* 28 A4
Puente la Reina de Jaca *E* 28 B4
Puentenansa *E* 36 B1
Puente Viesgo *E* 36 B1
Puerta de Segura (La) *E* 48 C1
Puerto Castilla *E* 41 F1
Puerto de la Encina *E* 47 E3
Puerto de Mazarrón *E* 49 E2
Puerto de San Vicente *E* 41 F3
Puerto de Santa María (El) *E* 47 D3
Puerto Lápice *E* 42 C3
Puertollano *E* 42 B4
Puerto Lumbreras *E* 49 D2
Puerto Real *E* 47 D3
Puerto Serrano *E* 47 E3
Puget-Théniers *F* 31 F2
Puhos *FIN* 109 E3
Puhos *FIN* 115 F4
Puig-reig *E* 38 C3
Puigcerdà *E* 29 E4
Puiseaux *F* 21 E3
Puisserguier *F* 30 A3
Pujols *F* 28 C1
Pukë *AL* 128 B3
Pukkila *FIN* 121 D3
Pula *I* 82 B4
Pula *HR* 77 D1
Pulborough *GB* 14 B4
Pulkau *A* 65 D4
Pulkkila *FIN* 115 D2
Pulpí *E* 49 D2
Pulsnitz *D* 58 A4
Puławy *PL* 126 B2
Pułtusk *PL* 126 A1
Punkaharju *FIN* 121 F2
Punkalaidun *FIN* 120 C3
Punta Ala *I* 76 A4
Punta Umbría *E* 46 C2
Puokio *FIN* 115 D1
Puolanka *FIN* 115 D1
Purbach am Neusierdler See *A* 69 E1
Purchena *E* 48 C3
Purgstall *A* 68 C1
Purkersdorf *A* 69 D1
Purmerend *NL* 54 B3
Purnu *FIN* 121 C2
Purullena *E* 48 B3
Puškin *RUS* 125 D1
Pustoška *RUS* 125 D2
Pusula *FIN* 120 C4
Putanges-Pont-Écrepin *F* 19 F2
Putbus *D* 51 F2
Putgarten *D* 51 E1
Putignano *I* 81 D2
Putlitz *D* 51 E4
Puttelange-aux-Lacs *F* 23 D2
Putten *NL* 54 C3
Puttgarden *D* 51 D2
Putyv'l *UA* 127 F1
Puumala *FIN* 121 E2
Le Puy-en-Velay *F* 26 B4
Puy-Guillaume *F* 26 A3
Puy-l'Évêque *F* 29 E1
Puylaurens *F* 29 F1
Puymirol *F* 29 D2
Püspökladány *H* 126 B4
Pwllheli *GB* 10 A3
Pyhäjärvi *FIN* 115 D2
Pyhäjoki *FIN* 120 B3
Pyhäjoki *FIN* 114 C1
Pyhältö *FIN* 121 E3
Pyhäntä *FIN* 115 D2
Pyhäntä *FIN* 115 E1
Pyhäranta *FIN* 120 B3
Pyhäsalmi *FIN* 115 D2
Pyhäselkä *FIN* 115 F3
Pyhtää / Pyttis *FIN* 121 E3
Pyla-sur-Mer *F* 28 B1
Pylkönmäki *FIN* 114 C3
Pyrjatyn *UA* 127 F1
Pyrzyce *PL* 52 B4

Q

Quakenbrück *D* 55 E2
Quarré-les-Tombes *F* 22 A4
Quarteira *P* 46 A2
Quarto d'Altino *I* 72 B4
Quartu S. Elena *I* 82 B4
Les Quatre Chemins *F* 24 B2
Quatretonda *I* 43 F4
Quedlinburg *D* 57 D4
Queenborough *GB* 15 D3
Queensferry *GB* 10 C3
Queluz *P* 40 A3
Queralbs *E* 39 D2
Querfurt *D* 57 E4
Quérigut *F* 29 F4
Quero *E* 42 C3
Quesada (Estación de) *E* 48 B2
Le Quesnoy *F* 17 D3
Questembert *F* 19 D4
Quettehou *F* 19 E1
Quiberon *F* 18 C4
Quickborn *D* 50 B3
Quiévrain *B* 17 D2
Quigley's Point *IRL* 3 D1
Quillan *F* 29 F4
Quilleboeuf-sur-Seine *F* 16 A4
Quimper *F* 18 B3
Quimperlé *F* 18 B3
Quincinetto *I* 27 F3
Quincoces de Yuso *E* 36 C1
Quingey *F* 27 D1
Aldea Quintana *E* 47 F2
Quintana de la Serena *E* 41 F4
Quintana del Puente *E* 36 B3
Quintana-Martín Galíndez *E* 36 C2
Quintanar de la Orden *E* 42 C3
Quintanar de la Sierra *E* 36 C3
Quintanar del Rey *E* 43 E3
Quintana Redonda *E* 37 D3
Quintanilha *P* 35 E3
Quintanilla de Onésimo *E* 36 A3
Quintin *F* 18 C3
Quinto *E* 37 F4
Quinzano d'Oglio *I* 71 E4
Quiroga *E* 32 C4
Quissac *F* 30 B2

R

Raab *A* 68 A1
Raabs an der Thaya *E* 64 C4
Raahe *FIN* 114 C1
Raajärvi *FIN* 109 E2
Rääkkylä *FIN* 115 F4
Raalte *NL* 55 D3
Raanujärvi *FIN* 109 D2
Raattama *FIN* 108 C1
Rab *HR* 77 E1
Rábade *E* 32 C3
Rabastens *F* 29 E2
Rabastens-de-Bigorre *F* 28 C3
Rabat *M* 85 F4
Rábida (Monasterio de la) *E* 46 C2
Rábita (La) *E* 48 B3
Rabka *PL* 126 A3
Racconigi *I* 27 F4
Rače *SLO* 73 F2
Rachiv *UA* 126 C3
Racibórz *PL* 126 A2
Rădăuți *RO* 127 D3
Råde *N* 117 D2
Rade *D* 50 B4
Radeberg *D* 58 A4
Radebeul *D* 58 A4
Radeburg *D* 58 A4
Radeče *SLO* 73 E2
Radechiv *UA* 126 C2
Radenci *SLO* 73 F1
Radenthein *A* 68 B3
Radevormwald *D* 61 F1
Radicondoli *I* 76 A4
Radlje *SLO* 73 E2
Radolfzell *D* 66 B2
Radom *PL* 126 B2
Radomsko *PL* 126 A2
Radomyšl' *UA* 127 E2
Radovljica *SLO* 73 D2
Radstadt *A* 68 A2
Radstock *GB* 13 E2
Radviliškis *LT* 124 B3
Radzyń Podlaski *PL* 126 B1
Raesfeld *D* 55 D4
Raffadali *I* 84 C3
Rafina *GR* 94 B4
Rágama *E* 35 F4
Ragaz, Bad *CH* 66 C4
Raglan *GB* 13 E1
Raguhn *D* 57 E4
Ragunda *S* 112 C2
Ragusa *I* 85 D4
Rahačoŭ *BY* 125 D4
Rahden *D* 55 F3
Ráhes *GR* 93 E2
Rahlstedt *D* 50 C3
Rain a. Lech *D* 67 D1
Räisälä *FIN* 109 E2
Raisio *FIN* 120 B4
Raittijärvi *FIN* 104 C3
Raja Jooseppi *FIN* 105 F3
Rajadell *E* 38 C4
Rajamäki *FIN* 121 D3
Raka *SLO* 73 E3
Rakitna *SLO* 73 D3
Rakkestad *N* 117 D2
Rakvere *EST* 124 C1
Ramacca *I* 85 D3
Ramales de la Victoria *E* 36 C1
Ramallosa *E* 32 A3
Ramallosa (A) *E* 32 A4
Ramberg *N* 107 E1
Rambervillers *F* 23 D3
Rambla (La) *E* 47 F2
Rambouillet *F* 21 E2
Rambucourt *F* 22 C2
Ramnoús *GR* 94 B4
Ramsau b. Berchtesgaden *D* 68 A2
Ramsau am Dachstein *A* 68 B2
Ramsele *S* 112 C2
Ramsey *GB* 11 F4
Ramsey *GB* 3 F3
Ramsgate *GB* 15 D3
Ramsjö *S* 112 B3
Ramstein-Miesenbach *D* 23 E1
Ramsund *N* 104 A4
Ramundberget *S* 112 A2
Ramvik *S* 112 C2
Ranalt *A* 67 C3
Randaberg *N* 116 A2
Randalstown *GB* 3 E2
Randan *F* 26 A3
Randanne *F* 26 A3
Randazzo *I* 85 D2
Randers *DK* 122 B2
Råneå *S* 108 C3
Rangsdorf *D* 57 F3
Rankweil *A* 66 C3
Rantasalmi *FIN* 121 E2
Rantsila *FIN* 115 D1
Ranua *FIN* 109 E3
Raon-l'Étape *F* 23 D3
Rapallo *I* 75 D2
Rapla *EST* 124 B1
Rapolano Terme *I* 76 B3
Rapolla *I* 80 C3
Rapperswil *CH* 66 B3
Rapsáni *GR* 88 A4
Raptópoulo *GR* 96 B2
Räsälä *FIN* 115 E3
Rasbo *S* 119 E2
Rascafría *E* 42 B1
Rasdorf *D* 62 C2
Raseiniai *LT* 124 B3
Rasquera *E* 44 B1
Rastatt *D* 23 F2
Rastede *D* 50 A4
Rastenberg *D* 63 D1
Rastenfeld *A* 64 C4
Rasueros *E* 35 F4
Rätan *S* 112 B3
Ratece *SLO* 72 C2
Ratekau *D* 50 C3
Rates *P* 34 B3
Rath Luirc (Charleville) / An Ráth *IRL* 4 C1
Rathdowney *IRL* 5 D2
Rathdrum / Ráth Droma *IRL* 5 E2
Rathenow *D* 57 E2
Rathfriland *GB* 3 E3
Rathkeale / Ráth Caola *IRL* 4 C1
Rathmelton *IRL* 2 C1
Rathmore *IRL* 4 B3
Rathmullan *IRL* 2 C1
Rathnew *IRL* 5 E2
Ratingen *D* 61 E1
Ratten *A* 69 D2
Rattenberg *A* 67 F3
Rattersdorf-Liebing *A* 69 E2
Rattray *GB* 9 D1
Rättvik *S* 119 D1
Ratzeburg *D* 50 C3
Raubling *D* 67 F2
Raucourt-et-Flaba *F* 17 F4
Raudaskylä *FIN* 114 C1
Raufarhöfn *IS* 106 C1
Raufoss *N* 117 D1
Rauha *FIN* 121 E3
Rauhamäki *FIN* 121 D2
Rauland *N* 116 C1
Rauma *FIN* 120 B3
Rauris *A* 68 A3
Rautalampi *FIN* 115 D3
Rautas *S* 108 A1
Rautavaara *FIN* 115 E2
Rautio *FIN* 114 C1
Rautjärvi *FIN* 121 F2
Ravanusa *I* 84 C4
Ravello *I* 80 A3
Ravenna *I* 76 B2
Ravensbrück *D* 51 F4
Ravensburg *D* 66 C2
Ravne na K. *SLO* 73 E2
Rawicz *PL* 59 D3
Rawtenstall *GB* 10 C2
Rayleigh *GB* 14 C3
Rayol-Canadel-sur-Mer *F* 31 E3
Real de San Vicente (El) *E* 42 A2
Réalmont *F* 29 F2
Rebais *F* 21 F2
Rebordelo *P* 35 D3
Recanati *I* 77 D3
Recco *I* 75 D2
Recey-sur-Ource *F* 22 B4
Rechnitz *A* 69 E2
Recke *D* 55 E3
Recklinghausen *D* 55 E4
Recoaro Terme *I* 72 A4
Recuerda *E* 36 C4
Redalen *N* 111 D4
Redange *L* 61 E3
Redcar *GB* 11 E1
Redditch *GB* 14 A2
Redon *F* 19 D4
Redondela *E* 32 A4
Redondo *P* 40 C4
Redruth *GB* 12 B4
Rees *D* 55 D4
Reeth *GB* 11 D1
Refsnes *N* 104 A3
Reftele *S* 123 E1
Regalbuto *I* 85 D3
Regen *D* 64 A4
Regensburg *D* 63 F4
Regenstauf *D* 63 F4
Reggello *I* 76 A3
Reggio di Calabria *I* 83 D4
Reggio nell'Emilia *I* 75 F1
Reggiolo *I* 75 F1
Reghin *RO* 126 C4
Reguengos de Monsaraz *P* 40 C4
Rehau *D* 63 E2
Rehburg-Loccum *D* 56 B3
Rehden *D* 55 F3
Rehna *D* 50 C3
Reichenau *CH* 66 C4
Reichenau *A* 69 D2
Reichenbach *D* 58 B4
Reichenbach *D* 63 E1
Reichertshofen *D* 67 E1
Reichshoffen *F* 23 E2
Reigate *GB* 14 C3
Reignier *F* 27 D3
Reillanne *F* 31 D2
Reims *F* 17 E4
Reinach *CH* 23 F4
Reinbek *D* 50 C3
Reinberg *D* 51 F2
Reine *N* 107 E1
Reinfeld *D* 50 C3
Reinheim *D* 62 B3
Reinli *N* 111 D4
Reinosa *E* 36 B1
Reischenhart *D* 67 F2
Reisjärvi *FIN* 114 C2
Reiss *GB* 7 E2
Reit i. Winkl *D* 67 F2
Reitzenhain *D* 63 F1
Remagen *D* 61 F2
Rémalard *F* 20 C3
Remich *L* 23 D1
Remiremont *F* 23 D3
Remolinos *E* 37 D3
Remoulins *F* 30 C2
Rempstone *GB* 11 E4
Remscheid *D* 61 F1
Renazé *F* 19 E4
Renchen *D* 23 F2
Rende *I* 83 E2
Rendína *GR* 88 C2
Rendína *GR* 93 D3
Rendsburg *D* 50 B2
Renginío *GR* 93 E3
Rengsdorf *D* 61 F2
Reni *UA* 127 E4
Renko *FIN* 121 C3
Renkum *NL* 54 C4
Rennebu *N* 111 D2
Rennerod *D* 62 A2
Rennes *F* 19 E3
Rennes-les-Bains *F* 29 F4
Rennweg *A* 68 B3
Rensjön *S* 108 A1
Renwez *F* 17 E3
La Réole *F* 28 C1
Replot *FIN* 114 B3
Repojoki *FIN* 105 E4
Reposaari *FIN* 120 B2
Räyrinki *FIN* 114 C3
Repvåg *N* 105 E1
Requena *E* 43 F3
Réquista *F* 29 F2
Rerik *D* 51 D2
Resen *MK* 128 B3
Resende *P* 34 C4
Reşiţa *RO* 128 B1
Resmo *S* 123 F2
Ressons-l'Abbaye *F* 16 C4
Resuttano *I* 84 C3
Retford *GB* 11 E3
Rethel *F* 17 E4
Rethem (Leine) *D* 56 B3
Réthimno *GR* 100 C3
Retiers *F* 19 E3
Retortillo de Soria *E* 36 C4
Retournac *F* 26 B4
Retuerta del Bullaque *E* 42 A3
Retz *A* 65 D4
Reuilly *F* 25 F1
Reus *E* 38 B4
Reusel *NL* 17 F1
Reutlingen *D* 66 B1
Reutte *A* 67 D3
Revel *F* 29 F3
Revigny-sur-Ornain *F* 22 B2
Revin *F* 17 E3
Revonlahti *FIN* 114 C1
Revsnes *N* 110 B4
Reyðarfjörður *IS* 106 C1
Reykhólar *IS* 106 A1
Reykholt *IS* 106 A2
Reykjahlið *IS* 106 B1
Reykjavík *IS* 106 A2
Rīlezkene *LV* 124 C3
Rezzato *I* 71 F4
Rezzoaglio *I* 75 E2
Rhade *D* 50 B3
Rhayader / Rhaeadr *GB* 10 B4
Rheda-Wiedenbrück *D* 55 D4
Rhede *D* 55 D4
Rhede *D* 55 D4
Rheinbach *D* 61 F2
Rheinberg *D* 55 D4
Rheinböllen *D* 61 F3
Rheine *D* 55 E3
Rheinfelden *D* 23 E4
Rheinfelden *CH* 23 F4
Rheinhausen *D* 61 E1
Rheinsberg *D* 51 F4
Rhêmes-Notre Dame *I* 27 F3
Rhenen *NL* 54 C4
Rheydt *D* 61 E1
Rheydt *D* 61 E1
Rhinau *F* 23 E3
Rhinow *D* 57 E2
Rho *I* 71 D4
Rhodes *GB* 103 F1
Rhondda *GB* 13 D1
Rhosneigr *GB* 10 A3
Rhossili *GB* 12 C2
Rhüden *D* 56 C3
Rhyl *GB* 10 B3
Rhynern *D* 55 F4
Rhynie *GB* 7 E4
Riaillé *F* 19 E4
Riákia *GR* 88 A3
Rial *E* 32 A4
Rians *F* 31 D2
Rianxo *E* 32 A3
Riaño *E* 33 F3
Riaza *E* 36 B4
Ribadavia *E* 32 B4
Ribadelago *E* 33 D4
Riba de Saelices *E* 43 D1
Riba de Santiuste *E* 36 C4
Ribadesella *E* 33 F2
Ribas de Campos *E* 33 F4
Ribčev Laz *SLO* 73 D2
Ribe *DK* 122 A3
Ribeauvillé *F* 23 E3
Ribécourt *F* 16 C4
Ribeira de Pena *P* 34 C3
Ribemont *F* 17 D3
Ribera *I* 84 B3
Ribérac *F* 25 D4
Ribera de Cardós *E* 29 E4
Ribera del Fresno *E* 41 D4

Ribes de Freser E 39 D3
Ribiers F 31 D1
Ribnica SLO 73 D3
Ribnica SLO 73 E3
Ribnica na P. SLO 73 E2
Ribniţa MOL 127 E3
Ribnitz-Damgarten D. 51 E2
Ribolla I 76 A4
Riccia I 80 A2
Riccione I 76 C2
Les Riceys F 22 B1
Richelieu F 25 D1
Richmond GB 11 D1
Richmond-
    upon-Thames GB .. 14 B3
Richtenberg D 51 E2
Rickling D 50 C3
Ricla E 37 E4
Riec-sur-Belon F 18 B3
Riedenburg D 63 E4
Ried im Innkreis A 68 A1
Ried im Oberinntal A. 67 D3
Riedlingen D 66 C2
Riegel D 23 E3
Riegersburg A 69 D3
Riego de la Vega E 33 E4
Riesa D 57 F4
Riesi I 84 C3
Riestedt D 57 D4
Rietberg D 55 F4
Rieti I 79 E1
Rieumes F 29 E3
Rieupeyroux F 29 F1
Rieux F 29 E3
Riez F 31 E2
Riezlern A 67 D3

Rīga LV 124 B2
Rigáni GR 92 C3
Rígeo GR 93 E1
Rignac F 29 F1
Rignano Flaminio I ... 79 D1
Rihéa GR 97 E3
Riihimäki FIN 121 D3
Riistavesi FIN 115 E3
Rijeka HR 73 E4
Rijssen NL 55 D3
Riksgränsen S 104 B4
Rillo E 43 F1
Rillo de Gallo E 43 E1
Rimavská Sobota SK. 126 A3
Rimbo S 119 F2
Rimini I 76 C2
Rîmnicu Sărat RO 127 D4
Rîmnicu Vîlcea RO 128 C1
Rímnio GR 87 F3
Rimske Toplice SLO ... 73 E2
Rincón
    de la Victoria E ... 48 A3
Rincón de Soto E 37 E3
Rindal N 111 D2
Ringaskiddy IRL 4 C4
Ringe DK 122 B3
Ringebu N 111 D40
Ringford GB 8 C4
Ringkøbing DK 122 A2
Ringsaker N 111 D4
Ringstad N 110 A30
Ringsted DK 122 C3
Ringwood GB 13 F3
Rínia (Nissí) GR 98 C2
Rinkaby S 123 E3

Rinteln D 56 B3
Río GR 93 D3
Rio Marina I 75 F4
Riocavado
    de la Sierra E 36 C3
Ríogordo E 48 A3
Riola Sardo I 82 A3
Riolo Terme I 76 A2
Riom F 26 A3
Riom-
    ès-Montagnes F.... 25 F4
Riomaggiore I 75 E2
Rio Maior P 40 A2
Rionero in Vulture I .. 80 C3
Rioseco de Tapia E ... 33 E3
Rioveggio I 76 A2
Rioz F 23 D4
Riparbella I 75 E3
Ripatransone I 77 D4
Ripley GB 11 D3
Ripoll E 39 D3
Ripollet E 39 D4
Ripon GB 11 D2
Riquewihr F 23 E3
Risbäck S 107 E4
Risca GB 13 D2
Riscle F 28 C2
Risnes N 116 B3
Risør N 116 C3
Risøyhamn N 104 A3
Ristiina FIN 121 D3
Ristijärvi FIN 115 E1
Ristilampi FIN 109 E2
Risum-Lindholm D ... 50 A2
Ritíni GR 88 A3

Ritoniemi FIN 115 E3
Ritsóna GR 94 A3
Rittmannshausen D .. 62 C1
Ríumar E 44 B1
Riva del Garda I 71 F3
Rivarolo Canavese I .. 27 F4
Rive-de-Gier F 26 C3
Rives F 27 D4
Rivesaltes F 30 A4
La Rivière-
    Thibouville F 20 C2
Rívio GR 92 B2
Rivisondoli I 79 F1
Rivne UA 126 C2
Rivoli I 27 F4
Rivolta d'Adda I 71 E4
Ríza GR 92 C3
Ríza PL 92 C3
Rizário GR 87 F2
Rízia GR 91 E1
Rízoma GR 87 F4
Rizómilos GR 93 E1
Rizovoúni GR 93 D1
Rjånes N 110 B2
Rjukan N 116 C1
Roa de Duero E 36 B3
Roadside GB 7 E2
Roan N 111 D1
Roanne F 26 B3
Robbio I 75 D1
Robertsfors S 113 E1
Robertville B 61 E2
Robič SLO 72 C2
Robla (La) E 33 E3
Robledillo de Gata E . 41 E1
Robledo E 43 D4
Robledo (El) E 42 A3

Robledo de Chavela E 42 B1
Robres E 37 F3
Roca
    de la Sierra (La) E .. 41 D3
Roca del Vallès (La) E 39 D4
Rocamadour F 29 E1
Rocca di Mezzo I 79 F1
Rocca di Papa I 79 E2
Rocca S. Casciano I .. 76 B2
Rocca Sinibalda I 79 E1
Roccadaspide I 80 B4
Roccalbegna I 76 B4
Roccalumera I 83 D4
Roccamonfina I 79 F2
Roccapalumba I 84 C3
Roccaraso I 79 F1
Roccastrada I 76 A4
Roccella Ionica I 83 E4
Rocchetta
    S. Antonio I 80 B2
Rochdale GB 11 D2
La Roche-Bernard F . 19 D4
La Roche-Canillac F . 25 F4
La Roche-Chalais F ... 24 C4
La Roche-Derrien F .. 18 C2
Roche-en-Ardenne
    (La) B 17 F3
La Roche-Guyon F ... 21 D2
La Roche-Posay F 25 D1
La Roche-sur-Foron F 27 E2
La Roche-sur-Yon F .. 24 B1
Rochechouart F 25 D3
Rochefort F 24 B2
Rochefort B 17 F3
Rochefort-en-Terre F. 19 D4
Rochefort-
    Montagne F 26 A3
Rochefort-
    sur-Nenon F 27 D1
La Rochefoucauld F . 25 D3
Rochehaut B 17 F3
La Rochelle F 24 B2
Rochemaure F 30 C1
La Rochepot F 26 C1
Rocheservière F 24 B1
Rochester GB 14 B3
La Rochette F 27 E3
Rochlitz D 63 F1
Rociana
    del Condado E 47 D2

Rocío (El) E 47 D2
Rockenhausen D 23 E1
Rocroi F 17 E3
Róda GR 86 B4
Roda (La) E 43 D3
Rodach D 63 D2
Rodacherbrunn D 63 E2
Roda de Andalucía
    (La) E 47 F3
Roda de Isábena E ... 38 B3
Rodavgí E 92 B1
Rødberg N 116 C1
Rødby DK 122 C4
Rødbyhavn DK 122 C4
Rødding DK 122 B3
Rødding DK 122 B3
Rødeby S 123 F2
Rodeiro E 32 B3
Rødekro DK 122 B3
Rodel GB 6 A3
Rodellar E 38 A3
Roden NL 55 D2
Ródenas E 43 E1
Rodewisch D 63 F2
Rodez F 29 F1
Rodi Garganico I 80 C1
Rodiezmo E 33 E3
Roding D 63 F4
Roditís GR 89 F1
Rododáfni GR 93 D4
Rodohóri GR 87 F2
Rodolívos GR 89 D1
Rödön S 112 B2
Rodópoli GR 88 B1
Rodopós GR 100 A3
Ródos (Nissí) GR 103 F2
Rodováni GR 100 A3
Rodvattnet S 112 C1
Rødven N 110 C2
Rødvig DK 123 D3
Röbel D 51 E3
Rödermark D 62 B3
Römhild D 63 D2
Roermond NL 61 E1
Roeselare B 15 F4
Rötha D 57 E4
Röthenbach
    a. d. Pegnitz D 63 D3
Rötz D 63 F3
Rogätz D 57 E3
Rogaška
    Slatina SLO 73 F2
Rogatec SLO 73 F2
Rogatica BIH 128 A2
Roggendorf D 50 C3
Roggiano Gravina I .. 83 E2
Roggosen D 58 A3
Rogliano F 78 B2
Rogliano I 83 E2
Rognan N 107 E2
Rohan F 18 C3
Rohatyn UA 126 C2
Rohr D 62 C2
Rohrbach-
    lès-Bitche F 23 E2
Rohrbach in
    Oberösterreich A .. 64 B4
Rohrbrunn D 62 B3
Roisel F 17 D3
Roissy-en-France F... 21 D2
Rojales E 49 F1
Rök S 118 C3
Rokiškis LT 124 C3
Røkland N 107 E2
Røldal N 116 B1
Rolfstorp S 123 D1
Rollag N 116 C1
Rolle CH 27 E2
Roma I 79 D2
Romagnano Sesia I .. 70 C4
Roman RO 127 D4
Romana I 82 A2
Romangordo E 41 F2
Romans-sur-Isère F .. 26 C4
Romanshorn CH 66 C3
Rombas F 22 C1
Romeral (El) E 42 C3
Romilly-sur-Seine F . 22 A3
Romny UA 127 F1
Romont CH 27 E1
Romorantin-
    Lanthenay F 21 E4
Rompido (El) E 46 C2
Romsey GB 13 F3
Roncade I 72 B4
Roncal E 28 B4
Ronce-les-Bains F 24 B3
Roncegno I 72 A3
Ronchamp F 23 D4
Ronchi
    dei Legionari I 72 C3
Ronciglione I 79 D1
Roncobilaccio I 76 A2

ROMA
PERCORSI DI
ATTRAVERSAMENTO E
DI CIRCONVALLAZIONE

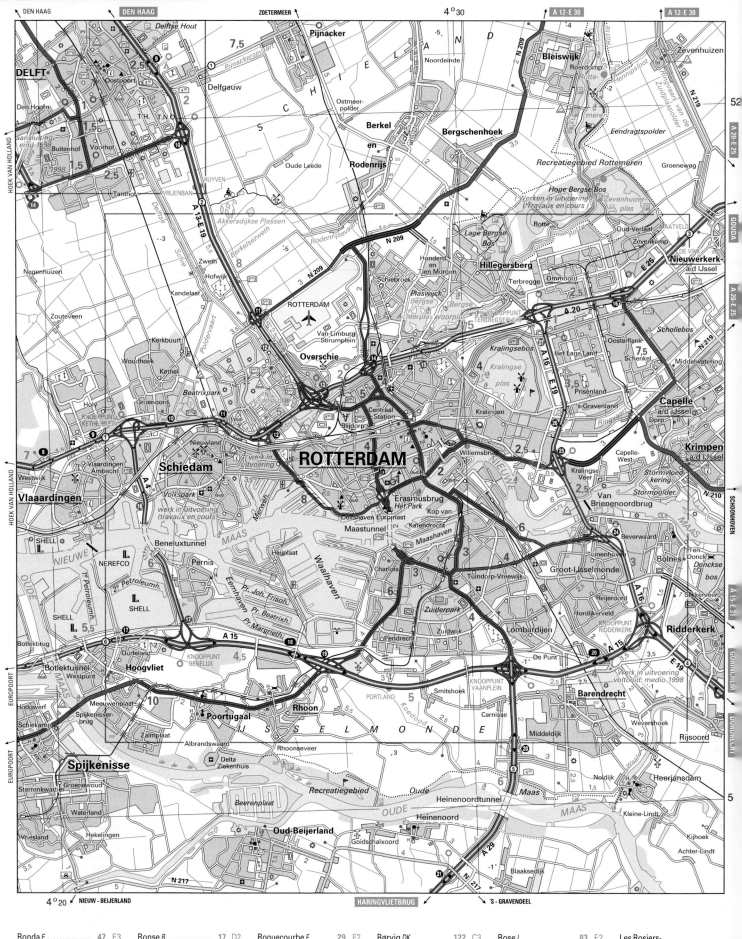

Ronda E	47	E3	Ronse B	17	D2	Roquecourbe F	29	F2	Rørvig DK	122	C3	Rose I	83	E2	Les Rosiers-
Rønde DK	122	C2	Roosendaal NL	17	E1	Roquefort F	28	C2	Rørvik N	106	C4	Rosegg A	68	B4	sur-Loire F	19	F4
Rondissone I	74	C1	Roperuelos			Roquefort-			Rørvik N	111	D1	Rosendal N	116	B1	Rosignano Marittimo I	75	F3
Rondvassbu N	111	D3	del Páramo E	33	E4	sur-Soulzon F	30	A2	Rosà I	72	A4	Rosenheim D	67	F2	Rosignano Solvay I	75	F3
Rönnäng S	118	A1	Ropinsalmi FIN	104	C3	Roquemaure F	30	C2	Rosal de la Frontera E	46	C1	Rosenthal D	64	A1	Roşiori de Vede RO	129	D1
Rønne DK	123	E4	La Roque-Gageac F	29	E1	Roquesteron F	31	F2	Rosans F	31	D1	Roses / Rosas E	39	E3	Roskilde DK	123	E3
Ronneburg D	63	E1	Roquebillière F	31	F2	Roquetas de Mar E	48	C3	Rosarno I	83	E3	Roseto degli Abruzzi I	77	E4	Roslavl' RUS	125	E2
Ronneby S	123	F2	Roquebrun F	30	A3	Roquevaire F	31	D3	Roscoff F	18	B2	Rosheim F	23	E2	Rosmaninhal P	41	D2
Rønnede DK	122	C3	Roquebrune-			Røros N	111	E3	Roscommon / Ros			La Rosière-1850 F	27	E3	Rosolina Mare I	72	B4
Rönnöfors S	112	A1	Cap-Martin F	31	F2	Rørøy N	107	D3	Comáin IRL	2	C4	Rosières-			Rosolini I	85	E4
Ronquillo (El) E	47	D1	La Roquebrussanne F	31	D3	Rorschach CH	66	C3	Roscrea / Ros Cré IRL	5	D2	en-Santerre F	16	C3	Rosporden F	18	B3

SALZBURG — 1/70000

Ross-on-Wye GB...... 13 E1
Rossano I............. 83 E2
Roßberg A....... 64 B40
Rosscarbery IRL...... 4 B4
Roßdorf D............ 62 B3
Rossell E............. 44 A1
Rosses Point IRL...... 2 B2
Roßhaupten D........ 67 D2
Rossio ao
  Sul do Tejo P....... 40 B2
Rosslare / Ros Láir IRL 5 E3
Rosslare Harbour /
  Calafort Ros Láir IRL 5 E3
Roßlau D............ 57 E3
Rosslea GB........... 3 D3
Rossön S............. 112 C1
Roßwein D........... 63 F1
Rosthwaite GB........ 10 C1
Røstlandet N.......... 107 D1
Rostock D............ 51 E2
Rostov RUS.......... 125 F1
Rostrenen F.......... 18 C3
Rostrevor GB......... 3 E3
Rosvik S............. 108 B4
Røsvik N............ 107 F1
Rota E............... 47 D3
Rotenburg D......... 50 B4
Rotenburg D......... 62 C1
Roth D.............. 63 D4
Rothbury GB.......... 9 E4
Rothenburg D........ 58 B4
Rothenburg
  o. d. Tauber D...... 62 C4
Rothéneuf F.......... 19 D2
Rotherham GB........ 11 D3
Rothes GB............ 7 E4
Rothesay GB.......... 8 B3
Rothwell GB.......... 11 E4
Rotonda I............ 80 C4
Rotondella I.......... 81 D4
Rott D.............. 67 D2
Rott a. Inn D......... 67 F2
Rottach-Egern D...... 67 E2
Rottenbach D........ 63 D2
Rottenburg
  a. d. Laaber D...... 67 F1
Rottenburg
  a. Neckar D........ 66 B1
Rottenmann A........ 68 B2
Rotterdam NL........ 54 B4
Rotterdam NL........ 54 B4
Rottne S............. 123 E1
Rottneros S.......... 118 C2
Rottweil D........... 23 F3
Roubaix F............ 15 F4
Rouen F.............. 16 A4
Rouffach F........... 23 E3
Rougé F.............. 19 E4
Rougemont F......... 23 D4
Rougemont-
  le-Château F....... 23 E4
Rouillac F............ 24 C3
Roujan F............ 30 A3
Roulans F............ 23 D4
Roundstone IRL...... 2 A4
Roússa GR........... 91 D1
Rovaniemi FIN........ 109 D2
Rovato I............. 71 E4
Rovereto I........... 71 F3
Roverud N........... 117 E1
Roviés GR............ 93 F2
Rovigo I............. 76 A1
Royal Leamington
  Spa GB............ 14 A2
Royal Tunbridge
  Wells GB........... 14 C4
Royan F............. 24 B3
Royat F............. 26 A3
Roybon F............ 26 C4
Roye F.............. 16 C4
Royère-
  de-Vassivière F..... 25 E3
Royo (El) E........... 37 D3
Røyrvik N........... 107 E4
Royston GB.......... 14 C2
Röyttä FIN........... 109 D3
Rozas
  de Madrid (Las) E... 42 B1
Rozay-en-Brie F...... 21 F2
Le Rozier F........... 30 A2
Rozoy-sur-Serre F.... 17 E4
Rožňava SK.......... 126 B3
Rrogozhinë AL........ 128 B3
Rúa (A) E............ 32 C4
Ruabon GB.......... 10 C3
Rubbestadneset N.... 116 A1
Rubena E............ 36 B2
Rubi E.............. 38 C4
Rubiães P............ 32 A4
Rubí
  de Bracamonte E... 36 A4
Rubielos de Mora E .. 43 F1

Rubiera I............. 75 F1
Rubio (El) E.......... 47 F2
Rudkøbing DK........ 122 C4
Rudn'a RUS.......... 125 E3
Rudolphstein D....... 63 E2
Rudolstadt D......... 63 D1
Rue F............... 16 B3
Rueda E............. 36 A4
Rueda de Jalón E..... 37 E4
Rüdersdorf D........ 58 A2
Rüdesheim a. Rhein D 62 A3
Rügen D............. 51 E2
Ruelle-sur-Touvre F... 25 D3
Rüsselsheim D....... 62 A3
Rüthen D............ 55 F4
Ruffec F............. 24 C3
Ruffieux F........... 27 D3
Rugby GB........... 11 D4
Rugeley GB.......... 11 D4
Rugles F............. 20 C2
Ruhla D............. 62 C1
Ruhland D........... 58 A4
Ruhpolding D........ 67 F2
Ruidera E............ 42 C4
Ruidoms E........... 38 B4
Ruka FIN............ 109 F2
Ruma YU............ 128 B1
Rumengol F.......... 18 B3
Rumigny F........... 17 E3
Rumilly F............ 27 D3
Runcorn GB......... 10 C3
Runde N............ 110 B2
Rundvik S........... 113 D2
Runni FIN............ 115 D2
Runtuna S........... 119 E3
Ruokojärvi FIN....... 121 F2
Ruokolahti FIN....... 121 F2
Ruokto S............ 108 A2
Ruoms F............. 30 B1
Ruotsinpyhtää /
  Strömfors FIN...... 121 E3
Ruovesi FIN.......... 120 C2
Rupt-sur-Moselle F... 23 D3
Ruse BG............. 129 D1
Ruše SLO........... 73 E2
Rush / An Ros IRL.... 3 E4
Rushden GB......... 14 B2
Rusko FIN........... 120 B4
Ruskele S........... 108 A4
Russenes N.......... 105 D1
Le Russey F.......... 27 E1
Russi I.............. 76 B2
Rust A.............. 69 E1
Rustefjelbma N....... 105 F1
Ruswil CH........... 66 A4
Rute E.............. 48 A2
Ruthin / Rhuthun GB.. 10 B3
Rüti CH............. 66 B3
Rutigliano I.......... 81 D2
Rutledal N........... 110 A4
Ruukki FIN........... 114 C1
Ruuponsaari FIN...... 115 D3
Ruurlo NL........... 55 D4
Ruvo di Puglia I...... 81 D2
Ruwer D............ 61 E3
Ruynes-
  en-Margeride F..... 26 A4
Ružomberok SK...... 126 A3
Ry DK.............. 122 B2
Rybinsk RUS......... 125 F1
Rybnik PL........... 126 A2
Ryd S.............. 123 E2
Ryde GB............ 13 F3
Rye GB............. 15 D4
Rygge N............ 117 D2
Rychnov nad
  Kněžnou CZ....... 65 D2
Rykene N........... 116 C3
Ryl'sk RUS.......... 127 F1
Rymättylä FIN....... 120 B4
Rypefjord N......... 105 D1
Rysjedalsvika N...... 110 A4
Ryttylä FIN.......... 121 D3
Rzeszów PL......... 126 B2
Ržev RUS........... 125 E2

S
Sa Calobra E........ 45 E3
Sa Pobla E.......... 45 E3
Sääksjärvi FIN....... 114 C3
Saal a. d. Donau D... 63 D4
Saalbach A.......... 67 F3
Saales F............ 23 E3
Saalfeld D........... 63 D1
Saalfelden A......... 68 A2
Saanen CH.......... 27 F2
Saarbrücken D....... 23 D1
Saarburg D.......... 23 D1
Saaremaa EST....... 124 A2
Saarenkylä FIN...... 109 D2

Saari FIN............ 121 F2
Saariharju FIN....... 109 E3
Saarijärvi FIN........ 115 D3
Saarikoski FIN....... 104 C3
Saariselkä FIN....... 105 F3
Saarlouis D.......... 23 D1
Saas Fee CH........ 70 C3
Šabac YU............ 128 A1
Sabadell E........... 39 D4
Sabaudia I........... 79 E4
Sabbioneta I......... 75 F1
Sabero E............ 33 F3
Sabiñánigo E........ 28 C4
Sabiote E............ 48 B1
Sablé-sur-Sarthe F... 19 F4
Les Sables-d'Olonne F 24 A2
Sables-d'Or-les-Pins F 19 D2
Sabóia P............ 46 A2
Sabres F............ 28 B2
Sabrosa P........... 34 C4
Sabugal P........... 41 D1
Sacavém P.......... 40 A3
Sacedón E........... 43 D1
Saceruela E......... 42 A4
Sacile I............. 72 B3
Sacramenia E........ 36 B4
Sada E.............. 32 B2
Sádaba E............ 37 E3
Sæbø N............. 110 B3
Sæby DK............ 122 C1
Sælvig DK........... 122 C3
Sævråsvåg N........ 110 A4
Safara P............ 46 C1
Säffle S............. 118 B2
Saffron Walden GB... 14 C2
Safonovo RUS....... 125 E3
Sagard D............ 51 F1
S'Agaró E........... 39 E3
Sagéika GR.......... 92 C4
Sagiáda GR.......... 86 C4
Sagres P............ 46 A20
Sagunt / Sagunto E.. 44 A3
Sagunto / Sagunt E.. 44 A3
Sagvåg N........... 116 A1
Sahagún E........... 33 F4
Sahalahti FIN........ 120 C2
Sahl DK............. 122 B2
Sahloinen FIN........ 121 D2
Saignelégier CH...... 23 E4

Saija FIN............ 109 E1
Saillagouse F........ 29 F4
Saillans F........... 30 C1
Saimaanranta FIN.... 121 E2
Sains-du-Nord F..... 17 E3
Sains-Richaumont F.. 17 D3
Saintes F............ 24 B3
Stes-Maries-
  de-la-Mer F........ 30 C3
Saintfield GB......... 3 E2
Saissac F............ 29 F3
Saky UA............ 127 F4
Säkylä FIN........... 120 B3
Sala S.............. 119 E2
Sala Consilina I...... 80 C3
Salacgriva LV........ 124 B2
Salamajärvi FIN...... 114 C3
Salamanca E......... 35 F4
Salamína GR......... 94 A4
Salamína (Nissí) GR .. 94 A4
Salándi GR........... 97 E2
Salar E.............. 48 A3
Salardú E........... 29 D4
Salas E............. 33 D2
Salas
  de los Infantes E ... 36 C3
Salbohed S.......... 119 D2
Salbris F............ 21 E4
Salceda (La) E....... 36 B4
Salcombe GB........ 12 C4
Saldaña E........... 33 F4
Saldus LV........... 124 B3
Sale I.............. 75 D1
Salem D............ 66 C2
Salemi I............. 84 A3
Sälen S............. 112 A4
Salen GB............ 8 B1
Salen GB............ 8 B1
Saler (El) E.......... 44 A3
Salernes F........... 31 E3
Salerno I............ 80 A3
Salers F............ 25 F4
Salgótarján H........ 126 A3
Salgueiro do Campo P 40 C2
Salice Terme I........ 75 D1
Salies-de-Béarn F.... 28 B3
Salies-du-Salat F..... 29 D3
Salignac-Eyvigues F . 25 E4
Salihli TR............ 129 F4

Salihorsk BY......... 125 D4
Salinas E............ 33 E2
Salindres F.......... 30 B2
Sälinkää FIN......... 121 D3
Salins-les-Bains F.... 27 D1
Salisbury GB......... 13 F2
Salla FIN............ 109 E2
Sallanches F......... 27 E3
Sallent E............ 38 C3
Sallent de Gállego E . 28 C4
Salmerón E.......... 43 D1
Salmoral E.......... 41 F1
Salo FIN............ 120 C4
Salò I.............. 71 F4
Salobral (El) E....... 43 D4
Salobreña E......... 48 B3
Salon-de-Provence F. 30 C2
Salorino E........... 41 D3
Salou E............. 44 C1
Salsbruket N......... 107 D4
Salses-le-Château F.. 30 A4
Salsomaggiore
  Terme I............ 75 E1
Salsta S............. 119 E1
Saltash GB.......... 12 C3
Saltburn-
  by-the-Sea GB..... 11 E1
Saltcoats GB......... 3 F1
Salto P............. 34 C3
Saltoluokta S........ 108 A1
Saltvik FIN.......... 120 A4
Saluggia I........... 74 C1
Saluzzo I............ 31 F1
Salvacañete E....... 43 E2
Salvagnac F......... 29 E2
Salvan CH.......... 27 F2
Salvaterra
  de Magos P........ 40 A3
Salvaterra de Miño E. 32 A4
Salvatierra E........ 37 D2
Salvatierra
  de los Barros E..... 41 D4
La Salvetat-Peyralès F 29 E2
La Salvetat-
  sur-Agout F........ 29 F3
Salviac F............ 29 E1
Salzburg A........... 68 A2

Salzburg A........... 68 A2
Salzgitter-Bad D...... 56 C3
Salzhausen D........ 50 C4
Salzkotten D......... 55 F4
Salzwedel D......... 51 D4
Sama de Langreo E .. 33 E2
Samariás (Farángi) GR 100 B3
Samarína GR......... 87 D3
Samatan F........... 29 D3
Sambatikí GR......... 97 E2
Sambiase I........... 83 E3
Sambir UA........... 126 D3
Samboal E........... 36 A4
Sambuca di Sicilia I.. 84 B3
Samedan CH........ 66 C4
Samer F............ 15 E4
Sámi GR............ 92 A4
Samikó GR.......... 96 B1
Sammatti FIN........ 120 C4
Sammichele di Bari I. 81 D2
Samnanger N........ 110 A4
Samoëns F.......... 27 E2
Samokov BG........ 128 C2
Samos E............ 32 C3
Sámos GR........... 99 F1
Sámos (Nissí) GR..... 99 F1
Samothráki GR....... 91 D3
Samothráki (Nissí) GR 91 D3
Samper de Calanda E 37 F4
Sampeyre I.......... 31 F1
Samtens D.......... 51 F2
Samugheo I......... 82 B3
Saná GR............ 88 C2
Sanary-sur-Mer F.... 31 D3
Sancergues F........ 26 A1
Sancerre F.......... 26 A1
Sanchidrián E....... 42 A1
Sancoins F.......... 26 A1
Sancti Petri E........ 47 D4
Sancti-Spíritus E..... 41 E1
Sancy F............ 26 A3
Sand N............. 116 B2
Sand N............. 117 E1
Sandane N.......... 110 B3
Sandanski BG....... 128 C3
Sandarne S......... 112 C4
Sandau D........... 51 E4
Sandbach GB....... 10 C3
Sande N............ 110 B2
Sande N............ 117 D2

Name	Page	Grid
Sande D	55	E1
Sande P.	34	B4
Sandefjord N.	117	D2
Sandeid N.	116	A1
Sandıklı TR	129	F4
Sandnes N.	116	A2
Sandness GB	7	F3
Sandnessjøen N.	107	D3
Sando E.	35	E4
Sandoméri GR	92	C4
Sandomierz PL.	126	B2
Sandown GB	13	F3
Sandrigo I.	72	A4
Sandstad N.	111	D2
Sandur DK.	106	A4
Sandviken S.	119	E1
Sandvikvåg N.	116	A1
Sandwich GB.	15	D3
Sandy GB	14	B2
Sangarcía E	36	A4
Sangerhausen D.	57	D4
Sangis S	108	C3
Sangüesa E	28	A4
Sanguinaires F.	74	C3
Sanguinet F.	28	B1
Sani GR	88	B3
Sanitz D.	51	E2
St-Olof S.	123	E3
Sanlúcar de Barrameda E	47	D3
Sanlúcar de Guadiana E.	46	B2
Sanlúcar la Mayor E.	47	D2
Sanluri I.	82	B3
Sannainen FIN	121	D4
Sannazzaro de' Burgondi I.	75	D1
Sannicandro di Bari I	81	D2
Sannicandro Garganico I.	80	B1
Sanok PL.	126	B3
Sanquhar GB.	8	C3
Sansepolcro I.	76	B3
Sanski Most BIH.	128	A1
Santaella E.	47	F2
Santana da Serra P.	46	A2
Santana P.	40	A4
Santander E.	36	B1
Santanyí E.	45	E3
Santarcangelo di Romagna I.	76	B2
Santarém P.	40	B3
Santas Martas E	33	E4
Santeramo in Colle I.	81	D2
Santhià I.	70	C4
Santiago de Alcántara E.	41	D2
Santiago de Compostela E.	32	A3
Santiago de la Espada E.	48	C1
Santiago de la Ribera E.	49	E2
Santiago do Cacém P	46	A1
Santiago do Escoural P.	40	B4
Santibáñez de Béjar E	41	F1
Santibáñez de la Peña E.	33	F3
Santibáñez de la Sierra E	41	E1
Santibáñez de Vidriales E.	33	D4
Santillana del Mar E.	36	B1
Santiponce E.	47	D2
Santoña E.	36	C1
Santos de Maimona (Los) E.	41	D4
Santos (Los) E.	41	F1
Santu Lussurgiu (Località) I.	82	B2
Santurtzi E.	36	C1
Sanxenxo / Sangenjo E	32	A4
Sanza I.	80	C4
Saorge F.	31	F2
Sapanca TR.	129	F3
Sápes GR	91	D2
Sapiéndza (Nissí) GR.	96	B3
Sappada I.	68	A4
Sappee FIN	120	C3
Sapri I.	80	C4
Säräisniemi FIN.	115	D1
Sarajärvi FIN.	109	E3
Sarajevo BIH.	128	A2
Sarakiní GR.	87	F1
Sarakíniko GR	94	A2
Saramon F.	29	D3
Sarandáporo GR	87	F3
Sarandë AL	128	B4
Saraváli GR	92	C4
Saray TR.	129	E3
Sarayköy TR.	129	F4
Sardara I.	82	B3
Sardínia GR.	92	C4
Sardoal P.	40	B2
S'Arenal E.	45	E3
Sarentino / Sarntal I.	67	E4
Sargans CH.	66	C4
Sari-d'Orcino F.	78	A3
Sariá (Nissí) GR	103	D3
Sariñena E.	38	A3
Särkisalmi FIN.	121	F2
Särkisalo FIN.	120	C4
Sarlat-la-Canéda F	25	E4
Särna S.	112	A4
Sarnano I.	77	D4
Sarnen CH.	66	B4
Sarnico I.	71	E4
Sarno I.	80	A3
Sarny UA.	127	D1
Särö S.	118	B4
Sarón E.	36	B1
Sarone I.	72	B3
Saronída GR.	98	A1
Saronno I.	71	D4
Sárospatak H.	126	B3
Sarpsborg N	117	D2
Sarracín E.	36	B2
Sarral E.	38	B4
Sarralbe F.	23	D2
Sarre-Union F.	23	E2
Sarrebourg F.	23	E2
Sarreguemines F.	23	E1
Sarria E.	32	C3
Sarrión E.	43	F2
Sarroch I.	82	B4
Sars-Poteries F.	17	E3
Sarsina I.	76	B2
Sarstedt D.	56	C3
Sarteano I.	76	B4
Sartène F.	78	A4
Sárti GR.	89	D3
Sartilly F.	19	E2
Sarule I.	82	B2
Sárvár H.	69	E2
Sarvsjö S.	112	A3
Sarzana I.	75	E2
Sarzeau F.	18	C4
Sarzedas P.	40	C2
Sassari I.	82	A4
Sassello I.	75	D2
Sassenage F.	27	D4
Sassenberg D.	55	F4
Sassenheim NL.	54	B3
Sassetta I.	75	F4
Sasso I.	79	D1
Sasso Marconi I.	76	A2
Sassoferrato I.	76	C3
Sassoleone I.	76	A2
Sassuolo I.	75	F2
Sástago E.	37	F4
Sátão P.	34	C4
Säter S.	119	D1
Satillieu F.	26	C4
Satolas-et-Bonce F.	26	C3
Sátoraljaújhely H.	126	B3
Satow D.	51	D3
Sátres GR.	89	F1
Satrup D.	50	B2
Sattel CH.	66	B4
Sattledt A.	68	B1
Satu Mare RO.	126	C3
Sauca E.	37	D4
Saucejo (El) E.	47	F3
Sauda N.	116	B1
Sauðárkrókur IS.	106	B1
Sauerlach D.	67	D2
Saugues F.	26	A4
Saujon F.	24	B3
Sauland N.	116	C2
Saulgau D.	66	C2
Saulieu F.	26	B1
Sault F.	31	D2
Saulx F.	23	D4
Saulxures-sur-Moselotte F.	23	D3
Saumur F.	24	C1
Saundersfoot GB	12	C1
Sauris I.	68	A4
Sauve F.	30	B2
Sauveterre-de-Béarn F.	28	B3
Sauveterre-de-Guyenne F.	28	C1
Sauveterre-de-Rouergue F.	29	F2
Sauvo FIN.	120	B3
Sauxillanges F.	26	A3
Le Sauze F.	31	E1
Sauze d'Oulx I.	27	E4
Sauzé-Vaussais F.	24	C2
Sauzon F.	18	C4
Sava I.	81	E3
Savália GR.	96	B1
Sävar S.	113	E1
Savelli I.	83	F2
Savenay F.	19	D4
Saverdun F.	29	E3
Saverne F.	23	E2
Savigliano I.	31	F1
Savignac-les-Églises F.	25	D4
Savignano Irpino I.	80	B2
Savignano sul Rubicone I.	76	B2
Savigny-sur-Braye F.	21	D4
Savines-le-Lac F.	31	E1
Saviñán E.	37	E4
Savitaipale FIN.	121	E2
Sävja S.	119	E2
Savognin CH.	66	C4
Savona I.	75	D2
Savonlinna FIN.	121	F2
Savonranta FIN.	115	F4
Sävsjö S.	123	E1
Savukoski FIN.	109	E1
Sawbridgeworth GB.	14	C2
Sax E.	49	E1
Saxmundham GB.	15	D2
Saxnäs S.	107	E4
Sayatón E.	42	C2
Säynätsalo FIN.	121	D2
Säyneinen FIN.	115	E3
Scaër F.	18	B3
Scafa I.	79	F1
Scafati I.	80	A3
Scalasaig GB.	8	A2
Scalby GB.	11	E1
Scalea I.	80	C4
Scalloway GB.	7	F3
Scandiano I.	75	F1
Scanno I.	79	F1
Scansano I.	76	A4
Scanzano Ionico I.	81	D3
Scarborough GB.	11	E1
Scardovari I.	76	B1
Scarinish GB.	8	A1
Scarriff / An Scairbh IRL.	4	C2
Ščekino RUS.	125	F3
Scey-sur-Saône-et-St-Albin F.	22	C4
Schachendorf A.	69	E2
Schärding A.	68	A1
Schaffhausen CH.	23	F4
Schafstädt D.	57	E4
Schagen NL.	54	B2
Schaprode D.	51	E2
Scharbeutz D.	50	C3
Scharnitz A.	67	E3
Scheeßel D.	50	B4
Scheggia I.	76	C3
Scheibbs A.	68	C1
Scheifling A.	68	C3
Scheinfeld D.	63	D3
Schenefeld D.	50	B3
Schenefeld D.	50	B3
Scherfede D.	56	B4
Schermbeck D.	55	D4
Scheßlitz D.	63	D3
Scheveningen NL.	54	B4
Schieder-Schwalenberg D.	56	B4
Schierling D.	63	F4
Schiermonnikoog NL.	55	D1
Schiers CH.	66	C4
Schifferstadt D.	23	F1
Schildau D.	57	F3
Schilpario I.	71	E3
Schiltach D.	23	F3
Schio I.	72	A4
Schirmeck F.	23	E2
Schirnding D.	63	E2
Schkeuditz D.	57	E4
Schkölen D.	63	E1
Schladming A.	68	B2
Schlagbrügge D.	50	C3
Schleching D.	67	F2
Schleiden D.	61	E2
Schleiz D.	63	E2
Schleswig D.	50	B2
Schleusingen D.	63	D2
Schlieben D.	57	F3
Schlitz D.	62	B2
Schlotheim D.	63	D1
Schluchsee D.	23	F3
Schlüchtern D.	62	B2
Schlüsselfeld D.	63	D3
Schlutup D.	50	C3
Schmalkalden D.	62	C1
Schmallenberg D.	62	A1
Schmidmühlen D.	63	E4
Schmilka D.	64	A1
Schmölln D.	52	A3
Schmölln D.	63	E1
Schnackenburg D.	51	D4
Schnaittenbach D.	63	E3
Schneeberg D.	63	F1
Schneverdingen D.	50	B4
Schönau D.	23	F4
Schönberg D.	63	F2
Schönberg D.	50	C2
Schönberg D.	64	A4
Schönebeck D.	57	E3
Schöneck D.	63	E2
Schönecken D.	61	E3
Schönewalde D.	57	F3
Schöningen D.	57	D3
Schönmünzach D.	23	F2
Schönsee D.	63	F3
Schönthal D.	63	F3
Schönwalde D.	50	C2
Schönwald i. Schwarzwald D.	23	F3
Schöppenstedt D.	57	D3
Schönberg im Stubaital A.	67	E3
Schönbrunn A.	69	D1
Schongau D.	67	D2
Schoonhoven NL.	54	B4
Schopfheim D.	23	F4
Schoppernau A.	66	C3
Schorndorf D.	66	C1
Schortens D.	55	E1
Schotten D.	62	B2
Schramberg D.	23	F3
Schrems A.	64	C4
Schrobenhausen D.	67	E1
Schröcken A.	67	D3
Schrozberg D.	62	C3
Schruns A.	66	C3
Schüttorf D.	55	E3
Schwaan D.	51	E3
Schwabach D.	63	D4
Schwabmünchen D.	67	D2
Schwäbisch-Gmünd D.	66	C1
Schwäbisch-Hall D.	62	C4
Schwaigern D.	62	B4
Schwalstadt-Treysa D	62	B1
Schwalstadt-Ziegenhain D.	62	B1
Schwandorf D.	63	E4
Schwanebeck D.	57	D3
Schwanenstadt A.	68	B1
Schwanewede D.	50	A4
Schwarmstedt D.	56	B2
Schwarza D.	63	D1
Schwarzach im Pongau A.	68	A3
Schwarzenbach a. d. Saale D.	63	E2
Schwarzenbek D.	50	C3
Schwarzenberg D.	63	F1
Schwarzenburg CH.	27	F2
Schwarzenfeld D.	63	E3
Schwarzheide D.	58	A4
Schwarzsee CH.	27	F1
Schwaz A.	67	E3
Schwechat A.	69	E1
Schwedt D.	52	A4
Schweich D.	61	F3
Schweinfurt D.	62	C2
Schweinitz D.	57	F3
Schwelm D.	61	F1
Schwendi D.	66	C2
Schwerin D.	51	D3
Schwerte D.	61	F1
Schwetzingen D.	23	F1
Schwyz CH.	66	B4
Sciacca I.	84	B3
Scicli I.	85	D4
Scilla I.	83	D4
Scole GB.	15	D2
Sconser GB.	6	B4
Scopello I.	70	C3
Scordia I.	85	D3
Scorzé I.	72	B4
Scourie GB.	6	C2
Scrabster GB.	7	D2
Ščučyn BY.	124	C4
Scunthorpe GB.	11	E2
Scuol / Schuls CH.	67	D4
Seaford GB.	14	C4
Seaham GB.	9	F4
Seaton GB.	13	D3
Seaton Delaval GB.	9	F4
Sebeş RO.	126	C3
Sebež RUS.	125	D3
Sebnitz D.	64	A1
Seca (La) E.	36	A4
Seckau A.	68	C3
Seclin F.	17	D2
Secondigny F.	24	C2
Sedan F.	17	F4
Sedano E.	36	B2
Sedbergh GB.	10	C1
Séderon F.	31	D2
Sedgefield GB.	11	D1
Sedico I.	72	B3
Sedini I.	82	B1
Sedlec I.	82	B2
Seebenau D.	51	D4
Seeboden A.	68	B3
Seebruck D.	67	F2
Seefeld in Tirol A.	67	E3
Seehaus A.	68	B2
Seehausen D.	51	D4
Seeheim-Jugenheim D.	62	B3
Seelisberg CH.	66	B4
Seelow D.	58	A2
Sées F.	20	C2
Seesen D.	56	C4
Seevetal D.	50	C4
Seewalchen A.	68	A2
Seewiesen A.	68	C2
Segesta I.	84	A3
Segni I.	79	E2
Segonzac F.	24	C3
Segorbe E.	43	F3
Segovia E.	36	B4
Segré F.	19	F4
Segura E.	41	D2
Segura de la Sierra E.	48	C1
Segura de Léon E.	47	D1
Segura de los Baños E.	43	F1
Sehnde D.	56	C3
Seia P.	41	D1
Seiches-sur-le-Loir F.	19	F4
Seierstad N.	106	C4
Seifhennersdorf D.	64	B1
Seignelay F.	22	A4
Seilhac F.	25	E4
Seinäjoki FIN.	114	B3
Seissan F.	29	D3
Seitenstetten Markt A	68	C1
Seixal P.	40	A4
Sékoulas GR.	96	C1
Selargius I.	82	B4
Selassía GR.	97	D2
Selb D.	63	E2
Selbekken N.	111	D2
Selbu D.	111	E2
Selby GB.	11	E2
Selçuk TR.	129	E4
Séléro D.	89	F1
Sélestat F.	23	E3
Selfoss IS.	106	A2
Séli GR.	87	F2
Selía GR.	100	C4
Selianítika GR.	93	D4
Seligenstadt D.	62	B3
Selínia GR.	94	A4
Selinunte I.	84	B3
Selje N.	110	B3
Seljord N.	116	C2
Selkirk GB.	9	D3
Sella Nevea I.	68	B4
Selles-sur-Cher F.	25	E1
Sellières F.	27	D1
Sellin D.	51	F2
Selm D.	55	E4
Selmsdorf D.	50	C3
Selommes F.	21	D4
Selongey F.	22	C4
Seløy N.	107	D3
Selsey GB.	14	B4
Selters D.	62	B2
Seltz F.	23	F2
Selva del Camp (La) E	38	B4
Selva di Val Gardena / Wölkenstein in Gröden I.	67	F4
Selvino I.	71	E4
Semič SLO.	73	E3
Seminara I.	83	E4
Semproniano I.	76	B4
Semur-en-Brionnais F.	26	B2
Sena E.	38	A4
Sénas F.	30	C2
Senden D.	66	C1
Sendim P.	35	E3
Senez F.	31	E2
Senftenberg D.	58	A4
Sénia (La) E.	44	A1
Senigallia I.	76	C3
Senise I.	81	D3
Senj HR.	73	E4
Senlis F.	16	C4
Sennen GB.	12	A4
Sennestadt D.	55	F4
Sennori I.	82	A1
Sennybridge GB.	13	D1
Senonches F.	21	D2
Senones F.	23	D3
Senorbì I.	82	B3
Senožeče SLO.	73	D3
Sens F.	21	F3
Senta YU.	128	B1
Sentilj SLO.	73	F1
Šentjernej SLO.	73	E3
Šentjur SLO.	73	E3
Šentvid na Slemenu SLO.	73	E2
Sépeaux F.	21	F3
Šepetivka UA.	127	D2
Sepino I.	80	A2
Sepúlveda E.	36	B4
Sequeros E.	41	E1
Seraing B.	17	F2
Seravezza I.	75	F3
Seregno I.	71	D4
Séres GR.	88	C1
Serfaus A.	67	D3
Serfopoúla (Nissí) GR	98	B2
Sergijev Posad RUS	125	F2
Seriate I.	71	E4
Sérifos GR.	98	B2
Sérifos (Nissí) GR.	98	B2
Sermaize-les-Bains F	22	B2
Sermide I.	76	A1
Sermoneta I.	79	E2
Sernancelhe P.	34	C4
Serón E.	48	C3
Serón de Nágima E.	37	D4
Serós E.	38	A4
Serpa P.	46	B1
Serpuchov RUS.	125	F3
Serra F.	44	A3
Serra S. Bruno I.	83	E3
Serracapriola I.	80	B1
Serrada E.	36	A4
Serra de Outes E.	32	A3
Serradifalco I.	84	C3
Serradilla E.	41	E2
Serramanna I.	82	B4
Serravalle Scrivia I.	75	D1
Serres F.	31	D1
Serrières F.	26	C4
Sersale I.	83	F2
Sertã P.	40	C2
Sérvia GR.	87	F3
Servian F.	30	A3
Servigliano I.	77	D4
Sesa E.	38	A3
Seseña E.	42	B2
Sesimbra P.	40	A4
Sesklío (Nissí) GR.	103	C1
Sesma E.	37	D2
Sessa Aurunca I.	79	F2
Sesta Godano I.	75	E2
Sestino I.	76	B3
Sesto / Sexten I.	67	F4
Sesto Calende I.	71	D4
Sesto Fiorentino I.	76	A3
Sesto S. Giovanni I.	71	D4
Sestola I.	75	F2
Sestri Levante I.	75	E2
Sestriere I.	27	E4
Sestu I.	82	B4
Séta GR.	94	B3
Setcases E.	39	D2
Sète F.	30	B3
Setenil E.	47	E3
Setermoen / Bardu N	104	B3
Settebagni I.	79	D1
Settimo Torinese I.	74	C1
Settle GB.	10	C2
Les Settons F.	26	B1
Setúbal P.	40	A4
Seu d'Urgell (La) / Seo de Urgel E	38	C2
Seui I.	82	B3
Seulo I.	82	B3
Seurre F.	26	C1
Sevastianá GR	87	F2
Sevenoaks GB.	14	C3
Sever do Vouga P.	34	B4
Sévérac-le-Château F	30	A1
Seveso I.	71	D4
Sevettijärvi FIN.	105	F2
Sevilla E.	47	D2
Sevilleja de la Jara E	42	A2
Sevlievo BG	129	D2
Sevnica SLO.	73	E2
Sévrier F.	27	D3
Sevsk RUS.	125	F4
Seyches F.	29	D1
Seyda D.	57	F3
Seyðisfjörður IS.	106	C1
Seyne F.	31	E1
La Seyne-sur-Mer F.	31	D3
Seyssel F.	27	D3

Sežana SLO 73 D3
Sézanne F 22 A2
Sezze I 79 E2
Sfáka GR 101 F4
Sfakiá GR 100 B4
Sfaktiría (Nissí) GR ... 96 B3
Sferracavallo I 84 B2
Sfintu Gheorghe RO .. 127 D4
Sforzacosta I 77 D3
Shaftesbury GB 13 E3
Shanklin GB 13 F3
Shap GB 10 C1
Sheerness GB 15 D3
Sheffield GB 11 D3
Shefford GB 14 B2
Shëngjin AL 128 B3
Shepshed GB 11 D4
Shepton Mallet GB ... 13 E2
Sherborne GB 13 E3
Shercock IRL 3 C3
Sheringham GB 15 D1
Shiel Bridge GB 6 C4
Shieldaig GB 6 B4
Shijak AL 128 B3
Shinás GR 88 A2
Shiniás GR 94 B4
Shínos GR 92 C3
Shinoússa (Nissí) GR .. 99 D3
Shipston-on-Stour GB 13 F1
Shizá (Nissí) GR 96 B3
Shkodër AL 128 B3
Sholári GR 88 B2
Shoreham GB 14 B4
Shrewsbury GB 10 C4
Shrewton GB 13 F2
Siátista GR 87 E3
Šiauliai LT 124 B3
Sibari I 81 D4
Sibbhult S 123 E2
Sibbo / Sipoo FIN 121 D4
Šibenik HR 77 F2
Sibiu RO 126 C4
Sicignano
degli Alburni I 80 B3
Sick D 50 B4
Šid YU 128 A1
Sidári GR 86 B4
Sideby FIN 114 B2
Sidensjö S 112 C2
Siderno I 83 E4
Sidiró GR 91 E1
Sidirókastro GR 88 C1
Sidirónero GR 90 A1
Sidmouth GB 13 D3
Siebenlehn D 63 F1
Siedlce PL 126 B1
Siegburg D 61 F2
Siegen D 62 A1
Siegsdorf D 67 F2
Siena I 76 A3
Sieppijärvi FIN 108 C2
Sieradz PL 126 A2
Sierck-les-Bains F 23 D1
Sierentz F............ 23 E4
Sierninghofen A 68 B1
Sierpc PL 126 A1
Sierra de Fuentes E .. 41 E3
Sierra de Yeguas E ... 47 F3
Sierra Nevada E 48 B3
Sierre CH............ 27 F2
Sievi FIN 114 C2
Sievin as FIN 114 C2
Sífnos (Nissí) GR...... 98 B3
Sigean F............. 30 A4
Sigerfjord N 104 A4
Siggjarvåg N.......... 116 A3
Sighetu Marmaţiei RO 126 C3
Sighişoara RO........ 126 C4
Siglufjörður IS 106 B1
Sigmaringen D 66 B2
Signy-l'Abbaye F 17 E4
Sígri GR 95 E1
Sigtuna S 119 E2
Sigüenza E 36 C4
Sigulda LV 124 B2
Siikainen FIN 120 B2
Siikajoki FIN 114 C1
Siilinjärvi FIN 115 E3
Sikaminiá GR......... 95 F1
Sikås S 112 B2
Siki GR 93 F1
Sikiá GR 89 D3
Sikiá GR 97 E3
Síkinos GR........... 98 C3
Síkinos (Nissí) GR..... 98 C3
Sikióna GR........... 93 E4
Sikoráhi GR.......... 91 D2
Sikoúrio GR.......... 88 A4
Sikovuono FIN 105 E3
Silandro /
Schlanders I 67 D4
Şile TR 129 F3
Siles E 48 C1

Siliqua I............... 82 B4
Silistra BG............ 129 E1
Silivri TR............. 129 E3
Siljan N.............. 117 D2
Siljansnäs S.......... 119 D1
Silkeborg DK 122 B2
Silla E 43 F3
Sillé-le-Guillaume F.. 19 F3
Silleda E 32 B3
Sillian A............. 67 F4
Silloth GB 9 D4
Sils E 39 D3
Siltakylä FIN 121 E3
Šilute LT 124 A3
Silvalen N 107 D3
Silvaplana CH 66 C4
Silvares P............ 40 C1
Silves P............. 46 A2
Silvi Marina I 77 E4
Silz A 67 E3
Simancas E........... 36 A3
Símandra GR.......... 88 B3
Simav TR 129 F4
Simaxis I 82 B4
Simbach D 67 F1
Simbach a. Inn D 68 A1
Sími GR 103 E1
Sími (Nissí) GR....... 103 E1
Simlångsdalen S 123 D2
Simmerath D.......... 61 E2
Simmern
(Hunsrück) D 61 F3
Simo FIN 109 D3

Simola FIN............ 121 E3
Simonsbath GB....... 13 D2
Simonswald D 23 F3
Simópoulo GR 96 B1
Simrishamn S 123 E3
Sinaia RO 129 D1
Sinalunga I 76 B4
Sinarádes GR......... 86 B4
Sinarcas E 43 E3
Sindelfingen D........ 66 B1
Sındırgı TR 129 E4
Síndos GR 88 B2
Sines P.............. 46 A1
Sinettä FIN 109 D2
Singen
(Hohentwiel) D 66 B2
Siniscola I 78 A4
Sinj HR 75 F1
Sinnicolau Mare RO .. 128 B1
Sinopoli I 83 E4
Sinsheim D........... 62 B4
Sintra P............. 40 A3
Sinzig D 61 F2
Siófok H 126 A4
Sion CH 27 F2
Sippola FIN 121 E3
Sira N 116 A3
Siracusa I 85 E4
Siret RO 127 D3
Sirevåg N............ 116 A3
Sirkka FIN 109 D1
Sirma N............. 105 E2

Sirmione I............ 71 F4
Sirna (Nissí) GR...... 99 F4
Sirolo I.............. 77 D3
Síros (Nissí) GR...... 98 C2
Siruela E 41 F4
Sisak HR 73 F3
Sisante E 43 D3
Síses GR 101 D3
Sissa I 75 F1
Sissach CH........... 23 F4
Sissonne F........... 17 E4
Sisteron F 31 D2
Sistiana I 72 C3
Sistranda N 111 D1
Sitges E 38 C4
Sithonía GR.......... 88 C3
Sitía GR 101 F4
Sittard NL 61 D1
Sittensen D 50 B4
Sittingbourne GB 15 D3
Siuntio /
Sjundeå FIN 120 C4
Siuro FIN 120 C2
Siurua FIN 109 E3
Siusi / Seis I 67 E4
Sivakkavaara GR..... 88 C3
Síviri GR 88 C3
Sívota GR 92 A1
Sívros GR 92 A3
Six-Fours-
les-Plages F 31 D3
Siziano I 71 D4
Sizun F 18 B2

Sjøåsen N 111 E1
Sjöbo S 123 E3
Sjøholt N 110 B2
Sjötorp S 118 C3
Sjoutnäset S 107 E4
Sjøvegan /
Salangen N 104 B3
Sjulsmark S 113 E1
Sjusjøen N 111 D4
Skåbu N 111 D3
Skadovs'k UA........ 127 F4
Skælskør DK......... 122 C3
Skærbæk DK 122 A2
Skafidiá GR.......... 96 B3
Skaftafell IS 106 B2
Skagaströnd IS 106 A1
Skage N............. 107 D3
Skagen DK.......... 122 C1
Skaill GB 7 E2
Skála GR 99 F2
Skála GR 93 F3
Skála GR 92 B4
Skála GR 97 D3
Skála GR 95 F2
Skála Eressoú GR..... 95 E2
Skála Kaliráhis GR.... 89 E2
Skála Oropoú GR 94 A4
Skála Potamiás GR ... 89 E2
Skála Rahoníou GR... 89 E2
Skála Volissoú GR ... 95 E2
Skaland / Berg N..... 104 A3
Skálavik DK 106 A4
Skálevik N 116 B3

Skalohóri GR 87 E3
Skalohóri GR 95 F1
Skalotí GR 90 A1
Skamnéli GR 87 D4
Skandáli GR 89 F4
Skanderborg DK 122 B2
Skandzoúra
(Nissí) GR 94 B2
Skånevik N 116 A1
Skåningsbukt N....... 104 C2
Skänninge S 119 D3
Skanör-
Falsterbo S 122 D3
Skara S 118 C3
Skaramangás GR 94 A4
Skarberget N......... 104 A4
Skåre S 118 C2
Skärfia GR 93 E2
Skärhamn S 118 A4
Skarnes N 117 E1
Skarplinge S 119 E1
Skarsvåg N 105 E1
Skärvången S 112 A1
Skarżysko-
Kamienna PL 126 A2
Skattungbyn S 112 B4
Skatval N 111 E1
Skaulo S 108 B1
Skaun N 111 D2
Skee S 118 A3
Skegness GB 11 F3
Skei N 110 B3
Skei N 111 D2

Sevilla

Skellefteå *S*	108	B4
Skelleftehamn *S*	108	B4
Skelmersdale *GB*	10	C2
Skepastó *GR*	88	C2
Skerries / Na Sceirí *IRL*	3	E4
Ski *N*	117	D2
Skíathos *GR*	94	A2
Skíathos (Nissí) *GR*	94	A1
Skibbereen / An Sciobairín *IRL*	4	B4
Skibby *DK*	122	C3
Skibotn *N*	104	C3
Skídra *GR*	87	F2
Skien *N*	116	C2
Skierniewice *PL*	126	A1
Skillingaryd *S*	118	C4
Skiniás *GR*	101	D4
Skinnarbu *N*	116	C1
Skinnskatteberg *S*	119	D1
Skipagurra *N*	105	F2
Skipton *GB*	11	D2
Skíros *GR*	94	C1
Skíros (Nissí) *GR*	94	C2
Skíti *GR*	88	B4

Skive *DK*	122	B2
Skjeberg *N*	117	D2
Skjelvik *N*	107	C2
Skjern *DK*	122	A2
Skjersholmane *N*	116	A1
Skjerstad *N*	107	E2
Skjervøy *N*	104	C2
Skjønhaug *N*	117	D2
Sklavopoúla *GR*	100	A3
Sklíthro *GR*	88	B4
Škloŭ *BY*	125	D2
Skodje *N*	110	B2
Škofja Loka *SLO*	73	D2
Škofljica *SLO*	73	E3
Skog *S*	112	C2
Skog *S*	112	C4
Skogar *IS*	106	B2
Skoghall *S*	118	C2
Skogstorp *S*	119	D2
Skokloster *S*	119	E2
Skollenborg *N*	117	D2
Skópelos *GR*	94	A2
Skópelos *GR*	95	F2
Skópelos (Nissí) *GR*	94	A1
Skopiá *GR*	93	E2

Skopje *MK*	128	B3
Skopós *GR*	87	E1
Skopun *DK*	106	A3
Skorovatn *N*	107	D4
Skorped *S*	112	C2
Skotína *GR*	88	A4
Skotterud *N*	117	E1
Skoulikariá *GR*	92	C1
Skoúra *GR*	97	D3
Skoúrta *GR*	94	A4
Skoútari *GR*	88	C1
Skoútari *GR*	97	D3
Skoutáros *GR*	95	F1
Skövde *S*	118	C3
Skrá *GR*	88	A1
Skreia *N*	117	D1
Skrolsvik *N*	104	A3
Skrydstrup *DK*	122	B3
Skudeneshavn *N*	116	A2
Skull / Schull *IRL*	4	B4
Skultuna *S*	119	D2
Skuodas *LT*	124	A3
Skurup *S*	123	D3
Skutskär *S*	119	E1
Skutvik *N*	107	E1

Skvyra *UA*	127	E2
Slagelse *DK*	122	C3
Slagnäs *S*	108	A3
Slǎnčev Brjag *BG*	129	E2
Slancy *RUS*	125	C1
Slane *IRL*	3	D4
Slangerup *DK*	123	D3
Slatina *RO*	128	C1
Slaŭharad *BY*	121	E4
Slavkov u Brna *CZ*	65	E3
Slavonski Brod *HR*	128	A1
Slavuta *UA*	127	D2
Sławno *PL*	52	C1
Sleaford *GB*	11	E3
Sliedrecht *NL*	54	B4
Sliema *M*	85	F4
Sligachan (Loch) *GB*	6	B4
Sligo / Sligeach *IRL*	2	B2
Slite *S*	119	F4
Sliven *BG*	129	D2
Slobozia *RO*	129	E1
Slonim *BY*	124	C4
Sloten *NL*	54	C2
Slough *GB*	14	B3

Slovenj Gradec *SLO*	73	E2
Slovenska Bistrica *SLO*	73	F2
Slovenske Konjice *SLO*	73	E2
Sluck *BY*	125	D4
Sluderno / Schluderns *I*	67	D4
Sluis *NL*	15	F3
Slunj *HR*	73	F4
Słupsk *PL*	52	C1
Smålandsstenar *S*	123	D1
Smaljaviči *BY*	125	D4
Smarhon' *BY*	124	C4
Šmarje *SLO*	73	F2
Šmarjeske Toplice *SLO*	73	E3
Šmartin *SLO*	73	E2
Smedby *S*	123	F2
Smederevo *YU*	128	B1
Smedjebacken *S*	119	D1
Smigáda *GR*	91	D1
Smila *UA*	127	F2
Smilde *NL*	55	D2

Smiltene *LV*	124	C2
Smolensk *RUS*	125	E3
Smoljan *BG*	129	D3
Smørhamn *N*	110	A3
Smygehamn *S*	123	D3
Snaith *GB*	11	E2
Snåsa *N*	111	F1
Sneek *NL*	54	C2
Sneem *IRL*	4	A3
Snihurivka *UA*	127	F3
Snillfjord *N*	111	D2
Soave *I*	72	A4
Sobrado dos Monxes *E*	32	B3
Sobral da Adiça *P*	46	C1
Sobral de Monte Agraço *P*	40	A3
Sobreira Formosa *P*	40	C2
Søby *DK*	122	B4
Soča *SLO*	72	C2
Soccia *F*	78	A3
Sochaczew *PL*	126	A1
Sochaux *F*	23	D4
Socovos *E*	49	D1

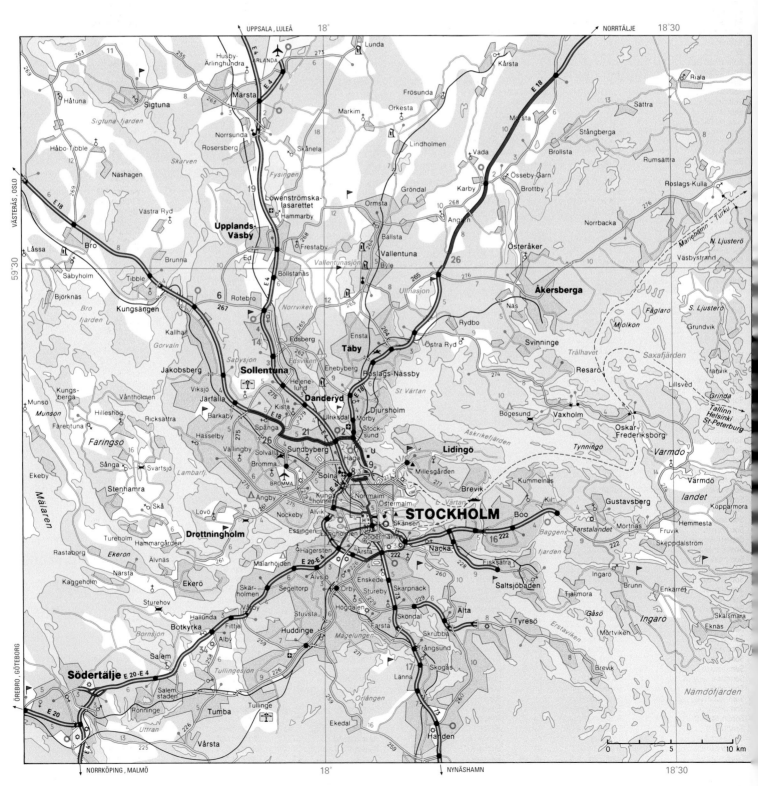

Socuéllamos E.... 42 C3
Sodankylä FIN.... 109 D1
Söderåkra S.... 123 F2
Söderbärke S.... 119 D1
Söderfors S.... 119 E1
Söderhamn S.... 112 C4
Söderköping S.... 119 D3
Södertälje S.... 119 E2
Sodražica SLO.... 73 E3
Sodupe E.... 36 C1
Sögel D.... 55 E2
Söll A.... 67 F2
Sömmerda D.... 63 D1
Soest NL.... 54 C3
Soest D.... 55 F4
Soestdijk NL.... 54 C3
Sofádes GR.... 93 D1
Sofia BG.... 128 C2
Sofiero S.... 123 D2
Sofikó GR.... 97 E1
Sofó GR.... 93 E1
Sogliano al Rubicone I.... 76 B2
Soglio CH.... 71 E3
Søgne N.... 116 B3
Soham GB.... 14 C2
Sohós GR.... 88 C2
Soignies B.... 17 E2
Soini FIN.... 114 C3
Soinlahti FIN.... 115 D2
Soissons F.... 17 D4
Söke TR.... 129 E4
Sokna N.... 117 D1
Soko Banja YU.... 128 D2
Sokołów Podlaski PL.... 126 B1
Sola N.... 116 A2
Solana (La) E.... 42 C4
Solana de los Barros E.... 41 D4
Solana del Pino E.... 48 A1
Solares E.... 36 B1
Solberg S.... 112 C1
Solčava SLO.... 73 E2
Sol'cy RUS.... 125 D1
Solda / Sulden I.... 67 D4
Sölden A.... 67 E3
Solenzara F.... 78 B4
Solesmes F.... 17 D3
Solesmes F.... 19 F4
Solevåg N.... 110 B2
Solf FIN.... 114 B3
Solferino I.... 71 F4
Solholmen N.... 110 C2
Solignac F.... 25 E3
Solignac-sur-Loire F.... 26 B1
Solihull GB.... 11 D4
Solingen D.... 61 F1
Sollana E.... 44 A3
Sollefteå S.... 112 C2
Sollenau A.... 69 D1
Sollentuna S.... 119 E2
Sóller E.... 45 E3
Sollerön S.... 118 C1
Søllested DK.... 122 C4
Solliès-Pont F.... 31 E3
Solnečnogorsk RUS.... 125 F2
Solofra I.... 80 B3
Solosancho E.... 42 A1
Solothurn CH.... 27 F1
Solre-le-Château F.... 17 E3
Solrød DK.... 123 D3
Solsona E.... 38 C3
Šolta HR.... 128 A2
Soltau D.... 50 B4
Sölvesborg S.... 123 E3
Solvorn N.... 110 B4
Soma TR.... 129 E4
Sombernon F.... 26 C1
Sombor YU.... 128 A1
Someren NL.... 17 F1
Somero FIN.... 120 C3
Sommarøy N.... 104 B2
Sommatino I.... 84 C3
Sommesous F.... 22 A2
Sommières F.... 30 B2
Somolinos E.... 36 C4
Soncillo E.... 36 B1
Soncino I.... 71 E4
Søndeled N.... 117 C3
Sønder Felding DK.... 122 A2
Sønderborg DK.... 122 B4
Sønderby DK.... 122 B4
Sondershausen D.... 57 D2
Søndersø DK.... 122 B3
Sondrio I.... 71 E3
Songeons F.... 16 B4
Sonkajärvi FIN.... 115 E2
Sonneberg D.... 63 D2
Sonnewalde D.... 58 A3
Sonsbeck D.... 55 D4
Son Servera E.... 45 E3

Sonthofen D.... 67 D3
Sontra D.... 62 C1
Sopeira E.... 38 B3
Sopot PL.... 124 A4
Sopron H.... 69 E1
Sør-Flatanger N.... 106 C4
Sora I.... 79 F2
Soragna I.... 75 E1
Söráker S.... 112 C3
Sørarnøy N.... 107 E2
Sorbas E.... 49 D3
Sore F.... 28 B1
Soresina I.... 71 E4
Sörfors S.... 113 D1
Sorga D.... 62 C1
Sorgono I.... 82 B3
Sorgues F.... 30 C2
Sørgutvik N.... 107 D4
Soria E.... 37 D3
Soriano nel Cimino I.... 79 D1
Sørkjosen N.... 104 C2
Sorø DK.... 122 C3
Soroca MOL.... 127 D3
Soroní GR.... 103 F2
Sørreisa N.... 104 B3
Sorrento I.... 80 A3
Sørrollnes N.... 104 A3
Sorsakoski FIN.... 115 E4
Sorsele S.... 107 F4
Sorso I.... 82 A1
Sort E.... 38 B2
Sortino I.... 85 E4
Sortland N.... 104 A3
Sorunda S.... 119 E3
Sørvær N.... 104 C1
Sørværøy N.... 107 D1
Sørvågen N.... 107 D1
Sørvagur DK.... 106 A3
Sørvattnet S.... 112 D4
Sørvik N.... 104 A3
Sos del Rey Católico E.... 28 B4
Soses E.... 38 A4
Sosnovyj Bor RUS.... 124 C1
Sosnowiec PL.... 126 A2
Sospel F.... 31 F2
Šoštanj SLO.... 73 E2
Sóstis GR.... 89 F1
Šostka UA.... 127 F1
Sotaseter N.... 110 C3
Sotillo de la Adrada E.... 42 A1
Sotíra GR.... 87 F2
Sotkamo FIN.... 115 E2
Soto del Barco E.... 33 E2
Soto de los Infantes E.... 33 D2
Soto de Luiña E.... 33 D2
Soto de Sajambre E.... 33 F3
Sotogrande E.... 47 E4
Sotopalacios E.... 36 B2
Sotrondio E.... 33 E3
Sottomarina I.... 72 B4
Sottrum D.... 50 B4
Sottunga FIN.... 120 A4
Sotuélamos E.... 43 D4
Soúda GR.... 100 B3
Souesmes F.... 21 E4
Soufflenheim F.... 23 F2
Souflí GR.... 91 E2
Soúgia GR.... 100 A3
Sougné-Remouchamps B.... 17 F2
Souillac F.... 25 E4
Souilly F.... 22 C2
Soulac-sur-Mer F.... 24 B3
Soulaines-Dhuys F.... 22 B3
Soulinári GR.... 96 B3
Soulópoulo GR.... 86 C4
Soultz-Haut-Rhin F.... 23 E3
Soultz-sous-Forêts F.... 23 E2
Soúnio GR.... 98 A1
Soúnio (Akr.) GR.... 98 A1
Souppes-sur-Loing F.... 21 F3
Sourdeval F.... 19 F2
Soure P.... 40 B1
Sournia F.... 29 F4
Sourotí GR.... 88 B2
Soúrpi GR.... 93 F2
Sousceyrac F.... 29 F1
Sousel P.... 40 C3
Soustons F.... 28 B2
Soutelo E.... 32 B3
La Souterraine F.... 25 E2
South Molton GB.... 13 D2
South Queensferry GB.... 9 D2
South Shields GB.... 9 F4
Southam GB.... 13 E4
Southampton GB.... 13 F3
Southborough GB.... 14 C4
Southend GB.... 3 E1
Southend-on-Sea GB.... 14 C3

Southport GB.... 10 C2
Southsea GB.... 13 F3
Southwell GB.... 11 E3
Southwold GB.... 15 E2
Souvála GR.... 97 F1
Souvigny F.... 26 A2
Sovata RO.... 126 C4
Sövdeborg S.... 123 E3
Soverato I.... 83 E3
Soveria Mannelli I.... 83 E2
Søvik N.... 110 B2
Sozopol BG.... 129 E2
Sp. Brnik SLO.... 73 D2
Spa B.... 61 D2
Spaichingen D.... 66 B2
Spakenburg NL.... 54 C3
Spalding GB.... 11 F4
Spandau D.... 57 F2
Spangenberg D.... 62 B1
Sparlösa S.... 118 B3
Spárta GR.... 93 F4
Spárti GR.... 97 D2
Spárto GR.... 92 B2
Spas-Demensk RUS.... 125 F3
Spáta GR.... 94 B4
Spatharéi GR.... 99 F1
Spean Bridge GB.... 8 C1
Spello I.... 76 C4
Spennymoor GB.... 11 D1
Sperhiáda GR.... 93 D2
Sperlonga I.... 79 F2
Spétses GR.... 97 E2
Spétses (Nissí) GR.... 97 E2
Spetsopoúla (Nissí) GR.... 97 E2
Speyer D.... 23 F1
Spezzano Albanese Terme I.... 81 D4
Spezzano della Sila I.... 83 E2
Spiddal / An Spidéal IRL.... 2 A4
Spiekeroog D.... 55 E1
Spielfeld A.... 69 D3
Spiez CH.... 27 F1
Spijkenisse NL.... 54 B4
Spili GR.... 100 C4
Spiliá GR.... 88 A4
Spilimbergo I.... 72 C3
Spilsby GB.... 11 F3
Spinalónga (Hers.) GR.... 101 E3
Spinazzola I.... 80 C3
Spincourt F.... 22 C1
Spišská Nová Ves SK.... 126 B3
Spital am Pyhrn A.... 68 B2
Spittal an der Drau A.... 68 B3
Spitz A.... 68 C1
Spjelkavik N.... 110 B2
Split HR.... 128 A2
Splügen CH.... 66 C4
Spodsbjerg DK.... 122 C4
Špola UA.... 127 F2
Spoleto I.... 76 C4
Sportnitz D.... 51 D4
Spotorno I.... 75 D2
Spremberg D.... 58 A4
Spresiano I.... 72 B3
Springe D.... 56 B3
Squillace I.... 83 E3
Squinzano I.... 81 F3
Srbobran YU.... 128 A1
Središče SLO.... 73 F2
Sremska Mitrovica YU.... 128 A1
Środa Wielkopolska PL.... 59 D2
Stade D.... 50 B3
Stádio GR.... 97 D1
Stadskanaal NL.... 55 D2
Stadthagen D.... 56 B3
Stadtilm D.... 63 D1
Stadtkyll D.... 61 E2
Stadtlohn D.... 55 D4
Stadtoldendorf D.... 56 B4
Stadtroda D.... 63 E1
Stadtsteinach D.... 63 E2
Stadt Wehlen D.... 64 A1
Staffanstorp S.... 123 D3
Staffelstein D.... 63 D2
Staffin GB.... 6 B3
Stafford GB.... 11 D4
Stágira GR.... 88 C2
Stahle D.... 56 B4
Stahovica SLO.... 73 E2
Staines GB.... 14 B3
Stainz A.... 69 D3
Štalcerji SLO.... 73 E3
Stalída GR.... 101 E3
Stall A.... 68 A3
Stalowa Wola PL.... 126 B3
Stamford GB.... 11 E4
Stamnes N.... 110 B4

Stams A.... 67 E3
Stamsund N.... 107 E1
Stange N.... 117 E1
Stanley GB.... 9 E4
Stános GR.... 92 B2
Stanós GR.... 88 C2
Stans CH.... 66 B4
Stansstad CH.... 66 B4
Stansted Mountfitched GB.... 14 C2
Stara Zagora BG.... 129 D2
Starachowice PL.... 126 B2
Staraja Russa RUS.... 125 D1
Stargard Szczeciński PL.... 52 B3
Stårheim N.... 110 B3
Stari Log SLO.... 73 E3
Starica RUS.... 125 F2
Starigrad Paklenica HR.... 77 F1
Starnberg D.... 67 E2
Starodub RUS.... 125 E4
Starogard Gdański PL.... 124 A4
Starokostjantyniv UA.... 127 D2
Starý Smokovec SK.... 126 A3
Staßfurt D.... 57 D3
Stathm. Angístis GR.... 89 D1
Statland N.... 106 C4
Stavanger N.... 116 A2
Staveley GB.... 11 D3
Stavelot B.... 61 E2
Stavenhagen Reuterstadt D.... 51 E3
Stavenisse NL.... 17 E1
Stavern N.... 117 D2
Stavoren NL.... 54 C2
Stavrodrómi GR.... 92 C4
Stavrohóri GR.... 101 F4
Stavrós GR.... 92 A3
Stavrós GR.... 94 A3
Stavrós GR.... 100 B3
Stavrós GR.... 93 D1
Stavrós GR.... 88 A2
Stavrós GR.... 88 C2
Stavroúpoli GR.... 89 E1
Stavsjo N.... 111 D4
Steckborn CH.... 66 B3
Steeg A.... 67 D3
Steenbergen NL.... 17 E1
Steenvoorde F.... 15 E4
Steenwijk NL.... 55 D2
Stefáni GR.... 94 A4
Stefáni GR.... 92 B1
Stefaniná GR.... 88 C2
Stefanovíkio GR.... 93 E1
Stege DK.... 123 D4
Stegersbach A.... 69 E2
Steibis D.... 66 C3
Steigen N.... 107 E1
Stein A.... 65 D4
Stein N.... 111 D4
Stein am Rhein CH.... 66 B3
Stein D.... 63 D3
Steinach D.... 63 D2
Steinach A.... 67 E3
Steinau a. d. Straße D.... 62 B2
Steinbach-Hallenberg D.... 63 D1
Steine N.... 110 A4
Steinfeld A.... 68 A4
Steinfeld (Oldenburg) D.... 55 F3
Steinfurt D.... 55 E3
Steingaden D.... 67 D2
Steinhausen D.... 66 C2
Steinheim D.... 56 B4
Steinheim D.... 67 D2
Steinkjer N.... 111 E1
Steinshamn N.... 110 B2
Steinsland N.... 116 A1
Stekene B.... 17 E1
Stenay F.... 17 F4
Stendal D.... 57 E2
Stení GR.... 94 A3
Stenlille DK.... 122 C3
Stenløse DK.... 123 D3
Stenness GB.... 7 E2
Stenó GR.... 97 D1
Sténoma GR.... 92 C2
Stenudden S.... 107 F2
Stenungsund S.... 118 B4
Sterkrade D.... 55 D4
Stérna GR.... 97 D1
Stérna GR.... 91 E1
Stérna GR.... 89 E1
Sternberg D.... 51 D3
Stérnes GR.... 100 B3
Sterup D.... 50 B2
Stevenage GB.... 14 C2
Stewarton GB.... 8 C3
Steyr A.... 68 B1

Steyrermühl A.... 68 B1
Stia I.... 76 B3
Stigliano I.... 80 C3
Stigtomta S.... 119 E3
Stiklestad N.... 111 E1
Stilída GR.... 93 E2
Stilo I.... 83 E3
Stimfalía (L.) GR.... 97 D1
Stintino I.... 82 A1
Štip MK.... 128 C3
Stípsi GR.... 95 F1
Stíra GR.... 94 B4
Stirling GB.... 8 C2
Stjärnhov S.... 119 E3
Stjärnsund S.... 119 D3
Stjørdal N.... 111 E2
Stockach D.... 66 B2
Stockbridge GB.... 13 E3
Stockelsdorf D.... 50 C3
Stockerau A.... 65 D4
Stockholm S.... 119 E2
Stockport GB.... 11 D3
Stocksbridge GB.... 11 D3
Stockton-on-Tees GB.... 11 D1
Stöde S.... 112 C3
Stoke-on-Trent GB.... 10 C3
Stokke N.... 117 D2
Stokmarknes N.... 104 A4
Stolberg D.... 57 D4
Stolberg D.... 61 E2
Stolin BY.... 127 D1
Stollberg D.... 63 F1
Stöllet S.... 118 C1
Stolpen D.... 58 A4
Stolzenau D.... 56 B3
Stómio GR.... 88 A4
Stone GB.... 11 D4
Stonehaven GB.... 9 E1
Stonglandet N.... 104 A3
Storå S.... 119 D2
Stora Blåsjön S.... 107 E4
Stora Skedvi S.... 119 D1
Stora Sundby S.... 119 D2
Storby FIN.... 120 A4
Stordal N.... 110 C2
Store Heddinge DK.... 123 D3
Store Molvik N.... 105 F1
Storebø N.... 116 A1
Storebro S.... 119 D4
Støren N.... 111 D2
Storfors S.... 118 C2
Storforshei N.... 107 E2
Storkow D.... 58 A3
Stormi FIN.... 120 C3
Stornoway GB.... 6 A2
Storo I.... 71 F3
Storožynec' UA.... 127 D3
Storsjö S.... 112 A2
Storslett / Nordreisa N.... 104 C2
Storsteinen N.... 104 C2
Storsteinnes N.... 104 B3
Storuman S.... 107 F4
Storvik N.... 104 C2
Storvik S.... 119 E1
Stotel D.... 50 A4
Stoúbcy BY.... 124 C4
Stoúpa GR.... 96 C2
Stournaréika GR.... 92 C1
Stourport-on Severn GB.... 10 C4
Støvring DK.... 122 B1
Stow-on-the-Wold GB.... 13 F1
Stowmarket GB.... 15 D2
Strà I.... 72 B4
Strabane GB.... 2 C2
Stradella I.... 75 D1
Stradsett GB.... 11 F4
Straelen D.... 55 D4
Strakonice CZ.... 65 A3
Stralsund D.... 51 E2
Stranda N.... 110 B3
Strandebarm N.... 116 B1
Strandhill IRL.... 2 B3
Strangford GB.... 3 E3
Strängnäs S.... 119 E2
Stranice SLO.... 73 E2
Stranorlar IRL.... 2 C2
Stranraer GB.... 3 F2
Strasbourg F.... 23 E2
Strasburg D.... 51 E3
Straßburg A.... 68 B3
Straßwalchen A.... 68 A2
Stratford-upon-Avon GB.... 13 E1
Strathaven GB.... 8 C3
Stratóni GR.... 88 C2
Stratoníki GR.... 88 C2
Strátos GR.... 92 B2
Stratton GB.... 12 C3

Straubing D.... 63 F4
Straumen N.... 107 F1
Straumen N.... 111 E1
Straumen N.... 107 E2
Straumsjøen N.... 104 A3
Straumsnes N.... 107 E2
Straupitz D.... 58 A3
Strausberg D.... 58 A2
Straußfurt D.... 63 D1
Streatley GB.... 13 F2
Street GB.... 13 E3
Strehaia RO.... 128 C1
Strehla D.... 57 F4
Streitberg D.... 63 D3
Strengberg A.... 68 C1
Stresa I.... 70 C4
Strimonikó GR.... 88 C1
Strobl A.... 68 A2
Strofádes (Nissiá) GR.... 96 A2
Strofiliá GR.... 94 A2
Strokestown IRL.... 2 C3
Stromberg D.... 62 A3
Stromeferry GB.... 6 B4
Strömfors FIN.... 121 E3
Stromness GB.... 7 E2
Strömsbruk S.... 112 C4
Strömsnasbruk S.... 123 E2
Strömstad S.... 118 A3
Strömsund S.... 112 B1
Strongoli I.... 83 F2
Strontian GB.... 8 B1
Stroud GB.... 13 E1
Strovlés GR.... 100 A3
Struer DK.... 122 A2
Struga MK.... 128 B3
Struge SLO.... 73 E3
Strumica MK.... 128 C3
Stryj UA.... 126 C3
Stryn N.... 110 B3
Strzelce Krajeńskie PL.... 52 B4
Stubbekøbing DK.... 122 C4
Stühlingen D.... 23 F4
Stugun S.... 112 B2
Stuhr D.... 50 A4
Stupino RUS.... 125 F2
Sturehov S.... 119 E2
Sturminster Newton GB.... 13 E3
Sturup S.... 123 D3
Stuttgart D.... 66 B1
Stykkishólmur IS.... 106 A1
Suances E.... 33 F2
Subbiano I.... 76 B3
Subiaco I.... 79 E1
Subijana E.... 36 C2
Subotica YU.... 128 A1
Suceava RO.... 127 D3
Sucevița RO.... 127 D3
Suchiniči RUS.... 125 F3
Sucina E.... 49 E2
Sudbury GB.... 11 D4
Sudbury GB.... 15 D2
Suddesjaur S.... 108 A3
Sudža RUS.... 127 F1
Sueca E.... 44 A4
Süchteln D.... 61 E1
Süderbrarup D.... 50 B2
Sueros de Cepeda E.... 33 E4
Süßen D.... 66 C1
Suhl D.... 63 D2
Suinula FIN.... 120 C2
Suippes F.... 22 B2
Sukeva FIN.... 115 E2
Sulina RO.... 127 E4
Sulingen D.... 55 F2
Sulitjelma N.... 107 F2
Sulkava FIN.... 121 E2
Sully-sur-Loire F.... 21 E4
Sulmona I.... 79 F1
Sultanhisar TR.... 129 F4
Sulz a. Neckar D.... 66 B1
Sulzbach (Saar) D.... 23 D1
Sulzbach a. d. Murr D.... 62 C4
Sulzbach-Rosenberg D.... 63 E3
Sulzemoos D.... 67 E1
Sumba N.... 106 A4
Sumburgh GB.... 7 F3
Sümeg H.... 69 F2
Šumen BG.... 129 E2
Sumiainen FIN.... 115 D3
Sumiswald CH.... 27 F1
Šumperk CZ.... 65 E2
Sumy UA.... 127 F1
Sund FIN.... 120 A4
Sunde N.... 116 A1
Sunde N.... 111 D1
Sunderland GB.... 9 F4
Sundern (Sauerland) D.... 62 A1
Sundom FIN.... 114 B3

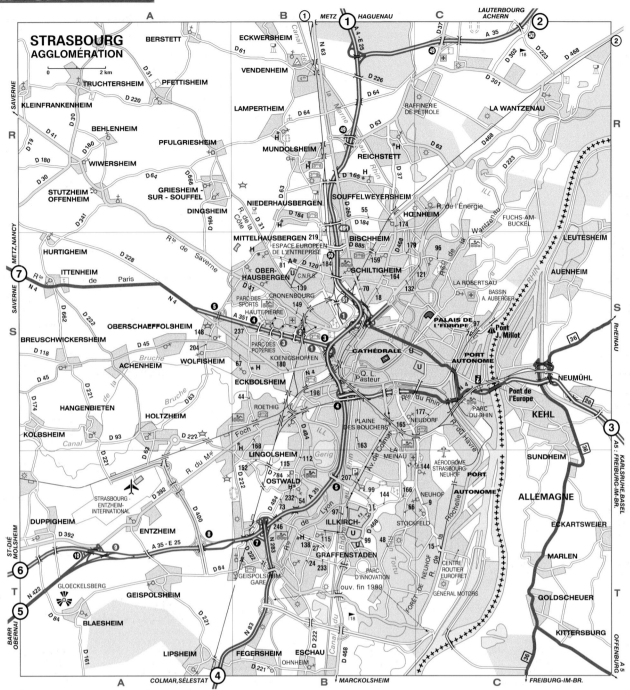

STRASBOURG
AGGLOMÉRATION

Sundsvall S 112 C3
Suni I 82 A2
Sunnansjö S 119 D1
Sunndalsøra N. 110 C2
Sunne S 112 B2
Sunne S 118 C2
Sunnemo S 118 C2
Suodenniemi FIN 120 B2
Suolahti FIN 115 D4
Suolijoki FIN. 109 D3
Suomenlinna FIN 121 D4
Suomenniemi FIN 121 E2
Suomusjärvi FIN 120 C4
Suomussalmi FIN. 115 E1
Suonenjoki FIN. 115 E3
Suopelto FIN 121 D2
Suopelto FIN 115 D3
Super-Besse F 26 A3
Super Molina E 38 C3
Supino I 79 E2
Surahammar S 119 D2
Suraž RUS. 125 E4
Surbo I. 81 F3
Surdulica YU 128 C2
Surenenpass CH 66 B4
Surgères F 24 B2
Súria E 38 C3
Surnadalsøra N. 111 D2
Sursee CH 66 A3
Survilliers F 21 E2
Susa I 27 F4
Susch CH 67 D4

Susurluk TR 129 E3
Sutri I 79 D1
Sutterton GB 11 F4
Sutton Coldfield GB .. 11 D4
Sutton GB. 14 C3
Sutton-in-Ashfield GB 11 D3
Suvereto I 75 F4
Suwałki PL 124 B4
La Suze-sur-Sarthe F. 20 C1
Suzzara I. 75 D1
Svaljava UA 126 B3
Svalöv S 123 D3
Svaneke DK. 123 E4
Svanstein S 108 C2
Svanvik N 105 F2
Svappavaara S 108 B1
Svärdsjö S. 119 D1
Svarstad N 117 D2
Svartå S 118 C2
Svartevatn N. 116 B3
Svedala S. 123 D3
Sveg S 112 A3
Svelgen N 110 B3
Svelvik N 117 D2
Svenljunga S. 118 B4
Svensby N. 104 B2
Svenstavik S 112 B2
Svetlahorsk BY. 125 D4
Svetlogorsk RUS 124 A4
Svetozarevo YU 128 B2
Svidník SK. 126 B3

Svilengrad BG. 129 D2
Svingvoll N. 111 D4
Svinoy DK 106 A3
Svištov BG. 129 D2
Svitavy CZ 65 D3
Svitlovods'k UA 127 F2
Svolvær N. 104 A4
Svorkmo N 111 D2
Svoronáta GR 92 A4
Svorónos GR 88 A3
Swadlincote GB. 11 D4
Swaffham GB 11 F4
Swalmen NL. 61 E1
Swanage GB 13 E3
Swanley GB 14 C3
Swanlinbar IRL 2 C3
Swansea /
  Abertawe GB 12 C1
Świdnica PL 59 D4
Świdwin PL 58 B2
Świebodzin PL 58 B2
Świecie PL. 126 A1
Swindon GB. 13 F2
Swinford / Béal Atha
  na Muice IRL 2 B3
Świnoujście PL. 52 A2
Swords / Sord IRL 3 D4
Syčovka RUS 125 E2
Sykäräinen FIN 114 C2
Syke D 55 F2
Sykkylven N. 110 B2
Sylling N. 117 D1
Sylt-Ost D 50 A1

Syltefjord N 105 F1
Synod Inn GB 12 C1
Syötekylä FIN. 109 E3
Syre GB 7 D2
Sysmä FIN 121 D2
Sysslebäck S 118 B1
Syväjärvi FIN 109 D1
Syvde N 110 B3
Syvdsnes N 110 B3
Syyspohja FIN. 121 F2
Szarvas H. 126 B40
Szczecin PL 52 A3
Szczecinek PL 52 C2
Szczytno PL. 124 A4
Szécsény H. 126 A3
Szeged H 126 B4
Székesfehérvár H. ... 126 A4
Szekszárd H. 126 A4
Szentendre H 126 A4
Szentes H. 126 B4
Szigetvár H. 128 A1
Szolnok H. 126 B4
Szombathely H 69 E2

Saint

St-Affrique F 30 A2
St-Agnant F 24 B3
St-Agrève F 26 B4
St-Aignan F 25 E1
St-Aignan-sur-Roë F. 19 E4

St-Alban-
  sur-Limagnole F ... 30 A1
St. Albans GB 14 B3
St-Amand-
  en-Puisaye F. 21 F4
St-Amand-les-Eaux F. 17 D2
St-Amand-Longpré F 21 D4
St-Amand-
  Montrond F. 25 F1
St-Amans F. 30 A1
St-Amans-des-Cots F 29 F1
St-Amans-Soult F ... 29 F3
St-Amant-
  Roche-Savine F 26 B3
St-Amant-Tallende F. 26 A3
St-Amarin F. 23 E3
St-Ambroix F. 30 B1
St-Amé F. 23 D3
St-Amour F 27 D2
St-André-
  de-Cubzac F. 24 C4
St-André-de-l'Eure F. 21 D2
St-André-
  de-Valborgne F. ... 30 B2
St-André-les-Alpes F. 31 E2
St. Andrews GB 9 D2
St-Anthème F. 26 B3
St-Antonin-
  Noble-Val F. 29 E2
St-Arnoult-
  en-Yvelines F. 21 E2
St. Asaph GB 10 B3

St-Astier F. 25 D4
St-Auban F. 31 E2
St-Aubin-
  d'Aubigné F 19 E3
St-Aubin-
  du-Cormier F. 19 E3
St-Aubin-sur-Mer F . 19 F1
St-Aulaye F. 24 C4
St. Austell GB 12 B3
St-Avold F. 23 D1
St-Aygulf F. 31 E3
St-Béat F. 29 D4
St-Beauzély F. 30 A2
St-Benin-d'Azy F. ... 26 A1
St-Benoît-du-Sault F. 25 E2
St-Benoît-
  sur-Loire F. 21 E4
St-Bertrand-de-
  Comminges F 29 D3
St-Blin F. 22 C3
St-Bonnet-de-Joux F. 26 B2
St-Bonnet-en-
  Champsaur F. 31 E1
St-Bonnet-
  le-Château F. 26 B4
St-Brevin-les-Pins F. 19 D4
St-Briac-sur-Mer F. .. 19 D2
St-Brice-en-Coglès F. 19 E3
St-Brieuc F. 19 D2
St-Calais F. 20 C4
St-Cast-le-Guildo F. . 19 D2
St-Céré F. 29 E1

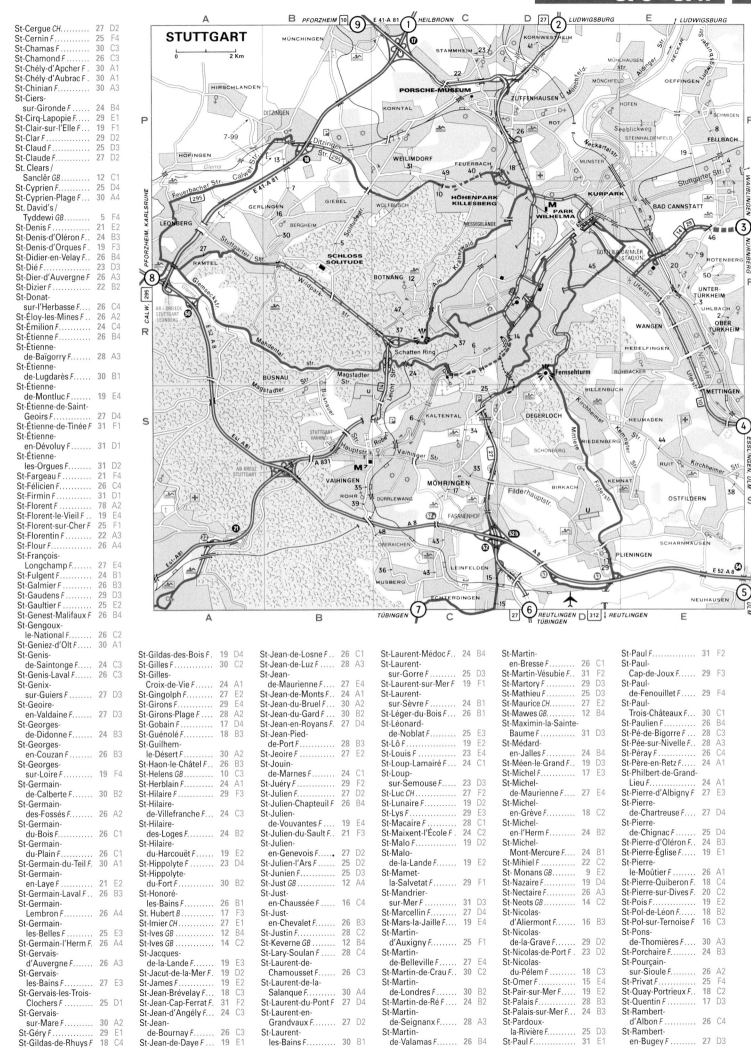

St-Cergue CH......... 27 D2
St-Cernin F............ 25 F4
St-Chamas F.......... 30 C3
St-Chamond F......... 26 C3
St-Chély-d'Apcher F.. 30 A1
St-Chély-d'Aubrac F . 30 A1
St-Chinian F........... 30 A3
St-Ciers-
  sur-Gironde F 24 B4
St-Cirq-Lapopie F..... 29 E1
St-Clair-sur-l'Elle F .. 19 F1
St-Clar F 29 D2
St-Claud F 25 D3
St-Claude F 27 D2
St. Clears /
  Sanclêr GB.......... 12 C1
St-Cyprien F........... 25 D4
St-Cyprien-Plage F .. 30 A4
St. David's /
  Tyddewi GB......... 5 F4
St-Denis F............. 21 E2
St-Denis-d'Oléron F.. 24 B3
St-Denis-d'Orques F . 19 F3
St-Didier-en-Velay F.. 26 B4
St-Dié F 23 D3
St-Dier-d'Auvergne F 26 A3
St-Dizier F 22 B2
St-Donat-
  sur-l'Herbasse F.... 26 C4
St-Éloy-les-Mines F .. 26 A2
St-Émilion F........... 24 C4
St-Étienne F 26 B4
St-Étienne-
  de-Baïgorry F....... 28 A3
St-Étienne-
  de-Lugdarès F....... 30 B1
St-Étienne-
  de-Montluc F........ 19 E4
St-Étienne-de-Saint-
  Geoirs F............. 27 D4
St-Étienne-de-Tinée F 31 F1
St-Étienne-
  en-Dévoluy F........ 31 D1
St-Étienne-
  les-Orgues F......... 31 D2
St-Fargeau F 21 F4
St-Félicien F 26 C4
St-Firmin F 31 D1
St-Florent F 78 F2
St-Florent-le-Vieil F .. 19 E4
St-Florent-sur-Cher F 25 F1
St-Florentin F 22 A3
St-Flour F 26 A4
St-François-
  Longchamp F........ 27 E4
St-Fulgent F 24 B1
St-Galmier F 26 B3
St-Gaudens F.......... 29 D3
St-Gaultier F 25 E2
St-Genest-Malifaux F 26 B4
St-Gengoux-
  le-National F........ 26 C2
St-Geniez-d'Olt F 30 A1
St-Genis-
  de-Saintonge F..... 24 C3
St-Genis-Laval F...... 26 C3
St-Genix-
  sur-Guiers F 27 D3
St-Geoire-
  en-Valdaine F....... 27 D3
St-Georges-
  de-Didonne F........ 24 B3
St-Georges-
  en-Couzan F 26 B3
St-Georges-
  sur-Loire F 19 F4
St-Germain-
  de-Calberte F....... 30 B2
St-Germain-
  des-Fossés F 26 A2
St-Germain-
  du-Bois F............ 26 C1
St-Germain-
  du-Plain F............ 26 C1
St-Germain-du-Teil F. 30 A1
St-Germain-
  en-Laye F 21 E2
St-Germain-Laval F .. 26 B3
St-Germain-
  Lembron F........... 26 A4
St-Germain-
  les-Belles F 25 E3
St-Germain-l'Herm F. 26 A4
St-Gervais-
  d'Auvergne F........ 26 A3
St-Gervais-
  les-Bains F.......... 27 E3
St-Gervais-les-Trois-
  Clochers F........... 25 D1
St-Gervais-
  sur-Mare F........... 30 A2
St-Géry F 29 E1
St-Gildas-de-Rhuys F 18 C4

St-Gildas-des-Bois F. 19 D4
St-Gilles F 30 C2
St-Gilles-
  Croix-de-Vie F 24 A1
St-Gingolph F.......... 27 E2
St-Girons F 29 E4
St-Girons-Plage F 28 A2
St-Gobain F 17 D4
St-Guénolé F 18 B3
St-Guilhem-
  le-Désert F 30 A2
St-Haon-le-Châtel F .. 26 B3
St-Helens GB.......... 10 C3
St-Herblain F 24 A1
St-Hilaire F 29 F3
St-Hilaire-
  de-Villefranche F .. 24 C3
St-Hilaire-
  des-Loges F......... 24 B2
St-Hilaire-
  du-Harcouët F...... 19 E2
St-Hippolyte F......... 23 D4
St-Hippolyte-
  du-Fort F............. 30 B2
St-Honoré-
  les-Bains F.......... 26 B1
St. Hubert B 17 F3
St-Imier CH........... 27 E1
St-Ives GB............. 12 B4
St-Ives GB............. 14 C2
St-Jacques-
  de-la-Lande F....... 19 E3
St-Jacut-de-la-Mer F. 19 D2
St. James F 19 E2
St-Jean-Brévelay F.... 18 C3
St-Jean-Cap-Ferrat F. 31 F2
St-Jean-d'Angély F.... 24 C3
St-Jean-
  de-Bournay F........ 26 C3
St-Jean-de-Daye F ... 19 E1

St-Jean-de-Losne F .. 26 C1
St-Jean-de-Luz F 28 A3
St-Jean-
  de-Maurienne F..... 27 E4
St-Jean-de-Monts F.. 24 A1
St-Jean-du-Bruel F... 30 A2
St-Jean-du-Gard F.... 30 B2
St-Jean-en-Royans F. 27 D4
St-Jean-Pied-
  de-Port F............. 28 B3
St-Jeoire F 27 E2
St-Jouin-
  de-Marnes F........ 24 C1
St-Juéry F 29 F2
St-Julien F............. 27 D2
St-Julien-Chapteuil F 26 B4
St-Julien-
  de-Vouvantes F..... 19 E4
St-Julien-du-Sault F.. 21 F3
St-Julien-
  en-Genevois F....... 27 D2
St-Julien-l'Ars F 25 D2
St-Junien F............ 25 D3
St-Just GB 12 A4
St-Just-
  en-Chaussée F 16 C4
St-Just-
  en-Chevalet F 26 B3
St-Justin F 28 C2
St-Keverne F........... 12 B4
St-Lary-Soulan F 28 C4
St-Laurent-de-
  Chamousset F....... 26 C3
St-Laurent-de-la-
  Salanque F.......... 30 A4
St-Laurent-du-Pont F 27 D4
St-Laurent-en-
  Grandvaux F......... 27 D2
St-Laurent-
  les-Bains F.......... 30 B1

St-Laurent-Médoc F.. 24 B4
St-Laurent-
  sur-Gorre F 25 D3
St-Laurent-sur-Mer F 19 F1
St-Laurent-
  sur-Sèvre F.......... 24 B1
St-Léger-du-Bois F... 26 B1
St-Léonard-
  de-Noblat F.......... 25 E3
St-Lô F 19 E2
St-Louis F 23 E4
St-Loup-Lamairé F ... 24 C1
St-Loup-
  sur-Semouse F 23 D3
St-Luc CH 27 F2
St-Lunaire F 19 D2
St-Lys F 29 E3
St-Macaire F 28 C1
St-Maixent-l'École F . 24 C2
St-Malo F 19 D2
St-Malo-
  de-la-Lande F....... 19 E2
St-Mamet-
  la-Salvetat F 29 F1
St-Mandrier-
  sur-Mer F 31 D3
St-Mars-la-Jaille F ... 19 E4
St-Martin-
  d'Auxigny F......... 25 F1
St-Martin-
  de-Belleville F 27 E4
St-Martin-de-Crau F . 30 C2
St-Martin-de-Ré F ... 24 B2
St-Martin-
  de-Seignanx F...... 28 A3
St-Martin-
  de-Valamas F....... 26 B4

St-Martin-
  en-Bresse F......... 26 C1
St-Martin-Vésubie F.. 31 F2
St-Martory F 29 D3
St-Mathieu F 25 D3
St-Maurice CH........ 27 E2
St-Mawes GB.......... 12 B4
St-Maximin-la-Sainte-
  Baume F 31 D3
St-Médard-
  en-Jalles F 24 B4
St-Méen-le-Grand F.. 19 D3
St-Michel F 17 E3
St-Michel-
  de-Maurienne F 27 E4
St-Michel-
  en-Grève F 18 C2
St-Michel-
  en-l'Herm F 24 B2
St-Michel-
  Mont-Mercure F.... 24 B1
St-Mihiel F 22 C2
St-Monans GB........ 9 E2
St-Nazaire F 19 D4
St-Nectaire F 26 A3
St-Neots GB 14 C2
St-Nicolas-
  d'Aliermont F........ 16 B3
St-Nicolas-
  de-la-Grave F 29 D2
St-Nicolas-de-Port F . 23 D2
St-Nicolas-
  du-Pélem F 18 C3
St-Omer F 15 E4
St-Pair-sur-Mer F ... 19 E2
St-Palais F 28 B3
St-Palais-sur-Mer F .. 24 B3
St-Pardoux-
  la-Rivière F 25 D3
St-Paul F............... 31 E1

St-Paul F............... 31 F2
St-Paul-
  Cap-de-Joux F....... 29 F3
St-Paul-
  de-Fenouillet F..... 29 F4
St-Paul-
  Trois-Châteaux F... 30 C1
St-Paulien F 26 B4
St-Pé-de-Bigorre F ... 28 C3
St-Pée-sur-Nivelle F.. 28 A3
St-Péray F 26 C4
St-Père-en-Retz F 24 A1
St-Philbert-de-Grand-
  Lieu F 24 A1
St-Pierre-d'Albigny F 27 E3
St-Pierre-
  de-Chartreuse F 27 D4
St-Pierre-
  de-Chignac F 25 D4
St-Pierre-d'Oléron F . 24 B3
St-Pierre-Église F..... 19 E1
St-Pierre-
  le-Moûtier F 26 A1
St-Pierre-Quiberon F. 18 C4
St-Pierre-sur-Dives F. 20 C2
St-Pois F 19 E2
St-Pol-de-Léon F 18 B2
St-Pol-sur-Ternoise F 16 C3
St-Pons-
  de-Thomières F..... 30 A3
St-Porchaire F......... 24 B3
St-Pourçain-
  sur-Sioule F 26 A2
St-Privat F 25 F4
St-Quay-Portrieux F.. 18 C2
St-Quentin F 17 D3
St-Rambert-
  d'Albon F............. 26 C4
St-Rambert-
  en-Bugey F 27 D3

St-Raphaël F 31 E3
St-Rémy-
de-Provence F...... 30 C2
St-Rémy-
sur-Durolle F...... 26 A3
St-Renan F 18 A2
St-Riquier F 16 B3
St-Romain-
de-Colbosc F...... 16 A4
St-Rome-de-Tarn F.. 30 A2
St-Saëns F............ 16 B4
St-Satur F 21 F4
St-Saulge F 26 A1
St-Sauveur-
en-Puisaye F....... 21 F4
St-Sauveur-
le-Vicomte F........ 19 E1
St-Sauveur-Lendelin F 19 E1
St-Sauveur-
sur-Tinée F.......... 31 F2
St-Savin F 24 C4
St-Savin F 25 D2
St-Savinien F......... 24 B3
St-Seine-l'Abbaye F.. 22 B4
St-Sernin-
sur-Rance F......... 29 E2
St-Servan-sur-Mer F. 19 D2
St-Sever F 28 B2
St-Sever-Calvados F. 19 E2
St-Sulpice-
les-Feuilles F 25 E2
St-Symphorien F 28 C1
St-Symphorien-
de-Lay F............ 26 B3
St-Symphorien-
d'Ozon F 26 C3
St-Symphorien-sur-
Coise F 26 C3
St-Thégonnec F...... 18 B2
St-Trivier-
de-Courtes F........ 26 C2
St-Trivier-
sur-Moignans F 26 C2
St-Trojan-les-Bains F. 24 B3
St-Tropez F........... 31 E3
St-Vaast-la-Hougue F 19 E1
St-Valery-en-Caux F.. 16 A3
Saint-Valery-
sur-Somme F....... 16 B3
St-Vallier F........... 26 C4
St-Vallier-de-Thiey F. 31 F2
St-Varent F........... 24 C1
St-Vaury F 25 E2
St-Véran F........... 31 E1
St. Vincent I 27 F3
St-Vincent-
de-Tyrosse F........ 28 B2
St-Vivien-de-Médoc F 24 B4
St-Wandrille-
Rançon F........... 16 A4
St-Yorre F............. 26 A3
St-Yrieix-la-Perche F. 25 E3

Sainte
Ste-Adresse F......... 20 C1
Ste-Anne-d'Auray F.. 18 C4
Ste-Croix CH......... 27 E1
Ste-Croix-du-Mont F. 28 C1
Ste-Croix-Volvestre F 29 E3
Ste-Enimie F 30 A1
Ste-Foy-la-Grande F. 28 C1
Ste-Foy-
l'Argentière F....... 26 C3
Ste-Geneviève-sur-
Argence F........... 30 A1
Ste-Hélène F 24 B4
Ste-Hermine F 24 B2
Ste-Livrade-sur-Lot F 29 D1
Ste-Lucie-
de-Tallano F 78 A4
Ste-Marie-
aux-Mines F........ 23 E3
Ste-Marie-Sicché F... 78 A4
Ste-Maure-
de-Touraine F....... 25 D1
Ste-Maxime F......... 31 E3
Ste-Menehould F..... 22 B2
Ste-Mère-Église F ... 19 E1
Ste-Sévère-
sur-Indre F 25 F2
Ste-Suzanne F........ 19 F3
Ste-Tulle F............ 31 D2

San
S. Bartolomeo
in Galdo I 80 B2
S. Benedetto
del Tronto I........ 77 D4
S. Benedetto in Alpe I 76 B2

S. Benedetto Po I..... 75 F1
S. Biagio Platani I.... 84 C3
S. Bonifacio I......... 72 A4
S. Candido /
Innichen I.......... 67 F4
S. Casciano
in Val di Pesa I..... 76 A3
S. Cataldo I........... 84 C3
S. Cataldo I........... 81 F3
S. Cipirello I.......... 84 B3
S. Clemente
a Casauria
(Abbazia) I 79 F1
S. Colombano
al Lambro I 75 E1
S. Damiano d'Asti I... 74 C1
S. Daniele del Friuli I. 72 C3
S. Daniele Po I........ 75 F1
S. Demetrio Corone I 83 D4
S. Donà di Piave I..... 72 B4
S. Donaci I............ 81 F3
S. Fele I.............. 80 B3
S. Felice a Cancello I. 80 A3
S. Felice Circeo I...... 79 E3
S. Felice sul Panaro I. 76 A1
S. Ferdinando
di Puglia I.......... 80 C2
S. Fratello I........... 85 D2
S. Gavino Monreale I 82 B3
S. Gemini I........... 76 C4
S. Giacomo /
St. Jakob I.......... 67 E4
S. Gimignano I........ 76 A3
S. Ginesio I........... 77 D4
S. Giorgio Canavese I 74 C1
S. Giorgio
del Sannio I......... 80 A3
S. Giorgio di Nogaro I 72 C3
S. Giorgio Ionico I.... 81 E3
S. Giorgio
Piacentino I........ 75 E1
S. Giovanni a Piro I... 80 B4
S. Giovanni di Sinis I. 82 A3
S. Giovanni in Fiore I. 83 E2
S. Giovanni
in Persiceto I....... 76 A1
S. Giovanni
Lupatoto I.......... 71 F4
S. Giovanni
Rotondo I.......... 80 B1
S. Giovanni Suergiu I 82 A4
S. Giovanni
Valdarno I.......... 76 A3
S. Giuliano Terme I... 75 F3
S. Giustino I.......... 76 B3
S. Lazzaro di Savena I 76 A1
S. Leo I.............. 76 B2
S. Leonardo in Passiria /
St. Leonhard in
Passeier I 67 E4
S. Lorenzo Nuovo I... 76 B4
S. Marcello I.......... 76 C3
S. Marcello
Pistoiese I.......... 75 F2
S. Marco Argentano I 83 E2
S. Marco dei Cavoti I. 80 A2
S. Marco in Lamis I... 80 B1
S. Martino
di Castrozza I....... 72 A3
S. Mauro Forte I...... 80 C3
S. Michele all'Adige I 71 F3
S. Miniato I........... 76 A3
S. Nicolò I............ 76 A1
S. Nicolò Gerrei I..... 82 B3
S. Pancrazio
Salentino I......... 81 E3
S. Pellegrino Terme I. 71 E4
S. Piero a Sieve I...... 76 A2
S. Pietro in Casale I... 76 A1
S. Pietro Vernotico I.. 81 F3
S. Polo d'Enza I....... 75 F1
S. Quirico d'Orcia I... 76 B4
S. Rufo I............. 80 B3
S. Salvo I............ 80 A1
S. Sebastiano
Curone I............ 75 D1
S. Severino
Marche I 76 C3
S. Severo I........... 80 B1
S. Valentino
alla Muta /
St. Valentin
a. d. Haide I....... 67 D4
S. Vigilio di Marebbe /
St. Vigil I 67 F4
S. Vincenzo I......... 75 F4
S. Vito I 82 C3
S. Vito
al Tagliamento I.... 72 C3
S. Vito Chietino I...... 80 A1
S. Vito
dei Normanni I..... 81 E3
S. Vito di Cadore I.... 67 F4

S. Vito lo Capo I....... 84 A2
S. Vito sullo Ionio I... 83 E3
S. Vittore del Lazio I.. 79 F2
San Adrián E 28 A4
San Agustín
del Guadalix E...... 42 B1
San Amaro E 32 B4
San Andrés del
Rabanedo E........ 33 E4
San Bartolomé de las
Abiertas E.......... 42 A2
San Bartolomé de la
Torre E 46 C2
San Bernardino CH... 71 D3
San Bernardino (Passo
del) CH............ 66 C4
San Carlos del Valle E 42 C4
San Clemente E...... 43 D3
San Cosme E......... 32 C2
San Cristóbal de
Entreviñas E........ 35 F3
San Cristóbal
de la Vega E........ 36 A4
S. Elia a Pianisi I...... 80 A2
S. Elpidio a Mare I.... 77 D3
San Emiliano E........ 33 E3
San Esteban E........ 33 E2
San Esteban
del Valle E.......... 42 A1
San Esteban
de Gormaz E........ 36 C4
San Esteban
del Molar E 35 F3
S. Eufemia Lamezia I. 83 E3
San Felices de los
Gallegos E.......... 35 D4
San Fernando E....... 47 D4
San Ildefonso-
La Granja E......... 42 B1
San Isidro E 49 D3
San Javier E........... 49 E2
San José E 49 E2
San Juan del Olmo E. 42 A1
San Juan
de los Terreros E ... 49 D3
San Juan
del Puerto E......... 46 C2
San Leonardo
de Yagüe E 36 C3
San Lorenzo de
Calatrava E 48 A1
San Lorenzo
de la Parrilla E...... 43 D2
S. Lucido I............ 83 E2
San Luis
de Sabinillas E 47 E4
San Marino RSM...... 76 B2
San Martín
de Castañeda E..... 33 D4
San Martín
de la Vega E........ 42 B2
San Martín de
Mondoñedo E....... 32 C2
San Martín de
Montalbán E........ 42 A2
San Martín de
Valdeiglesias E...... 42 A1
San Mateo
de Gállego E........ 37 F3
San Miguel
de Escalada E....... 33 E4
San Miguel
del Arroyo E........ 36 A4
San Miguel
de Salinas E 49 E2
San Millán
de la Cogolla E 36 C2
San Millán
de Lara E........... 36 C3
San Nicolás
del Puerto E........ 47 E1
San Pedro E.......... 43 D4
San Pedro
de Alcántara E...... 47 F4
San Pedro
del Arroyo E........ 42 A1
San Pedro
de Latarce E 35 F3
San Pedro
del Pinatar E........ 49 E2
San Pedro
de Mérida E........ 41 E3
San Pedro
Manrique E......... 37 D3
San Rafael E.......... 42 B1
San Remo I........... 74 C3
San Roque E 47 E4
San Roque E 32 A2
San Sadurniño E 32 B2
San Salvador de
Cantamuda E....... 33 F3
San Sebastián /
Donostia E.......... 28 A3

San Silvestre
de Guzmán E 46 C2
S. Sperate I........... 82 B4
San Telmo E.......... 46 C1
San Vicente de la
Barquera E.......... 33 F2
San Vicente
de Alcántara E 41 D3
San Vincente de la
Cabeza E 35 E3
San Vitero E.......... 35 E3

Sankt
St-Aegyd A........... 69 D1
St-Andrä A 68 C3
St-Andreas-berg D ... 56 C4
St-Anton
am Arlberg A....... 67 D3
St-Blasien D 23 F4
St-Christophen A..... 69 D1
St-Gallen A........... 68 C2
St-Gallen CH......... 66 C3
St-Gallenkirch A...... 66 C4
St-Georgen D 23 E3
St-Georgen
am Längsee A 68 C3
St-Georgen
im Attergau A 68 A2
St-Gilgen A........... 68 A2
St-Goar D............ 62 A3
St-Goarshausen D.... 62 A3
St-Ingbert D.......... 23 E1
St-Jakob
i. Rosental A........ 68 B4
St-Johann
im Pongau A........ 68 A3
St-Johann in Tirol A.. 67 F2
St-Lambrecht A...... 68 B3
St-Leonhard
a. Forst A........... 68 C1
St-Leonhard
im Pitztal A......... 67 D3
St-Lorenzen
im Lesachtal A...... 68 A4
St-Märgen D 23 F3
St-Margarethen D.... 50 B3
St-Michael
im Lungau A........ 68 B3
St-Michael in
Obersteiermark A.. 68 C2
St-Michaelisdonn D.. 50 A3
St. Moritz CH........ 66 C4
St. Niklaus CH........ 27 F2
St-Oswald A.......... 68 B3
St-Paul
im Lavanttal A...... 68 C3
St-Peter
in der Au Markt A .. 68 C1
St-Peter-Ording D.... 50 A2
St. Peterburg RUS.... 125 D1
St-Pölten A........... 69 D1
St-Valentin A......... 68 B1
St-Veit
an der Glan A....... 68 C3
St. Vith B............ 61 E2
St-Wendel D......... 23 E1
St-Wolfgang im
Salzkammergut A.. 68 A2

Sant
Sant Agustí
de Lluçanès E....... 39 D3
Sant Andreu de
Llavaneres E........ 39 D4
Sant Antoni
de Portmany /
San Antonio
de Portmany E 44 C4
Sant Antoni
de Calonge E 39 E3
Sant Boi
de Lluçanès E....... 39 D3
Sant Carles
de la Ràpita E....... 44 B1
Sant Celoni E......... 39 D4
Sant Cugat
del Vallès E 39 D4
Sant Esteve
d'En Bas E 39 D3
Sant Feliu
de Guixols /
San Feliú
de Guixols E........ 39 E3
Sant Francesc E...... 44 C4
Sant Hilari Sacalm E. 39 D3
Sant Hipòlit
de Voltregà E 39 D3
Sant Joan
d'Alacant E......... 49 F1

Sant Joan
de Labritja E........ 44 C4
Sant Joan de les
Abadesses E........ 39 D3
Sant Josep E......... 44 C4
Sant Llorenç
de Morunys E 38 C3
Sant Lluís E.......... 45 F3
Sant Mateu E......... 44 A2
Sant Miquel E........ 44 C4
Sant Pau
de Segúries E....... 39 D3
Sant Pol de Mar E.... 39 D4
Sant Quirze
de Besora E......... 39 D3
Sant Quirze Safaja E. 39 D4
Sant Ramon E........ 38 C4
Sant Sadurní
d'Anoia E 38 C4
Sant Salvador
(Monestir) E 45 E3
Sant Vicent
del Raspeig E....... 49 F1

Santa
S. Agata de' Goti I.... 80 A3
S. Agata di Militello I. 85 D2
S. Agata di Puglia I... 80 B2
S. Andrea Frius I...... 82 B3
S. Angelo
dei Lombardi I...... 80 B3
S. Angelo in Vado I... 76 B3
S. Angelo Lodigiano I 75 E1
S. Antioco I.......... 82 A4
S. Antonio
di Gallura I......... 82 B1
S. Apollinare
in Classe I.......... 76 B2
Sta Caterina
di Pittinuri I 82 A2
Sta Caterina
Valfurva I............ 67 D4
Sta Cesarea Terme I.. 81 F3
Sta Cristina
Valgardena /
St. Christina
in Gröden I......... 67 F4
Sta Croce
di Magliano I....... 80 A1
Sta Lucia del Mela I.. 83 D4
Sta Margherita I...... 82 B4
Sta Margherita
di Belice I.......... 84 B3
Sta Margherita
Ligure I............ 75 D2
Sta Maria
Capua Vetere I...... 80 A3
Sta Maria
degli Angeli I....... 76 C4
Sta Maria
della Versa I 75 D1
Sta Maria Maggiore I 72 C3
Sta Marinella I........ 78 C1
Sta Sofia I........... 76 B2
Sta Sofia d'Epiro I.... 83 E2
Santa Amalia E........ 41 E3
Santa Ana E.......... 43 D4
Santa Bárbara E 44 B1
Santa Bárbara
de Casa E 46 C1
Santa Catarina
da Fonte
do Bispo P......... 46 B2
Santa Clara-a-Velha P 46 A1
Santa Coloma
de Faners E 39 D3
Santa Coloma
de Queralt E 38 C4
Santa Colomba de
Somoza E 33 D4
Santa Comba E 32 A2
Santa Comba Dão P.. 40 C1
Santa Comba
de Rosas E 35 D3
Santa Cristina
de Lena E 33 E3
Santa Cruz
de la Sierra E 41 E3
Santa Cruz
de la Zarza E 42 C2
Santa Cruz
del Retamar E....... 42 B2
Santa Cruz de Moya E 43 E2
Santa Cruz
de Mudela E........ 42 B3
Santa Elena E........ 48 B1
Santa Eufemia E...... 41 F4
Santa Eugenia E...... 32 A3

Santa Eulália P........ 40 C3
Santa Eulalia E........ 43 E1
Santa Eulalia
de Oscos E 32 C2
Santa Eulària
des Riu /
Santa Eulalia
del Río E 44 C4
Santa Fé E 48 A3
Sta Fiora I 76 B4
Sta Gertrude / St.
Gertraud I.......... 67 E4
Sta Giusta I........... 82 B3
Santa Liestra y San
Quílez E 38 A3
Santa Luzia P......... 46 A1
Santa Magdalena de
Polpís E 44 A2
Santa Margalida E.... 45 E3
Santa Margarida do
Sádão P 46 A1
Santa Margarida i els
Monjós E........... 38 C4
Santa Maria
da Feira P 34 B4
Santa María
de Huerta E 37 D4
Santa María
del Campo E........ 36 B3
Santa María
del Campo Rus E... 43 D3
Santa María
del Páramo E 33 E4
Santa María
de Nieva E.......... 49 D2
Santa María
de Valverde E 35 E3
Santa María la Real de
Nieva E 36 A4
Santa María
La Real de Oseira
(Monasterio) E 32 B3
Santa Marina
del Rey E 33 E4
Santa Marina
de Valdeón E 33 F3
Santa Marta E........ 41 D4
Santa Marta de
Penaguião P........ 34 C4
Santa Marta
de Tormes E 35 F4
Sta Ninfa I 84 B3
Santa Olalla E........ 42 A2
Santa Olalla
del Cala E 47 D1
Santa Pau E 39 D3
Santa Pola E.......... 49 F1
Santa Ponça E 45 D3
Sta Severa I........... 79 D1
Santa Susanna E 39 D4
Sta Teresa di Riva I... 83 D4
Sta Teresa Gallura I.. 82 B1

Santo
Santo Domingo de la
Calzada E 36 C2
Santo Domingo
de Silos E 36 C3
Santo Estêvão P...... 41 D1
Santo Estêvão P...... 40 A3
Santo-Pietro-
di-Tenda F 78 A3
Sto Stefano d'Aveto I 75 E2
Sto Stefano
di Cadore I 72 B2
Sto Stefano
di Camastra I....... 84 C2
Sto Stefano
Quisquina I......... 84 B3
Sto Stino di Livenza I 72 B3
Santo Tirso P......... 34 B3
Santo Tomé E........ 48 B1
S. Onofrio I........... 83 E3

São
São Bartolomeu de
Messines P......... 46 A2
São Brás
de Alportel P........ 46 B2
São Cristóvão P...... 40 B4
São Domingos P...... 46 A1
São Gregório P 32 B4
São Jacinto P 34 B4
São João
da Madeira P 34 B4
São João
da Pesqueira P 34 C4
São João
de Tarouca P........ 34 C4

São João dos Caldeireiros P 46 B1
São José da Lamarosa P 40 B3
São Leonardo P 40 C4
São Manços P 40 C4
São Marcos da Serra P 46 A2
São Marcos do Campo P 40 C4
São Martinho das Amoreiras P 46 A1
São Martinho do Porto P 40 A4
São Matias P 46 B1
São Miguel de Machede P 40 C4
São Pedro da Torre P ... 32 A4
São Pedro de Moel P ... 40 A2
São Pedro do Sul P ... 34 B4
São Romão P 40 C1
São Teotónio P 46 A1
São Vicente da Beira P 40 C2

Sint

St-Niklaas B 17 E1
St-Oedenrode NL 17 F1
St-Truiden B 17 F2

T

Tábara E 35 E3
Taberg S 118 C4
Tabernas E 48 C3
Taboada E 32 B2
Tábor CZ 64 B3
Tábua P 40 C1
Tabuaço P 34 C4
Tabuenca E 37 E3

Täby S 119 E2
Tadcaster GB 11 D2
Tafalla E 28 A4
Tafjord N 110 C3
Taggia I 74 C3
Tagliacozzo I 79 E1
Taglio di Po I 76 B1
Tahal E 48 C3
Tahkvuori FIN 115 E3
Tailfingen D 66 B2
Tain GB 7 D3
Tain-l'Hermitage F ... 26 C4
Taipadas P 40 B3
Taipalsaari FIN 121 E3
Taivalkoski FIN 109 E3
Taivassalo / Tövsala FIN 120 B4
Taktikoúpoli GR 97 F1
Tálanda GR 97 E3
Talarrubias E 41 F3
Talaván E 41 E2
Talavera de la Reina E ... 42 A2
Talavera la Real E 41 D4
Talayuela E 41 F2
Talayuelas E 43 E2
Taldom RUS 125 F2
Talgarth GB 13 D1
Talla I 76 B3
Tallante E 49 E3
Tallard F 31 E1
Tällberg S 119 D1
Tallinn EST 124 B1
Talloires F 27 E3
Tallow IRL 4 C3
Talluskylä FIN 115 D3
Talmont-St-Hilaire F .. 24 A2
Tal'ne UA 127 E2
Talsi LV 124 B2
Talvik N 105 D2
Tamames E 41 E1
Támara E 33 F4
Tamarinda E 45 F2
Tamarite de Litera E .. 38 A3

Tamási H 126 A4
Tåme S 108 B4
Tammela FIN 120 C3
Tampere FIN 120 C3
Tamsweg A 68 B3
Tamworth GB 11 D4
Tana N 105 F2
Tanágra GR 94 B3
Tandådalen S 112 A4
Tandragee GB 3 D3
Tandsbyn S 112 B2
Tandsjöborg S 112 B2
Tanganheira P 46 A1
Tangerhütte D 57 E2
Tangermünde D 57 E2
Tanhua FIN 109 E1
Taninges F 27 E2
Tanlay F 22 A4
Tann D 62 C2
Tännäs S 112 A3
Tänndalen S 112 A3
Tannheim A 67 D3
Tannila FIN 109 D3
Tanumshede S 118 A3
Taormina I 85 E2
Tapa EST 124 B1
Tapia de Casariego E .. 33 D2
Taracena E 42 C1
Tarancón E 42 C2
Taranto I 81 E3
Tarare F 26 B3
Tarašča UA 127 E2
Tarascon F 30 C2

Tarascon-sur-Ariège F 29 E4
Tarazona E 37 E3
Tarazona de la Mancha E 43 E3
Tarbert IRL 4 B2
Tarbert GB 8 B2
Tarbert GB 6 A3
Tarbes F 28 C3
Tarbet GB 8 C2
Tarcento I 68 A4
Tardets-Sorholus F ... 28 B3
Tardienta E 37 F3
Tärendö S 108 C2
Targon F 28 C1
Tlârgoviste BG 129 D2
Târgu Mureş RO 126 C4
Tarifa E 47 E4
Tarm DK 122 A2
Tarmstedt D 50 B4
Tärnaby S 107 E3
Tarnobrzeg PL 126 C2
Tarnos F 28 A3
Tarnów PL 126 B2
Tarouca P 34 C4
Tarp D 50 B2
Tarporley GB 10 C3
Tarquinia I 78 C1
Tarragona E 44 C1
Tarrasa / Terrassa E ... 38 C4
Tàrrega E 38 B4
Tårs DK 122 A4
Tarsia I 83 E2

Tartas F 28 B2
Tartu EST 124 C2
Tarvasjoki FIN 120 B3
Tarvisio I 68 B2
Täsch CH 27 F2
Tåsjö S 112 B1
Tåstrup DK 123 D3
Tata H 126 A4
Tatabánya H 126 A4
Tatarbunary UA 127 E4
Tau N 116 A2
Tauberbischofsheim D 62 B2
Taucha D 57 E4
Taufkirchen D 67 F1
Taulé F 18 B2
Taunton GB 13 D3
Taunusstein-Neuhof D 62 A3
Tauplitz A 68 B2
Tauragė LT 124 B3
Taurianova I 83 E4
Tauste E 37 F3
Tauves F 25 F3
Tavannes CH 27 F1
Tavarnelle Val di Pesa I 76 A3
Tavastila FIN 121 E3
Tavaux F 27 D1
Taverna I 83 E3
Tavernelle I 76 B4

Tavernes F 31 E2
Tavernes de la Valldigna E ... 44 A4
Tavira P 46 B2
Tavistock GB 12 C3
Tavşanlı TR 129 F3
Taxenbach A 68 A3
Taxiárhis GR 88 C3
Tayinloan GB 8 B3
Taynuilt GB 8 B1
Tayport GB 9 D2
Tazones E 33 E2
Tczew PL 124 A4
Teano I 79 F2
Teba E 47 F3
Tebay GB 10 C1
Techendorf A 68 A4
Tecklenburg D 55 E3
Tecuci RO 127 D4
Teeriranta FIN 109 F3
Teféli GR 101 D4
Tegéa GR 97 D1
Tegelen NL 61 E1
Tegernsee D 67 E2
Teggiano I 80 C4
Teignmouth GB 13 D3
Teijo FIN 120 C4
Le Teil F 30 C1
Le Teilleul F 19 F2
Teisendorf D 68 A2
Teisko FIN 120 C2
Teixeiro E 32 B2
Teixoso P 40 C1

Torino

Tekirdağ TR	129	E3
Telavåg N	116	A1
Telč CZ	64	C3
Télendos (Nissí) GR	99	F3
Telese I	80	A2
Telford GB	10	C4
Telfs A	67	E3
Telgte D	55	E4
Tellingstedt D	50	B2
Telšiai LT	124	B3
Telti I	82	B1
Teltow D	57	F2
Témbi GR	88	A4
Tembleque E	42	B3
Temerin YU	128	B1
Temmes FIN	115	D1
Tempio Pausania I	82	B1
Templemore / An Teampall Mór IRL	5	D2
Templin D	51	F4
Temse B	17	E1
Tenala / Tenhola FIN	120	C4
Tenbury Wells GB	10	C4
Tenby / Dinbych-y-pysgod GB	12	C1
Tence F	26	B4
Tende F	31	F2
Tendilla E	42	C1
Tennes N	104	B3
Tensta S	119	E2
Tenterden GB	14	C4
Teolo I	72	A4
Tepasto FIN	108	C1
Tepelenë AL	128	B4
Teplice CZ	64	A1
Tepsa FIN	109	D1
Teramo I	77	D4
Terebovlja UA	126	C2
Terena P	40	C4
Terespol PL	126	B1
Tergnier F	17	D4
Terjärv FIN	114	C2
Terlizzi I	81	D2
Termas de Monfortinho P	41	D2
Terme Luigiane I	83	D2
Termini Imerese I	84	C2
Terminillo I	79	E1
Termoli I	80	A1
Terneuzen NL	17	D1
Terni I	79	D1
Ternitz A	69	D2
Ternopil' UA	126	C2
Térovo GR	92	B1
Térpilos GR	88	B1
Terpní GR	88	C1
Terpsithéa GR	93	D3
Terracina I	79	E2
Terråk N	107	D4
Terralba I	82	B3
Terranova di Pollino I	81	D4
Terranuova Bracciolini I	76	A3
Terras de Bouro P	34	B3
Terrassa / Tarrasa E	38	C4
Terrasson-Lavilledieu F	25	E4
Terrenoire F	26	C4
Terriente E	43	E2
Teruel E	43	F2
Tervakoski FIN	120	C3
Tervo FIN	115	D3
Tervola FIN	109	D3
Tervuren B	17	E2
Terzaga E	43	E1
Teslić BIH	128	A1
Tessin D	51	E3
Tessy-sur-Vire F	19	E2
La Teste-de-Buch F	28	B1
Tetbury GB	13	E2
Teterow D	51	E3
Tetíïv UA	127	E2
Tetovo MK	128	B3
Tetrákomo GR	92	C1
Tettnang D	66	C2
Teuchern D	63	E1
Teufen CH	66	C2
Teulada I	82	B4
Teupitz D	57	F3
Teuva FIN	114	B4
Tewkesbury GB	13	E1
Tezze I	72	B3
Thale D	57	D4
Thalfang D	61	F3
Thalgau A	68	A2
Thalheim D	63	F1
Thalmässing D	63	E4
Thalwil CH	23	F4
Thame GB	14	B3
Thann F	23	E4
Thannhausen D	67	D1
Thaon-les-Vosges F	23	D3
Tharandt D	64	A1
Tharsis E	46	C2
Thássos GR	89	E2
Thássos (Nissí) GR	89	E2
Thèbes GR	93	F3
Le Theil F	20	C3
Themar D	63	D2
Thénezay F	24	C1
Thenon F	25	D4
Theológos GR	89	E2
Theológos GR	93	F3
Théoule-sur-Mer F	31	F3
Thermá GR	88	C1
Thérma GR	91	D3
Thérma GR	99	E1
Thérma Lefkádas GR	99	E1
Thérmi GR	88	B2
Thérmi GR	95	F1
Thermissía GR	97	E2
Thérmo GR	92	C3
Thermopíles GR	93	E2
Thérouanne F	15	E4
Thespiés GR	93	F4
Thesprotikó GR	92	B1
Thessaloníki GR	88	B2
Thetford GB	11	F4
Theux B	61	D2
Thèze F	28	C3
Thiaucourt-Regniéville F	22	C2
Thiberville F	20	C2
Thiéblemont-Farémont F	22	B2
Thiendorf D	58	A4
Thiene I	72	A4
Thiers F	26	A3
Thiesi I	82	B2
Thiessow D	51	F2
Le Thillot F	23	D3
Thimariá GR	91	E2
Thímena GR	99	F1
Thímena (Nissí) GR	99	E1
Thionville F	22	C1
Thíra GR	99	D4
Thíra (Nissí) GR	99	D4
Thirassía (Nissí) GR	98	C4
Thirsk GB	11	D1
Thisted DK	122	B1
Thiviers F	25	D4
Thizy F	26	B3
Thoissey F	26	C2
Tholey D	23	D1
Thollon-les-Mémises F	27	E2
Tholó GR	96	B2
Tholopotámi GR	95	F4
Tholós GR	88	C1
Thomastown / Baile Mhic Andáin IRL	5	D3
Thônes F	27	E3
Thonon-les-Bains F	27	E2
Thorens-Glières F	27	E3
Thorikó GR	98	A1
Thorne GB	11	E2
Thornhill GB	8	C4
Thouarcé F	24	C1
Thouars F	24	C1
Thouría GR	96	C2
Thoúrio GR	91	E1
Thrapston GB	11	E4
Threshfield GB	11	D2
Thüringen A	66	C3
Thueyts F	30	B1
Thuile (la) I	27	E3
Thuin B	17	E3
Thuir F	30	A4
Thum D	63	F1
Thun CH	27	F1
Thurles / Durlas IRL	5	D2
Thursby GB	9	D4
Thurso GB	7	E2
Thury-Harcourt F	19	F2
Thusis CH	66	C4
Thyborøn DK	122	A1
Tibro S	118	C3
Tichvin RUS	125	E1
Tidö S	119	D2
Tiefenbronn D	23	F2
Tiefencastel CH	66	C4
Tiefensee D	52	A4
Tiel NL	54	C4
Tielt B	15	F4
Tiemblo (El) E	42	A1
Tienen B	17	F2
Tiercé F	19	F4
Tierga E	37	E4
Tierp S	119	E1
Tigharry GB	6	A3
Tighnabruaich GB	8	B2
Tignes F	27	E3
Tiheró GR	91	E2
Tihío GR	87	E2
Tiistenjoki FIN	114	C3
Tíjola E	48	C3
Tikkakoski FIN	115	D4
Tikkala FIN	115	F3
Tilburg NL	17	F1
Tilbury GB	14	C3
Tílissos GR	101	D3
Tillberga S	119	E2
Tillières-sur-Avre F	21	D2
Tilly-sur-Seulles F	19	F1
Tílos (Nissí) GR	102	D2
Tilsit RUS	124	B4
Timbáki GR	100	C4
Tímbano GR	89	E1
Timfristós GR	93	D2
Timişoara RO	128	B1
Timmendorfer Strand D	50	C3
Timoleague IRL	4	C4
Timrå S	112	C3
Tinahely IRL	5	E2
Tinchebray F	19	F2
Tineo E	33	D2
Tingáki GR	103	D1
Tinglev DK	122	B3
Tingsryd S	123	E2
Tingvoll N	110	C2
Tinnoset N	116	C2
Tínos GR	98	C1
Tínos (Nissí) GR	98	C1
Tintagel GB	12	C3
Tinténiac F	19	E3
Tiñosillos E	36	A4
Tione di Trento I	71	F3
Tipasoja FIN	115	E2
Tipperary / Tiobraid Árann IRL	4	C3
Tiranë AL	128	B3
Tirano I	71	E3
Tiraspol MOL	127	E4
Tire TR	129	E4
Tîrgovişte RO	129	D1
Tîrgu Frumos RO	127	D4
Tîrgu Jiu RO	128	C1
Tîrgu-Neamţ RO	127	D4
Tîrgu Secuiesc RO	127	D4
Tírig E	44	A2
Tírintha GR	97	D1
Tiriolo I	83	E3
Tírnavos GR	88	A4
Tirós GR	97	E2
Tirrenia I	75	F3
Tirschenreuth D	63	F3
Tirstrup DK	122	C2
Tisvildeleje DK	123	D2
Tiszafüred H	126	B4
Tiszavasvári H	126	B3
Titisee-Neustadt D	23	F3
Tito I	80	C3
Titov Veles MK	128	C3
Titran N	110	C1
Tittmoning D	67	F1
Tivenys E	44	B1
Tiverton GB	13	D3
Tivissa E	44	B1
Tivoli I	79	E1
Tjåmotis S	108	A2
Tjällmo S	119	D3
Tjeldstø N	110	A4
Tjøme N	117	D2
Tjong N	107	E2
Tjørnuvik DK	106	A3
Tjøtta N	107	D3
Tobarra E	49	D1
Tobercurry / Tobar an Choire IRL	2	B3
Tobermore GB	3	D2
Tobermory GB	8	A1
Toberonochy GB	8	B2
Toboso (El) E	42	C3
Tocha P	40	B3
Tocina E	47	E2
Todi I	76	C4
Todmorden GB	11	D2
Todtmoos D	23	F4
Todtnau D	23	F3
Tönning D	50	A2
Töpen D	63	E2
Toft GB	7	F2
Tofte N	117	D2
Toftir DK	106	A3
Toftlund DK	122	B3
Tohmajärvi FIN	115	F4
Toholampi FIN	114	C2
Toijala FIN	120	C3
Toivakka FIN	121	D2
Toivala FIN	115	E3
Tokaj H	126	B3
Toledo E	42	B2
Tolentino I	77	D3
Tolfa I	79	D1
Tolga N	111	E3
Tollarp S	123	E3

TOULOUSE

Tølløse DK 122 C3
Tolmezzo I 68 A4
Tolmin SLO 72 C2
Toló GR 97 E1
Tolosa P 40 C2
Tolosa E 28 A3
Tolox E 47 F3
Tolva FIN 109 F2
Tolve I 80 C3
Tomar P 40 B2
Tomaszów Lubelski PL 126 C2
Tomaszów Mazowiecki PL 126 A2
Tombebœuf F 29 D1
Tomelilla S 123 E3
Tomelloso E 42 C3
Tomintoul GB 7 D4
Tomiño E 32 A4
Tømmervåg N 110 C2
Tomra N 110 C2
Tona E 39 D3
Tonara I 82 B3
Tonbridge GB 14 C4
Tondela P 40 C1
Tønder DK 122 A3
Tongeren B 17 F2
Tongue GB 7 D2
Tonnay-Boutonne F 24 B3
Tonnay-Charente F 24 B3
Tonneins F 29 D1
Tonnerre F 22 A4
Tønsberg N 117 D2
Tonstad N 116 B2
Topeno FIN 120 C3
Topla SLO 73 E2
Toplița RO 127 D4
T'oploje RUS 125 F3
Toploú GR 101 F3
Topolčany SK 126 A3
Topólia GR 100 C3
Torà E 38 C3
Torano Castello I 83 E2
Torbole I 71 F3
Torcello I 72 B4
Torchiarolo I 81 F3
Torcy F 21 F2
Tordera E 39 D4
Tordesillas E 36 A3
Tordesilos E 43 E1
Töre S 108 C3
Tore GB 7 D4
Töreboda S 118 C2
Torella del Sannio I 80 A2
Toreno E 33 D3
Torgau D 57 F4
Torgelow D 52 A3
Torhout B 15 F4
Torigni-sur-Vire F 19 F2
Torija E 42 C1
Torino I 27 F4
Torla E 28 C4
Törmänen FIN 105 F3
Törmänmäki FIN 115 E1
Tormos E 37 F3
Tornavacas E 41 F1
Tornio FIN 109 D3
Toro E 35 F3
Toróni GR 89 D4
Toropec RUS 125 D1
Torpo N 110 C4
Torpoint GB 12 C3
Torpshammar S 112 B4
Torquay GB 13 D3
Torquemada E 36 A3
Torralba de Calatrava E 42 B4
Torrão P 40 B4
Torre Annunziata I 80 A3
Torre Beretti e Castellaro I 75 D1
Torre Canne I 81 E2
Torre de' Passeri I 79 F1
Torre del Greco I 80 A3
Torre dell'Impiso I 84 A2
Torre d'en Besora (La) I 44 A2
Torre Faro I 83 D4
Torre la Cárcel E 43 E1
Torre Orsaia I 80 C4
Torre Pellice I 27 F4
Torrebaja E 43 E2
Torreblanca E 44 A2
Torrecaballeros E 36 B4
Torrecampo E 42 A4
Torrecilla en Cameros E 37 D2
Torrecillas de la Tiesa E 41 F3
Torre de Dom Chama P 35 D3
Torre de Juan Abad E 42 C4
Torre de la Higuera E 47 D3

Torre del Bierzo E 33 D4
Torre del Campo E 48 A2
Torre del Mar E 48 A3
Torre del Valle (La) E 33 E4
Torredembarra E 38 C4
Torre de Moncorvo P 35 D4
Torredonjimeno E 48 A2
Torregrossa E 38 B4
Torreira P 34 B4
Torrejoncillo E 41 E2
Torrejoncillo del Rey E 43 D2
Torrejón de Ardoz E 42 C1
Torrejón de la Calzada E 42 B2
Torrejón el Rubio E 41 E2
Torrelaguna E 42 C1
Torrelapaja E 37 D4
Torrelavega E 36 B1
Torrellano E 49 F1
Torrelobatón E 36 A3
Torrelodones E 42 B1
Torremaggiore I 80 B1
Torremegía E 41 E4
Torremocha E 41 E3
Torremolinos E 47 F4
Torrent E 43 F3
Torrente de Cinca E 38 A4
Torrenueva E 42 C4
Torre Pacheco E 49 E2
Torreperogil E 48 B1
Torres del Río E 37 D2
Torres Novas P 40 B2
Torres Vedras P 40 A3
Torrevieja E 49 F2
Torri del Benaco I 71 F4
Torridon GB 6 C4
Torriglia I 75 D2
Torrijas E 43 F2
Torrijo E 37 D4
Torrijos E 42 A2
Tørring DK 122 B2
Torrita di Siena I 76 B4
Torroella de Montgrí E 39 E3
Torröjen S 118 C3
Torrox E 48 A3
Torsås S 123 F2
Torsby S 118 C1
Torshälla S 119 D2
Torshavn DK 106 A3
Torsminde DK 122 A2
Tórtoles de Esgueva E 36 B3
Tortoli I 82 C3
Tortona I 75 D1
Tortorici I 85 D2
Tortosa E 44 B1
Tortosendo P 40 C1
Toruń PL 126 A1
Torup S 123 D1
Tørvikbygd N 116 B1
Toržok RUS 125 E2
Tosbotn N 107 D4
Toscolano-Maderno I 71 F4
Tosno RUS 125 D1
Tossa de Mar E 39 E4
Tostedt D 50 B4
Totana E 49 E2
Tôtes F 16 A4
Tøtlandsvik N 116 B2
Totnes GB 13 D3
Toucy F 21 F4
Toul F 22 C2
Toulon F 31 D3
Toulon-sur-Arroux F 26 B2
Toulouse F 29 E3
Toumbítsi GR 96 C1
Le Touquet-Paris-Plage F 16 B2
La Tour-d'Auvergne F 25 F3
La Tour-du-Pin F 27 D3
La Tour-Fondue F 31 E3
Tourcoing F 15 F4
Tourlída GR 92 C3
Tournai B 15 F4
Tournan-en-Brie F 21 F2
Tournay F 28 C3
Tournon-d'Agenais F 29 D1
Tournon-St-Martin F 25 D1
Tournon-sur-Rhône F 26 C4
Tourouvre F 20 C2
Tours F 20 C4
Toury F 21 E3
La Toussuire F 27 E4
Le Touvet F 27 D4
Töysä FIN 114 C2
Törökszentmiklós H 126 B4
Trabanca E 35 E4
Trabazos E 35 E3

Traben-Trarbach D 61 F3
Trabia I 84 C2
Tracino I 84 A4
Trafaria P 40 A3
Trafoi I 67 D4
Tragacete E 43 E2
Trahiá GR 97 E1
Trahíli GR 94 B3
Traiguera E 44 A1
Traisen A 69 D1
Traiskirchen A 69 D1
Traismauer A 69 D1
Trakai LT 124 C4
Tralee / Trá Lí IRL 4 B3
Tramagal P 40 B2
Tramariglio I 82 A2
Tramatza I 82 B3
Tramonti di Sopra I 68 A4
Tramore / Trá Mhór IRL 5 D3
Trľaln BG 128 C2
Tranås S 119 D4
La Tranche-sur-Mer F 24 B2
Trancoso P 34 C4
Tranebjerg DK 122 C3
Tranemo S 118 B4
Tranent GB 9 D2
Trani I 80 C2
Tranóvalto GR 87 E3
Trápeza GR 93 D4
Trappstadt D 63 D2
Trasacco I 79 F1
Trassem D 23 D1
Traun A 68 B1
Traunkirchen A 68 B2
Traunreut D 67 F2
Traunstein D 67 F2
Travemünde D 50 C3
Travnik BIH 128 A2
Le Trayas F 31 F3
Trbovlje SLO 73 E2
Trebbin D 57 F3
Trébeurden F 18 C2
Trebinje BIH 128 A2
Trebisacce I 81 D4
Trebišov SK 126 B3
Trebnje SLO 73 E3
Tréboul F 18 B3
Trebsen D 57 F4
Trebujena E 47 D3
Trecastagni I 85 E3
Trecate I 71 D4
Tredegar GB 13 D1
Tredozio I 76 B2
Treffort F 27 D2
Treffurt D 62 C1
Tregaron GB 10 B4
Trégastel F 18 C2
Tregnago I 72 A4
Tregony GB 12 B4
Tréguier F 18 C2
Trehörningsjö S 113 D1
Treia D 50 B2
Treia I 77 D3
Treignac F 25 E3
Trelleborg DK 122 C3
Trelleborg S 123 D3
Trélon F 17 E3
La Tremblade F 24 B3
Tremestieri I 83 D4
Tremezzo I 71 D3
Tremp E 38 B3
Trenčín SK 126 A3
Trendelburg D 56 B4
Trento I 71 F3
Le Tréport F 16 B3
Trepuzzi I 81 F3
Trescore Balneario I 71 E4
Tresenda I 71 E3
Tresfjord N 110 C2
Tresjuncos E 42 C3
Trespaderne E 36 C2
Trets F 31 D3
Tretten N 111 D4
Treuchtlingen D 63 D4
Treuen D 63 E1
Treuenbrietzen D 57 F3
Treungen N 116 C2
Trevélez E 48 B3
Trèves F 30 A2
Trevi I 76 C4
Trévières F 19 F1
Treviglio I 71 E4
Trevignano Romano I 79 D1
Treviño E 37 D2
Treviso I 72 B4
Trévoux F 26 C3
Trezzo sull'Adda I 71 E4
Tría Nissiá (Nissiá) GR 99 F4
Triánda GR 103 F2

Triaucourt-en-Argonne F 22 B2
Triberg D 23 F3
Tribsees D 51 E2
Tricarico I 80 C3
Tricase I 81 F4
Tricesimo I 68 A4
Trichiana I 72 B3
Trie-sur-Baïse F 29 D3
Trieben A 68 C2
Trier D 61 F3
Trieste I 73 D3
Trifíli GR 91 E2
Trigóna GR 87 E4
Trigueros E 46 C2
Trijueque E 42 C1
Trikala GR 88 A2
Tríkala GR 93 E4
Trikala GR 93 D1
Trikeri GR 93 F2
Trílofo GR 93 D2
Trillevallen S 112 A4
Trillo E 43 D1
Trílofo GR 93 D2
Trim / Baile Átha Troim IRL 3 D4
Trindade P 35 D3
Tring GB 14 B2
Trinità d'Agultu e Vignola I 82 B1
Trinitapoli I 80 C2
La Trinité-Porhoët F 19 D3
La Trinité-sur-Mer F 18 C4
Trino I 74 C1
Triora I 74 C3
Trípi GR 97 D2
Tripití GR 89 D3
Trípoli GR 97 D1
Triponzo I 76 C4
Tripótama GR 96 C1
Triptis D 63 E1
Trittau D 50 C3
Trittenheim D 61 F3
Trivento I 80 A1
Trizína GR 97 F1
Trnava SK 126 A3
Trnovo SLO 72 C2
Troarn F 19 F1
Trofa P 34 B3
Trofaiach A 68 C2
Trofors N 107 D3
Trogir HR 128 A2
Troia I 80 B2
Troina I 85 D3
Les Trois-Épis F 23 E3
Les Trois-Moutiers F 24 C1
Troisdorf D 61 F2
Trois-Ponts B 61 D2
Trojan BG 129 D2
Trojane SLO 73 E2
Trollhättan S 118 B3
Tromsdalen N 104 B2
Tromsø N 104 B2
Trondheim N 111 D1
Tronö S 112 C4
Troo F 20 C4
Troon GB 3 F1
Trópea GR 96 C1
Tropea I 83 E3
Trosa S 119 E2
Trostberg D 67 F2
Trostjanec' UA 127 F1
Trouville F 16 A4
Trowbridge GB 13 E2
Troyes F 22 A3
Trubčevsk RUS 125 F4
Trubia E 33 E2
Truchas E 33 D4
Truchtersheim F 23 E2
Trujillo E 41 E3
Trun F 20 C2
Truro GB 12 B4
Trutnov CZ 64 C1
Truva TR 129 E3
Tryde S 123 E3
Tržič SLO 73 D2
Třebíč CZ 65 D3
Třeboň CZ 64 B4
Třinec CZ 65 F2
Tsamandás GR 86 C4
Tsangaráda GR 93 F1
Tsangário GR 92 A1
Tsarítsani GR 87 F4
Tsarkassiános GR 87 E3
Tsotíli GR 87 E3
Tsoukaládes GR 92 A2
Tuam / Tuaim IRL 2 B4
Tubilla del Agua E 36 B2
Tubre / Taufers im Münstertal I 67 D4
Tuchan F 29 E4
Tudela E 37 D3
Tudela de Duero E 36 A3

Türkheim D 67 D2
Tuffé F 20 C3
Tuhkakylä FIN 115 E2
Tui I 32 A4
Tukums LV 124 B2
Tula RUS 125 F1
Tulcea RO 127 E4
Tul'čyn UA 127 E3
Tulla IRL 4 C2
Tullamore / Tulach Mhór IRL 2 C4
Tulle F 25 E4
Tullgarn S 119 E3
Tullins F 27 D4
Tulln A 69 D1
Tullow / An Tulach IRL 5 E2
Tulppio FIN 109 E1
Tulsk IRL 2 C3
Tumba S 119 E2
Tuohikotti FIN 121 E3
Tuoro sul Trasimeno I 76 B4
La Turballe F 19 D4
La Turbie F 31 F2
Turckheim F 23 E3
Turda RO 126 C4
Turégano E 36 B4
Turenki FIN 120 C3
Turgutlu TR 129 E4
Türi EST 124 B1
Turi I 81 D2
Turinge S 119 E2
Turís E 43 F3
Turjak SLO 73 E3
Turku / Åbo FIN 120 B4
Turmiel E 43 D1
Turnberry GB 3 F1
Turnhout B 17 E1
Türnitz A 69 D1
Turnov CZ 64 B1
Turnu Măgurele RO 129 D2
Turriff GB 7 E4
Turriers F 31 E1
Tursi I 81 D4
Turtola FIN 108 C2
Tuscania I 78 C1
Tuse DK 122 C3
Tutajev RUS 125 F1
Tutrakan BG 129 D1
Tuttlingen D 66 B2
Tuturano I 81 F3
Tutzing D 67 E2
Tuulos FIN 121 D3
Tuupovaara FIN 115 F3
Tuusniemi FIN 115 E3
Tuusula FIN 121 D4
Tuxford GB 10 C3
Tuzla BIH 128 A1
Tvedestrand N 116 C3
Tver' RUS 125 F1
Tvøroyri DK 106 A4
Twimberg A 68 C3
Twist D 55 E3
Twistringen D 55 F2
Tydal N 111 E2
Tyin N 110 C4
Tyndaris I 83 D4
Tyndrum GB 8 C2
Tynemouth GB 9 F4
Tynkä FIN 114 C2
Tynset N 111 E3
Tyresö S 119 E2
Tyringe S 123 E3
Tyristrand N 117 D1
Tyrnävä FIN 115 D1
Tysse N 116 A1
Tyssebotn N 110 A4
Tyssedal N 116 B1
Tywyn GB 10 A4

U

Úbeda E 48 B1
Ublá SK 126 B3
Ubrique E 47 E3
Uchte D 55 F3
Uckange F 22 C1
Uckfield GB 14 C4
Uclés E 42 C2
Udbyhøj DK 122 B2
Uddevalla S 118 B3
Uddheden S 118 B2
Uden NL 54 C4
Udine I 72 C3
Überlingen D 66 B2
Uebigau D 57 F4
Ueckermünde D 52 A3
Uelsen D 55 E3
Uelzen D 50 C4
Uetersen D 50 B3
Uetze D 56 C3
Uffenheim D 62 C3
Ugento I 81 F4
Ugíjar E 48 B3
Ugine F 27 E3
Uglič RUS 125 F1
Uherské Hradiště CZ 65 C3
Uhingen D 66 C1
Uhrsleben D 57 D3
Uig GB 6 B4
Uimaharju FIN 115 F3
Uithoorn NL 54 B3
Uithuizen NL 55 D1
Ukkola FIN 115 F3
Ukmergė LT 124 C3
Ulcinj YU 128 A3
Ulefoss N 116 C2
Uleila del Campo E 49 D3
Ulfborg DK 122 A2
Ul'janovka UA 127 E3
Ullånger S 112 C2
Ullapool GB 6 C3
Ullared S 123 D1
Ullava FIN 114 C2
Ulldecona E 44 B1
Ulm (Donau) D 66 C1
Ulmen D 61 F3
Ulricehamn S 118 C4
Ulrichsberg A 64 B4
Ulsberg N 111 D2
Ulsta GB 7 F2
Ulsteinvik N 110 B2
Ulverston GB 10 C1
Ulvik N 116 B1
Ulvila FIN 120 B3
Ulvsjö S 112 A4
Uman' UA 127 E3
Umbertide I 76 B3
Umbukta N 107 E3
Umeå S 113 D1
Umhausen A 67 E3
Unari FIN 109 E2
Uncastillo E 37 E2
Undersåker S 112 A2
Undredal N 110 B4
Uneča RUS 125 E4
Ungheni MOL 127 D3
Ungilde E 33 D4
Unhais da Serra P 40 C1
Unión (La) E 49 E2
Unna D 55 E4
Unnaryd S 123 E1
Unquera E 36 A1
Unterach A 68 A2
Unterhaching D 67 E2
Unterschleißheim D 67 E2
Unterwasser CH 66 C3
Unterweißenbach A 68 C1
Upavon GB 13 E2
Upinniemi FIN 120 C4
Uppingham GB 11 E4
Upplands-Väsby S 119 E2
Uppsala S 119 E2
Upton-upon-Severn GB 13 E1
Uras I 82 B3
Urbania I 76 C3
Urbe I 75 D2
Urbino I 76 C3
Urda E 42 B3
Urdos F 28 B4
Urepel F 28 A3
Urfahr A 68 B1
Urfeld D 67 E2
Uri I 82 A2
Uriage-les-Bains F 27 D4
Urjala FIN 120 C3
Urk NL 54 C3
Urla TR 129 E4
Urlingford IRL 5 D2
Urnäsch CH 66 C3
Urnes N 110 C4
Urshult S 123 E2
Ururi I 80 A1
Ury F 21 F3
Urziceni RO 129 D1
Usagre E 41 E4
Uşak TR 129 F4
Usedom D 51 F2
Useres (Les) E 44 A2
Usingen D 62 A2
Usk / Brynbuga GB 13 E1
Üsküdar TR 129 F3
Uslar D 56 B4
Ussat F 29 E4
Ussé F 25 D1
Usseglio I 27 E4
Ussel F 25 F3
Usselln D 62 A1
Ustaoset N 116 C1
Ustaritz F 28 A3
Uster CH 66 B3
Ústí nad Labem CZ 64 A1
Ustka PL 52 C1
Ust'užna RUS 125 F1
Utajärvi FIN 115 D1

Utåker N	116	A1
Utbjoa N	116	A1
Utebo E	37	F3
Utelle F	31	F2
Utena LT	124	C3
Utiel E	43	F3
Utne N	116	B1
Utrecht NL	54	C4
Utrera E	47	E2
Utrillas E	43	F1
Utsjoki FIN	105	E2
Uttendorf A	68	A1
Uttendorf A	67	F3
Utting D	67	E2
Uttoxeter GB	11	D4
Uukuniemi FIN	121	F2
Uurainen FIN	115	D4
Uusikaupunki FIN	120	B3
Uvdal N	116	C1
Uzel F	18	C3
Uzerche F	25	E4
Uzès F	30	C2
Užhorod UA	126	B3
Užice YU	128	B2
Uzunköprü TR	129	E3
Uzyn UA	127	E2

V

Vä S	123	E3
Vaajakoski FIN	115	D4
Vääkiö FIN	115	E1
Vaala FIN	115	D1
Vaalajärvi FIN	109	D1
Vaalimaa FIN	121	E3
Vaals NL	61	E2
Vaaraslahti FIN	115	D3
Vaasa / Vasa FIN	114	B3
Vaassen NL	54	C3
Vabre F	29	F2
Vác H	126	A40

Vacha D	62	C1
Väddö S	119	F2
Vadheim N	110	B4
Vado Ligure I	75	D2
Vadsø N	105	F2
Vadstena S	118	C3
Væggerløse DK	122	C4
Vaféika GR	89	F1
Vafiohóri GR	88	A1
Vågaholmen N	107	E2
Vågåmo N	111	D3
Vågan N	107	E2
Våge N	116	A1
Vaggeryd S	118	C4
Vágia GR	93	F3
Vagioniá GR	101	D4
Vagnhärad S	119	E3
Vagos P	40	B1
Vagur DK	106	A4
Vähäkyrö FIN	114	B3
Vahto FIN	120	B3
Väï GR	101	F3
Vaiano I	76	A2
Vaiges F	19	F3
Vaihingen a. d. Enz D	62	B4
Vailly-sur-Aisne F	17	D4
Vailly-sur-Sauldre F	21	F3
Vainikkala FIN	121	E3
Vaisaluokta S	107	F1
Vaison-la-Romaine F	30	C1
Vaksdal N	110	A4
Le Val-André F	19	D2
Le Val-d'Ajol F	23	D3
Val-de-Reuil F	16	B4
Val-d'Isère F	27	F3
Val-Thorens F	27	E4
Vålådalen S	112	A2
Valadares P	34	B4
Valamen FIN	115	E3
Valareña E	37	E3
Valašské Meziříčí CZ	65	F2
Valax FIN	121	D4

Valbella CH	66	C4
Vålberg S	118	C2
Valberg F	31	F2
Valbo S	119	E1
Valbondione I	71	E3
Valbonnais F	27	D4
Valcarlos E	28	A3
Valdagno I	72	A4
Valdahon F	27	E1
Valdaj RUS	125	E1
Valdaora / Olang I	67	F4
Valdecaballeros E	41	F3
Valdecabras E	43	D2
Valdecarros E	41	F1
Valdedíos E	33	E2
Valdefuentes E	41	E3
Valdeganga E	43	E4
Valdelacasa de Tajo E	41	F2
Valdelinares E	43	F2
Valdemarsvik S	119	E4
Valdemeca E	43	E2
Valdemorillo E	42	B1
Valdemoro E	42	B2
Valdenoceda E	36	B1
Valdepeñas E	42	C4
Valdepeñas de Jaén E	48	A2
Valderas E	35	F3
Valderiès F	29	F2
Valderrobres E	44	A1
Valdestillas E	36	A4
Valdeverdeja E	41	F2
Valdevimbre E	33	E4
Valdezcaray E	36	C2
Valdieri I	31	F1
Valdobbiadene I	72	B3
Vale de Açor P	46	B1
Vale de Cambra P	34	B4
Vale de Estrela P	41	D1
Vale de Prazeres P	40	C1
Valeggio sul Mincio I	71	F4
Valença do Minho P	32	A4
Valençay F	25	E1

Valence F	26	C4
Valence-d'Agen F	29	D2
Valence-d'Albigeois F	29	F2
Valence-sur-Baïse F	29	D2
València E	44	A3
Valencia de Alcántara E	41	D3
Valencia de Don Juan E	33	E4
Valencia de las Torres E	41	E4
Valencia del Ventoso E	47	D1
Valenciennes F	17	D3
Valensole F	31	D2
Valentano I	78	C1
Valentigney F	23	D4
Valenza I	75	D1
Valevåg N	116	A1
Valfabbrica I	76	C4
Valga EST	124	C2
Valgorge F	30	B1
Valgrisenche I	27	F3
Valguarnera I	85	D3
Valhelhas P	41	D1
Valimítika GR	93	D4
Valíra GR	96	C2
Valjevo YU	128	B2
Valjok N	105	E2
Valjunquera E	44	A1
Valkeakoski FIN	120	C3
Valkeala FIN	121	E3
Valkenburg aan de Geul NL	61	D2
Valkenswaard NL	17	F1
Valko FIN	121	D3
Vall d'Uixó (La) E	44	A3
Valladolid E	36	A3
Vallata I	80	B3

Vallbo S	112	A2
Valldal N	110	C3
Vall d'Alba E	44	A2
Valldemossa E	45	E3
Valle N	116	B2
Valle Castellana I	77	D4
Valle Mosso I	70	C4
Valleberga S	123	E3
Valle de Abdalajís E	47	F3
Valle de la Serena E	41	E4
Valle de los Caídos E	42	B1
Valle de Matamoros E	41	D4
Vallentuna S	119	E2
Valleraugue F	30	B2
Vallet F	24	B1
Valletta M	85	F4
Vallgrund FIN	114	B3
Vallø DK	123	D3
Vallo della Lucania I	80	B4
Valloire F	27	E4
Vallombrosa I	76	A3
Vallon-en-Sully F	25	F2
Vallon-Pont-d'Arc F	30	B1
Vallorbe CH	27	E1
Vallorcine F	27	E3
Vallouise F	27	E4
Valls E	38	B4
Vallsta S	112	B4
Valmiera LV	124	B2
Valmojado E	42	B2
Valmont F	16	A4
Valmontone I	79	E3
Valmorel F	27	E3
Valognes F	19	E1
Valongo P	34	B4
Valoria la Buena E	36	A3
Valøya N	106	C4
Valožyn BY	124	C4
Valpaços P	35	D3
Valpalmas E	37	F3
Valprato Soana I	27	F3
Valras-Plage F	30	A3

Valréas F	30	C1
Vals-les-Bains F	30	B1
Valsamónero GR	104	C4
Valsavarenche I	27	F3
Valset N	111	D1
Valsjöbyn S	112	A1
Valtessiníko GR	96	C1
Valtierra E	37	E3
Valtimo FIN	115	E2
Váltos GR	91	E1
Valtotópi GR	88	C1
Valtournenche I	27	F3
Valvasone I	72	C3
Valverde de Cervera E	37	E3
Valverde de Júcar E	43	D3
Valverde del Camino E	46	C2
Valverde de Leganés E	41	D4
Valverde del Fresno E	41	D1
Våmb S	118	C3
Våmhus S	112	A4
Vamlingbo S	119	F4
Vammala FIN	120	B3
Vampula FIN	120	B3
Vamvakoú GR	97	D2
Vamvakoú GR	93	E1
Vandellós E	44	B1
Vänersborg S	118	B3
Vangsnes N	110	B4
Vangsvik N	104	B3
Vanha Vaasa FIN	114	B3
Vännäs S	113	D1
Vannavålen N	104	C4
Vannes F	18	C4
Les Vans F	30	B1
Vansbro S	118	C1
Vantaa / Vanda FIN	121	D4
Vanttauskoski FIN	109	E2
Vaour F	29	E2

Valencia

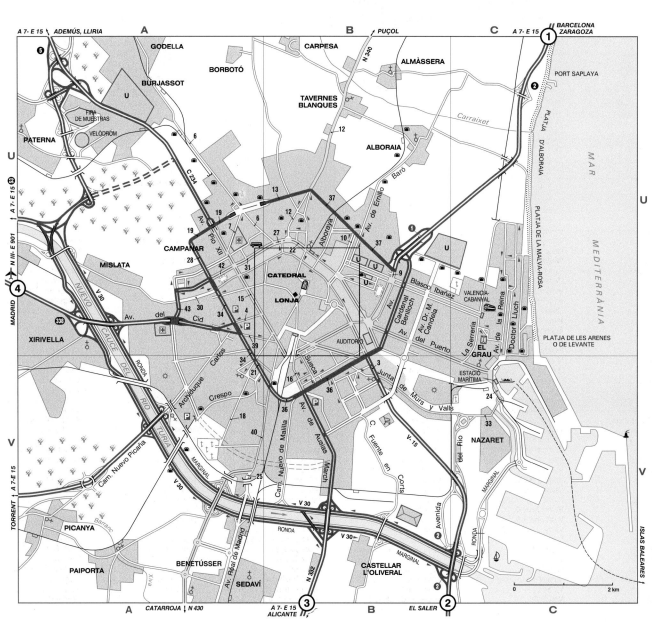

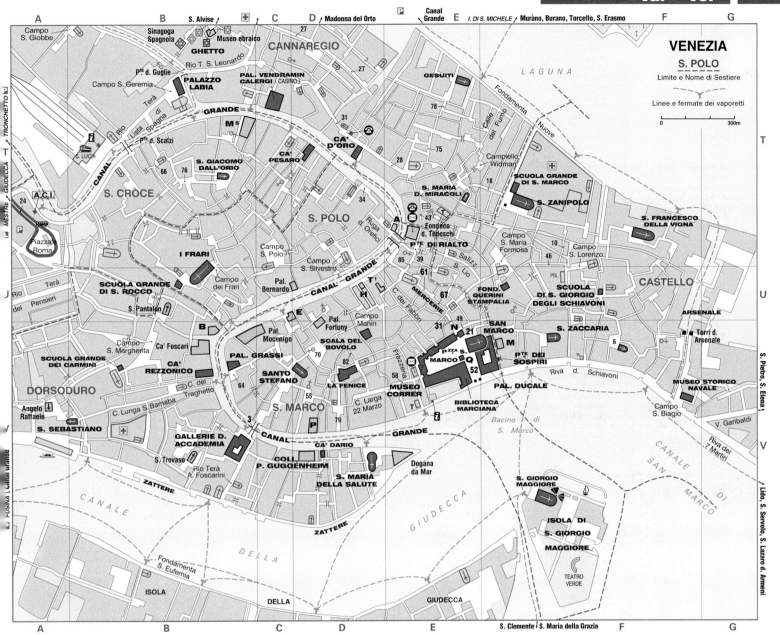

VENEZIA
S. POLO
Limite e Nome di Sestiere
Linee e fermate dei vaporetti
0   300m

Name	Page	Grid
Vara S	118	B3
Varades F	19	E4
Varallo I	70	C4
Varangerbotn N	105	F2
Varano de Melegari I	75	E1
Varazze I	75	D2
Varberg S	123	D1
Várda GR	92	C4
Varde DK	122	A3
Vårdø FIN	120	A4
Vardø N	105	F1
Varel D	50	A4
Vareleíi GR	94	B4
Varengeville-sur-Mer F	16	A3
Varenna I	71	D3
Varennes-en-Argonne F	17	F4
Varennes-sur-Allier F	26	A2
Varennes-sur-Amance F	22	C4
Varese I	71	D4
Varese Ligure I	75	E2
Vårgårda S	118	B3
Vargas E	36	B1
Varhaug N	116	A2
Vári GR	98	C2
Vári GR	97	E3
Varilhes F	29	E4
Varimbómbi GR	94	A4
Váris GR	87	E3
Varkaus FIN	115	E1
Várkiza GR	97	F1
Varmahlíð IS	106	B1
Varmo I	72	C3
Varna BG	129	E2
Värnamo S	123	E1
Varnhem S	118	C3
Värö S	123	D1
Varpaisjärvi FIN	115	E3
Várpalota H	126	A4
Vars F	31	E1
Vartholomió GR	92	B4
Vartius FIN	115	F1
Varvára GR	88	C2
Varzi I	75	D1
Varzy F	21	F4
Vasaraperä FIN	109	E2
Vásárosnamény H	126	B3
Vaskio FIN	120	C4
Vaskivesi FIN	120	C2
Vaslui RO	127	D1
Vassarás GR	97	D2
Vassés GR	96	C2
Vassieux-en-Vercors F	27	D4
Vassiliká GR	94	A2
Vassiliká GR	88	B2
Vassiliká GR	95	F2
Vassilikí GR	92	A3
Vassilikí GR	87	E4
Vassilikó GR	94	A3
Vassilikós GR	96	A1
Vassilís GR	93	E1
Vassy F	19	F2
Västanfjärd FIN	120	B4
Västenbäck S	112	B2
Västerås S	119	D2
Västervik S	119	E4
Vasto I	80	A1
Vasyl'kiv UA	127	E2
Vatan F	25	E1
Väte S	119	F4
Vaterá GR	95	F2
Vateró GR	87	F3
Váthi GR	94	A3
Váthi GR	88	B1
Váthi GR	92	B3
Váthi GR	99	F3
Váthia GR	97	D4
Vathílakos GR	88	A2
Vathílakos GR	89	D1
Vathílakos GR	87	E3
Vathípetro GR	101	D4
Vathís GR	99	F4
Vatne N	110	B2
Vatólakos GR	87	E3
Vatra Dornei RO	126	C4
Vattholma S	119	E2
Vaucouleurs F	22	C2
Vaŭkavysk BY	124	C4
Vauvert F	30	B2
Vauvillers F	23	D3
Vávdos GR	88	C3
Växjö S	123	E2
Växtorp S	123	D2
Vayrac F	25	E4
V'az'ma RUS	125	F3
Veberöd S	123	D3
Vechta D	55	F2
Vecilla (La) E	33	E3
Vecinos E	41	F1
Vedelago I	72	B4
Veendam NL	55	D2
Veenendaal NL	54	C4
Vega de Espinareda E	33	D3
Vegadeo E	32	C2
Vega de Valcarce E	32	C3
Vegarienza E	33	E3
Vegårshei N	116	C3
Vegas del Condado E	33	E3
Vegesack D	50	A4
Veghel NL	54	C4
Veguellina de Órbigo E	33	E4
Veguillas (Las) E	41	F1
Vehkalahti FIN	121	E3
Vehmaa FIN	120	B3
Vehmersalmi FIN	115	E3
Veidnesklubben N	105	E1
Veiga (A) E	32	C4
Veikkola FIN	120	C3
Veinge S	123	D2
Veiros P	40	C3
Vejen DK	122	B3
Vejer de la Frontera E	47	D4
Vejle DK	122	B3
Vel. Lašče SLO	73	E3
Velada E	42	A2
Velanídia GR	97	E4
Velayos E	42	A1
Velbert D	61	F1
Velburg D	63	F2
Velden A	68	B4
Velden D	67	F1
Velden D	63	E3
Veldhoven NL	17	F1
Velenje SLO	73	E2
Velestíno GR	93	E1
Vélez Blanco E	49	D2
Vélez de Benaudalla E	48	B3
Vélez Málaga E	48	A3
Vélez Rubio E	49	D2
Veliés GR	97	E3
Veliki Preslav BG	129	D2
Velikije Luki RUS	125	D2
Veliko Tărnovo BG	129	D2
Velilla del Río Carrión E	33	F3
Vélines F	24	C4
Velingrad BG	128	C2
Veliž RUS	125	E3
Velkua FIN	120	B4
Vellahn D	50	C4
Vellés (La) E	35	F4
Velletri I	79	E2
Vellinge S	123	D3
Vélos GR	94	B3
Velpke D	57	D3
Velten D	57	F2
Velvendós GR	87	F3
Velyka Lepetycha UA	127	F3
Vemdalen S	112	A3
Vemdalsskalet S	112	A3
Vemhån S	112	A3
Véna GR	91	D2
Venaco F	78	A3
Venarey-les-Laumes F	22	B4
Venaria I	27	F4
Vence F	31	F2
Venda Nova P	34	C3
Vendas Novas P	40	B4
Vendel S	119	E1
Vendeuvre-sur-Barse F	22	B3
Vendôme F	21	D4
Vendrell (El) E	38	C4
Veneheitto FIN	115	D1
Venezia I	72	B4
Vengjaneset N	116	A1
Venialbo E	35	F4
Venjan S	112	A4
Venlo NL	61	E1
Vennesla N	116	B3
Vennesund N	107	D4
Venosa I	80	C3
Venray NL	55	D4
Venta Nueva E	33	D3
Ventas con Peña Aguilera E	42	B3
Ventas de Huelma E	48	A3
Ventimiglia I	31	F2
Ventnor GB	13	F3
Ventspils LV	124	A2
Venturina I	75	F4
Vera N	111	E1
Vera E	49	D3
Verbania I	70	C4
Verberie F	16	C4
Verbicaro I	80	C4
Verbier CH	27	F2
Vercel-Villedieu-le-Camp F	27	F2
Vercelli I	74	C1
Verchnjadzvinsk BY	124	C3
Verchn'odniprovs'k UA	127	F2
Verdalsøra N	111	E1
Verde I	75	D2
Verden D	56	B2
Verdikoússa GR	87	F4
Le Verdon-sur-Mer F	24	B3
Verdun F	17	F4
Verdun-sur-Garonne F	29	E2
Verdun-sur-le-Doubs F	26	C1
Vergato I	76	A2
Vérgi GR	88	C1
Vergiate I	71	D4

Name	Page	Ref
Vergína GR	88	A2
Vergína GR	88	A2
Vergio F.	75	D2
Vergt F.	25	D4
Véria GR.	87	F2
Verín E	32	C4
Verl D	55	F4
Vermand F.	17	D3
Vermenton F.	22	A4
Vernet-les-Bains F.	29	F4
Verneuil-sur-Avre F	21	D2
Vernon F.	21	D2
Vernoux-en-Vivarais F	26	C4
Verny F.	23	D2
Veroli I.	79	E2
Verona I.	71	F4
La Verpillière F.	26	C3
Verran N	111	E1
Verrès I.	27	F3
Versailles F.	21	E2
Versmold D.	55	F4
Verteillac F	25	D4
Vertientes (Las) E	48	C2
Vertus F.	22	A2
Verucchio I.	76	B2
Verviers B	61	D2
Vervins F.	17	E3
Verzuolo I.	31	F1
Verzy F.	22	A2
Vesanto FIN.	115	D3
Vescovato F.	78	B3
Vesilahti FIN	120	C3
Vesivehmaa FIN	121	D3
Vesjegonsk RUS.	125	F1
Veskoniemi FIN	105	F3
Vesoul F	23	D4
Véssa GR.	95	F4
Vestby N.	117	D2
Vestbygda N	116	A2
Vesterø Havn DK.	122	C1
Vestertana N	105	F1
Vestmanna DK.	106	A3
Vestnes N.	110	C2
Vestone I.	71	F4
Vestre jakobselv N.	105	F2
Veszprém H	126	A4
Veteli FIN.	114	C3
Vetlanda S.	123	F1
Vetralla I.	79	D1
Vetriolo Terme I.	72	A3
Vetschau D.	58	A3
Veules-les-Roses F	16	A3
Veulettes-sur-Mer F .	16	A3
Veurne B.	15	F4
Vevey CH.	27	E2
Vévi GR.	87	E2
Veynes F.	31	D1
Veyre-Monton F	26	A3
Veyrier-du-Lac F	27	E3
Vezdemarbán E.	35	F3
Vézelay F.	22	A4
Vézelise F.	22	C3
Vézénobres F.	30	B2
Vézins-de-Lévézou F.	30	A1
Vezzani F.	78	A3
Vezzano I.	71	F3
Viadana I.	75	F1
Viana E.	37	D2
Viana do Alentejo P ..	40	B4
Viana do Bolo E.	32	C4
Viana do Castelo P	34	B3
Vianden L.	61	E4
Vianen NL.	54	C4
Viareggio I	75	F3
Vias F.	30	A3
Vibo Valentia I.	83	E3
Viborg DK.	122	B2
Vibraye F.	20	C3
Vic E.	39	D3
Vič SLO.	73	E2
Vic-en-Bigorre F.	28	C4
Vic-Fezensac F.	29	D2
Vic-le-Comte F.	26	A3
Vic-sur-Aisne F.	17	D4
Vic-sur-Cère F.	25	F4
Vicálvaro E.	42	B1
Vicdessos F.	29	E4
Vicebsk BY.	125	D3
Vicenza I.	72	A4
Vichy F.	26	A2
Vico F.	78	A3
Vico del Gargano I.	80	C1
Vico Equense I.	80	A3
Victoria M.	85	F40
Vidago P.	34	C3
Vidareidi DK.	106	A3
Vidauban F.	31	E3
Viddal N.	110	B3
Videbæk DK.	122	A2
Videm SLO.	73	E3
Vidiáki GR.	96	C1
Vidigueira P.	40	C4
Vidin BG	128	C2
Vidreres E	39	D3
Vidsel S.	108	B3
Viechtach D	63	F4
Viechtwang A	68	B2
Vieira de Leiria P.	40	A2
Vieira do Minho P	34	C3
Vielha E.	29	D4
Vielle-Aure F.	28	C4
Vielmur-sur-Agout F.	29	F3
Vielsalm B.	61	E2
Vienenburg D.	56	C3
Vienne F.	26	C3
Vieremä FIN	115	D2
Viernheim D.	23	F1
Vierraden D.	52	A4
Viersen D.	61	E1
Vierumäki FIN	121	D3
Vierzon F.	25	F1
Vieste I.	80	C1
Vietas S.	108	A1
Vietri di Potenza I.	80	B3
Vietri sul Mare I.	80	A3
Vieux-Boucau-les-Bains F.	28	A2
Vif F.	27	D4
Vig DK.	122	C3
Le Vigan F.	30	B2
Vigeland N.	116	B3
Vigeois F.	25	E4
Vigevano I.	71	D4
Viggiano I.	80	C3
Vígla GR.	92	B2
Vignale Monferrato I.	74	C1
Vignola I.	76	A2
Vignole Borbera I.	75	D1
Vignory F.	22	B3
Vigo di Fassa I	67	F4
Vigo E.	32	A4
Vigone I.	27	F4
Vigonza I.	72	B4
Vihanti FIN	114	C1
Vihiers F.	24	C1
Vihtavuori FIN	115	D4
Vihtijärvi FIN	120	C3
Vihti FIN.	120	C3
Viiala FIN.	120	C3
Viiksimo FIN.	115	F1
Viinijärvi FIN.	115	E3
Viitasaari FIN	115	D3
Vik IS.	106	B2
Vik N.	116	C3
Vik N.	107	D4
Vik N.	110	B4
Vika S.	119	D1
Vikajärvi FIN	109	D2
Vikedal N.	116	A1
Vikersund N.	117	D1
Vikeså N.	116	A2
Vikevåg N.	116	A2
Vikingstad S.	119	D3
Víkou GR.	87	D4
Vikran N	104	B3
Viksdalen N.	110	B3
Viksjö S.	112	C2
Viksta S.	119	E1
Vila de Cruces E.	32	B3
Vila Nova de Santo André P.	46	A1
Vila-real / Villarreal E.	44	A2
Vila-rodona E.	38	C4
Vila Boim P.	40	C3
Vilada E.	38	C3
Viladamat E.	39	E3
Vila de Rei P.	40	B2
Vila do Bispo P.	46	A2
Vila do Conde P.	34	B3
Viladrau E.	39	D3
Vilafamés E.	44	A2
Vila Fernando P.	40	C3
Vila Flor P.	35	D4
Vilafranca E.	44	A2
Vila Franca das Naves P	35	D4
Vilafranca del Penedès E.	38	C4
Vila Franca de Xira P.	40	A3
Vila Fresca de Azeitão P	40	A4
Vilagarcía de Arousa E.	32	A3
Vila Joiosa (La) / Villajoyosa E.	49	F1
Vilalba / Villalba E.	32	C2
Vilaller E.	29	D4
Vilallonga E.	44	A4
Vilamarxant E.	43	F3
Vilanova d'Alcolea E.	44	A2
Vilanova E.	32	C2
Vila Nova da Barquinha P.	40	B2
Vilanova de Arosa E.	32	A3
Vila Nova de Cerveira P.	32	A4
Vila Nova de Famalicão P.	34	B3
Vila Nova de Foz Côa P.	35	D4
Vila Nova de Gaia P ..	34	B4
Vila Nova de Milfontes P.	46	A1
Vila Nova de Paiva P.	34	C4
Vila Nova de Poiares P.	40	B1
Vila Nova de São Bento P.	46	C1
Vilanova de Sau E.	39	D3
Vilanova i la Geltrú / Villanueva y Geltrú E.	38	C4
Vila Pouca de Aguiar P.	34	C3
Vila Praia de Âncora P.	32	A4
Vilar de Barrio E.	32	B4
Vilar Formoso P	41	D1
Vila Real P.	34	C3
Vila Real de Santo António P.	46	B2
Vila-seca E.	44	C1
Vila Velha de Ródão P	40	C2
Vila Verde P.	34	B3
Vila Verde da Raia P ..	35	D4
Vila Verde de Ficalho P.	46	C1
Vila Viçosa P .	40	C4
Vilches E.	48	B1
Vilejka BY.	124	C4
Vilhelmina S	107	F1
Vília GR	93	F4
Viljakkala FIN.	120	C2
Viljandi EST.	124	B2
Vilkaviškis LT.	124	B4
Villa Adriana I.	79	E1
Villa Bartolomea I.	72	A4
Villa Literno I.	79	F3
Villa Minozzo I.	75	F2
Villa Opicina I.	73	D3
Villa Potenza I.	77	D3
Villa Santina I.	68	A4
Villa S. Giovanni I.	83	D4
Villa Sta Maria I.	80	A1
Villa Vomano I.	77	D4
Villabassa / Niederdorf I.	67	F4
Villablanca E.	46	C2
Villablino E.	33	D3
Villabona E.	28	A3
Villabrágima E.	35	F3
Villabuena del Puente E.	35	F4
Villacañas E.	42	C3
Villacarriedo E.	36	B1
Villacarrillo E.	48	B1
Villacastín E.	42	A1
Villach A.	68	B4
Villacidro I.	82	B4
Villada E.	33	F4
Villa de Don Fadrique (La) E.	42	C3
Villa del Prado E.	42	B2
Villa del Río E.	48	A1
Villadiego E.	36	B2
Villadossola I.	70	C3
Villaescusa de Haro E	43	D3
Villafáfila E.	35	F3
Villaflores E.	35	F4
Villafranca di Verona I.	71	F4
Villafranca in Lunigiana I.	75	E2
Villafranca Piemonte I.	27	F4
Villafranca Tirrena I.	83	D4
Villafranca E.	44	A2
Villafranca del Bierzo E.	33	D3
Villafranca de los Barros E.	41	E4
Villafranca de los Caballeros E.	42	C3
Villafranca-Montes de Oca E.	36	C2
Villafranco del Guadalquivir E.	47	D2
Villafrati I.	84	B3
Villafrechós E.	35	F3
Villafruela E.	36	B3
Villafuerte E.	36	B3
Villager de Laciana E.	33	D3
Villaggio Mancuso I..	83	E2
Villaharta E.	47	F1
Villahermosa E	42	C4
Villahoz E.	36	B3
Villaines-la-Juhel F.	19	F3
Villala FIN.	115	F4
Villalba de los Barros E.	41	D4
Villalba del Rey E.	43	D2
Villalcázar de Sirga E.	33	F4
Villalgordo del Marquesado E.	43	D3
Villalón de Campos E	36	A3
Villalpando E.	35	F3
Villalpardo E.	43	E3
Villaluenga E.	37	E4
Villamanrique E.	42	C4
Villamanrique de la Condesa E.	47	D2
Villamañan E.	33	E4
Villamartín E.	47	E3
Villamartín de Campos E.	36	A3
Villamayor de Campos E.	35	F3
Villamayor de Santiago E.	42	C3
Villandraut F.	28	C1
Villandry F.	20	C4
Villanova Monteleone I.	82	A2
Villanubla E.	36	A3
Villanueva de Alcardete E.	42	C3
Villanueva de Alcorón E.	43	D1
Villanueva de Algaidas E.	47	F3
Villanueva de Argaño E.	36	B2
Villanueva de Bogas E.	42	B3
Villanueva de Cameros E.	37	D3
Villanueva de Córdoba E.	47	F1
Villanueva de Franco E.	42	C4
Villanueva de Gállego E.	37	F3
Villanueva de la Concepción E.	47	F3
Villanueva de la Fuente E.	42	C4
Villanueva de la Jara E.	43	D3
Villanueva de la Reina E.	48	A1
Villanueva del Arzobispo E.	48	C1
Villanueva de la Serena E.	41	E4
Villanueva de la Sierra E.	41	E1
Villanueva de las Torres E.	48	B2
Villanueva de la Vera E.	41	F2
Villanueva del Campo E.	35	F3
Villanueva del Duque E.	47	F1
Villanueva del Fresno E.	40	C4
Villanueva del Huerva E.	37	F4
Villanueva de los Castillejos E.	46	C2
Villanueva de los Infantes E.	42	C4
Villanueva del Rey E .	47	F1
Villanueva del Río y Minas E.	47	E2
Villanueva del Trabuco E.	48	A3
Villanueva de San Carlos E.	42	B4
Villaquejida E.	33	E4
Villaquilambre E.	33	E4
Villar de Peralonso E.	35	E4
Villarcayo E.	36	C1
Villard-de-Lans F.	27	D4
Villar de Arnedo (El) E	37	D2
Villar de Cañas E.	43	D3
Villarde Domingo García E.	43	D2
Villardefrades E.	35	F3
Villar del Arzobispo E	43	F3
Villar del Rey E.	41	D3
Villarejo de Fuentes E.	43	D3
Villarejo de Salvanés E.	42	C2
Villarente E.	33	E4
Villares (Los) E.	48	A2
Villares de la Reina E.	35	E4
Villares del Saz E.	43	D2
Villargarcía del Llano E.	43	E3
Villargordo del Cabriel E.	43	E3
Villaricos E.	49	D3
Villarino E.	35	E4
Villaroya E.	37	D3
Villaroya de los Pinares E.	43	F1
Villarquemado E.	43	F1
Villarramiel E.	36	A3
Villarrín de Campos E	35	F3
Villarrobledo E.	43	D3
Villarroya de la Sierra E.	37	E4
Villarrubia de los Ojos E.	42	B3
Villarrubia de Santiago E.	42	C2
Villarrubio E.	42	C2
Villars-les-Dombes F.	26	C3
Villars-sur-Ollon CH ..	27	F2
Villarta de San Juan E	42	C3
Villasalto I.	82	C3
Villasana de Mena E..	36	C1
Villasandino E.	36	B2
Villasante de Montija E.	36	C1
Villasarracino E.	33	F4
Villaseco de los Reyes E.	35	E4
Villasequilla de Yepes E.	42	B2
Villasimius I.	82	C4
Villasor I.	82	B4
Villatobas E.	42	C2
Villatoya E.	43	E3
Villava E.	28	A4
Villaverde del Río E.	47	E2
Villaviciosa E.	33	E2
Villaviciosa de Córdoba E.	47	F1
Villaviciosa de Odón E.	42	B1
Villavieja de Yeltes E.	35	E4
Villé F.	23	E3
Ville-en-Tardenois F.	17	D4
Ville-sur-Tourbe F.	17	F4
Villebois-Lavalette F.	25	D3
La Villedieu-du-Clain F.	25	D2
Villedieu-les-Poêles F	19	E2
Villefagnan F.	24	C3
Villefort F.	30	B1
Villefranche-d'Albigeois F.	29	F2
Villefranche-de-Lauragais F.	29	E3
Villefranche-de-Lonchat F.	24	C4
Villefranche-de-Rouergue F.	29	F1
Villefranche-du-Périgord F.	29	D1
Villefranche-sur-Cher F.	25	E1
Villefranche-sur-Mer F.	31	F2
Villefranche-sur-Saône F.	26	C3
Villel E.	43	F2
Villemur-sur-Tarn F .	29	E2
Villena E.	43	F4
Villenauxe-la-Grande F.	22	A2
Villeneuve F.	29	F1
Villeneuve-d'Ascq F..	15	F4
Villeneuve-de-Berg F	30	C1
Villeneuve-de-Marsan F.	28	C2
Villeneuve-l'Archevêque F.	22	A3
Villeneuve-lès-Avignon F.	30	C2
Villeneuve-sur-Lot F .	29	D1
Villeneuve-sur-Yonne F.	21	F3
Villeréal F.	29	D1
Villers-Bocage F.	16	C3
Villers-Bocage F.	19	F2
Villers-Bretonneux F.	16	C3
Villers-Cotterêts F.	17	D4
Villers-devant-Orval B.	17	F4
Villers-Farlay F.	27	D1
Villers-la-Ville B.	17	E2
Villers-le-Lac F.	27	E1
Villers-sur-Mer F.	20	C1
Villersexel F.	23	D4
Villerupt F.	22	C1
Villerville F.	20	C1
Villetta Barrea I.	79	F2
Villiers-St-Georges F.	21	F2
Villingen-Schwenningen D ..	23	F3
Villoldo E.	33	F4
Villoria E.	35	F4
Villotta I.	72	B3
Vilnius LT.	124	C4
Vil'nohirs'k UA	127	F3
Vilppula FIN	120	C2
Vilsbiburg D.	67	F3
Vilseck D.	63	E3
Vilshofen D.	64	A4
Vilvoorde B.	17	E2
Vimercate I.	71	D4
Vimianzo E.	32	A2
Vimieiro P.	40	C3
Vimioso P.	35	E3
Vimmerby S.	119	D4
Vimoutiers F.	20	C2
Vímpeli / Vindala FIN	114	C2
Vinadio I.	31	F1
Vinaixa E.	38	B4
Vinaròs E.	44	B2
Vinay F.	27	D4
Vinça F.	29	F4
Vinchiaturo I.	80	A2
Vinci I.	76	A3
Vindeln S.	113	D1
Vinderup DK.	122	B2
Vindsvik N.	116	B2
Vingåker S.	119	D3
Vingelen N.	111	E3
Vinhais P.	35	D3
Vinica SLO.	73	E3
Vinje N.	116	C2
Vinkovci HR.	128	A1
Vinnycja UA	127	D2
Vinsternes N.	110	C2
Vinstra N.	111	D3
Vinuesa E.	36	C3
Viñas (Las) E	48	A1
Viñuelas E.	42	C1
Vipava SLO.	73	D3
Vipiteno / Sterzing I. ..	67	E4
Vire F.	19	F2
Vireux-Wallerand F.	17	E4
Virgen A.	67	F3
Virgen de la Cabeza (Santuario) E.	48	A1
Virgen del Camino (La) E ..	33	E4
Virginia IRL	3	D4
Virieu F.	27	D3
Virieu-le-Grand F.	27	D3
Virkkala / Virkby FIN	120	C4
Virkkula FIN.	109	F2
Virmutjoki FIN.	121	F2
Virolahti FIN.	121	E3
Virónia GR.	88	B1
Virovitica HR.	128	A1
Virrat FIN.	120	C4
Virsbo S.	119	D2
Virserum S.	123	F1
Virtasalmi FIN.	121	E2
Virton B.	17	F4
Virtsu EST.	124	B2
Vis HR.	128	A2
Visby S.	119	F4
Visé B.	17	F2
Višegrad BIH.	128	A2
Viserba I.	76	C2
Viseu P.	34	C4
Viso (El) E.	47	F1
Viso del Alcor (El) E.	47	E2
Viso del Marqués E.	42	B4
Visp CH.	70	C3
Visselhövede D.	50	B4
Vissenbjerg DK.	122	B3
Vissiniá GR.	87	E2
Visso I.	76	C2
Vistabella del Maestrat E.	44	A2
Vistheden S.	108	B3
Visuvesi FIN.	120	C2
Vitaby S.	123	E3
Vítala GR.	94	B3
Viterbo I.	79	D1
Vitigudino E.	35	D4
Vitína GR.	96	C1
Vitoli GR.	93	D2
Vitoria / Gasteiz E.	37	D2
Vitré F.	19	E3
Vitrey-sur-Mance F.	22	C4
Vitriola I.	75	F2
Vitry-en-Artois F.	17	D3
Vitry-le-François F.	22	B2

Vítsa *GR*	87	D4	Vlahópoulo *GR*	96	B2	Volissós *GR*	95	E3
Vitsand *S*	118	C1	Vlasenica *BIH*	128	A2	Volkach *D*	62	C3
Vittangi *S*	108	B1	Vlássio *GR*	92	C1	Volkmarsen *D*	56	B4
Vitteaux *F*	22	B4	Vlásti *GR*	87	E2	Volmunster *F*	23	E1
Vittel *F*	22	C3	Vlihó *GR*	92	A3	Voločys'k *UA*	127	D2
Vittoria *I*	85	D4	Vlissingen *NL*	17	D1	Volodymyr-		
Vittorio Veneto *I*	72	B3	Vlorë *AL*	128	B4	Volyns'kyj *UA*	126	C2
Vittoriosa *M*	85	F4	Vlotho *D*	55	F3	Volokolamsk *RUS*	125	F2
Vittsjö *S*	123	E2	Vobbia *I*	75	D2	Volonne *F*	31	D2
Vitznau *CH*	66	B4	Voe *GB*	7	F3	Vólos *GR*	93	F1
Viù *I*	27	F4	Vöcklabruck *A*	68	A1	Volpiano *I*	27	F4
Vivaro *I*	72	B3	Vöhringen *D*	66	C1	Volta Mantovana *I*	71	F4
Viveiro *E*	32	C2	Völkermarkt *A*	68	C3	Volterra *I*	76	A3
Vivel del Río Martín *E*	43	F1	Völklingen *D*	23	D1	Voltri *I*	75	D2
Viver *E*	43	F2	Vogatsikó *GR*	87	E3	Volturara Appula *I*	80	B3
Viverols *F*	26	B4	Vogelsdorf *D*	58	A2	Volvic *F*	26	A3
Viveros *E*	43	D4	Voghera *I*	75	D1	Volx *F*	31	D2
Le Vivier-sur-Mer *F*	19	E2	Vohenstrauß *D*	63	F3	Vónitsa *GR*	92	B3
Viviers *F*	30	C1	Void *F*	22	C2	Vonnas *F*	26	C2
Vivonne *F*	25	D2	Voikka *FIN*	121	E3	Voorschoten *NL*	54	B4
Vizille *F*	27	D4	Voikoski *FIN*	121	E3	Voorst *NL*	55	D3
Vizítsa *GR*	93	F1	Voiron *F*	27	D4	Voorthuizen *NL*	54	C3
Vizzavona *F*	78	A3	Voiteur *F*	27	D1	Vopnafjörður *IS*	106	C1
Vizzavona *F*	75	D2	Voitsberg *A*	68	C3	Vöra / Vöyri *FIN*	114	B3
Vizzini *I*	85	D4	Vojakkala *FIN*	108	C3	Vorau *A*	69	D2
Vlaardingen *NL*	54	B4	Vojens *DK*	122	B3	Vorchdorf *A*	68	B1
Vlagtwedde *NL*	55	E2	Vojnik *SLO*	73	E2	Vordernberg *A*	68	C2
Vlaháva *GR*	87	E4	Vókas *GR*	89	D1	Vorderriß *D*	67	E2
Vlahéma *GR*	96	C1	Volchov *RUS*	125	D1	Vordingborg *DK*	122	C3
Vlahérna *GR*	92	B1	Volda *N*	110	B3	Voreppe *F*	27	D4
Vlahiótis *GR*	97	D3	Volders *A*	67	A3	Vorey *F*	26	B4
Vlahokerassiá *GR*	97	D2	Volendam *NL*	54	C3	Vóri *GR*	100	C4
Vlahomándra *GR*	92	C3	Volímes *GR*	92	A4	Vormsi *EST*	124	B1

Vorna *FIN*	115	D2	Vrams-			Vuoskojaure *S*	104	C4
Voroneţ *RO*	127	D3	Gunnarstorp *S*	123	D2	Vuostimo *FIN*	109	E2
Vorsfelde *D*	57	D3	Vranje *YU*	128	C2	Vuotso *FIN*	105	F4
Vru *EST*	124	C2	Vransko *SLO*	73	E2	Vylkove *UA*	127	E4
Voss *N*	110	B4	Vrástama *GR*	88	C3	Vyšnij Voloček *RUS*	125	E1
Votonóssi *GR*	87	D4	Vrbas *YU*	128	A1	Vyškov *CZ*	65	E3
Voúdia *GR*	98	B3	Vravróna *GR*	94	B4			
Vouhorína *GR*	87	E3	Vreden *D*	55	D4	**W**		
Vouillé *F*	24	C2	Vresse-sur-Semois *B.*	17	F3			
Voukoliés *GR*	100	A3	Vrésthena *GR*	97	D2	Waalwijk *NL*	54	C4
Voúla *GR*	97	F1	Vreta Kloster *S*	119	D3	Waasmunster *B.*	17	E1
Vouliagméni *GR*	97	F1	Vrhnika *SLO*	73	D3	Wabern *D*	62	B1
Voúlpi *GR*	92	C2	Vría *GR*	88	A3	Wachow *D*	57	E2
La Voulte-			Vrínena *GR*	93	E2	Wadebridge *GB*	12	B3
sur-Rhône *F*	30	C1	Vríssa *GR*	95	F2	Wädenswil *CH.*	66	B3
Vouraïkós *GR*	93	D4	Vrísses *GR*	100	B3	Wächtersbach *D*	62	B2
Vourkári *GR*	98	A1	Vrissiá *GR*	93	E1	Wagenfeld *D*	55	F3
Vourliótes *GR*	99	F1	Vrissoúla *GR*	92	B1	Wageningen *NL*	54	C4
Voúrvoura *GR*	97	D2	Vrnjačka Banja *YU*	128	B2	Waging a. See *D*	67	F2
Vourvouroú *GR*	88	C3	Vrondádos *GR*	95	F3	Wagrain *A*	68	A3
Voutás *GR*	93	F2	Vrondamás *GR*	97	D3	Wahlstedt *D*	50	C3
Vouvant *F*	24	B2	Vronderó *GR*	87	D2	Waiblingen *D*	66	B1
Vouvray *F*	20	C4	Vrondissí *GR*	101	D4	Waidhaus *D*	63	F3
Vouzela *F*	34	B4	Vrondoú *GR*	88	A3	Waidhofen		
Vouziers *F*	17	E4	Vrossína *GR*	86	C4	an der Thaya *A*	64	C4
Voves *F*	21	D3	Vrouhás *GR*	101	E4	Waidhofen		
Vovoússa *GR*	87	D4	Vukovar *HR*	128	A1	an der Ybbs *A*	68	C1
Voznesens'k *UA*	127	F3	Vuohijärvi *FIN*	121	E3	Waidring *A*	67	F2
Vrå *DK*	122	B1	Vuokatti *FIN*	115	E2	Waischenfeld *D*	63	E3
Vrådal *N*	116	C2	Vuoksenniska *FIN*	121	F2	Waizenkirchen *A*	68	B1
Vraca *BG*	128	C2	Vuolijoki *FIN*	115	D2	Wakefield *GB*	11	D2
Vrahti *GR*	93	E4	Vuollerim *S*	108	B2	Wałbrzych *PL*	65	D1
Vrahnéika *GR*	92	C4	Vuonislahti *FIN*	115	F3			

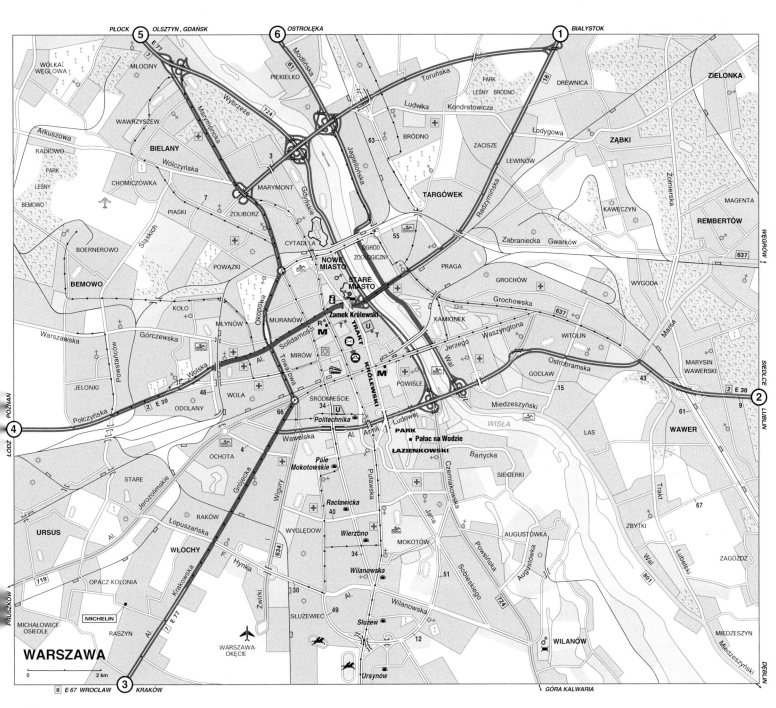

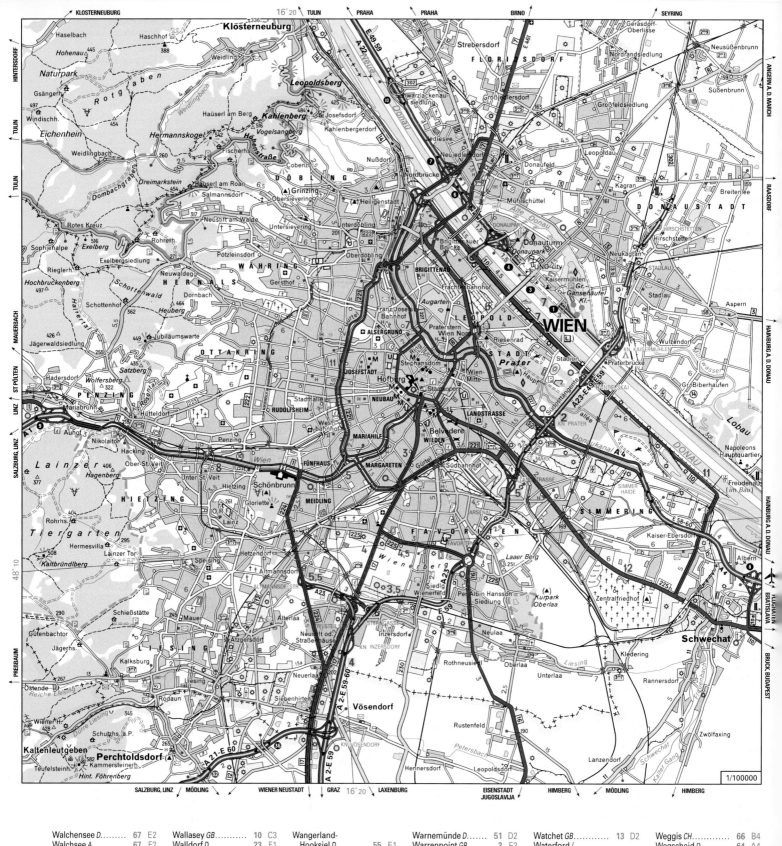

Walchensee D	67 E2	Wallasey GB	10 C3	Wangerland-		
Walchsee A	67 F2	Walldorf D	23 F1	Hooksiel D	55 E1	
Wald CH	66 B3	Walldürn D	62 B3	Wangerooge D	55 E1	
Waldbröl D	61 F1	Wallenfels D	63 E2	Wängi CH	66 B3	
Waldeck D	62 B2	Wallersdorf D	63 F4	Wanna D	50 A3	
Waldenbuch D	66 B1	Wallerstein D	63 D4	Wanne-Eickel D	55 E4	
Waldenburg D	63 F1	Wallingford GB	13 F2	Wantage GB	13 F2	
Waldfischbach-		Walls GB	7 F3	La Wantzenau F	23 E2	
Burgalben D	23 E1	Walsall GB	11 D4	Wanzleben D	57 D3	
Waldheim D	63 F1	Walsrode D	56 B2	Warburg D	56 B4	
Waldkappel D	62 C1	Walsum D	55 D4	Wardenburg D	50 A4	
Waldkirch D	23 F3	Waltershausen D	62 C1	Ware GB	14 C2	
Waldkirchen D	64 A4	Walton-		Waregem B	15 F4	
Waldkraiburg D	67 F1	on-the-Naze GB	15 D2	Wareham GB	13 E3	
Wald-		Waltrop D	55 E4	Waremme B	17 F2	
Michelbach D	23 F1	Wałcz PL	52 C3	Waren D	51 E3	
Waldmünchen D	63 F3	Wanderup D	50 B2	Warendorf D	55 F4	
Waldsassen D	63 F2	Wandlitz D	51 E4	Warin D	51 D3	
Waldshut-		Wanfried D	62 C1	Warkworth GB	9 F4	
Tiengen D	23 F4	Wangenbourg F	23 E2	Warmenstein ach D	63 E2	
Walenstadt CH	66 C3	Wangen i. Allgäu D	66 C2	Warminster GB	13 E2	

Warnemünde D	51 D2	Watchet GB	13 D2
Warrenpoint GB	3 E3	Waterford /	
Warrington GB	10 C3	Port Láirge IRL	5 D3
Warstein D	55 F4	Waterloo B	17 E2
Warszawa PL	126 A1	Waterville /	
Warth A	67 D3	An Coireán IRL	4 A3
Wartha D	62 C1	Watford GB	14 B3
Warwick GB	13 F1	Wattens A	67 E3
Washington GB	9 F4	Watton GB	15 D1
Wasselonne F	23 E2	Wattwil CH	66 B3
Wassen CH	66 B4	Waulsort B	17 F3
Wassenaar NL	54 B4	Wavre B	17 E2
Wassenberg D	61 E1	Waxweiler D	61 E3
Wasseralfingen D	62 C4	Wągrowiec PL	53 D2
Wasserbillig D	61 E3	Wedel (Holstein) D	50 B3
Wasserburg		Wedemark D	56 B3
a. Inn D	67 F2	Weener D	55 E2
Wassertrüdingen D	63 D4	Weert NL	17 F1
Wassigny F	17 D3	Weferlingen D	57 D3
Wassy F	22 B3	Wegberg D	61 E1
Wasungen D	62 C2	Wegeleben D	57 D3

Weggis CH	66 B4
Wegscheid D	64 A4
Wehr D	23 F4
Weibersbrunn D	62 B3
Weichshofen D	63 F4
Weida D	63 E1
Weiden	
i. d. Oberpfalz D	63 E3
Weikersheim D	62 C4
Weil der Stadt D	66 B1
Weilburg D	62 A2
Weilheim a. d. Teck D	66 C1
Weilheim	
i. Oberbayern D	67 E2
Weimar D	63 D1
Weinfelden CH	66 B3
Weingarten D	66 C2
Weinheim D	23 F1
Weinsberg D	62 B4
Weismain D	63 D2
Weißbriach A	68 A4

Weißenbach		
a. Lech A	67	D3
Weißenberg D	58	B4
Weißenburg D	63	D4
Weißenfels D	57	E4
Weißenhorn D	66	C1
Weißenkirchen in der		
Wachau A	68	C1
Weißensee D	63	D1
Weißenstadt D	63	E2
Weißkirchen A	68	C3
Weißwasser D	58	B4
Weitra A	64	C4
Weiz A	69	D2
Wejherowo PL	53	D1
Weldon GB	11	E4
Wellin B	17	F3
Wellingborough GB	14	B2
Wellington GB	13	D3
Wellington		
Bridge IRL	5	E3
Wells GB	13	E2
Wells-next-		
the-Sea GB	15	D1
Wels A	68	B1
Welshpool /		
Trallwng GB	10	B4
Weltenburg D	63	E4
Welwyn		
Garden City GB	14	C3
Welzheim D	66	C1
Welzow D	58	A4
Wem GB	10	C4
Wemding D	63	D4
Wemyss Bay GB	8	B2
Wenden D	56	C3
Wengen CH	66	A4
Wenns A	67	D3
Werben D	51	E4
Werdau D	63	E1
Werder D	57	F2
Werdohl D	61	F1
Werfen A	68	A2
Werl D	55	F4
Werlte D	55	E2
Wermelskirchen D	61	F1
Wermsdorf D	57	F4
Wernberg-Köblitz D	63	E3
Werne D	55	E4
Werneck D	62	C3
Werneuchen D	57	F2
Wernigerode D	57	D4
Wertach D	67	D3
Wertheim D	62	C3
Werther D	55	F3
Wertingen D	67	D1
Wervik B	15	F4
Wesel D	55	D4
Wesenberg D	51	F4
Wesendorf D	56	C2
Wesselburen D	50	A2
Wessobrunn D	67	E2
West Auckland GB	11	D1
West Bridgford GB	11	E4
West Kilbride GB	8	B3
West Linton GB	9	D3
West Looe GB	12	C3
West Mersea GB	15	D3
West-Terschelling NL	54	C1
Westbury GB	13	E2
Westendorf A	67	F3
Westenholz D	56	B2
Westerburg D	62	A2
Westerholt D	55	E1
Westerland D	50	A1
Westerlo B	17	F1
Westernbödefeld D	62	A1
Westerstede D	55	E1
Westhofen D	62	A3
Weston-		
super-Mare GB	13	D2
Westport / Cathair na		
Mart IRL	2	A3
Wetherby GB	11	D2
Wetter (Ruhr) D	61	F1
Wetteren B	17	D1
Wettin D	57	E4
Wettringen D	55	E3
Wetwang GB	11	E2
Wetzikon CH	66	B3
Wetzlar D	62	A2
Wexford /		
Loch Garman IRL	5	E3
Weyer Markt A	68	C2
Weyhausen D	56	C2
Weyhill GB	13	F2
Weymouth GB	13	E3
Weyregg		
a. Attersee A	68	A2
Węgorzewo PL	124	B4
Whaley		
Bridge GB	11	D3
Whitburn GB	9	D3
Whitby GB	11	E1
Whitchurch GB	10	C3
White Bridge GB	6	C4
Whitehaven GB	10	B1
Whitehead GB	3	E2
Whiteness GB	7	F3
Whithorn GB	8	C4
Whitland GB	12	C1
Whitley Bay GB	9	F4
Whitstable GB	15	D3
Whittlesey GB	11	F4
Wick GB	7	E2
Wickford GB	14	C3
Wicklow /		
Cill Mhantáin IRL	5	E3
Widnes GB	10	C3
Wiefelstede D	50	A4
Wiehe D	57	D4
Wiek D	51	F1
Wieluń PL	126	A2
Wien A	69	D1
Wien-Schwechat A	69	D1
Wiener Neudorf A	69	D1
Wiener Neustadt A	69	D1
Wies A	69	D3
Wiesau D	63	E3
Wiesbaden D	62	A3
Wieselburg A	68	C1
Wiesenburg D	57	E3
Wiesensteig D	66	C1
Wiesentheid D	62	C3
Wiesenttal D	63	D3
Wiesing A	67	F3
Wiesloch D	23	F1
Wiesmath A	69	E2
Wiesmoor D	55	E1
Wigan GB	10	C2
Wigston GB	11	E4
Wigton GB	9	D4
Wigtown GB	8	C4
Wijhe NL	55	D3
Wil CH	66	B3
Wildalpen A	68	C2
Wildbad		
i. Schwarzwald D	23	F2
Wildeck D	62	C10
Wildeck D	62	C1
Wildeshausen D	55	F2
Wildon A	69	D3
Wilfersdorf A	65	E4
Wilhelmsburg A	69	D1
Wilhelmshaven D	50	A4
Wilhemsburg D	50	B4
Wilhering A	68	B1
Wilkau-Haßlau D	63	F1
Willebroek B	17	E1
Willemstad NL	54	B4
Willingen D	62	A1
Williton GB	13	D2
Wilmslow GB	10	C3
Wilnsdorf D	62	A1
Wilsdruff D	64	A1
Wilster D	50	B3
Wilton GB	13	F2
Wiltz L	61	E3
Wimborne		
Minster GB	13	E3
Wimereux F	15	D4
Wincanton GB	13	E2
Winchcombe GB	13	F1
Winchelsea GB	14	C4
Winchester GB	13	F3
Windeck D	61	F2
Windermere GB	10	C1
Windischeschen-		
bach D	63	E3
Windischgarsten A	68	B2
Windsbach D	63	D4
Windsor GB	14	B3
Winkleigh GB	12	C3
Winklern A	68	A3
Winnenden D	66	C1
Winnigstedt D	57	D3
Winnweiler D	23	E1
Winschoten NL	55	D2
Winsen D	50	C4
Winsen (Aller) D	56	C2
Winsford GB	10	C3
Winsum NL	55	D1
Winterberg D	62	A1
Winterswijk NL	55	D4
Winterthur CH	66	B3
Wintzenheim F	23	E3
Wipperfürth D	61	F1
Wisbech GB	11	F4
Wischhafen D	50	B3
Wishaw GB	8	C3
Wismar D	51	D3
Wissant F	15	E4
Wissembourg F	23	E1
Wissen D	61	F2
Witham GB	14	C3
Withernsea GB	11	F2
Witney GB	13	F1
Wittdün D	50	A2
Witten D	61	F1
Wittenberg D	57	F3
Wittenberge D	51	D4
Wittenburg D	51	D3
Wittichenau D	58	A4
Wittingen D	56	C2
Wittlich D	61	F3
Wittstock D	51	F4
Witzenhausen D	56	C4
Włocławek PL	53	F4
Władysławowo PL	53	E1
Włodawa PL	126	B1
Wöllersdorf A	69	D1
Woensdrecht NL	17	E1
Woerden NL	54	B4
Wörgl A	67	F3
Wörlitz D	57	E3
Wörrstadt D	62	A3
Wlrth F	23	E3
Wörth a. d. Donau D	63	F4
Wörth a. Main D	62	B3
Wörth a. Rhein D	23	F1
Wohlen CH	23	F4
Woippy F	22	C1
Woking GB	14	B3
Wokingham GB	14	B3
Woldegk D	51	F3
Wolfach D	23	F3
Wolfegg D	66	C2
Wolfen D	57	E3
Wolfenbüttel D	56	C3
Wolfhagen D	62	B1
Wolfratshausen D	67	E2
Wolfsberg A	68	C3
Wolfsburg D	56	C3
Wolgast D	51	F2
Wolkersdorf A	65	E4
Wollersheim D	61	E2
Wollin D	57	E3
Wolmirstedt D	57	D3
Wolnzach D	67	E1
Wolsingham GB	11	D1
Wolsztyn PL	58	C2
Wolvega NL	54	C2
Wolverhampton GB	14	A1
Wolverton GB	14	B2
Woodbridge GB	15	D2
Woodhall Spa GB	11	E3
Woodstock GB	13	F1
Wooler GB	9	E3
Worb CH	27	F1
Worbis D	56	C4
Worcester GB	13	E1
Workington GB	9	D4
Worksop GB	11	E3
Workum NL	54	C2
Wormerveer NL	54	B3
Wormhout F	15	E4
Worms D	23	F1
Worthing GB	14	B4
Wragby GB	11	E3
Wrexham /		
Wrecsam GB	10	C3
Wriezen D	52	A4
Wrocław PL	59	D4
Wroughton GB	13	F2
Wünnenberg D	55	F4
Wünsdorf D	57	F3
Würzburg D	62	C3
Wulfen D	55	E4
Wullowitz A	64	B4
Wunsiedel D	63	E2
Wunstorf D	56	B3
Wuppertal D	61	F1
Wurzen D	57	F4
Wusterhausen D	51	E4
Wustrow D	51	E2
Wuustwezel B	17	E1
Wyk a. Föhr D	50	A2
Wymondham GB	15	D1
Wöbbelin D	51	D4

X

Xàbia / Jávea E	44	A4
Xanten D	55	D4
Xánthi GR	89	E1
Xeresa E	44	A4
Xert E	44	A1
Xerta E	44	B1
Xertigny F	23	D3
Xifianí GR	87	F1
Xilagani GR	89	F1
Xiliki GR	93	E3
Xilókastro GR	93	E4
Xilopáriko GR	92	C1
Xilópoli GR	88	B1
Xilóskalo GR	100	B3
Xiniáda GR	93	E2
Xinó Neró GR	87	E2
Xinzo de Limia E	32	B4
Xirokámbi GR	97	D3
Xirókambos GR	99	F2
Xirolímni GR	87	E3
Xixona E	49	F1
Xubia E	32	B2
Xunqueira		
de Ambía E	32	B4

Y

Yalova TR	129	F3
Yanguas E	37	D3
Yarmouth GB	13	F2
Ybbs an der Donau A	68	C1
Yébenes (Los) E	42	B3
Yebra E	42	C2
Yecla E	49	E1
Yeovil GB	13	E3
Yepes E	42	B2
Yerville E	16	A4
Yesa E	28	B4
Yesa (La) E	43	F2
Yeste E	48	C1
Ylämaa FIN	121	E3
Ylämylly FIN	115	F3
Yläne FIN	120	B3
Yli-Ii FIN	109	D3
Yli-Kärppä FIN	109	D3
Yli-Muonio FIN	108	C1
Yli Nampa FIN	109	D2
Yli-Olhava FIN	109	D3
Ylihärmä FIN	114	B3
Ylikiiminki FIN	115	D3
Ylistaro FIN	114	B3
Ylitornio FIN	108	C3
Ylivieska FIN	114	C2
Ylläsjärvi FIN	108	C1
Ylöjärvi FIN	120	C2
York GB	11	E2
Youghal / Eochaill IRL	5	D3
Yoxford GB	15	D2
Ypäjä FIN	120	C3
Yport F	16	A4
Yppäri FIN	114	C2
Yseure F	26	A2
Yssingeaux F	26	B4
Ystad S	123	E3
Ytterhogdal S	112	B3
Yttermalung S	118	C1
Yuncos E	42	B2
Yunquera E	47	F3
Yunquera		
de Henares E	42	C1
Yuste		
(Monasterio de) E	41	F2
Yverdon-		
les-Bains CH	27	E1
Yvetot F	16	A4
Yvoir B	17	F3
Yvoire F	27	E2

Z

Zaandam NL	54	B3
Žabljak YU	128	A2
Zadar HR	77	F2
Zafarraya E	48	A3
Zafóra (Nissí) GR	101	C2
Zafra E	41	D4
Žaga SLO	72	C2
Zagorá GR	93	F1
Zagória GR	87	D4
Zagorje SLO	73	E2
Zagreb HR	73	F3
Zahara		
de los Atunes E	47	D4
Zaháro GR	96	B1
Zahinos E	41	D4
Zahna D	57	F3
Záhony H	126	B30
Zaidín E	38	A3
Zaječar YU	128	C2
Zákinthos GR	96	A4
Zákinthos (Nissí) GR	96	A1
Zakopane PL	126	A3
Zákros GR	101	F4
Zalaegerszeg H	69	E30
Zalamea		
de la Serena E	41	F4
Zalamea la Real E	47	D2
Zalău RO	126	C4
Zalec SLO	73	E2
Zališčyky UA	126	C3
Zalla E	36	C1
Zálongo GR	92	A1
Zaltbommel NL	54	C4
Zambrana E	36	C2
Zamora E	35	F3
Zamość PL	126	B2
Zandvoort NL	54	B3
Zanglivéri GR	88	B2
Zaorejas E	43	D1

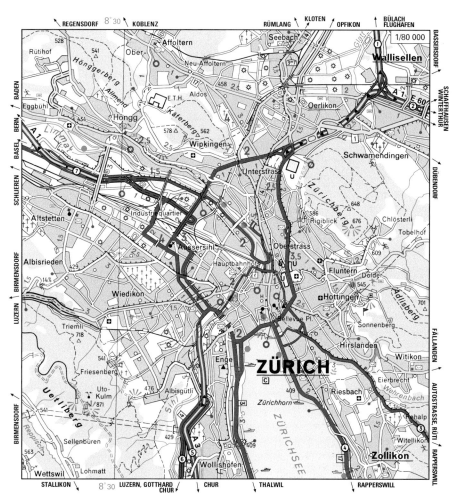

Zapadnaja
    Dvina *RUS* 125 E2
Zápio *GR* 93 E1
Zapponeta *I* 80 C2
Zaragoza *E* 37 F4
Zárakes *GR* 94 B4
Zaratán *E* 36 A3
Zarautz *E* 37 D1
Zarcilla de Ramos *E* .. 49 D2
Zárkos *GR* 87 F4
Zarós *GR* 101 D4
Zaroúhla *GR* 93 D4
Zarrentin *D* 50 C3
Zarza la Mayor *E* 41 D2
Žaškiv *UA* 127 E2
Zavattarello *I* 75 D1
Zawiercie *PL* 126 A2
Zbaraž *UA* 126 C2
Zduńska Wola *PL* 126 A2
Zebreira *P* 41 D2
Zeebrugge *B* 15 F3
Zefiría *GR* 98 B3
Zehdenick *D* 51 F4
Zeist *NL* 54 C4
Zeitz *D* 63 E1

Zejtun *M* 85 F4
Žekovec *SLO* 73 E2
Zele *B* 17 E1
Zelenogorsk *RUS* 124 C1
Železniki *SLO* 73 D2
Železnogorsk *RUS* 125 F4
Želin *SLO* 73 D3
Zélio *GR* 93 F3
Zell (Mosel) *D* 61 F3
Zella-Mehlis *D* 63 D2
Zell am See *A* 68 A3
Zell am Ziller *A* 67 F3
Zell an der Pram *A* 68 A1
Zeltweg *A* 68 C3
Zelzate *B* 17 D1
Zenica *BIH* 128 A2
Zerbst *D* 57 E3
Zerf *D* 23 D1
Zeri *I* 75 E2
Zermatt *CH* 27 F2
Zernez *CH* 67 D4
Zestoa *E* 37 D1
Zetel *D* 55 E1
Zeulenroda *D* 63 E1

Zeven *D* 50 B4
Zevenaar *NL* 55 D4
Zevgaráki *GR* 92 C3
Zevgolatió *GR* 96 C2
Zevio *I* 72 A4
Zicavo *F* 78 A4
Zicavo *F* 75 D3
Ziegenrück *D* 63 E1
Zielona Góra *PL* 58 B3
Zierikzee *NL* 54 A4
Ziersdorf *A* 65 D4
Zierzow *D* 51 D4
Ziesar *D* 57 E3
Zimnicea *RO* 129 D2
Zinal *CH* 27 F2
Zingst *D* 51 E2
Zin'kiv *UA* 127 E1
Zinnowitz *D* 51 F2
Zinnwald *D* 64 A1
Zirchow *D* 52 A2
Žiri *SLO* 73 D3
Zirl *A* 67 E3
Zirndorf *D* 63 D3
Ziros *GR* 101 F4
Zistersdorf *A* 65 E4

Zittau *D* 64 B1
Žizdra *RUS* 125 F3
Zlatica *BG* 128 C2
Zlatni Pjasĺaĺci *BG* 129 E2
Zlín *CZ* 65 F3
Žlobin *BY* 125 E4
Žmerynka *UA* 127 D2
Znam"janka *UA* 127 D2
Znojmo *CZ* 65 D4
Zöblitz *D* 63 F1
Zörbig *D* 57 E4
Zoetermeer *NL* 54 B4
Zollikofen *CH* 27 F1
Zoločiv *UA* 126 C2
Zolotonoša *UA* 127 D2
Zonguldak *TR* 129 F2
Zóni *GR* 91 E1
Zonianá *GR* 100 C3
Zonza *F* 78 A4
Zoodóhos Pigí *GR* 97 F1
Zoodóhos Pigí *GR* 87 F3
Zorita *E* 41 F3
Zossen *D* 57 F3
Zoutkamp *NL* 55 D1
Zoutleeuw *B* 17 F2

Zoúzouli *GR* 87 D3
Žovkva *UA* 126 C2
Žovti Vody *UA* 127 F2
Zrenjanin *YU* 128 B1
Zschopau *D* 63 F1
Zubcov *RUS* 125 F2
Zucaina *E* 44 A2
Zudar *D* 51 F2
Zülpich *D* 61 E2
Zuera *E* 37 F3
Zürs *A* 67 D3
Zufre *E* 47 D1
Zug *CH* 66 B3
Zuidlaren *NL* 55 D2
Zújar *E* 48 C2
Zundert *NL* 17 E1
Zuoz *CH* 67 D4
Zürich *CH* 23 F4
Zurrieq *M* 85 F4
Zurzach *CH* 23 F4
Žukovka *RUS* 125 F4
Zumaia *E* 37 D1
Zumarraga *E* 37 D1
Zusmarshausen *D* 67 D1
Zutphen *NL* 55 D3

Zvenyhorodka *UA* 127 E2
Zvolen *SK* 126 A30
Zvornik *BIH* 128 A1
Žužemberk *SLO* 73 E3
Zweibrücken *D* 23 E1
Zweisimmen *CH* 27 F2
Zwenkau *D* 57 E4
Zwettl *A* 64 C4
Zwettl
    an der Rodl *A* 68 B1
Zwickau *D* 63 F1
Zwiefalten *D* 66 C2
Zwiesel *D* 64 A4
Zwijndrecht *NL* 54 B4
Zwönitz *D* 63 F1
Zwolle *NL* 55 D3
Žytkavičy *BY* 127 D1
Žytomyr *UA* 127 D2
Žd'ár
    nad Sázavou *CZ* 65 D3
Žilina *SK* 126 A3
Zagań *PL* 58 B3
Žary *PL* 58 B3
Žyrardów *PL* 126 A1
Żywiec *PL* 126 A3